# STREET ATLAS

# Northamptonshire

## Corby, Daventry, Kettering, Northampton, Wellingborough

First published in 1999 by

Philip's, a division of
Octopus Publishing Group Ltd
2-4 Heron Quays, London E14 4JP

Third edition 2007
First impression 2007
NHPCA

ISBN-10  0-540-09086-7 (spiral)
ISBN-13  978-0-540-09086-0 (spiral)

© Philip's 2007

This product includes mapping data licensed
from Ordnance Survey® with the permission of
the Controller of Her Majesty's Stationery Office.
© Crown copyright 2007. All rights reserved.
Licence number 100011710.

Data for the speed cameras provided by
PocketGPSWorld.com Ltd.

Ordnance Survey and the OS Symbol are
registered trademarks of Ordnance Survey, the
national mapping agency of Great Britain.

Printed by Toppan, China

## Contents

| | |
|---|---|
| II | **List of mobile speed cameras** |
| III | **Key to map symbols** |
| IV | **Key to map pages** |
| VI | **Route planning** |
| X | **Administrative and Postcode boundaries** |
| 1 | **Street maps** at 3½ inches to 1 mile |
| 240 | **Index** of towns, villages, streets, hospitals, industrial estates, railway stations, schools, shopping centres, universities and places of interest |

## Digital Data

The exceptionally high-quality mapping found in this atlas is available as digital data in TIFF format, which is easily convertible to other bitmapped (raster) image formats.

The index is also available in digital form as a standard database table. It contains all the details found in the printed index together with the National Grid reference for the map square in which each entry is named.

For further information and to discuss your requirements, please contact james.mann@philips-maps.co.uk

# Mobile speed cameras

The vast majority of speed cameras used on Britain's roads are operated by safety camera partnerships. These comprise local authorities, the police, Her Majesty's Court Service (HMCS) and the Highways Agency.

This table lists the sites where each safety camera partnership may enforce speed limits through the use of mobile cameras or detectors. These are usually set up on the roadside or a bridge spanning the road and operated by a police or civilian enforcement officer. The speed limit at each site (if available) is shown in red type, followed by the approximate location in black type.

In addition to the routes below, mobile speed enforcement can also take place in local areas of concern requested by residents or as determined by the Police.

**A5**
60 DIRFT to County Boundary
60 Norton/Whilton Crossroads
30/40 Towcester Racecourse to A43

**A6**
60 Burton Latimer Bypass

**A14**
70 Kelmarsh
70 Kelmarsh Junctions 7-10

**A43**
60 Laxton Turn to A47 Duddington
60 Mawsley to A14 Junc 8 (inc Mawsley Spur)
70 Towcester to M1 Junc 15a

**A45**
60 M1 Junc 16 to Weedon
60 Stanwick to Raunds

**A361**
60 Byfield to Chipping Warden

**A422**
60 Brackley West to A43

**A428**
60 East Haddon
30/60 Great Houghton to Yardley Hastings

**A508**
30 Northampton, Plough Gyratory
30 Northampton, St Georges Avenue to Holly Lodge Rd
30 Northampton, St Peters Way to St Georges Avenue
30/60 Stoke Bruerne to A5
70 Wootton Flyover to M1 Junc 15

**A509**
60 Wellingborough to Isham

**A605**
40/60 Thrapston to Warmington

**A4256**
30 Daventry, Eastern Way

**A4500**
40/60 Great Billing to Earls Barton
30 Northampton, Abington Park to York Rd
30 Northampton, Park Avenue to Booth Lane South
30 Northampton, Weedon Rd to Duston Rd

**A5076**
40 Mere Way
40 Northampton, Great Billing Way South

**A5193**
30/40 Wellingborough, London Rd

**A6003**
50/60 Kettering to Corby

**A6014**
40/60 Corby, Oakley Rd

**B569**
50 Irchester to Rushden

**B576**
60 Desborough to Rothwell

**B4038**
30/60 Kilsby, Rugby Rd

**B4525**
40/60 Welsh Lane

**B5385**
60 Watford to West Haddon

**UNCLASSIFIED**
30 Brackmills Industrial Estate
30 Northampton, Grange Rd

| | |
|---|---|
| **Motorway** with junction number | |
| **Primary route** – dual/single carriageway | |
| **A road** – dual/single carriageway | |
| **B road** – dual/single carriageway | |
| **Minor road** – dual/single carriageway | |
| **Other minor road** – dual/single carriageway | |
| **Road under construction** | |
| **Tunnel, covered road** | |
| **Speed cameras - single, multiple** | |
| **Rural track, private road or narrow road in urban area** | |
| **Gate or obstruction to traffic** (restrictions may not apply at all times or to all vehicles) | |
| **Path, bridleway, byway open to all traffic, road used as a public path** | |
| **Pedestrianised area** | |
| **Postcode boundaries** | |
| **County and unitary authority boundaries** | |
| **Railway, tunnel, railway under construction** | |
| **Tramway, tramway under construction** | |
| **Miniature railway** | |
| **Railway station** | |
| **Private railway station** | |
| **Metro station** | |
| **Tram stop, tram stop under construction** | |
| **Bus, coach station** | |

| | |
|---|---|
| ◆ | **Ambulance station** |
| ◆ | **Coastguard station** |
| ◆ | **Fire station** |
| ◆ | **Police station** |
| ✚ | **Accident and Emergency entrance to hospital** |
| Ⓗ | **Hospital** |
| + | **Place of worship** |
| ℹ | **Information Centre** (open all year) |
| 🛒 | **Shopping Centre** |
| Ⓟ | **Parking** |
| P&R | **Park and Ride** |
| PO | **Post Office** |
| ⛺ | **Camping site** |
| 🚐 | **Caravan site** |
| ▶ | **Golf course** |
| ✕ | **Picnic site** |
| Prim Sch | **Important buildings, schools, colleges, universities and hospitals** |
| | **Built up area** |
| | **Woods** |
| River Medway | **Water name** |
| | **River, weir, stream** |
| | **Canal, lock, tunnel** |
| | **Water** |
| | **Tidal water** |
| *Church* | **Non-Roman antiquity** |
| ROMAN FORT | **Roman antiquity** |
| 87 / 58 | **Adjoining page indicators** |

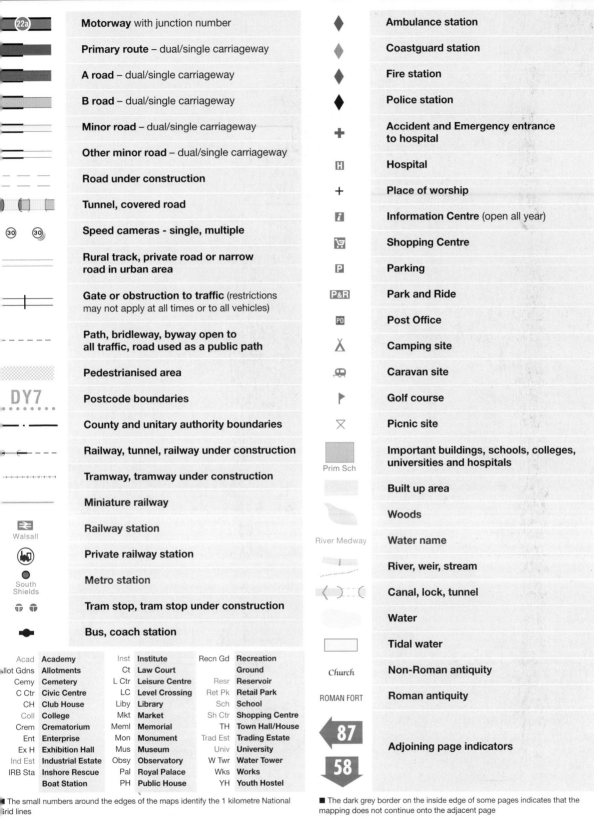

| | | | | | | |
|---|---|---|---|---|---|---|
| Acad | Academy | Inst | Institute | Recn Gd | Recreation Ground |
| Allot Gdns | Allotments | Ct | Law Court | | |
| Cemy | Cemetery | L Ctr | Leisure Centre | Resr | Reservoir |
| C Ctr | Civic Centre | LC | Level Crossing | Ret Pk | Retail Park |
| CH | Club House | Liby | Library | Sch | School |
| Coll | College | Mkt | Market | Sh Ctr | Shopping Centre |
| Crem | Crematorium | Meml | Memorial | TH | Town Hall/House |
| Ent | Enterprise | Mon | Monument | Trad Est | Trading Estate |
| Ex H | Exhibition Hall | Mus | Museum | Univ | University |
| Ind Est | Industrial Estate | Obsy | Observatory | W Twr | Water Tower |
| IRB Sta | Inshore Rescue Boat Station | Pal | Royal Palace | Wks | Works |
| | | PH | Public House | YH | Youth Hostel |

■ The small numbers around the edges of the maps identify the 1 kilometre National Grid lines

■ The dark grey border on the inside edge of some pages indicates that the mapping does not continue onto the adjacent page

**The scale of the maps on the pages numbered in blue is 5.52 cm to 1 km • 3½ inches to 1 mile • 1: 18103**

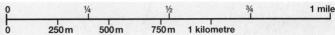

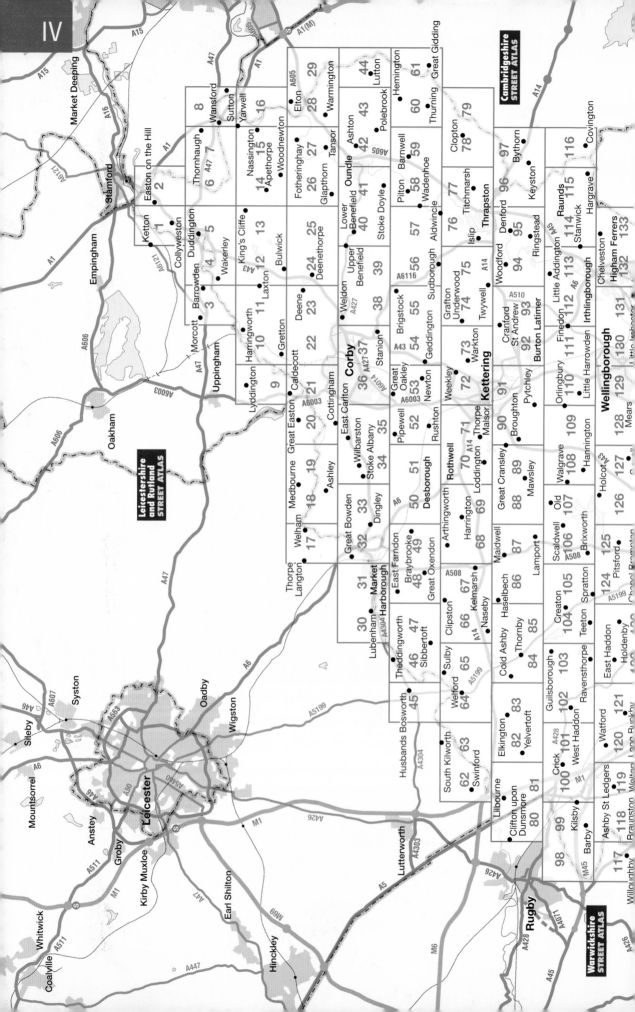

# Key to map pages

**Map pages at 3½ inches to 1 mile**

122

**Scale**

0    5    10
0    5    10    15 km
        10 miles

Bedfordshire STREET ATLAS
Buckinghamshire STREET ATLAS
Oxfordshire STREET ATLAS

Newton Bromswold

Wymington 148 149 Knotting Green
Irchester 146 147 Podington Wollaston
144 145 Earls Barton Great Doddington

Clapham
Bedford
Kempston
Cranfield

Luton
Dunstable
Leighton Buzzard
Winslow
Bicester
Buckingham

Strixton 164 165 Bozeat Hinwick
Warrington 180 Olney 195
Yardley Hastings 178 179 Ravenstone 194
Denton
162 163 Grendon Castle Ashby
Cogenhoe 160 161 Great Houghton
142 143 Ecton Boothville
Horton 176 177 Quinton
193 Hartwell 192
207 Hanslope 206 Long Street
218 Castlethorpe Cosgrove
229 Old Stratford
235 Thornton
228 Wicken 235

Church Brampton 140 141 Kingsthorpe
Northampton 158 159 Far Cotton
Rothersthorpe 174 175 Collingtree
Blisworth 190 191 Roade
204 205 Alderton Stoke Bruerne
216 45 217 Pottersbury Paulerspury
227 Lillingstone Lovell
226 Lillingstone Dayrell

Great Brington 138 139 Harlestone
Harpole 156 157 Kislingbury
Nether Heyford
Bugbrooke 172 173 Gayton Pattishall
Astcote 186 187 Grimscote Maidford
Tiffield 188 189
Greens Norton 202 203 Towcester
Pury End 214 215 Whittlebury
Silverstone
224 225 Dadford
234 Evenley

Whiton 136 137 Brockhall Norton
Dodford 154 155 Weedon Flore
Everdon 170 171 Farthingstone Litchborough
Hinton 184 185 Canons Ashby Eydon
Woodend 200 201 Weston Abthorpe
Wappenham 212 213 Helmdon
Syresham 224
Halse 222 223 Whitfield
Brackley 232 233 Hinton-in-the-Hedges
Croughton 238 239 Cottisford

134 135 Daventry
Staverton 152 153 Badby Newnham
168 169 Charwelton Preston Capes
Byfield 182 183 Aston le Walls
Chipping Warden 196 197 Wardington
Sulgrave 210 211 Greatworth
Middleton Cheney
Thenford 220 221 Farthinghoe
Kings Sutton 230 231 Charlton Adderbury
Aynho 236 237 Clifton Souldern

Southam
150 151 Helidon
Priors Marston 166 167 Priors Hardwick
Wormleighton 181 Claydon
208 209 Chacombe Williamscott
Warkworth 219

A421 A603 A600 A6 A428 A422 A509 M1 A5 A4146 A4012 A505 A4146 A418 A413 A421 A423 A425 A45 A5130 A4012 A508 A43 A361 A422 A4260 A4095 M40 A34 A44 A423

Scale

0     5     10 km

0  1  2  3  4  5  6 miles

## Major administrative and Postcode boundaries

County and unitary authority boundaries

District boundaries

Postcode boundaries

Area covered by this atlas

**Scale**

0 — 5 — 10 — 15 km

0 — 5 — 10 miles

Lincolnshire

SK | TF

Rutland

City of Peterborough

SK
SP

Leicestershire

Easton on the Hill
PE9
LE15
Wansford
PE6
TF
TL
PE5
Lyddington
Wakerley
King's Cliffe
NN17
Deene
Warmington
PE7
Market Harborough
LE16
Wilbarston
Corby
Corby
PE8
Oundle
Great Oakley
NN18
East Northamptonshire
PE28
Braybrooke
Desborough
Brigstock
LE17
Rothwell
Kettering
NN16
Woodford
Thrapston
Welford
Kettering
NN15
Warwickshire
Maidwell
Burton Latimer
CV21
CV22
Yelvertoft
NN6
Raunds
Guilsborough
Irthlingborough
NN9
CV23
Barby
Brixworth
Northamptonshire
Higham Ferrers
Daventry
Moulton
Wellingborough
NN8
Rushden
Wellingborough
NN10
Daventry
Wollaston
Cambridgeshire
NN2
NN3
NN29
CV47
Harpole
NN5
NN1
Bozeat
NN11
Northampton
NN4
Bugbrooke
Hackleton
Byfield
NN7
Roade
MK46
South Northamptonshire
MK16
Towcester
MK19
Culworth
NN12
Milton Keynes
Silverstone
Bedfordshire
OX17
Syresham
Cosgrove
MK12
OX16
Stony Stratford
MK11
Farthinghoe
Brackley
NN13
MK18
King's Sutton
Croughton
MK17
OX15
OX27
Herts
OX25
Oxfordshire
Buckinghamshire
Luton
SP | TL

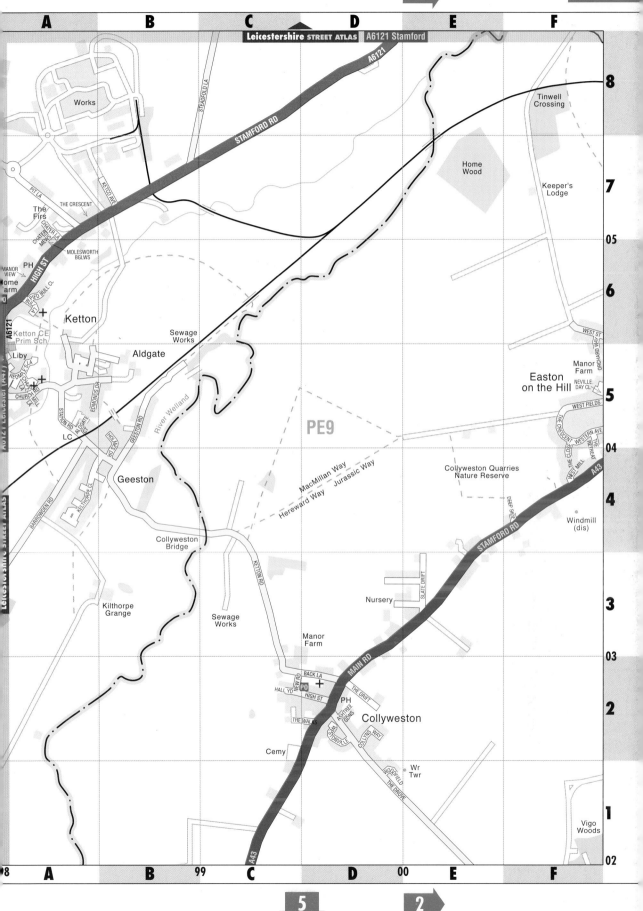

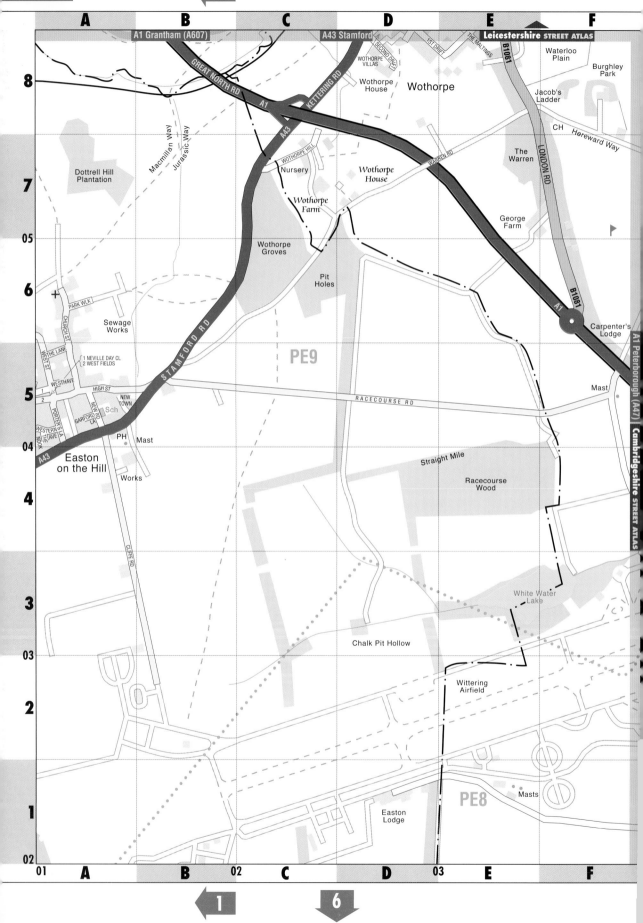

**Leicestershire** STREET ATLAS

A1 Grantham (A607)

A43 Stamford

GREAT NORTH RD

KETTERING RD

Wothorpe
Villas

Wothorpe
House

Wothorpe

Waterloo
Plain

Burghley
Park

Jacob's
Ladder

THE MALTINGS

B1081

CH   Hereward Way

1ST DRIFT

SECOND DRIFT

A1

A43

WOTHORPE HILL

Nursery

Wothorpe
Farm

Wothorpe
House

WARREN RD

The
Warren

LONDON RD

Dottrell Hill
Plantation

Macmillan Way

Jurassic Way

Wothorpe
Groves

George
Farm

Pit
Holes

A1

B1081

Carpenter's
Lodge

PARK WLK

Sewage
Works

STAMFORD RD

PE9

CHURCH ST

THE LANE

WEST ST

WESTHAVE

1 NEVILLE DAY CL
2 WEST FIELDS

HIGH ST

NEW
TOWN

RACECOURSE RD

Mast

1

2

Sch

PORTER'S LA

GARFORD LA

NEW RD

WESTERN AVE

THE NOOK

A43

PH   Mast

Easton
on the Hill

Works

CLIFFE RD

Straight Mile

Racecourse
Wood

White Water
Lake

Chalk Pit Hollow

Wittering
Airfield

Easton
Lodge

PE8

Masts

A1 Peterborough (A47)    Cambridgeshire STREET ATLAS

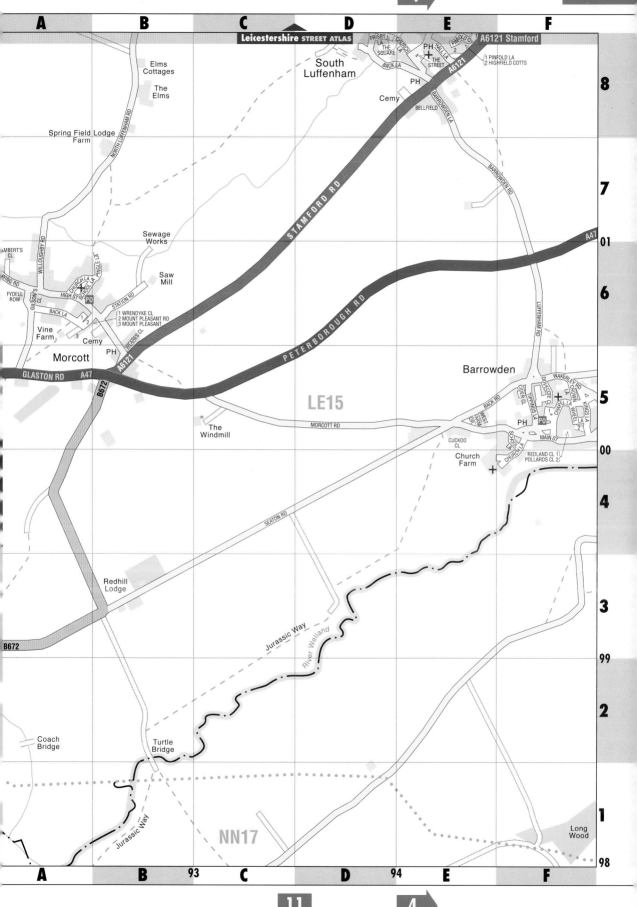

Leicestershire STREET ATLAS

South Luffenham

1 PINFOLD LA
2 HIGHFIELD COTTS

A6121 Stamford

Elms Cottages

The Elms

Spring Field Lodge Farm

Sewage Works

Saw Mill

STAMFORD RD

PETERBOROUGH RD

A47

01

Bellfield

BARROWDEN LA

BARROWDEN RD

LUFFENHAM RD

MBERT'S CL
WING RD
WILLOUGHBY RD
FYDELL ROW
GILSON'S CL
High St
CHURCH LA
SCHOOL LA
ANGLE LA
PO
BACK LA
Vine Farm
Cemy
PH
STATION RD
NEARES CL
A6121

1 WRENDYKE CL
2 MOUNT PLEASANT RD
3 MOUNT PLEASANT

Morcott

GLASTON RD    A47

B672

LE15

The Windmill

MORCOTT RD

Barrowden

WAKERLEY RD
DOVECOTE CL
CIDER CL
TIPPINGS LA
CHAPEL LA
CROWN LA
KINGS LA
WHEEL LA
PO
Main St
BACK RD
WEST FARM
CUCKOO CL
REDLAND CL 1
POLLARDS CL 2
PH
SCHOOL LA
CHURCH LA

Church Farm

00

4

SEATON RD

Redhill Lodge

Jurassic Way

River Welland

3

B672

99

2

Coach Bridge

Turtle Bridge

Long Wood

1

Jurassic Way

NN17

98

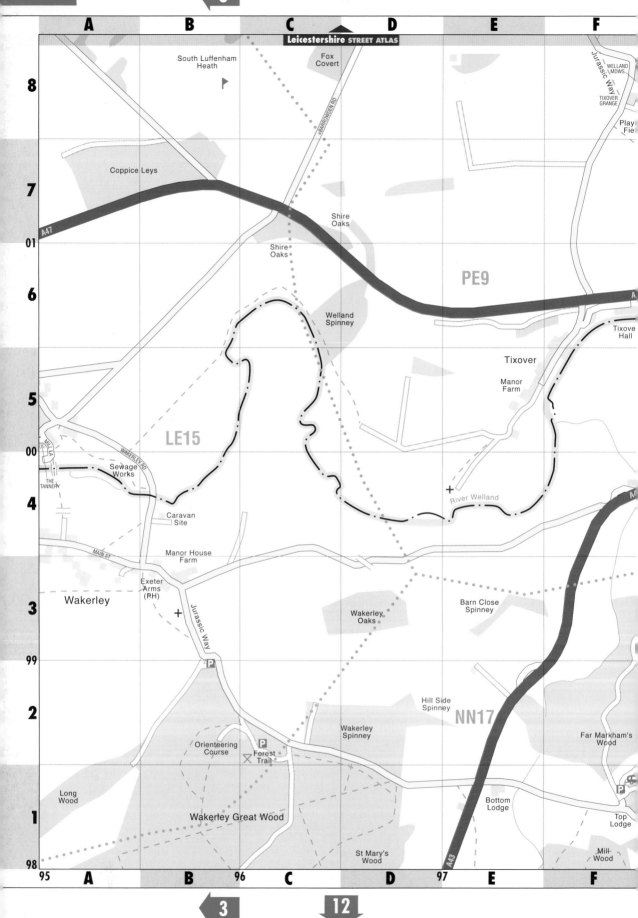

| A | B | C | D | E | F |

**Leicestershire** STREET ATLAS

South Luffenham Heath

Fox Covert

Jurassic Way

WELLAND MDWS

TIXOVER GRANGE

Play Fie

Coppice Leys

A47

Shire Oaks

Shire Oaks

PE9

Welland Spinney

Tixove Hall

Tixover

Manor Farm

LE15

MILL LA

WAKERLEY RD

Sewage Works

THE TANNERY

River Welland

Caravan Site

MAIN ST

Manor House Farm

Exeter Arms (PH)

Wakerley

Jurassic Way

Barn Close Spinney

Wakerley Oaks

P

Hill Side Spinney

NN17

Far Markham's Wood

Orienteering Course

P

Forest Trail

Wakerley Spinney

Long Wood

Wakerley Great Wood

Bottom Lodge

Top Lodge

Mill Wood

A43

St Mary's Wood

| 95 | A | B | 96 | C | D | 97 | E | F |

A   B   C   D   E   F

Sewage
Works

River Welland

Vigo
Woods

THE DROVE

Cuckoo
Lodge

**8**

A43

A47

Quarry

Little
Wood

**01**

Collyweston Great Wood

**7**

HIGHFIELD RD

STAMFORD RD

GREEN LA

MILL ST

CHURCH LA

TODD'S HILL

**PE9**

**6**

Duddington

Manor
House

HIGH ST

GREEN LA

PH

Gregory's
Lodge

Cemy

The
Assarts

**5**

Gore
Piece

**00**

North
Spinney

**4**

Long
Spinney

Jurassic Way

Little
Wood

**PE8**

Noses
Halt

Cunnington's
Spinney

**3**

Dales
Wood

Peter's
Nook

**99**

Dumb Bob
Spinney

Buxton
Wood

Westhay Wood

**2**

The
Gullet

**NN17**

Great
Watkinson

Old
Sale

**1**

TOP
LODGE

Stockings

**98**

Hither
Hazelwood

A   B   99   C   D   00   E   F

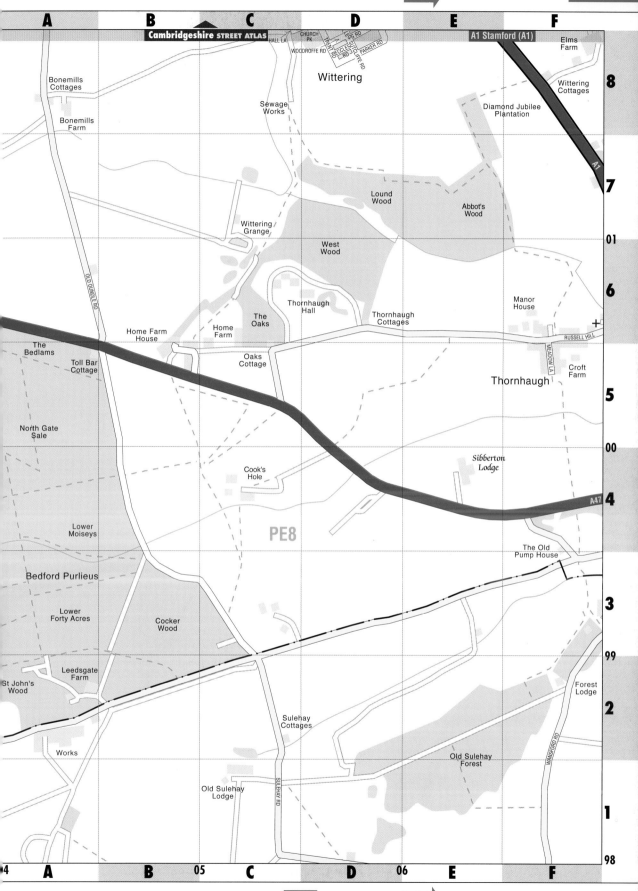

**Cambridgeshire** STREET ATLAS

Wittering

A1 Stamford (A1)

Elms Farm

Bonemills Cottages

Bonemills Farm

Sewage Works

CHURCH PK
WOODROFFE RD
HALL LA
TRENT RD
ECCLES RD
CLIFFE RD
PARKER RD
B26 RD

Diamond Jubilee Plantation

Wittering Cottages

Lound Wood

Abbot's Wood

OLD DUMBLE RD

Wittering Grange

West Wood

Manor House

Thornhaugh Hall

The Oaks

Thornhaugh Cottages

RUSSELL HILL

Home Farm House

Home Farm

MEADOW LA

The Bedlams

Toll Bar Cottage

Oaks Cottage

Thornhaugh

Croft Farm

North Gate Sale

Sibberton Lodge

Cook's Hole

A47

Lower Moiseys

PE8

The Old Pump House

Bedford Purlieus

Lower Forty Acres

Cocker Wood

St John's Wood

Leedsgate Farm

Forest Lodge

Sulehay Cottages

Works

WANSFORD RD

Old Sulehay Forest

SULEHAY RD

Old Sulehay Lodge

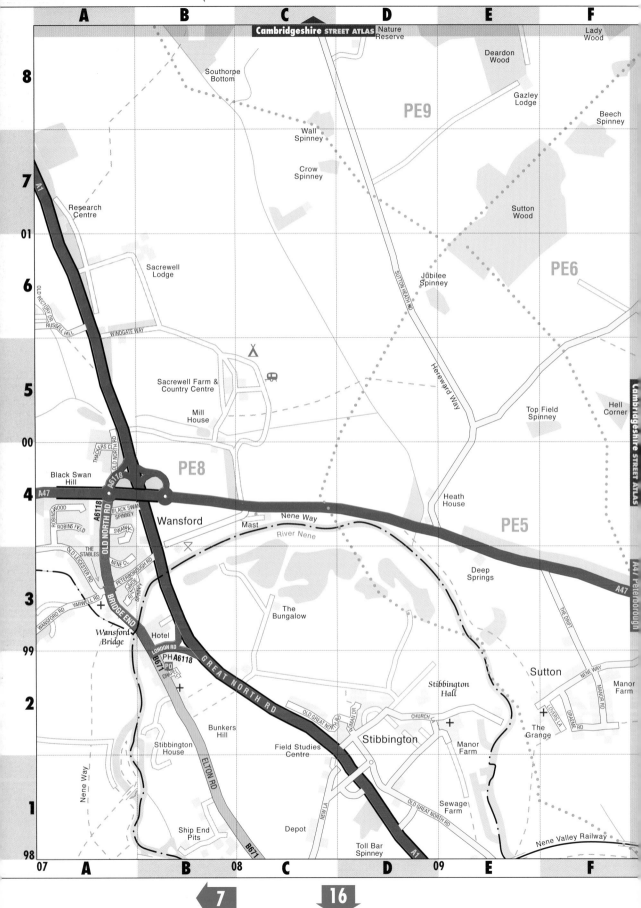

Cambridgeshire STREET ATLAS

Nature
Reserve

Lady
Wood

Deardon
Wood

PE9

Gazley
Lodge

Beech
Spinney

8

Southorpe
Bottom

Wall
Spinney

7

Crow
Spinney

Sutton
Wood

Research
Centre

01

Sacrewell
Lodge

PE6

Jubilee
Spinney

6

WINDGATE WAY

OLD RECTORY DR
RUSSELL HILL

SUTTON HEATH RD

Sacrewell Farm &
Country Centre

Hereward Way

Top Field
Spinney

Hell
Corner

5

Mill
House

00

THACKERS CL
OLD NORTH RD

PE8

Black Swan
Hill

A6118

4

A47

A6118
OLD NORTH RD

BLACK SWAN
SPINNEY

Heath
House

PE5

A47

A47 Peterborough

ROBINS
WOOD

ROBINS FIELD

SWAIN

Wansford

Mast

Nene Way

Nene Cl.

River Nene

THE
STABLES

OLD LEICESTER RD

NENE CL.

PETERBOROUGH RD

Deep
Springs

3

WANSFORD RD
YARWELL RD

BRIDGE END

GATE
PIT SPINNEY

The
Bungalow

THE DRIFT

Wansford
Bridge

Hotel

LONDON RD

A6118

GREAT NORTH RD

99

B671

PH
PO
CHAPEL

Stibbington
Hall

Sutton

NENE WAY
MANOR RD

Manor
Farm

2

Bunkers
Hill

OLD GREAT NOR

ROMAN DR

CHURCH LA.

LOVERS LA.
GRANGE RD

The
Grange

Stibbington
House

ELTON RD

Field Studies
Centre

Stibbington

Manor
Farm

Nene Way

1

NEW LA.

Depot

OLD GREAT NORTH RD

Sewage
Farm

Ship End
Pits

B671

Toll Bar
Spinney

A1

Nene Valley Railway

98

A    B    C    D    E    F

A6003 Oakham

Leicestershire STREET ATLAS

8

Colley Rise

Hotel

Manor Farm

Prestley Hill

7

Lyddington

Main St

Stoke Rd

The Green

Bluecoat La

PH

Bede House

Church La

97

Windmill Way

6

Thorpe Rd

Bee Hill

Gretton Rd

Sewage Works

LE15

B672

5

96

4

Lyddington Rd

3

95

LE16

Uppingham Rd

Middle Bridge

Mill Rd

2

The Old Vicarage

River Weiland

NN17

1

B672

94

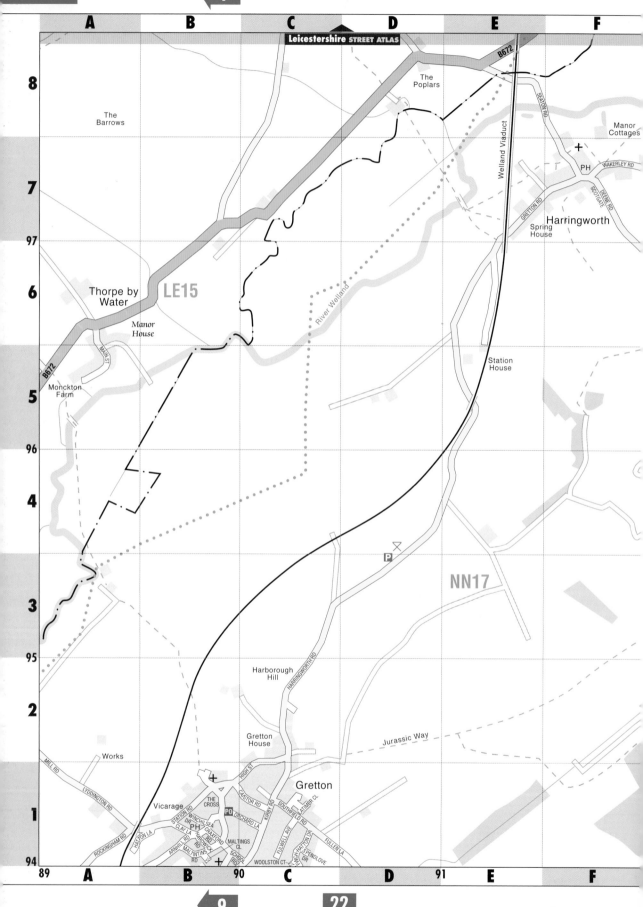

Leicestershire STREET ATLAS

The Poplars

The Barrows

B672

Manor
Cottages

PH

WAKERLEY RD

DENE RD

SCOTGATE

SEATON RD

Harringworth

GRETTON RD

Spring
House

Welland Viaduct

Thorpe by
Water

LE15

Manor
House

MAIN ST

B672

Monckton
Farm

River Welland

Station
House

P

NN17

Harborough
Hill

HARRINGWORTH RD

Jurassic Way

Works

MILL RD

LYDDINGTON RD

Gretton
House

High St

Gretton

LATIMER CL

ROCKINGHAM RD

Vicarage

THE
CROSS

STATION RD

WINCHILSEA
DR

CRAXFORD
RD

HADDOCK
RD

CAISTOR RD

KIRBY RD

SOUTHFIELD RD

FINCH LA

SPENDLOVE
DR

FULLEN LA

PO

ORCHARD LA

PH

CLAY LA

HATTON LA

ARBULL RD

MALTINGS
CL

MALTINTING
RD

SCHOOL
RD

FUSWELL LANE

WOOLSTON CT

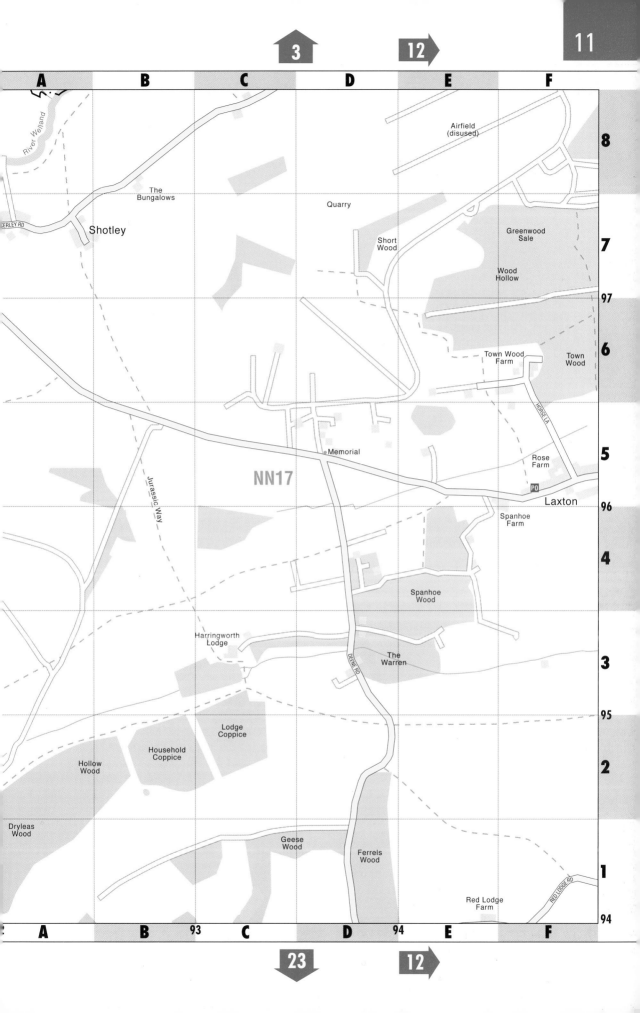

A    B    C    D    E    F

River Welland

The Bungalows

ERLEY RD

Shotley

8

Airfield (disused)

Quarry

Greenwood Sale

Short Wood

Wood Hollow

7

97

Town Wood Farm

Town Wood

6

HORSE LA

Memorial

NN17

Rose Farm

Laxton

PO

5

96

Spanhoe Farm

Jurassic Way

4

Spanhoe Wood

Harringworth Lodge

DEENE RD

The Warren

3

95

Lodge Coppice

Household Coppice

Hollow Wood

2

Dryleas Wood

Geese Wood

Ferrels Wood

Red Lodge Farm

RED LODGE RD

1

94

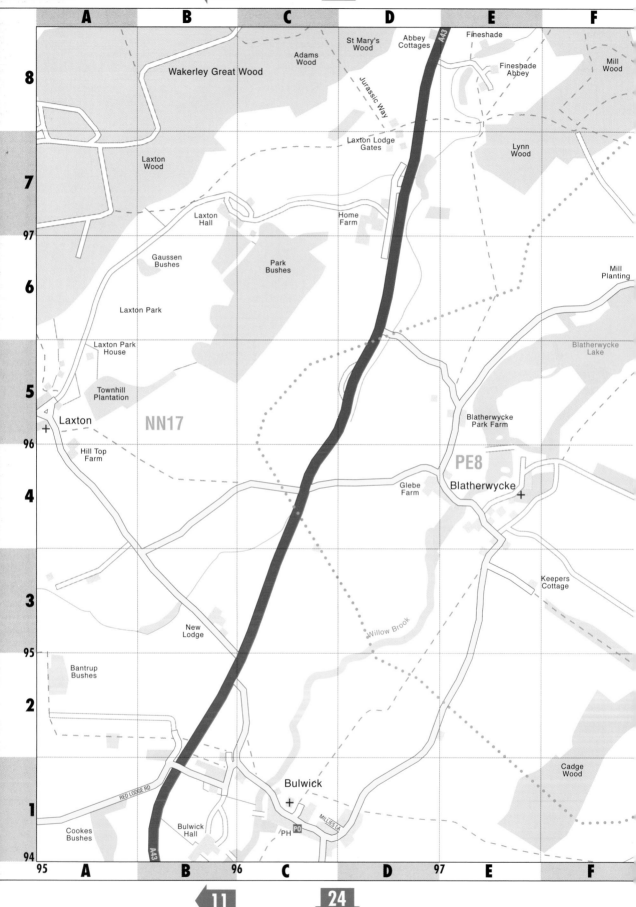

A   B   C   D   E   F

8   Wakerley Great Wood
Adams Wood
St Mary's Wood
Abbey Cottages
Fineshade
Fineshade Abbey
Mill Wood

Laxton Wood
Jurassic Way
Laxton Lodge Gates
Lynn Wood

7

97
Laxton Hall
Home Farm

Gaussen Bushes
Park Bushes
Mill Planting

6
Laxton Park
Blatherwycke Lake

Laxton Park House

5
Townhill Plantation
Blatherwycke Park Farm

NN17
Laxton

96
Hill Top Farm
PE8
Blatherwycke

4
Glebe Farm

Keepers Cottage

3
New Lodge
Willow Brook

95
Bantrup Bushes

2

Cadge Wood

1
Bulwick

RED LODGE RD
MILLIES LA
PH  PO
A43

Cookes Bushes
Bulwick Hall

94
95   A   B   96   C   D   97   E   F

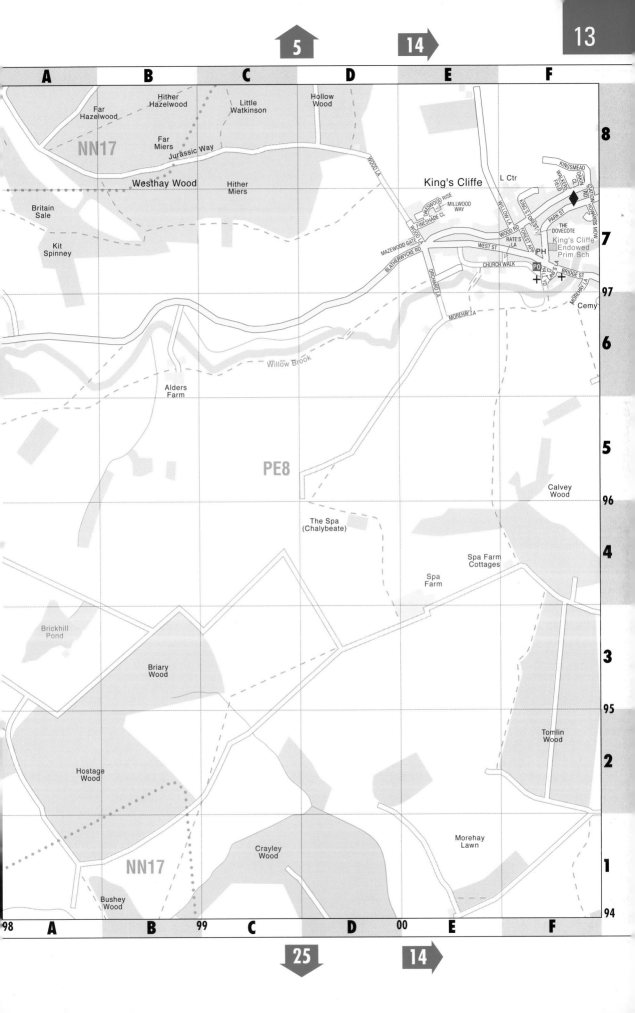

A    B    C    D    E    F

8

Rosary
Farm

Huskisson's
Lodge

Airfield
(disused)

Great Byards
Sale

Jack's
Green

PARK CL

PARK ST

Sewage
Works

7

Great Morton
Sale

Cornforth
Holmes

97

BRIDGE ST

Cemy

6

Bluefield
Farm

Quarry
Cottages

Bushrubs
Wood

APETHORPE RD

PE8

5

Willowbrook
Lodge

96

KINGS CLIFFE RD

PH    MANOR FARM

BRIDGE ST

4

THE ORCHARD    MAIN ST

HUNTING WAY    LAUNDRY RD

✛

Priors
Haw

Apethorpe

Apethorpe
Hall

3

Willow Brook

95

New
Wood

2

Conegar
Farm

ORCHARD CRES

PADDMORE CL

Woodnewton

ST MARYS CL

ST MARYS

ST HILLS

MEADOW
GATE

ORCHARD LA

Cheeseman's
Wood

THE PADDOCK    MAIN ST

WADES CL

PH

LINDSEY CL

NASSINGTON RD

1

Lodge
Farm

OUNDLE RD

Willowbrook
Farm

94

Fisher's Close
Spinney

Sewage
Works

A   B   C   D   E   F

Whiteland's
Coppice

SULEHAY RD

OLD SULEHAY RD

MAIN ST

Yarwell

PREBENDAL GN

Ring
Haw

Prebendel
Farm

**8**

Fair Oak
Sale

NASSINGTON RD

Cemy

**7**

**97**

Little Morton
Sale

APETHORPE RD

New
Sulehay

Pygrene

Ford

SEWTER
GDNS

EAST FIELDS

THE GROVE

NORTHFIELD LA

ST MARY'S WAY

MILL RD

**6**

Shortwood
Lodge

FENN CL

ST MARY'S

Nassington

PARKWAY CL

RUNNELL LA

PO

STATION RD

PH

Home
Farm

**5**

WESTMORELAND CL

ST MARY'S

Nassington
Prim Sch

PARKWAY

RUNNELL LA

PH

**PE8**

Manor
House

CHURCH ST

Manor
Farm

**96**

WOODNEWTON RD

FOTHERINGHAY RD

**4**

Newton
Hill

Newton
Spinney

Swan's
Nest

**3**

**95**

Nene Way

**2**

Park
Spinney

Park
Lodge

**1**

Willow Brook

**94**

A   05   B   C   06   D   E   F

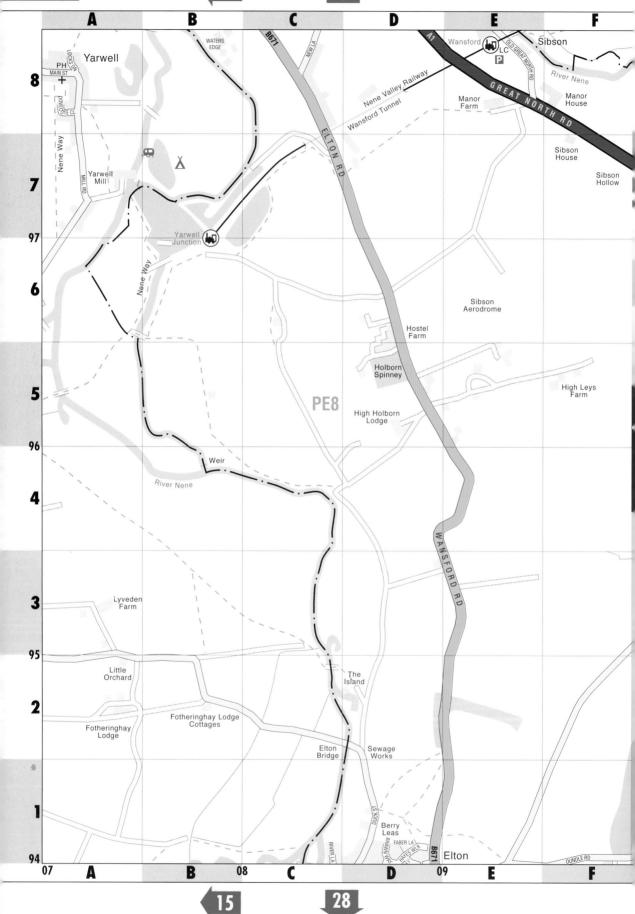

15
8

A B C D E F

8

Yarwell
Wansford
Sibson
PH
MAIN ST
Nene Valley Railway
Manor House
DOVECOTE CL
Wansford Tunnel
Manor Farm
GREAT NORTH RD
7
Yarwell Mill
Sibson House
Sibson Hollow
97
Yarwell Junction

6
Sibson Aerodrome
Hostel Farm

5
Holborn Spinney
High Leys Farm
High Holborn Lodge

96
Weir
River Nene
4

3
Lyveden Farm
WANSFORD RD

95
Little Orchard
The Island
2
Fotheringhay Lodge Cottages
Sewage Works
Fotheringhay Lodge
Elton Bridge

1
Berry Leas
Elton
94
A B 08 C D 09 E F

PE8

ELTON RD
B671
KEW LA
A1
OLD GREAT NORTH RD
River Nene
Nene Way
MILL RD
LOCKS GN
Nene Way
WATERS EDGE
DUCK ST
BRAWN WAY
HAYES WLK
FABER LA
B671
RIVER LA
OUNDLE RD

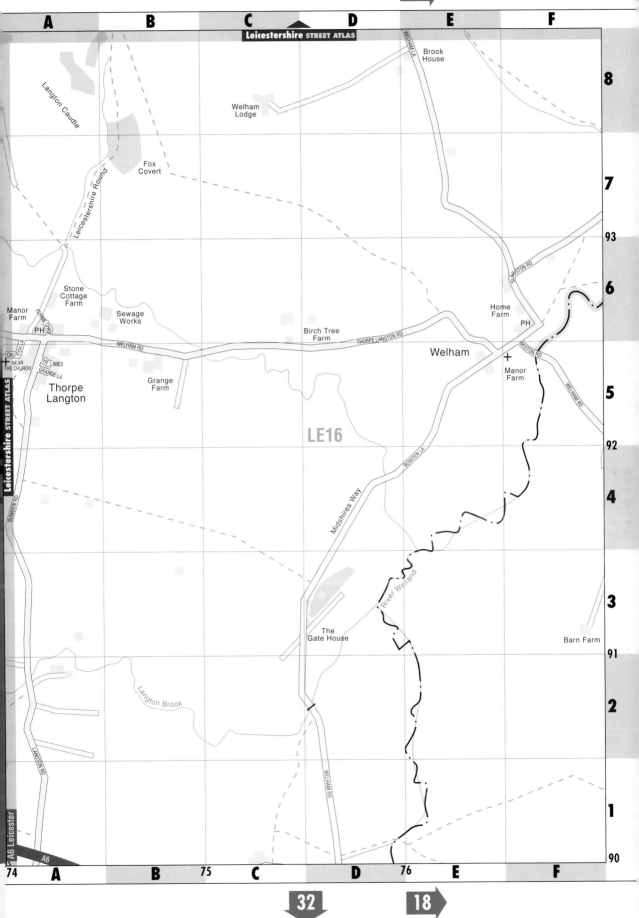

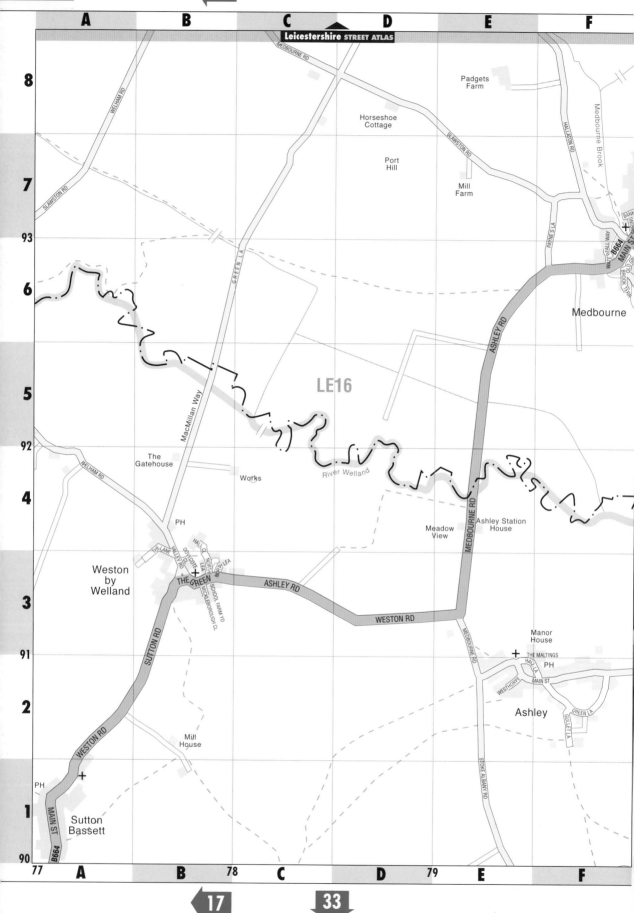

Leicestershire STREET ATLAS

A B C D E F

8

Padgets
Farm

Horseshoe
Cottage

Port
Hill

Mill
Farm

Medbourne

7

SLAWSTON RD

SLAWSTON RD

GREEN LA

PAYNE'S LA

ASHLEY RD

WATERY WAY

B664

MAIN ST

Medbourne Brook

HALLATON RD

BANK

BROOK TERR

93

6

MacMillan Way

**LE16**

River Welland

Medbourne

5

92

The
Gatehouse

Works

MEDBOURNE RD

Meadow
View

Ashley Station
House

4

PELHAM RD

WELHAM RD

PH

Weston
by
Welland

THE LANE

VALLEY RD

HALL CL

DOVECOTE
CL

NORTH
LEA

SOUTH LEA

THE GREEN

SCHOOL FARM YD

MICKLEBOROUGH CL

ASHLEY RD

WESTON RD

Manor
House

THE MALTINGS

HALL LA

PH

3

91

SUTTON RD

MEDBOURNE RD

WESTHORPE

MAIN ST

GULLET LA

GREEN LA

Ashley

2

WESTON RD

Mill
House

STOKE ALBANY RD

1

PH

MAIN ST

B664

Sutton
Bassett

90

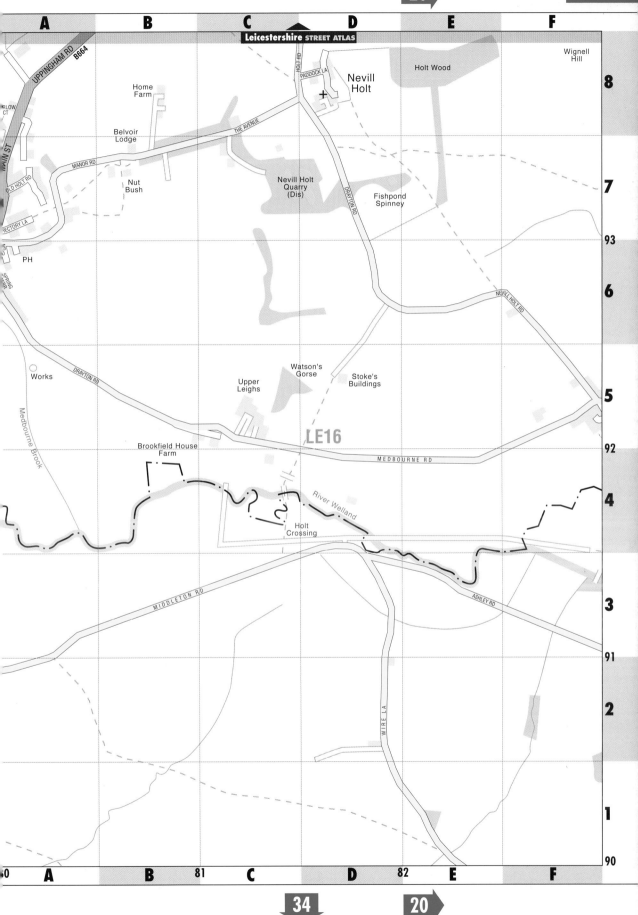

Leicestershire STREET ATLAS

UPPINGHAM RD
B664

Home
Farm

Nevill
Holt

Holt Wood

Wignell
Hill

8

HARLOW
CT

MAIN ST

Belvoir
Lodge

THE AVENUE

PADDOCK LA

HOLT RD

OLD HOLT RD

MANOR RD

Nut
Bush

Nevill Holt
Quarry
(Dis)

Fishpond
Spinney

DRAYTON RD

7

RECTORY LA

93

PH

SPRING CRESCENT

NEVILL HOLT RD

6

Works

DRAYTON RD

Watson's
Gorse

Stoke's
Buildings

Medbourne Brook

Upper
Leighs

5

Brookfield House
Farm

LE16

92

River Welland

Holt
Crossing

4

MIDDLETON RD

ASHLEY RD

3

91

WIRE LA

2

1

90

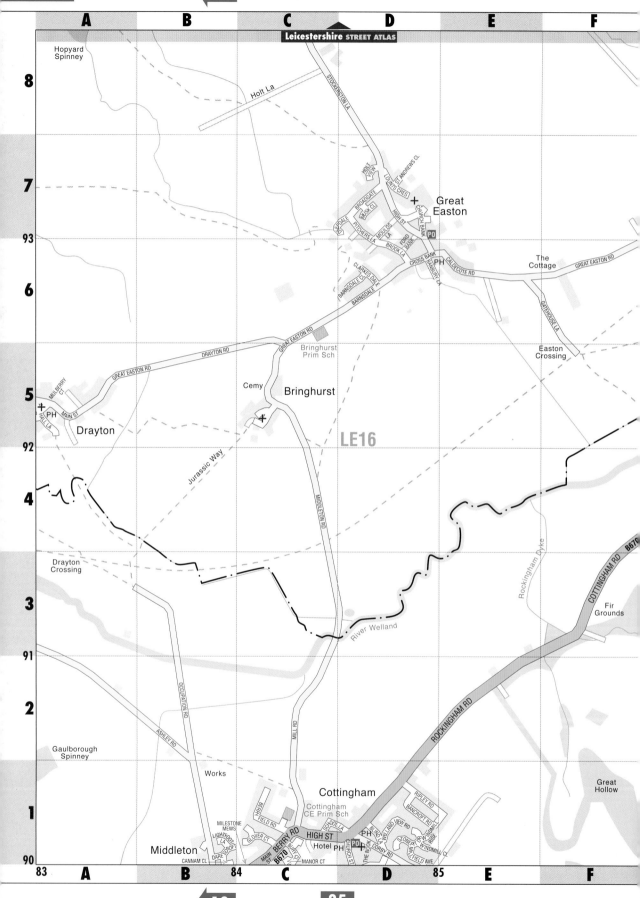

**Leicestershire** STREET ATLAS

Hopyard Spinney

Holt La

STOCKERSTON LA

HOLT VIEW

ST ANDREWS CL

LOUNTS CRES

**Great Easton**

BROADGATE

MASK CL

SPDALE

PICKERS LA

HIGH ST

MOULDS LA

CHURCH BANK

PO

BROOK LA

POND BANK

PH

CROSS BANK

CALLICOTE RD

BANBURY LA

CLARKES DALE CT

BARNSDALE CT

BARNSDALE

The Cottage

GREAT EASTON RD

GATEHOUSE LA

GREAT EASTON RD

DRAYTON RD

Bringhurst Prim Sch

Easton Crossing

MULBERRY CT

Cemy

**Bringhurst**

GREAT EASTON RD

MAIN ST

HALL LA

PH

**Drayton**

Jurassic Way

**LE16**

Drayton Crossing

MIDDLETON RD

Rockingham Dyke

Fir Grounds

OCCUPATION RD

River Welland

COTTINGHAM RD

B670

Gaulborough Spinney

ASHLEY RD

ROCKINGHAM RD

Great Hollow

Works

**Cottingham**

RIPLEY RD

MILL RD

BERRY RD

B670

MILESTONE MEWS

LIGHTFOOT LA

DARE CROFT

GLOVER CT

MAIN ST

SCHOOL LA

HIGH ST

Hotel

PH

Cottingham CE Prim Sch

BANCROFT RD

WELLAND VIEW RD

PH

PO

CHURCH ST

THE HOOK

STONEY

CORBY RD

WINDMILL RISE

WINDMILL CL

FIELD AVE

**Middleton**

CANNAM CL

MANOR CT

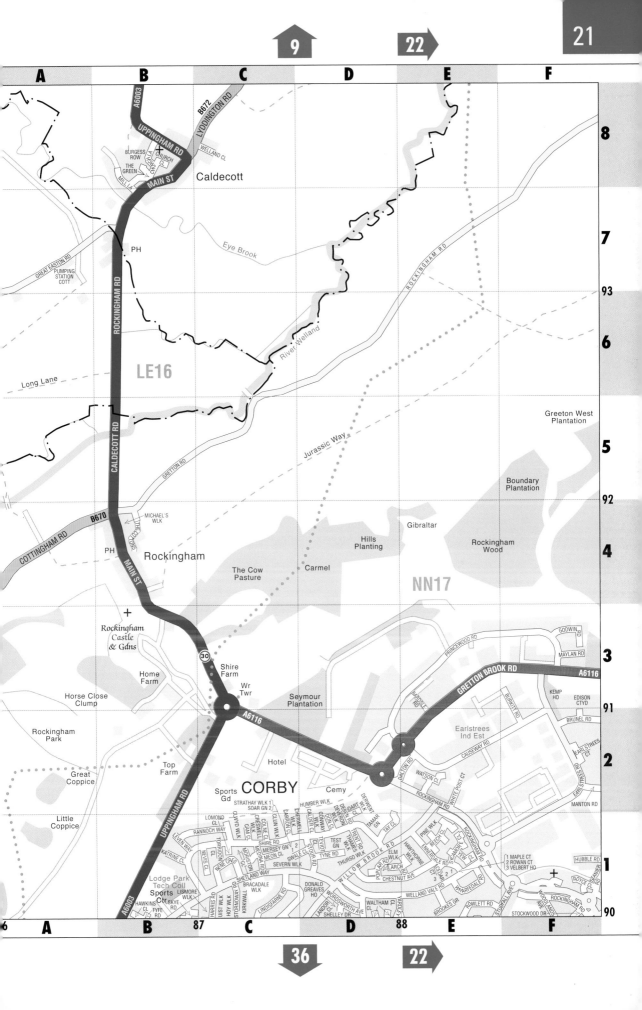

A  B  C  D  E  F

8

Rockingham Rd
NORTHERN CL
KIRBY RD
WELLAND CL
Wr Twr
STAFFORD RD
FINCH-HATTON DR
Gretton Prim Sch
Jurassic Way
South Lodge
FULLEN LA
Kirby Hall Farm

7

93

CORBY RD

6

Greeton East Plantation

Corby Tunnel

5

NN17
Keepers Lodge Farm
Kirby Lodge

92

Brookfield Plantation
Forest Nursery
KIRBY LA

GRETTON BROOK RD

4

Rockingham Motor Speedway

GRETTON RD

P

Factory
P
P
Weldon Lodge

3

Greeton Brook Plantation
A6116

91

MITCHELL RD
PHOENIX PARKWAY
HERITAGE WAY
Willowbrook East Ind Est
SHELTON CT

2

FLEMING RD
BRUNEL RD
ALEXANDER CT
BRUNEL CT
Earlstrees Ind Est
MANTON RD
SHELTON RD
PYWELL CT
PYWELL RD
SONDES RD
PRIORS CT 1
ADELAIDE HO 2
MELBOURNE HO 3
PERTH HO 4
DARWIN HO 5
CANBERRA HO 6
ARNSLEY RD 7
BIRCHINGTON RD

CORBY

STOCKBRIDGE RD
MACADAM RD
MARCONI CTYD
RUTHERFORD CT
BAIRD RD
PRIESTLEY CT
ARKWRIGHT RD
CULVERT WAY
STEEL RD
BARON CT
SALLOW RD
CAVENDISH CTYD
Weldon North Ind Est
Corby Gate Bsns P
VENTURE C

1

HUBBLE RD
STANIER RD
CRICK CL
PARSONS GR
LISTER CT
JAMES WATT AVE
STEPHENSON WAY
NEWTON GR
GENNER RD
GAYDON HO
DARWIN
BOYLE RD
DARWIN RD
HUNTERS RD
BRACEY RD
Enterprise Ind Pk
CORBY CT
A6116

90

89  A  B  90  C  D  91  E  F

A   B   C   D   E   F

Mavis Wood

Bamford Spinney

8

Sweethill Spinney

7

93

Gretton Brook

Kirby Spinney

Parker's Spinney

Manor Farm

Deene   Deene Hall

6

Kirby Hall

KIRBY LA

Home Farm

Deene Park

5

The Rookery

Fir Plantation

NN17

92

4

Dibbin's Wood

Hollow Wood

Bangrave Wood

Weldon Little Wood

CH

Priors Hall Quarry

Priors Hall Plantation

A43

3

91

Shire Cottage

Lodge Farm

2

CHINGTON

GRETTON RD

RS HAW RD

PRIORS CT

STAMFORD RD

Weldon Park

1

ARNSLEY RD

A43

90

A   B   93   C   D   94   E   F

A  B  C  D  E  F

8

Kennel
Coppice

Gretton Brook

7

Great
Spinney

Bulwick
Lodge

93

NN17

Glebe
Farm

+

6

The
Lake

Barratt's
Coppice

Rough
Close

DEENETHORPE LA

5

OSIER BED LA

92

Forest
Lodge

4

Deenethorpe

BENEFIELD RD

Burn
Coppice

STAMFORD RD

A43

3

Home
Farm
Lodge

91

Langley
Coppice

2

Airfield
(dis)

PE8

1

Mast

90

95  A  B  96  C  D  97  E  F

A B C D E F

Holey
Brookes

Boar's
Head
Cottage

Blackmore
Thick Farm

Boar's
Head
Farm

NN17

Shire
Hill
Lodge

**93**

Stone
Hill

**6**

Frere Hill
Wood

Great
Old
Sale

Little
Old
Sale

New Hall

**5**

Frere
Hill

Crossway
Hand
Farm

Vicarage
Farm

**92**

Crossway
Hand
Cottages

**4**

Wymond
Hill

PE8

Tottenhoe
Lodge

**3**

**91**

Westwood
Lodge

Provost
Lodge

**2**

Glapthorn Cow
Pasture

Sandy
Forth
Lodge

**1**

**90**

'8 A B 99 C D 00 E F

25
14

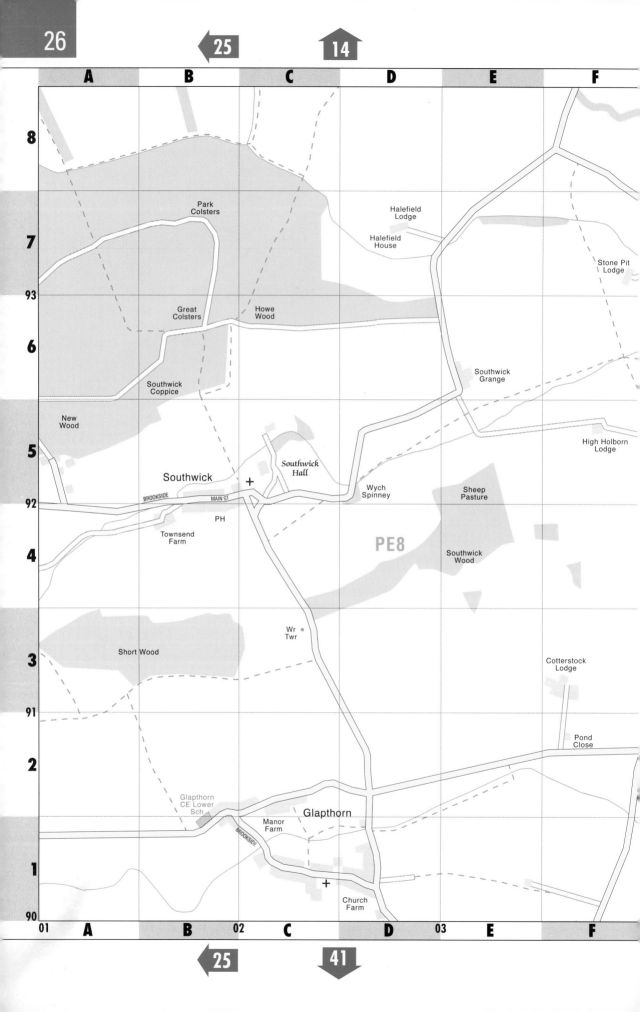

A B C D E F

8

Park
Colsters

Halefield
Lodge

7

Halefield
House

Stone Pit
Lodge

93

Great
Colsters

Howe
Wood

6

Southwick
Coppice

Southwick
Grange

New
Wood

High Holborn
Lodge

5

Southwick

Southwick
Hall

Wych
Spinney

Sheep
Pasture

92

BROOKSIDE      MAIN ST

PE8

PH

Southwick
Wood

4

Townsend
Farm

Wr
Twr

3

Short Wood

Cotterstock
Lodge

91

Pond
Close

2

Glapthorn
CE Lower
Sch

Glapthorn

Manor
Farm

BROOKSIDE

1

Church
Farm

90

01      A      B      02      C      D      03      E      F

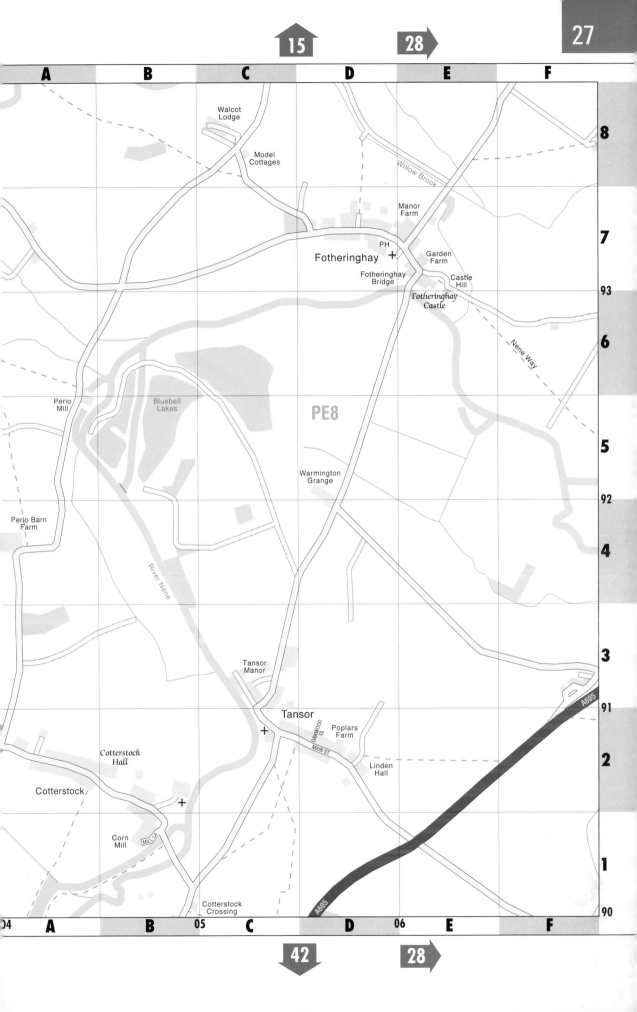

PE8

A  B  C  D  E  F

CH

Elton
Furze

Lodge
Farm

Furze
Farm

Rectory
Farm

Elton Lodge
Farm

GREENHILL RD

A605

60

Greenhill
Lodge

Bate's
Lodge

GREENHILL RD

Lawrence's
Lodge

PE7

BULLOCK RD

Bonser's
Lodge

Stockhill
Lodge

Tookey
Farm

Billing Brook

Field End
Close

Morborne
Hill

PE8

Mast

Mast

Radio
Station

Papley
Gorse

Long Spinney

Horse Close
Hovel

America
Farm

Morborne
Hill Top

8

7

93

6

5

92

4

3

91

2

1

90

10  A  B  11  C  D  12  E  F

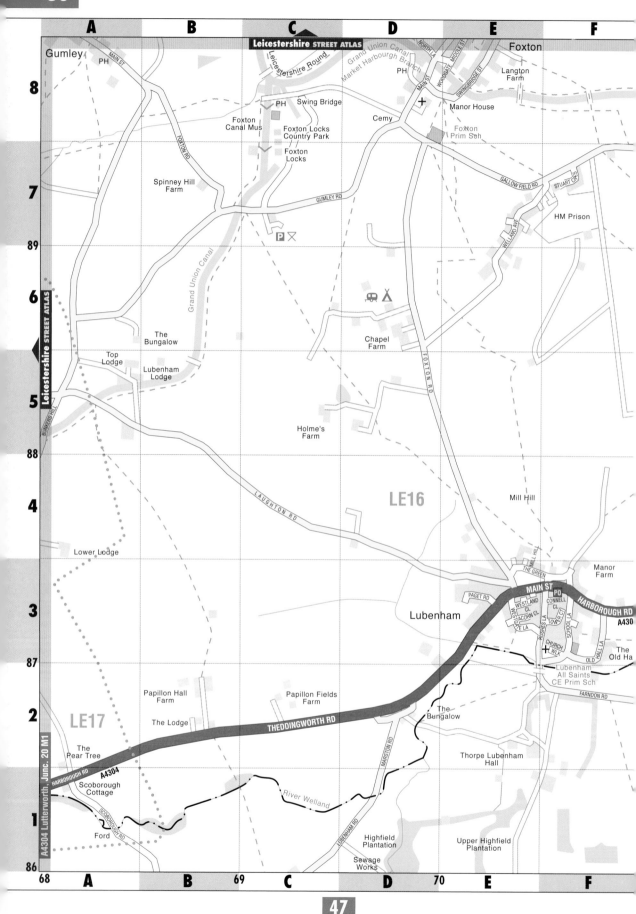

Gumley

Foxton

LE16

LE17

Lubenham

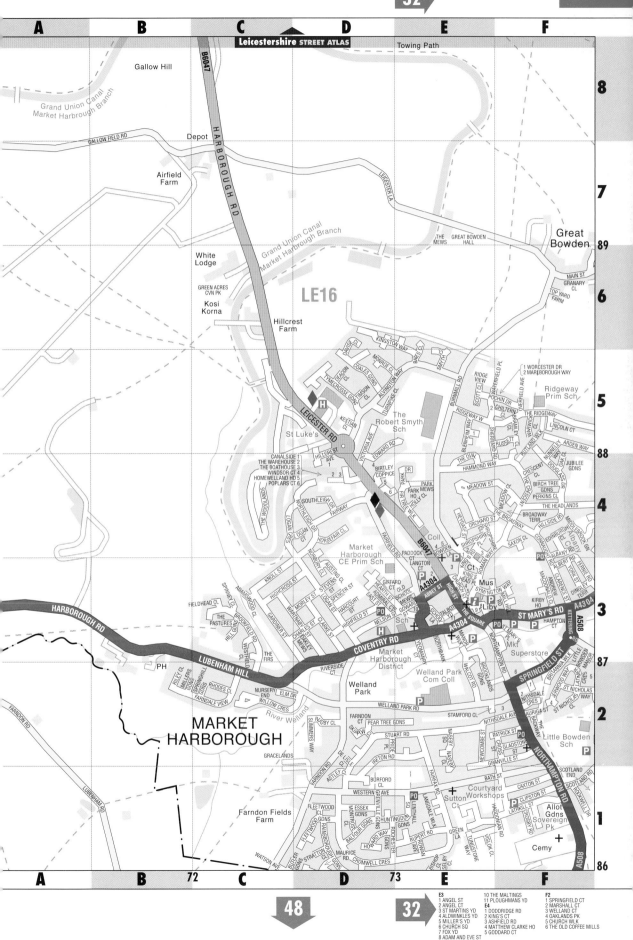

**Leicestershire** STREET ATLAS

Towing Path

8

Gallow Hill

Grand Union Canal
Market Harbrough Branch

Depot

7

Airfield
Farm

Great
Bowden

89

White
Lodge

Grand Union Canal
Market Harbrough Branch

THE
MEWS

GREAT BOWDEN
HALL

MAIN ST

GREEN ACRES
CVN PK

**LE16**

GRANARY
CL

6

Kosi
Korna

TOP YARD
FARM

Hillcrest
Farm

Kingston Way

1 WORCESTER DR
2 MARLBOROUGH WAY

Ridgeway
Prim Sch

5

St Luke's

The
Robert Smyth
Sch

88

CANALSIDE 1
THE WAREHOUSE 2
THE BOATHOUSE 3
WINDSOR CT 4
HOMEWELLAND HO 5
POPLARS CT 6

Birtley
Coppice

THE HEADLANDS

4

Market
Harborough
CE Prim Sch

Coll

A4304

Mus

Liby

St Mary's Rd

A4304

A508

3

**HARBOROUGH RD**

Coventry Rd

Market
Harborough
District

Mkt
Superstore

87

**LUBENHAM HILL**

PH

Welland Park
Com Coll

Welland Park

Little Bowden
Sch

2

**MARKET
HARBOROUGH**

River Welland

Farndon
Ct

NORTHAMPTON RD

GRACELANDS

Courtyard
Workshops

1

Farndon Fields
Farm

Sutton
Ct

Allot
Gdns
Sovereign
Pk

Cemy

86

E3
1 ANGEL ST
2 ANGEL CT
3 ST MARTINS YD
4 ALDWINKLES YD
5 MILLER'S YD
6 CHURCH SQ
7 FOX YD
8 ADAM AND EVE ST
9 FACTORY LA

10 THE MALTINGS
11 PLOUGHMANS YD
E4
1 DODDRIDGE RD
2 KING'S CT
3 ASHFIELD RD
4 MATTHEW CLARKE HO
5 GODDARD CT

F2
1 SPRINGFIELD CT
2 MARSHALL CT
3 WELLAND CT
4 OAKLANDS PK
5 CHURCH WLK
6 THE OLD COFFEE MILLS

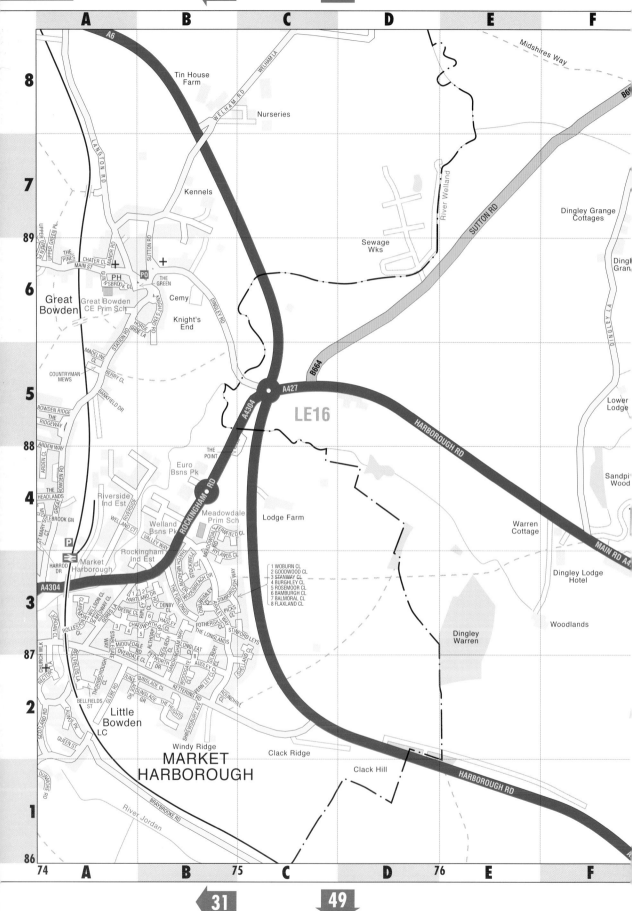

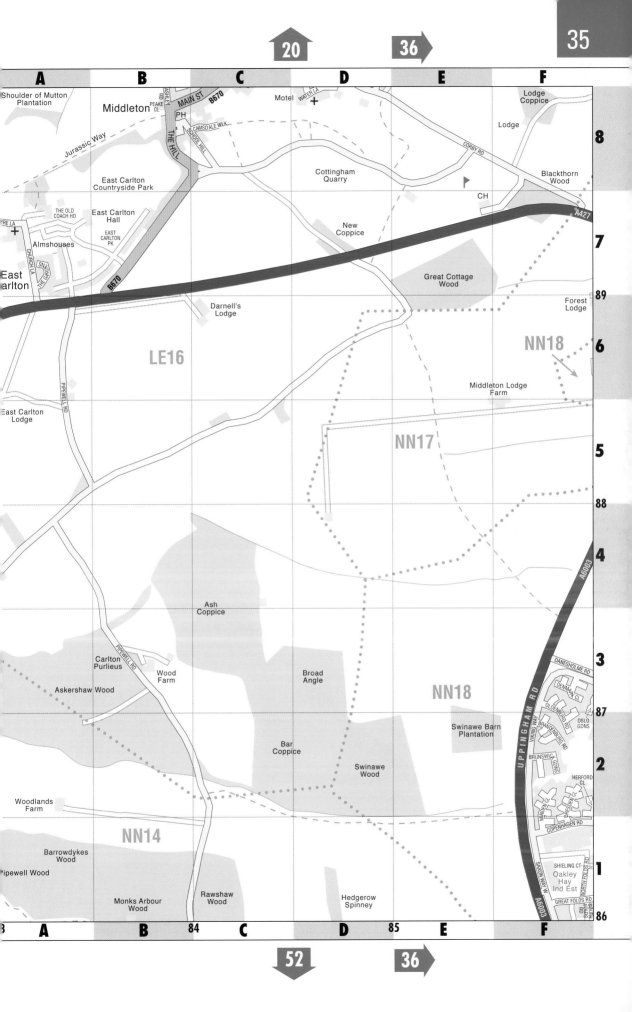

A  B  C  D  E  F

Shoulder of Mutton
Plantation

Middleton

Jurassic Way

East Carlton
Countryside Park

THE OLD
COACH HO

East Carlton
Hall

EAST
CARLTON
PK

Almshouses

East
Carlton

PIPEWELL RD

LE16

East Carlton
Lodge

Motel

Lodge
Coppice

Lodge

CORBY RD

Blackthorn
Wood

CH

A427

New
Coppice

Cottingham
Quarry

Great Cottage
Wood

Forest
Lodge

Darnell's
Lodge

NN18

Middleton Lodge
Farm

NN17

Ash
Coppice

Carlton
Purlieus

Wood
Farm

PIPEWELL RD

Askershaw Wood

Broad
Angle

NN18

Swinawe Barn
Plantation

Bar
Coppice

Swinawe
Wood

DANESHOLME RD

DENMARK CL

OLDENBURG RD

OSLO
GDNS

VIKING WAY

BRANDENBURG RD

BRUNSWICK GDNS

HERFORD
CL

DRESDEN CL

MUNICH CL

COPENHAGEN RD

UPPINGHAM RD

A6003

Woodlands
Farm

NN14

Barrowdykes
Wood

Pipewell Wood

Monks Arbour
Wood

Rawshaw
Wood

Hedgerow
Spinney

SHIELING CT

Oakley
Hay
Ind Est

GREAT FOLDS RD

SAXON WAY

NORTH FOLDS RD

SOUTH
FOLDS
RD

A6003

8

7

89

6

5

88

4

87

3

2

86

1

A  B  84  C  D  85  E  F

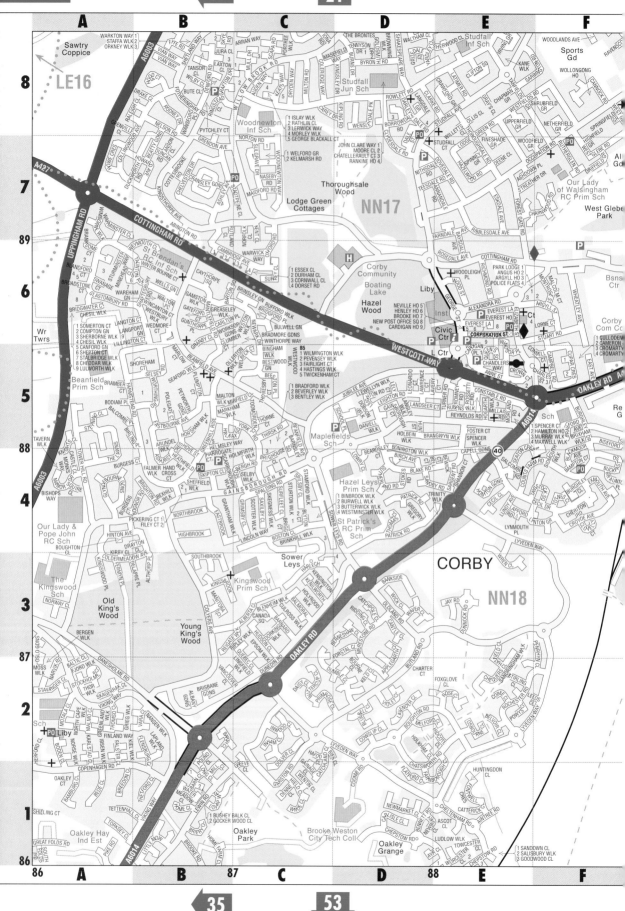

A | B | C | D | E | F

**8**

AINSLEY RD    Ind Est
A427
LARRATT RD    WALNUT CL.
BRAMBLEWOOD RD
GRETTON RD    Ind Est
HALL'S CL    BRANSON MEWS
CHAPEL RD    DOBBIN CL    DEENESIDE
ROMAN CL    PH
STAMFORD RD A427
DEENE END
CRICKETERS GM
EAST CRCS
Weldon
WATER LA    DASH PRM CL    KINGS RD VIEW    ROSE AVE    BRIDGE ST    HIGH ST    ROSE CT    ORCHARD CT    CHURCH    SCHOOL LA
Weldon CE Prim Sch    PO
THE ASHES
GANDER LA    ORCHARD
CORBY RD
HILLSIDE CRES
Manor House
CHURCH WLK
Mast
A427
ROUNDLE RD

**7**

Weldon Stone Quarry
CHURCH ST
WOODLANDS DR
Allot Gdns
SPINNEY RD
WOODSIDE PK

PE8

**89**

STAMFORD RD

**6**

NN17

**5**

**88**

**4**

Harry's Wood
Upper Laundimer Wood
Harry's Park Wood

**3**

Middle Laundimer Wood
NN14
Meadow Leys
Bushylawn Lodge

**87**

A6116    BRIGSTOCK RD

**2**

Works
Nether Laundimer Wood
Old Dry Hills
Old Dry Bushes

STANION RD
Brigstock Camp
OLD DRY LA

**1**

Stanion Lodge
Red Piece
STANION RD
Maltley Farm
A6116

**86**

92 | A | B | 93 | C | D | 94 | E | F

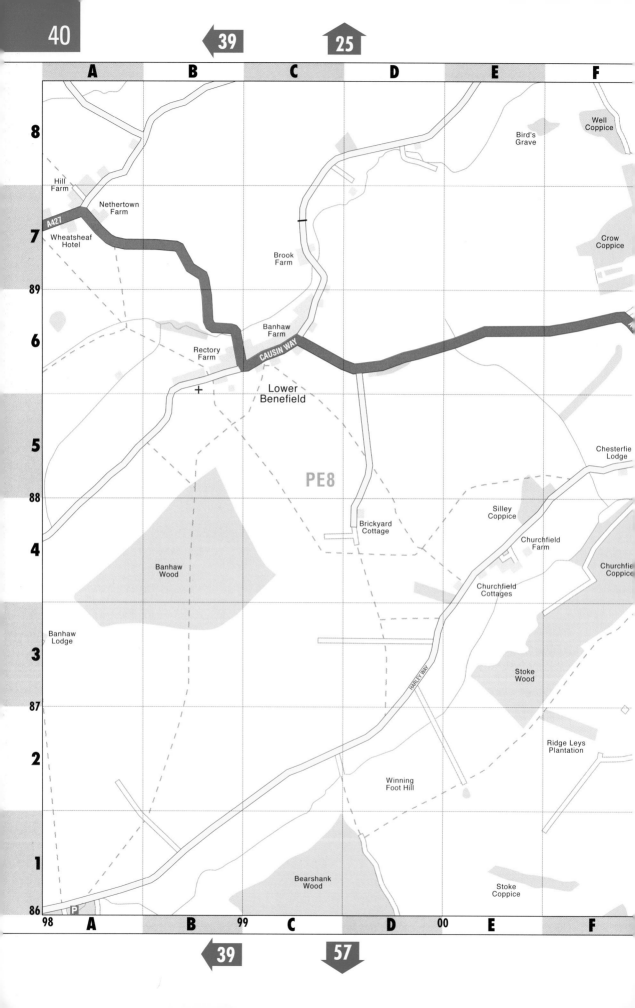

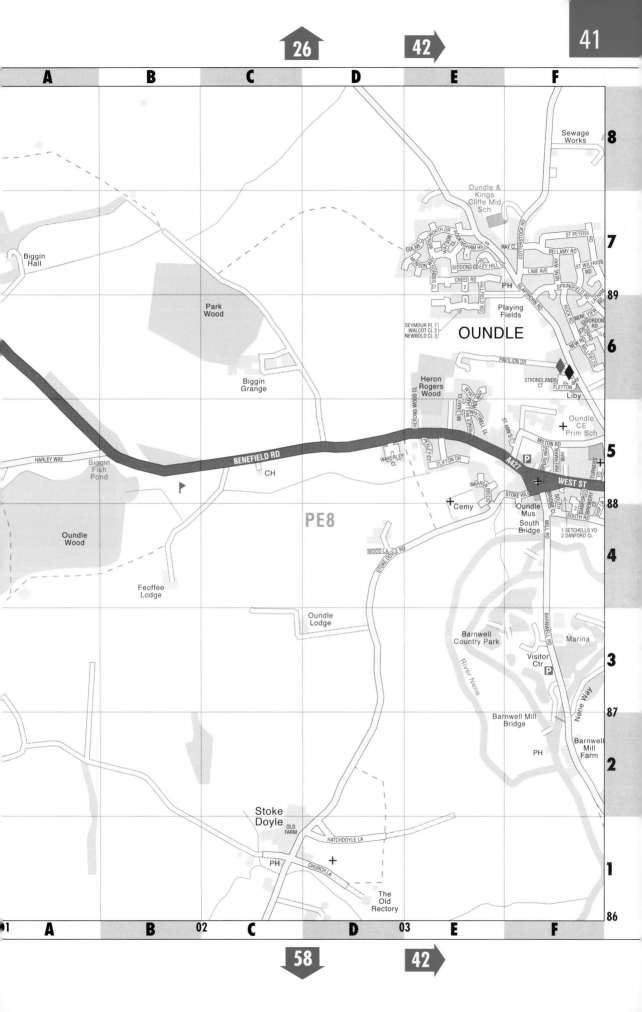

A   B   C   D   E   F

8

Tansor Lodge

A605

ELMINGTON COTTS   Elmington Lodge

Elmington

7

Elmington Top Lodge

Rifle Range

1 DERWENT HO
2 SEVERN HO
3 MEDWAY HO
4 TRENT HO

OCCUPATION RD

SPRINGFIELD RD

89

Oundle Wharf

ST PETERS RD

NEW RD

LAXTON RD

STATION RD   A427

North Bridge

Nene Way

RIVERSIDE M.

2 3 4

6

BRIDGE LA

VICTORIA RD

OUNDLE

Nene Way

FOTHERINGHAY MEWS

Chapel Farm

Ashton

Entrance Lodge

VINE CL

EAST RD

NORTH ST

Laxton Jun Sch

Brickyard Wood

HARPOOL LA

HAVELOCK COTTS

HALFMOON MEWS

Oundle Sch

PH

5

Ashton Green Farm

BLACKPOT LA

NEW ST

CHURCH

A427

DUCK LA

Nene Valley Bsns Pk

ASHTON RD

Manor House

DRUMMING WELL LA

WEST ST

MASON'S

TANEY CT

WEBB CL

ST CHRISTOPHER'S DR

PE8

88

Art Gall

GALLERY LA

CROWN CT

Herne Lodge

ROWELL WAY

BRAMSTON CL

BASSETT PL

BASSETT FORD RD

SOUTH RD

4

RIVERSIDE CL

Prince William Sch

HERNE RD

River Nene

3

New Lodge Farm

HIGHFIELDS

CHURCH ROW

Nene Way

Red Lodge Farm

PH

KINGS ARMS LA

MAIN ST

DUKE ST

POLEBROC

87

CHURCH ST

HEMINGTON RD

CIRCUS GR

2

Sands Barn

ROBERT'S LA

Sewage Works

1

Horse Close Spinney

A605

Sweetley Spinney

86

A   B   C   D   E   F

8

7

89

6

Rectory
Farm

Tansor Wold
Farm

Tansor
Wold

Miriam's Cover

Stamford
Hovels

Stamford
Cover

Toll Bar
Gate

5

Warmington Spinney
Plantation

The
Gorse

**PE8**

Ashton Wold
Farm

West
Lodge

Ashton Wold
House

88

Greenhouse
Corner

4

Ashton Wold

The
Common

Lutton
Hovels

Water Gap
Field

Allard's
Home

Lake Fields

Bluestone
Covert

**Polebrook**

Lutton Road
Cottages

3

FERGUSON'S CL

MORGAN'S CL

MAIN ST

Polebrook Airfield
Nature Reserve

87

HALL
GDNS

Polebrook
CE Prim
Sch

LUTTON RD

Polebrook
Lodge

Rectory
Farm

2

Airfield
(disused)

1

86

**A** **B** **C** **D** **E** **F**

8

Cold
Harbour

New Farm

Ongutein Manor
Farm

7

Lodge
Farm

89

PE7

Papley
Cottages

Papley

6

Field
Farm

Papley
Coppice

WASHINGLEY LA

Papley
Farm

Ringmoor
Spinney

5

BULLOCK RD

88

Grange
Farm

Lutton Farm

Woodbine
Farm

MILTON TERR

Chapel
End

4

Lutton

Manor
Farm

The Old
Rectory

PE8

3

Lutton Lodge
Farm

87

2

High Holborn
Farm

Long
Plantation

PE28 →

1

Top
Lodge

86

**A** **B** 11 **C** **D** 12 **E** **F**

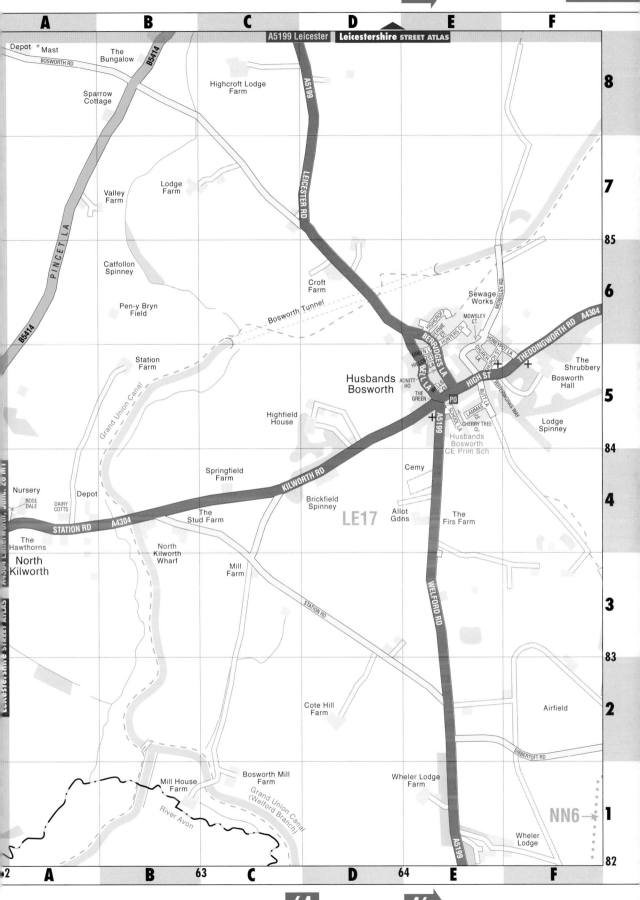

A5199 Leicester | **Leicestershire** STREET ATLAS

A    B    C    D    E    F

8

7

85

6

5

84

4

83

3

2

82

Depot  • Mast
BOSWORTH RD
The Bungalow
B5414

Sparrow
Cottage

Highcroft Lodge
Farm

A5199

Valley
Farm

Lodge
Farm

PINCET LA

Catfollon
Spinney

LEICESTER RD

Pen-y Bryn
Field

Croft
Farm

B5414

Bosworth Tunnel

Sewage
Works

MOWSLEY RD

HIGHCROFT
FERNIE CT
Hunters Cl
Mowsley
CT

THEDDINGWORTH RD  A4304

Station
Farm

Grand Union Canal

BERRIDGES LA

GREEN LA
HILLCREST
WELLS CL

HONEYPOT LA
CHURCH LA
CHURCH

The
Shrubbery
Bosworth
Hall

Husbands
Bosworth

HIGH ST

PO

WATERWORKS WAY

Highfield
House

ADNITT
HO
THE
GREEN

A5199

BUTT LA

LAMMAS
CL
CHERRY TREE
CL

SCHOOL LA

Lodge
Spinney

Husbands
Bosworth
CE Prim Sch

LE17

Springfield
Farm

Cemy

Brickfield
Spinney

Allot
Gdns

The
Firs Farm

Nursery
ROSE
DALE
DAIRY
COTTS

Depot

The Stud Farm

North
Kilworth
Wharf

KILWORTH RD

WELFORD RD

STATION RD  A4304

The
Hawthorns

North
Kilworth

Mill
Farm

STATION RD

Airfield

SIBBERTOFT RD

Cote Hill
Farm

Wheler Lodge
Farm

NN6 →

Mill House
Farm

Bosworth Mill
Farm

Grand Union Canal
(Welford Branch)

River Avon

A5199

Wheler
Lodge

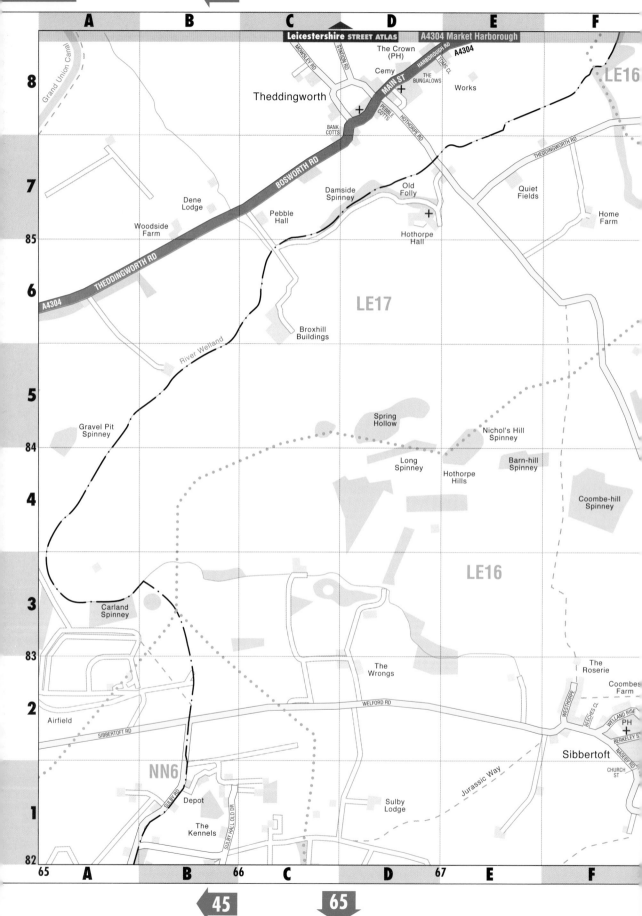

Leicestershire STREET ATLAS    A4304 Market Harborough

LE16

The Crown (PH)

Cemy

MORNSLEY RD
STATION RD

MAIN ST
HARBOROUGH RD
A4304
TOMS CL

THE BUNGALOWS
Works

Theddingworth

PEBBLE COTTS
HOTHORPE RD

BANK COTTS

BOSWORTH RD

Dene Lodge

Damside Spinney

Old Folly

THEDDINGWORTH RD

Quiet Fields

Pebble Hall

Hothorpe Hall

Home Farm

Woodside Farm

THEDDINGWORTH RD

A4304

LE17

Broxhill Buildings

River Welland

Gravel Pit Spinney

Spring Hollow

Nichol's Hill Spinney

Long Spinney

Barn-hill Spinney

Hothorpe Hills

Coombe-hill Spinney

Carland Spinney

LE16

The Wrongs

The Roserie

Coombes Farm

WELFORD RD

WESTHORPE
BEECHES CL
WELAND RISE
PH
BERKELEY ST

Airfield

SIBBERTOFT RD

NASEBY RD

Sibbertoft

NN6

SILBY RD

Depot

SULBY HALL OLD DR

Jurassic Way

CHURCH ST

The Kennels

Sulby Lodge

47 31

A B C D E F

8

LUBENHAM RD
THE LEALAND
HARBOROUGH RD
COUNCIL HO'S
HOME FARM CL

Brierley Farm

Harrison Cl

Watson Ave
Maurice Rd
Barnard Gdns
Hopton Fields
Gerrard Gdns
Rainsborough Gdns
Bishop Cl
Lindsey Gdns
Ritche Pk
Argyle Pk
Jackson
Vaughan Cl
Selby Cl
Dallison Cl

Leisure Ctr

TORCH WAY

NORTHAMPTON RD A508

New House Farm

Farndon Fields Prim Sch

Oxendon Lodge Farm

Oxendon Lodge Cottages

JUSTIN PARK CVN SITE

7

MARSTON LA

The Dales

East Farndon Hall

BACK LA
MAIN ST

East Farndon

CH

85

Jurassic Way

6

RECTORY CT

Farn Wood

OXENDON RD

Jurassic Way

Allot Gdns

CLIPSTON RD

The Lodge

Little Oxendon

LE16

84

FARNDON RD

Waterloo House

4

HARBOROUGH RD

The Spinney

West End

CLIPSTON LA

MEWS COTTS
OXENDON HALL
Main St

PH

BRAYBROOKE RD

Oxendon House

Great Oxendon

Midshires Way

83

2

HARBOROUGH RD

CLIPSTON RD

Sewage Works

NORTHAMPTON RD

Station Cottage
OXENDON RD

1

SIBBERTOFT RD

OXENDON RD

A508

82

71 A B 72 C D 73 E F

47 67

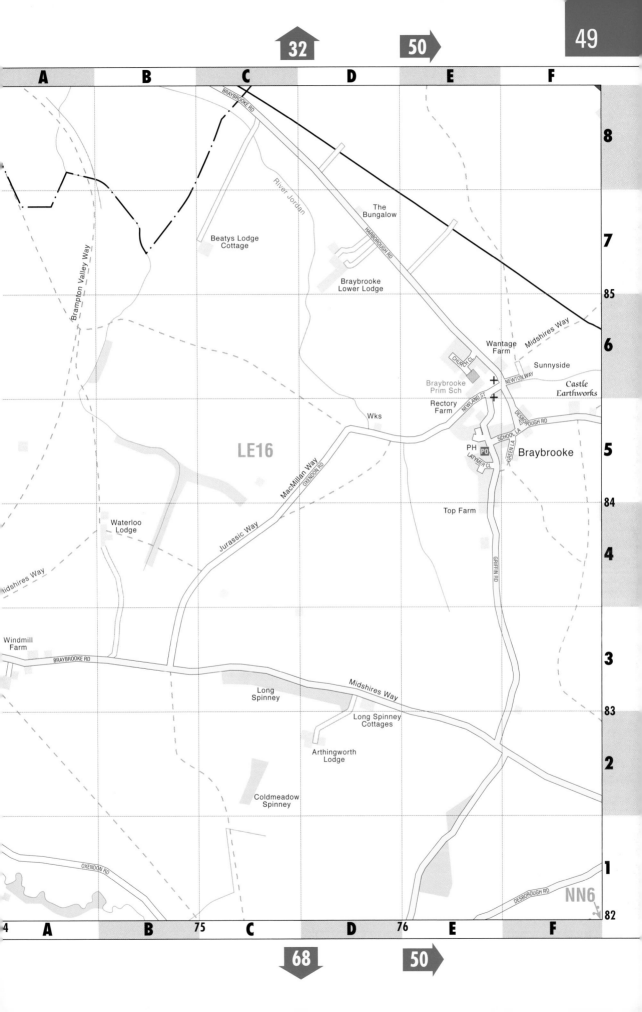

A | B | C | D | E | F

8
7
85
6

River Jordan

Braybrooke Rd

The Bungalow

Beatys Lodge Cottage

Brampton Valley Way

Harborough Rd

Braybrooke Lower Lodge

Wantage Farm

Sunnyside

Midshires Way

Church Cl

Braybrooke Prim Sch

Newton Way

Castle Earthworks

Rectory Farm

Newland St

Wks

LE16

MacMillan Way

Oxendon Rd

Desborough Rd

School La

Green La

Braybrooke

PH

PO

Latymer Cl

5
84
4

Top Farm

Waterloo Lodge

Jurassic Way

Griffin Rd

Midshires Way

Windmill Farm

Braybrooke Rd

3
83

Long Spinney

Midshires Way

Long Spinney Cottages

Arthingworth Lodge

2

Coldmeadow Spinney

1

Oxendon Rd

Desborough Rd

NN6

82

A | B | C | D | E | F

**8** Commons Farm

Hermitage Wood

Birch Quarter

LE16

Rogu Quar

Brampton Wood

Midshires Way

Hermitage Cottages

The Hermitage

B576

**7** HARBOROUGH RD

Pond Quarter

Tires Quarter

Jurassic Way
Midshires Way
Macmillan Way

Hotel

Glebe Cottage

**85**

Eckland Lodge Farm

Garden Ctr

BRAMPTON WOOD LA

Park Hill Farm

Eckland Lodge Bsns Pk

Dob Hall Farm

**6**

Factory

B669

STOKE RD

B5

The Gran

**5** The Bungalow

LE16

Smallholding

Wyndie Rydge Farm

A6

NN14

B5

**84**

Humfrey's Lodge

ASHFORD LEA 1
BIRCHVALE CT 2
EDALE GN 3
HEATHCOTE GR 4
TIDESWELL CL 5
CHELMORTON VALE 6
HATHERSAGE CL 7
DOVEDALE CL 8
HOWDEN GN 9

**4** Lodge Farm

Upper Lodge

Wr Twr

Loatlands Prim Sch

**3**

Lodge Farm

GREEN LA

Harrington Rd

**83**

**2**

Monkfield Coll

WOODWELL HILL

ROYAL GDNS

FEDERATION AVE

WINDSOR AVE

PIONEER AVE

**1** DESBOROUGH RD

NN6

Loatland Lodge Farm

A6

**82**

77 | A | 78 | B | C | 79 | D | E | F

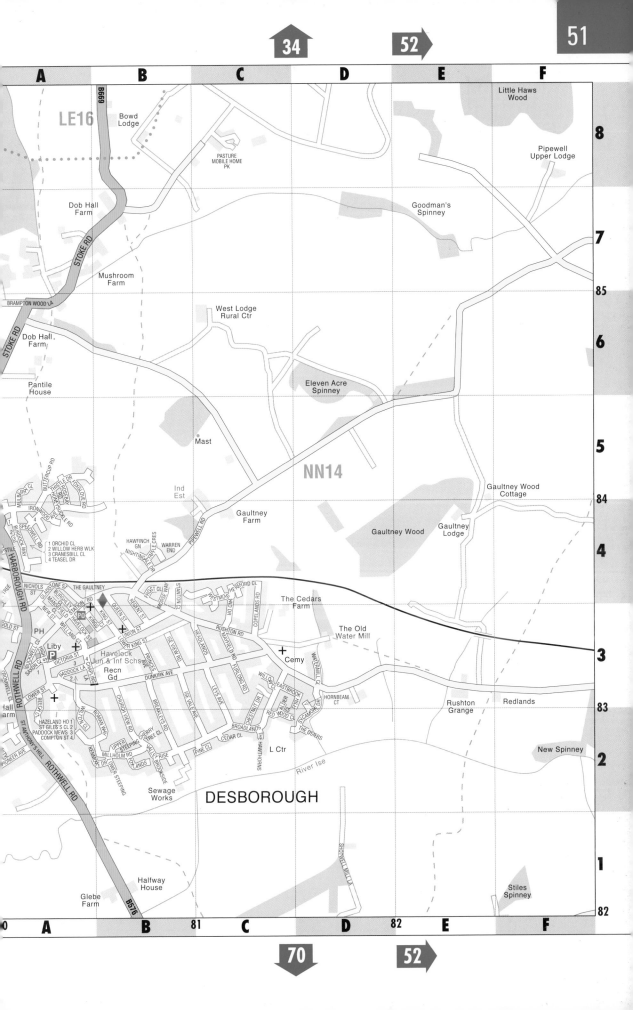

A B C D E F

8

Rawshaw
Wood

Hedgerow
Spinney

The Old
Red House

Harper's Brook

Home
Farm

OAKLEY RD

A6003

RYDER C

SAXON

Oa
H I
Ir E

Lower Lodge
Farm

UPPINGHAM RD

NN18

Pipewell
Hall

Pipewell

SAXON WAY W

7

Shangri-La

Pipewell
Lodge

White Lodge
Farm

85

UPPINGHAM RD

6

Hilton's End
Spinney

Alder
Wood

Storefield
Wood

Town's Close
Lodge

Forty Acre
Spinney

OAKLEY RD

5

New
Wood

NN14

Storefield
Lodge

84

Lady Mary's
Spinney

Rectory
Farm

4

3

MIDLAND
COTTS

Rushton
Prim Sch

BESWICK
CL

White Gates
Farm

83

DESBOROUGH RD

Manor
Farm

MATTHEWS CL

STATION RD

CHAPEL LA

MANOR RD

Rushton Triangular
Lodge

The
Privet

The
Wilderness

PH

HIGH ST

2

RNIB Rushton
Hall Sch

Rushton

Whitegate
Farm

Glendon
Sidings

Birch
Spinney

Hovel
Spinney

Sewage
Works

River Ise

1

Glendon Iron Or
Works

Crownest
Spinney

Hogs Hole
Spinney

Kettering North
Junction

82

83 A B 84 C D 85 E F

A   B   C   D   E   F

8
7
85
6
5
84
4
84
3
83
2
1
82

**Oakley Hay Ind Est**
MEDLICOTT CL
SAXON WAY E
PH
A6014
OAKLEY RD
LOWER LEAH CL
LEWIN RD
HOPPET CL
HARDEN CL
HEADWAY
HEADWAY
HORSELEASE CL
HAY CL
BRECK RD
OAKLEY POND
HEMPLAND CL
BROOKE RD
Oakley CL
HARPERS CL
HOME FARM CL
FIELD COTTS
CHUR.
Oakley Hall
Bridge Farm
WOODLANDS LA
Great Oakley
Woodlands
MILL HILL
Brooklyn Farm
Station Cotts
CHEPSTOW RD
KEMPTON CL
HARCOURT

**Ash Plantation**

NN18

Oakley Bushes

Storefield Cotts

ROCKINGHAM RD
50
A6003

Barford Bridge

NN14

Newton
River Ise
Dovecote Farm
Mill Farm
NEWTON RD
SKEFFINGTON CL

Geddington Grange Farm

GRANGE RD
Grange Road Workshops

Glebe Farm

Weekley Hall Wood

Square Spinney

Bolt Wood Coppice

**A** | **B** | **C** | **D** | **E** | **F**

FEATHERBED LA

A43

**8**

Little Oakley

Moat Farm

The Manor Farm

Rising Bridge

Start Wood

NN18

**7**

Great Hames Sale

Birch Tree Lawn

**85**

Cobley Lodge Farm

Woodlands

Great Brand

Geddington Chase

Pedlar's Wells

**6**

Newton Spinney

STAMFORD RD

Crab Tree Hills

Langley Quarter

Little Brand

Pale Hill

Clay Dick

**5**

Chase Lodge

**84**

Lardours Wood

Cotton Hills

**4**

Red House

Bright Trees

NN14

BRIGHT TREES RD

FERN DALE CL

CHASE VIEW RD

THE WOODLANDS

QUEEN ELEANOR RD

WOOD ST

HALL CL

**3**

NEWTON RD

Geddington

1 LEE'S WAY
2 WORMLEIGHTON WAY
3 BAKEHOUSE HILL
4 CHURCH HILL
5 CASTLE GDNS

WEST ST

MALTING LA

MAGDALENE CL

**83**

DALLINGTON CL

SKEFFINGTON CL

NEW RD

Queen Eleanor's Cross

PH

BRIDGE ST

CHASE FARM

Geddington CE Prim Sch

Round Coppice

Pitmans Sale

Sedge Hills

CHAPEL LA

QUEEN ST

PO

Ford

PRIORY CL

GRAFTON RD

**2**

GRANGE RD

Sawmill

MILBY LA

30

THOMAS RIPPIN CL

Kennel Quarter

Boughton Wood

KETTERING RD

Bancroft Wood

**1**

Sewage Works

Boughton Wood Lodge

Thorny Coppice

A43 STAMFORD RD

New Ground Spinney

**82**

A    B    C    D    E    F

BELLS CL
SWAN AVE
STANION RD
NEWTOWN
OLD DRY LA
A6116 RD

Harpers Brook

Playing Field

DUSTHILL RD

Chase Farm

FERMYN CL
WOODYARD CL
BENEFIELD

PO
PH
HIGH ST
BACK LA
CAUSIN CL

1 WOODLANDS MEWS
2 WOODLANDS CL
3 HALL HILL

BRIDGE ST
LATHAM ST
Sch
MILL
KENNEL HL
KENNEL HL
STABLE HILL
Brigstock
CHURCH ST
THE DYKE
MONTERLY GATE

The Manor House

HARPER'S CT
MAUNTLEY CT
SANDLANDS AVE
LYVEDEN RD

PARK WLK
SUDBOROUGH RD

SANDLANDS CL

Sewage Works

Park Farm

**NN14**

Bullymore's Lodge

Old Lodge Farm

GRAFTON RD

Park Cottages

Hillside Farm

Breakhill Cottage

Long Sale

Fox Earth

Roadside Quarter

Barn Quarter

Old Head Wood

Snapes Wood

Great Bull Sedge

Schich's Corner

Stevenson's Quarter

8

85

7

6

5

84

4

3

83

2

1

82

A    B    C    D    E    F
92   93   94
74 56

A    B    C    D    E    F

8

BENEFIELD RD

Mounterley
Wood

HARLEY WAY

Luscote
Lodge

Harley Way
Lodge

7

A6116

Stephen Oak
Riding

Cherry
Lap

Royal
Coppice

Fermyn
Woods

Sling's
Nook

PE8

Fermyn Woods
Country Park

85

LYVEDEN RD

BARNARD'S WAY

P

Tresham
Coppice

Assart's
Coppice

Lady Wood
Head

Lady
Wood

6

SUDBOROUGH RD

Manor
Farm

5

Sudborough Green
Lodge

84

Cat's Head
Wood

Souther
Wood

4

Catshead
Farm

NN14

Green Side
Wood

3

Green
Lodge

Titchmarsh
Wood

Belle
Vue

83

Harper's Brook

Snapes
Lodge

2

1

Snapes
Wood

Sudborough

Grange
Farm

PH
MAIN ST

BREWERY
YD

A6116

82

SLIPTON
LA

95    A    B    96    C    D    97    E    F

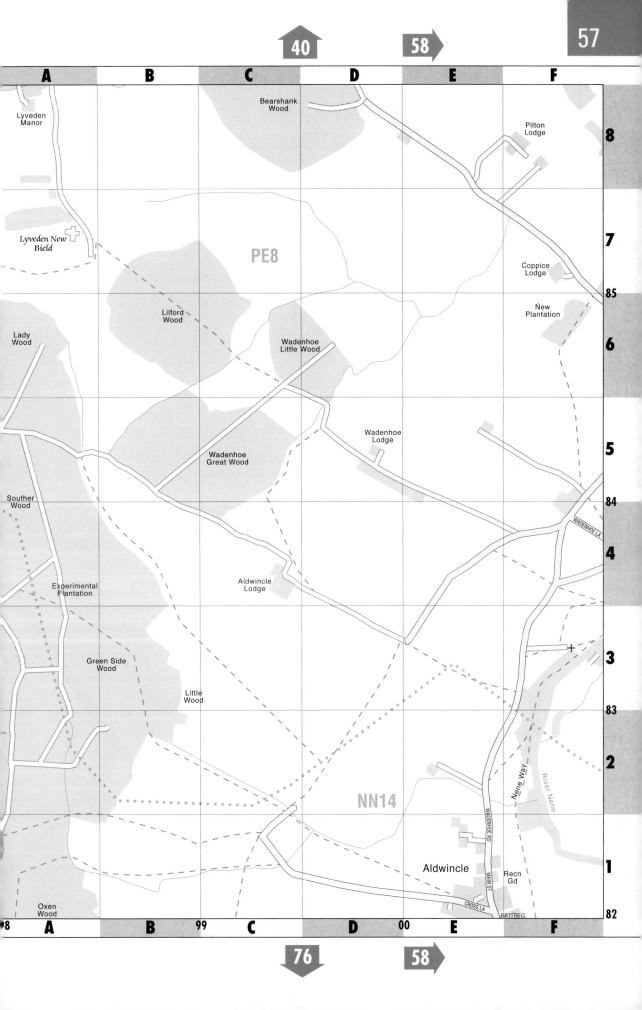

A B C D E F

Lyveden
Manor

Bearshank
Wood

Pilton
Lodge

Lyveden New
Bield

PE8

Coppice
Lodge

New
Plantation

Lilford
Wood

Wadenhoe
Little Wood

Lady
Wood

Wadenhoe
Lodge

Wadenhoe
Great Wood

Souther
Wood

WADENHOE LA

Experimental
Plantation

Aldwincle
Lodge

Green Side
Wood

Little
Wood

NN14

Nene Way

River Nene

WADENHOE RD

Aldwincle

MAIN ST

Recn
Gd

Oxen
Wood

CROSS LA

FULLERS CL

8
7
85
6
5
84
4
3
83
2
1
82

8    A    B    99    C    D    00    E    F

**A** **B** **C** **D** **E** **F**

8

Manor House

Great Ground Spinney

7

**PE8**

85

Pilton Lodge Farm

6

Petty Fields Plantation

Lilford Lodge Farm

Pilton Grange

Manor House +

Pilton

River Nene

Lilford Woods

5

Boat Houses

Lilford Park

Wr Twr

84

Lilford Hall

Lilford Woods

Lilford Bridge

Lilford Home Farm

WADENHOE

THE GREEN

Meml

GLEBE CT.

PILTON RD

4

MAIN ST

PO

Lilford

Wadenhoe

Wadenhoe House

OAKLEE CL.

MILL LA.

The Linches

CHURCH ST

Sudden's Plantation

PH

3

P

Nene Way +

Ratling Irons Plantation

83

Achurch

B662

2

Rectory Farm

River Nene

1

B662

**NN14**

A605

82

01 **A** **B** 02 **C** **D** 03 **E** **F**

A B C D E F

Wks

White Lodge

Barnwell Workshops

New Fox Convert

Armston

Burray Spinney

Empty Spinney

Armston Grove

Blind Spinney

Barnwell Castle

Barnwell Manor

Fox Convert

CASTLE VIEW LA

WELL LA

CHURCH LA

CHURCH HILL

CHURCH RD

ARMSTON RD

A605

PO

Barnwell St Andrew

LATHAM'S COTTS

PH

Barnwell

MONTAGU TERR

Castle Farm

Barnwell All Saints

MAIN ST

CHANCEL TERR

Nene Way

Friars Close Farm

Lower Farm

Broadway Corner

PE8

Barnwell Brook

West Lodge Farm

Barnwell Lodge Farm

Bright Pitts Farm

Wigsthorpe

Hall Farm

South Lodge Farm

B662

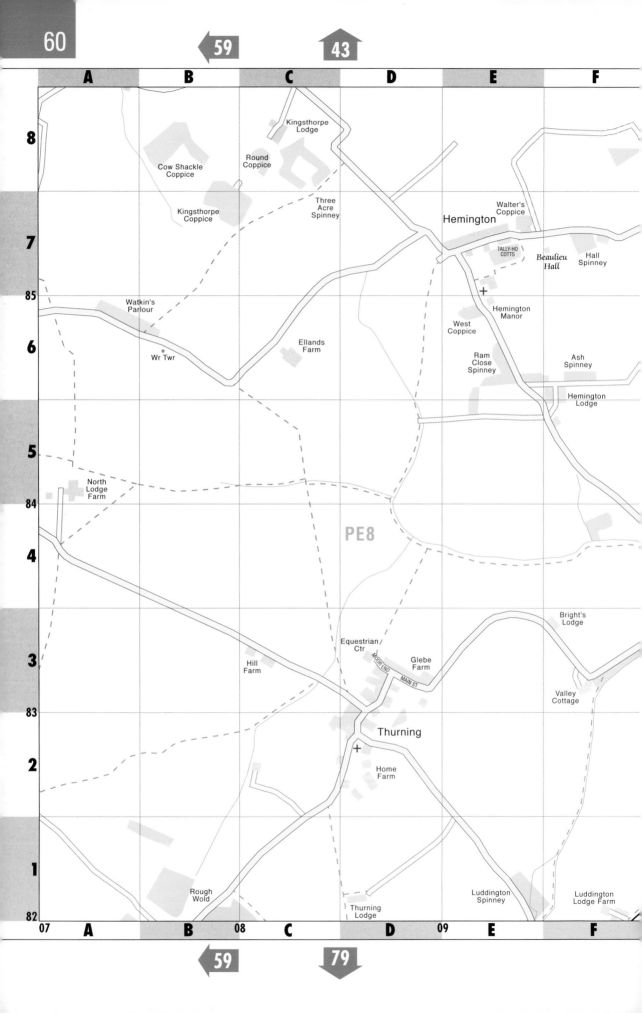

A    B    C    D    E    F

8

Kingsthorpe
Lodge

Round
Coppice

Cow Shackle
Coppice

Three Acre
Spinney

Walter's
Coppice

Hemington

7

TALLY-HO
COTTS

Beaulieu
Hall

Hall
Spinney

Kingsthorpe
Coppice

85

Watkin's
Parlour

West
Coppice

Hemington
Manor

6

Wr Twr

Ellands
Farm

Ram
Close
Spinney

Ash
Spinney

Hemington
Lodge

5

North
Lodge
Farm

84

PE8

4

Bright's
Lodge

3

Hill
Farm

Equestrian
Ctr

MOOR END

MAIN ST

Glebe
Farm

Valley
Cottage

83

Thurning

2

Home
Farm

1

Rough
Wold

Thurning
Lodge

Luddington
Spinney

Luddington
Lodge Farm

82

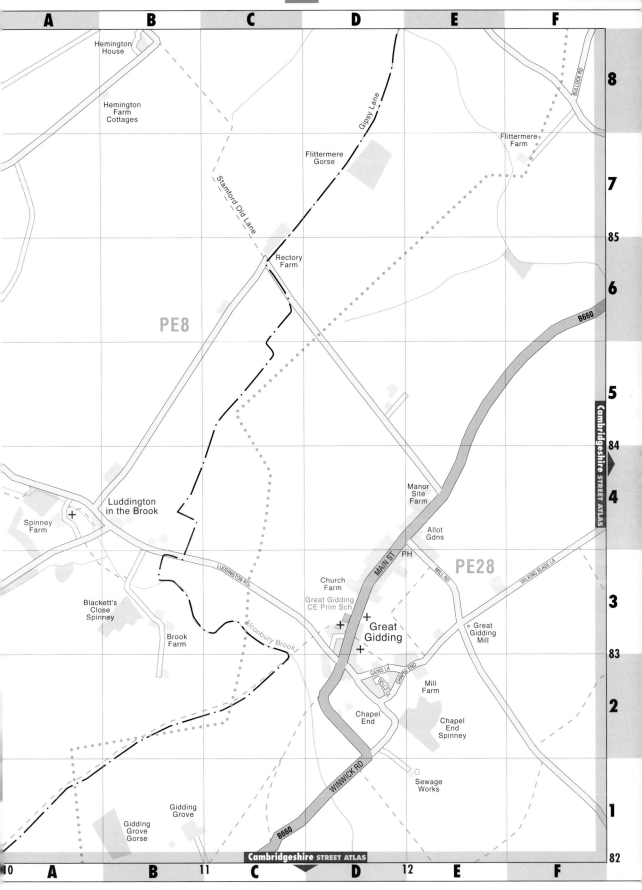

A    B    C    D    E    F

Hemington House

Hemington Farm Cottages

Gipsy Lane

Flittermere Gorse

Flittermere Farm

Stamford Old Lane

BULLOCK RD

PE8

B660

Cambridgeshire STREET ATLAS

Rectory Farm

Manor Site Farm

Luddington in the Brook

Allot Gdns

MAIN ST

PH

MILL RD

PE28

MILKING SLADE LA

Spinney Farm

Church Farm

Great Gidding CE Prim Sch

Great Gidding

Great Gidding Mill

Blackett's Close Spinney

LUDDINGTON RD

Brook Farm

Alconbury Brook

GAINS LA

BELLS CL

CHAPEL END

Mill Farm

Chapel End

Chapel End Spinney

WINWICK RD

Sewage Works

Gidding Grove

B660

Gidding Grove Gorse

10    A    B    11    C    D    12    E    F

8
85
6
5
84
4
3
83
2
1
82

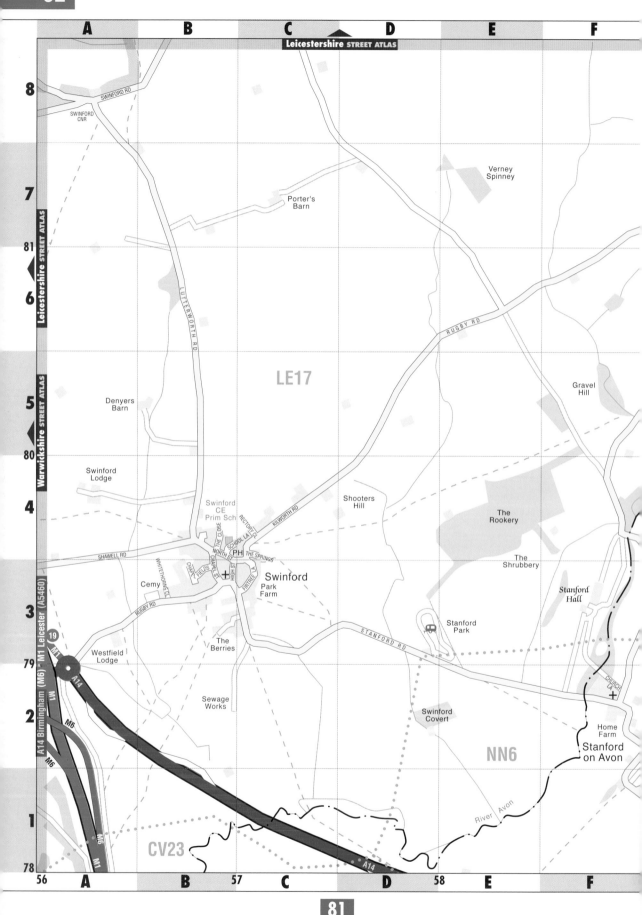

A  B  C  D  E  F

8
7
81
6
5
80
4
3
79
2
1
78

56  A  B  57  C  D  58  E  F

Leicestershire STREET ATLAS

Warwickshire STREET ATLAS

A14 Birmingham (M6) · M1 Leicester (A5460)

SWINFORD RD
SWINFORD CNR

Porter's Barn

Verney Spinney

LUTTERWORTH RD

RUGBY RD

LE17

Gravel Hill

Denyers Barn

Swinford Lodge

Swinford CE Prim Sch

THE CLOSE
RECTORY CL
SCHOOL LA
KILWORTH RD

Shooters Hill

The Rookery

The Shrubbery

SHAWELL RD

NORTH ST
FIELDS
CHAPEL ST
WHITETHORNS CL
PH
THE SPRINGS
FIRTREE LA
HIGH ST

Cemy

Swinford Park Farm

Swinford

Stanford Hall

RUGBY RD

The Berries

STANFORD RD

Stanford Park

Stanford on Avon

19

M1
A14
M6
M6
M1

Westfield Lodge

Sewage Works

Swinford Covert

NN6

CHURCH LA
Home Farm

CV23

River Avon

A14

A B C D E F

South Kilworth
CE Prim Sch

TANSER
COTT

PO

PH

South
Kilworth

THE SYCAMORES

WALCOTE RD

CHURCH LA

NORTH RD

DOG LA

WELFORD RD

River Avon

LE17

Top Barn
Farm

RUGBY RD

Old
Covert

Sybole
Farm

81

New
Covert

Downton
Farm

SOUTH KILWORTH RD

ovel
Hill

Stanford
Resr

6

Downtown
Hill

80

Pleasure
Gd

5

4

Mon

Grand Union Canal

NN6

79

Old
Hemplow

2

Wood
Cottage

Jurassic Way

Park
Farm

Half Moon
Spinney

1

78

8

7

3

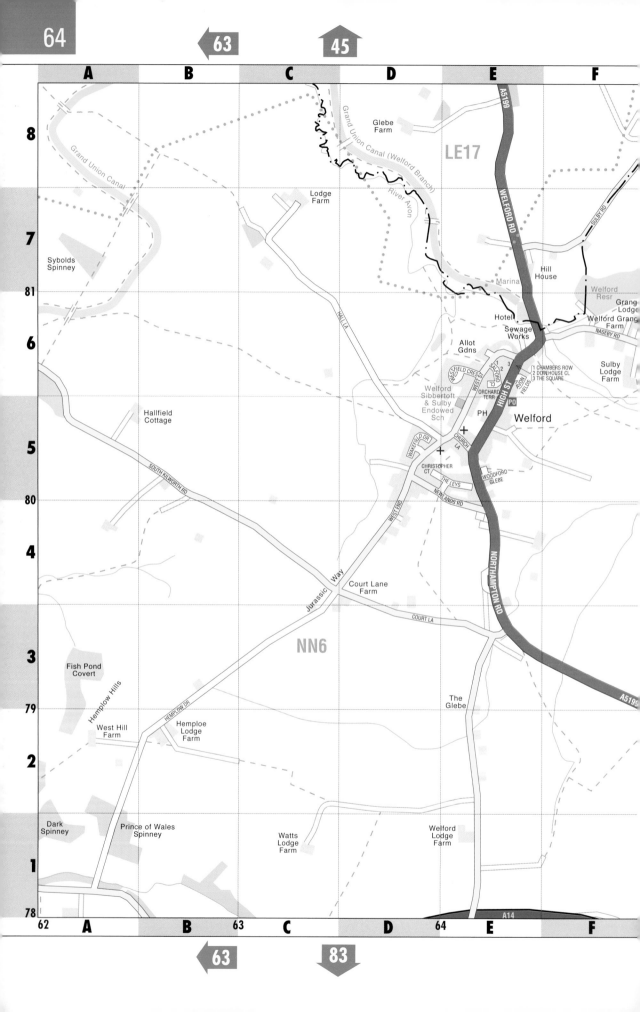

Grand Union Canal

Glebe Farm

Grand Union Canal (Welford Branch)

LE17

A5199

WELFORD RD

SULBY RD

Sybolds Spinney

River Avon

Lodge Farm

HALL LA

Hill House

Marina

Welford Resr

Grang Lodge

Hotel

Sewage Works

Allot Gdns

Welford Grang Farm

NASEBY RD

Sulby Lodge Farm

WESTFIELD CRES

SALFORD

1 CHAMBERS ROW
2 DOVEHOUSE CL
3 THE SQUARE

Hallfield Cottage

Welford Sibbertoft & Sulby Endowed Sch

ORCHARD TERR

HIGH ST

AVON FIELDS

PO

PH

Welford

SOUTH KILWORTH RD

WAKEFIELD DR

CHURCH LA

CHRISTOPHER CT

THE LEYS

WEST END

NEWLANDS RD

WOODFORD GLEBE

Jurassic Way

NN6

Court Lane Farm

COURT LA

NORTHAMPTON RD

Fish Pond Covert

Hemplow Hills

HEMPLOW DR

The Glebe

A5199

West Hill Farm

Hemploe Lodge Farm

Dark Spinney

Prince of Wales Spinney

Watts Lodge Farm

Welford Lodge Farm

A14

LE16

NN6

**Map labels:**

Sulby
Home Farm
Dunster House
Sulby Gardens
Sulby Covert
Park House
Park Farm
SULBY RD
SULBY HALL OLD DR
Jurassic Way
Sulbyhall Farm
Sulby Resr
Sulby Grange
Broadmoor Farm
NASEBY RD
Sulby Abbey Farm
The Lodge
Red Hill Farm
Fenny Hill
River Avon
Lake House
Naseby Hall
Welford Lodge
Abbotts Lodge
Portly Ford Farm
Woolley's Farm
Shuckburgh Farm
NORTHAMPTON RD
Pilshong Farm
Portly Ford Lodge
Portly Ford Bridge
A5199
A14
Carvells La

**Grid references (right margin):** 8, 81, 7, 6, 5, 80, 4, 3, 79, 2, 1, 78

**Grid references (bottom margin):** 65, A, B, 66, C, D, 67, E, F

A B C D E F

8

The Old Manse

Clipston

The Paddocks

NOBOLD CT

PEG'S LA

The Chestnuts

Longhold Lodge

LE16

7

81

Prince Rupert's Farm

Dust Hill

Dust Hill Farm

Long Hold Spinney

6

5

The Plantation

Mon

P

80

Naseby Covert

4

Paisnell Spinney

Naseby Field

Mill Hill

3

New-House Farm

A14

NN6

Mill Hill Farm

79

Mast

2

A14

Clothill Spinney

1

Obelisk

Naseby

PH

HALL CL

NEWLANDS

Carvells La

CHURCH ST

HIGH ST

Naseby CE Prim Sch

78

NASEBY RD

COTT LA

MARCROFT

CHAPEL LA

NASEBY RD

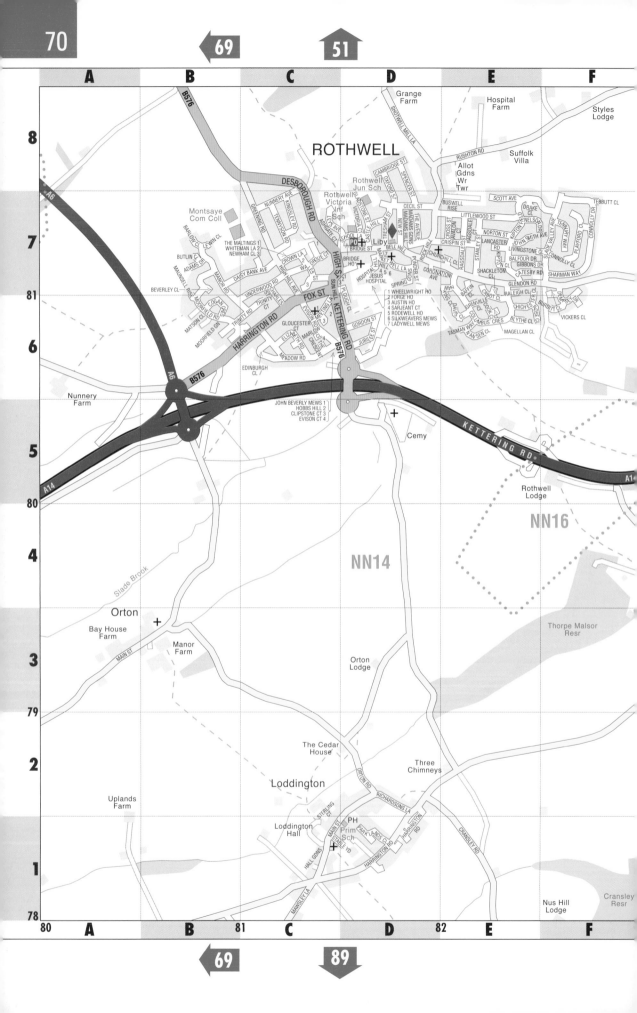

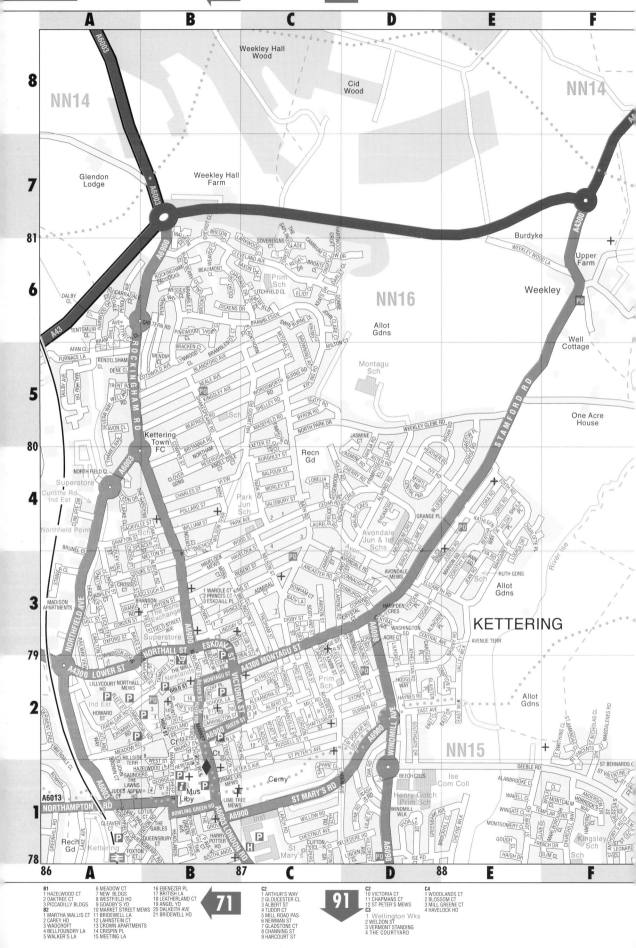

**B1**
1 HAZELWOOD CT
2 OAKTREE CT
3 PICCADILLY BLDGS
**B2**
1 MARTHA WALLIS CT
2 CAREY HO
3 WADCROFT
4 BELLFOUNDRY LA
5 WALKER'S LA

6 MEADOW CT
7 NEW BLDGS
8 WESTFIELD HO
9 GOADBY'S YD
10 MARKET STREET MEWS
11 BRIDEWELL CT
12 LAHNSTEIN CT
13 CROWN APARTMENTS
14 CRISPIN PL
15 MEETING LA

16 EBENEZER PL
17 BRITISH LA
18 LEATHERLAND CT
19 ANGEL YD
20 DALKEITH AVE
21 BRIDEWELL HO

**C2**
1 ARTHUR'S WAY
2 GLOUCESTER CT
3 ALBERT ST
4 TUDOR CT
5 MILL ROAD PAS
6 NEWMAN ST
7 GLADSTONE CT
8 CHANNING ST
9 HARCOURT ST

**C2**
10 VICTORIA CT
11 CHAPMANS CT
12 ST PETER'S MEWS
**C3**
1 Wellington Wks
2 WELDON ST
3 VERMONT STANDING
4 THE COURTYARD

**C4**
1 WOODLANDS CT
2 BLOSSOM CT
3 MILL GREENE CT
4 HAVELOCK HO

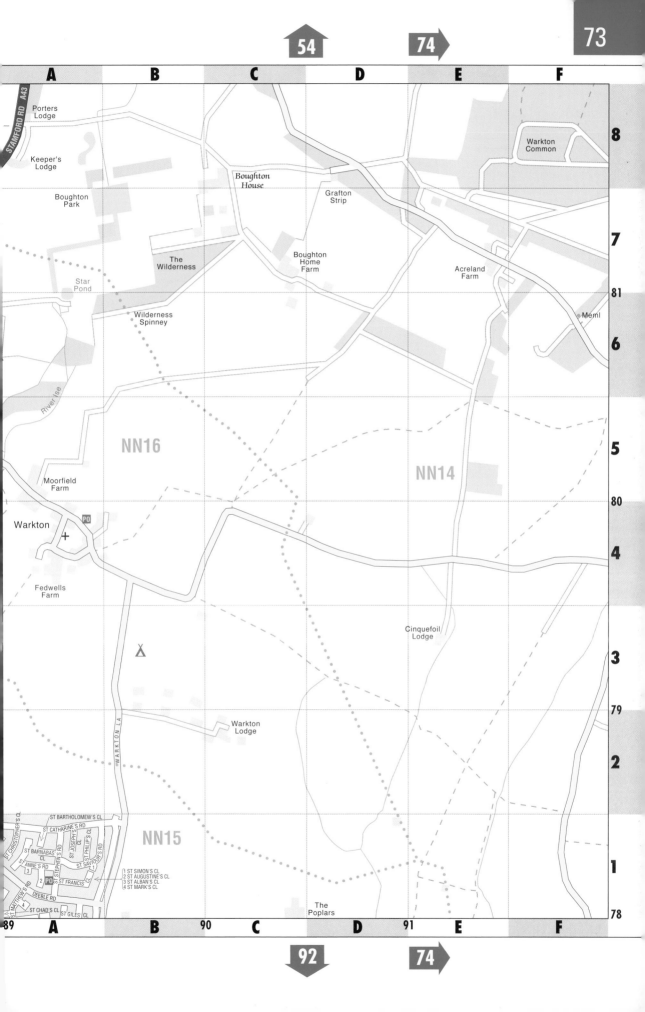

A B C D E F

STAMFORD RD A43

Porters
Lodge

Keeper's
Lodge

Boughton
Park

Boughton
House

Grafton
Strip

Warkton
Common

The
Wilderness

Boughton
Home
Farm

Acreland
Farm

Star
Pond

Wilderness
Spinney

Meml

River Ise

NN16

NN14

Moorfield
Farm

Warkton

PO

Fedwells
Farm

Cinquefoil
Lodge

Warkton
Lodge

WARKTON LA

NN15

ST BARTHOLOMEW'S CL

ST CATHARINE'S RD

ST CHRISTOPHER'S RD

ST JOSEPH'S CL

ST PHILIP'S RD

ST BARNABAS
CL

ST ANNE'S RD

ST STEPHEN'S RD

ST SAVIOUR'S CL

3

1 ST SIMON'S CL
2 ST AUGUSTINE'S CL
3 ST ALBAN'S CL
4 ST MARK'S CL

ST FRANCIS CL

PO

ST MATTHEW'S RD

DEEBLE RD

4

ST CHAD'S CL

ST GILES CL

The
Poplars

58

78

A  B  C  D  E  F

PE8

8

Thorpe Fox
Covert

7

81

6

NN14

5

80

Sewage
Works

Titchmarsh

4

Thorpe Brook

3

79

Townhill
Coppice

2

1

78

A14

01  A  B  02  C  D  03  E  F

96

78

Brancey
Bridge

THORPE RD

Marina

Titchmarsh
Mill

Thorpe
Waterville

Brook
Farm

LILFORD RD

PH

A605

40

Cricket
Gd

THORPE CT

ISLINGTON

CHURCH ST

Titchmarsh
CE Prim Sch

MANOR
FARM CT

SCHOOL LA

PARK RD

DRYDEN S CL

THE GREEN

CHAPEL ST

NORTH ST

Rectory
Farm

PH

PARK FARM
CT

HIGH ST

TOFTS

ST ANDREWS LA

ST ANDREW'S
CL

LONDON END

LOBBY CL

POLOPIT

Newbrook
Farm

The
Bungalow

Castle Manor
Farm

PE8

PE8

A B C D E F

8

Towcester Hill
Spinney

Bull Nose
Coppice

Alvaston

7

Long Thong
Coppice

Long Thong
Farm

81

Blackthorn
Coppice

6

Ash Pole
Coppice

BERRY GREEN PK

Home
Farm

PO

Clopton

NN14

5

Skulking Dudley
Copse

Clopton
Hall

B662

80

4

Ringdales
Wood

Crows
Nest
Farm

Bidwell
Farm

3

79

Foxholes
Farm

2

Fayway

WARREN LA

Chequer
Hill
Coppice

1

Warren
Lodge
Farm

78

A   B   C   D   E   F

Middle
Copse

Barnwell
Wold

Common
Wold

PE8

Gumwells
Wold

THURNING RD

8

7

81

6

Winwick
Lodge

Broad Lane

Cambridgeshire STREET ATLAS

5

80

NN14

4

Grange
Farm

PE28

Fieldbarn
Farm

3

Cockbrook
Farm

Ash
Copse

79

South Farm

Mariner's
Gorse

2

COCKBROOK LA

Sewage
Works

B662

Cockbrook
Lodge

1

78

07   A   B   08   C   D   09   E   F

**Warwickshire** STREET ATLAS

LE17

Newton Ct

Mill Farm

Newton Manor La

St Thomas Cross (PH)

Newton Rd

Lilbourne Furze

Lilbourne Gorse

Station

Dunsmore Farm

Buckwell La

Cemy

Clifton upon Dunsmore

North Rd

Manor La

Manor Farm

Dunsmore

Almond Bank

Magpie Lodge Farm

Rugby Rd

PH

Church St

Robert's Wk

Howard Cl

Lilbourne Rd

Allan's La

Main St

PO

Orchard

Evergreen

Goodacre

Dunsmore House

Hillmorton La

Clifton Hall Farm

CV23

Masts

South Rd

Allan's Dr

Dunsmore Home Farm

76

Hotel

Clifton Hall

The Meadows

Hillmorton La

Grange Farm House

Masts

Home Farm

Clifton Brook

Oxford Canal

CV21

Masts

Oxford Canal Walk

A1
1 BROMWICH RD
2 PETTIVER CRES
3 WIGSTON RD
4 THE MEWS
5 LOWER HILLMORTON RD

The Kent

RUGBY

Waverley Rd

The Kent

Robert Hill Cl

Pine Gr

The Locks

Brindley Rd

Hillmorton Locks

Normandy Farm

Rugby Radio Station

Gibson Cl

Featherbed La

Jenkins Rd

Coton Rd

School Cl

Gainsborough Cres

Constable Rd

1 BONNINGTON CL
2 LANDSEER CL

Dyson Cl

Jackson Rd

Cleves Rd

School Gdns

Lower St

Fox Cl

Reynolds

Lower St

Masts

A    B    C    D    E    F

A14

A14

8

7

77

Sewage
Works

STATION RD

M1

The
Green
Farm

GREEN FARM
CL

RIGBY RD

THE HORSEPOOL

THE GREEN

CHAPEL LA

STONEHOUSE CT

Stonehouse
Farm

Lilbourne

HILLMORTON LA

Lilbourne
Lodge

Clarkes
Farm

6

YELVERTOFT RD

Lilbourne
Fields
Farmhouse

Lodge
Farm

CV23

Mast

Mast

Mast

Mast

Mast

5

76

4

Mast

Mast

Mast

Radio
Station

Mast

Mast

Mast

Mast

Mast

Mast

Mast

NN6

Shenley
Farm

3

75

2

New House
Farm

Crick
Lodge

Mast

Mast

A5

M1

1

74

A B C D E F

8

7

77

6

A14

A14

A5199

Naseby
Resr

Fulbrook
Farm

Reservoir
Farm

STANFORD RD
STANFORD CL
WEST HADDON RD
BRIDLE LA
CRABTREE LA
MAIN ST
CHURCH LA
PARK SPINNEY CL
THORNBY RD
PH

5

Cold Ashby

NN6

Lodge Farm

76

Park
Spinney

WELFORD RD

Thornby
Hall

4

COLD ASHBY RD

Thornby House
Farm

ST HELENS CL
CHURCH LA
PH

NASEBY RD

STONE HOUSE
MEWS

Thornby

Doebank
Spinney

Lovells
Lodge

Firetail
Covert

3

Firetail

75

Thornby
Grange

Grange
Farm

2

Rabbit
Spinney

Nortoft
Lodge

Ashbylane
Farm

1

West Lodge

74

A5199

A  B  C  D  E  F

Mast

8

Bassetts Lodge
Farm

MAIDWELL RD

Haselbech
Grange

Haselbech

Manor
Farm

Scotland Wood
Farm

NASEBY RD

7

Haselbech
Hall

The
Rectory

77

Dale
Wood

Maidwell
Dale

6

Black
Hall

Haselbech
Hill

Dale
Farm

5

Shutterdown
Spinney

Maidwell
Lodge

76

NN6

4

Blueberry
Lodge

Mitley
Spinney

Houseground
Spinney

Macmillan Way

3

75

Moss Hall
Spinney

Gamboro
Plantation

2

Rickleboro Hill
Spinney

Blueberry
Grange

Park
Spinney

1

74

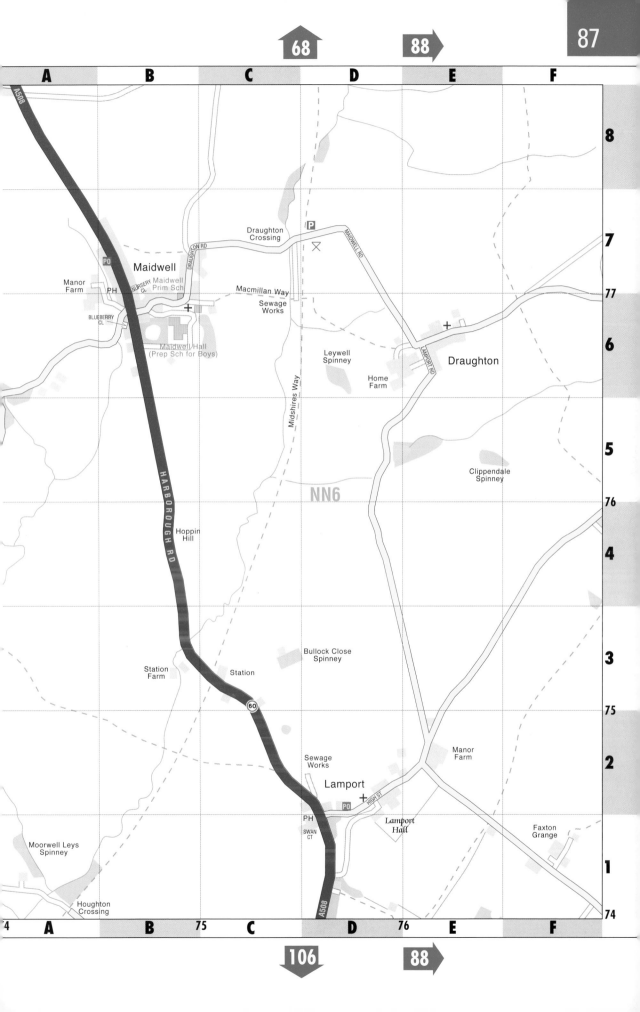

A  B  C  D  E  F

8

7

77

6

5

76

4

3

75

2

1

74

Manor
Farm

PH

PO

Maidwell

NURSERY
CL

Maidwell
Prim Sch

BLUEBERRY
CL

DRAUGHTON RD

Draughton
Crossing

P

Macmillan Way

Sewage
Works

MAIDWELL RD

LAMPORT RD

Draughton

Leywell
Spinney

Home
Farm

Maidwell Hall
(Prep Sch for Boys)

Midshires Way

HARBOROUGH RD

Hoppin
Hill

NN6

Clippendale
Spinney

Station
Farm

Station

60

Bullock Close
Spinney

Manor
Farm

Sewage
Works

Lamport

PO

HIGH ST

Lamport
Hall

Faxton
Grange

PH

SWAN
CT

Moorwell Leys
Spinney

Houghton
Crossing

A508

A508

A  B  C  D  E  F

4  75  76

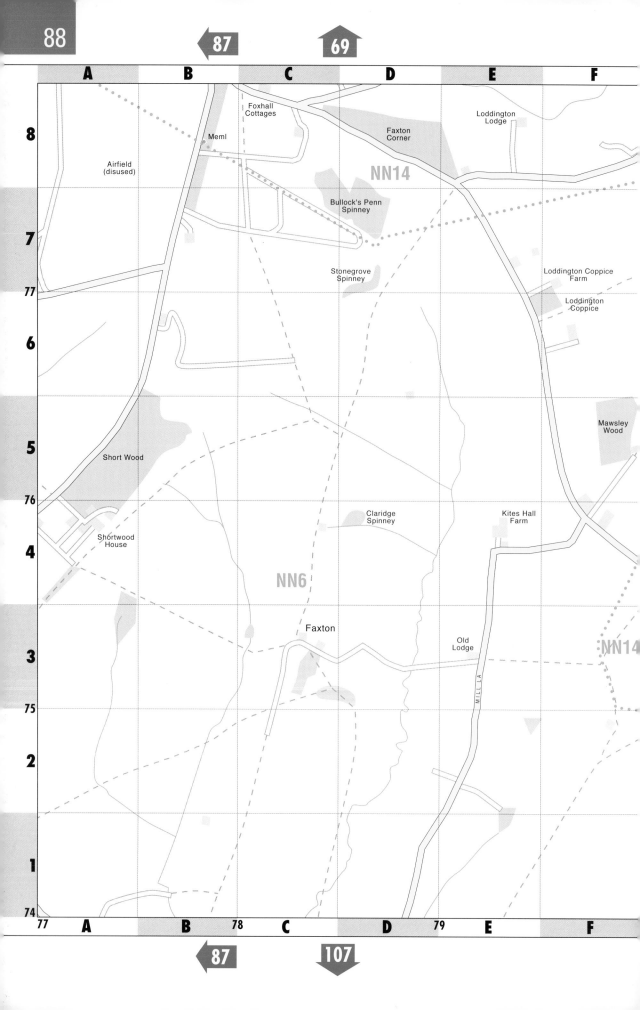

A  B  C  D  E  F

8

Foxhall
Cottages

Loddington
Lodge

Faxton
Corner

Meml

Airfield
(disused)

NN14

7

Bullock's Penn
Spinney

77

Stonegrove
Spinney

Loddington Coppice
Farm

Loddington
Coppice

6

Mawsley
Wood

5

Short Wood

76

Claridge
Spinney

Kites Hall
Farm

Shortwood
House

4

NN6

Faxton

Old
Lodge

NN14

3

MILL LA

75

2

1

74

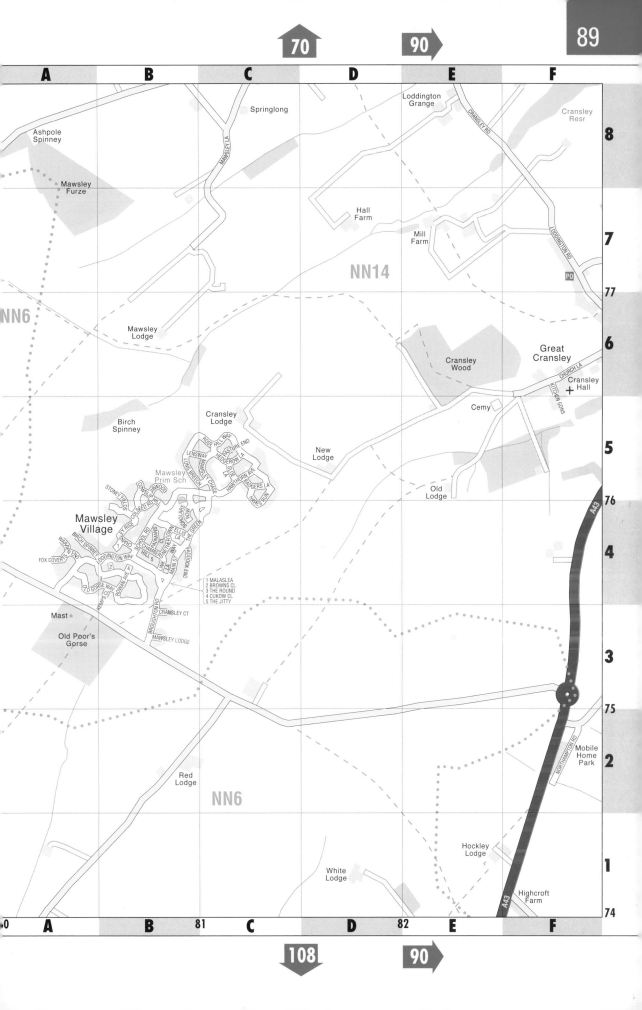

A B C D E F

Loddington
Grange

Cransley
Resr

Ashpole
Spinney

8

Mawsley
Furze

CRANSLEY RD

MAWSLEY LA

LODDINGTON RD

Hall
Farm

Mill
Farm

7

PO

NN14

77

NN6

Mawsley
Lodge

Great
Cransley

6

Cransley
Wood

CHURCH LA

Cransley
Hall

KITCHEN GDNS

Birch
Spinney

Cransley
Lodge

Cemy

ROSE HILL WAY

PASTURE END

HEDGEROW LA

5

Lensway

LONG BREECH

Mawsley
Prim Sch

HAWTHORN AVE

New
Lodge

STONEY FIELDS

LONGSLIP

IPSWOOD

BADGERS LA

HARE'S RUN

Old
Lodge

76

A43

Mawsley
Village

BIRCH SPINNEY

SCHOOL RD

NETHERTOWN LA

THE GREEK

PADDOCK END

1 MALASLEA
2 BROWNS CL
3 THE ROUND
4 CUKOW CL
5 THE JITTY

4

FOX COVERT'S

WARREN END

LODDINGTON WAY

HILL 5

2

3

4

GORSE WAY

KEMPS CL

ROWAN AVE

CRANSLEY CT

BROUGHTON RD

MAWSLEY LODGE

Mast

Old Poor's
Gorse

3

75

NORTHAMPTON RD

Mobile
Home
Park

2

NN6

Red
Lodge

Hockley
Lodge

1

White
Lodge

A43

Highcroft
Farm

74

A  B  C  D  E  F

8

White Hill
Lodge

Allotment
Spinney

7

77

6

77

The
Gorse

Sewage
Works

NN15

Broughton
Grange

5

PH
CHURCH LA
BRIDLE WAY
BROUGHTON HILL
HOLLY
LA

Allot
Gdns

GRANGER RD
THURIBURN RD
KETTERING RD

Little
Cransley

A43

CRANE CL
THE BANKS

Allot
Gdns

76

CHAPEL
VIEW
COX'S LA  SILVER ST
WEST ST  TERR
CRANSLEY HILL
HIGH ST
BROOKHAVEN
GATE LA
MANOR FARM CL
4

Manor
Farm

Recn
Gd

Broughton
Prim Sch

ST ANDREWS

Cemy

Rathmine
Farm

ASHBROOK
CL

3
2  ST ANDREW'S CT
1  CHURCH ST

Pytchley
Lodge

4

ST ANDREWS WAY 1
CHURCH VIEW 2
DAWKINS CT 3
BAKEHOUSE MEWS 4
PO

BURTONE
CL
OAK CL
GLEBE AVE

Broughton

HUTCHINSON AVE

WELLINGBOROUGH RD
GLEBE AVE

NN14

Underwood's Hill
Spinney

3

NORTHAMPTON RD
MEACHAM CL
DONALDSON AVE
PODMORE WAY
BAKER AVE
MACKAY CL
RIGGALL CL
CARTER AVE

KERLEY CL
LENTON CL

Headlands
Farm

New
Covert

75

Pytchley New
Covert

Manor Farm
House

2

BLACKSMITH'S
LA

Pytchley

Stud
Farm

Pytchley
Endowed CE
Prim Sch

BROUGHTON RD

1

Spencer
Lodge

74

83  A  B  84  C  D  85  E  F

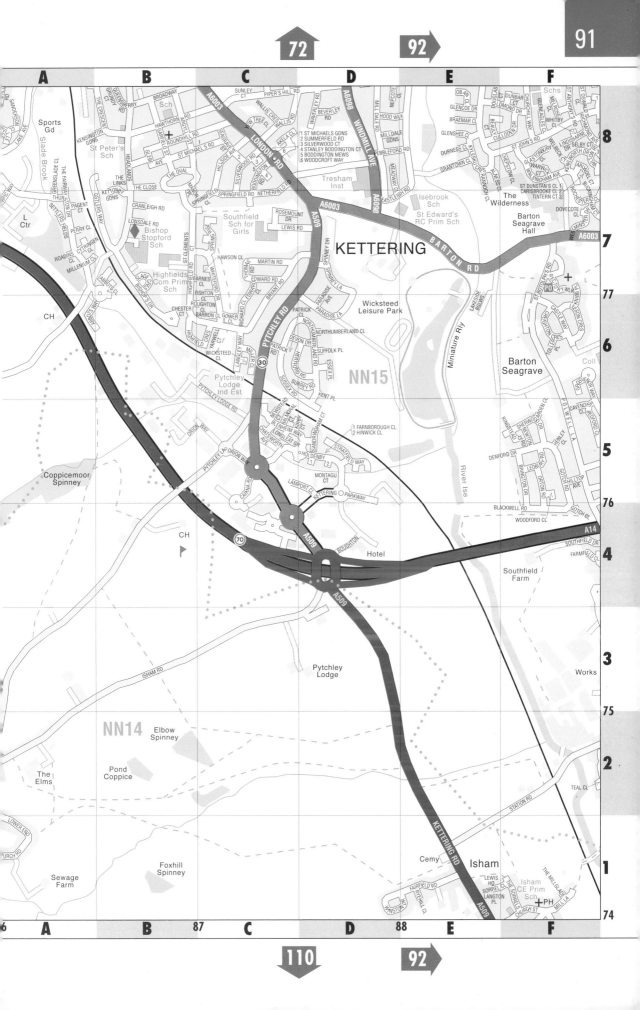

A B C D E F

8

Warkton
Spinney

St James Cl
St Matthew's Rd
St John's Rd
Westleigh Rd
Ridgway Rd

Shaft Field
Spinney

7

KETTERING

The Osier
Bed

Stubbs
Spinney

TOP DYSON

A6003
1 BUCKINGHAM CT
2 WATERHOUSE GDNS
3 BEARDSLEY GDNS

Barton
Seagrave

The Grange

NN14

77

Latimer Com
Arts Coll

The Lodge

Hayfield
Lodge

6

BARTON RD

Cranford Rd

1 RUFFORD CL
2 GROSVENOR CL
3 TAVISTOCK RD
4 BELGRAVE CL
5 SALCEY CL
6 EPPING CL
7 ROSSENDALE DR
8 QUANTOCK CL
9 BOWLAND DR

Blackbridge
Farm

5

Sch

A6003

CRANFORD RD

76

A14

A6

WINDMILL
COTTS

4

Mast

NN15

ELM RD
ACORN
PK

Altendiez Way

Rectory
Plantation

Double
Dug Spinney

Burton
Latimer
Hall

3

Football
Gd

WOODCOCK ST

NORTH
AVE

BIRD ST
GEORGE ST

75

Recn
Ctr

STATION RD

Sturgess
Ct

WOLD RD

2

Meadowside
Jun & Inf
Schs

Sch

PO

Cemy

1 HERON CL
2 SWAN CL
3 BRENT CL

1 BURTON HO
2 CROXEN CL

Pigott's
La Liby

BURTON
LATIMER

1

Hog's
Hole

1 BARLOW CT
2 MACKINTOSH CT
3 MEADS CT
4 MORBY CT

White Lodge
Farm

A6

NN14

GRACE CT 1
HAWTHORN RD 2
HILLCREST AVE 3

74

89 A 90 B C 91 D E F

**A** **B** **C** **D** **E** **F**

A14

**8**

Woodwell

WOODWELL COTTS

Hill Farm

KETTERING RD

THRAPSTON RD

**7**

MILL RD

1 CONSTABLE WLK
2 SUNNYSIDE
3 ROSE PADDOCK
4 THE SHRUBBERIES
5 WHITTLESEA TERR

VICTORIA CT

ORCHARD CT

WEST ST

HIGHFIELD

EADY'S ROW

NEWTOWN

LONG NEWTOWN ROW

HIGH ST

PLEASANT ROW

FIRST TERR

THE LEYS

TRAILLI LA

Woodford Shrubbery

**77**

PH

Woodford CE Prim Sch

BAKERS LA

THE MOORINGS

Woodford

WALNUT TREE CL

ADDINGTON RD

THE GREEN

DE LACLE

CHURCH GN

RECTORY LA

CHURCH ST

**6**

Wr Twr

**NN14**

Ham La

**5**

River Nene

Three Hills

**76**

**4**

Glebe Farm

Nene Way

Rectory Farm

CRANFORD RD

Rush Glen Farm

WOODFORD RD

Woodford Mill

**3**

RUSHWELL CL

Great Addington CE Prim Sch

MEADOW VIEW

**75**

The Manor House

MAIN ST

PH

RINGSTEAD RD

MANOR CL

CHAPEL CL

Great Addington

Home Farm

**2**

LOWER ST

STATION RD

Shooter's Hill

Nene Way

Ringstead Grange

WOODFORD RD

**1**

**NN9**

**74**

**A** **B** **C** **D** **E** **F**

95 96 97

A  B  C  D  E  F

8

7

77

6

Woodford
Grange

Nene Way

/River Nene

Westfield
Spinney

CHILD'S
ST
MEADOW LA
PEG'S LA
FREEMAN'S LA
CHURCH LA
HIGH ST
CHAPEL LA
SPINNEY
DUCK END
PH
SCHOOL LA
FRONT ST
BROWN'S LA
RISE
RIVERVIEW
GDNS
CHURCH WLK

Rose
Hill
Farm

Brawn's
Spinney

Denford

RINGSTEAD RD

NN14

5

Newleys
Farm

76

Vicarage
Spinney

4

Allot
Gdns

Tithe Farm

HAM LA

Brigg's Lodge
Farm

DENFORD RD

Ringstead

BROOK WLK 1
THE GROVE 2
BRAMBLE CL 3
CHURCH WLK 4

PEACOCK DR
BURNELL CL
NEWELL RD
GREENBANK TERR
BATES
AVE
NORTHFIELD AVE
ORCHARD
BRAYBROOKE CL
MOUNTBATTEN DR

Ringstead
Farm

Raunds Lodge
Farm

BONSOR GDNS
CARLOW RD
YEOMAN
PO
BACK LA
HIGH ST
CHERRY ST
MEADOW CL
CARLOW
TITHE CL
PH
CHAPEL ST
MIDDLEFIELD CL
CHURCH ST
PH
POUND LA
RISEBRY ST
GLADSTONE ST
SPENCER ST

Football
Gd

inewell Lake
Nature Trail
P

Ringstead
CE Prim
Sch

3

75

STATION RD
KINGFISHER
CL

Cemy

NN9

2

Blotts
Barn

BROOKS RD

A45

1

74

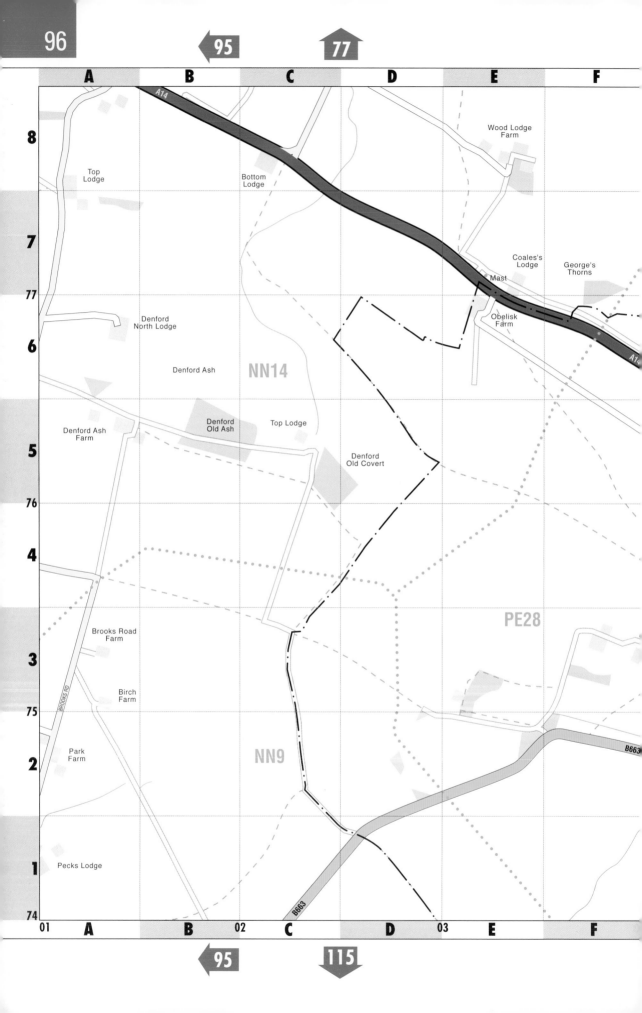

A B C D E F

8

Top
Lodge

Bottom
Lodge

A14

Wood Lodge
Farm

7

Coales's
Lodge

George's
Thorns

77

Mast

Denford
North Lodge

Obelisk
Farm

6

Denford Ash

NN14

A14

Denford Ash
Farm

Denford
Old Ash

Top Lodge

5

Denford
Old Covert

76

4

PE28

Brooks Road
Farm

3

Birch
Farm

BROOKS RD

75

B663

Park
Farm

NN9

2

B663

1

Pecks Lodge

74

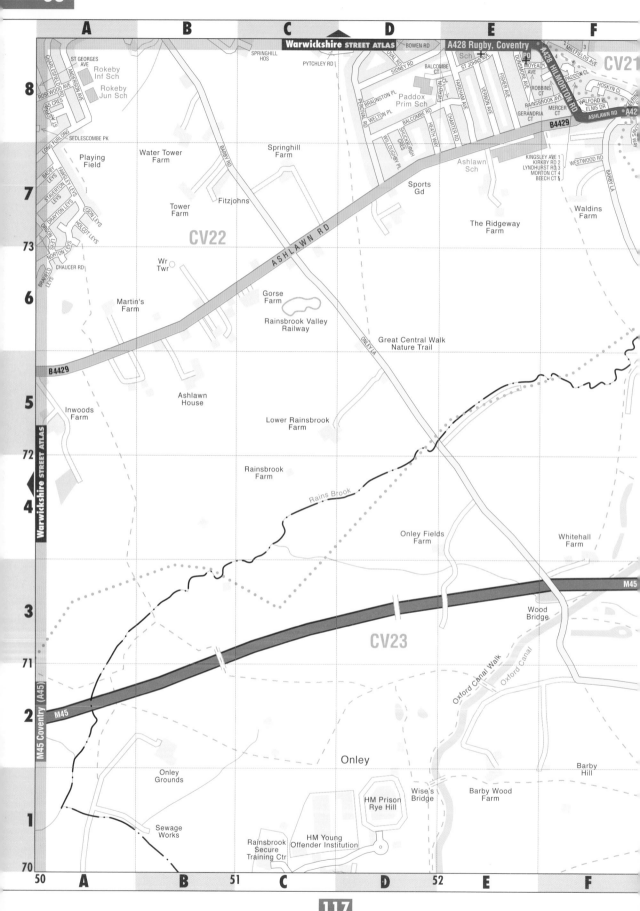

Warwickshire STREET ATLAS

CV21

CV22

CV23

**Labels on map (selected):**

St Georges Ave, Rokeby Inf Sch, Rokeby Jun Sch, Rosewood Ave, Anderson Ave, Charlesfield, Sedlescombe Pk, Long Furlong, Playing Field, Water Tower Farm, Springhill Farm, Springhill Hos, Bowen Rd, Pytchley Rd, Oval Rd, Sidney Rd, Balcombe Ct, A428 Rugby, Coventry, St Johns Rd, Sch, A428, Millfields Ave, Paddox Cl, Hoskyn Cl, Walford Pl, Elms Dr, Ashlawn Rd, Braunston Pl, Percival Rd, Welton Pl, Balcombe Rd, Charter Rd, Heath Way, Fisher Rd, Vernon Ave, Fareham Ave, Dunsmore Ave, Robbins Ct, Rainsbrook Ave, Gerandria Ct, Mercer Ct, B4429, Paddox Prim Sch, Willoughby Pl, Stuckeys Rch Cres, Ashlawn Sch, Kingsley Ave 1, Kirby Rd 2, Lyndhurst Rd 3, Morton Ct 4, Beech Ct 5, Westwood Rd, Barby La

Fawsley Leys, Staverton Leys, Drayton Leys, Eden Leys, Holgot Leys, Morton Leys, Chaucer Rd, Bromeld Leys, Tower Farm, Fitzjohns, Sports Gd, The Ridgeway Farm, Waldins Farm, Martin's Farm, Wr Twr, Gorse Farm, Rainsbrook Valley Railway, Great Central Walk Nature Trail, Onley La, Inwoods Farm, Ashlawn House, Lower Rainsbrook Farm, Rainsbrook Farm, Rains Brook, Onley Fields Farm, Whitehall Farm, M45, Wood Bridge, Oxford Canal Walk, Oxford Canal, M45 Coventry (A45), Onley, Onley Grounds, Barby Hill, Sewage Works, Rainsbrook Secure Training Ctr, HM Young Offender Institution, HM Prison Rye Hill, Wise's Bridge, Barby Wood Farm

Warwickshire STREET ATLAS

A | B | C | D | E | F

A  B  C  D  E  F

8

Flinthill

Crackshill
Farm

Heygates
Farm

The
Bungalow

Crack's
Hill

7

Grand Union Canal

Glebe
Farm

Wold
Farm

73

Mount
Pleasant

6

LOWFIELDS
RD

Nursery

Wold
Farm

MONKS WAY

WEST HADDON RD

NN6

A428  CRICK RD

5

Crick

Crick
Wharf

Cottage
Farm

MAIN RD  PO

HATHERLEY
CL

1 COLEMAN CL
2 THORNTON CL
3 ASHWORTH CL
4 WOLSEY CL

BOAT HORSE LA

72

West
Lodge

Montrose
Fam

4

Crick Tunnel

Silsworth
Lodge

3

Jurassic Way

Flavell's
Lodge

71

Limes
Farm

WATFORD RD

2

Grand Union Canal

The
Old Lodge

Watford
Covert

Heygate
Farm

1

Home
Farm

Poole's
Lodge

Northingworth
Lodge

70

A  B  60  C  D  61  E  F

A B C D E F

8

Winwick

Warren
Covert

White House
Farm

Mill House

Springfield
Farm

7

73

Pasture
Farm

Glebe
Farm

Wayside
Farm

Manor
Farm

6

Bungalow
Farm

Jurassic Way

NN6

Marrowell
Farm

West Haddon
Grange

5

A428        CRICK RD

SYLES CT

NELVERTOFT RD

WEST END

WORCESTER
CL

CHURCH
CL

PARNELL CL

MORRISON
CL

LATTIMORE CL

MUNCASTER
WAY

MORRISON PARK RD

ELEANOR

GUILSBOROUGH RD

THE
OLD BRICKYARD

72

ALMSHOUSES

West Haddon
Endowed CE
Prim Sch

THE
GREEN

VICTORIA CL

ELIZABETH RD

PITCHLEY CL

WESTFIELD
CT

FIELD CL

ATTERBURY CL

DAIRY CL

CROWN

PH

PO

FORGE DR

4

STAFFORDS LA RD

HARDAYS LA

HILLSIDE

FITZROY
CT

STATION RD

HIGH ST

SPENCER
CT

NORTHAMPTON RD

West Haddon

The Hall

FOXHILL RD

Torkington
Lodge

Lodge
Farm

3

WATFORD RD

Washbrook
Spinney

Hungerwell
Barn

71

2

Home Farm

Grove Farm

Park House

Foxhill

1

A428

70

62        A        63        B        C        D        64        E        F

**A** **B** **C** **D** **E** **F**

8

Blackpits
Spinney

Square Hedge
Spinney

Cottesbrooke

7

Oak
Spinney

Lodges
Spinney

Cottage
Farm

The Green Lane

73

Hollowell
Resr

Hollowell
Grange

6

Great Creaton
Lodge

NN6

5

Neaturn
Lodge

Hollowell
Lodge

Hollowell

Home
Farm

HOME FARM YD.

WELFORD RD

HOME FARM CL.
LANGHAM CT.
BRIXWORTH RD

72

GUILSBOROUGH HILL

ORCHARD CL.

CREATON RD

Hollowell Rd

LITCHFIELD LA.
HIGH HORSESHOE CL.
THE JETTY
THE HOUSE

THE GREEN
SPRING CL.

HIGHFIELD PK

PO

VIOLET LA.

Great Creaton
Prim Sch

4

CHURCH HILL

Sewage
Works

Creaton

PH

Blackberry
Hill
Farm

JUDGES
CT

Highgate
House

3

Pastures
Farm

Macmillan Way

TEETON LA.

71

2

Ravensthorpe
Lodge

Landymoors
Farm

Ravensthorpe
Resr

A5199

1

Water
Works

Teeton
Lodge

FIVEWAYS

Hall

Teeton

70

**68** **A** **B** **69** **C** **D** **70** **E** **F**

86
106

A B C D E F

8

Cottesbrooke Hall

Cottesbrooke Hall Gdns

Cottesbrooke Grange

Old School Cotts

Main St

Station Rd

Home Farm

Pitmorehill Spinney

7

73

Beck Dairy

Gullivers

6

Macmillan Way

Creaton Covert

5

Badge Lodge

NN6

72

Sewage Works

Brixworth Rd

Glebe Farm

Corn Mill

Station Rd

4

Grooms La

Creaton Grange Farm

Sewage Works

Little Creaton

3

Matts Cottages

Midshires Way

71

Folly Farm

2

Spratton Rd

Welford Rd

Spratton Hall Sch

Erskin Wood

Cemy

Brixworth Rd

Ash Tree Farm

Smith St

A5199

Spratton CE Prim Sch

Gorse Rd

Stavford Cl

High St

Smithills

Manor Rd

School Rd

PH

PO

1

Bakers La 1
Haynes La 2
The Piece 3
Blackthorn Cl 4

Church Rd

Glebelands

St Lukes Cl

Yew Tree La

Ye Olde Hall Cl

Church La

Spratton

70

1 A 72 B C 73 D E F

124
106

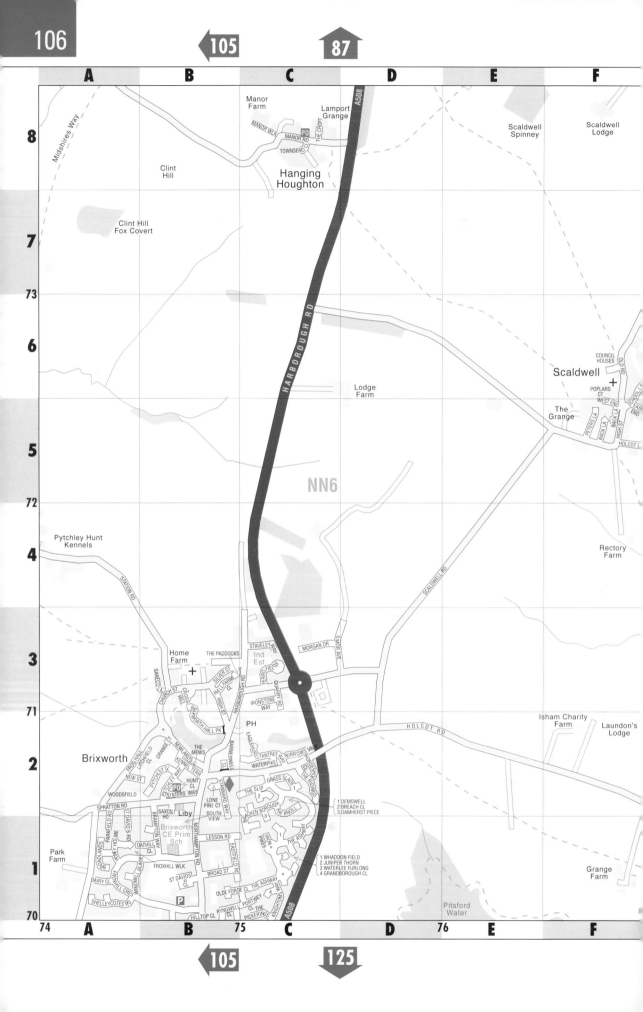

88
108

**A** **B** **C** **D** **E** **F**

8

7

73

6

5

72

4

3

71

2

1

70

Oak
Spinney

OLD RD

CHAPEL LA

SCALDWELL RD
or LAMPORT RD

TOWNSON CL

BARNES CL

CHARLES CL

CLEAVERS LA

HARRINGTON RD

BRIXLE RD

FAXTON
END

Wold Farm
Ind Pk

MILL LA

BROUGHTON RD

Old

Grange
Farm

PH

WALGRAVE RD

CHERRY HILL

EAST END

HOLCOT LA

NN6

Ford

TOWNSEND RD

SPRINGFIELD RD

OLD RD

HILL
CL

ORCHARD
CL

Mill
Farm

HOLCOT RD

Cemy

Rectory
Farm

Works

Brixworth
Fox Covert

Pitsford Water

Grange Farm
Cottages

HOLCOT RD

New Grange
Farm

Causeway

BRIXWORTH RD

WALGRAVE RD

The
Lodge

P

**A** **B** **C** **D** **E** **F**

7  78  79

126
108

107
89

| | A | B | C | D | E | F |
|---|---|---|---|---|---|---|

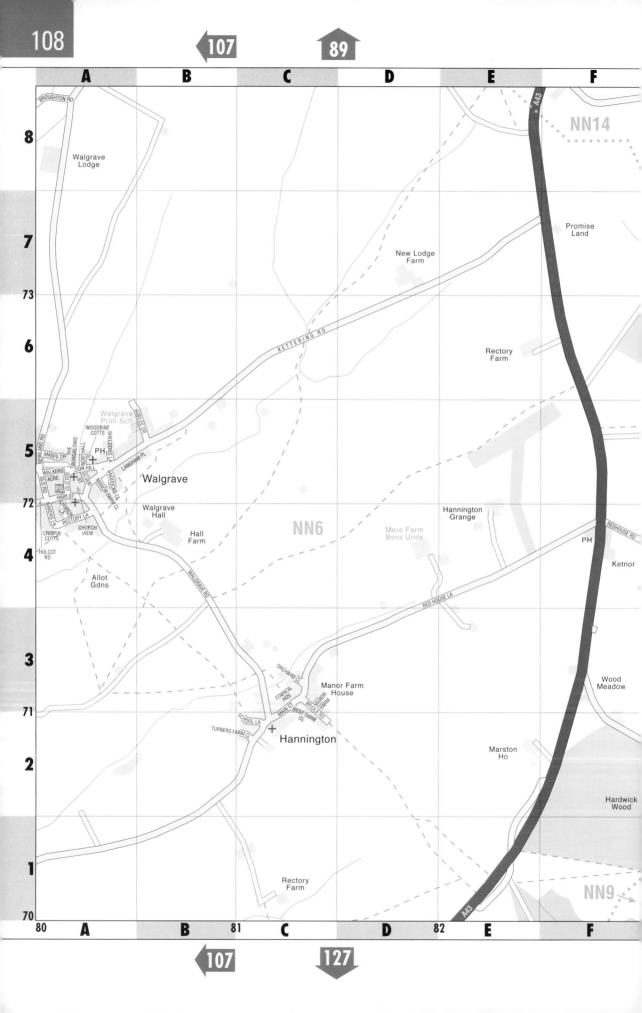

BROUGHTON RD

NN14

8

Walgrave Lodge

7

73

KETTERING RD

New Lodge Farm

Promise Land

6

Rectory Farm

Walgrave Prim Sch

JUBILEE DR

WOODBINE COTTS

SHELDONS LA

LANGHAM PL

NEWLAND RD

AMBER DR

THE BUNGALOWS

NORTHALL

PH

ZION HILL

PADDOCKS CL

MANOR FARM CL

5

Walgrave

WALKERS ACRE

SILVER ST

OLD RD

HIGH ST

PO

CHURCH

Walgrave Hall

Hannington Grange

Mere Farm Bsns Units

NN6

72

BAKERS LA

RECTORY LA

CRISPIN COTTS

CHURCH VIEW

Hall Farm

PH

Ketnor

HOLCOT RD

REDHOUSE RD

4

Allot Gdns

WALGRAVE RD

RED HOUSE LA

Wood Meadow

3

ORCHARD CL

Manor Farm House

COUNCIL HOS

MAIN ST

MANOR FARM

BRIDLE RD

WEST FARM CL

71

SCHOOL LA

TURNERS FARM CL

Hannington

Marston Ho

2

Hardwick Wood

1

Rectory Farm

A43

NN9

70

107
127

**A** **B** **C** **D** **E** **F**

Pytchley
Lodge

8

Pytchley
Grange

7

73

Badsaddle
Farm

Badsaddle
Wood

Moorfield
Lodge

6

NN14

Orlingbury
Hold

PYTCHLEY RD

THE
GREEN

TAGGIES YD

5

NN6

NORTHAMPTON RD

THE PADDOCKS

72

Withmale
Park Wood

Wythemail
Park Farm

4

Bush
Walk

REDHOUSE RD

Rectory
Farm

3

71

2

NN9

1

Hardwick
Lodge

70

**A** **B** 84 **C** **D** 85 **E** **F**

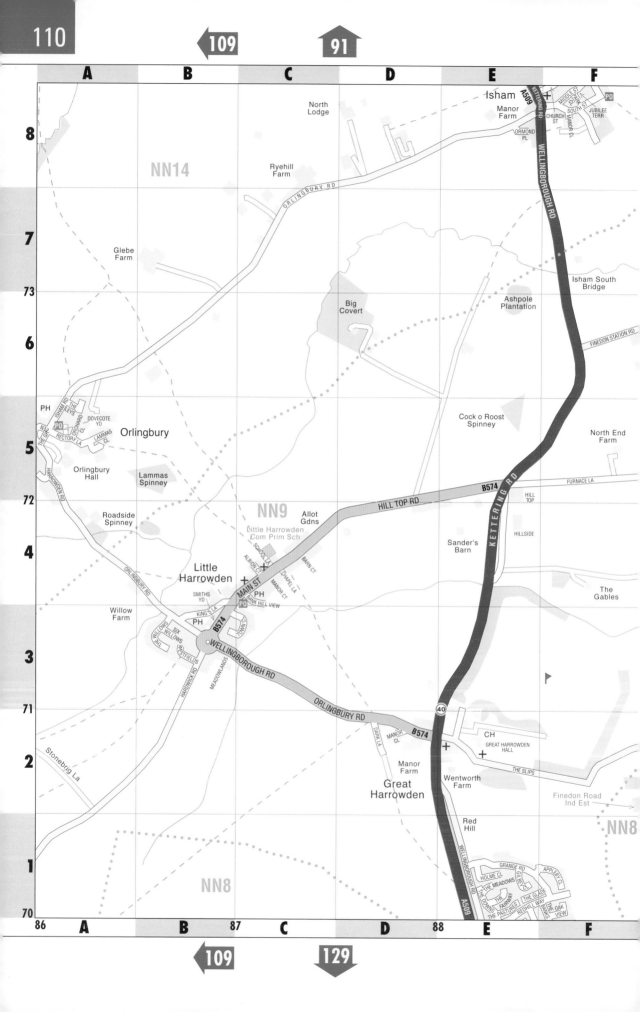

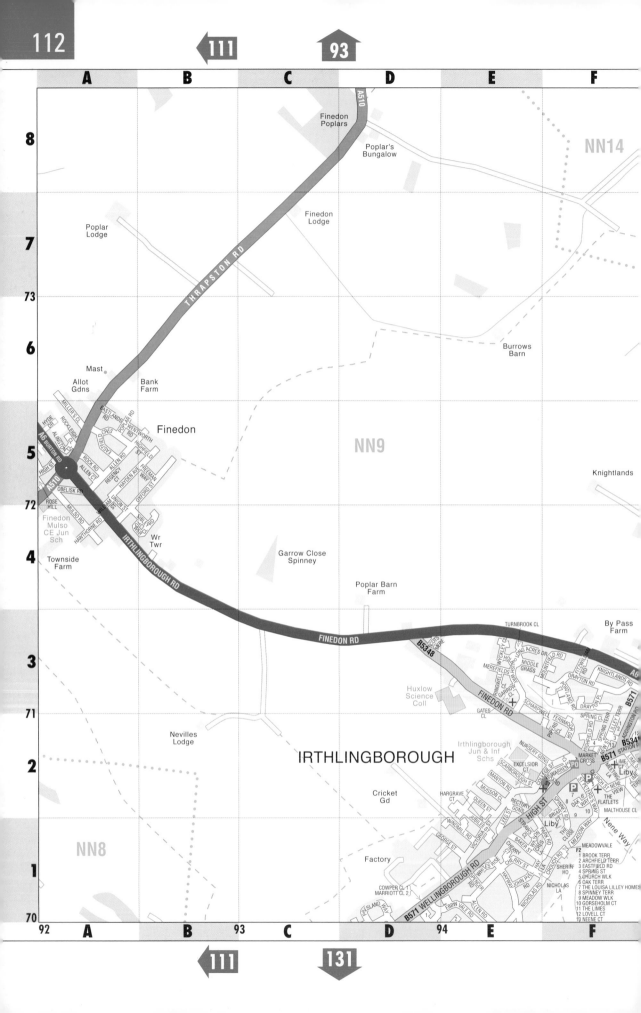
**A**   **B**   **C**   **D**   **E**   **F**

8

NN14

Finedon
Poplars

Poplar's
Bungalow

A510

7

Poplar
Lodge

Finedon
Lodge

THRAPSTON RD

73

6

Burrows
Barn

Mast

Allot
Gdns

Bank
Farm

NN9

5

MILLER'S CL
ROCKLEIGH
ALLINGTON RD
HYDE DR
EASTLANDS RD
POPLAR RD
WENTWORTH RD
CRES
EASTFIELD
HIGHFIELD
RD
Finedon
ROCK RD
ALLEN RD
ALLEN CT
REGENCY CT
HAYDEN AVE
FREEMAN WAY
OXFORD ST

Knightlands

A6 BURTON RD

72

A510
HIGH ST
OBELISK RD
ROSE
HILL
MULSO RD
HAWTHORNE RD
WILLIAM ST
UNION ST
SIBLEY
CLOSE
WEST

Finedon
Mulso
CE Jun
Sch

IRTHLINGBOROUGH RD

Wr
Twr

4

Townside
Farm

Garrow Close
Spinney

Poplar Barn
Farm

FINEDON RD

TURNBROOK CL

By Pass
Farm

3

B5348
SCOTS
INFRE

Huxlow
Science
Coll

FINEDON RD

WICKLEY CL
DINGWELL CL
GARROW CL
MIDDLE
GRASS
ACRES DR
RD RD
MOUNTFIELD RD
SCHARPWELL
MEREFIELDS
PORTLAND RD
DRAYTON RD
KNIGHTLANDS RD
FITZWILLIAM RD
DRAY

B571

A6

71

GATES
CL

PIPERS CL
FERNMOOR DR
SPRING CLOSE
SPRING TERR
LILLEY TERR
ADDINGTON RD

NURSERY GDNS

B571

B5341

Nevilles
Lodge

IRTHLINGBOROUGH

Irthlingborough
Jun & Inf
Schs

EXCELSIOR

MARKET
CROSS

STATION RD
Liby

LIME
CT

2

SCARBOROUGH ST
MANTON RD
MUSSON CL
QUEEN ST
RECTORY
GDNS
WARREN RD
HIGH ST
BRIAR HILL
NENE
OAK ST
NEW
MEADOW WAY

NENE WAY

THE
FLATLETS

Cricket
Gd

HARGRAVE
CT

MALTHOUSE CL

Liby

MEADOWVALE

F2
1 BROOK TERR
2 ARCHFIELD TERR
3 EASTFIELD RD
4 SPRING ST
5 CHURCH WLK
6 OAK TERR
7 THE LOUISA LILLEY HOMES
8 SPINNEY TERR
9 MEADOW WLK
10 GORSEHOLM CT
11 THE LIMES
12 LOVELL CT
13 NEENE CT

1

NN8

WINDMILL RD
VICTORIA ST
LEES ST
JUBILEE ST
GEORGE ST
BAKERS ST
CHERRY ST
CHERRY ST
PARK RD
CROUCH RD
NICHOLAS RD

SHERIFF
HO

Factory

NICHOLAS
LA

B571 WELLINGBOROUGH RD
HAYDEN RD
JOHN PYEL
ALLEN RD
BBW VALE RD
GRESLAND WAY
WHALES RISE

COWPER CL 1
MARRIOTT CL 2

70

92   A   B   93   C   D   94   E   F

A   B   C   D   E   F

8

Top
Lodge

Sewage
Works

WATERVILL
WAY
AMEN PL
WEEKLY CL
HIGH ST
AMEN
CNR

THE
GREEN
BACK LA
BAKEHOUSE HILL
BURROWS FARM LA
PH

Burrows
Farm

Burrows
Farm

CHURCH
WLK

DOVECOT DR
CHAPEL HILL
EVERGREEN DR
UP END
ROSE
COTTS
IRTHLINGBOROUGH RD

Little
Addington

**NN14**

Mallows
Cotton

7

Addington Park
Ind Est

HILL FARM
EST

Hog Dyke

A45

73

MEADOW LA

6

Freestones
Lodge

PH

**NN9**

5

WELFORD CL 1
FESTIVAL CL 2

BUGBY DR
FETTEDENE RD
GARDENFIELDS CL

CHURCHILL AVE
LANGLEY
CRES
WELFORD AVE

NOBLE AVE

ADDINGTON RD
THE SHORTLANDS
CLAIRE
CL
PALMER AVE

Nene Way

72

ALEXANDER RD
ALEXANDER PL
PO

River Nene

4

Needham Rd

ALFRED ST
LAURENCE
WAY
RECTORY
CL

Stanwick

JOHN
EAGLE
CL

Ford

DOLBEN AVE
GREEN LA
MANSFIELD ST
SPENCER PAR
PARK
ST

Crow
Hill

Diamonds
Bsns Ctr

MARSH LA

WEST ST

HILLSTONE
CT

VILLA CL
SAMUELS CL
HIGHWAY RD
HIGH GRANGE RD

3

The
Hall

DOVEHOUSE CL
DOVEHOUSE GDNS

B571

ATTLEY WAY
DIAMOND WAY

Hall
Farm

71

B5348
STATION RD

Nene Park
(Rushden &
Diamonds FC)

Factory

STATION RD

STATION RD

Netherfield

2

Dieren

Caravan
Site

Redlands
Farm

The
Quarries

1

Nene Way

Chowns Mill
Bsns Pk

A6
A45

**NN10**

STANWICK RD

70

A   B   C   D   E   F

**RAUNDS**

**Stanwick**

NN9

A45
B663
BRICK KILN RD
MIDLAND RD
NORTH ST
HIGH ST
BROOK ST
GROVE ST
WELLINGTON RD
CHELVESTON RD
WARTH PARK WAY
MEADOW LA

Scalley Farm
Kepwick
Scalley Farm
Sewage Works
Hog Dyke
Mast
Windmill Prim Sch
Cemy

New Barn Farm
Northdale Farm
1 Chestnut Ct
2 Penny La
3 Bridge St
4 Tithe Barn Cl
5 Dovecote Cl
Blotts Barn Bsns Ctr
Brooks Farm
BROOKS RD

Liby
Church
Manor House
Manor Farm
Thorpe House Farm
Darsdale Farm
Schs

SHELTON RD

Stanwick Prim Sch
Cemy
The Avenue
Brookside
East St
The Hollow
The Woodlands

Pastures Lodge Farm
Kiriandra House
Pasture Barn
New Covert
Stanwick Pastures

PRETORIA COTTS

98   A   99   B   C   00   D   E   F

70   71   72   73   6   5   4   3   2   1   8   7

A B C D E F

Bedfordshire STREET ATLAS

PE28

8

7

73

6

NN9

5

72

4

3

71

2

1

70

B663

Napleton Lodge Farm

Station House

Inn

Napleton Cottage

Raunds Plantation

STATION RD

Friendly Lodge

Old Meadow

Railway Lodge

Raunds Grange

Black Lodge

Red Lodge

Mere Farm

SHELTON RD

Bottom Farm

BROOK ST

Hillstone House

Rose Cottage

The Gables

Top Farm

Hargrave Riding Centre

New England Farm

CHURCH ST

NAGS HEAD LA

PH

Hargrave

ELM CL

CHURCH RD

PO

Grange Farm

The Grove

Hargrave Hall

B645

PE28

Mill View Farm

B645

115
97

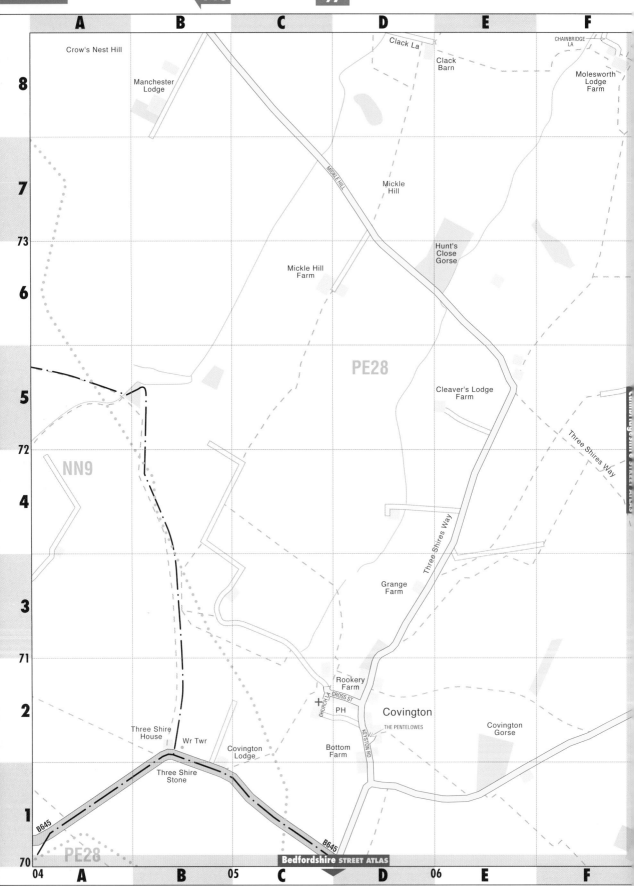

Crow's Nest Hill

Clack La

Clack Barn

CHAINBRIDGE LA

Molesworth Lodge Farm

Manchester Lodge

MICKLE HILL

Mickle Hill

Hunt's Close Gorse

Mickle Hill Farm

PE28

Cleaver's Lodge Farm

Three Shires Way

NN9

Three Shires Way

Grange Farm

Rookery Farm

CROSS ST

Covington

CHURCH LA

PH

THE PENTELOWES

Covington Gorse

Three Shire House

Wr Twr

Covington Lodge

Bottom Farm

KEYSTON RD

Three Shire Stone

B645

B645

PE28

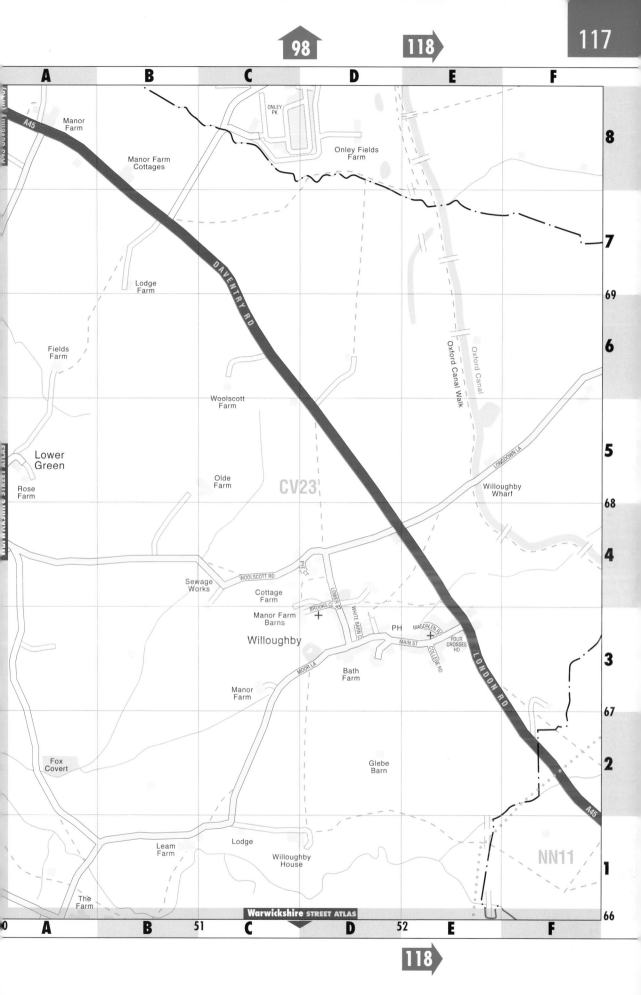

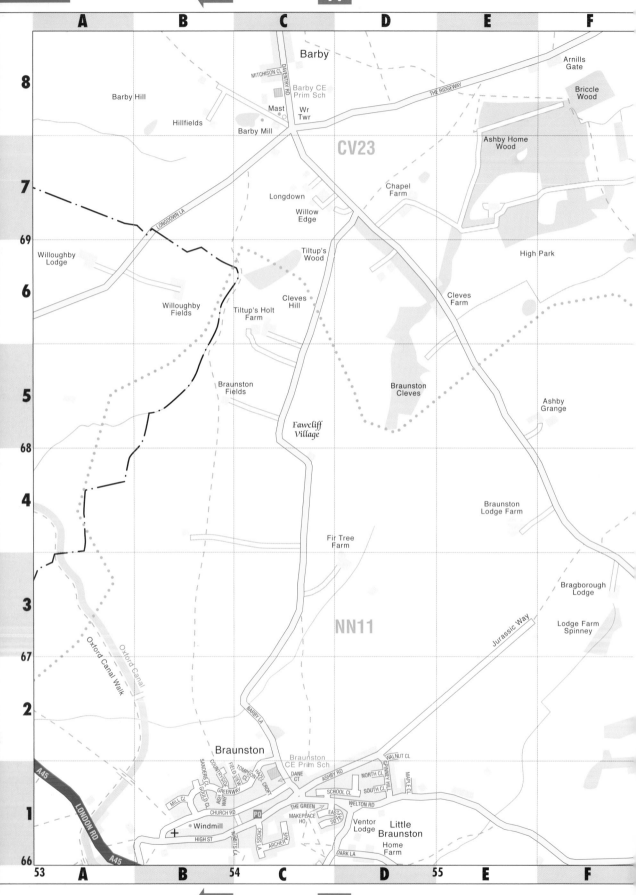

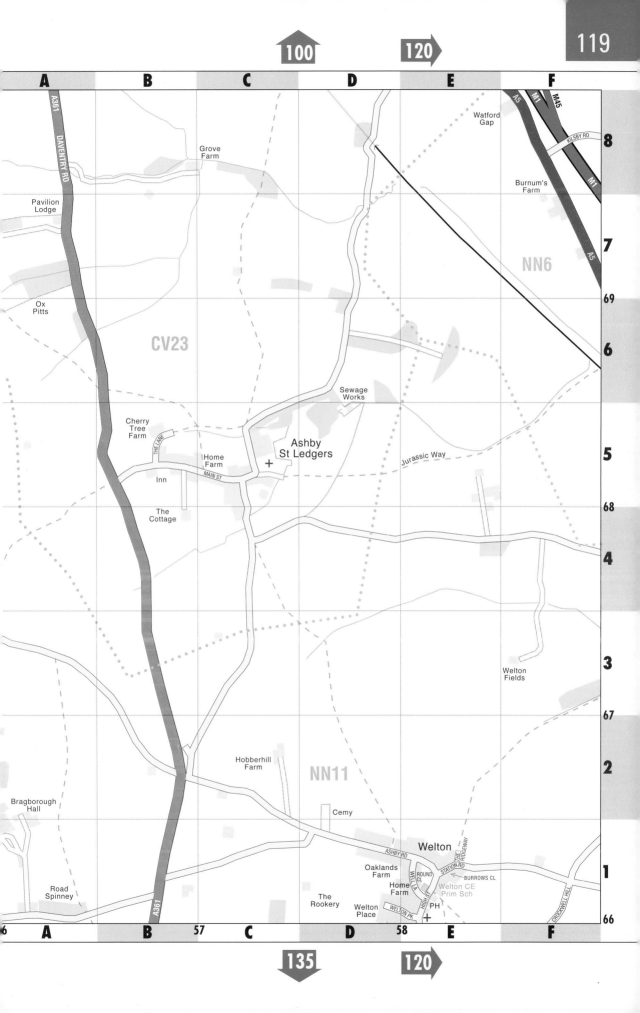

119
101

**A** **B** **C** **D** **E** **F**

8

WATFORD RD

Long Spinney

Barleypiece Spinney

Watford Lodge Farm

KILSBY RD

Jurassic Way

7

WEST HADDON RD

Cemy

Park House

69

Bluebell Spinney

WOODLANDS CT

CHURCH ST

MAIN ST

Jurassic Way

PARK LA

PARK CL

HEMLEY CT

PO

EDEN CL

Watford

6

Watford Locks

Grand Union Canal

Sewage Works

Watford Lodge

LONG BUCKBY RD

STATION RD

5

Foxholes

Watford Gap Service Area

NN6

Mast

Murcott

68

B5385

FOG COTTS

Brockhill Lodge

B5386

4

Langborough Barn

Welton Lodge Farm

3

Mill House

67

NN11

2

Sewage Works

Welton Grange

Ryehill Lodge

White Barn Farm

1

Welton Hythe

A5

M1

Greenhill Farm

66

59 **A** **B** 60 **C** **D** 61 **E** **F**

102
122

A  B  C  D  E  F

8

7

69

6

NN6

5

68

Foxhill
Farm

Buckby
Lodge

A428

Leighton
Lodge

Paynes
Lodge

Gale
House

Gale
Lodge

Covert
Barn

A428

B5385

Hinde Mills
Barn

Grange
Farm

Vanderplank's
Covert

Mast

Highfields

Uplands
Farm

Lodge LA

Mast

Old
Coopers

Lodge Farm

Long
Buckby
Pocket
Park

MURCOTT
CL

MURCOTT

WEST ST

Church
Farm

Long Buckby

LAWRENCE CT

THE BANKS

THE CHASE

GRIMLEY CL

TOWING END

STENHOUSE CL

ORCHARD RISE

COTTON
END

4

PARKFIELD RD

SYERS GREEN CL

JUBILEE CL

SYERS LA

HOLMFIELD
TERR

HARBIDS

KING ST

SHARPES
LA

SANDERS
TERR

CHURCH ST

THE
MEWS

MARKET PL

HIGH ST

PYTCHLEY DR

TEBBUT CL

THE LEYS

LEYS CL

MILL

MULTOAKE TERR

THE
APPLEGARTH

BERRYFIELD

THE

LIME AVE

Inf
Sch

EAST ST

GROVE FARM CL

Rye Close

Liby

THE MOUNTS

STATION CL

PITLAMS CL

WILLIAM RD

SKINYARD LA

HAL DR

WITSSON

KINGSTON
WAY

CLIFTON CL

PHILLIPS

ASHMORE

HAMMAS LEYS

High Stack

MARRIOTS RD

The
Mounts

SALEM CL

LUCY
RD

THE POPLARS

SOUTH CL

HADRY CL

SPENCER RD

BRINGTON RD

WATTS WAY

Oak Lodge
Farm

3

GRASS CROFT

GREENHILL

RYEHILL CL

GREENHILL
CT

COOK
WAY

SOUTH CL

WRIGHT
RD

WINDSOR CL

1 CHARLES CL
2 CHESTNUT CL

Long Buckby
Jun Sch

ROCKHILL
RD

COOK CL

FOX'S CL

STATION RD

WATSON RD

Gravel Pit
Lodge

Lodge LA

67

2

Hoborough
Hill

P

Long
Buckby

Floyers
Farm

Panther's
Lodge

Patford
Bridge

1

Brook's
Barn

Perkin's
Lodge

NN7

66

62  A  B  63  C  D  64  E  F

137
122

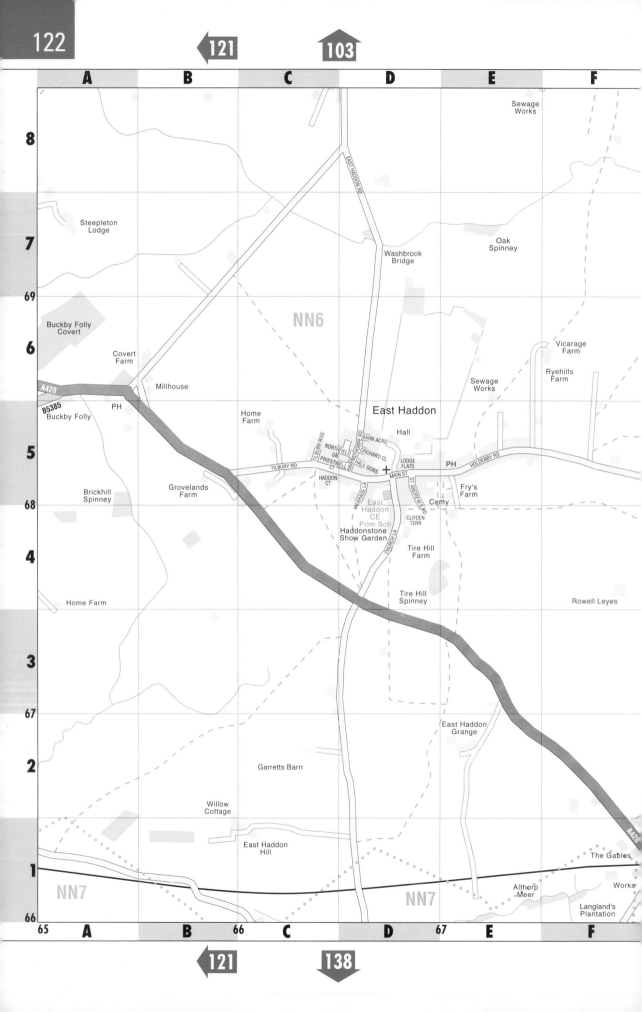
A | B | C | D | E | F

8

7

69

**NN6**

6

Sewage Works

Steepleton Lodge

Oak Spinney

East Haddon Rd

Washbrook Bridge

Buckby Folly Covert

Covert Farm

Millhouse

A428

B5385

Buckby Folly

PH

Home Farm

Vicarage Farm

Ryehills Farm

Sewage Works

East Haddon

Hall

5

TILBURY RD

TILBURY RISE

NORTHFIELD

ORCHARD CL

RAVENSTHORPE RD

BARN ACRE

GM

PRIESTWELL CT

HALL GDNS

LODGE FLATS

PH

HOLDENBY RD

Grovelands Farm

HADDON CT

VICARAGE LA

MAIN ST

ST ANDREW'S RD

Fry's Farm

Brickhill Spinney

68

East Haddon CE Prim Sch

CLIFDEN TERR

Cemy

Haddonstone Show Garden

CHURCH LA

Tire Hill Farm

4

Home Farm

Tire Hill Spinney

Rowell Leyes

3

67

East Haddon Grange

2

Garretts Barn

Willow Cottage

A428

East Haddon Hill

The Gables

1

**NN7**

**NN7**

Althorp Meer

Works

Langland's Plantation

66

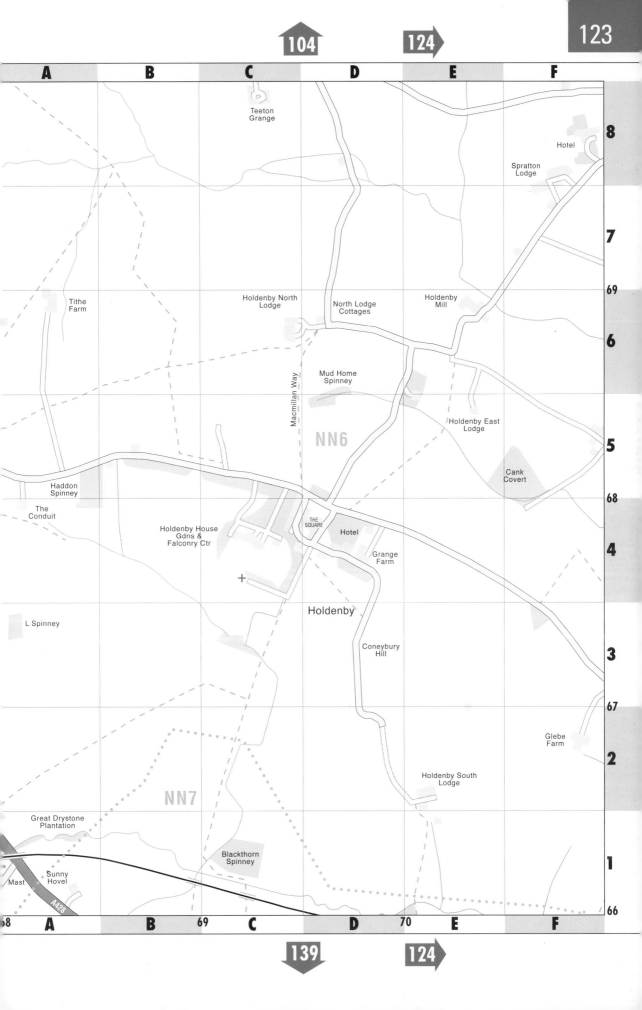

**A** **B** **C** **D** **E** **F**

8

Teeton
Grange

Hotel

Spratton
Lodge

7

69

Tithe
Farm

Holdenby North
Lodge

North Lodge
Cottages

Holdenby
Mill

6

Macmillan Way

Mud Home
Spinney

Holdenby East
Lodge

NN6

5

Haddon
Spinney

Cank
Covert

68

The
Conduit

Holdenby House
Gdns &
Falconry Ctr

THE
SQUARE

Hotel

Grange
Farm

+

Holdenby

L Spinney

Coneybury
Hill

3

67

Glebe
Farm

2

NN7

Holdenby South
Lodge

Great Drystone
Plantation

Blackthorn
Spinney

1

Mast

Sunny
Hovel

A428

66

68 **A** **B** 69 **C** **D** 70 **E** **F**

A   B   C   D   E   F

8

7

Spratton Grange Farm

Spratton Lodge

69

Spratton Grange

Long Spinney

6

Cank Farm

NN6

Midshires Way

5

Spratton Bridge

WELFORD RD

Merry Tom Crossing

68

Circular Spinney

Circular Spinney

P

4

Sander's Covert

Hoe Hill

Merry Tom La

Brampton Valley Way

Pitsford Lodge Farm

3

Damsel's Barn

Sedgebrook Home Farm

67

Spinney Farm

Sedgebrook Hall

Brampton Hill

The Red House

2

Brampton Hill Farm

Pitsford & Brampton

P

Brampton La

PH

Chapel Brampton

Humphrey Farm

Hamilton St

CEDAR LA

BACK LA

GREAT CL

LITTLE CL

PO

Pitsford Rd

Northampton & Lamport Rly

NN2

1

Church Farm

HALFWAY THORN

HARLESTONE RD

SPENCER CL

NORTHAMPTON RD

PH

A5199

STABLES LA

The Bramptons Prim Sch

66

WILLOW CL

A5199

GORSE RD

ORCHARD CL

RYEFIELDS CL

CHURCH RD

YEW TREE LA

HOLDENBY RD

THE WAY

Circular Spinney

HILLTOP CL
STONEHILL WAY
HITS
SAXON POPH LEYS
FAR BROOK
KNIGHTONS WAY
SALT PIKES
HIGH SLADE

A508

8

THE ASHWAY 1
WHEATENS CL 2
2

South Lodge

Brixworth Country Park

P
Visitor Ctr

7

NORTHAMPTON RD

Pitsford Hill

Northampton Sailing Club

Pitsford Water

Moulton Grange Cottages

69

Hill Farm

NN6

Moulton Grange

6

Mon

P
GRANGE LA

RESERVOIR HOS

Springhill Farm

THE DOVECOTE
CHURCH LA
GLEBE LA
ORCHARD COTTS

Pitsford

Pitsford Prim Sch

MANOR RD
BROADLANDS
THE CHASE

5

The Dairy Farm

68

Longman's Hill

THE SQUARE
PO
HIGH ST

PH

DRUMMOND CL

4

HOME FARM LA

Northamptonshire Gram Sch

STABLE CT

Sedgebrook Grange

Home Farm

Mast

Hillcrest

BRAMPTON LA

MOULTON RD

3

Pitsford Ctr

67

Duke's Clump

Fox Covert Hall

PITSFORD RD

NN3

Grotto Spinney

NN2

Bunkers Hill Farm

2

SPECTACLE LA

Sedgebrook Lodge Farm

Butcher's Spinney

Ford

Brickhill Spinney

Boughton Park

BUTCHER'S LA

Moulton Mill

1

A508

PH

BUTCHER'S LA
SPRING CL

66

← 125    107

A  B  C  D  E  F

8

Lower Brixworth
Lodge

Pitsford Water

BRIXWORTH RD

Manor
Farm

RECTORY LA
MAIN ST
PO
FARM CL
GLEBE CL
WINSLAND CT
WALGRAVE RD
POLLARDS LA
PH
BACK LA
BRITTENS
VIEW
SUNNY
BANK
Holcot
The
Hawthorns
Equestrian
Ctr
SYWELL RD

NN6

7

Northfields

Moulton Grange
Farm

MOULTON RD

TITHE CL

Hospital
Bungalow

69

Hillcrest

Moulton Lodge
Farm

Tithe
Farm

6

North
Farm

South
Lodge

5

HOLCOT RD

Overstone
Old Rectory

68

Slade
Farm

Grange
Cottages

Overstone
Grange

4

Moulton
Lodge

BOUGHTON FAIR LA

NN3

A43

3

Hog Hole
Spinney

Marsh
Spinney

KETTERING RD

67

PITSFORD RD

2

Holcot
Centre

Cemy

THE GROVE

BROWNS CL

Grove
Farm

GROVE FARM LA

Sandy Hill
Farm

SANDY HILL LA

PARK VIEW

Moulton

THE HOLLIES
THE COLLEGE
GROUNDS
Moulton
Coll
Moulton
Prim Sch
CHURCH VIEW
CHURCH
PARADE
CHURCH HILL
Moulton
CHURCH
MEWS
NN6

Sewage
Works

THE LAURELS
SEWELL CL
WEST ST
SCHOOL LA
HIGH ST
SIDDONS WAY
TARRANT CL
PYTCHLEY
VIEW
HOMESTEAD CL
THE CRESCENT
Overstone Rd
EADY CL
WANTAGE CL
PARK
VIEW CL
Overstone
Farm

ARNSBY CRES

JEFFS CL
LYTHON CL
THE PADDOCKS
POUND CT
AND LA
CROSS ST
BARLOW LA
NORTHAMPTON
LA
ASHBY
PH
PO
Liby
DOVE S LA
OAKLEY DR
PRINCE DE WALES ROW
TARRANT WAY
ASHLEY LA
A43
OVERSTONE LA
Overstone LA
SYWELL RD
THE AVENUE
BILLING LA

1

Carey CT

BOUGHTON RD

Moulton
Sch & Coll

LUNCHFIELD GDNS
LUNCHFIELD LA

66

C1
1 LEONARD LA
2 BLUEBELL PK CVN PK
3 THE NURSERIES
4 ASHBY GDNS
5 CHAPPELL HO
6 WELLS CT
7 LUNCHFIELD WLK
8 STOCKS HILL

A B C D E F

8

Hardwick Short
Wood

NN9

Sywell
Wood

7

Rifle Range

69

New College
Farm

SYWELL RD

White
House

Teacaddy
Farm

A43

6

Sywell
Grange

NN6

New Inn
Spinney

Sywell Lodge
Farm

5

Northampton
(Sywell)
Airport

KETTERING RD

Rectory
Farm

68

Overstone
Grange

Ind
Est

Sywell Airport
Bsns Pk

Hotel

4

NN3

WELLINGBOROUGH RD

Park
Pond

HOLCOT LA

Sywell

WEBBS LA

Rectory
Farm

WESTLEA RD

S STONELEA RD

PH

Sywell
Hall

3

PIE CNR

OVERSTONE
HTS

CHURCH LA

The
Rectory

Sywell
House

HORSE SHOE
COTTS

67

Cowpasture Spinney

WOODFORD CHASE

PARK CL

BREAMBRIDGE CL

Sywell CE
Prim Sch

Bonfire
Bank

2

Lavender Hill
Farm

PO

Ass
Bank

OVERSTONE RD

ECTON LA

Ferny
Bank

New
Plantation

Long Spinney

Overstone
Prim Sch

SYWELL RD

OVERSTONE CRES

WOODLAND AVE

Highlands

Large
Quarter

Cottage
Farm

1

Overstone

Parson's
Wood

Young
Spinney

ASHDALE CL

WOODSIDE

PINE CRES

PINE AVE

New Hayes
Wood

Hayes
Wood

Gashouse
Spinney

WOODSIDE AVE

PARKLANDS

HIGH WOODS

66

127
109

A B C D E F

8

**Hardwick**

Hardwick
Grange

Hardwick
House

Manor
House

Merrydale
Farm

HARDWICK RD

7

NN9

69

Sywell
Wood

Appleby
Gate

SYWELL RD

6

Cheesecake
Spinney

MOONSHINE GAP

Appleby
Lodge

Highfield
Lodge

5

Wood Lodge
Farm

Wilby
Hall

68

Corries
Spinney

4

HIGHFIELD RD

The
Rookery

NN6

NN8

Wr Twr

The
Grange

3

Poultry
Farm

Manor
Farm

67

GLEBE RD

Mears Ashby
Prim Sch

Mears
Ashby

NORTH ST

NURSERY CT

2

TINKERS
CRES

EARLS BARTON RD

MANOR RD

CHURCH ST

BAKEHOUSE
LA

WELLINGBOROUGH RD

VICARAGE LA

DALE FARM
COTTS

DALE CL

Sywell
Bottom

Recn
Gd

PADDOCK

AXIS LA

THE BARNS

DUCHESS END

WILBY RD

Mast

MEARS ASHBY RD

Glebe
Barn

SYWELL RD

Hill
Farm

PH

1

66

83 A 84 B C 85 D E F

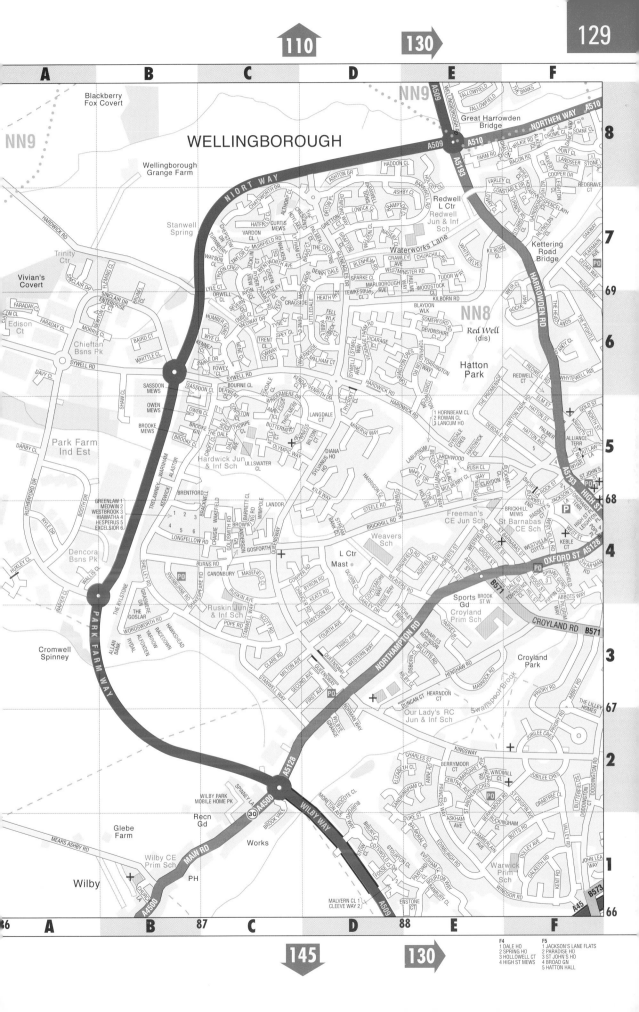

A4
1 CHURCH WAY
2 ANGEL LA
3 MARKET SQ
4 PEBBLE LA
5 CHEESE LA
6 SWANS LA
7 CORN LA
8 SPRING LA
9 The Swansgate Ctr

A5
1 CHARNWOOD
2 ALLIANCE CT
3 BAKER ST
4 PERKINS CT
5 BELL CT
6 LITTLE PARK ST
7 UPPER HAVELOCK ST
8 PARK CRES
9 SALEM LA

10 BENGEWORTH CT
11 HERRIOTTS CT

B5
1 LODGE CT
2 MANOR CT
3 HOWARD CT
4 LAUREL CT
5 STANLEY MEWS

112
132

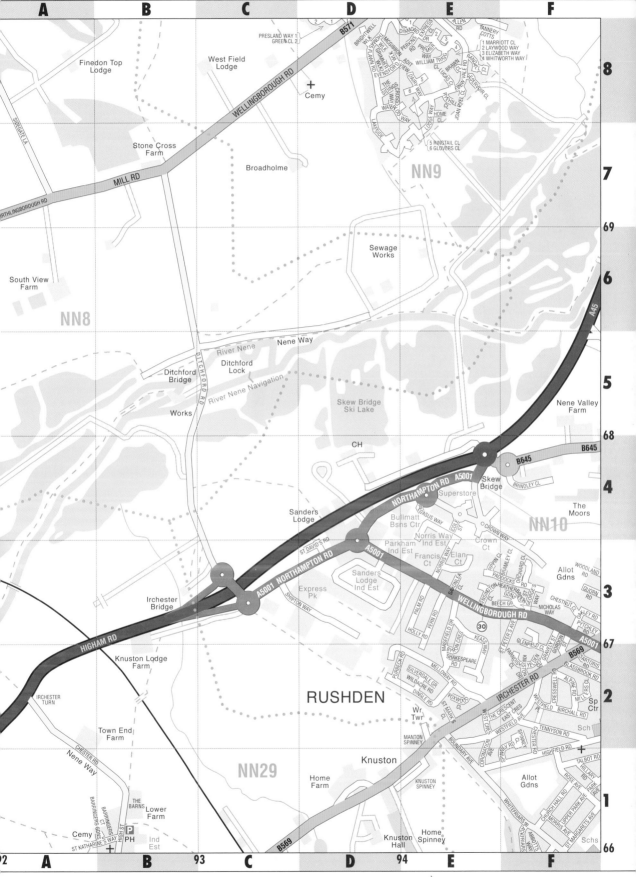

**A** **B** **C** **D** **E** **F**

Finedon Top Lodge

SIDEGATE LA

IRTHLINGBOROUGH RD

MILL RD

South View Farm

NN8

West Field Lodge

Stone Cross Farm

Broadholme

WELLINGBOROUGH RD

Cemy

PRESLAND WAY 1
GREEN CL 2

B571

BRIGHTWELL

NN9

1 MARRIOTT CL
2 LAYWOOD WAY
3 ELIZABETH WAY
4 WHITWORTH WAY

TANNERY COTTS

LAKESIDE

5 RINGTAIL CL
6 GLOVERS CL

Sewage Works

River Nene

Nene Way

Ditchford Bridge

DITCHFORD RD

Ditchford Lock

River Nene Navigation

Works

Skew Bridge Ski Lake

CH

Sanders Lodge

ST DAVID'S RD

A5001 NORTHAMPTON RD

SHIPTON WAY

Express Pk

Sanders Lodge Ind Est

Northampton Rd

NORTHAMPTON RD

A5001

Superstore

Skew Bridge

BRINDLEY CL

B645

B645

Nene Valley Farm

The Moors

NN10

Bullmatt Bsns Ctr

PEGASUS WAY

Parkham Ind Est

Norris Way Ind Est

Francis Ct

Elan Ct

Crown Ct

CROWN WAY

Allot Gdns

WOODLAND

QUORN RD

CHESTNUT

NICHOLAS WAY

PYTCHLEY RD

WELLINGBOROUGH RD

30

A5001

B569

Sp Ctr

Irchester Bridge

HIGHAM RD

IRCHESTER TURN

Knuston Lodge Farm

CHESTER RD

Nene Way

Town End Farm

BARRINGERS GDNS

BARRINGERS CT

THE BARNS

Lower Farm

P PH

Ind Est

Cemy

ST KATHARINE'S WAY

ST HIGH

NN29

RUSHDEN

PALM RD

FERN RD

HOLLY RD

MASEFIELD DR

SHAKESPEARE RD

PURBECK RD

SILVERDALE GR

WILDACRE RD

DINGLE RD

FOXWOOD

MELLOWAY RD

KEATS

ST MARK'S

Wr Twr

MANTON SPINNEY

Home Farm

Knuston

KNUSTON SPINNEY

Knuston Hall

Home Spinney

B569

IRCHESTER RD

BOUNDARY AVE

WEST CRES

THE CRESCENT

EAST CRES

CORONATION AVE

WESTFIELD AVE

CRESSWELL RD

ALPINE RD

SPINNEY RD

CHESTER RD

TENNYSON RD

HIGHFIELD RD

HILLARY

ROSE AVE

Allot Gdns

TALBOT RD

CHURCH HALL RD

WHITEFRIARS

UPPER PARK AVE

MORRIS AVE

FOXHALLS

ST MARGARETS AVE

ABBOTS

Schs

A45

**A** **B** **C** **D** **E** **F**

2 93 C D 94 E F

8 7 69 6 5 68 4 3 67 2 1 66

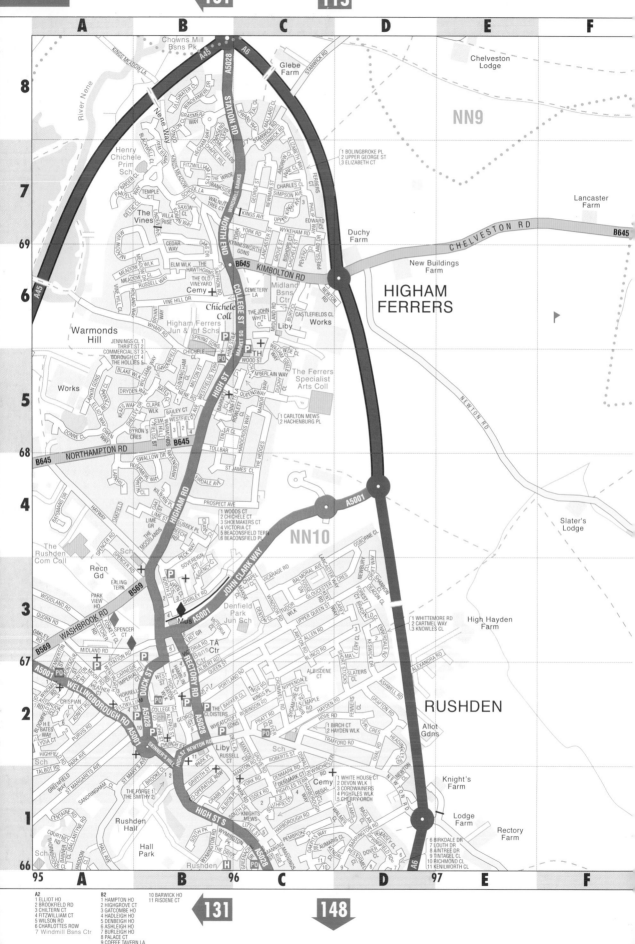

A B C D E F

8

7

69

6

5

68

4

3

67

2

1

66

NN9

Chelveston
Lodge

Lancaster
Farm

CHELVESTON RD

B645

HIGHAM
FERRERS

New Buildings
Farm

Duchy
Farm

NEWTON RD

Slater's
Lodge

NN10

High Hayden
Farm

RUSHDEN

Knight's
Farm

Lodge
Farm

Rectory
Farm

River Nene

Henry Chichele
Prim Sch

The Vines

Warmonds
Hill

Works

The Rushden
Com Coll

Chowns Mill
Bsns Pk

Glebe
Farm

NENE WAY

STATION RD

NORTH END

A5028

KIMBOLTON RD

Midland
Bsns Ctr

COLLEGE ST

Chichele
Coll

Cemy

HIGH ST

HIGHAM RD

NORTHAMPTON RD

The Ferrers
Specialist
Arts Coll

Higham Ferrers
Jun & Inf Schs

JOHN CLARK WAY

A5001

WASHBROOK RD

B569

WELLINGBOROUGH RD

A5001

DUCK ST

RECTORY RD

A5028

Denfield
Park Juh Sch

Mus

HIGH ST S

A5028

Rushden
Hall

Hall
Park

Rushden

A6

A2
1 ELLIOT HO
2 BROOKFIELD RD
3 CHILTERN CT
4 FITZWILLIAM CT
5 WILSON RD
6 CHARLOTTES ROW
7 Windmill Bsns Ctr

B2
1 HAMPTON HO
2 HIGHGROVE CT
3 GATCOMBE HO
4 HADLEIGH HO
5 DENBEIGH HO
6 ASHLEIGH HO
7 BURLEIGH HO
8 PALACE CT
9 COFFEE TAVERN LA
10 BARWICK HO
11 RISDENE CT

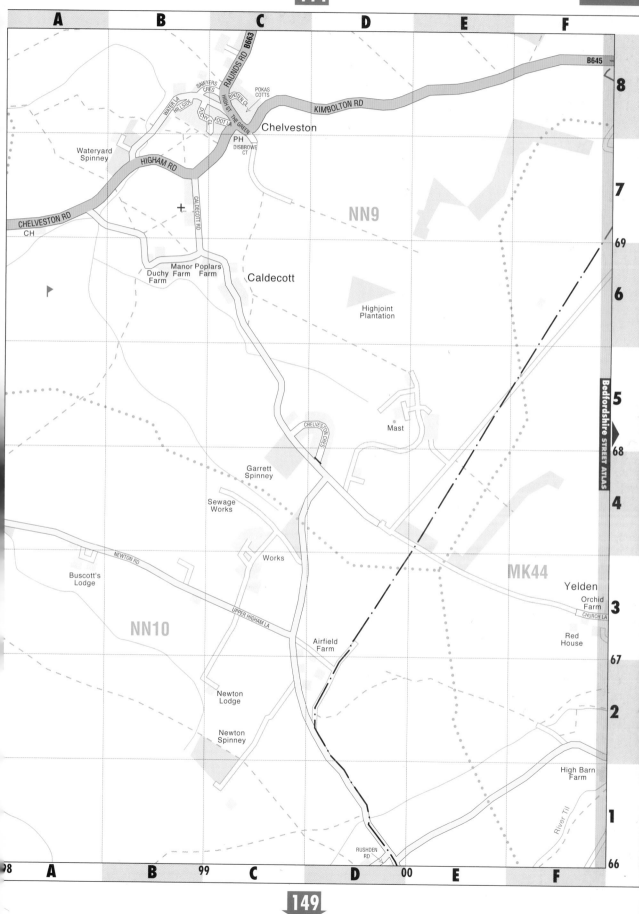

| | A | B | C | D | E | F |
|---|---|---|---|---|---|---|

B663

RAUNDS RD

B645

8

SAWYERS CRES

BRUTEN CL

POKAS COTTS

KIMBOLTON RD

WATER LA

HILLSIDE

HIGH ST THE GREEN

DUCHY CL

FOOT LA

Chelveston

PH

DISBROWE CT

Wateryard Spinney

HIGHAM RD

7

CHELVESTON RD

CH

CALDECOTT RD

NN9

+

69

Manor Poplars Farm

Duchy Farm

Farm

Caldecott

6

Highjoint Plantation

5

CHELVESTON CRES

Mast

68

Garrett Spinney

4

Sewage Works

Newton Lodge

NEWTON RD

Works

Buscott's Lodge

MK44

Yelden

Orchid Farm

3

NN10

UPPER HIGHAM LA

CHURCH LA

Red House

Airfield Farm

67

Newton Lodge

2

Newton Spinney

High Barn Farm

River Til

1

RUSHDEN RD

66

| | A | | B | 99 | C | | D | 00 | E | | F |
|---|---|---|---|---|---|---|---|---|---|---|---|

98

Bedfordshire STREET ATLAS

118

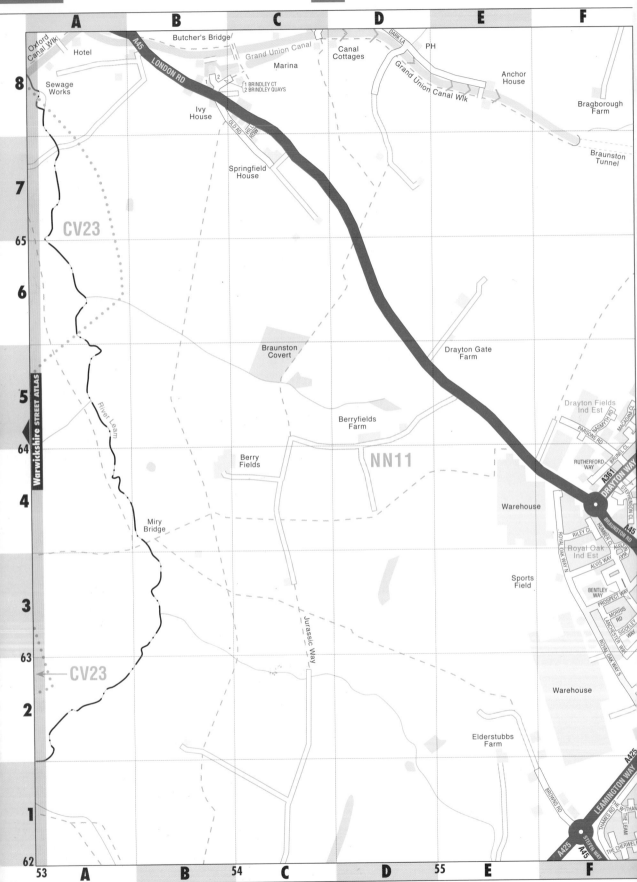

152

A · B · C · D · E · F

8

Crockwell
Farm

Cornerhill
Spinney

Norton
Junction

Buckby
Top Lock

Rye Hill
Farm

NN6

Grand Union Canal

Grand Union Canal Wlk

Swing
Bridge

PH

NEWBRIDGE

A5

M1

Surney
Cottage

THE
COUNCIL HOS

Surney
Farm

7

Thrupp
Grounds

B4036

Long
Buckby Wharf

+

Thrupp
Lodge

65

Thrupp
Covert

Norton
Lodge
Farm

WHILTON
LODGE

6

Whilton
Locks

B4036

5

NN11

Marina

SPOTTED CON LA

Sewage
Works

DAVENTRY RD

Beehive
Lodge

64

EAGLESFIELD
HOME FARM LTD
BAKERS

MANOR GDNS

Norton Hall
Farm

Pant Y Owen
Farm

4

PH

+

Norton

Watling
Lodge

WEEDON LA

THE BROADWAY

Allot
Gdns

3

Noborough
Lodge

63

The
Woodyard

2

Underhill
Spinney

Heart of The Shires
Sh Village

NN7

Mast

Noborough
Farm

Noborough
Spinney

Ivy House
Farm

Borough Hill
Plantation

1

62

59    A    B    60    C    D    61    E    F

121
138

**A** **B** **C** **D** **E** **F**

8

Surney
Bridges

The
Bungalow

Elm
Lodge

Perkin's
Lodge

NN6

NN7

7

Sewage
Works

65

NN11

SOUTH
VIEW

THE GREEN

WARD CLOSE LA

6

THE
GARDENS

LANGTON RISE

MANOR LA

Whilton

Roughmoor
Grounds

Whilton
Mill

Hill
Top

Home
Farm

5

Gipsy
Spinney

64

Windmill
Barn

4

Greenclose
Spinney

Violet
Spinney

Gazewell
Farm

Ashpole
Spinney

3

Muscott

Muscott
House

Gazewell
Spinney

Acre
Spinney

63

NN7

Whiltonbrook
Spinney

Grand Union Canal

Diamond
Bridge

THE
MEWS

Brockhall

Brockhall
Manor

2

The
Hall

Grand Union Canal Wlk

Burton
Wood

Flore Fields
Farm

Flore Fields
Spinney

Butlin's
Farm

Flore Fields
House

1

The
Dial
House

A5

M1

62

**A** **B** **C** **D** **E** **F**

52    63    64

A B C D E F

NN6

8

Moor Farm
Glebe Farm
Hazel Tree Farm
Langlands Plantation

Sewage Works
Sir John's Wood

Brickfield Spinney

7

Thornburrow Hill

Bedford Cotts
WHILTON RD
Great Brington

Gawburrow Hill
WARDLE'S CL
THE GREEN
BACK LA
MAIN ST

65

The Bushes
THE POUND
PO PH
Birchfield Farmhouse
Chinkwell Spinney

HAMILTON LA
Almshouses

NN11

6

Macmillan Way

Church Spinney

Chinkwell Belts

5

Brington Prim Sch

Harlestone Forest

64

Foxinhole Spinney

PYE CT
NN7

4

White House
FOLLY LA
FERMOY CT PH
MAIN ST

Church Farm

Little Brington
BLACKSMITHS LA

Harlestone Thicket

3

Hillcrest Cotts
Nobottle Wood

Waydale Hill
Townsend Farm
Midshires Way
Grove House
Short Wood

63

Grange Farm
Nobottle
Nobottle House

2

Flore Lodge

Range
West Lodge

1

62

65 A B 66 C D 67 E F

A  B  C  D  E  F

8  7  65  6  5  64  4  3  63  2  1  62

Delf Spinney

NN6

Millholme Plantation

Pedigree Buildings Farm

Lucas's Field Plantation

East Lodge

Glebe Farm

Althorp

Old Lodge Plantation

Glebe Cotts

GLEBE LA

Althorp Park

Dog Pond

Three Corner Plantation

New Park Plantation

Oaktree Stew

Obelisk

PARK FARM BARNS

CHURCH LA

Mill

Great Stew

HARLESTONE RD

CH

Harlestone Prim Sch

Lower Harlestone

PH
30

The Paddocks

Chinkwell Clumps

PO

Harlestone

Midshires Way

Yew Tree Farm

THE GREEN

Sand Pit

Yewtree Spinney

Upper Harlestone

SWEDISH HOS

Standingwell Spinney

Round Oak Plantation

NN5

Broadgow Spinney

NN7

Fleetland Farm

PORT RD

Sowditch Thicket

BERGERAC CL

ANJOU CT

Nobottle Belt

Oldfield Thicket

Heath Farm

SANDY LA
ALSACE CL
INGON CL
TOURAINE CT
ROCHELLE WAY
BEAUVAIS CT
VELOCETTE WAY
PROVENS CT
BEAUNE CL

Wr Twr

Lodge Barn

NORTHAMPTON

MARSEILLES CL 1
HIRONDELLE CL 2

ST EMILION CT
BLOSSAC CT
POITIERS CT
ANGER CL
AQUITAINE CL
TRIUMPH GDNS
WEGGS FARM RD
BORDEAUX CL
BORDEAUX CT
BROUGH
GREENS
BORDEAUX

The Lodge

8  69  70

A B C D E F

NN3

8

Boughton Grange
Grange Farm
Boughton Hall
Boughton Prim Sch
Butcher's La
Spring Cl
Church St
PO
Boughton Green Rd
Church (remains of)
Holly Lodge
St John's Spring

Boughton

NN6
Rectory Farm
Westview Farm
BRAMPTON LA

7

Obelisk
White Hills
HARBOROUGH RD N
LYNTON AVE
TIVERTON AVE
OBELISK RISE
ASH RISE
REYNARD WAY
HUNTERS
Westleigh Pk 1
Rowley Way 2
Jackson Cl 3
Jacobin Cl 4
Briscoe Cl 5
Duncan Cl
Lower Farm Rd
Ind Est

RED HOUSE RD A5076
65

White Hills Way
Whitehills Prim Sch
Greenhills Rd
Sandhills Rd
Sandhills Cl
St Mark's Ave
HOLLY LODGE DR
SUTTON CL
DIXON RD
Mast
All Saints CE Mid Sch
Northants Ent Pk
Northampton Science Pk
KYOTO CL
Regal Cl
Kings Park Rd
North Cl

6

Spring Park
DELTA WAY
PLOUGHMANS WLK
Edward Watson Cl
Pasteur
MORETON WAY
A5076
HINTON RD
BLAKESLEY RD
COSGROVE WAY
CROUGHTON RD
WHITFIELD WAY
Cemy
Hill Top
Sunnyside
Kingsthorpe Com Coll
1 Spens Ho
2 Rhymer Ho
3 Berwick Ho
4 Silverstone Cl
5 Bradden Cl
6 Courteenhall Cl
Nene Univ Coll Northampton
NN3

5

1 Haycroft Wlk
2 Larwood Cl
3 Shepherd Cl
4 Coleraine Cl
1 Cheviot Ho
2 Yarrow Ho
3 Hamilton Ho
4 Aynho Wlk
5 Usher Ho
6 Middleton Cl
7 Radstone Way
8 Charlton Cl
9 Syresham Way
10 Kingsthorpe Ho
HARBOROUGH RD
WALLSECK CL
HINTON CL
JENNER CRES
ST MARTINS
WINDMILL
Hill Terr
Allot Gdns
64

WELFORD RD
FOXGROVE AVE
NN2
Princess Anne Bldg 1
Mescalero 2
Newland Sq 3
P
BECTIVE VIEW
RUSKIN RD
WHISTON RD
NEWNHAM RD
GROSVENOR GDNS
Grosvenor Ho
Sch
HOLDENBY RD
BROCKHALL CL
1 Churchfield Cl
2 Badby Cl
3 Helidon Cl
Northampton Sch for Girls

4

NORTH WESTERN AVE
KINGSWAY
BARONS WAY
BISHOPS DR
30
A5199
YELVERTOFT RD
BARNWELL RD
HASTINGS RD
WEST RIDGE
NBC DEPOT
WALTON HEATH WAY
HEATHERDALE WAY
HOLLINGSIDE DR
BRACKENHILL CL
LYTHAM RD
AINSDALE RD
HOYLAKE DR
BANKSIDE
Allot Gdns

3

VICARAGE CL
Kingsthorpe Village Prim Sch
Kingsthorpe
GARFIELD
NORTON RD
CRANFORD RD
DORSET RD
DORSET GDNS
MORRIS RD
WIND RIDGE
KINGSLAND AVE
KINGSLAND CL
ROSEDALE RD
LANGDALE RD
WESTWORTH WAY
THISTLEHOLME CL
Schs
63

Manor Ct 1
Old Yew Ct 2
High Gn 3
Tyebeck Ct 4
Garfield Ho 5
THE GREEN
GREEN END
THE LEYS
ST DAVID'S RD
QUEENSLAND GDNS
Sch
CROCKET CL
FURZE WLK
Malcolm Terr 1
Wallace Terr 2
KENMUIR AVE
ROTHERSAY TERR
Schs

NN5
FREMEAUX TERR
MILL LA
A5095
Northgate Sch
KINGSTHORPE GR
NORTHAMPTON
CH
Allot Gdns
ROTHERSAY RD
BROOKFIELD RD
Kingsley Park
A5123
2

WINDRUSH WAY
WELLAND WAY
Kingsthorpe Bsns Ctr
Allot Gdns
Queens Park Ind Est
QUEEN'S PARK PAR
CLARENCE AVE
CECIL RD
EDINBURGH RD
Edinburgh Mews
BALMORAL RD
FAIRWAY
MASFIELD WAY
SUMMINGDALE CL
ROMANY RD
CARLTON RD
RAEBURN RD
30
NN1

Kingsheath Workshops
Kingsfield Bsns Pk
HEATHFIELD WAY
Queen's Park
Northgate Sch
BALMORAL CL
BALFOUR RD
Fairfields Sch
Unity Coll
TRINITY AVE
Webbs Factory
Univ Coll Northampton
HOMESTEAD WAY
ST GEORGE'S AVE
A5123 KETTERING RD
Phippsville

1

Kingsfield Bsns Pk
K2 Ho
GLADSTONE RD
HORSLEY RD
CARTWRIGHT
BURLEIGH
ARTHUR ST
Monarch Ind Est
Kingsthorpe Hollow
WITHAM HO
RADLEIGH
MILTON ST
OLIVERS RD
A5095
PO
CEDAR RD
BROADWAY
62

4 A 75 B C 76 D E F

C3
1 Cranford Ho
2 Kingsthorpe Sh Ctr
3 Eton Ct
4 Stable Ct
5 Alexandra Terr
6 Cranford Terr
**159**
**142**
E1
1 Bethany Homestead
2 Dardis Cl
3 Kingsley Gdns
4 Methodist Homestead

A B C D E F

8 NN2

7

65

6

5

64

4

63

2

1

62

**NORTHAMPTON**

Moulton
New Manor Farm
Moulton Park
Moulton Park Bsns Ctr
Northampton Sch for Girls
Thomas Becket RC Sch
NN6
Coleman Leys
Round Spinney
Hotel
Boothville
Boothville Prim Sch
Thorplands Prim Sch
Billing Arbours
NN3
Eastfield Park
The Arbours
Spinney Hill
The Arbours Prim Sch
St Gregory's RC Prim Sch
Weston Favell Sch
Northampton Coll
Parklands Prim Sch
Northampton Sch for Girls
Billing Brook Sch
Lumbertubs Prim Sch
Headlands Prim Sch
Sheraton Mews
Cottarville
Weston Favell CE Prim Sch
Cedar Road Prim Sch
Liby
NN1
Western Favell Ctr
L Ctr
Northampton Acad
Quartercroft

RED HOUSE RD
A5076
TALAVERA WAY
A5123
BOOTH RISE
KETTERING RD N
KETTERING RD
PARK AVE N
A5101
A5123
LUMBERTUBS WAY
WELLINGBOROUGH RD
A4500
A43
PARK VIEW
A43
THORPEVILLE

Fire HQ
Ind Est

77 78 79

A B C D E F

C4
1 PATTERDALE WLK
2 APPLEBY WLK
3 BORROWDALE WLK
4 SKELTON WLK
5 CALDBECK WLK
6 DALSTON WLK
7 KIRKSTONE WLK
8 LANERCOST WLK
9 AMBLESIDE CL

E3
1 MOUNTS CT
2 FULLERBURN CT
3 PENISTONE WLK
4 BAUKEWELL CT

F1
1 GROUNDWELL CT
2 MIDDLEWELL CT
3 THEBWELL RD
4 WALLEDWELL CT
5 RUNNEYMEDE GDNS

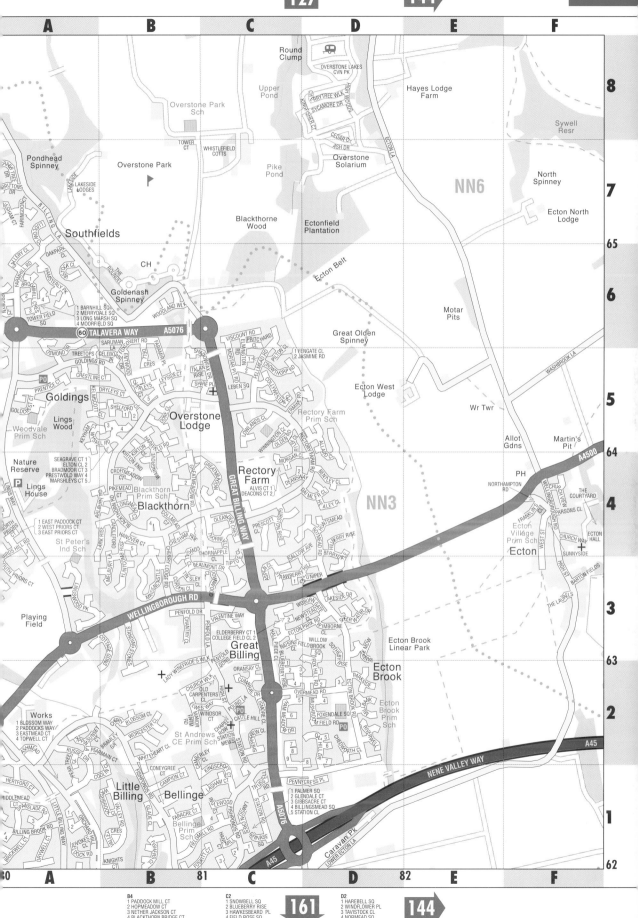

**B4**
1 PADDOCK MILL CT
2 HOPMEADOW CT
3 NETHER JACKSON CT
4 BLACKTHORN BRIDGE CT
5 MIDDLEMARCH

**C2**
1 SNOWBELL SQ
2 BLUEBERRY RISE
3 HAWKESBEARD PL
4 FIELD ROSE SQ
5 SALTWELL SQ
6 HORSEMOOR SQ
7 CLIPSTON FIELD PL
8 GREEN DALE SQ
9 LONG MALLOWS RISE

**D2**
1 HAREBELL SQ
2 WINDFLOWER PL
3 TAVISTOCK CL
4 NORMEAD SQ
5 BELLROPES SQ
6 LOCKCROFT SQ
7 SHARROW PL
8 THURSPIT PL

143
128

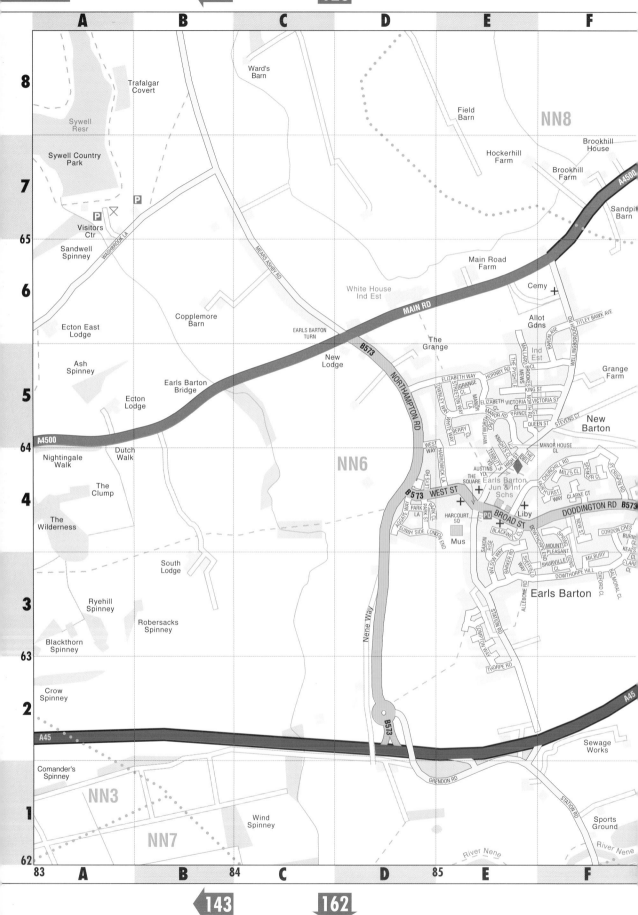

143
162

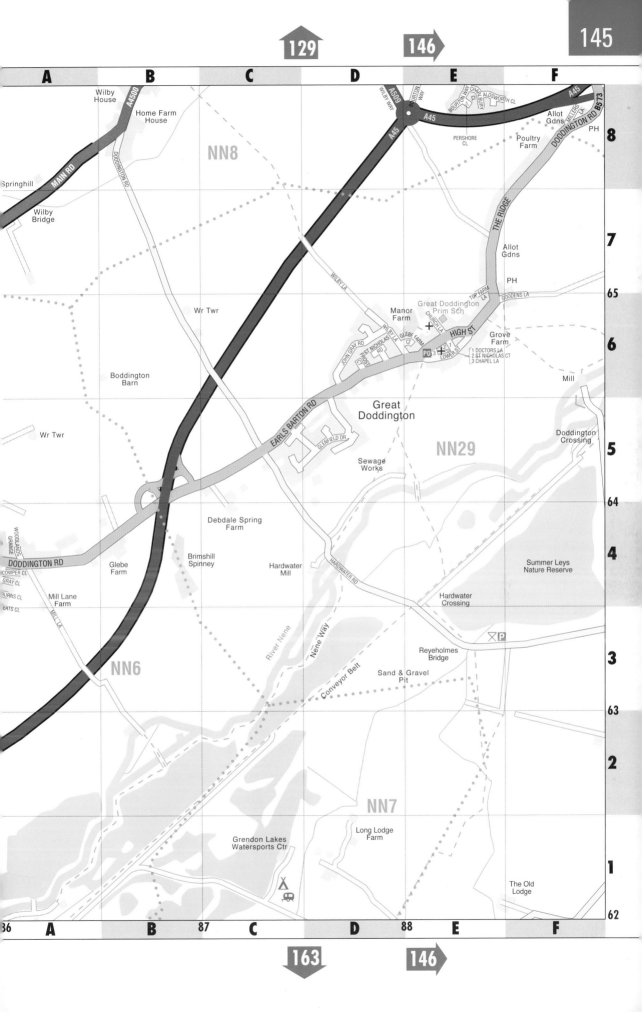

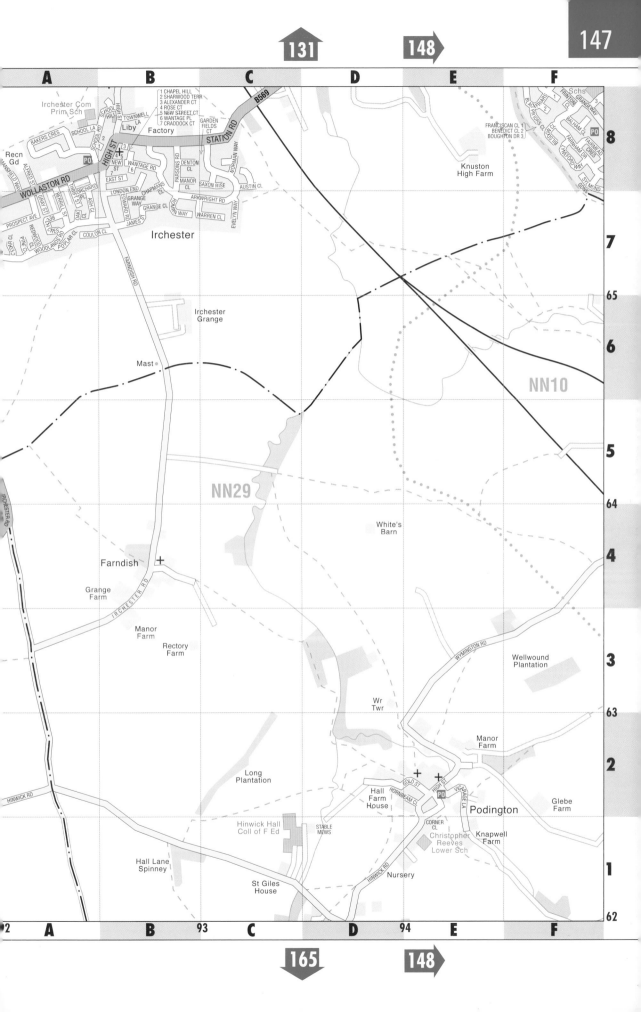

131
148
165
148

A B C D E F

1 CHAPEL HILL
2 SHARWOOD TERR
3 ALEXANDER CT
4 ROSE CT
5 NEW STREET CT
6 WANTAGE PL
7 CRADDOCK CT

FRANCISCAN CL 1
BENEDICT CL 2
BOUGHTON DR 3

B569

Irchester Com Prim Sch

School La

Baker's Cres

Liby

Factory

STATION RD

Garden Fields Ct

Knuston High Farm

8

Recn Gd

High St

New St

East St

Wantage Rd

Parsons Rd

Denton Cl

Saxon Rise

Manor Cl

Austin Cl

Norman Way

Wollaston Rd

Mansfield Way

Alfred St

Gray St

Berrill St

Thrift St

Orchard

Ash Cl

London End

Edward Rd

Grange Way

Chapmans Rd

James St

Arkwright Rd

Warren Cl

Evelyn Way

7

Prospect Ave

Redwood Cl

Pine Cl

Woodlands Rd

Poplar Cl

Coulon Cl

Irchester

65

Farndish Rd

Irchester Grange

6

Mast

NN10

Irchester Rd

NN29

5

64

White's Barn

Farndish

4

Grange Farm

Irchester Rd

Manor Farm

Rectory Farm

Wymington Rd

Wellwound Plantation

3

63

Wr Twr

Manor Farm

2

Hinwick Rd

Long Plantation

Hall Farm House

Hornbeam Cl

Gold St

High St

Vicarage La

PO

Podington

Glebe Farm

Hinwick Hall Coll of F Ed

Stable Mews

Corner Cl

Christopher Reeves Lower Sch

Knapwell Farm

1

Hall Lane Spinney

St Giles House

Hinwick Rd

Nursery

62

A 93 B C 94 D E F

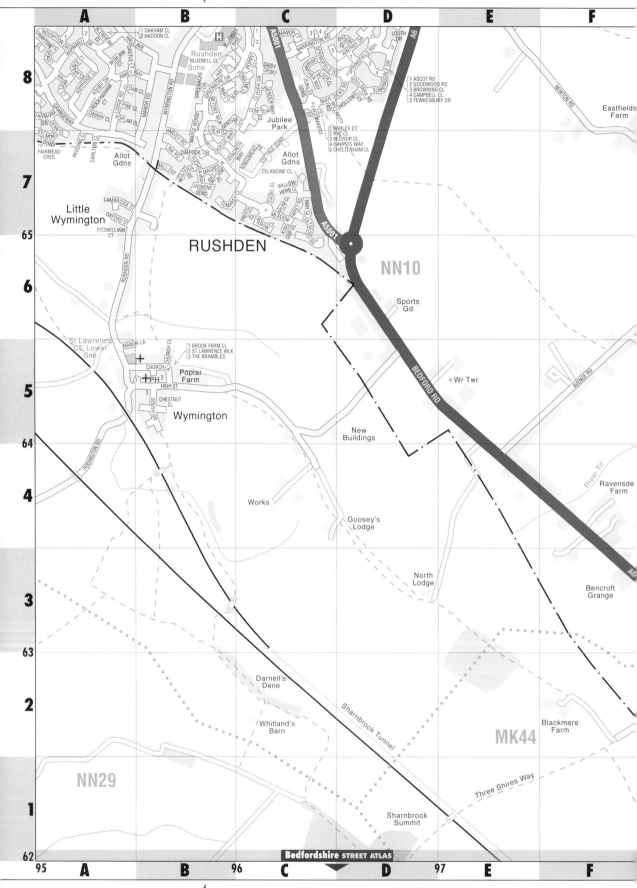

8

1 OAKHAM CL
2 HADDON CL

H

Rushden
Bluebell Cl.
Schs

Jubilee
Park

Allot
Gdns

1 ASCOT RD
2 GOODWOOD RD
3 BROWNING CL
4 CAMPBELL CL
5 TEWKESBURY DR

1 BARLEY CT.
2 RYE CL.
3 BELVOIR CL.
4 OAKPITS WAY
5 CHELTENHAM CL

Eastfields
Farm

Allot
Gdns

FAIRMEAD
CRES

7

Little
Wymington

CAMBRIDGE ST
OXFORD ST
FITZWILLIAM
CT

RUSHDEN

65

6

NN10

St Lawrence
CE Lower
Sch

MANOR LA

1 BROOK FARM CL
2 ST LAWRENCE WLK
3 THE BRAMBLES

Sports
Gd

CHURCH
PH
HIGH ST

Poplar
Farm

5

CHESTNUT
CL

Wymington

BEDFORD RD

• Wr Twr

AVENUE RD

New
Buildings

64

River Til

Ravensden
Farm

4

PODINGTON RD

Works

Goosey's
Lodge

North
Lodge

Bencroft
Grange

3

63

Darnell's
Dene

Sharnbrook Tunnel

MK44

2

Whitland's
Barn

Blackmere
Farm

Three Shires Way

NN29

1

Sharnbrook
Summit

62

A   B   C   D   E   F

8

7

65

6

NN10

5

64

MK44

4

3

63

2

1

62

8   A   B   99   C   D   00   E   F

Manor
Lodge

NEWTON RD

RUSHDEN RD

Manor
Farm

PH
Newton
Bromswold

CHURCH WLK

CHURCH LA

Rectory
Farm

Newton
Gorse

Yelden
Wold

PO

venue
Farm

AVENUE RD

River Til

IIGHAM PARK RD

Higham
Park

Knotting

Manor
Farm

MELCHBOURNE RD

BEDFORD RD

Three Shires Way

West
Wood

Strawberry
Hill Farm

STRAWBERRY HILL COTTS

FORTY FOOT LA

Knotting
Fox Farm

Sheeprack
Wood

The
Cottage

Knotting
Green Farm

Knotting
Green

A6

A6 Bedford

Bedfordshire STREET ATLAS

Bedfordshire STREET ATLAS

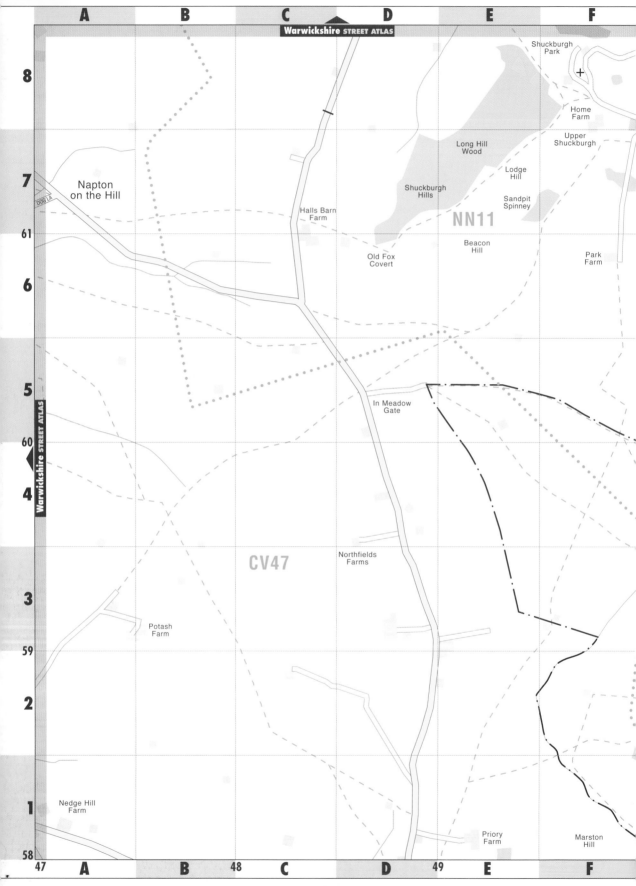

Shuckburgh
Park

Home
Farm

Long Hill
Wood

Upper
Shuckburgh

Lodge
Hill

Shuckburgh
Hills

Sandpit
Spinney

**NN11**

Beacon
Hill

Park
Farm

Napton
on the Hill

DOG LA

Halls Barn
Farm

Old Fox
Covert

In Meadow
Gate

**CV47**

Northfields
Farms

Potash
Farm

Nedge Hill
Farm

Priory
Farm

Marston
Hill

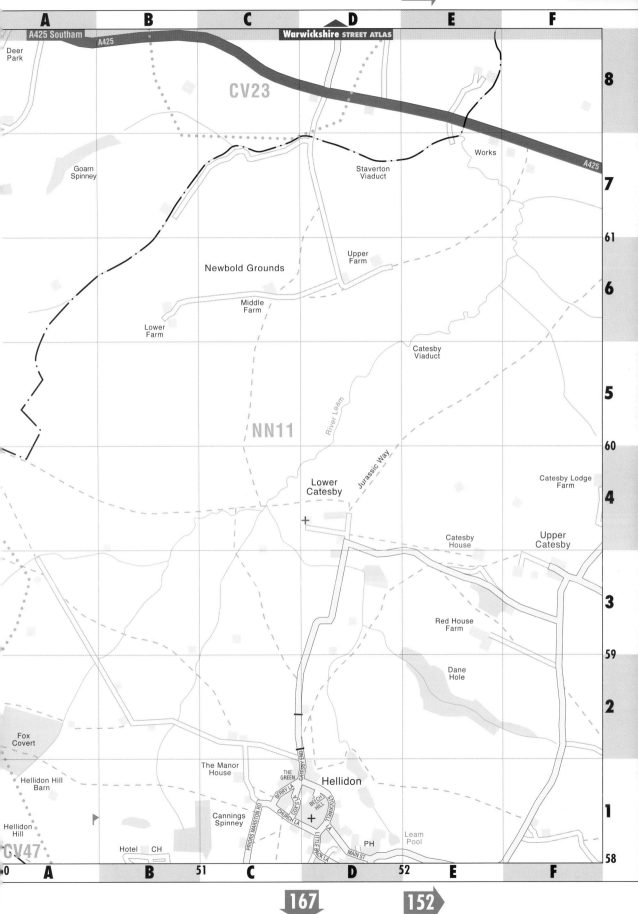

A B C D E F

A425 Southam  A425  Warwickshire STREET ATLAS

Deer Park

CV23

8

Goarn Spinney

Staverton Viaduct

Works

A425

7

61

Newbold Grounds

Upper Farm

6

Middle Farm

Lower Farm

Catesby Viaduct

5

River Leam

NN11

60

Lower Catesby

Jurassic Way

Catesby Lodge Farm

4

Catesby House

Upper Catesby

Red House Farm

3

59

Dane Hole

2

Fox Covert

Hellidon Hill Barn

The Manor House

THE GREEN

Hellidon

Leam Pool

Hellidon Hill

Cannings Spinney

BERRY LA

FOX'S LA

CHURCH LA

BEECH HILL

STOCKWELL LA

UPR CATESBY LA

LITTLE PACK LA

MAIN ST

PH

1

CV47

Hotel  CH

PRIORS MARSTON RD

58

A B 51 C D 52 E F

151 134

**A** **B** **C** **D** **E** **F**

8

A425 WELLAND CL 1
THAMES RD 2
A45
STEFEN L
TYHL

STAVERTON RD

Drayton
Lodge

CH

Woodhollow
Cottages

Stepnell
Spinney

Hall
Farm

Sewage
Works

HOME CL

Staverton CE
Prim Sch

Hotel

Oak
Spinne

Manor
House

CROFT LA

BRAUNSTON LA

Compton
Cottage

MANOR RD

GLEBE LA

OAKHAM LA

7 A425

THE WOODLANDS

WELL LA

THE GREEN
THE ORCHARD

PO

DAVENTRY RD

CHURCH

1 WINDMILL LA
2 WINDMILL GDNS
3 CHURCH FIELDS
2

Staverton
Clump

Staverton Wood

Staverton Hill
Farm

Big Hill

Pond
Spinney

PH
DAVENTRY RD

3

Staverton
Acres

Staverton

Mast

61

Broiler Breeder
Farm

Vine Tree
Farm

Sports
Gd

Badby Lodge
Farm

Bates
Farm

Jurassic Way

Staverton
Fields

6

Badby
Fields

Markleys

NN11

5

60

Bridge Hill
Farm

4

Studborough
Hill

Studborough
Clump

NESIDI
CL

3

Longridge
Farm

Staverton
Lodge

Barehill
Farm

PINGLO

PH

ORCHARD
CL

POUND LA

Badby
Sch

SCHOOL LA

59

Arbury
Hill

STONEWAY
VICARAGE
HILL

WMN ST

CHURCH HILL

2

BUNKERS HILL

Highfield
Farm

Haycock Hill
Farm

Konigssee
Farm

The
Beeches

Badby
Plantation

1

A361

Badby
Down

58

53 **A** 54 **B** **C** 54 **D** 55 **E** **F**

151 168

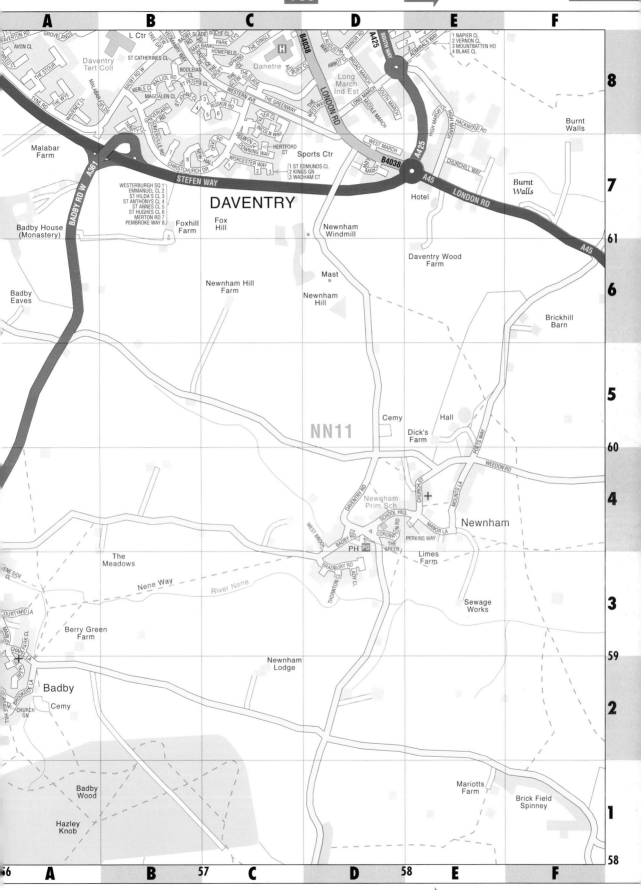

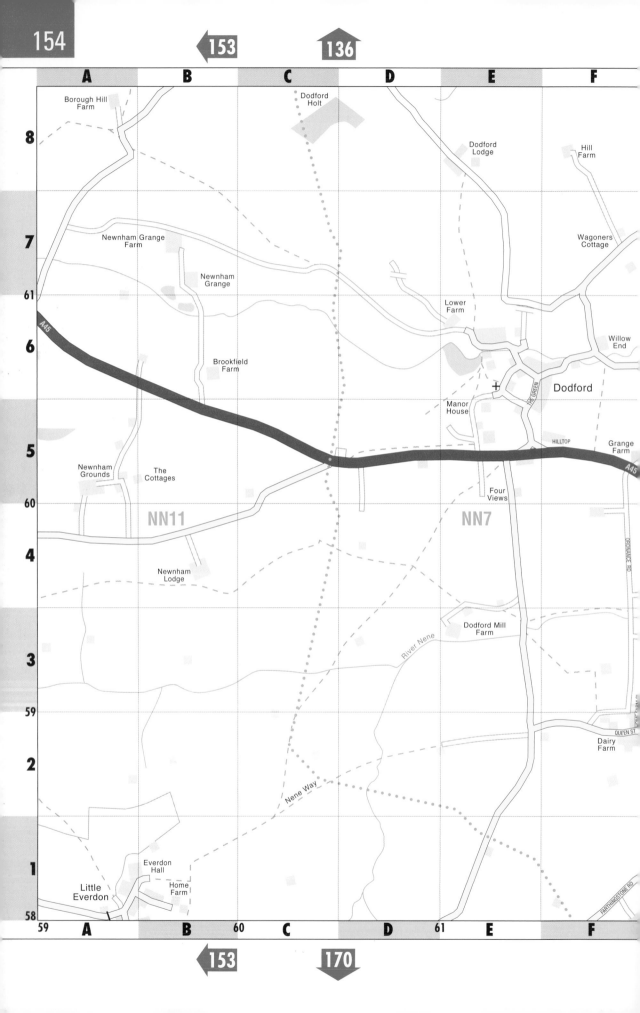

153
136

A B C D E F

8

7

61

6

5

60

4

59

3

2

1

58

Borough Hill
Farm

Dodford
Holt

Dodford
Lodge

Hill
Farm

Newnham Grange
Farm

Wagoners
Cottage

Newnham
Grange

Lower
Farm

Willow
End

Brookfield
Farm

Dodford

THE GREEN

Manor
House

HILLTOP

Grange
Farm

A45

Newnham
Grounds

The
Cottages

Four
Views

NN11

NN7

Newnham
Lodge

Dodford Mill
Farm

River Nene

ORDNANCE RD

QUEEN ST

Dairy
Farm

Nene Way

FARTHINGSTONE RD

Everdon Hall

Home
Farm

Little
Everdon

59 A B 60 C D 61 E F

153
170

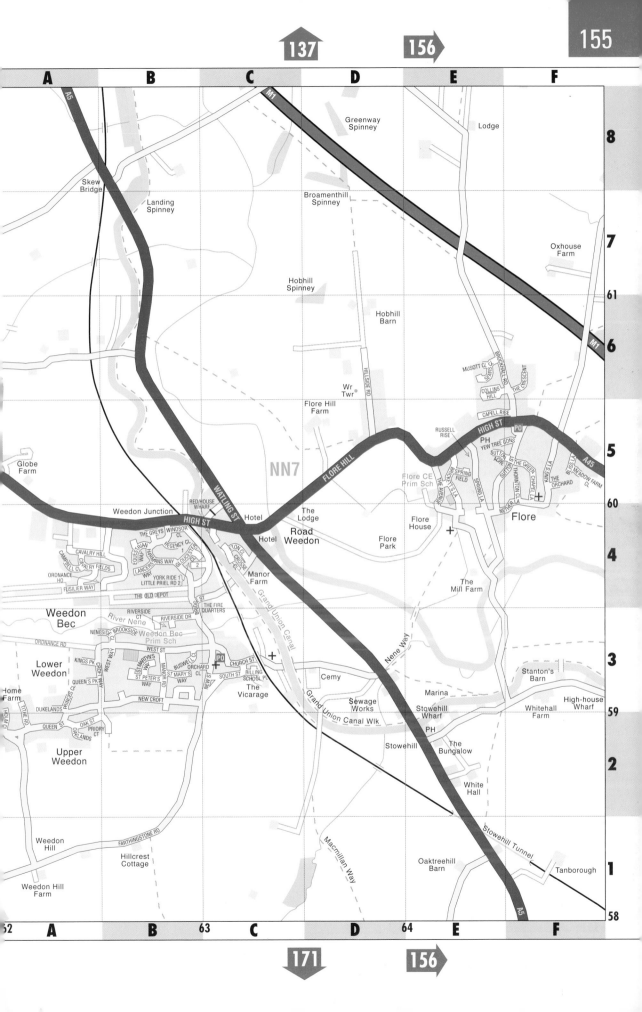

A   B   C   D   E   F

8

Skew Bridge

Landing Spinney

Greenway Spinney

Lodge

7

Broamenthill Spinney

Oxhouse Farm

61

Hobhill Spinney

6

M1

Hobhill Barn

Wr Twr

Musott Cl
Brockhall Rd
Collins Hill
The Crescent
Capell Rise
HIGH ST
PO

5

Globe Farm

Flore Hill Farm

HILLSIDE RD

FLORE HILL

Flore CE Prim Sch

NN7

Russell Rise

PH
Yew Tree Gdns
SPRING FIELD
BRICKKILN LA
SUTTON CL
ACRE
LS THORNTON CL
THE GREEN
CHAPEL LA
KING'S LA
NETHER CL
THE ORCHARD
BLISS LA
MEADOW FARM CL
A45

Flore

60

Weedon Junction

WATLING ST

Red House Wharf

HIGH ST

Hotel

The Lodge

Road Weedon

Hotel

Flore House

Flore Park

+

4

THE GREYS
WINDSOR CL
REGENCY CL
HARMANS WAY
LANCERS WAY
CAVALRY HILL
CAVALRY FIELDS
CAMPBELL CL
ORDNANCE HQ
FUSILIER WAY
YORK RIDE 1
Little Priel Rd 2
THE OLD DEPOT
EQUESTRIAN WAY
GLOUCESTER CL
2
ELTON CL
CROSSE CL
BRIDGE ST
Manor Farm

The Mill Farm

Weedon Bec

River Nene

RIVERSIDE CT
RIVERSIDE DR
THE FIRE QUARTERS
Weedon Bec Prim Sch

Grand Union Canal

Nene Way

3

ORDNANCE RD
NENESIDE
BROOKSIDE
WEST WAY
WEST ST
MARTYNS WAY
ST PETER'S CL
CROFT WAY
KINGS PK
MANOR RD
BUSWELL CL
ST MARY'S CL
PO
ORCHARD
NEW ST
CHURCH ST
SOUTH ST
BILLING WAY
SCHOOL PL
+

Lower Weedon

Queen's Pk
PRINCES CL

The Vicarage

Cemy

Sewage Works

Grand Union Canal Wlk

Marina

Stowehill Wharf

Stanton's Barn

Whitehall Farm

High-house Wharf

59

Home Farm

TITHE RD
HOLLY CL
DUKELANDS
QUEEN ST
OAK ST
PRIORY CT
OAKLANDS

Stowehill

PH

The Bungalow

2

Upper Weedon

White Hall

Weedon Hill

FARTHINGSTONE RD

Hillcrest Cottage

Macmillan Way

Oaktreehill Barn

Stowehill Tunnel

Tanborough

1

Weedon Hill Farm

A5

58

52   A   B   63   C   D   64   E   F

← 155
138

**A** **B** **C** **D** **E** **F**

8

Vicarage Farm

Dundas Covert

Lower Glassthorpe

New Covert

Harpole Covert

Cloverlea

7

Harpole Hill Farm

Macmillan Way

61

GLASSTHORPE LA

Flitnell Barn

Lakes Farm

6

M1

Glassthorpehill

Climatological Sta

NN7

5

A45

60

Upper Heyford Lodge

A4500

4

Dovecote Farm

The Cottages

MAIN RD

16

A45

Nene Way

Heyford Mill

Hill Farm

M1

Home Farm

Hipwells

3

Simon's Cottage

Upper Heyford

59

River Nene

Chapmans Close

Bugbrooke Mill

2

Grand Union Canal

Midshires Way
Grand Union Canal Wlk

MANOR PK

CHURCH LA

Cemy

MANOR WLK

MIDDLE ST

WATERY LA

BROOKSIDE

Nene Way

WEEDON RD

PARSONS CL

PH

BROOKSIDE PL

Sch

PO

WAKEFIELD WAY

THE GREEN

BUGBROOKE RD

Nether Heyford

THE POUND

ROBERTS FIELD

HILLSIDE RD

1

WINSTON CL

FURNACE LA

WESTERN AVE

LEE CRES

CLOSE RD

THE PLAY

HILLSIDE RD

Sewage Works

SOUTH VIEW

58

65 **A** **B** 66 **C** **D** 67 **E** **F**

← 155
172

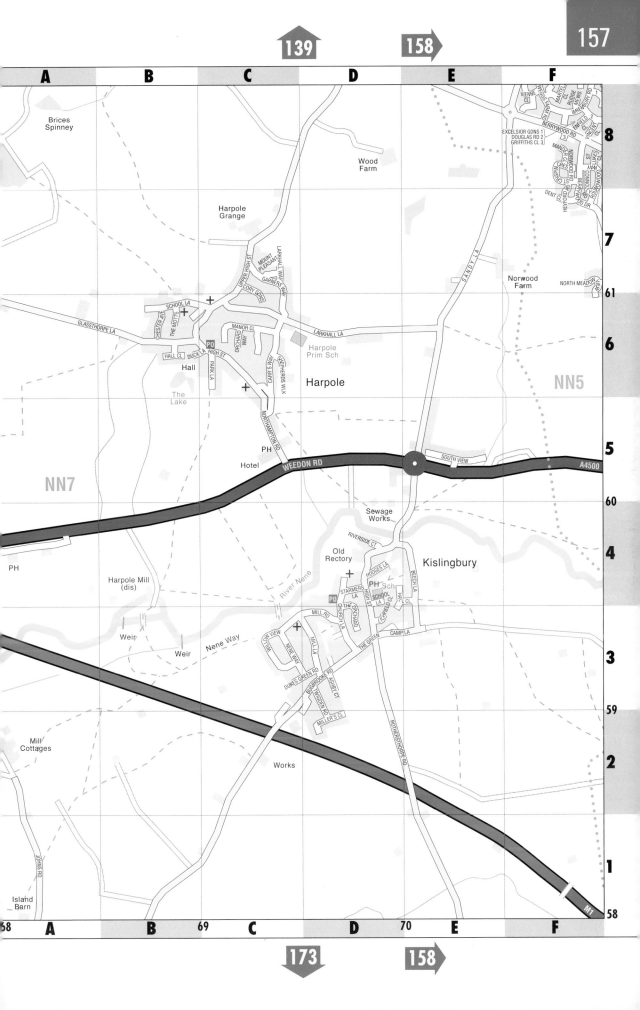

A  B  C  D  E  F

Brices
Spinney

Wood
Farm

Harpole
Grange

8

7

61

VIENNE CL
EMFIELD
BERRYWOOD RD
EXCELSIOR GDNS 1
DOUGLAS RD 2
GRIFFITHS CL 3

NORTH MEADOW

Norwood
Farm

NN5

SANDY LA

UPPER HIGH ST
MOUNT PLEASANT
LARKHALL WAY
GARNERS WAY
CORY GDNS
SCHOOL LA
CHESTER AVE
THE MOTTS

GLASSTHORPE LA

MANOR CL
ORCHARD WAY
LARKHALL LA

Harpole
Prim Sch

PO

HALL CL  DUCK LA  HIGH ST

Hall

PARK LA

CARR'S WAY

SHEPHERDS WLK

Harpole

The
Lake

NORTHAMPTON RD

NN7

PH

Hotel  WEEDON RD

SOUTH VIEW

A4500

5

60

4

Sewage
Works

RIVERSIDE CT

Old
Rectory

Kislingbury

PH

River Nene

Harpole Mill
(dis)

STARMERS LA
THE ORCHARD
CHURCH LA
MILL RD

PH  Sch
SCHOOL

HODGES LA
HIGH ST
BEECH LA
LA

PO

LOCKFIELD CL

PH

Weir

Weir

Nene Way

WILLOW VIEW

NENE WAY

MILL LA

THE GREEN

CAMP LA

3

59

DUKES GREEN RD
BUGBROOKE RD
ASHBY CT
TWIGDEN RD
MILLER'S CL

Mill
Cottages

Works

ROTHERSTHORPE RD

2

1

Island
Barn

JOHNS RD

M1

58

157  140

F8
1 GLEBELAND WLK
2 DALLINGTON GN
3 TENNYSON CL
4 CARDIGAN CL
5 DALLINGTON HAVEN

A B C D E F

8

The Duston Sch
GALAHAD CT
Cemy
Liby
Duston
1 EDINBURGH HO
2 LIMEHURST SQ
3 WINDSOR HO
4 GIFFORD CT
5 STEPHEN BENNETT CL
6 ROSETTE CL
Ingleborough Way
Dallington

Chiltern Prim Sch
Park View
The Lawns

7
St Crispin Dr
Berry Wood
North Meadow View
1 BEECHWOOD RD
2 POND FARM CL
3 STARMER'S YD
4 SQUIRREL LA
5 GOUGHS COTTS
WEDMORE CL
Lyncrest Prim Sch
Windsor Cres
Warwick Ho 1
Harlestone Ct 2

61
THOMPSON CL
Hospital Farm
St Luke's CE Prim Sch
Millway Prim Sch
Westfield RD

6
Upton Lodge
Princess Marina
Westgate RD
Ind Est
Superstore
Ind Est
The Bsns Ctr

5
A4500
Quinton House Sch
Upton
NN5
Hotel
WEEDON RD
A5076
P
Sixfields L Complex
Northampton Town FC
Sixfields Stad
Edgar Mobbs Way
P

60
Park House
FARADAY CL
TELFORD WAY
CLICKERS PL
CLICKERS DR
BLACK CAT DR

4
Upton Hall Farm
Bottom Spinney
Works
Duston Mill (dis)
Rainsborough Cres
Newstone Cres

NN7
Upton Mill
UPTON WAY
1 TOWER HILL CL
2 TALLYFIELD END
3 CHEVIOT CT
4 LANGLEY CL
5 LIMLOW CL
Briar Hill
NN4

3
Bly La
River Nene
Grand Union Canal Northampton Arm
Canal Wlk

59
DANES CAMP WAY

2
Pineham Barn
MILLSTONE CL 1
COBBLESTONE CT 2
BRINDLESTONE CL 3
DAPPLESTONE CL 4
QUARTERSTONE 5
A5123
A5076
MILLER HILL 1
FARRAXTON SQ 2
Hunsbury Hill Spinney
Camp Hill
Mus
Hupsbury Park Prim Sch

WHITESANDS WAY 6
CAULDECOTT CL 7
LYNMORE CL 8
KEYSTONE 9
Hunsbury Hill
Hunsbury Hill Country Park

1
SWAN VALLEY WAY
LADYMEAD
A5123

58
M1

71 A B 72 C D 73 E F

157  174

I15A

F2
1 ARCHANGEL SQ
2 ARCHANGEL RD
3 MARNOCK SQ
4 HASELRIG SQ
5 DAYRELL SQ
6 BENJAMIN SQ
7 PLANTAGENET SQ
8 BROCADE CL
9 ROTHERHITHE CL

F3
1 SPRINGER STRAIGHT
2 FRENSHAM CL
3 ROSENELLA CL
4 DICKSON CL

**A6**
1 CALEDONIAN HO
3 ORCHARD ST
4 MELBOURNE HO
5 ABBEY HO
6 DEVONSHIRE HO

7 EYELETTER HO
8 STITCHMAN HO
**C6**
1 ST MARTINS HO
2 ST GEORGES HO
3 CLAREMONT CT
4 LATYMER CT

2 SANDHILL RD

**B6**
5 ST BARTHOLEMEWS HO
6 SUSSEX CT
7 ST MARKS HO
8 ST JOHN'S HO
9 ST STEPHENS HO
10 ST BARNABAS HO

11 LOWER HARDING ST
12 ST LUKE'S HO
13 CRISPIN ST
14 CRISPIN ST
15 NEWLIFE APARTMENTS
16 ALTHORP ST

17 SIMON'S WLK
18 UPPER CROSS ST
19 BLACKFRIARS HO
20 ST PETER'S HO
21 DODDRIDGE ST
22 ST MARY'S CT
23 PHOENIX ST

24 DODDRIDGE ST
25 ST KATHERINE'S CT
26 BERKELEY HO
27 ST KATHERINE SQ
28 COLLEGE ST MEWS
29 BRADSHAW ST
30 DRUM LA

**C7**
1 ADELAIDE TERR
2 LEICESTER TERR
3 ALLISTON GDNS
4 SEMILONG HO
5 ADELAIDE HO
6 MILL HO

**C7**
7 UPPER PRIORY ST
8 FRANCIS ST
9 ARUNDEL ST
10 GRAFTON PL
11 ST PATRICK ST
12 ALBURY ST

**E7**
1 THE PLAZA 2 & 4
2 SHAKESPEARE HO

13 BELMONT CT
14 CHALFONT CT
15 CROMWELL CT
16 DARENTH CT
17 IDEAL BLDGS
18 WELLINGTON PL
19 ELM ST

20 OAK ST
21 TEMPLE BAR
22 LAWRENCE CT
23 GIBRALTAR CT
24 NELSON ST

141
160

**A** **B** **C** **D** **E** **F**

NN2
NN5
NN1
NORTHAMPTON
NN4

**A2**
1 BLACKWALL CL
2 DARTFORD CL
**A3**
1 NICHOLLS HO
2 BROOM CT
3 THISTLE CT
4 HUNSBARROW RD
5 FURZE CT

**C5**
1 DODDRIDGE
2 ST KATHERINE'S CT
3 MERCER'S ROW
4 WOOLMONGER ST
5 ST PETERS WLK
6 GOLD STREET MEWS
7 ADELAIDE PL
8 GREGORY ST
9 FREESCHOOL ST

**C6**
10 THE GREEN
11 COURT RD
12 ST PETERS SQ
13 FOUNDRY ST
14 GAS ST

**D6**
1 CAMPBELL SQ
2 MINSTER HO
3 NOTRE DAME MEWS
4 PRINCES WLK
5 NEWLAND WLK
6 PEACOCK PL
7 NORTHAMPTON HO

**E6**
1 CHAPEL PL
2 KETTERING GDNS
3 WILBERFORCE ST
4 PALMERSTON HO
5 PALMERSTON CT
6 STOCKLEY ST
7 WOODFORD ST
8 THE WORKS
9 WOODFORD WLK

10 HAROLD ST
11 ECTON ST
12 ST LAWRENCE CT
**F6**
1 BOUVERIE RD
2 NEW TOWN RD
3 MELBOURNE ST
4 MELBOURNE WLK
5 BOUVERIE WLK
6 ELIZABETH WLK

7 VERNON WLK
8 AMBRIDGE CT
9 ST ANDREW'S HO
10 VERNON CT
11 CLIFTONVILLE CT
12 WOODSTOCK
13 THRIFT MEWS

**F7**
1 MARTONIA

175
160

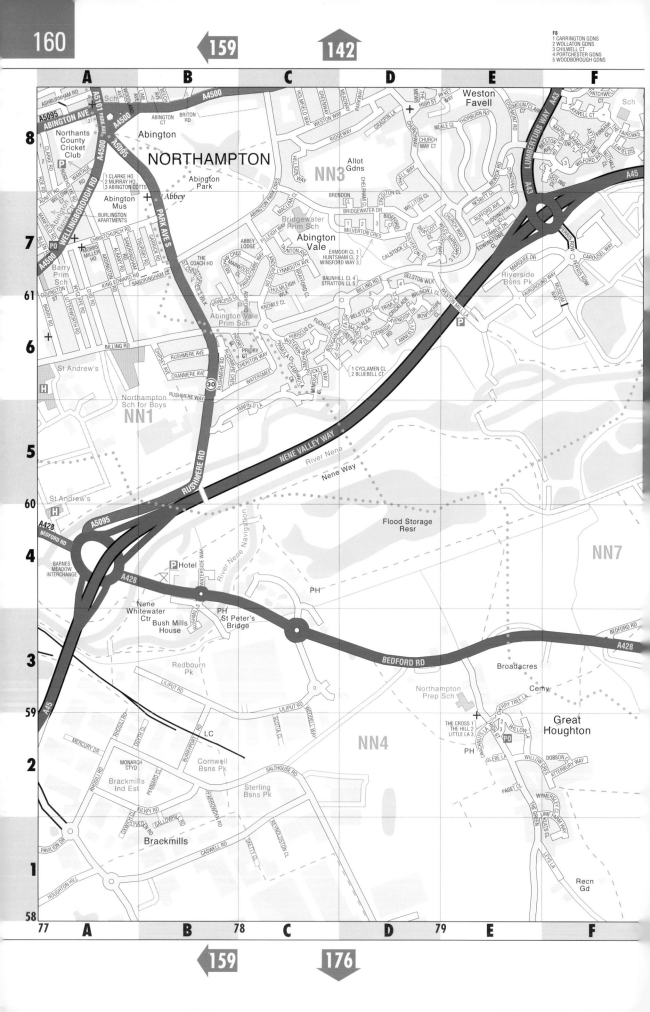

**A8**
1 SLADESWELL CT
2 PADWELL CT
3 BESTWELL CT
4 LEYSWELL CT
5 MARSHWELL CT
6 WALLINGFORD END
7 TWYFORD CL
8 BROMFORD CL

143  162

161

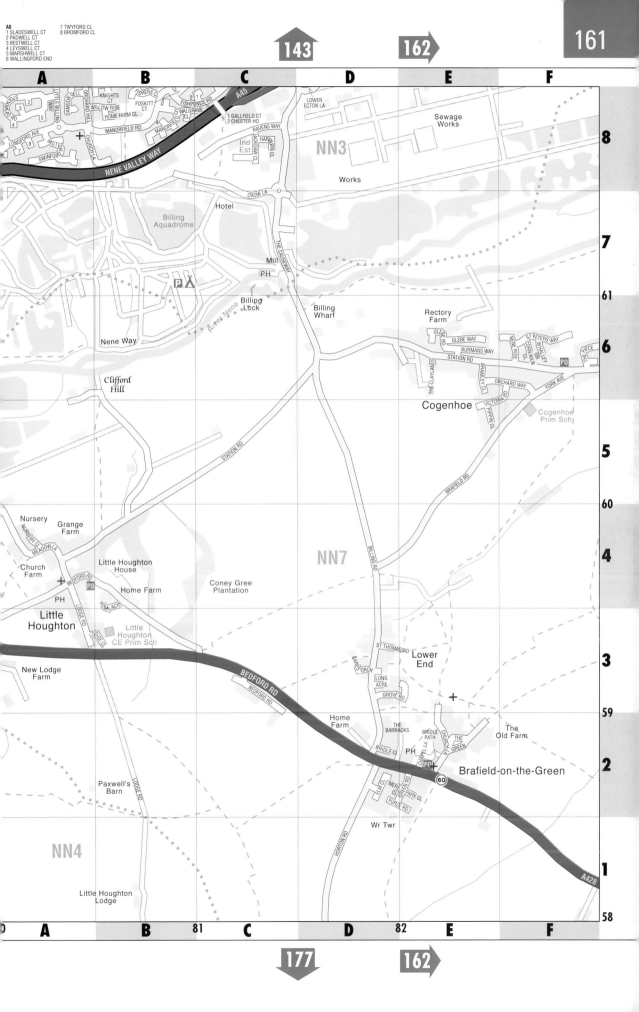

NN3

Sewage
Works

8

Billing
Aquadrome

Hotel

NENE VALLEY WAY

Works

7

Mill
PH

P

Billing
Lock

Billing
Wharf

Rectory
Farm

61

Nene Way

GLEBE RD
GLEBE WAY
BURMANS WAY
STATION RD
ST PETERS WAY
WHALLEY
NENE RISE
CORN KILN CL
THE PIECE
PO

6

Clifford
Hill

THE CLAYLANDS
BRAMLEY CL
ORCHARD WAY
YORK AVE

Cogenhoe

Cogenhoe
Prim Sch

STATION RD

VICTORIA RD
PIPPIN CL

5

BRAFIELD RD

60

Nursery
Grange
Farm

NURSERY CL
MEADOW LA

NN7

BILLING RD

4

Church
Farm

Little Houghton
House

Home Farm

Coney Gree
Plantation

Little
Houghton

BEDFORD RD
PO
PH
LODGE RD
HOM. ACRE

Little
Houghton
CE Prim Sch

3

New Lodge
Farm

BEDFORD RD
BEDFORD RD

St Thomas Rd
CAREY CH.
LONG
ACRE
GROVE RD

Lower
End

59

Home
Farm

THE
BARRACKS
BRIDLE CL
BRIDLE PATH
PH
CHAPEL LA
PO
CHURCH LA
THE GREEN

The
Old Farm

2

Paxwell's
Barn

LODGE RD

ELM CL
MERE CL
GREEN PARK CL
FURZE RD

60

Brafield-on-the-Green

NN4

HORTON RD

Wr Twr

A428

1

Little Houghton
Lodge

58

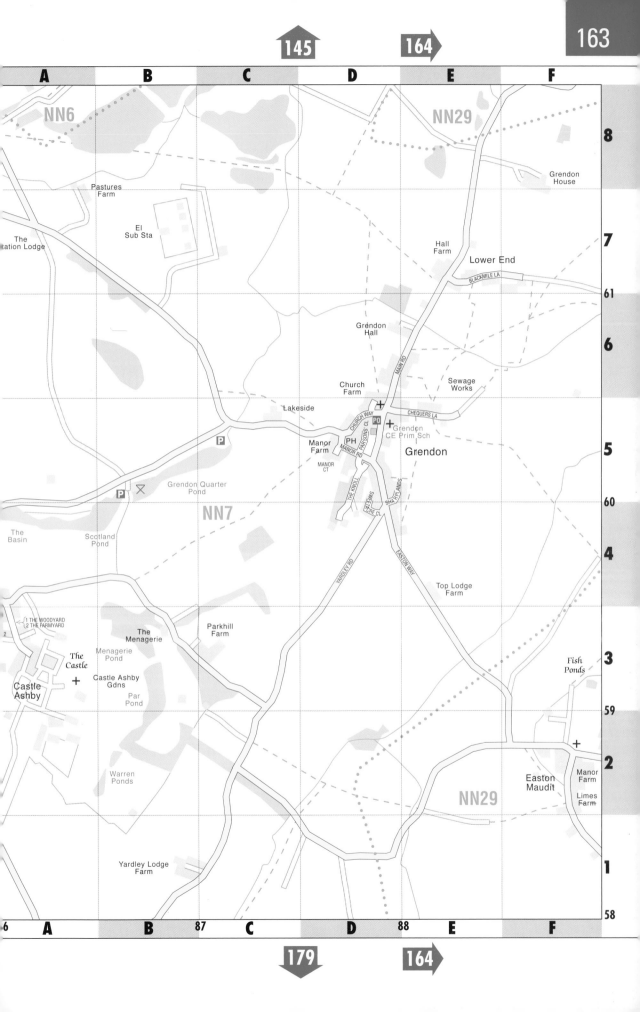

A   B   C   D   E   F

NN6

NN29

8

Grendon House

Pastures Farm

El Sub Sta

The Station Lodge

7

Hall Farm

Lower End

BLACKMILE LA

61

6

Grendon Hall

MAIN RD

Church Farm

Sewage Works

Lakeside

CHURCH WAY

CHEQUERS LA

PO

Grendon CE Prim Sch

Manor Farm

PH

PARSONS CL

MANOR RD

Grendon

5

MANOR CT

60

Grendon Quarter Pond

THE KNOLL

SWEETBRI.RE CL.

SHEEPLANDS

NN7

The Basin

Scotland Pond

YARDLEY RD

EASTON WAY

4

Top Lodge Farm

1 THE WOODYARD
2 THE FARMYARD

2

Parkhill Farm

Fish Ponds

3

The Menagerie

The Castle

Menagerie Pond

Castle Ashby Gdns

Par Pond

Castle Ashby

59

Manor Farm

2

Warren Ponds

Easton Maudit

Limes Farm

NN29

Yardley Lodge Farm

1

58

6   A   B   87   C   D   88   E   F

A   B   C   D   E   F

8

Hillmount
Spinney

Manor
Farm

Church Farm

Strixton Manor
Bsns Ctr

**Strixton**

Shepherds Hill

Lodge
Farm

7

Strixton
Plantation

**NN7**

Poplars
Farm

61

6

Greenfield
Lodge

5

WOLLASTON RD

**NN29**

60

4

Red Gables
Farm

FULLWELL RD

HOPE ST

COUNCIL ST

BULL CL

Church
Farm

**Bozeat**

Glebe
Farm

Three Fields
Farm

1 CHURCH FARM CL
2 PUDDING BAG LA
3 THE ORCHARD
4 BURTON TERR

3

Slype
Farm

Spring Vale
Farm

PEAR TREE CL

ALLENS HILL

MALLOWS CL

CHURCH WLK

HARROLD RD

Bozeat Com
Prim Sch

Cemy

HENSMANS LA

LONDON RD

1
MILE ST

BURLEIGH
TERR

2

4

CHURCH LA

MANOR CL

DYCHURCH LA

59

EASTON LA

HIGH ST

PH 5

6

PO 7

East Farm
Spring Hill Farm

GOFFS
YD

Park
Farm

STONEY
PIECE
CL

SELBY
GDNS

HEWETT'S CL

WYMAN CL

KNIGHTS CL

BROOKSIDE

DAG LA

2

REED ST

ABBEY CL

MILL RD

ST MARY'S RD

FIR TREE GR

HILLSIDE CL

5 WARNERS HILL
6 CAMDEN SQ
7 WHEELWRIGHTS YD
8 SPENCER GDNS
9 COBBLER'S PL

CLAYLAND
CL

ROBERTS ST

9
LITTLE CL

1

Low Farm

White House
Farm

Home
Farm

58

89   A   90   B   C   91   D   E   F

A509

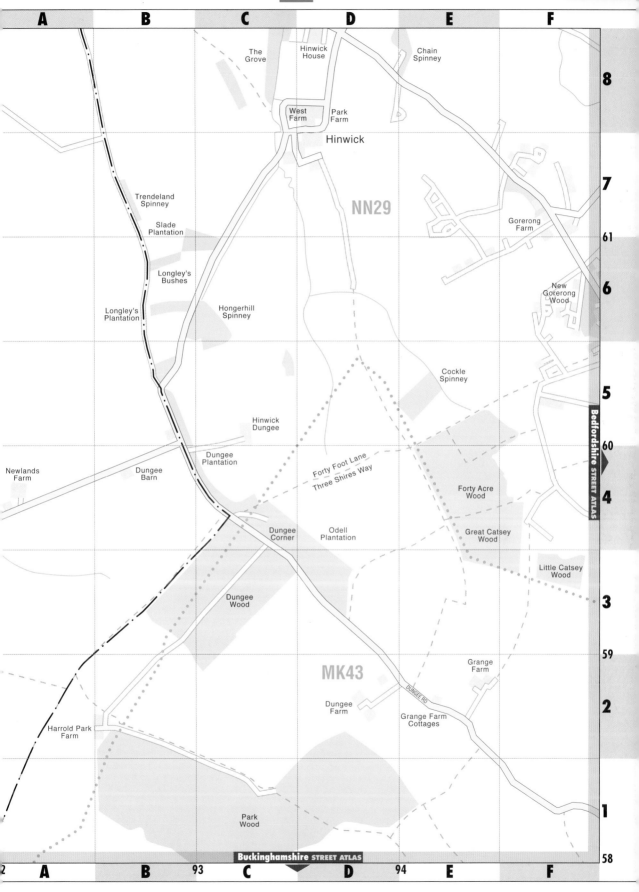

A | B | C | D | E | F

8
7
61
6
5
60
4
3
59
2
1
58

The Grove

Hinwick House

Chain Spinney

West Farm

Park Farm

Hinwick

NN29

Trendeland Spinney

Slade Plantation

Gorerong Farm

Longley's Bushes

New Gorerong Wood

Longley's Plantation

Hongerhill Spinney

Cockle Spinney

Hinwick Dungee

Dungee Plantation

Newlands Farm

Dungee Barn

Forty Foot Lane

Three Shires Way

Forty Acre Wood

Dungee Corner

Odell Plantation

Great Catsey Wood

Little Catsey Wood

Dungee Wood

MK43

Grange Farm

DUNGEE RD

Dungee Farm

Grange Farm Cottages

Harrold Park Farm

Park Wood

93 | 94

A | B | C | D | E | F

The Meadows

TURVINS MDW

SCABURGH RD

PO

VICARAGE LA

KEYS LA

Priors Marston

Hill Farm

Marston Hill

The Priors Sch

1

ST LEONARDS CL 1
WESTFIELD BARNS 2

THE HOLLOWAY

THE GREEN

HOLLYBUSH

SCHOOL LA

2

PH

MARSTON HILL

SOUTHAM RD

HELIDONS RD

PRIORS CT

Westover Farm

Chestnuts Farm

Manor Farm

HARDWICK RD

BYFIELD RD

CV47

Sewage Works

ST MARY'S CL

Church End

THE CLOISTERS

Priors Hardwick

PH

AGRICULTURAL HOS

Grange Farm

London End

WELSH RD

The Old Vicarage

Rump Hall

Fields Farm

NN11

Warwickshire STREET ATLAS

151
168

A   B   C   D   E   F

**8**

Hillcrest

PRIORS MARSTON RD

LITTLE BACK LA

Little Down Hill

Windmill

CHARWELTON LA

Windmill Hill Farm

Windmill Hill

Jurassic Way

CV47

Fir Trees Farm

Attlefield Farm

**7**

Cherwell Farm

Steppington Hill

**57**

Shutwell

Bromtrees Farm

Steppington Farm

Manor Farm

**6**

Mast
Radio Sta

NN11

**5**

**56**

Stirch

Blackdown Covert

Blackdown Farm

**4**

Hill Farm

A361

Hill Farm

**3**

Charwelton Hill

**55**

Iron Hill Farm

Ludwell Farm

IRON CROSS

**2**

Dodds Cottage

Pitwell Farm

Butterwell

Manor Farm

**1**

A361

**54**

0   A   B   51   C   D   52   E   F

183
168

167
152

| | A | B | C | D | E | F |

**8**

Beeches
Farm

Rytonhill
Farm

Grove
Spinney

Sharman's
Hill

Long Furlong
Farm

**7**

Horseground
Clump

**57**

Steppington
Spinney

Little
Fawsley

**6**

Sharmans
Farm

Fawsley
Farm

The
Dingle

Barley Field
Farm

Charwelton

**5**

Charwelton
Hall

NN11

PARTRIDGE
CL

**56**

PH

COUNCIL
HOS

CHAPEL ST

CHURCH ST

**4**

HIGH ST

MANOR CL

A361

Sewage
Works

Jurassic Way

The
Angles

River Cherwell

Church
Charwelton

**3**

Holywell
Pool

**55**

**2**

Blindpool
Spinney

Preston Fields
Farm

Charwelton
Lodge

Hollingwood
House

**1**

Hinton
House

Hinton
Hill

Hintonhill
Farm

**54**

| 53 | A | | B | 54 | C | | D | 55 | E | | F |

167
184

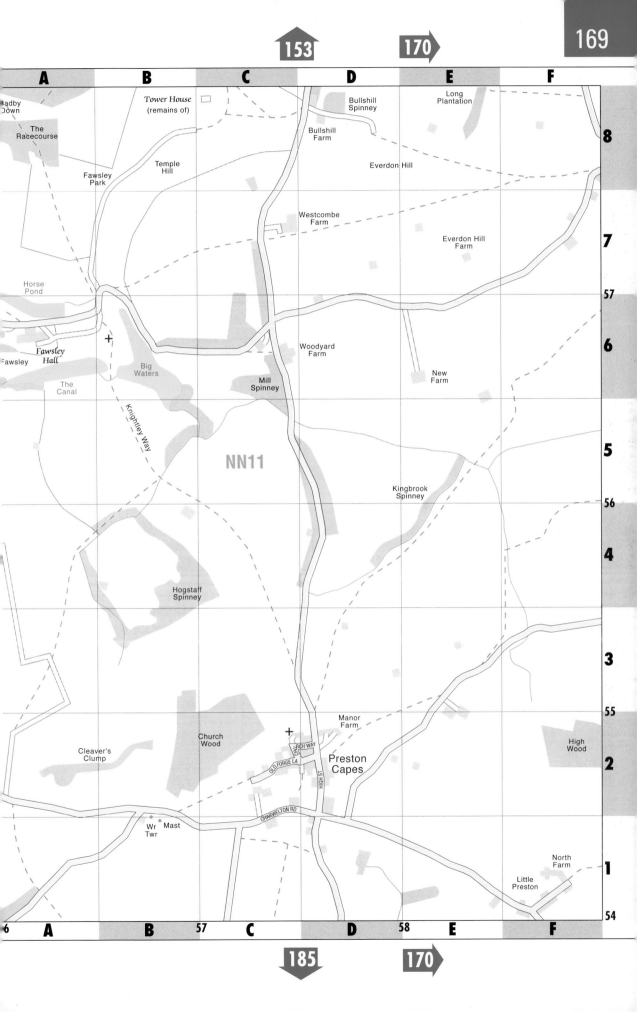

169
154

**A  B  C  D  E  F**

8

Nene Way

Weedon Villa

Sewage Works

Everdon

Fern Hollow

NN7

Weedon Lodge Cottage

Weedon Lodge

LONG ROW CL.

THE GREEN

FAWSLEY RD

SCHOOL LA

HIGH ST

PH

College Farm

The Manor House

STUBBS RD

BETHEL LA

WELL LA

7

Wood Farm

Joban

57

Everdon Wood

6

Castle Dykes

Snorscomb Mill

Everdon Stubbs Nature Trail

Everdon Stubbs Woodland Trust Wood

Castle Dyke Farm

Meg Spinney

NN11

Wr Twr

Farthingstone Heath

FARTHINGSTONE RD

5

Snorscomb

56

Snorscomb Farm

Cockcrow Spinney

4

Hen Wood

Fernhill Lodge

Mantles Heath

Knightley Way

NN12

Manor Farm

3

COUNCIL HOS 1
MANOR GDNS 2
CATTLE END 3

WEEDON RD

LITCHBOROUGH RD

Hotel

CH

Park Farm

PH

Earls Farm

EVERDON RD

MAIN ST

55

High Wood

Church Farm

Farthingstone

2

Macmillan Way

Little Court

Littlecourt Yard

Knightley Wood

Little Court Farm

MIDFORD RD

Cemy

Glebe Farm

1

54

**59  A  B  60  C  D  61  E  F**

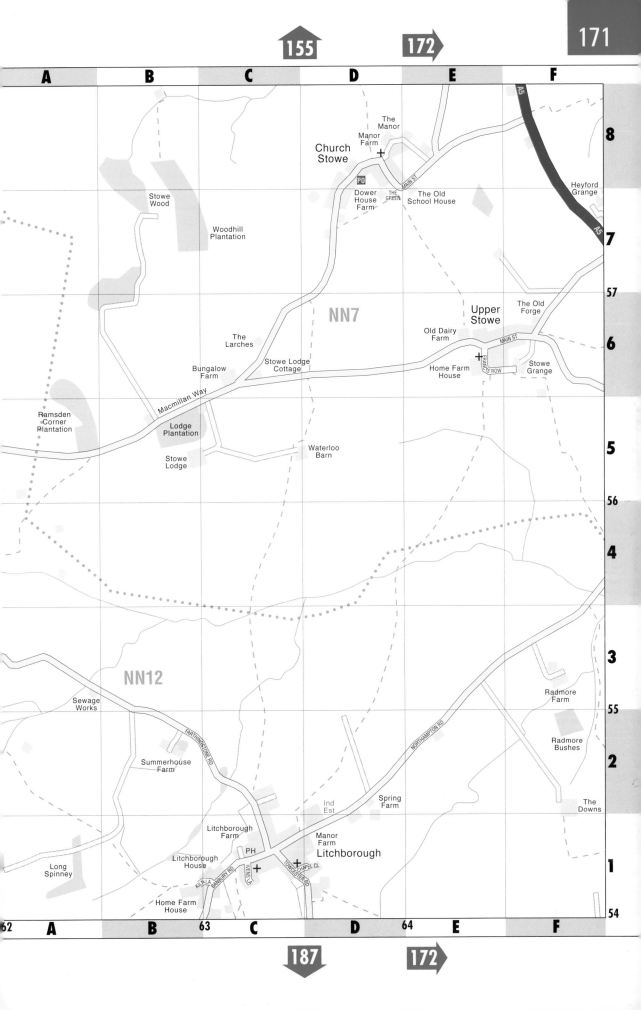

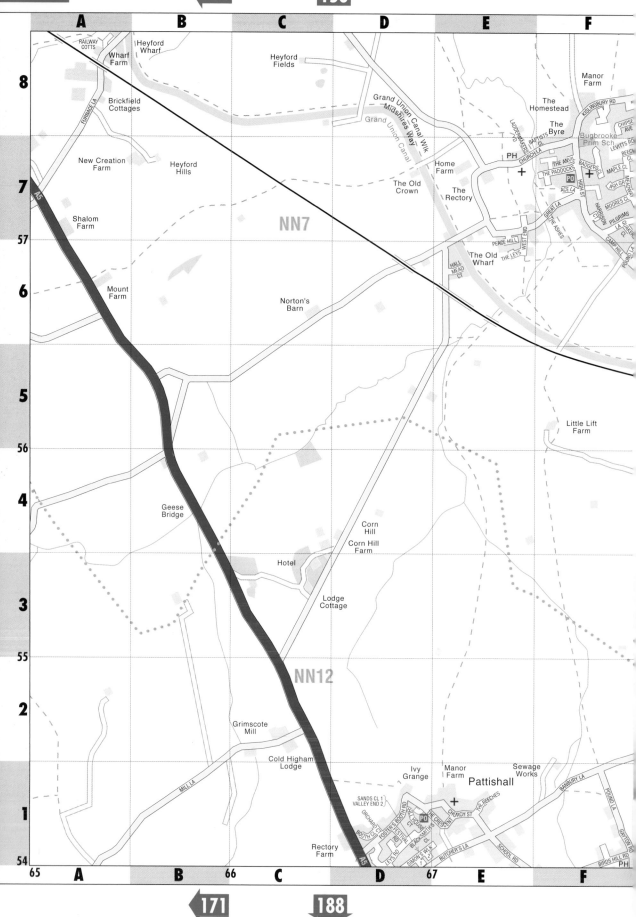

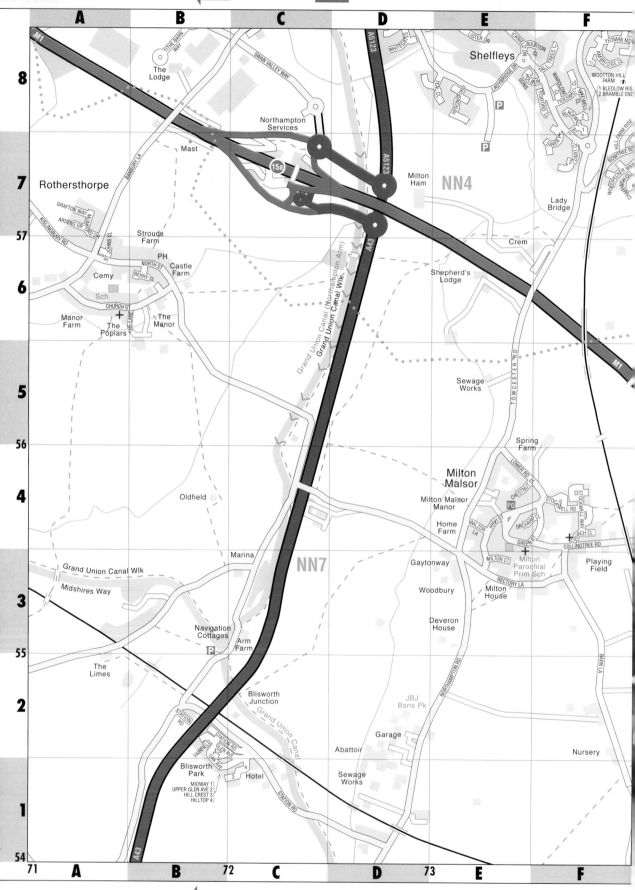

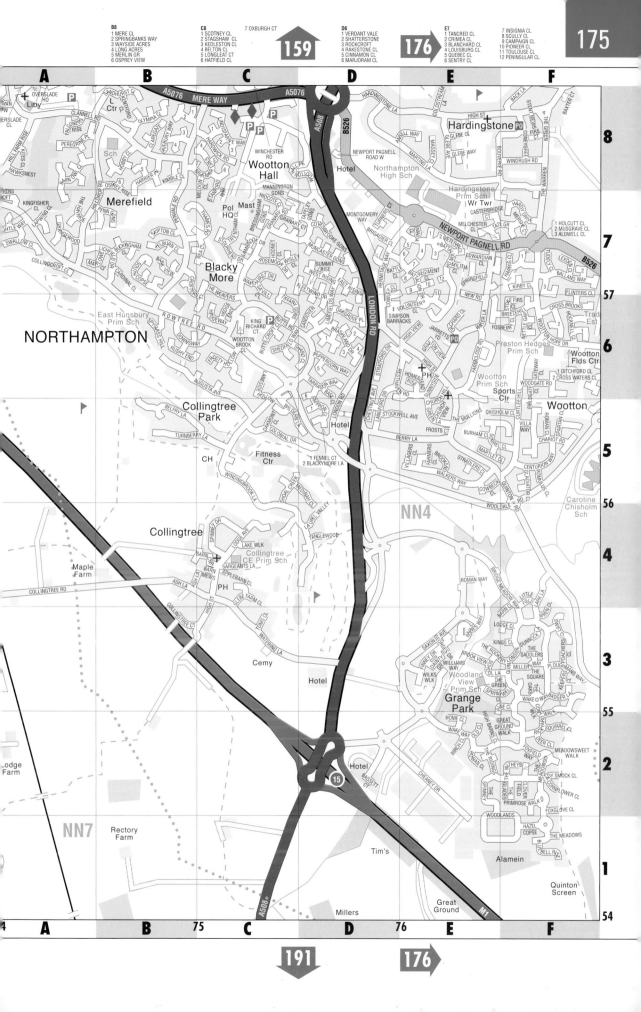

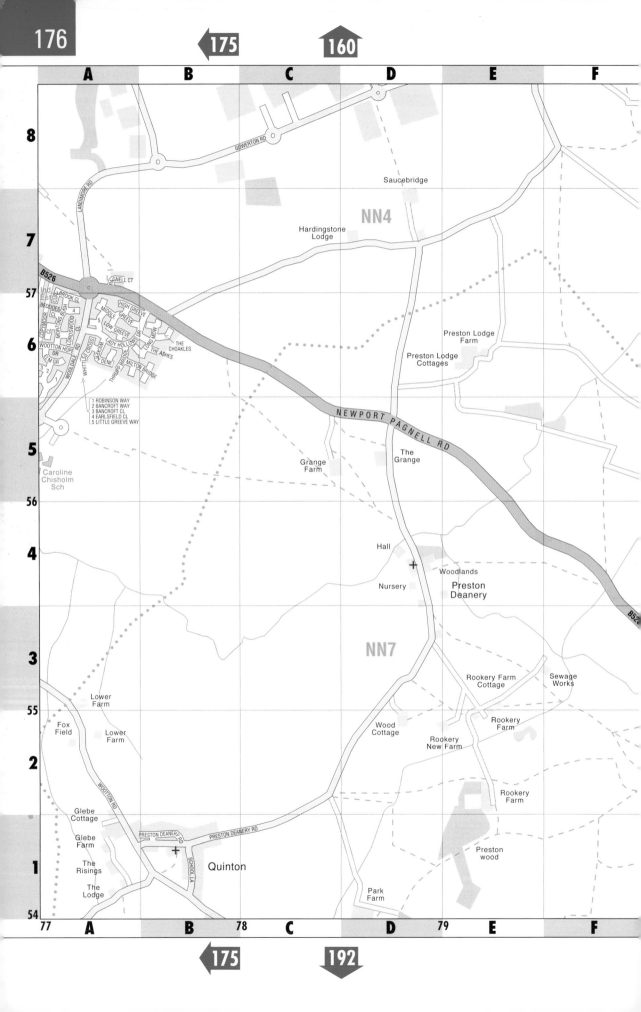

**A** **B** **C** **D** **E** **F**

8

Gowerton Rd

Saucebridge

NN4

Hardingstone
Lodge

7

B526

PAGNELL CT

BROOK CL
BEDDOES
CL
COPYMOOR
CL
Ind
Est

HIGH GREEVE

MIDDLE
GREEVE

LOW GREEVE

Preston Lodge
Farm

57

MORTONS
CL
CHIDSWOOD
CL

WOOTTON HOPE
DR
ELM GR

WOODVALE RD

WHITTLES DRIVE

LADY HOLLOWS DR

LONG ROW

THE CHOAKLES

THE ASHES

Preston Lodge
Cottages

6

CROSS
DENE

THRUPP BRIDGE

MILTON BRIDGE

1 ROBINSON WAY
2 BANCROFT WAY
3 BANCROFT CL
4 EARLSFIELD CL
5 LITTLE GREEVE WAY

NEWPORT PAGNELL RD

The
Grange

5

Caroline
Chisholm
Sch

Grange
Farm

56

Hall

4

Woodlands

Nursery

Preston
Deanery

NN7

3

Rookery Farm
Cottage

Sewage
Works

Lower
Farm

55

Fox
Field

Lower
Farm

Wood
Cottage

Rookery
Farm

2

Rookery
New Farm

Rookery
Farm

WOOTTON RD

Glebe
Cottage

Preston Deanery Rd

Preston Deanery Rd

Glebe
Farm

1

The
Risings

SCHOOL LA

Quinton

Preston
wood

The
Lodge

Park
Farm

54

**77** **A** **B** **78** **C** **D** **79** **E** **F**

B526

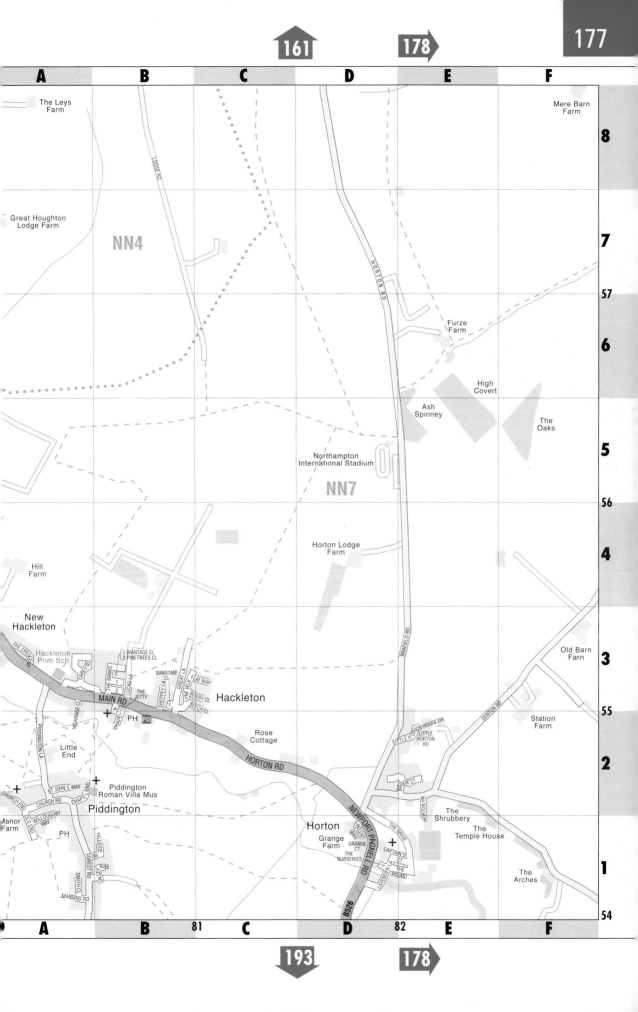

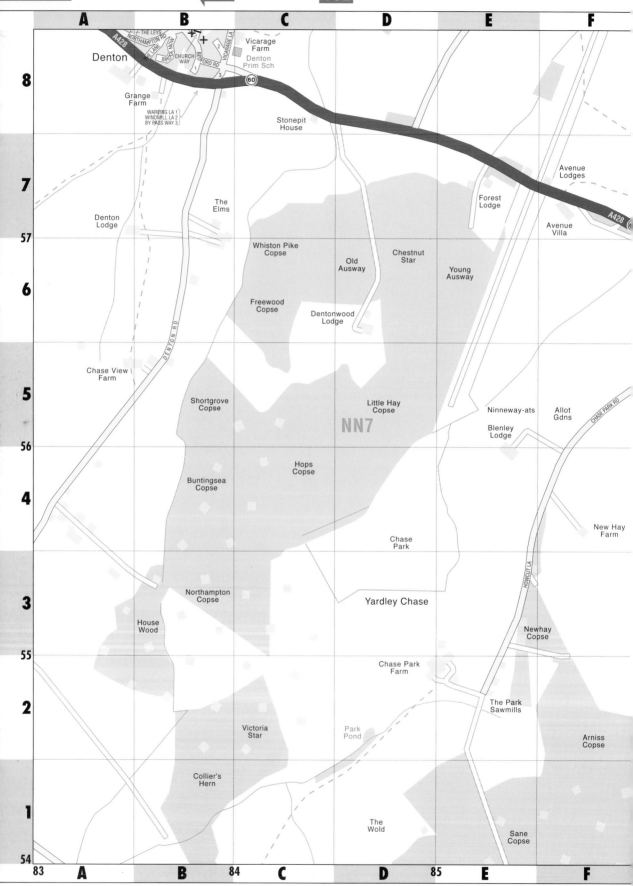

A   B   C   D   E   F

Denton

A428
NORTHAMPTON RD
THE LEYS
THE LANE
BRICK WAY
CHURCH WAY
ROXFORD RD
VICARAGE LA

Vicarage Farm
Denton Prim Sch
60

Grange Farm

WAREING LA 1
WINDMILL LA 2
BY PASS WAY 3

Stonepit House

Avenue Lodges

The Elms

Forest Lodge

A428

Denton Lodge

Avenue Villa

Whiston Pike Copse

Old Ausway

Chestnut Star

Young Ausway

Freewood Copse

Dentonwood Lodge

Chase View Farm

DENTON RD

Shortgrove Copse

Little Hay Copse

Ninneway-ats

Allot Gdns

Blenley Lodge

CHASE PARK RD

NN7

Buntingsea Copse

Hops Copse

New Hay Farm

Chase Park

Northampton Copse

HOWGUT LA

Yardley Chase

Newhay Copse

House Wood

Chase Park Farm

The Park Sawmills

Victoria Star

Park Pond

Arniss Copse

Collier's Hern

The Wold

Sane Copse

83   A   B   84   C   D   85   E   F

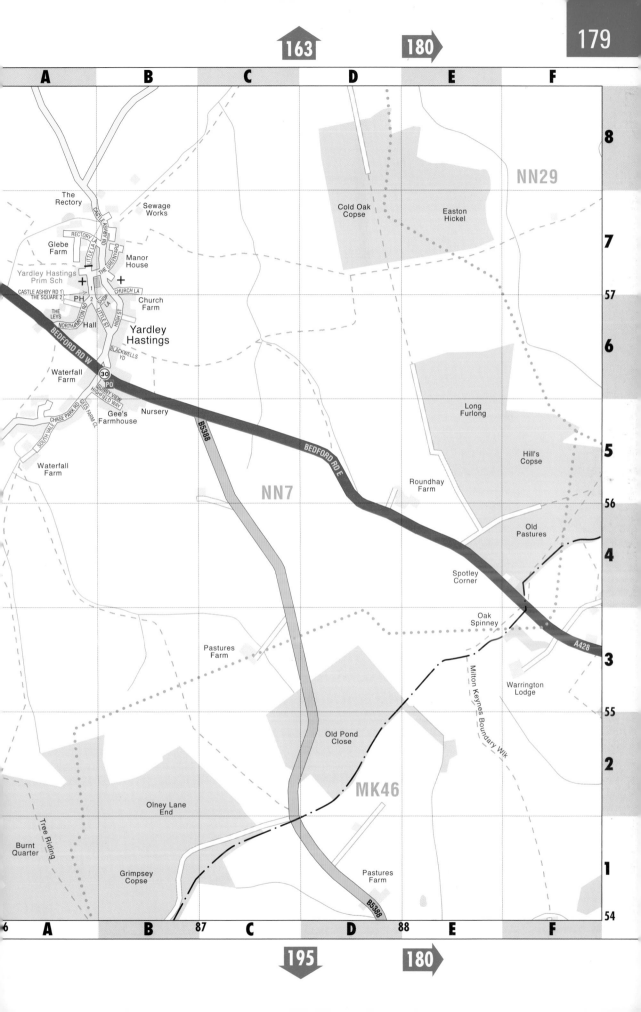

A   B   C   D   E   F

8

7

57

6

NN29

Stocking
Hollow

The
Belts

Horn
Wood

A509

Wold
Barn

Santon
Barn

The Lodge

The
Slipe

Bozeat
Wood

Bozeat
Grange

Nunwood
Barn

MK43

5

Mast

The Oaks
Wood

56

Northey
Farm

Milton Keynes Boundary Wlk

Nun
Wood

Three Shires Way

4

New Pastures
Farm

Threeshire
Wood

Lavendon Lodge
Farm

Barslay
Spinney

3

A428

Broadlane
Spinney

Warrington
House

55

Nursery

Park
Farm

2

Nuniron
Spinney

Nunirons

A428

MK46

Castle
Farm

Castle Rd

The Nest
Farm

Lower
Farm

1

Brickfield
Plantation

A509

Warrington

Lavendon

Warrington House
Farm

Home
Farm

54

89   A   B   90   C   D   91   E   F

Bedfordshire STREET ATLAS

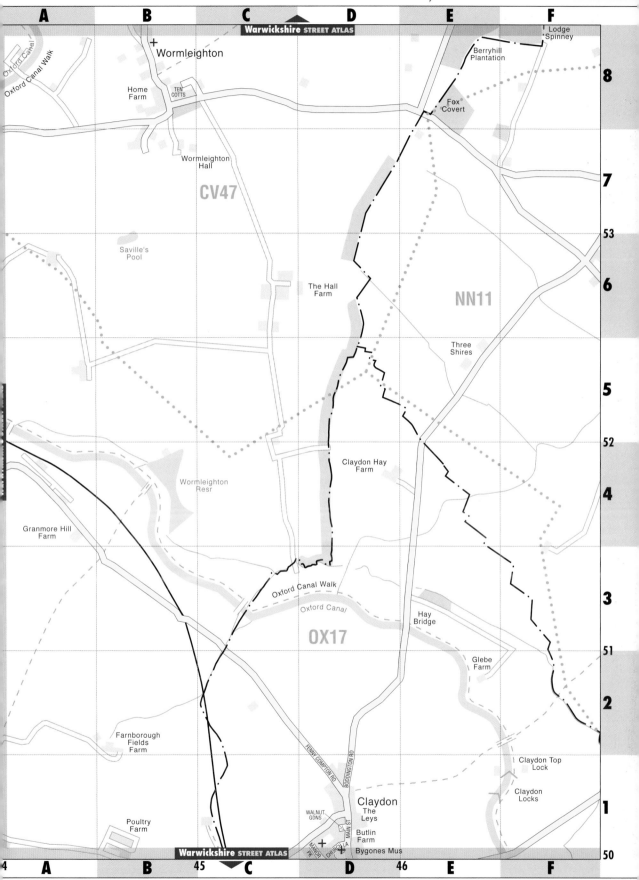

A B C D E F

Lodge
Spinney

Berryhill
Plantation

+ Wormleighton

8

Oxford Canal Walk

Oxford Canal

Home
Farm

TEN
COTTS

Fox
Covert

Wormleighton
Hall

CV47

7

53

Saville's
Pool

The Hall
Farm

NN11

6

Three
Shires

5

52

Claydon Hay
Farm

Wormleighton
Resr

4

Granmore Hill
Farm

3

Oxford Canal Walk

Oxford Canal

OX17

Hay
Bridge

Glebe
Farm

51

2

Farnborough
Fields
Farm

Claydon Top
Lock

Claydon
Locks

1

Poultry
Farm

FENNY COMPTON RD

BODDINGTON RD

WALNUT
GDNS

Claydon
The
Leys

MANOR
PK

CHURCH LA

MAIN ST

+

Butlin
Farm

+

Bygones Mus

50

4 A B 45 C D 46 E F

181
166

A  B  C  D  E  F

8

CV47

Highland Farm

Townsend Farm

Upper Boddington

Playing Field

TOWNSEND LA

FROG LA

WARWICK RD

THE ORCHARD

PRIORS HARDWICK RD

LONDON END

FARM STILE

THE LEYS

PH

7

Boddington CE Sch

CHURCH RD

PO

Manor Farm

P

P

53

Spella House

Boddington Resr

6

NN11

The Manor House

The Grange

HILL RD

Sewage Works

WELSH RD

5

THE GREEN

PH

THE PADDOCK

OWL END WAY

OWL END LA

Boddington Ct

MILLERS CL

Lower Boddington

52

Cedars Farm

BANBURY RD

4

Paradise Farm

3

Springfield House

Sewage Works

SUTTON CL

BUTTERS CL

51

BLACKSMITH'S LA

MAIN ST

PLOWDEN CL

OX17

Manor House

St Mary's RC Prim Sch

2

Aston le Walls

APPLETREE LA

Lawn Hill

Field's Cottages

1

Highfurlong Brook

50

47  A  B  48  C  D  49  E  F

181
196

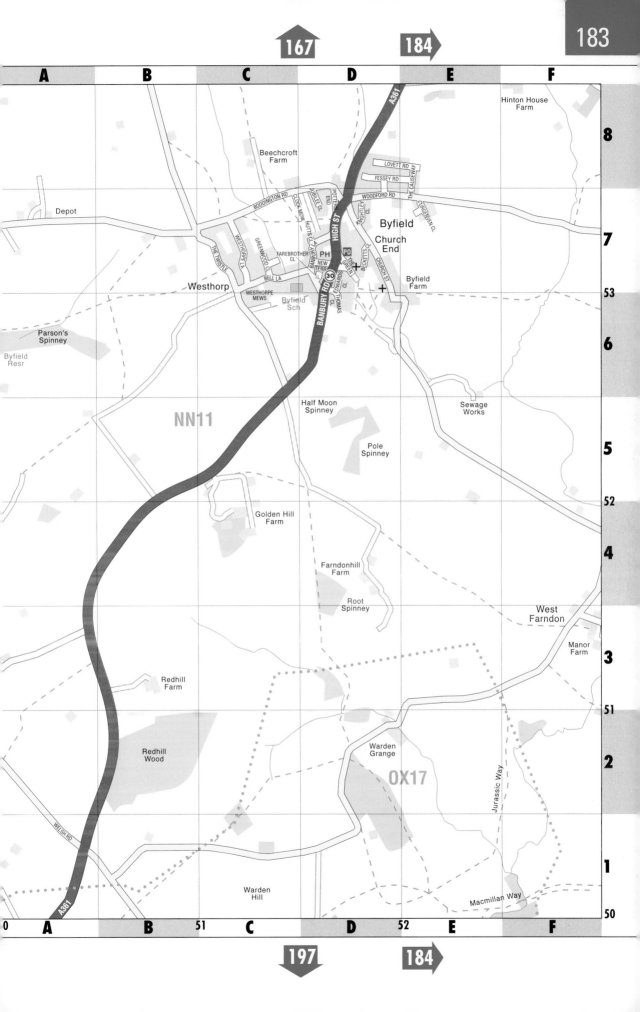

167
184

A B C D E F

8
7
53
6
5
52
4
51
3
2
1
50

Hinton House Farm

Beechcroft Farm

LOVETT RD
FESSEY RD
Woodford RD
THE CAUSEWAY
CURGENVEN CL

Byfield
Church End

BODDINGTON RD
CLOCK MDW
JUBILEE CL
NUTTS CL
POTTERS END
HIGH ST
WIGHTLEY CL
BECKETTS CL
CHURCH ST

Depot

THE THISTLE
WESTHORPE LA
GREENWOOD CL
BELL LA
FAREBROTHER CL
BANBURY
NEW TERR
EDWARDS THOMAS CL
ST THOMAS GREEN

PH
PO
30

Westhorp
WESTHORPE MEWS
Byfield Sch

Byfield Farm

BANBURY RD

Parson's Spinney

Byfield Resr

NN11

Half Moon Spinney

Sewage Works

Pole Spinney

Golden Hill Farm

Farndonhill Farm

Root Spinney

West Farndon

Manor Farm

Redhill Farm

Warden Grange

OX17

Jurassic Way

Redhill Wood

A361

WELSH RD

Warden Hill

Macmillan Way

A361

0 A 51 B C 52 D E F
50

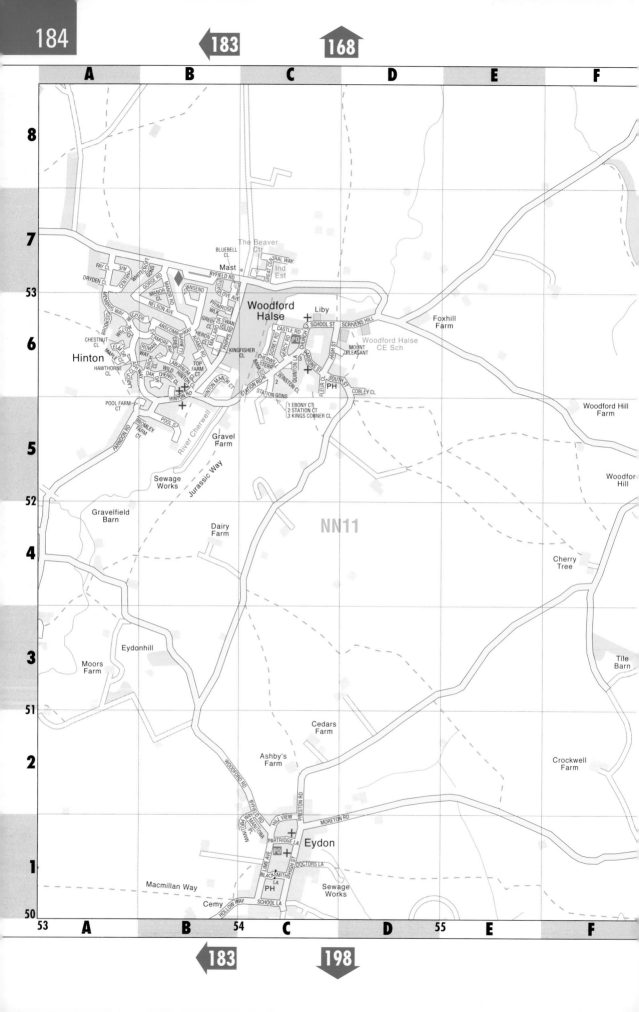

A   B   C   D   E   F

8
7
53
6
5
52
4
3
51
2
1
50

**Woodford Halse**

**Hinton**

The Beaver Ctr

BLUEBELL CL

Mast

BYFIELD RD

Ind Est

GREAT CENTRAL WAY

FAY CL

DRYDEN CL

WHITECROFT

CENTURY AVE

GORSE RD

MANOR RD

BARRETT CL

TANNSEND

FOXGLOVE AVE

PRIMROSE WLK

NELSON AVE

ANSCOMB WAY

GREBE CL

SWAN CL

Liby

SCHOOL ST

SCRIVENS HILL

Foxhill Farm

CHESTNUT CL

ELM DR

MAPLE CL

BROOKSIDE WAY

MEWBROS WAY

BEECHCR

WILLOW CL

SYCAMORE AVE

ADAMS RD

MALLARD

PHIPPS

HERON CL

KINGFISHER CL

CASTLE RD

SIDNEY RD

PERCY RD

CHERWELL TERR

SWAN CL

Woodford Halse CE Sch

MOUNT PLEASANT

HIGH ST

HAWTHORNE CL

ROW WAY

BIRCH

OAK

CHERRY CL

ASH WAY

LABURNUM CL

WILD CL

TOP FARM CT

HINTON RD

HINTON MANOR CT

STATION RD

STATION GDNS

CHERWELL BANK

WINSTON CL

QUINTON CL

FLEUR CL

SOUTH ST

PH

COBLEY CL

POOL FARM CT

BROMLEY FARM CT

Hinton RD

POOL ST

FARNDON RD

River Cherwell

Gravel Farm

1 EBONY CT
2 STATION CT
3 KINGS CORNER CL

Woodford Hill Farm

Woodford Hill

Sewage Works

Jurassic Way

Gravelfield Barn

Dairy Farm

**NN11**

Cherry Tree

Eydonhill

Moors Farm

Cedars Farm

Ashby's Farm

WOODFORD RD

BYFIELD RD

MANTON WAY

HILL VIEW

PRESTON RD

MORETON RD

Crockwell Farm

Tile Barn

Macmillan Way

LIME AVE

PARTRIDGE LA

BLACKSMITHS LA

HIGH ST

DOCTORS LA

**Eydon**

PH

SCHOOL LA

HOLLOW WAY

Cemy

Sewage Works

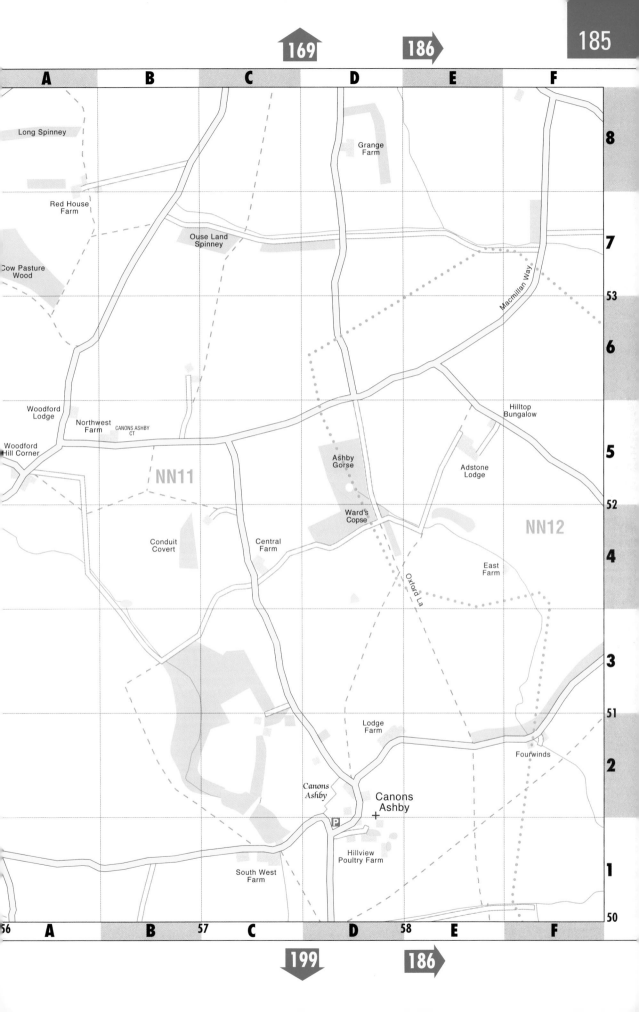

169
186

**A** **B** **C** **D** **E** **F**

8

Long Spinney

Grange
Farm

Red House
Farm

7

Cow Pasture
Wood

Ouse Land
Spinney

Macmillan Way

53

6

Woodford
Lodge

Hilltop
Bungalow

Northwest
Farm

CANONS ASHBY
CT

Woodford
Hill Corner

Ashby
Gorse

Adstone
Lodge

5

**NN11**

52

Ward's
Copse

**NN12**

Conduit
Covert

Central
Farm

East
Farm

4

Oxford La

3

Lodge
Farm

51

Fourwinds

2

Canons
Ashby

Canons
Ashby

P

Hillview
Poultry Farm

South West
Farm

1

50

199
186

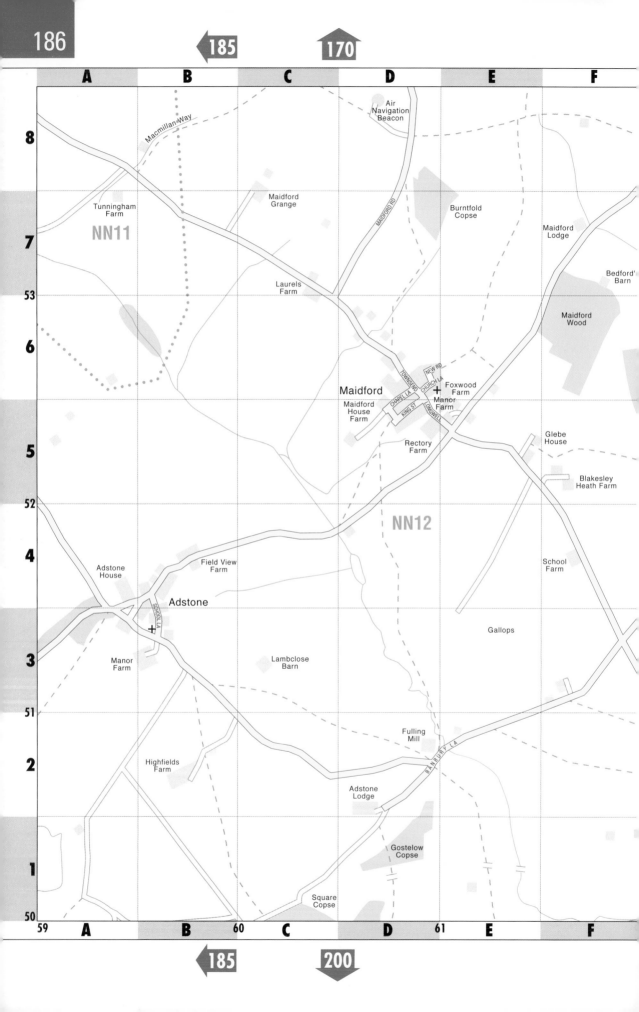

185
170

**A** **B** **C** **D** **E** **F**

8

Macmillan Way

Air
Navigation
Beacon

Tunningham
Farm

NN11

Maidford
Grange

MAIDFORD RD

Burntfold
Copse

Maidford
Lodge

7

Bedford'
Barn

53

Laurels
Farm

Maidford
Wood

6

NEW RD

TOWNSEND RD

CHURCH LA

Foxwood
Farm

Maidford

CHAPEL LA

Manor
Farm

Maidford
House
Farm

KING ST

LONGWELL

Glebe
House

5

Rectory
Farm

Blakesley
Heath Farm

52

NN12

4

Field View
Farm

Adstone
House

School
Farm

Adstone

SCHOOL LA

3

Manor
Farm

Lambclose
Barn

Gallops

51

Fulling
Mill

2

BANBURY LA

Highfields
Farm

Adstone
Lodge

Gostelow
Copse

1

Square
Copse

50

59 **A** **B** 60 **C** **D** 61 **E** **F**

185
200

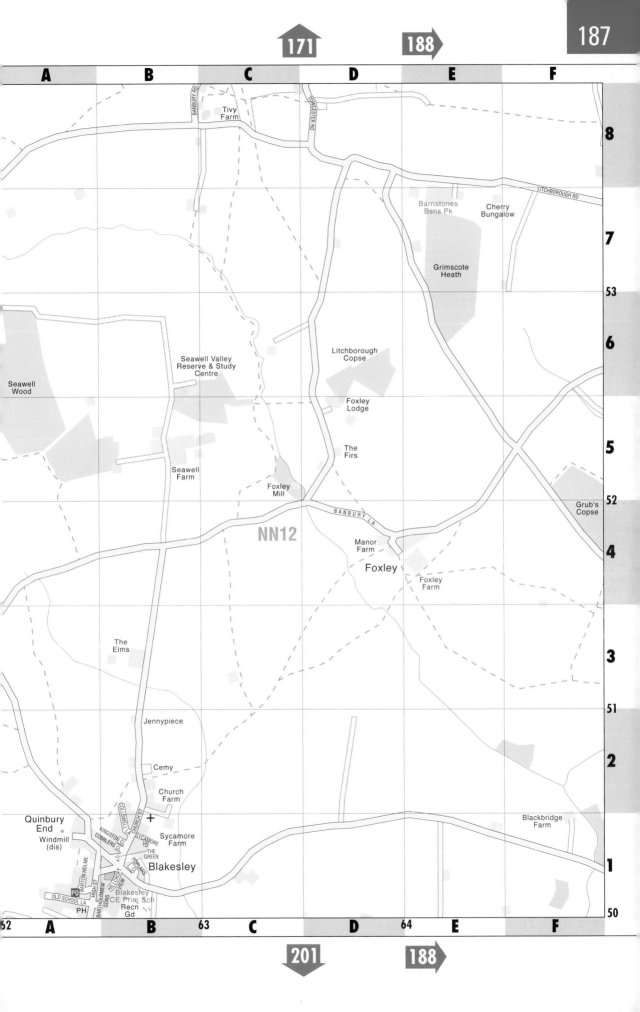

A  B  C  D  E  F

8
7
53
6
5
52
4
3
51
2
1
50

Tivy Farm

BANBURY RD
TOWCESTER RD

LITCHBOROUGH RD

Barnstones Bsns Pk

Cherry Bungalow

Grimscote Heath

Litchborough Copse

Seawell Valley Reserve & Study Centre

Seawell Wood

Foxley Lodge

The Firs

Seawell Farm

Foxley Mill

NN12

BANBURY LA

Grub's Copse

Manor Farm

Foxley

Foxley Farm

The Elms

Jennypiece

Cemy

Church Farm

Quinbury End

Windmill (dis)

COLLWELL CL
KINGSTON CL
COBBLERS CL
CHURCH ST
SYCAMORE YD
THE GREEN
PERRANS CL

Sycamore Farm

BARTON HOLME
HIGH ST
BARTHOLOMEW GDNS
HILCROFT
D VIEW

Blakesley

PO

Old School La

PH

Blakesley CE Prim Sch Recn Gd

Blackbridge Farm

62  A  B  63  C  D  64  E  F

50

187 172

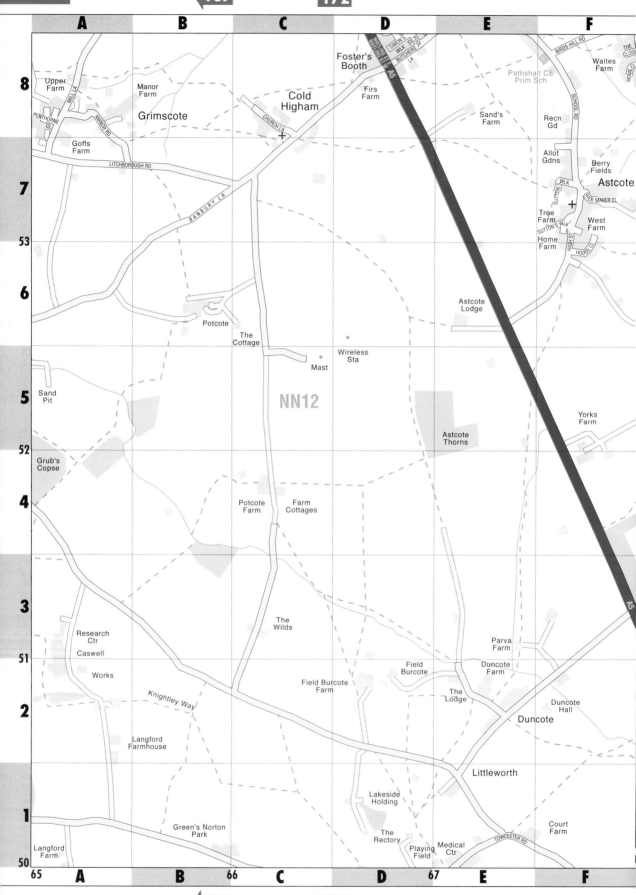

NN12

Foster's Booth

Cold Higham

Grimscote

Upper Farm

Manor Farm

Goffs Farm

LITCHBOROUGH RD

BANBURY LA

Potcote

The Cottage

Mast

Wireless Sta

Sand Pit

Grub's Copse

Potcote Farm

Farm Cottages

The Wilds

Research Ctr Caswell

Works

Knightley Way

Langford Farmhouse

Green's Norton Park

Langford Farm

Firs Farm

Sand's Farm

Pattishall CE Prim Sch

Waites Farm

Recn Gd

Allot Gdns

Berry Fields

Astcote

Tree Farm

West Farm

Home Farm

Astcote Lodge

Yorks Farm

Astcote Thorns

Parva Farm

Duncote Farm

Field Burcote

Field Burcote Farm

The Lodge

Duncote Hall

Duncote

Littleworth

Lakeside Holding

The Rectory

Playing Field

Medical Ctr

Court Farm

TOWCESTER RD

SCHOOL RD

MILL LA

MANOR RD

PENTHORNE CL

CHURCH LA

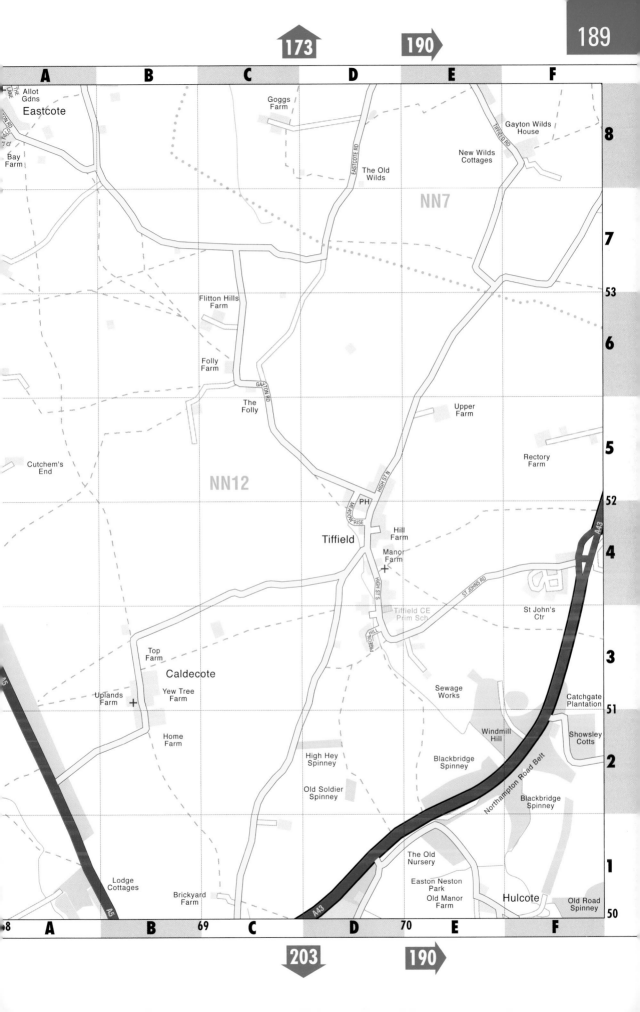

189
174

**A** **B** **C** **D** **E** **F**

BLISWORTH RD

Hill Farm

GAYTON RD

Highcliffe Farm

NORTHAMPTON RD

CHAPEL LA

LITTLE LA

Blisworth Com Prim Sch

8

Blisworth Lodge

PH

POND BANK

WEST BROOK

HIGH ST

PO

COURTEENHALL RD

Gayton Wood Farm

Blisworth Mill

CHURCH LA

ASHLEY CT

EASTFIELD

HOME CL

WELLSPRING

WINDMILL AVE

BUTTMEAD

GREENAWAY CL

CONNEGAR LEYS

7

GREENSIDE

**Blisworth**

Rectory Farm

TOWCESTER RD

Grand Union Canal

Stone Works Farm

53

Glebe Farm

**NN7**

Tunnel Hill Farm

6

Tunnel Hill Cottages

70

Wood Cottage Farm

KNOCK LA

5

Grand Union Canal Wlk

Windmill Cottage

A43

Blisworth Hill

52

Wood Farm

STOKE RD

Blisworth Hill Farm

4

Top Farm

Burn Wood

Blisworth Tunnel

Buttermilk Hall Farm

3

Midshires Way

Nun Wood

51

Stoke Plain Lodge

**NN12**

Showsley Belt

Station House

2

Showsley Grounds

SHOWSLEY RD

HIGH ST

1

Hill Farm

Stoke Plain

Nettle Spinney

MAIN RD

SHUTLANGER RD

50

**71** **A** **B** **72** **C** **D** **73** **E** **F**

189
204

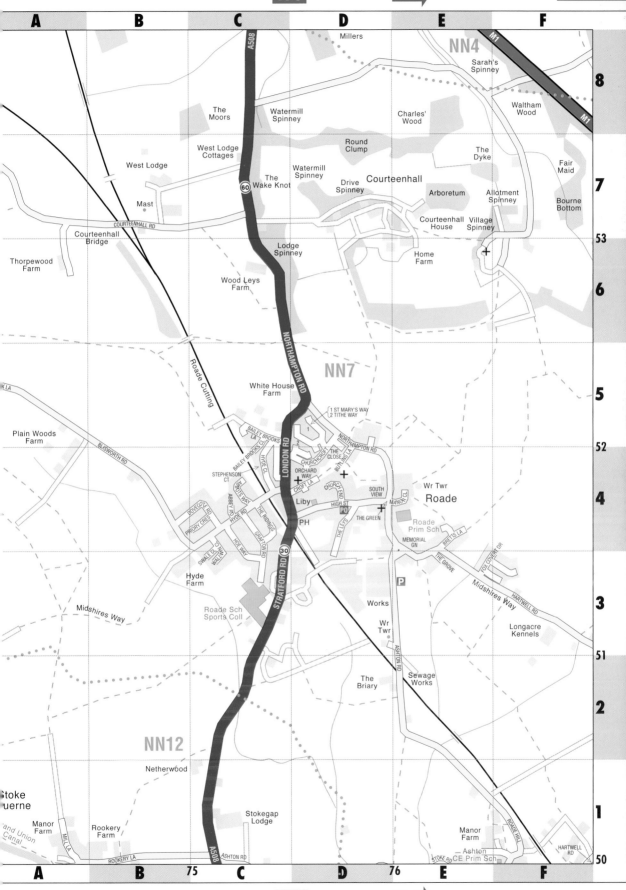

191 176

| | A | B | C | D | E | F |
|---|---|---|---|---|---|---|

**8**

NN4

Manor Farm

Manor Cottages

West Hall

**M1**

**7**

Liddell Wood

Quinton Green Cotts

Quinton Green

Midshires Way

**53**

East Lodge

**6**

**5**

Fox Covert

Villach

Stoneway Copse

Crabtree Thick

Forest Close

Hollow Quarter

Shrubby Copse

**52**

NN7

**4**

Ashwood Farm

Forest Lodge

Salcey Forest Trail

Rush Copse

Midshires Way

Hartwell Clear Copse

Seven Oaks

Pound Riding

**3**

Rawlesmere Copse

**51**

Rowley Wood

Vicarage

FOREST GLADE

Sandpit Copse

CRABTREE CL

Ashton Lodge Farm

HARTWELL RD

Woodland View Farm

MEADSLADE

FOREST VIEW

FOREST RD

WOOD

OAK CL

STONEWAY

SALCEY CL

RUSH CL

LIME CL

**2**

Colmarel Kennels

Ashton House

CHURCH CL

HILLSIDE

SCHOOL LA

GRAFTON CL

ROSE CL

Hartwell CE Prim Sch

ASHTON RD

MALTING WAY

STOCKING CL

SWIMCOMBE

BLACKSMITHS

ROBINS CL

PH

**Hartwell**

HARTWELL RD

LOWER END

PARK RD

PARK LA

AMBERLEY RD 1
STONEHURST CL 2

**1**

MK1

Laythick Copse

**Lower End**

FOLLY LA

**50**

| 77 | A | B | 78 | C | D | 79 | E | F |
|---|---|---|---|---|---|---|---|---|

A   B   C   D   E   F

8

The Paddock

Cross Maples

Manor Farm

Hay Copse

Church Slade

7

NN7

Cowpers Oak Lodge

Biggin Lodge

53

Ravenstone Road Copse

Milton Keynes Boundary Wlk

Great Wood

Barnstaple Wood

6

Dinglederry

Ash Beds

Roadley's Brake

5

Hanger's Spinney

Woodlands

52

4

MK16

Cheyney Farm

3

Parkfield Farm

MK46

Northend Farm

Northend

Cemy

51

Parkfield Spinney

Milton Keynes Boundary Wlk

THE ALMSHOUSES

Horseshoe Farm

2

CHASEPORT CL

BAY LA

ABBEY WAY

WESTON RD

Spring Barn

Ravenstone

MEADOW CT

COMMON ST

Yew Tree Farm

1

B526

Mannings Farm

50

83   A   B   84   C   D   85   E   F

8

NN7

7

53

Howbrook
Copse

Olney Park
Farm

Milton Keynes Boundary Wlk

B5388

Olney
Hyde

Smith's
Farm

Court
Farm

Iwick
Wood

6

Allot
Gdns

Sewage
Works

Warrington
Road
Farm

Ind
Est

STILEBROOK RD

WARRINGTON
RD

DRIFT
WAY

Hungary
Hall

Dickens
Spinney

MK46

YARDLEY RD

Olney Mid Sch

KIPPELL
ALL SS
MOSS'S
WAY
KING'S
MEAD
LILY HILL
FERNE
FURLONG

5

KENSINGTON
PL

MIDLAND RD

NEWTON
ST

52

Milton Keynes Boundary Wlk

Olney

Long La

SHORT MASSEY 1
CRAB TREE CL 2
HAWKSWOOD 3
FISHERMANS CL 4

WHYGHILL
ASPREYS
ASPREYS
MASSEY
TALBOTS
HYDE
GUINEA
ORCH
MAYBUSH
WLK
MOORES HILL
TRNELL
3
2
1
CLICKERS
YD
B5388

DARTMOUTH RD

HIGH ST

HOLES

Pheasants
Nest

The
Alcove

STOCKEN CL 1
WHITMEES CL 2

FLAGGS
SHILLS
ASPREYS
DIXEYS
2
1
SILLSWOOD
DICKENS
SPINNEY
CHERRY
ORCH
RIV
ST
JOSEPH'S
CL
RISE
WEST ST
Long La
SPRINGFIELD
RD
DELLS
WEST ST
COBBS
GDN

LACE
MEWS

LIBY

4

ANDING
CL
BACON
HILL
COURT
CNR
ASHLEA
THORNLEA
ST
CROFT
SPRING LA
ORCHARD
RISE
12
11
10

Overbrook
Spinney

Olney
Inf Sch

HOLLY
WOOD
SPINNEY HILL RD
DAGNALL RD
THE PYGHTLE
WESTON
CL

THE PYGHTLE

NLEA
Mus
P
PO
P

3

Weston
Park

Flamingo Gardens
& Zoo Park

STONE PIT
CL
BEECH AVE
WESTON RD
Recn
Gd

OAKDOWN
CRES

LIME ST

4
3

HIGH ST

51

The
Wilderness

Laundry
Cottage

Goosey
Bridge

CLAY PIT LA 1
WAGSTAFF WAY 2
PEBODY PL 3
STONEMASONS CL 4
CHANTRY RISE 5
PEMBROKE HO 6
CHURCH ST 7
DSBORN'S CT 8
MARKET PL 9
ROSE CT 10
BERRELL'S CT 11
FOUNTAIN CT 12

Works

2

BRIDGE ST

Weston
Underwood

PH
WOOD LA
HIGH ST
CROSS LA

COWPERS ORCH

Church
Farm
PO
PEYERS LA

THE CLOSE

River Great Ouse

Otter
Pool

Heron
Water

Grebe
Lake

The
Willows

Emberton
Country Park
& Visitor Centre

Snipe
Pool

A509

Emberton

1

HARVEY DR

A509
Milton Keynes

50

A509 Wellingborough

Buckinghamshire STREET ATLAS

A   B   C   D   E   F

NN11

8

Stone
House

Macmillan Way

7

Calves
Close
Spinney

WELSH RD

Job's
Hill

Wardenhill
Covert

Horseclose
Spinney

Wardenhill
Farm

Bush Hill
Spinney

Bush Hill
Barn

River Cherwell

Trafford
Cottage

49

CULWORTH RD

Drunken
Meadow
Spinney

Roundhill
Spinney

Trafford House
Farm

6

Blackgrounds

River Cherwell

Home
Farm

Jurassic Way

5

The
Pool

48

Edgcote

Edgcote
House

Trafford
Bridge

Mire
Spinney

OX17

4

EDGCOTE
DRIVE COTTS

Trafford Bridge
Farm

Wadground
Barn

3

Ladshill
Spinney

Edgcote
Hill

Danesmoor
Spinney

47

Danes
Moor

Hay
Spinney

Orchard
Spinney

Ashbed
Spinney

Old
Spinney

2

Edgcote
Lodge

1

46

A   51   B   C   D   52   E   F

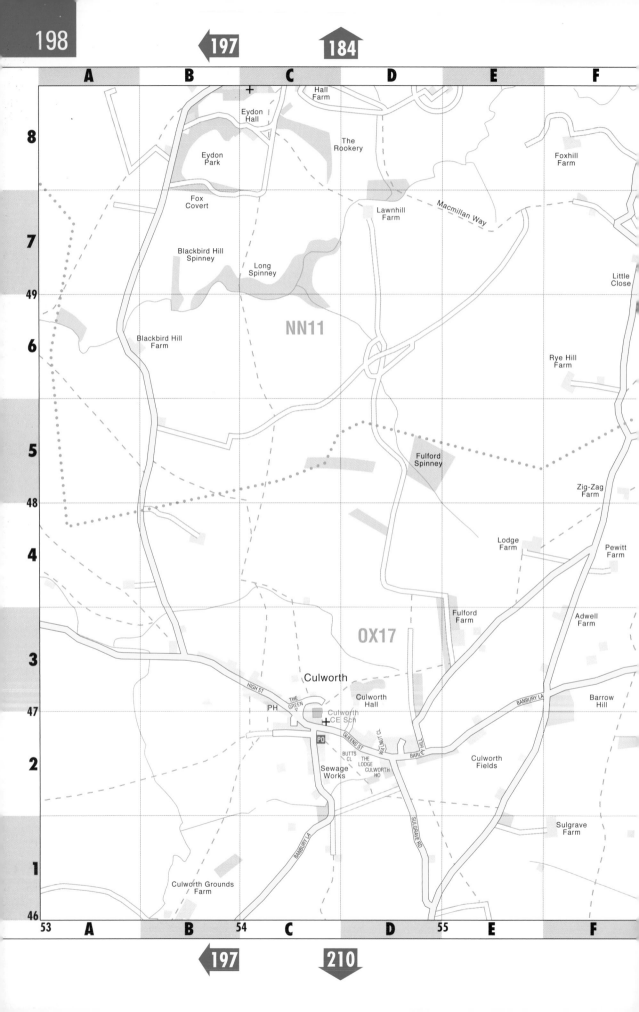

A B C D E F

8

Eydon Hall

Hall Farm

Eydon Park

The Rookery

Foxhill Farm

Fox Covert

7

Blackbird Hill Spinney

Lawnhill Farm

Macmillan Way

Long Spinney

49

Little Close

NN11

6

Blackbird Hill Farm

Rye Hill Farm

5

Fulford Spinney

Zig-Zag Farm

48

Lodge Farm

4

Pewitt Farm

Fulford Farm

Adwell Farm

OX17

3

Culworth

Barrow Hill

HIGH ST

THE GREEN

Culworth Hall

BANBURY LA

47

PH

Culworth CE Sch

QUEENS ST

WATLING TO

PO

BARL

2

BUTTS CL

THE LODGE CULWORTH HO

CULWORTH

Culworth Fields

Sewage Works

BANBURY LA

SULGRAVE RD

Sulgrave Farm

1

Culworth Grounds Farm

46

53  A  B  54  C  D  55  E  F

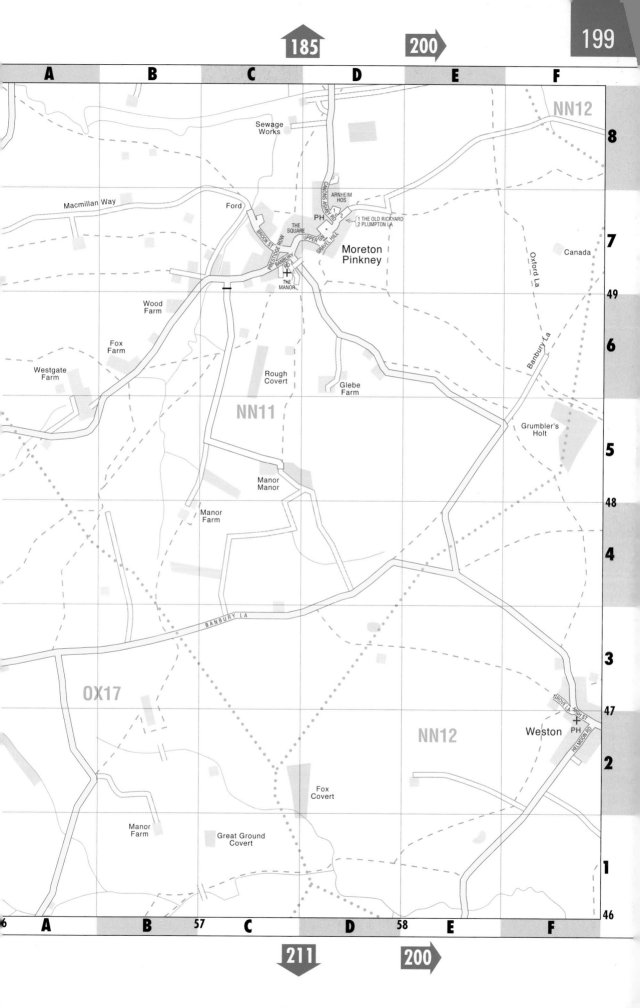

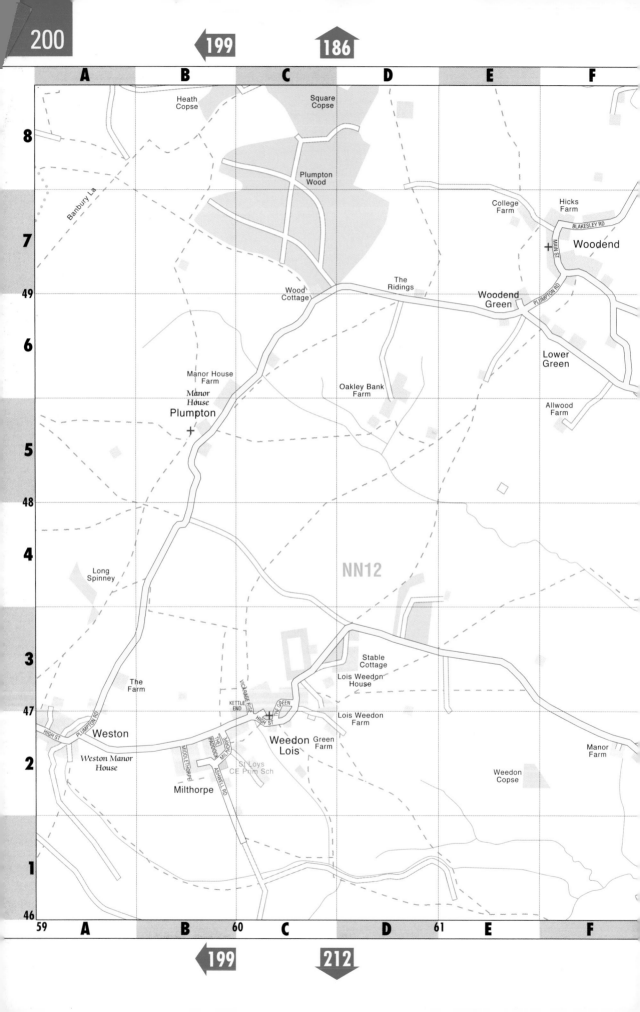

**A**   **B**   **C**   **D**   **E**   **F**

Heath Copse

Square Copse

Plumpton Wood

Banbury La

College Farm

Hicks Farm

BLAKESLEY RD

MAIN ST

Woodend

8

7

49

Wood Cottage

The Ridings

Woodend Green

PLUMPTON RD

6

Manor House Farm

Manor House

Plumpton

Oakley Bank Farm

Lower Green

Allwood Farm

5

48

Long Spinney

4

NN12

3

The Farm

Stable Cottage

Lois Weedon House

47

KETTLE END

VICARAGE RISE

THE GREEN

HIGH ST

Lois Weedon Farm

High St

PLUMPTON RD

Weston

Weedon Lois

Green Farm

Manor Farm

2

Weston Manor House

MIDDLETHORPE

THE PADDOCKS

THE MILK

ASHWELL RD

St Loys CE Prim Sch

Weedon Copse

Milthorpe

1

46

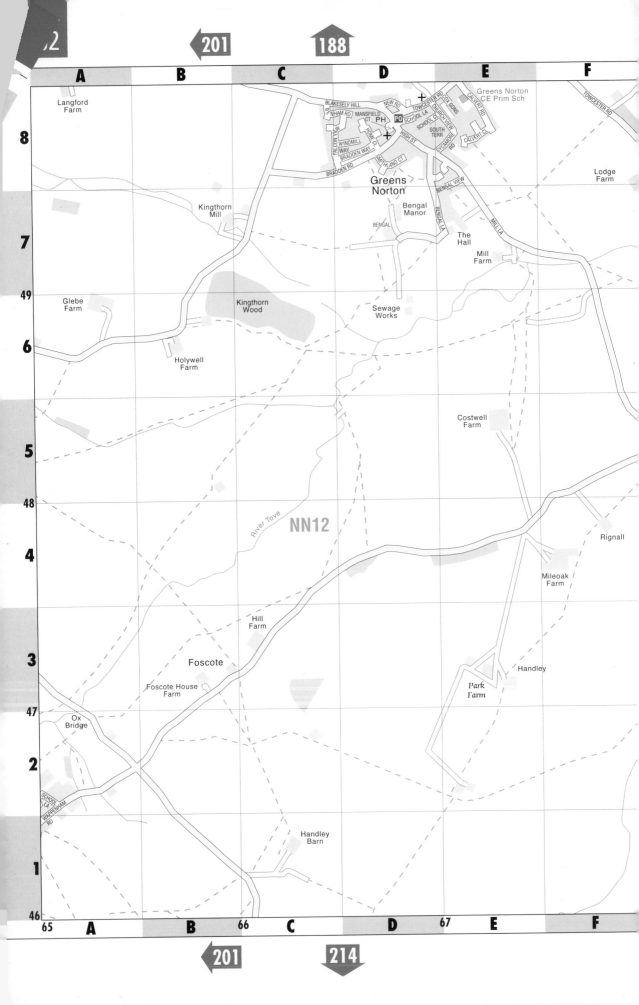

A B C D E F

8

Langford
Farm

Greens Norton
CE Prim Sch

Lodge
Farm

BLAKESELY HILL
BLENHAM RD
MANSFIELD CT
HOME CT
FALCON VIEW
WINDMILL WAY
BRADDEN WAY
BRADDEN RD
NEW RD
TOWCESTER RD
SCHOOL LA
SCHOOL CT
CHURCH VIEW
SCHOOL CT
SOUTH TERR
HIGH ST
COT GDNS
CALVERT GDNS
SYCAMORE RD
CALVERT CL
TOWCESTER RD

PH
PO

SMITH LAND CT

Greens
Norton

Kingthorn
Mill

Bengal
Manor

Bengal

Bengal View
BENGAL LA
BENGAL LA

The
Hall

MILL LA

Mill
Farm

7

Glebe
Farm

Kingthorn
Wood

Sewage
Works

49

6

Holywell
Farm

Costwell
Farm

5

48

River Tove

NN12

Rignall

4

Mileoak
Farm

Hill
Farm

3

Foscote

Handley

Foscote House
Farm

Park
Farm

47

Ox
Bridge

2

SCHOOL LA
WAPPENHAM RD

Handley
Barn

1

46

65    A         B      66    C         D      67    E         F

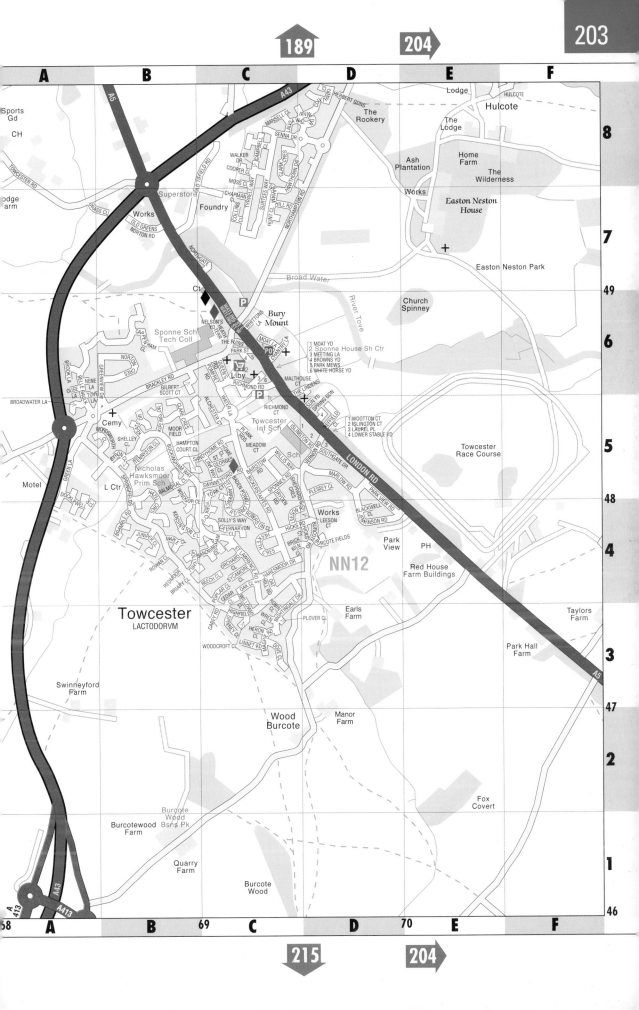

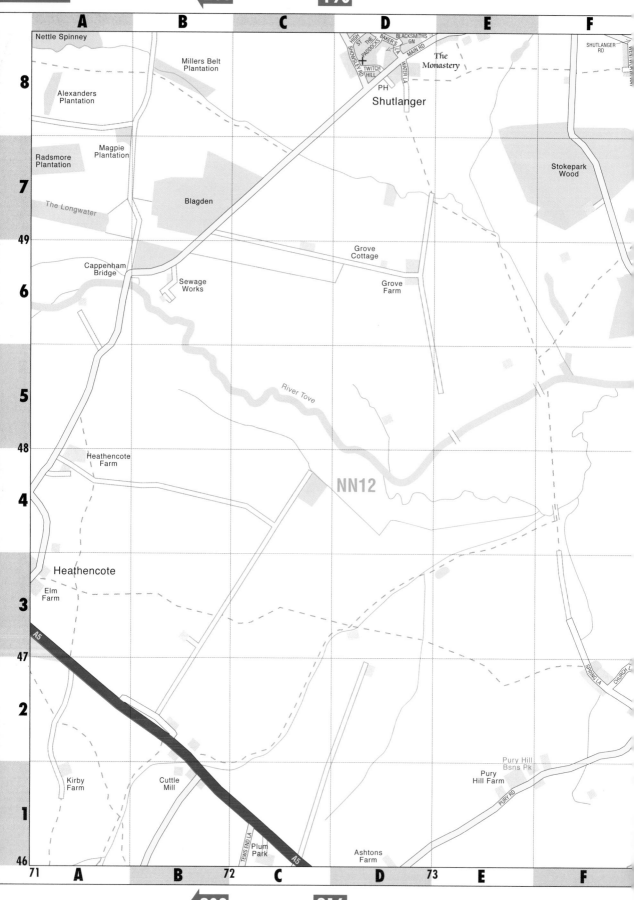

| A | B | C | D | E | F |

Nettle Spinney

Millers Belt
Plantation

HIGH
ST
THE
PADDOCKS

SNOWSLEY RD

BAKER'S

BLACKSMITHS
GN

MAIN RD

SHUTLANGER
RD

WEN PLATE WY

8

Alexanders
Plantation

TWITCH
HILL

WATER LA

The
Monastery

PH

Shutlanger

Radsmore
Plantation

Magpie
Plantation

Stokepark
Wood

7

The Longwater

Blagden

49

Grove
Cottage

6

Cappenham
Bridge

Sewage
Works

Grove
Farm

River Tove

5

48

Heathencote
Farm

NN12

4

Heathencote

Elm
Farm

3

A5

47

SPRING LA

CHURCH

2

Pury Hill
Bsns Pk

Kirby
Farm

Cuttle
Mill

Pury
Hill Farm

PURY RD

1

TEWS END LA

Plum
Park

A5

Ashtons
Farm

46

| 71 | A | | B | 72 | C | | D | 73 | E | | F |

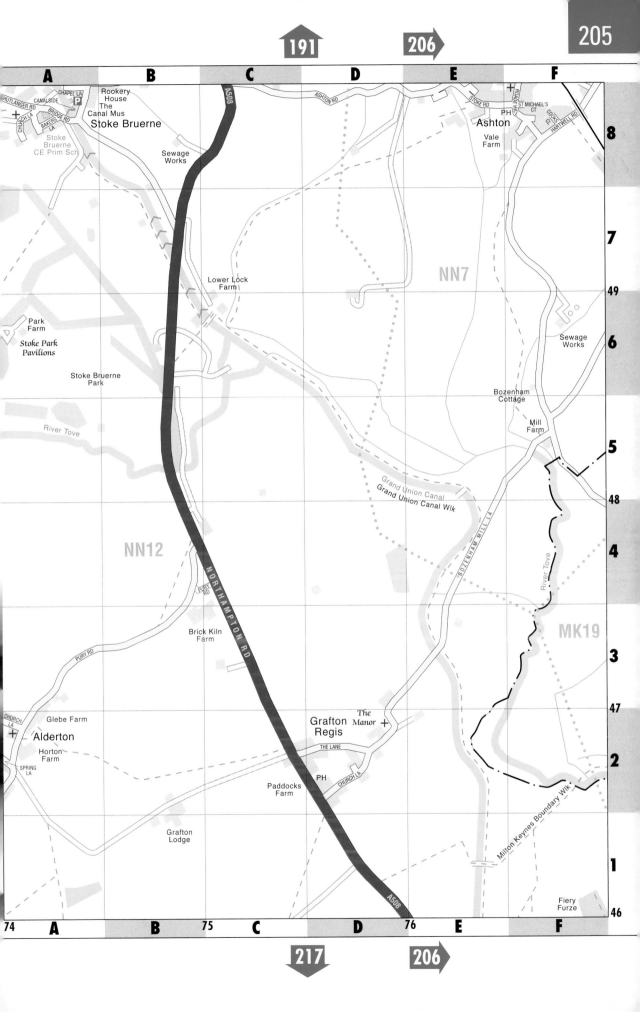

205
192

**A** **B** **C** **D** **E** **F**

**8**

Park Farm

Ravenshead Farm

FOLLY LA

PARK RD

Elms Farm

Hartwell End Farm

Hartwell End House

**7**

NN7

Stonepit Farm

**49**

Chapel Farm

**6**

Gorden's Lodge

ROSE LA

Roselane Farm

**5**

Glebe Farm

FOREST RD

**48**

Model Farm

GLEBE LA

Long Street

HARTWELL RD

PH

+

**4**

Milton Keynes Boundary Walk

Chantry Farm

RHYMER CL

HOLIDAY LA

Folly Farm

Halfway Houses

LONG STREET

Pindon Manor

Pindon End

HIGHAM CROSS RD

Sewage Works

WILLIAMS CL

**3**

New Farm

Pindon Manor Farm

Higham Cross

MK19

Badger's Balney

**47**

Green End La

Grange Farm

Mast

**2**

Huntgate End

Huntgate End Farm

Cuckoo Hill Farm

**1**

River Tove

Cuckoos' Hill

Maltmill Lane Farm

CASTLETHORPE RD

**46**

NN12

Lincoln Lodge Cottage

**77** **A** **B** **78** **C** **D** **79** **E** **F**

205
218

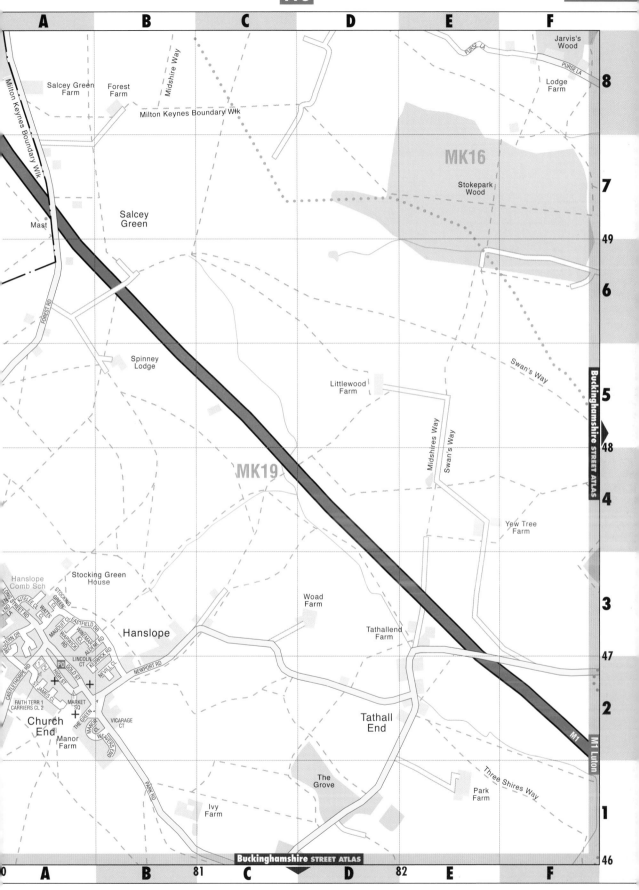

Jarvis's Wood

PURSE LA

PURSE LA

Salcey Green Farm

Forest Farm

Milton Keynes Boundary Wlk

Midshire Way

Milton Keynes Boundary Wlk

Lodge Farm

**8**

MK16

Stokepark Wood

**7**

**49**

Salcey Green

Mast

FOREST RD

**6**

Spinney Lodge

Swan's Way

Littlewood Farm

Midshires Way

Swan's Way

**5**

**48**

MK19

Yew Tree Farm

**4**

Hanslope Comb Sch

Stocking Green House

Woad Farm

Tathallend Farm

**3**

STOCKING GREEN

WATTS

KITELEE CL

LONG'S STREET RD

LONG'S END LA

MANDUIT CL

EASTFIELD DR

WARWICK RD

WINEMAR CL

ALDERIE RD

Hanslope

**47**

STERN DR

LINCOLN CT

KESWICK RD

NEVILL CL

NEWPORT RD

PO GOLD ST

CASTLETHORPE RD

HIGH ST

ST JAMES CL

FAITH TERR 1

CARRIERS CL 2

MARKET SQ

THE GREEN

VICARAGE CT

Church End

Manor Farm

MANOR

WEAVERS END

Tathall End

**2**

PARK RD

The Grove

Park Farm

Three Shires Way

M1

M1 Luton

Ivy Farm

**1**

**46**

Milton Keynes Boundary Wlk

0  A  B  81  C  D  82  E  F

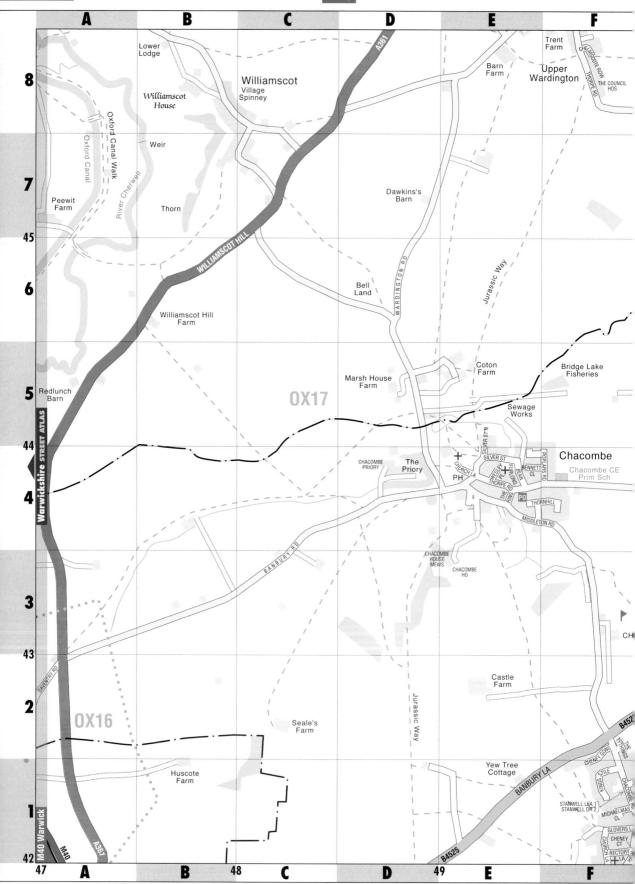

197
210

A B C D E F

8
7
45
6
5
44
4
3
43
2
1
42

New Barn
Gypsy Barn
Archers House
Hangland Farm
Fern Hill
The Hill
Hanginghill Barn
Hill Farm
Thorpe Hill
TOWNSEND LA
Thorpe Lodge Farm
Mast
BANBURY LA
OX17
Chacombe Lodge Farm
40
Thenford Hill
B4525
Chinnor Farm
Jeff's Farm
Thenford Hill Farm
Grange Farm
Chacombe Hill Farm
BANBURY LA
Thenford Grounds Farm
Stanwell Farm
Field Barn
Rectory Farm
Cold Harbour
WATERS LA
CHENWELL LEA
Chenderit Sch
STANWELL CL
Middleton Cheney
Cemy
BULL BAULK
THENFORD RD

A B C D E F
51 52

A B C D E F

8
7
45
6
5
44
4
43
3
2
42
1

NN12

Sewage Works

WESTON RD

Sulgrave Manor

Rectory Farm

LITTLE ST

Coolington Farm

Allithorne Wood

Peter's Farm

Stuchbury Lodge

College Farm

Home Farm

Stuchbury Manor Farm

Stuchbury

Stuchbury Hall Farm

OX17

Washbrook Spinney

Stuchbury Fox Covert

WRIGHTONS HILL

WAPPENHAM RD

Helmdon

THE GREEN

BARN CT

Helmdon Prim Sch

STATION RD

PH

BELL CL

HINTON'S CL

SHORTLANDS CL

CHURCH ST

Sewage Works

NN13

Grange Farm Barn

HELMDON RD

Fatlands Farm

Greatworth Hall

Spring Farm

B4525

Bungalow Farm

Redlands House

Glebe Farm

Ash Vale Farm

Blackpits Barn

Halse Copse

Greatworth Fields

6 57 58

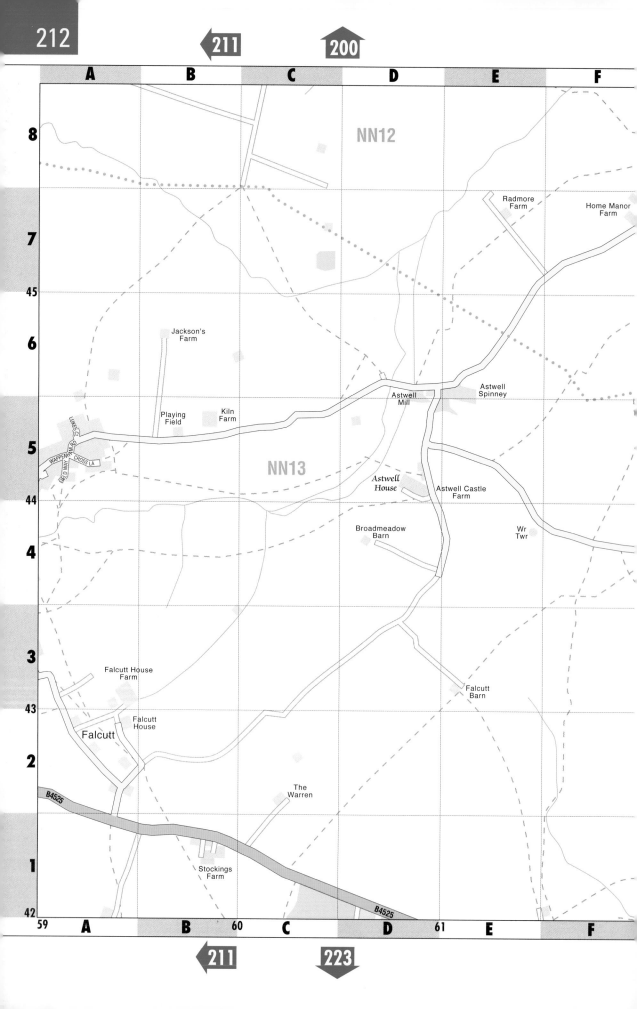

NN12

Radmore Farm

Home Manor Farm

Jackson's Farm

Astwell Spinney

Playing Field

Kiln Farm

Astwell Mill

LUKES CL

WAPPENHAM RD

BREDO WAY

CROSS LA

NN13

Astwell House

Astwell Castle Farm

Broadmeadow Barn

Wr Twr

Falcutt House Farm

Falcutt Barn

Falcutt House

Falcutt

The Warren

B4525

Stockings Farm

B4525

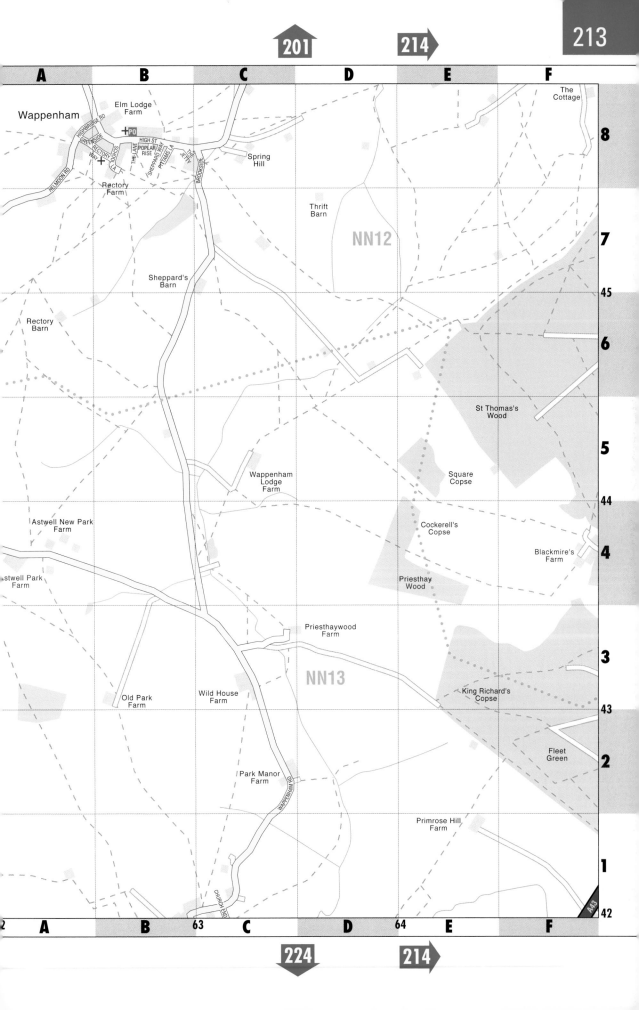

A B C D E F

The Cottage

Wappenham

Elm Lodge
Farm

HIGHBRIDGE RD
GREENSIDE
RECTORY
WAY
SCHOOL LA
ST JOHN'S
THE LANE
SHEPPARD WAY
POPLAR RISE
PYTTANS LA
HIGH ST
THE JETTY
BROOKSIDE

PO

Spring
Hill

HELMDON RD

Rectory
Farm

Thrift
Barn

NN12

8

7

45

Sheppard's
Barn

Rectory
Barn

6

St Thomas's
Wood

5

Wappenham
Lodge
Farm

Square
Copse

44

Astwell New Park
Farm

Cockerell's
Copse

Blackmire's
Farm

4

stwell Park
Farm

Priesthay
Wood

Priesthaywood
Farm

3

NN13

King Richard's
Copse

Old Park
Farm

Wild House
Farm

43

Fleet
Green

2

Park Manor
Farm

WAPPENHAM RD

Primrose Hill
Farm

1

CHURCH END

A43

42

A B C D E F
63 64

215
204

A B C D E F

8

Tew's End

CAREYS RD

Paulerspury

Plum Park

Grafton Park

SCRIVENERS LA

Paulerspury CE Prim Sch

NEW POU CL

TEWS END LA

STONY HILL

LONGCROFT LA

GRAYS CL

GRAYS LA

PVRY RD

PLUM PARK LA

7

LOWER ST

PO

THE GREEN

PARK LA

PH

FAIRFIELD RD

LUMBER LA

HIGH ST

Kingstons Farm

Plumpton End

45

Plum Park Farm

6

Park Farm

The Gullet

Stollage Farm

Bradlem Pond

5

NN12

King's Copse

44

Bear's Copse

Lady Copse

4

Say's Copse

Old Tun Copse

Kennels Cottages

KENNELS DR

Wakefield Little Lodge

3

Smalladine Copse

43

Wakefield Lawn

MK18

2

Wakefield Lodge

MAINT

Home Farm

The Pheasantry

DEANSHANGER DR

1

Briary Wood

Hill Cops

42

71 A B 72 C D 73 E F

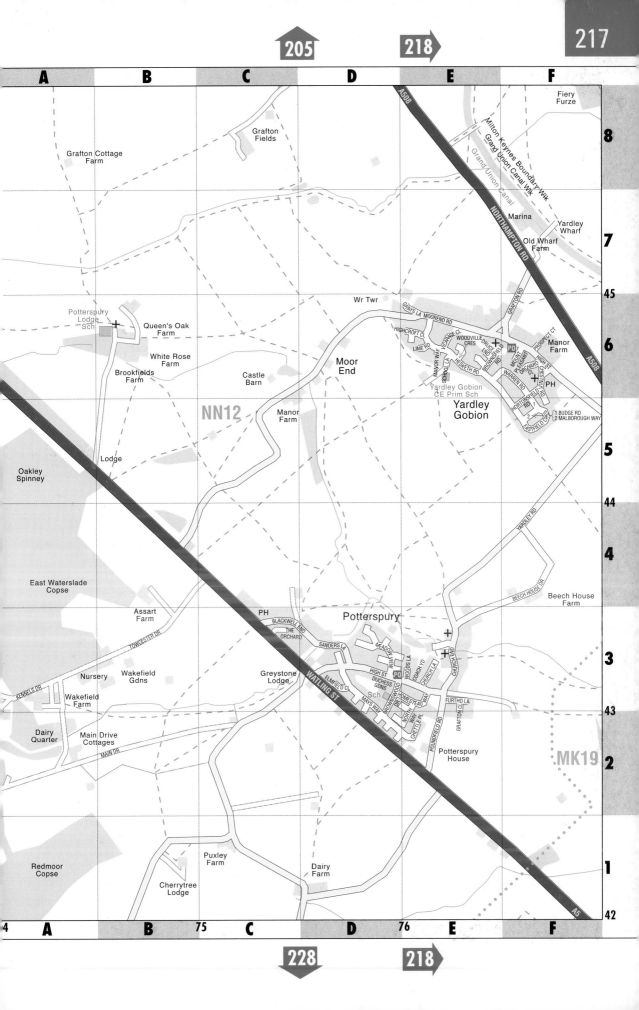

205
218

**A** **B** **C** **D** **E** **F**

8

Fiery Furze

Grafton Fields

Grafton Cottage Farm

Milton Keynes Boundary Wlk
Grand Union Canal Wlk
Grand Union Canal

NORTHAMPTON RD

Marina

Yardley Wharf

7

45

Old Wharf Farm

Potterspury Lodge Sch

Queen's Oak Farm

White Rose Farm

Brookfields Farm

Castle Barn

Moor End

Wr Twr

GRAYS LA   MOOREND RD

HIGHCROFT CL

LIME RD

VICARAGE CL

WOODVILLE CRES

BROWNSFIELD

DRUCE END

MOUNT PLEASANT

GRAFTON RD

PROSPECT CT

HIGH ST   CHESTNUT CL

Manor Farm

6

MANOR WAY   SCHOOL LA

HESKETH RD

WARREN RD

ORCHARD CL

PH

A508

Yardley Gobion CE Prim Sch

Yardley Gobion

HORTONSFIELD RD

CASTFIELD CL

1 BUDGE RD
2 MALBOROUGH WAY

NN12

Manor Farm

Lodge

Oakley Spinney

5

44

4

East Waterslade Copse

Assart Farm

TOWCESTER DR

PH

BLACKWELL END

THE ORCHARD

SANDERS LA

Potterspury

YARDLEY RD

BEECH HOUSE DR

Beech House Farm

3

KENNELS DR

Nursery

Wakefield Gdns

Greystone Lodge

ELMFIELD CL

WATLING ST

MEADOW VIEW

HIGH ST   DUCHESS Sch

WOODS LA

COACH YD

CHURCH LA

CHURCH END

FURTHO LA

MK19

Wakefield Farm

MAYS WAY

NORTH WAY   HOMESTEAD WAY

CHETTLE PL

GRAFTON RD

POUNDFIELD RD

43

Dairy Quarter

Main Drive Cottages

MAIN DR

Potterspury House

2

Redmoor Copse

Puxley Farm

Cherrytree Lodge

Dairy Farm

A5

1

42

**A** 75 **B** **C** **D** 76 **E** **F**

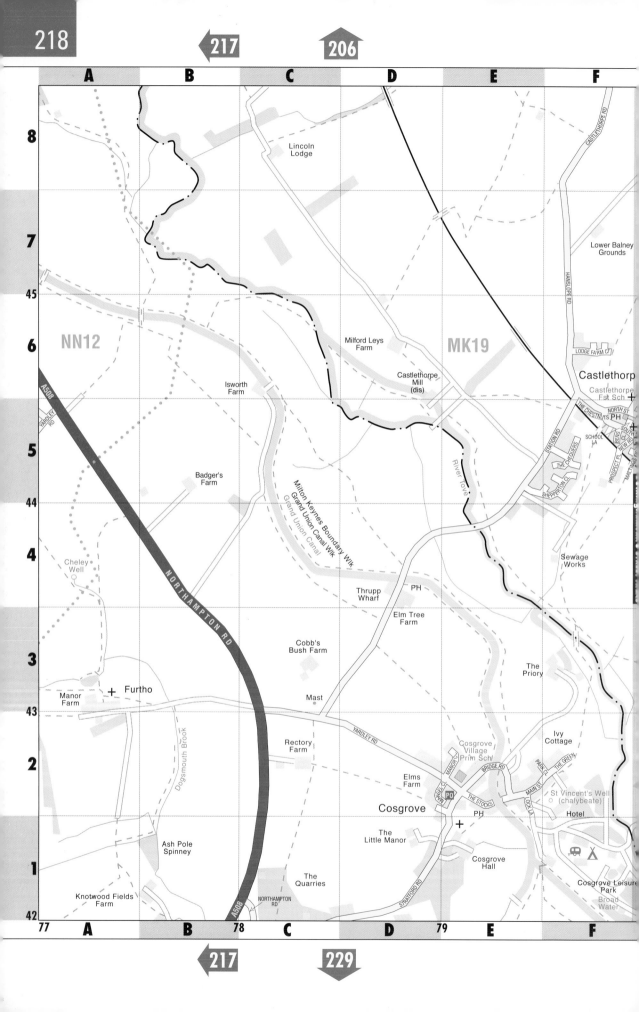

217
206

A B C D E F

8

7

45

6

NN12

5

44

4

43

2

1

42

77 A B 78 C D 79 E F

Lincoln
Lodge

Lower Balney
Grounds

Milford Leys
Farm

Castlethorpe
Mill
(dis)

MK19

Castlethorpe

Castlethorpe
Fst Sch

THE CHESTNUTS

NORTH ST

PH

SCHOOL LA

STATION RD

PROSPECT PL

THE CHEQUERS

SHEPPERTON CT

NEW ST

SOUTH

MATTINGS

Isworth
Farm

Badger's
Farm

River Tove

Sewage
Works

Cheley
Well

NORTHAMPTON RD

A508

Milton Keynes Boundary Wlk
Grand Union Canal Wlk
Grand Union Canal

Thrupp
Wharf

PH

Elm Tree
Farm

The
Priory

Cobb's
Bush Farm

Mast

Manor
Farm

Furtho

Dogsmouth Brook

Ivy
Cottage

Rectory
Farm

YARDLEY RD

Cosgrove
Village
Prim Sch

Elms
Farm

MANOR CT

BRIDGE RD

PARK CL

THE GREEN

MAIN ST

LOCK LA

St Vincent's Well
(chalybeate)

PO

THE STOCKS

PH

Hotel

Cosgrove

YARDLEY RD

The
Little Manor

Cosgrove
Hall

Ash Pole
Spinney

The
Quarries

STRATFORD RD

Cosgrove Leisure
Park

Broad
Water

Knotwood Fields
Farm

A508

NORTHAMPTON
RD

YARDLEY RD

HANSLOPE RD

LODGE FARM CT

CASTLETHORPE RD

217
229

← 219
209

A B C D E F

8

**Lower Middleton Cheney**

THENFORD RD
ASH TREE CT
SLADE LEAS
WATERS LA
LEXTON CONS
MAIN RD
ROSE HALL LA
ROYAL OAK LA
POPLARS
BRAGGINTONS LA
ONGBORGES
SALKINS
MANOR CL
HAILSHAM CT
WASPHE DR
ASHLADE
HORTON CRES
HORTON DR
HORTON RD
HORTON CL
KINGSTON
NORTON DR
THE AVENUE
DANDS DR
DANDS CL
BULL BAULK CL
PEACOCKS
ARROW CL
YEW TREE CL
MIDWAY
BOWMAN CL
HORTON

Thenford House
Gardener's Cottage
STABLE YD
**Thenford**

A422

TULBROOK STONES

Sewage Works

Burgess Farm

Thenford Lodge

41

OX17

6

Middleton Lodge Farm

Thenford Grange

Works

Avenue Bridge

5

Farthinghoe Stream

A422

40

Baldwin's Spinney

4

Great Purston

NN13

Little Purston

3

Farthinghoe Park

39

2

Buston Farm

Buston Farm Cottages

Sandy La

1

Astrophill Farm

Coldharbour

38

Rosamond's Bower

50 A B 51 C D 52 E F

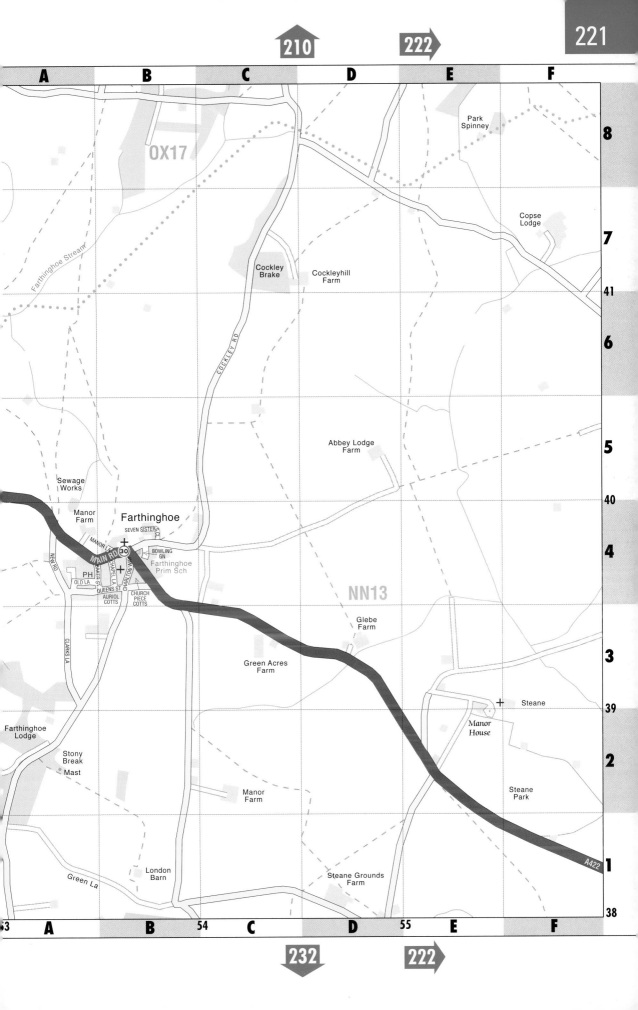

A B C D E F

8
7
41
6
5
40
4
3
39
2
1
38

Park
Spinney

Copse
Lodge

OX17

Farthinghoe Stream

Cockley
Brake

Cockleyhill
Farm

COCKLEY RD

Abbey Lodge
Farm

Sewage
Works

Manor
Farm

Farthinghoe

SEVEN SISTERS
CT

MANOR LA

MAIN RD
30

CHAPEL LA

PALMER ST

BOWLING
GN

Farthinghoe
Prim Sch

CHARLTON RD

NN13

NENE RD

PH
OLD LA

QUEENS ST

AURIOL
COTTS

CHURCH
PIECE
COTTS

Glebe
Farm

CLARKS LA

Green Acres
Farm

Steane

Manor
House

Farthinghoe
Lodge

Stony
Break

Mast

Manor
Farm

Steane
Park

Green La

London
Barn

Steane Grounds
Farm

A422

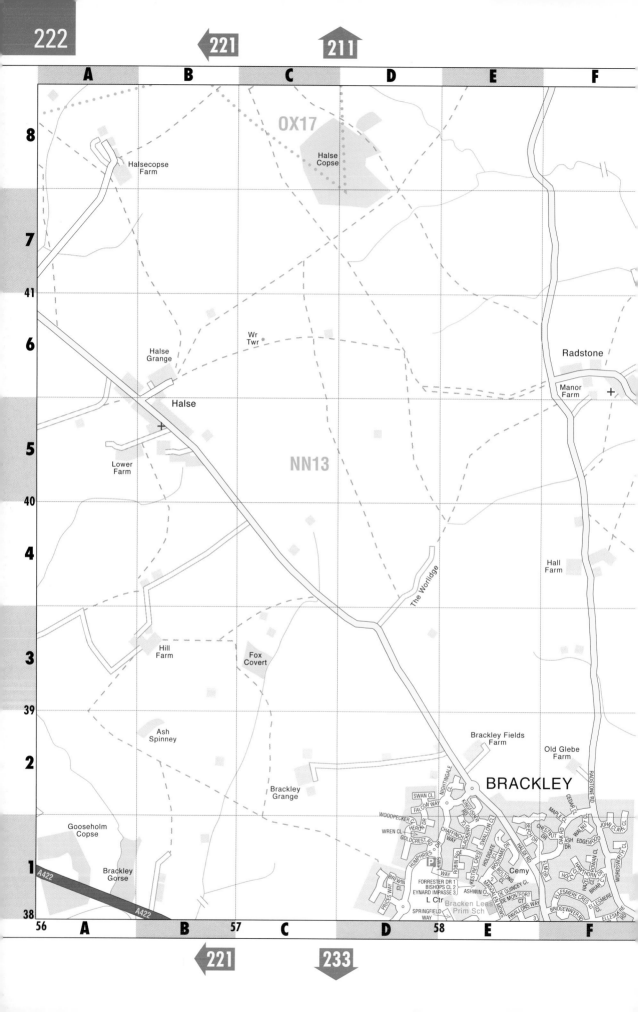

A  B  C  D  E  F

OX17

8

Halsecopse
Farm

Halse
Copse

7

41

Wr
Twr

6

Radstone

Halse
Grange

Manor
Farm

Halse

NN13

5

40

Lower
Farm

The Worlidge

4

Hall
Farm

Hill
Farm

Fox
Covert

3

39

Ash
Spinney

Brackley Fields
Farm

Old Glebe
Farm

2

Brackley
Grange

BRACKLEY

SWAN CL

NIGHTINGALE CL

FALCON WAY

WOODPECKER CL

KINGFISHER CL

CEDAR CL

MAPLE CL

CHESTNUT

JOHN CLARK CL

Gooseholm
Copse

WREN CL

HERON DR

CHAFFINCH
WAY

SWALLOW CL

BEECH DR

ASH
DR

WALNUT

EDGEWOOD

HAZEL

GOLDCREST RD

ROBIN RISE

BLACKBIRD

HOLDGATE

POTHAMS DR

OAK DR

BROWNLOW DR

HAWTHORN DR

HOLLY

1

A422

Brackley
Gorse

HUMPHRIES
WAY

P

KESTREL CL

HIMS

PARLOUR MDWS

Cemy

ELM CL

BRIAR

WORDSWORTH CL

ELLESMERE

Brackley Leas
Prim Sch

FORRESTER DR 1
BISHOPS CL 2
EYNARD IMPASSE 3

ASHWIN CL

DE QUINCEY WAY

DE MONTFORT

ELLESMERE CRES

BRIDGEWATER WAY

ELLESMERE RD

L Ctr

SPRINGFIELD
WAY

PAVILIONS WAY

38

A422

56  A  B  57  C  D  58  E  F

A B C D E F

8

Falcutt
Hall

Crowfield
B4525

Staplegate
Farm

Crowfield

Shortgrove
Wood

Whistley
Wood

Pimlico
Farm

B4525

7

41

Pimlico

6

Kiln
Farm

Hoppersford
Farm

Wrighton's
Barn

A43

Hoppersford
Bridge

NN13

5

Coldharbour
Farm

40

4

Whitfield House
Farm

Fox
Covert

THE AVENUE

CHESTNUT LN

MILL RD

FARRER CT

TRENGOTHAL
CT

Inn

CHAPEL LA

Whitfield

Mill
Bridge

Manor
Farm

Ilett's
Farm

Sewage
Works

River Great Ouse

3

Sundale

39

Bushey End
Wood

Foxhill
Spinney

2

Saw
Mill

NORTHAMPTON RD

Airstrip

Versions
Farm

1

A43

TURWESTON RD

38

9 A B 60 C D 61 E F

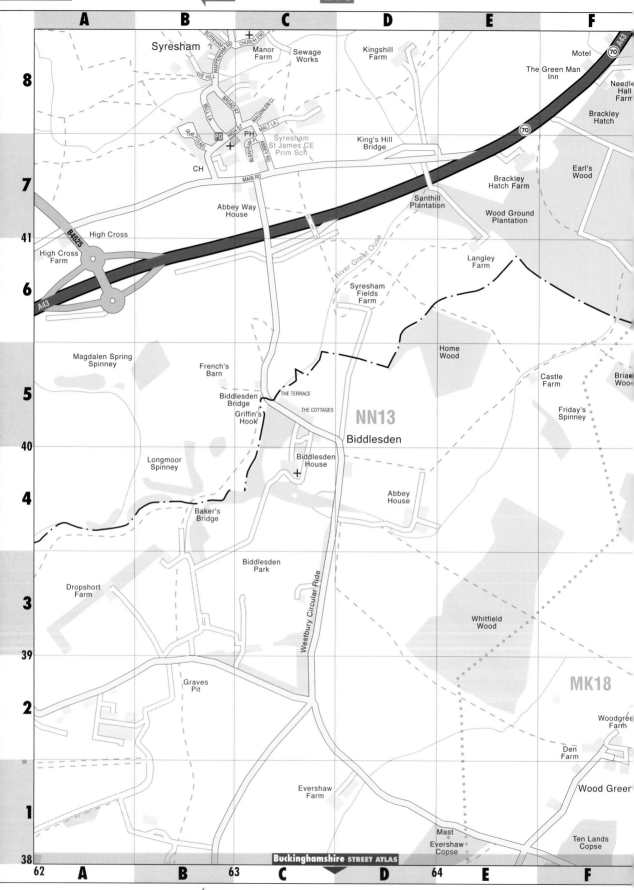

A    B    C    D    E    F

8

Silverstone
Motor Racing
Circuit

Airstrip

NN12

Pentimore
Wood

Mary
Wood

NN13

Farthing
Wood

7

41

Buttockspire
Wood

Wetley's
Wood

The
Fogs

Stowe
Corner

CH

6

Swallowtail
Wood

Old Red
Ditch

Red Ditches
Farm

Hollyhill
Wood

Point
Copse

Sawpit
Wood

5

Thatcham Ponds
Farm

Blackpit
Farm

40

Stowe
Woods

4

Parkfields

Woodlands
Farm

MK18

DADFORD RD

Three Parks
Wood

3

39

2

NORTH
HILL

Wolfe's
Obelisk

Dadford

Gorrell
Farm

1

Vancouver
Lodge

Stowe
Park

38

5    A    B    66    C    D    67    E    F

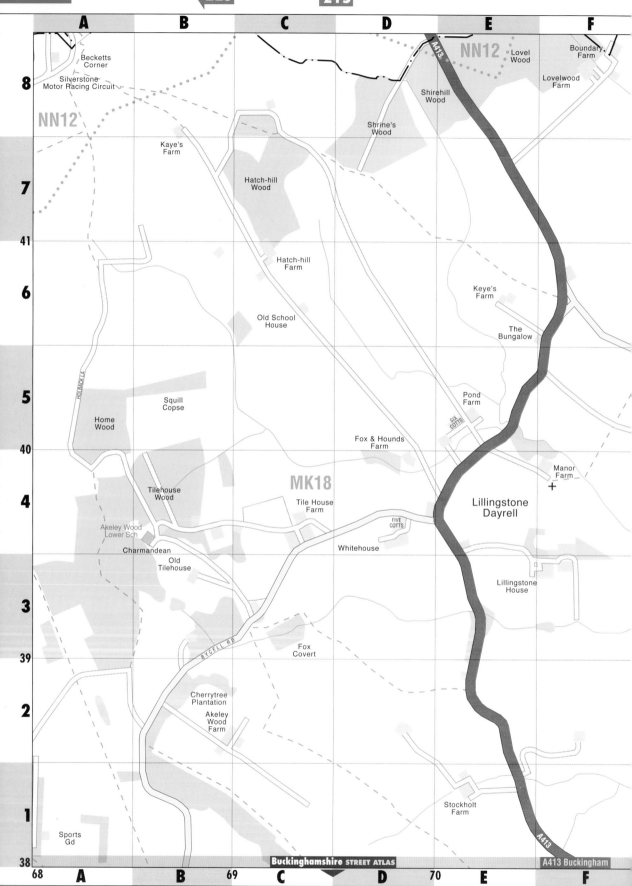

**A** **B** **C** **D** **E** **F**

MK19

8

Point's Copse

Green
Farm

Steeple
Oak

Grange
Farm

Shrob
Spinney

7

Puxley

NN12

Old Copse
Spinney

Hanger
Lodge

41

Poultry
Farm

Stollage
Lodge

6

Hurst
Farm

Folly Fields
Farm

The
Folly

Hurst
Cottage

5

Wr
Twr

PUXLEY RD

HIGH ST

GLEBE RD

NORTH WAY

RIDGMONT
BEAUMONT
THE RIDING

ELM DR

WESTFIELD AVE

WOOD CL
MANOR
KINGSHILL CR
BROOK WAY
HONEY HILL DR

FOXGOLES CL

SEAMH

40

Liby

PORTER'S CL
PARKS CL

Northfields

FOLLY RD

SPRINGFIELD GDNS

LITTLE LONDON

BOSWELL LA

ROBERTS CL

WOODMANS CL

CANAL LA

4

Deanshanger

BROOKWAY

CHURCH LA

PO

HIGH ST

THE SMITHY

STRATFORD RD

Hotel

POUND ST

ST JOHN'S LA

CHURCH CL

BRIDE WLK

PATRICKS LA

PH

Kingsbrook Sch

PH

CROSS TREE RD

DEANSHANGER RD

QUARRY GREEN CL

Silver Spinney
Farm

DOVEHOUSE
CT

THE GREEN

THE BEECHES

Deanshanger
Prim Sch

3

Home Farm

Wicken

Dagnall
Cottages

MK19

LECKHAMPSTEAD RD

Dagnall
Farm

Hotel

39

WICKEN PARK RD

Sparrow
Lodge

Grand Union Canal Buckingham Arm (dis)

BUCKINGHAM RD

A422

2

Pightle
Farm

New Barn

MK18

Mount Mill
Cottages

1

Akeley Wood
Jun Sch

Jack's
Copse

Bedlam
Copse

A422

38

74 **A** **B** 75 **C** **D** 76 **E** **F**

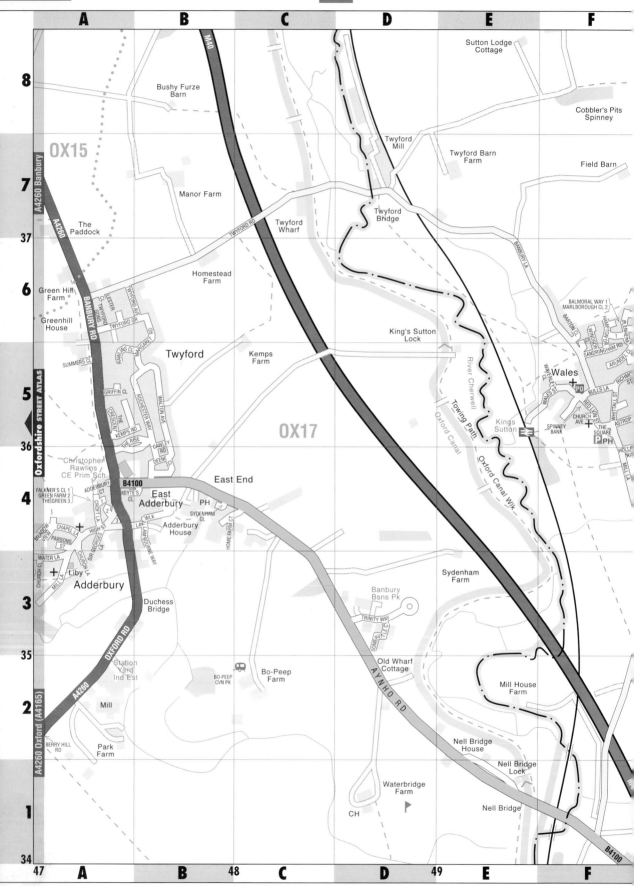

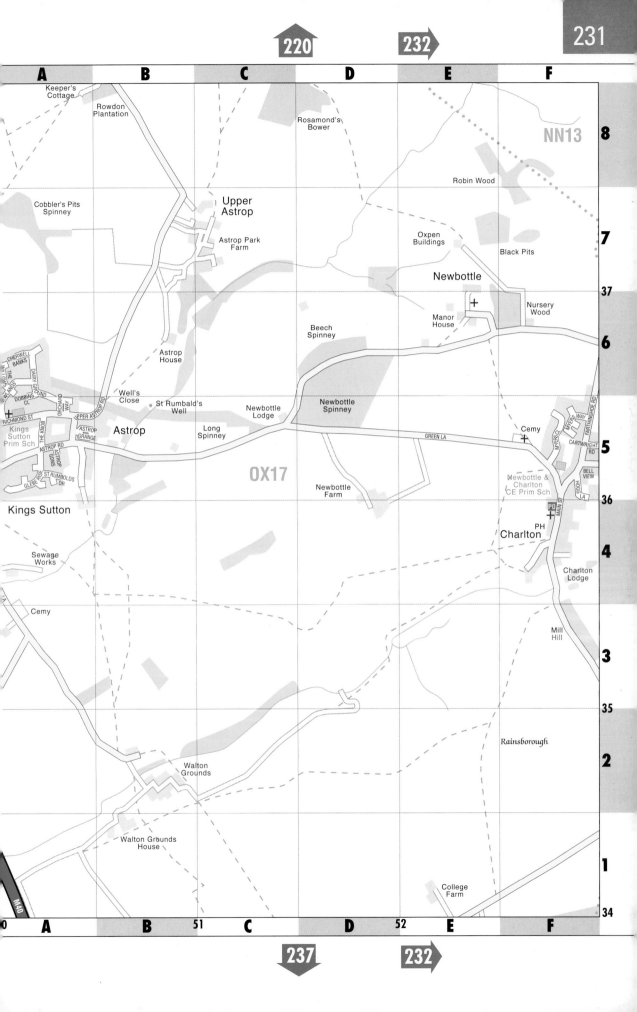

Keeper's Cottage
Rowdon Plantation
Rosamond's Bower
NN13
8
Robin Wood
Cobbler's Pits Spinney
Upper Astrop
Astrop Park Farm
Oxpen Buildings
Black Pits
7
Newbottle
37
Manor House
Nursery Wood
Beech Spinney
6
CHERWELL BANKS
THE MITTINS
DAIRY GROUND
Astrop House
DOBBINS CL
ORCHARD WAY
UPPER ASTROP RD
Well's Close
St Rumbald's Well
Newbottle Lodge
Newbottle Spinney
MYERS CL
MYERS WAY
FARTHINGHOE RD
CARTWRIGHT RD
RICHMOND ST
Kings Sutton Prim Sch
THE KNOB
ASTROP GRANGE
Astrop
Long Spinney
GREEN LA
Cemy
BELL VIEW
5
ASTROP RD
ASTROP GDNS
GLEBE RISE
ST RUMBOLDS DR
OX17
Newbottle Farm
Newbottle & Charlton CE Prim Sch
BELL LA
HIGH ST
36
Kings Sutton
PO
Charlton
PH
4
Sewage Works
Charlton Lodge
MAIN ST
Cemy
Mill Hill
3
35
Rainsborough
Walton Grounds
2
Walton Grounds House
1
M40
College Farm
34

**A** **B** **C** **D** **E** **F**

Colready
Farm

Coleready
Plantation

Hinton Grounds
Farm

8

Forceleap
Close

7

THE
CHESTNUTS

Walltree
Farm

37

NORRIS
ACRE

Airfield

Forceleap
Farm

Hinton-in-the-
Hedges

6

PH

BADGER
DUCK EA

FARTHINGHOE RD

Sports
Gd.

Washbrook
Farm

Charlton House
Farm

5

CARTWRIGHT RD

NN13

36

4

Charlton
Firs

The
Cabin

The
Dower House

3

College Barn
Spinney

Camp Farm

35

Rowler

OX17

Myers'
Copse

Rowler's
Covert

2

1

Cross
Stones

34

222
234

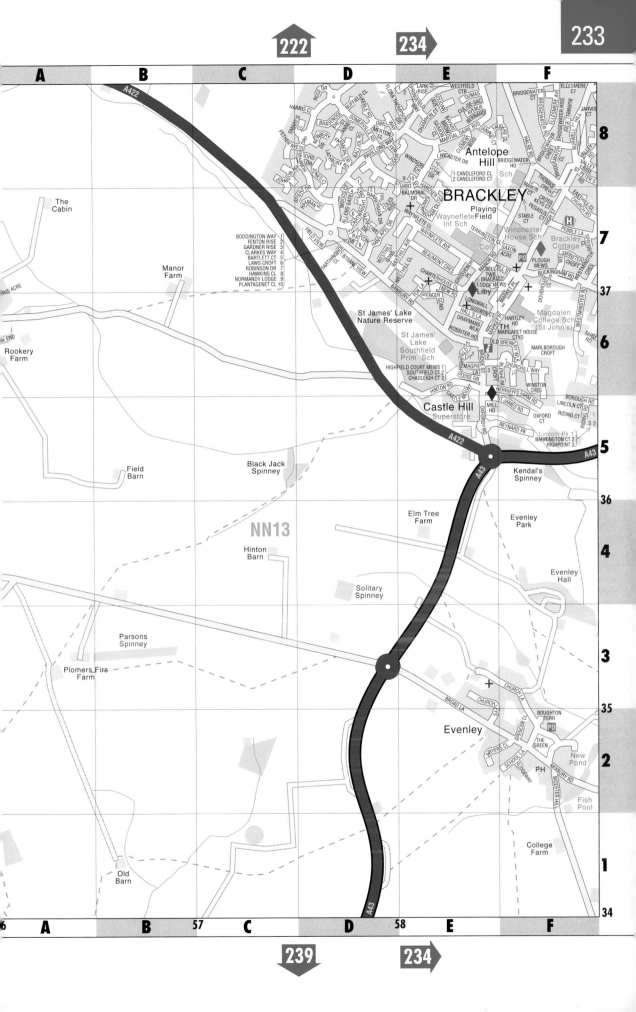

A   B   C   D   E   F

The Cabin

A422

Antelope Hill

1 CANDLEFORD CL
2 CANDLEFORD CT

BRACKLEY

Playing Field

Wayneflete Inf Sch

Winchester House Sch

Brackley Cottage

8

7

Manor Farm

BODDINGTON WAY 1
FENTON RISE 2
GARDNER RISE 3
CLARKES WAY 4
BARTLETT CT 5
LAWS CROFT 6
ROBINSON DR 7
HAWKINS CL 8
NORMANDY LODGE 9
PLANTAGENET CL 10

St James' Lake Nature Reserve

37

Rookery Farm

St James' Lake

Southfield Prim Sch

Magdalen College Sch (St John's)

Marlborough Croft

6

HIGHFIELD COURT MEWS 1
SOUTHFIELD CT 2
CHADLEIGH CT 3

Castle Hill

Superstore

A422

A43

Kendal's Spinney

A43

5

Field Barn

Black Jack Spinney

36

NN13

Elm Tree Farm

Evenley Park

4

Hinton Barn

Evenley Hall

Solitary Spinney

Parsons Spinney

3

Plomers Firs Farm

Church La

BOUGHTON TERR

35

Evenley

New Pond

2

Old Barn

College Farm

Fish Pool

1

A43

34

6   A   B   57   C   D   58   E   F

239
234

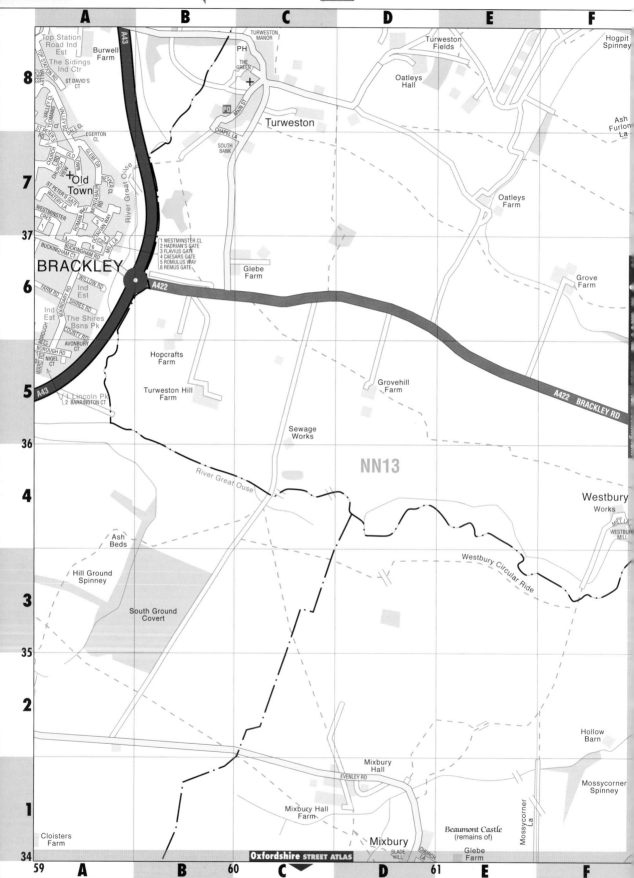

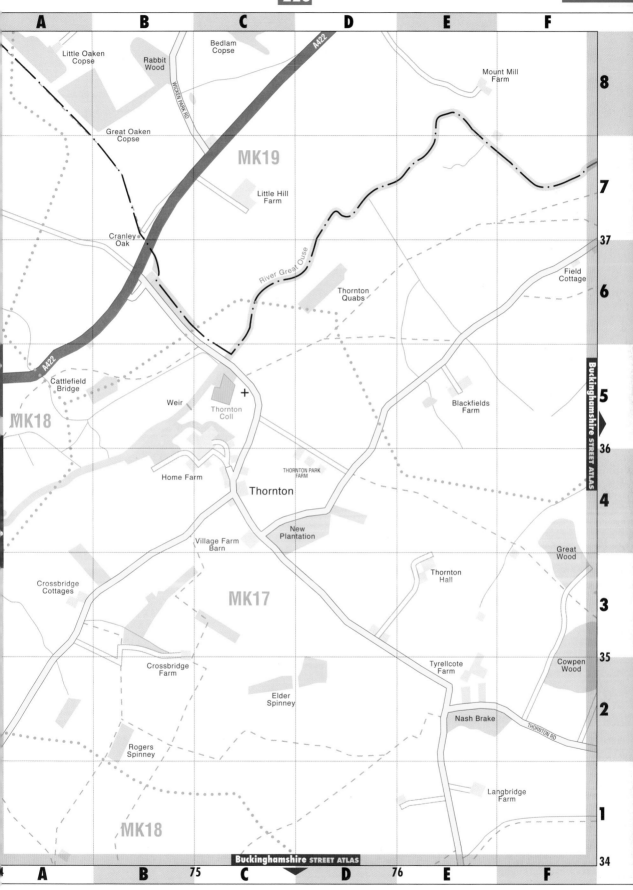

Little Oaken
Copse

Rabbit
Wood

Bedlam
Copse

Mount Mill
Farm

8

Great Oaken
Copse

MK19

Little Hill
Farm

7

Cranley
Oak

37

River Great Ouse

Thornton
Quabs

Field
Cottage

6

Cattlefield
Bridge

MK18

Weir

Thornton
Coll

Blackfields
Farm

5

36

Home Farm

THORNTON PARK
FARM

Thornton

4

Village Farm
Barn

New
Plantation

Great
Wood

Crossbridge
Cottages

MK17

Thornton
Hall

3

35

Crossbridge
Farm

Tyrellcote
Farm

Cowpen
Wood

Elder
Spinney

Nash Brake

THORNTON RD

2

Rogers
Spinney

Langbridge
Farm

1

MK18

34

Buckinghamshire STREET ATLAS

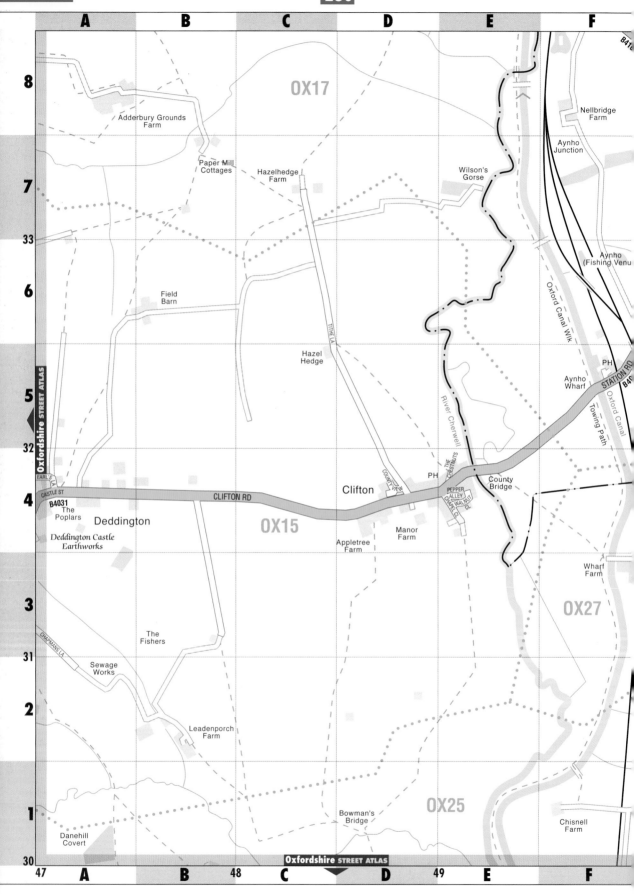

OX17

Adderbury Grounds Farm

Paper Mill Cottages

Hazelhedge Farm

Wilson's Gorse

Nellbridge Farm

Aynho Junction

Aynho (Fishing Venu

Field Barn

Hazel Hedge

TITHE LA

Oxford Canal Wlk

Aynho Wharf

STATION RD

PH

B40

Oxford Canal

Towing Path

River Cherwell

THE CHESTNUTS

County Bridge

PH

Clifton

COUNTY VIEW

PEPPER ALLEY

CHAPEL CL

WALNUT

Wharf Farm

OX27

EARL'S LA

CASTLE ST

CLIFTON RD

OX15

B4031

The Poplars

Deddington

Deddington Castle Earthworks

Appletree Farm

Manor Farm

CHAPMANS LA

The Fishers

Sewage Works

Leadenporch Farm

Bowman's Bridge

OX25

Chisnell Farm

Danehill Covert

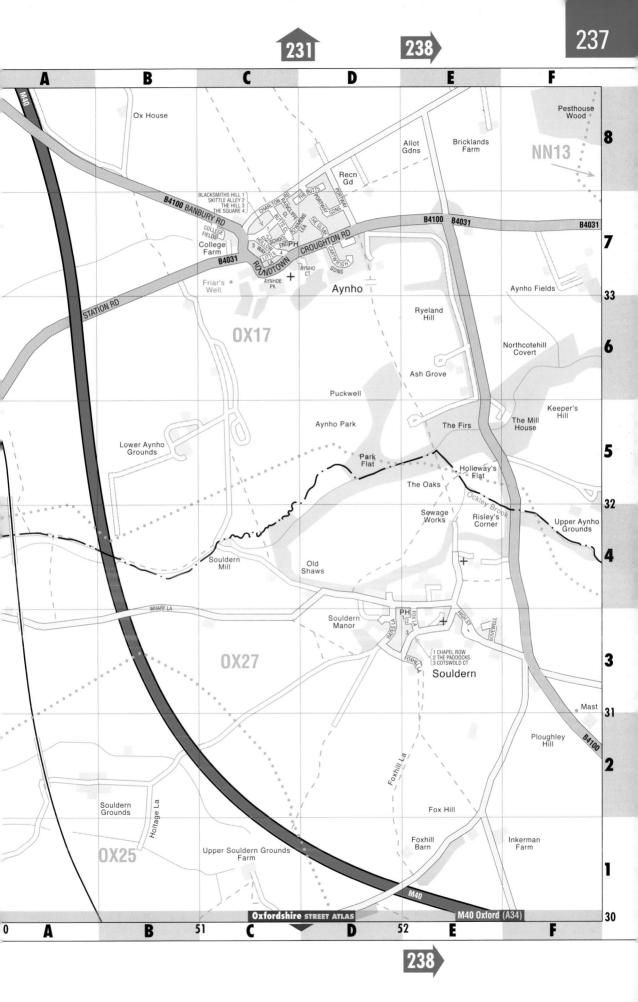

A B C D E F

8

Ox House

Pesthouse Wood

Allot Gdns

Bricklands Farm

NN13

BLACKSMITHS HILL 1
SKITTLE ALLEY 2
THE HILL 3
THE SQUARE 4

B4100 BANBURY RD

Recn Gd

THE BUTTS

CHARLTON RD

RUNCLIFFE

BOWMENS

PORTWAY

B4100

B4031

B4031

7

COLLEGE FIELDS

College Farm

B4031

BUTTS CL

SCHOOL END PH

HOLTOM WAY

LITTLE LA

THE GLEBE

PORTWAY GDNS

CROUGHTON RD

ROUNDTOWN

AYNHOE PK

AYNHO CT

CARTWRIGHT GDNS

Aynho

STATION RD

Friar's Well

Aynho Fields

33

OX17

Ryeland Hill

6

Northcotehill Covert

Ash Grove

Puckwell

Keeper's Hill

Aynho Park

The Firs

The Mill House

5

Lower Aynho Grounds

Park Flat

Holloway's Flat

32

The Oaks

Ockley Brook

Sewage Works

Risley's Corner

Upper Aynho Grounds

4

Souldern Mill

Old Shaws

WHARF LA

Souldern Manor

PH

FOX LA

HIGH ST

BOVEWELL

BATES LA

1 CHAPEL ROW
2 THE PADDOCKS
3 COTSWOLD CT

FOXHILL LA

3

OX27

Souldern

Mast

31

Ploughley Hill

B4100

2

Souldern Grounds

HOLTAGE LA

Foxhill La

Fox Hill

Inkerman Farm

1

OX25

Upper Souldern Grounds Farm

Foxhill Barn

M40

M40 Oxford (A34)

30

A     B     C     D     E     F

OX17

Cemy
Croughton
Croughton
All Saints
CE Prim Sch

8

Warren
Farm

Recn
Gd
PH
HIGH ST
MANOR
FARM
COTTS

WHEELER'S RISE
MILL LA
CHAPEL END

BRACKLEY RD
YEW TREE RISE

The
Moors

CHURCH
END
CHURCH
LA
PARK END
PO
B40

BLENHEIM

7

B4031

The
Green

Park End
Works

PORTWAY CRES
PORTWAY
PORTWAY DR

Old Down
Pond

33

Old Down
Covert

Sewage
Works

Park
Farm

SIXTH ST
FIFTH AVE
FIFTH ST E
FIFTH ST
FOURTH AVE
BIRKSCALE AVE
FOURTH ST
THIRD
ST
SECOND ST
ST ANDREWS AVE
FIRST ST

Padbury's
Bottom

6

NN13

New
Buildings

Smanhill
Covert

OX17

Masts

Middle
Covert

5

32

4

Ockley Brook

Pimlico
Farm

Crook's
Firs

3

OX27

Thriftwood
House

31

Tower
Fields

Roundhill
Farm

Lower
Rookery

B4100

Horwell
Corner

Round Hill

2

A43

1

Horwell
Farm

Park Farm

Hermitage
Belt

B4100

Oxford
Lodge

30

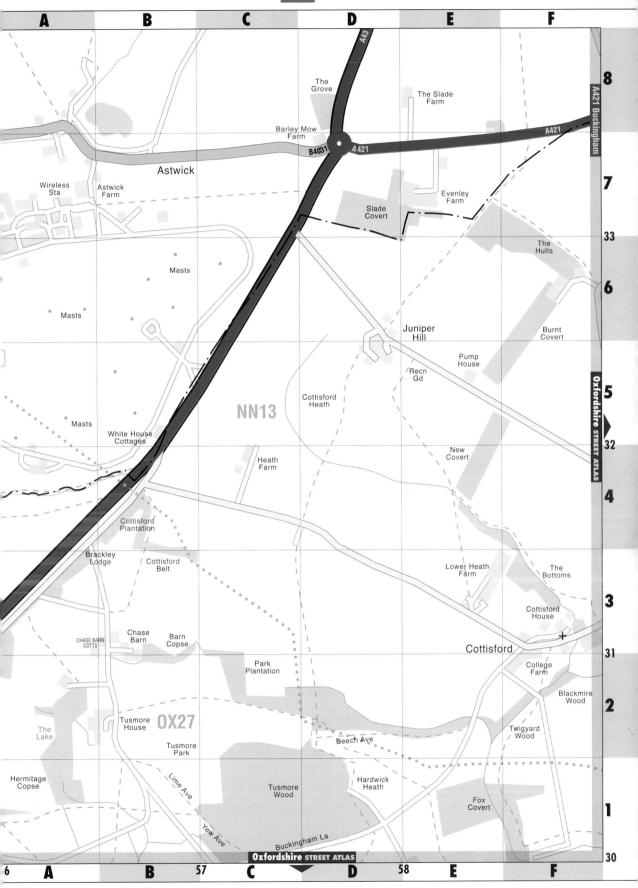

A  B  C  D  E  F

8

7

33

6

5

32

4

3

31

2

1

30

The Grove

The Slade Farm

Barley Mow Farm

B4031  A421

A421 Buckingham

Astwick

A43

Wireless Sta

Astwick Farm

Evenley Farm

Slade Covert

The Hulls

Masts

Juniper Hill

Burnt Covert

Pump House

Masts

Recn Gd

NN13

Cottisford Heath

New Covert

Masts

White House Cottages

Heath Farm

Cottisford Plantation

Brackley Lodge

Cottisford Belt

Lower Heath Farm

The Bottoms

Cottisford House

CHASE BARN COTTS

Chase Barn

Barn Copse

Cottisford

Park Plantation

College Farm

Blackmire Wood

The Lake

Tusmore House

OX27

Twigyard Wood

Tusmore Park

Beech Ave

Hermitage Copse

Lime Ave

Tusmore Wood

Hardwick Heath

Fox Covert

Yew Ave

Buckingham La

# Index

**Place name** May be abbreviated on the map

**Location number** Present when a number indicates the place's position in a crowded area of mapping

**Locality, town or village** Shown when more than one place has the same name

**Postcode district** District for the indexed place

**Page and grid square** Page number and grid reference for the standard mapping

**Church Rd** **6** Beckenham BR2.........**53** C6

Cities, towns and villages are listed in CAPITAL LETTERS

Public and commercial buildings are highlighted in magenta    Places of interest are highlighted in blue with a star★

## Abbreviations used in the index

| | | | | | | | | | |
|---|---|---|---|---|---|---|---|---|---|
| Acad | **Academy** | Comm | **Common** | Gd | **Ground** | L | **Leisure** | Prom | **Promenade** |
| App | **Approach** | Cott | **Cottage** | Gdn | **Garden** | La | **Lane** | Rd | **Road** |
| Arc | **Arcade** | Cres | **Crescent** | Gn | **Green** | Liby | **Library** | Recn | **Recreation** |
| Ave | **Avenue** | Cswy | **Causeway** | Gr | **Grove** | Mdw | **Meadow** | Ret | **Retail** |
| Bglw | **Bungalow** | Ct | **Court** | H | **Hall** | Meml | **Memorial** | Sh | **Shopping** |
| Bldg | **Building** | Ctr | **Centre** | Ho | **House** | Mkt | **Market** | Sq | **Square** |
| Bsns, Bus | **Business** | Ctry | **Country** | Hospl | **Hospital** | Mus | **Museum** | St | **Street** |
| Bvd | **Boulevard** | Cty | **County** | HQ | **Headquarters** | Orch | **Orchard** | Sta | **Station** |
| Cath | **Cathedral** | Dr | **Drive** | Hts | **Heights** | Pal | **Palace** | Terr | **Terrace** |
| Cir | **Circus** | Dro | **Drove** | Ind | **Industrial** | Par | **Parade** | TH | **Town Hall** |
| Cl | **Close** | Ed | **Education** | Inst | **Institute** | Pas | **Passage** | Univ | **University** |
| Cnr | **Corner** | Emb | **Embankment** | Int | **International** | Pk | **Park** | Wk, Wlk | **Walk** |
| Coll | **College** | Est | **Estate** | Intc | **Interchange** | Pl | **Place** | Wr | **Water** |
| Com | **Community** | Ex | **Exhibition** | Junc | **Junction** | Prec | **Precinct** | Yd | **Yard** |

## Index of towns, villages, streets, hospitals, industrial estates, railway stations, schools, shopping centres, universities and places of interest

### 240 1st–Amb

1st Drift PE9 ★........... 2 D8
78 Derngate ★ NN1 .....159 D5

### A

A6 Bsns Ctr NN16........ 71 E4
Abbey Cl NN29...........164 C2
**Abbey Ct**
  **11** Daventry NN11.......135 C2
  Wollaston NN29........146 D3
Abbey Ho **5** NN5 .......159 A6
Abbey Lo NN3 ...........160 C7
Abbey Prim Sch The
  NN4.................159 C1
**Abbey Rd**
  Northampton NN4 ......159 B3
  Roade NN7 ...........191 C4
  Syresham NN13........224 C2
  Wellingborough NN8 ...129 F3
Abbey Rise NN29 .......146 D3
**Abbey St**
  Daventry NN11 ........135 C2
  Market Harborough LE16 .. 31 E3
  Northampton NN5 ......159 A6
**Abbey Way**
  Ravenstone MK46 ......194 E2
  Rushden NN10.........148 A8
Abbot Cl NN11...........153 D8
Abbots Cl NN15..........91 B7
**Abbots Way**
  Kettering NN15 ........91 A6
  Northampton NN5 ......158 F6
  Roade NN7 ...........191 C4
  Wellingborough NN8 ...129 F4
Abbotts Cl NN14.......... 77 D3
Abbotts Way NN10 .....131 F1
Aberdare Rd NN5 .......159 A8
Aberdeen Terr NN5 .....159 A6
**ABINGTON** ............160 B8
Abington Ave NN3 ......160 A8
Abington Bsns Ctr
  NN1.................160 A7
Abington Cotts NN1.....160 A8
Abington Ct NN3........160 B8
Abington Gr NN1 .......159 F8
Abington Mus ★ NN1.....160 A7
Abington Park Cres
  NN3 .................160 C7
Abington Rd NN17.......36 B7

Abington Sq NN1 .......159 E6
Abington St NN1........159 D6
**ABINGTON VALE** ........160 C7
Abington Vale Prim Sch
  NN3.................160 C6
Ablett Cl NN14............ 76 D2
**ABTHORPE** ............201 F1
Abthorpe Ave NN2 ......141 D5
**Accurate Boot The**
  NN1.................159 E7
Ace La NN7..............172 E7
**ACHURCH** ..............58 C2
**Acorn Cl**
  Islip NN14.............76 B3
  Kettering NN15 ........92 B5
  Lubenham LE16 ........30 E3
Acorn Ind Est NN14 .....76 B3
Acorn Pk NN15 ..........92 D4
Acorn Way NN12........214 E4
Acre Cl NN11 ...........135 C6
Acre Ct NN16 ...........72 D3
Acre La NN7............141 A6
Acremead PE8........... 28 B3
Acre St NN16 ........... 72 D3
Adam Bsns Ctr NN16....71 F5
Adam & Eve St **8** LE16.. 31 E3
Adams Ave NN1 ........159 F7
**Adams Cl**
  Stanwick NN9 .........114 A5
  Wellingborough NN8 ...130 B5
Adams Dr NN14......... 70 B7
Adams Rd NN11 ........184 B6
Adamswood Cl LE16 .....31 C3
**ADDERBURY** ...........230 A3
Adderbury Ct OX17 .....230 A4
**Addington Park Ind Est**
  NN14.................113 C7
**Addington Rd**
  Irthlingborough NN9 ....113 A5
  Woodford NN14.........94 D6
Addis Cl NN15 ...........92 C1
**Addison Rd**
  Desborough NN14...... 50 F3
  Northampton NN3 ......142 B2
Addlecroft Cl NN2 ......141 B3
**Adelaide Ho**
  Corby NN17............ 22 F1
  **5** Northampton NN2 ...159 C7
Adelaide Pl **7** NN1 ....159 C5
Adelaide St NN2 ........159 C7
Adelaide Terr **1** NN2 ..159 C7
Adit View NN9 ..........131 D8

**Admiral Ct**
  Kettering NN16 ........ 72 C3
  Market Harborough
  LE16................. 31 D3
Admirals Way NN11.....135 E2
Adnitt Ho LE17.......... 45 E5
**Adnitt Rd**
  Northampton NN1 ......159 F7
  Rushden NN10.........132 A2
**ADSTONE** .............186 B4
Afan Cl NN16 ...........72 A5
Affleck Bridge NN9 .....111 F4
Aggate Way NN6........144 D4
Agnes Rd NN2 ..........159 C8
**Agricultural Hos**
  CV47.................166 A5
Ainsdale Cl NN2 ........141 F3
**Aintree Dr** NN10 .......148 D8
**Aintree Rd**
  Corby NN18 ........... 36 E1
  Northampton NN3 ......141 F4
Aislable Ho OX16 .......219 A7
Akela Cl NN15 ..........91 C8
**Akeley Wood Jun Sch**
  MK19................228 A1
**Akeley Wood Lower Sch**
  MK18................226 B4
Alanbrooke Cl NN15 ....72 E1
Alastor NN8 ............129 B5
**Albany Rd**
  Market Harborough
  LE16................. 31 F4
  Northampton NN1 ......160 A7
Albany The **6** NN11....135 C2
Alberta Cl NN18 ........36 C3
Albert Pl NN1...........159 D6
**Albert Rd**
  Finedon NN9 ..........111 F5
  Market Harborough LE16 .. 31 F3
  Rushden NN10.........132 B2
  Wellingborough NN8 ...130 B5
Albert St **3** NN16......72 C2
**Albion Ct**
  Little Harrowden NN9 ...110 C4
  Northampton NN1 ......159 D5
Albion Ho NN1..........159 D5
**Albion Pl**
  Northampton NN1 ......159 D5
  Rushden NN10.........132 B1
Albion Rd NN16.........72 B3
Albisdene Ct NN10......132 C2

**Alchester Ct** NN12 .....203 C5
Alcombe Rd NN1 .......159 E7
Alcombe Terr NN1......159 E7
Aldbury Ct **12** NN1 .....159 C7
Aldene Rd MK19 .......207 B3
Alder Cl NN14 .......... 51 C3
Alder Ct NN3 ..........142 F5
Alderley Cl NN5........158 B8
**ALDERTON** ............205 A2
Aldgate ...............1 B5
Aldgate Ct PE9 .........1 A5
Aldsworth Cl NN8......145 E8
Aldwell Cl NN4 .........175 F7
**ALDWINCLE** ...........76 F8
Aldwincle Rd NN14 .....76 A6
Aldwinkles Yd **4** LE16.. 31 E3
**Alexander Ct**
  Corby NN17............ 22 A2
  Irchester NN29 ........147 B8
  Northampton NN3 ......142 A3
Alexander Pl NN9 ......113 A4
Alexander Rd NN9 ......113 A4
**Alexandra Rd**
  Corby NN17............ 36 E6
  Desborough NN14...... 50 F3
  Northampton NN1 ......159 E6
  Rushden NN10.........132 D2
  Wellingborough NN8 ...130 B5
**Alexandra St**
  Burton Latimer NN15 ... 92 B2
  Kettering NN16 ........ 72 C2
Alexandra Terr **5**
  NN2.................141 C3
Alfoxden NN8 ..........129 B3
**Alfred St**
  Irchester NN29 ........147 A8
  Kettering NN16 ........ 72 C2
  Northampton NN1 ......159 F6
  Rushden NN10.........132 B2
  Stanwick NN9 .........113 F4
Alfred Street Jun Sch
  NN10................132 B2
Alibone Cl NN3 .........126 D1
Alice Ct NN6............100 F6
Alice Dr NN15 ..........92 B1
Alice Gdns NN16........ 72 D3
Alington Cl NN9 ........112 A5
Aiken Cl NN8 ...........129 F8
Allan Bank NN8.........129 B3
Allans Cl CV23 .........80 A5
Allans Dr CV23 .........80 A5
Allard Cl NN3...........143 D4
Allebone Rd NN6 .......144 E3

Alledge Dr NN14......... 94 D7
Allen Ct NN9 ...........112 A5
**Allen Rd**
  Finedon NN9 ..........112 A5
  Irthlingborough NN9....112 E1
  Northampton NN1 ......160 A7
  Rushden NN10.........132 A3
Allens Gate NN13 .......233 D7
Allens Hill NN29 ........164 D3
Allens Orch OX17 .......196 F6
**Alliance Ct** **2** NN8 .....130 A5
Alliance Terr NN8.......129 F5
Alliston Gdns **3** NN2...159 C7
All Saints CE Mid Sch
  NN2.................141 E6
All Saints' CE Prim Sch
  NN8.................130 B4
**Alma St**
  Northampton NN5 ......159 A6
  Wellingborough NN8 ...130 A5
**Almond Cl**
  Barby CV23 ...........99 C1
  Bugbrooke NN7 ........173 C1
Almond Gr NN3.........142 C1
Almond Rd NN16 .......72 D4
**Almshouses The**
  MK46.................194 E2
Alness Cl NN15 .........91 E8
Alpine Rd NN10.........131 F2
Alpine Way NN5 ........140 A3
Alsace Cl NN5 ..........139 F2
Altendiez Way NN15 ....92 B4
Althorp ★ NN7 ..........139 A7
**Althorp Cl**
  Market Harborough
  LE16................. 32 B3
  Wellingborough NN8 ...129 C2
Althorp Pl NN16 ........ 72 D3
Althorp Pl NN18 ........ 36 B3
Althorp Rd NN5.........159 A6
Alton St NN4 ...........159 B3
Alvington Way LE16 .....31 D5
Alvis Ct NN3............143 C4
Alvis Way NN11.........134 F3
Amber Dr NN6...........108 A5
Amberley Rd NN7 .......192 C1
**Ambleside Cl**
  **9** Northampton NN3 ...142 C4
  Wellingborough NN8 ...129 C4
Ambridge Cl NN4 .......174 F8
Ambridge Ct **8** NN1 ...159 F6

Ambush St NN5 159 B6
Amen Cnr NN14 113 C8
Amen Pl NN14 113 C8
Amundsen Cl NN11 135 B5
Ancell Rd MK11 229 E5
Anchor Dr NN2 141 B6
Anderson Ave CV22 98 A8
Anderson Dr NN15 72 F1
Anderson Gn NN8 129 C4
Anding Cl MK46 195 E4
Andrew Cl NN10 132 C7
Andrew Macdonald Cl
LE16 31 F3
Andrews Ave NN13 238 E6
Andrews Way NN9 114 B5
Angel Ct 2 LE16 31 E3
Angel La 2 NN8 130 A4
Angel St
1 Market Harborough
LE16 31 E3
Northampton NN1 159 D5
Angel Yd 19 NN16 72 B2
Anglian Rd NN11 135 B1
Anglia Way NN3 141 F6
Angus Ho NN17 36 F6
Anjou Ct NN5 139 F2
Annandale Rd NN17 36 E7
Anna's La NN12 173 B1
Anne Cl NN10 132 C7
Anne Rd NN8 129 E2
Annesley Cl NN3 160 D6
Anne St NN17 36 E5
Ann Sq NN16 72 E3
Anscomb Way NN11 184 B6
Ansell Way NN4 175 E8
Anson Cl
Corby NN17 36 B7
Daventry NN11 135 D1
ANTELOPE HILL 233 E8
Anthony Ct MK11 229 D5
Antona Cl NN9 114 B4
Antona Dr NN9 114 B4
Antona Gdns NN9 114 B4
Anvil The NN7 172 F7
APETHORPE 14 C3
Apethorpe Rd PE8 15 C6
Apollo Cl NN11 135 B3
Applebarn Cl NN4 175 C4
Appleby Cl NN9 110 F1
Appleby Wlk 2 NN3 142 C4
Appledore Cl NN2 141 C4
Applegarth Cl NN18 36 D3
Applegarth The NN6 121 C4
APPLETREE 196 C8
Appletree Ct NN9 111 F5
Appletree Ind Est
OX17 196 E7
Appletree La NN11 182 F2
Appletree Rd OX17 196 F6
Approach The NN5 158 F6
Aquitaine Cl NN5 139 F1
Arbour Ct NN3 142 E4
Arbours Prim Sch The
NN3 142 D3
Arbour View Ct NN3 142 E5
Arbury Banks OX17 196 F5
Archangel Rd 2 NN4 158 F2
Archangel Sq 1 NN4 158 F2
Archer Ave NN11 118 C1
Archers Cl NN2 141 B5
Archers Spinney CV21 99 B8
Archery Rd OX17 209 A1
Archfield NN8 129 F4
Archfield Terr 2 NN9 112 F2
Arden Cl
3 Daventry NN11 135 B4
Kettering NN15 91 F5
Market Harborough
LE16 32 A4
Ardens Gr NN7 174 A7
Arden Way LE16 31 F5
Ardington Rd NN1 160 A7
Argyle Pk LE16 48 E8
Argyle St NN5 159 A6
Argyll Ho NN17 36 E6
Argyll St
Corby NN17 36 F6
Kettering NN15 91 B8
Ariel Cl NN5 140 A1
Arkwright Rd
Corby NN17 22 C1
Irchester NN29 147 C7
Arlbury Rd NN3 143 B4
Armley Cl NN6 121 C4
ARMSTON 59 E8
Armston Rd PE8 59 B8
Arndale NN2 140 F5
Arnheim Hos NN11 199 D7
Arnhill Rd NN17 10 B1
Arnills Way CV23 100 A2
Arnold Cott MK19 229 B7
Arnold Rd NN2 159 C8
Arnsby Cres NN3 126 B1
Arnsley Rd NN17 23 A1
Arnull Cres NN11 135 B4
Arran Way NN17 36 C8
Arrow Cl OX17 220 A8
Arrow Head Rd NN4 158 F3
ARTHINGWORTH 68 C8
Arthingworth Rd NN14 50 E4
Arthur St
Northampton NN2 141 C1
Wellingborough NN8 129 E4
Arthur's Way 1 NN16 72 C2
Artizan Rd NN1 159 F7
Arum Cl NN10 148 C7
Arundel Cl
Kings Sutton OX17 230 F5
Arundel Cl *continued*
Thrapston NN14 76 F2
Arundel Ct
Kettering NN15 91 F8
Rushden NN10 148 A8
Arundel St 9 NN1 159 C7
Arundel Wlk NN18 36 B5
Ascot Cl NN18 36 E1
Ascot Rd NN10 148 D8
Ashbourne Dr NN14 50 E4
Ashbrook Cl NN14 90 A4
Ashbrow Rd NN4 158 F3
Ashburnham Rd NN1 159 F8
Ashby Cl NN8 129 E7
Ashby Ct
Guilsborough NN6 103 E7
Kislingbury NN7 157 D3
Moulton NN3 126 C1
Ashby Dr
Crick NN6 100 F5
Rushden NN10 148 A8
Ashby Fields Prim Sch
NN11 135 C5
Ashby Gdns 4 NN3 126 C1
Ashby Pk NN11 135 C4
Ashby Rd
Braunston NN11 118 C1
Daventry NN11 135 B4
Daventry NN11 135 B7
Daventry NN11 135 C2
Kilsby CV23 100 A2
Welton NN11 119 D1
ASHBY ST LEDGERS 119 D5
Ash Cl
Daventry NN11 135 C4
Irchester NN29 147 A7
Ashcroft Cl NN5 140 B1
Ashcroft Gdns NN3 142 A2
Ash Ct NN14 76 D1
Ashdale Cl NN6 127 D1
Ashdown Cl NN15 92 A5
Ashdown Pl NN17 36 E7
Ashdown Rd NN11 135 C4
Ash Dr
Brackley NN13 222 F1
Sywell NN6 143 D7
Ashes The
Bugbrooke NN7 172 F7
Northampton NN4 176 B6
Weldon NN17 38 C8
Ashfield Ave NN9 114 D6
Ashfield Rd
3 Market Harborough
LE16 31 E4
Wellingborough NN8 129 E4
Ashfield Rise NN9 114 C6
Ashford Cl NN3 160 C6
Ashford Lea NN14 50 E4
Ashgate Ct NN14 70 C7
Ash Gr
Bugbrooke NN7 172 F7
Desborough NN14 50 E4
Northampton NN2 141 B6
Ash La NN4 175 B4
Ashlade OX17 220 B7
Ashlawn Rd CV22 98 C7
Ashlawn Sch CV22 98 E7
Ashlea MK46 195 E3
Ashleigh Cl CV23 99 C2
Ashleigh Ho 6 NN10 132 B2
ASHLEY 18 E2
Ashley Ave NN17 36 B7
Ashley Ct
Blisworth NN7 190 D7
Kettering NN16 72 A3
Ashley La NN3 126 D1
Ashley Rd
Medbourne LE16 18 E6
Middleton LE16 20 B2
Stoke Albany LE16 34 A5
Weston by W LE16 18 C3
Ashley Way
Market Harborough
LE16 32 B3
Northampton NN3 142 E2
Ashmead NN3 143 A2
Ashmore NN6 121 C4
Ashpole Spinney NN4 158 C2
Ash Rd NN15 72 D1
Ashridge Cl NN10 148 A8
Ash Rise NN2 141 C6
Ash St NN1 159 C7
ASHTON
Oundle 42 D5
Roade 205 E8
Ashton CE Prim Sch
NN7 191 F1
Ashton Cl NN11 135 A3
Ashton Gr NN8 129 D8
Ashton Lodge Farm
NN7 192 A2
Ashton Rd
Hartwell NN7 192 C1
Oundle PE8 42 B5
Roade NN7 191 E2
Stoke Bruerne NN12 205 D8
Ash Tree Ct OX17 220 B8
Ashtree Gdns PE9 1 D2
Ashtree Way NN5 158 C7
Ashurst Cres NN18 36 B4
Ash Way
Braunston NN11 118 B1
Hinton NN11 184 A6
Ashway The
Brixworth NN6 106 C1
Brixworth NN6 125 B8
Ashwell Rd
Rushden NN10 132 D2
Ashwell Rd *continued*
Weedon Lois NN12 200 B2
Ashwells La NN6 82 B4
Ashwin Cl NN13 222 E1
Ashwood Rd NN5 158 C7
Ashworth Cl NN6 101 A6
Ashworth St NN11 135 C1
Askham Ave NN8 129 E1
Aspen Cl
Northampton NN3 143 C3
Rushden NN10 132 B3
Aspen Ho NN15 72 A1
Aspreys MK46 195 E4
Astbury Cl NN11 153 C8
ASTCOTE 188 F7
Aster Cl NN3 160 D6
Aster Rd NN16 72 D4
Astley Cl LE16 31 D1
Astley Pl CV21 99 B7
ASTON LE WALLS 182 F2
Aston Rise NN5 158 B8
Astral Row OX17 210 E2
ASTROP 231 B5
Astrop Gdns OX17 231 A5
Astrop Grange OX17 231 A5
Astrop Rd
Kings Sutton OX17 231 A5
Middleton Cheney
OX17 219 F6
ASTWICK 239 B7
Athelstan Rd NN16 72 D2
Atterbury Cl NN6 102 D4
Atterbury Way NN4 160 F2
Attlee Cl NN3 142 B4
Attley Ct NN8 129 C5
Attley Way NN9 113 A3
Auctioneers Ct NN1 159 D4
Auctioneers Way
NN1 159 D4
Auden Way NN17 36 C8
Audley Cl LE16 32 B2
Augusta Ave NN4 175 C6
Augustus Rd MK11 229 E4
Auriga St LE16 31 F2
Auriol Cotts NN13 221 B4
Austin Cl NN29 147 C8
Austin Ho NN14 70 D7
Austins Cl LE16 31 D3
Austins Pl NN12 214 E4
Austin St NN1 159 D7
Austins Yd NN6 144 E4
Austin Way NN11 134 F4
Avalon Ct NN14 70 E7
Avebury Way NN4 175 B8
Avenue Bernard
NN13 233 E8
Avenue Cl NN9 111 E5
Avenue Inf Sch The
NN8 130 A5
Avenue Rd
Finedon NN9 111 E5
Rushden NN10 148 F5
Wellingborough NN8 130 A5
Avenue Terr NN16 72 E3
Avenue The
Flore NN7 155 E5
Medbourne LE16 19 C8
Middleton Cheney
OX17 220 A8
Moulton NN3 142 E8
Northampton, Dallington
NN5 158 F7
Northampton, Meadow View
NN2 140 F6
Northampton NN1 159 F5
Northampton, Spinney Hill
NN3 142 A3
Rothwell NN14 70 D7
Stanwick NN9 114 A3
Wellingborough NN8 130 A5
Whitfield NN13 223 D4
Aviemore Gdns NN4 158 E1
Avignon Cl NN5 140 A2
Avonbury Ct NN13 234 A5
Avon Cl
Daventry NN11 153 A8
Kettering NN16 72 A5
Wellingborough NN8 129 C6
Avondale Jun & Inf Schs
NN16 72 D4
Avondale Mews NN16 72 D3
Avondale Rd NN16 72 D3
Avon Dr NN5 140 E1
Avon Fields NN6 64 E6
Avon Wks NN16 72 D3
Axe Head Rd NN4 158 F4
AYNHO 237 D7
Aynho Cres NN2 141 C5
Aynho Ct OX17 237 D7
Aynhoe Pk OX17 237 C7
Aynho (Fishing Venue)*
OX17 236 F6
Aynho Rd OX17 230 D2
Aynho Wlk NN2 141 D5
Aynsley Cl NN14 50 F3
Ayr Cl NN18 36 E1
Azalea Cl NN3 160 D6

B

Back La
Brigstock NN14 55 F8
Chapel Brampton NN6 124 D1
Collyweston PE8 1 D2
East Farndon LE16 48 B7
Elton PE8 28 D8
Gayton NN7 173 E2
Back La *continued*
Great Brington NN7 138 C6
Holcot NN6 126 E8
Little Addington NN14 113 B8
Morcott LE15 3 A6
Northampton NN4 175 F8
Ringstead NN14 95 B3
Scaldwell NN6 106 F5
South Luffenham LE15 3 D8
Backley Cl NN15 90 E8
Back Rd LE15 3 E5
Backway NN29 146 D2
Backway The LE16 31 F2
Bacon Hill MK46 195 E4
Bacon Rd NN8 129 F8
BADBY 153 A2
Badby Cl NN2 141 E4
Badby Leys CV22 98 A7
Badby Pk NN11 135 A5
Badby Rd
Daventry NN11 135 C1
Newnham NN11 153 D4
Badby Rd W
Daventry NN11 153 A7
Daventry NN11 153 B8
Badby Sch NN11 152 F3
Baden Powell Cres
NN12 203 C4
Badger La NN4 175 F3
Badgers Cl NN7 172 F7
Badgers Hyde NN13 232 F6
Badgers La NN14 89 C5
Badgers Wlk NN2 141 B5
Baffin Cl NN14 70 E7
Bailey Brooks Cl NN7 191 C5
Bailey Brooks La NN7 191 C5
Bailey Ct NN10 132 B5
Bailiff St NN1 159 D7
Baines Pl NN12 214 E4
Baines Way NN4 175 E3
Baird Ave NN5 158 D4
Baird Cl NN11 135 B5
Baird Ct NN8 129 B6
Baird Rd NN17 22 D1
Bairstow Rd NN12 203 C5
Bakehouse Hill
Geddington NN14 54 A3
Little Addington NN14 113 B8
Bakehouse La
Burton Latimer NN15 92 C3
Mears Ashby NN6 128 B2
Bakehouse Mews
NN14 90 B4
Bakehouse Rise NN6 85 B8
Baker Ave NN14 90 A3
Baker Ct NN14 76 D1
Bakers Cres NN29 147 A8
Bakers La
Norton NN11 136 C4
Spratton NN6 105 B1
Stoke Bruerne NN12 205 A8
Walgrave NN6 108 A4
Woodford NN14 94 D6
Baker's La NN12 204 D8
Baker St
Farthinghoe NN13 221 B4
Gayton NN7 173 E2
Irthlingborough NN9 112 E1
Northampton NN2 159 C8
3 Wellingborough
NN8 130 A5
Bakewell Cl NN4 174 F8
Balcombe Ct CV22 98 E8
Balcombe Pl NN18 36 A5
Balcombe Rd CV22 98 D8
Balding Cl CV23 99 C1
Baldwin Cl NN3 142 B4
Baler Cl NN11 135 C6
Balfour Cl NN2 141 C1
Balfour Dr NN14 70 E7
Balfour Gdns LE16 31 D1
Balfour Rd NN2 141 D1
Balfour St NN16 72 C4
Balham Cl NN10 147 F8
Balland Way NN4 175 F7
Ballantyne Rd NN10 132 A1
Balliol Rd
Brackley NN13 233 D8
Daventry NN11 153 B8
Balmoral NN18 36 C3
Balmoral Ave NN10 132 C3
Balmoral Cl
Earls Barton NN6 144 F3
Market Harborough LE16 32 B2
Towcester NN12 203 B5
Wellingborough NN8 129 E1
Balmoral Ct NN15 91 C5
Balmoral Dr NN13 233 E7
Balmoral Ho NN2 141 C1
Balmoral Rd NN2 141 C1
Balmoral Way OX17 230 F6
Baltic Cl NN18 36 A2
Bamburg Cl NN18 36 A1
Bamburgh Cl LE16 32 B3
Bampton Ct NN18 36 F4
BANBURY 219 A6
Banbury Bsns Pk
OX17 230 D3
Banbury Cl
Northampton NN4 158 D2
Wellingborough NN8 129 E1
Banbury La
Banbury OX17 219 B8
Banbury OX17 219 C8
Blakesley NN12 186 D2
Byfield NN11 183 D7
Cold Higham NN12 188 B7
Culworth OX17 198 E3
Banbury La *continued*
Foxley NN12 187 D4
Gayton NN7 173 D4
Great Easton LE16 20 D6
Kings Sutton OX17 230 E6
Middleton Cheney
OX17 209 C4
Northampton NN4 158 D1
Rothersthorpe NN7 174 B7
Thorpe Mandeville
OX17 210 B8
Weston NN12 199 C3
Banbury Rd
Aynho OX17 237 C7
Brackley NN13 233 E6
Byfield NN11 183 D7
Chacombe OX17 208 C3
Chipping Warden OX17 196 F6
Litchborough NN12 171 C1
Lower Boddington
NN11 182 C4
Moreton Pinkney NN11 199 C7
Twyford OX17 230 A6
Bancroft Cl NN4 176 A6
Bancroft Rd LE16 20 D1
Bancroft Way NN4 176 A6
Bangrave Rd NN17 37 F8
Bangrave Rd S NN17,
NN18 37 F6
Bank Cotts LE16 46 C8
Bankfield Dr LE16 32 A5
Bank Hill View NN9 110 C4
Bankside
Corby NN18 36 D3
Higham Ferrers NN10 132 B7
Northampton NN2 141 F3
Woodford Halse NN11 184 C6
Banks The
Broughton NN14 90 B5
Hackleton NN7 177 B3
Kilsby CV23 100 A2
Long Buckby NN6 121 B4
Wellingborough NN9 129 F8
Bank View NN4 175 B7
Banner Cl NN10 132 A1
Bannerman Dr NN13 233 D7
Bants La NN5 158 E7
Baptists Cl NN7 172 F7
BARBY 99 D1
Barby CE Prim Sch
CV23 118 C8
Barby La
Braunston NN11 118 C2
Rugby CV23 99 B5
BARBY NORTOFT 99 F6
Barby Rd
Kilsby CV23 99 F3
Rugby CV22 98 B7
Bardsley Rd NN17 21 E3
Barford MK11 229 F4
Baring Ho NN5 159 A7
Baring Rd NN5 159 A7
Barker Cl NN10 132 C2
Barker Rd NN6 144 E3
Barksdale Ave NN13 238 E6
Barley Cl
Daventry NN11 135 C6
Hartwell NN7 192 E2
Rugby CV21 99 A8
Barley Croft NN6 100 F6
Barley Ct NN10 148 C8
Barley Dr NN15 92 C2
Barley Hill OX17 198 D2
Barley Hill Rd NN3 142 F6
Barley La NN2 141 B5
Barlow Cl NN14 70 B7
Barlow Ct NN15 92 B1
Barlow La NN3 126 C1
Barlows La LE16 34 C5
Barn Acre NN6 122 D5
Barnard NN18 36 C3
Barnard Cl NN5 158 B8
Barnard Gdns LE16 48 D8
Barnard's Way NN14 56 A6
Barn Cl
Corby NN18 36 B1
Northampton NN4 175 F3
Barn Cnr NN4 175 C4
Barn Ct
Helmdon NN13 211 F4
Little Harrowden NN9 110 C4
Barnes Cl
Daventry NN11 135 B3
Kettering NN15 91 B7
Old NN6 107 D7
Barnes Mdw* NN4 159 F4
Barnes Meadow Intc
NN4 160 A4
Barneswell Cl NN6 106 B2
Barnet Cl NN4 159 A2
Barnett Cres NN11 184 B6
Barnett Rd OX17 219 F8
Barnfield Cl NN2 141 B4
Barnhill Sq NN3 143 A6
Barn La NN7 174 F2
Barn Mews NN4 175 C4
Barn Owl Cl NN4 175 A8
Barnsdale LE16 20 D6
Barnsdale Cl LE16 20 D6
Barnsley Sq NN18 36 C4
Barnstaple Cl NN3 160 E7
Barns The
Irchester NN29 131 B1
Mears Ashby NN6 128 C2

Barnstones Bsns Pk NN12 187 E7
Barn Way NN5 140 C2
BARNWELL 59 B6
Barnwell CE Prim Sch PE8 59 B6
Barnwell Cl NN14 76 E2
Barnwell Ctry Pk* PE8 41 E3
Barnwell Ctry Pk Visitor Ctr* PE8 41 F3
Barnwell Dr NN10 148 A8
Barnwell Gdns NN8 129 D7
Barnwell Rd
Northampton NN2 141 D4
Oundle PE8 41 F3
Wellingborough NN8 129 E7
Barnwell St NN16 72 D2
Barnwell Workshops PE8 59 B8
Baron Ave
Earls Barton NN6 144 F6
Kettering NN16 71 E3
Baron Ct
Corby NN17 22 E1
Northampton NN1 159 F8
Baronson Gdns NN1 159 F8
Barons Way NN2 141 A4
Barrack Rd NN1, NN2 159 C7
Barracks The NN7 161 D2
Barratt Cl NN10 132 B5
Barrett Cl NN8 129 C4
Barringers Ct NN29 131 B1
Barringers Gdns NN29 131 B1
Barrington Ct NN13 233 F5
Barrington Rd NN10 148 C8
Barron Cl NN15 91 C6
BARROWDEN 3 E5
Barrowden La LE15 3 E8
Barrowden Rd
Barrowden PE9 4 C8
Ketton PE9 1 A4
South Luffenham LE15 3 F7
Barry Prim Sch NN1 160 A7
Barry Rd NN1 160 A6
Barth Cl NN18 36 B2
Bartholomew Gdns NN12 187 A1
Bartlett Ct NN13 233 D7
Bartley Dr NN16 71 F4
Barton Cl OX17 230 F6
Barton Fields NN6 143 F3
Barton Holme NN12 187 A1
Barton Rd NN15 91 E7
Bartons Cl The 2 NN5 140 F1
BARTON SEAGRAVE 92 A7
Barton Seagrave Prim Sch NN15 92 A6
Barton Sq NN18 36 B6
Barwick Ho 10 NN10 132 B2
Basil Cl NN4 175 D6
Bassett Ct NN4 175 D2
Bassett Ford Rd PE8 42 A4
Bassett Lowke Ho NN1 159 D5
Bassett Pl PE8 42 A4
Bassett's Ct NN8 129 F4
Bassett Way LE16 67 A8
Bates Ave NN14 95 B3
Bates Cl
Higham Ferrers NN10 132 B5
Market Harborough LE16 31 E5
Bates La OX27 237 D3
Bath La NN16 72 C3
Bath Rd NN16 72 C4
Bath St LE16 31 E1
Batsmans Dr NN10 132 A4
Battalion Dr NN4 175 E7
Battle Cl
Cranford St John NN14 93 A6
Northampton NN4 175 D7
Baukewell Ct 4 NN3 142 E3
Baulmsholme Cl NN4 159 C4
Baunhill Cl NN3 160 D7
Baxter Ct NN4 175 F8
Bayard Brow NN13 233 E8
Bayes St NN16 72 A3
Bay La MK46 194 D2
Baysdale Ave NN17 36 E6
Beacon Ct NN4 158 E3
Beaconsfield Pl NN10 132 B3
Beaconsfield Terr
Northampton NN1 159 D7
Rushden NN10 132 B3
Beanfield Ave NN18 36 B5
Beanfield Prim Sch NN18 36 A5
Bean Furlong OX17 208 E4
Beardsley Ct NN18 36 D5
Beardsley Gdns NN15 92 A7
Beatrice Rd NN16 72 B5
Beatty Cl NN11 135 E1
Beatty Gdns NN17 36 B7
Beaufort Dr
Kettering NN15 92 A6
Northampton NN5 140 C1
Beauly Ct NN15 91 E8
Beaumaris Cl NN10 132 C1
Beaumont Cl NN16 72 B6
Beaumont Cres NN13 233 E7
Beaumont Dr NN3 143 C3
Beaune Cl NN5 139 F1
Beauvais Ct NN5 139 F1
Beaver Ctr The NN11 184 C7
Beck Ct NN8 129 D6
Becketts Cl NN11 183 D7
Beckett's View NN1 159 E5
Becket Way NN3 142 B4
Bective Rd NN2 141 C4
Bective View NN2 141 D4
Bedale Rd NN8 130 A6
Beddoes Cl NN4 176 A6
Bede Cl
Corby NN18 36 A1
Higham Ferrers NN10 132 C5
Bede Ho* LE15 9 D7
Bedford Cl NN15 91 F5
Bedford Cotts NN7 138 D7
Bedford Mans NN1 159 D5
Bedford Pl NN1 159 D5
Bedford Rd
Denton NN7 178 B8
Little Houghton NN7 160 F3
Northampton NN1 159 E4
Rushden NN10 148 D5
Bedford Rd E NN7 179 D5
Bedford Rd W NN7 179 A6
Beech Ave
Northampton NN3 142 A1
Olney MK46 195 E3
Beech Cl
Bugbrooke NN7 172 F7
Corby NN17 21 E1
Desborough NN14 51 A3
Hackleton NN7 177 B3
Towcester NN12 203 C4
Beech Cres
Irchester NN29 147 A7
Kettering NN15 72 D1
Beechcroft Gdns NN3 142 A2
Beech Ct
Rugby CV22 98 F8
Thrapston NN14 76 D2
Beech Dr
Brackley NN13 222 E1
Hinton NN11 184 B6
Wellingborough NN8 129 E5
Beeches Cl LE16 46 F2
Beeches The
Deanshanger MK19 228 E3
Pattishall NN12 172 E1
Beech Gr
Northampton NN3 142 D5
Rushden NN10 131 F3
Beech Hill NN11 151 D1
Beech House Dr NN12 217 F4
Beech La NN7 157 E4
Beech Rd NN10 132 B4
Beechwood Dr NN3 142 E1
Beechwood Rd NN5 158 C7
Beeston Ave NN3 160 F8
Beeston Pl NN18 36 C5
Belfield Cl NN3 142 B3
Belfry La NN4 175 B5
Belfry Way NN11 135 E2
Belgrave Cl NN15 92 A5
Bellamy Rd PE8 41 F7
Bell Cl NN13 211 F4
Bell Ct
Corby NN18 36 D4
5 Wellingborough NN8 130 A5
Belle Baulk NN12 203 A6
Bell End NN29 146 D2
Bellfield LE15 3 E8
Bellfields La LE16 32 A2
Bellfields St LE16 32 A2
Bellfoundry La 4 NN16 72 B2
Bell Hill
Finedon NN9 111 E4
Rothwell NN14 70 D7
BELLINGE 143 B1
Bellinge Prim Sch NN3 143 B1
Bell La
Byfield NN11 183 C7
Husbands Bosworth LE17 45 E5
Syresham NN13 224 B8
Bellropes Sq 5 NN3 143 D2
Bells Cl NN14 55 E8
Bell St NN8 130 A5
Bell Twr NN13 233 F7
Bell View OX17 231 F5
Bellway Cl NN16 72 A3
Bell Wlk CV21 99 A8
Belmont Ct 13 NN1 159 C7
Belmont Gdns NN9 114 C6
Belstead Rd NN3 160 D6
Belton Cl 4 NN4 175 C8
Belvedere Cl NN5 158 F7
Belvedere Rd NN15 72 D1
Belvoir Cl
Corby NN18 36 E2
Northampton NN5 140 B1
Rushden NN10 148 C8
Belvoir Dr NN15 92 A6
Bembridge Dr NN2 141 B1
Benbow Cl NN11 135 E2
Benedict Cl NN10 147 F8
Benefield Rd
Brigstock NN14 39 B2
Deenethorpe NN17 24 C4
Oundle PE8 41 C5
Bengal NN12 202 D7
Bengal La NN12 202 E7
Bengal View NN12 202 E8
Bengeworth Ct 10 NN8 130 A5
Benham Ct NN3 142 F3
Benham Rd NN12 202 D8
Benjamin Sq 6 NN4 158 F2
Bennett Cl
Chacombe OX17 208 E4
Daventry NN11 135 A4
Stony Stratford MK11 229 D4
Bennett Rd NN18 36 D1
Bens Cl MK19 218 F5
Bentley Cl NN3 143 D4
Bentley Ct NN9 111 B1
Bentley Way NN11 134 F3
Bentley Wlk NN18 36 C5
Bergen Wlk NN18 36 A2
Bergerac Cl NN5 139 F2
Berkeley Cl NN1 159 F6
Berkeley Ho 26 NN1 159 C6
Berkeley St LE16 46 F2
Berneshaw Cl NN18 36 D3
Bern Links NN4 159 A3
Bern Side NN4 159 A3
Berrell's Ct MK46 195 F3
Berridges La LE17 45 E5
Berrill St NN29 147 A7
Berrister Pl NN9 114 E7
Berry Cl
Earls Barton NN6 144 E5
Great Bowden LE16 32 A5
Hackleton NN7 177 B3
Rothersthorpe NN7 174 B6
Berrydale NN3 143 D4
Berryfield NN6 121 C4
Berry Field Rd LE16 20 C1
Berry Green Ct NN9 111 F5
Berry Green Pk NN14 78 E6
Berry Green Rd NN9 111 E5
Berry Hill Rd OX17 230 A2
Berry La
Hellidon NN11 151 C1
Northampton NN4 175 E5
Berrymoor Ct NN8 129 E2
Berrymoor Rd NN8 129 E2
Berry Rd LE16 20 C1
Berrywood Dr NN5 157 F7
Berrywood Rd NN5 158 A7
Bertha Way NN16 72 E4
Berwick Ho NN2 141 D5
Berwick Rd NN14 37 E3
Berwick Way NN15 92 A8
Bessemer Gr NN18 37 B6
Bestwell Ct 3 NN3 161 A8
Bestwood Cl NN14 50 F4
Bestwood Gn NN18 36 C5
Beswick Cl NN14 52 C3
Bethany Homestead 1 NN2 141 E1
Bethel La NN11 170 B7
Betjeman Cl
Daventry NN11 135 A3
Higham Ferrers NN10 132 A5
Betony Wlk NN10 148 B8
Bettycroft Cl NN6 103 E1
Bevan Cl
Warmington PE8 28 B3
Wellingborough NN8 130 C7
Beverley Cl NN14 70 B7
Beverley Cres NN3 142 C1
Beverley Rd NN15 91 D8
Beverley Wlk NN18 36 C5
Bewick Ct NN18 36 E4
Bewick Rd NN3 160 E8
Bexhill Wlk NN18 36 B4
Bibury Cl NN8 129 D1
Bibury Cres NN3 142 D6
Bicester Hill NN13 233 F2
Bickerstaffes Rd NN12 203 C5
Bidders Cl NN1 159 D4
BIDDLESDEN 224 D5
Bideford Cl NN3 160 D7
Bideford Sq NN18 36 F5
Bies Cl NN18 36 C2
Big Gn PE8 28 C3
Bignal Ct NN15 90 E8
Billing Aquadrome* NN7 161 B7
Billing Arbours Ho NN3 142 E4
Billing Brook Rd NN3 142 F4
Billing Brook Specl Sch NN3 142 F3
Billing La
Moulton NN6 126 F1
Northampton NN3, NN6 143 A7
Billing Rd
Brafield-on-t-G NN7 161 D4
Northampton NN1 159 F6
Billing Rd E NN3 160 D7
Billing School Pl NN7 155 C3
Billington St NN1 159 F7
Bilsdon Cl NN10 147 F8
Bilton Ct NN8 129 D5
Binbrook Wlk NN18 36 C4
Binder Cl NN10 132 A7
Binders Ct NN14 37 F2
Bingham Wlk NN18 36 C5
Birchall Rd NN10 131 F2
Birch Ave NN18 36 D4
Birch Barn Way NN2 141 B6
Birch Cl
Hinton NN11 184 B6
Northampton NN4 175 E2
Birch Ct NN10 132 C2
Birchfield Cres NN3 142 C2
Birchfield Ct NN3 142 B1
Birchfield Rd
Northampton NN1, NN3 142 A1
Wellingborough NN8 129 E4
Birchfield Rd E NN3 142 C1
Birchington Rd NN17 22 F2
Birch Rd
Kettering NN16 72 D3
Rushden NN10 132 C2
Birch Spinney NN14 89 A4
Birch Tree Gdns LE16 31 F4
Birchvale Ct NN14 50 E4
Birds Hill Rd
Eastcote NN12 188 F8
Northampton NN3 142 F3
Birds Hill Wlk NN3 142 F2
Bird St NN15 92 D3
Birkdale Cl
Daventry NN11 135 E2
Northampton NN2 141 F3
Birkdale Dr NN10 132 D1
Birling Pl NN18 36 B5
Birtley Coppice LE16 31 D4
Bishop Cl LE16 48 E8
Bishops Cl NN13 222 E1
Bishops Ct
4 Daventry NN11 135 C2
Higham Ferrers NN10 132 C7
Bishops Dr NN2 141 B3
Bishop's Dr NN15 91 B6
Bishop Stopford Sch NN15 91 B7
Bishops Way NN18 36 A4
Bitten Ct NN3 142 E3
Blackberry Cl NN16 72 B6
Blackberry La NN4 158 F3
Blackbird Cl NN13 222 E1
Blackbridge Ct NN14 76 C2
Black Cat Dr NN5 158 D4
Blackdown MK11 229 F4
Blackfriars NN10 147 F8
Blackfriars Ho 19 NN1 159 C6
Black Lion Hill NN1 159 B5
Blacklocks Hill OX17 219 B8
Blackmile La NN7 163 E7
Blackmires La NN12 214 B5
Blackmoor Ave NN18 36 F4
Blackpot La PE8 42 A5
Blacksmith's Cl NN12 172 D1
Blacksmiths Gn NN12 204 D8
Blacksmiths Hill OX17 237 C7
Blacksmiths La
Eydon NN11 184 C1
Little Brington NN7 138 B4
Blacksmith's La
Aston le W NN11 182 F2
Pytchley NN14 90 F2
Blacksmith's Way NN7 192 C1
Black Swan Spinney PE8 8 A4
BLACKTHORN 143 B4
Blackthorn Bridge Ct 4 NN3 143 B4
Blackthorn Cl
Kettering NN16 72 C6
Spratton NN6 105 A1
Blackthorn Prim Sch NN3 143 B4
Blackthorn Rd NN3 143 B4
Blackwall Cl 1 NN4 159 A2
Blackwell Cl
Earls Barton NN6 144 E4
Higham Ferrers NN10 132 B7
Towcester NN12 203 D4
Blackwell End NN12 217 C3
Blackwell Hill NN4 174 F8
Blackwell Rd NN15 91 F4
Blackwells Yd NN7 179 B6
BLACKY MORE 175 C7
Blackymore La NN4 175 D5
Bladon Cl NN3 142 C4
Blake Cl NN11 153 E8
Blake Ct NN15 92 A8
Blake Rd NN18 36 D4
Blakesely Hill NN12 202 D8
BLAKESLEY 187 B1
Blakesley CE Prim Sch NN12 187 B1
Blakesley Cl NN2 141 C5
Blakesley Rd NN12 200 F7
Blake Wlk NN10 132 A5
Blanchard Cl 3 NN4 175 E7
Blandford Ave NN16 72 B5
Blandford Ct NN18 36 A6
BLATHERWYCKE 12 E4
Blatherwycke Rd PE8 13 E7
Blaydon Wlk NN8 129 E6
Bleaklow Cl NN14 50 E3
Bledlow Rise NN4 174 F8
Blencowe Dr NN13 233 D7
Blenheim NN13 238 B7
Blenheim Ave MK11 229 E4
Blenheim Cl NN10 148 A8
Blenheim Croft NN13 233 F6
Blenheim Pl NN13 224 C7
Blenheim Rd
Northampton NN4 159 B2
Wellingborough NN8 129 D7
Blenheim Rise OX17 230 F6
Blenheim Way
Kettering NN15 91 C5
Market Harborough LE16 31 E5
Blenheim Wlk NN18 36 C3
Blinco Rd NN10 132 C3
Blind La LE16 20 D1
Bliss Charity Sch The NN7 156 C2
Bliss La NN7 155 F5
BLISWORTH 190 E7
Blisworth Cl NN4 159 A2
Blisworth Com Prim Sch NN7 190 D8
Blisworth Mill NN7 190 C7
Blisworth Rd
Gayton NN7 173 F1
Roade NN7 191 B4
Bloomfield Cl NN10 132 A2
Blossac Ct NN5 139 F1
Blossom Ct 2 NN16 72 C4
Blossom Way NN3 143 A1
Blotts Barn Bsns Ctr NN9 114 F8
Bluebell Cl
Corby NN18 36 D2
Hinton NN11 184 B7
Kettering NN16 72 E4
Rushden NN10 148 C8
Wellingborough NN8 130 B6
Bluebell Ct NN3 160 C6
Bluebell Pk Cvn Pk 2 NN3 126 C1
Bluebell Rise
Northampton NN4 175 F1
Rushden NN10 148 B8
Blueberry Cl NN6 87 B6
Blueberry Rise 2 NN3 143 C2
Bluecoat La LE15 9 D7
Blythe Cl NN14 70 E6
Blyton Ct NN18 36 C4
Boarden Cl NN3 142 A7
Boardman Rd NN15 90 F8
Board St NN9 112 F2
Boat Horse La NN6 101 A5
Boathouse The LE16 31 D4
Bobtail Ct NN5 140 C1
Boddington CE Sch NN11 182 C7
Boddington Ct NN11 182 C5
Boddington Mews NN15 91 C8
Boddington Rd
Byfield NN11 183 C7
Claydon OX17 181 D1
Kettering NN15 91 C8
Boddington Way NN13 233 D8
Boden Cl NN18 36 A2
Bodiam CL NN14 76 E2
Bodiam Pl NN18 36 A5
Bodleian Cl NN11 153 B8
Bognor Rd NN18 36 B4
Bolingbroke Pl NN10 132 C7
Bollinger Cl NN5 139 F1
Boltons Cl NN13 222 E1
Bondfield Ave NN2 141 D3
Bonham Ct NN16 72 C3
Bonington Wlk NN18 36 D5
Bonnington Cl CV21 80 B1
Bonsor Gdns NN14 95 A3
Boon Wlk NN17 37 B7
Booth Cl NN12 172 D1
Booth Dr NN8 129 A4
Booth La N NN3 142 C4
Booth La S NN3 142 D2
Booth Meadow Ct NN3 142 E5
Booth Rise NN3 142 D6
BOOTHVILLE 142 D5
Boothville Gn NN3 142 D5
Boothville Prim Sch NN3 142 C4
Bo-Peep Cvn Pk OX17 230 C2
Bordeaux Cl NN5 139 F1
Bordeaux Ct NN5 139 F1
BOROUGH 135 E2
Borough Ct
Brackley NN13 234 A5
Higham Ferrers NN10 132 B5
Borough Rd NN13 234 A5
Borrowdale Rd NN17 36 D8
Borrowdale Wlk 3 NN3 142 C4
Bostock Ave NN1 159 F7
Bostock Mews NN1 159 F7
Boston Cl NN18 36 C4
Boswell La MK19 228 E4
Bosworth Cl
Northampton NN4 159 A1
Warmington PE8 28 B3
Bosworth Independent Coll NN2 159 C8
Bosworth Rd
Husbands Bosworth LE17 45 A8
Theddingworth LE17 46 C7
Bothy The OX17 237 D7
Botmead Rd NN3 143 D4
Bottom La LE16 34 B5
Bougainvillea Dr NN3 160 C6
BOUGHTON 141 D8
Boughton NN15 91 D4
Boughton Cl NN18 36 A4
Boughton Dr NN10 148 A8
Boughton Fair La NN3 126 B4
Boughton Green Rd NN2, NN3 141 D5
Boughton Ho* NN14 73 C8
Boughton La NN3 141 F7
Boughton Prim Sch NN2 141 D8

**Boughton Rd**
Boughton NN2, NN3 141 F8
Corby NN18 36 D2
Moulton NN3 126 A1
**Boughton Terr** NN13 233 F2
**Boundary Ave** NN10 131 E1
**Boundary Cres** MK11 229 E6
**Boundary Rd** NN13 234 A6
**Bourne Cl**
Corby NN18 36 D2
Wellingborough NN8 129 C6
**Bourne Cres** NN5 140 E1
**Bourton Cl** NN4 174 E8
**Bourton Way** NN8 129 E1
**Bouverie Rd** NN4 175 E8
**Bouverie St** 1 NN1 159 F6
**Bouverie Wlk** 5 NN1 159 F6
**Bovewell** OX27 237 E3
**Bow Ct** NN4 158 E3
**Bowden La**
Market Harborough LE16 31 E4
Welham LE16 17 E4
**Bowden Rd**
Northampton NN5 159 A6
Thorpe Langton LE16 17 A4
**Bowden Ridge** LE16 32 A5
**Bowen Rd** CV22 98 D8
**Bowen Sq** 7 NN11 135 C1
**Bowhill** NN16 72 A1
**Bowland Dr** NN15 92 A5
**Bowling Gn** NN13 221 B4
**Bowling Green Ave** NN15 72 B1
**Bowling Green La** NN5 158 A6
**Bowling Green Rd** NN15 72 B1
**Bowman Cl** OX17 220 A8
**Bowmans Cl** NN4 158 D1
**Bowmens Lea** OX17 237 C7
**Bowness** NN8 129 D5
**Bowthorpe Cl** NN3 160 D6
**Box Gdns** NN8 130 A5
**Boxwood Dr** CV23 100 A3
**Boyle Rd** NN17 22 C1
**BOZEAT** 164 D3
Bozeat Com Prim Sch NN29 164 D3
**Bozenham Mill La** NN7 205 E4
**Brabham Cl** NN12 214 D4
**Bracadale Wlk** NN17 21 C1
**Bracken Borough** NN6 106 C2
**Bracken Cl** NN16 72 B5
**Brackendale Dr** CV23 99 C1
**Bracken Field Sq** NN3 142 F7
**Brackenhill Cl** NN2 141 E3
Bracken Leas Prim Sch NN13 222 E1
**BRACKLEY** 233 E7
Brackley CE Jun Sch NN13 233 F8
**Brackley Cl** NN2 141 D6
Brackley Cottage Hospl NN13 233 F7
Brackley Jun Sch NN13 233 E6
**Brackley La** NN12 201 F1
**Brackley Lodge Mews** NN13 233 F7
**Brackley Rd**
Croughton NN13 238 D8
Greatworth OX17 210 E1
Silverstone NN12 214 D3
Towcester NN12 203 B6
Westbury NN13 234 F5
Brackley Waynflete Inf Sch NN13 233 E7
**BRACKMILLS** 160 B1
Brackmills Ind Est NN4 160 A2
**Bracknell** NN8 129 C4
**Bradbury Rd** NN11 153 D3
**BRADDEN** 201 F6
**Bradden Cl** NN2 141 D5
**Bradden Rd** NN12 202 D8
**Bradden Way** NN12 202 D8
**Bradfield Cl**
Rushden NN10 132 D3
Wellingborough NN8 111 A1
**Bradfield Rd** NN8 111 A1
**Bradford Wlk** NN18 36 C5
**Bradgate Ho** NN1 159 E6
**Bradmoor Ct** NN3 143 B5
**Bradmore Gdns** NN18 36 C6
**Bradshaw St** 29 NN1 159 C6
**Bradshaw Way** NN29 146 F8
**Braemar Cl** NN15 91 E8
**Braemar Cres** NN4 175 C8
**Brafield Leys** CV22 98 A6
**BRAFIELD-ON-THE-GREEN** 161 E2
**Brafield Rd**
Cogenhoe NN7 161 E5
Horton NN7 177 E3
**Braggintons La** OX17 220 B8
**Braid Ct** NN8 129 D7
**Braithwaite Cl** NN15 90 F8
**Brakey Rd** NN17 37 F8
**Bramber Ct** NN18 36 A5
**Bramble Cl**
Kettering NN16 72 B6
Ringstead NN14 95 A3
**Bramble End** NN4 174 F8
**Bramble Rd** NN12 203 B4
**Brambleside**
Kettering NN16 72 C6
Thrapston NN14 76 D1
Brambleside Com Prim Sch NN16 72 C6
**Brambleside Ct** NN16 72 B6
**Brambles The** NN10 148 B5
**Bramblewood Rd** NN17 38 A8
**BraMCote Dr** NN3 160 F8
**Bramhall Rise** NN5 158 B8
**Bramley Cl**
Cogenhoe NN7 161 E6
Market Harborough LE16 31 F5
Rushden NN10 131 F3
**Bramley Ct** NN29 146 D3
**Bramley Gr** NN3 143 B2
**Bramley Ho** 7 NN11 135 C2
**Brammar Ho** NN5 158 F7
**BRAMPTON ASH** 33 E3
**Brampton Cl**
Kettering NN15 92 A5
Wellingborough NN8 129 D7
**Brampton Hill** LE16 33 F4
**Brampton La**
Boughton NN2, NN6 141 A7
Chapel Brampton NN6 125 A3
Bramptons Prim Sch The NN6 124 D1
Brampton Valley Way* NN6 124 E4
**Brampton Way** NN6 106 B1
**Brampton Wlk** NN3 141 F5
**Brampton Wood La** NN14 50 F7
**Bramshill Ave** NN16 72 A6
**Bramston Cl** PE8 42 A4
**Brandenburg Rd** NN18 35 F2
**Brangwyn Wlk** NN18 36 E5
**Branksome Ave** NN2 141 B1
**Branksome Ct** NN18 36 A6
**Branson Ct** NN16 72 A3
**Branson Mews** NN17 38 A8
**Brasenose Dr** NN13 233 D8
**Brashland Dr** NN4 175 D6
**BRAUNSTON** 118 C2
Braunston CE Prim Sch NN11 118 C1
**Braunston Cl** NN4 159 A2
**Braunston La** NN11 152 C8
**Braunston Pl** CV22 98 D8
**Braunston Rd** NN11 135 B2
**Braunton Pl** NN18 36 F4
**Brawn Cl** NN9 131 E8
**Brawn Way** PE8 16 D1
**BRAYBROOKE** 49 F5
**Braybrooke Cl** NN14 95 C3
Braybrooke Prim Sch LE16 49 E6
**Braybrooke Rd**
Arthingworth LE16 68 D8
Desborough NN14 50 F4
Dingley LE16 33 A3
Great Oxendon LE16 49 A3
Market Harborough LE16 32 B1
**Brayford Ave** NN18 36 F5
**Brayford Cl** NN3 160 C7
**Breach Cl** NN6 106 C2
**Breakleys Rd** NN14 51 B2
**Breck Cl** NN18 53 B8
**Brecon Cl** NN16 72 B6
**Brecon St** NN5 159 A8
**Breedon Cl** NN18 36 A1
**Breezehill** NN4 175 F6
**Brembridge Cl** NN6 127 D2
**Brendon Cl** NN3 160 D7
**Brent Cl** NN15 92 A2
**Brentford** NN8 129 B5
**Brer Ct** NN4 159 F5
**Bressingham Gdns** NN4 175 C7
**Breton** MK11 229 E6
**Bretton Cl** NN5 140 A1
**Bretts La** NN7 191 E4
**Brewery Ct** PE8 41 F4
**Brewery Yd** NN14 56 E1
**Brewin Cl** NN13 222 D1
**Briar Cl** NN13 222 F1
**Briar Ct** NN9 112 F2
**BRIAR HILL** 158 F3
Briar Hill Prim Sch NN4 158 F3
**Briar Hill Rd** NN4 159 B2
**Briar Hill Wlk** NN4 159 B2
**Briar Rd** NN16 72 E5
**Briars The** NN4 159 A3
**Briarwood Way** NN29 146 D1
**Briary Cl** NN12 203 B4
**Brickett's La** NN7 155 E5
**Brickhill Mews** NN8 129 E4
**Brickhill Rd** NN8 129 D4
**Brick Kiln Cl** NN12 203 D4
**Brick Kiln La** NN2 159 D8
**Brick Kiln Rd** NN9 114 D8
**Brickwell Ct** NN3 143 A1
**Brickyard Spinney Rd** NN3 142 B6
**Bridewell Ho** 21 NN16 72 B2
**Bridewell La** 11 NN16 72 B2
**Bridge Ct**
Corby NN17 37 A7
Thrapston NN14 76 C2
**Bridge End** PE8 8 A3
**Bridge Ho** NN14 70 D7
**Bridge Mdw** NN7 178 B8
**Bridge Meadow Way** NN4 175 F4
**Bridgend** NN6 82 B4
**Bridge Rd**
Cosgrove MK19 218 E2
Desborough NN14 50 F4
Stoke Bruerne NN12 205 A8
**Bridge St**
Apethorpe PE8 14 D4
Brackley NN13 233 E6
Brigstock NN14 55 E7
Geddington NN14 54 A2
Kettering NN16 72 C3
King's Cliffe PE8 14 A7
Northampton NN1 159 C5
Olney MK46 195 F2
Raunds NN9 114 D7
Rothwell NN14 70 D7
Thrapston NN14 76 C2
Weedon Bec NN7 155 B4
Weldon NN17 38 B8
**Bridge View** PE8 42 A6
**Bridgewater Cl** NN13 233 F8
**Bridgewater Cres** NN13 233 F8
**Bridgewater Ct** NN13 233 F8
**Bridgewater Dr** NN3 160 D7
**Bridgewater Ho** NN13 233 F8
Bridgewater Prim Sch NN3 160 C7
**Bridgewater Rd** NN13 233 F8
**Bridgewater Rise** NN13 233 F8
**Bridge Wlk** MK19 228 E4
**Bridgford Pl** NN18 36 C6
**Bridgwater Ct** NN18 36 A6
**Bridle Cl**
Brafield-on-t-G NN7 161 D2
Wellingborough NN8 111 A1
**Bridle La** NN6 84 B6
**Bridle Path** NN7 161 E2
**Bridle Rd**
Burton Latimer NN15 92 A2
Hannington NN6 108 C3
Old NN6 107 D7
**Bridle Way** NN14 90 A6
**Briery Cl** NN18 36 B1
**Brigadier Cl** NN4 175 D7
**Brigg Ct** NN18 36 C4
**Brighouse Cl** NN18 36 C4
**Brighton Rd** NN18 36 B4
**Bright Trees Rd** NN14 54 B3
**Brightwell Wlk** NN9 131 D8
**BRIGSTOCK** 55 E7
Brigstock Latham's CE Prim Sch NN14 55 F7
**Brigstock Rd** NN14 38 A2
**Brindlestone Cl** NN4 158 D2
**Brindley Cl**
Daventry NN11 135 A5
Rushden NN10 131 F4
**Brindley Ct** NN11 134 B8
**Brindley Quay** NN11 134 B8
**Brindley Rd** CV21 80 B1
**BRINGHURST** 20 C5
Bringhurst Prim Sch LE16 20 C6
**Brington Dr** NN15 91 F5
Brington Prim Sch NN7 138 C5
**Brington Rd** NN6 121 C3
**Brinkhill Wlk** NN18 36 C4
**Brinsley Gn** NN18 36 C6
**Brisbane Gdns** NN18 36 B2
**Briscoe Cl** NN2 141 E6
**BRITAIN** 173 F1
**Britain Cotts** NN7 173 F1
**Britannia Gdns** NN8 130 C4
**Britannia Rd** NN16 72 B5
Britannia Trad Ctr NN5 140 D2
**Britannia Wlk** LE16 31 F2
**British La** 17 NN16 72 B2
**Briton Gdns** NN3 142 B1
**Briton Rd** NN3 142 B1
**Briton Terr** NN3 142 B1
**Britten Cl** NN9 133 C8
**Brittens View** NN6 126 E8
**Brittons Dr** NN3 143 A7
**Brixham Wlk** NN18 36 F5
**BRIXWORTH** 106 A2
Brixworth CE Prim Sch NN6 106 B1
Brixworth Ctry Pk* NN6 125 C8
Brixworth Ctry Pk Visitor Ctr* NN6 125 C7
**Brixworth Hall Pk** NN6 106 B2
**Brixworth Rd**
Creaton NN6 104 F4
Holcot NN6 126 D8
Spratton NN6 105 D1
**Broadgate** LE16 20 D7
**Broadgate Way** PE8 28 C2
**Broad Gn** 4 NN8 129 F5
**Broadhurst Dr** NN3 161 A8
**Broad La** NN13 233 E3
**Broadlands**
Brixworth NN6 106 A1
Desborough NN14 51 C2
Pitsford NN6 125 D5
Raunds NN9 114 E6
**Broad March** NN11 153 D8
**Broadmead Ave** NN3 142 B2
**Broadmead Ct** NN3 142 B2
**Broad St**
Brixworth NN6 106 B1
Earls Barton NN6 144 E4
Northampton NN1 159 C6
Syresham NN13 224 B8
**Broadstone Ct** NN18 36 A6
**Broadwater La** NN12 203 A5
**Broadway**
Kettering NN15 91 B8
Northampton NN1, NN3 142 A1
Wellingborough NN8 130 A3
**Broadway E** NN3 142 B1
**Broadway Terr** LE16 31 F4
**Broadway The**
Market Harborough LE16 31 F4
Norton NN11 136 C4
**Brocade Cl** 8 NN4 158 F2
**BROCKHALL** 137 D2
**Brockhall Cl** NN2 141 E4
**Brockhall Rd**
Flore NN7 155 E6
Northampton NN2 141 E4
**Brockhill Cl** NN15 72 E1
**Brockton St** NN2 141 D1
**Brockwood Cl** NN5 140 A1
**Bromford Cl** 8 NN3 161 A8
**Bromley Farm Ct** NN11 184 B5
**Bromwich Rd** 1 CV21 80 A1
**Bronte Cl** NN16 72 C6
**Brontes The** NN17 36 D8
**Brook Ct**
Horton NN7 177 E2
Silverstone NN12 214 D5
**Brooke Cl**
Rushden NN10 132 B1
Wellingborough NN8 129 B5
**Brooke Gn** NN8 129 B5
**Brooke Ho** NN17 36 E6
Brooke House Coll LE16 31 E4
**Brooke Mews** NN8 129 B5
**Brookend** NN4 175 E5
**Brooke Rd** NN18 53 B8
**Brookes Gr** NN17 21 E1
**Brookes Mews** NN6 144 E5
Brooke Weston City Tech Coll NN18 36 D1
**Brook Farm Cl** NN10 148 B5
**Brookfield Rd**
Market Harborough LE16 31 C3
Northampton NN2 141 E2
2 Rushden NN10 132 A2
**Brookhaven** NN14 90 B4
**Brook La**
Great Easton LE16 20 D6
Northampton NN5 158 F8
Towcester NN12 203 A6
**Brookland Cres** NN1 142 A1
**Brookland Rd** NN1, NN3 142 A1
**Brooklands Cl** NN11 135 C1
**Brooklands Gdns** LE16 31 E2
**Brook St E** NN8 130 B4
**Brook St W** NN8 129 F4
**Brooks Cl**
Burton Latimer NN15 92 C1
Willoughby CV23 117 D4
**Brooksdale Cl** NN16 72 B6
**Brookside**
Bozeat NN29 164 D2
Desborough NN14 51 B2
Glapthorn PE8 26 C1
Hinton NN11 184 A6
Lillingstone Lovell MK18 227 A6
Southwick PE8 26 B5
Stanwick NN9 114 A3
Wappenham NN12 213 C8
Weedon Bec NN7 155 B3
**Brookside Cl**
Old Stratford MK19 229 B6
Yelvertoft NN6 82 B4
**Brookside La** NN11 153 A2
**Brookside Mdws** NN5 140 E1
**Brookside Mews** NN6 82 B4
**Brookside Pl** NN7 156 C2
**Brooks Rd** NN9 114 F8
**Brook St**
9 Daventry NN11 135 C2
Hargrave NN9 115 E3
Moreton Pinkney NN11 199 C7
Northampton NN1 159 B7
Raunds NN9 114 D6
**Brook Terr**
1 Irthlingborough NN9 112 F2
Medbourne LE16 18 F6
**Brook Vale** NN8 129 C2
**Brook View** NN4 175 E3
**Brookway** MK19 228 E4
**Brook Wlk** NN14 95 A3
**Broom Ct** 2 NN4 159 A3
**Broomhill Cres** NN3 143 A6
**Broom Way** NN15 90 F8
**Brough Cl** NN5 139 F1
**BROUGHTON** 90 B4
**Broughton Hill** NN14 90 A6
**Broughton Pl** NN3 142 B3
Broughton Prim Sch NN14 90 A4
**Broughton Rd**
Mawsley Village NN14 89 B3
Old NN6 107 E8
Pytchley NN14 90 E2
**Browning Ave** NN16 72 C5
**Browning Cl**
8 Daventry NN11 135 B4
Rushden NN10 148 D8
**Browning Rd**
Rugby CV21 99 B8
Wellingborough NN8 129 C4
**Browning Wlk** NN17 36 D8
**Brownlow Ct** NN3 142 E4
**Browns Cl**
Mawsley Village NN14 89 B4
Moulton NN3 126 D2
**Brownsfield Rd** NN12 217 E6
**Brown's La** NN14 95 C6
**Browns Rd** NN11 134 F1
**Brown's Way** NN1 159 E5
**Brownswood Dr** NN12 217 D3
**Browns Yd** NN12 203 C6
**Bruce St** NN5 158 F6
**Brundall Cl** NN3 160 D7
**Brunel Cl**
Daventry NN11 134 F4
Kettering NN16 72 A3
Wellingborough NN8 129 B6
**Brunel Ct** NN17 22 A2
**Brunel Dr** NN5 158 D5
**Brunel Rd** NN17 22 A2
**Brunswick Gdns** NN18 35 F2
**Brunswick Pl** NN1 159 E7
**Brunswick Wlk** NN1 159 E7
**Brunting Rd** NN3 142 C8
**Bryant Rd** NN15 91 C7
**Bryant Way** NN10 132 B6
Bsns Ctr The NN5 158 F6
Bsns Exchange The NN16 72 B3
**Buccleuch St** NN16 72 B3
**Buchanan Cl** NN4 159 A3
**Buckfast Sq** NN18 36 F4
**Buckingham Cl**
Northampton NN4 175 B7
Wellingborough NN8 129 E1
**Buckingham Ct**
Brackley NN13 234 A6
Kettering NN15 91 F7
**Buckingham Rd**
Brackley NN13 234 A6
Deanshanger MK19 228 F3
**Buckingham Way** NN12 203 B5
**Buckle Ho** NN5 159 B5
**Buckley Ct** MK11 229 F4
Bucknell Wood Forest Wlk* NN12 214 B6
**Bucknill Cres** CV21 99 B7
**Bucknills La** NN6 100 F5
**Buckwell Cl**
Desborough NN14 51 A3
Wellingborough NN8 129 E5
**Buckwell End** NN8 129 F4
**Buckwell La** CV23 80 B6
**Budge Rd** NN12 217 F5
**BUGBROOKE** 173 A7
Bugbrooke Com Prim Sch NN12 172 F7
**BUGBROOKE DOWNS** 173 C4
**Bugbrooke Rd**
Gayton NN7 173 D2
Kislingbury NN7 157 D3
Nether Heyford NN7 156 C1
**Bugby Dr** NN9 113 B5
**Bugby Way** NN9 114 D7
**Bull Baulk** OX17 220 A8
**Bull Cl** NN29 164 D3
**Bull La** PE9 1 A6
Bullmatt Bsns Ctr NN10 131 E4
**Bullock Rd** PE7 29 D5
**Bulls La** OX17 230 F5
**Bulwell Gn** NN18 36 C6
**BULWICK** 12 C1
**Bungalows The**
Theddingworth LE17 46 D8
Walgrave NN6 108 A5
**Bunkers Hill**
Badby NN11 152 F2
Foxton LE17 30 A5
**Bunsty Ct** MK11 229 F5
**Bunting Cl** NN15 92 A2
**Bunting Rd** NN2 141 D1
**Bunting's La** PE8 28 B3
**Burcote Fields** NN12 203 D4
**Burcote Rd** NN12 203 D4
Burcote Wood Bsns Pk NN12 203 B1
**Burditt Cl** NN14 70 F6
**Burdock Way** NN14 51 A4
**Burford Ave** NN3 142 D5
**Burford Cl** LE16 31 D1
**Burford Way** NN8 129 D1
**Burgess Ct** NN18 36 A4
Burgess Farm OX17 220 B7
**Burgess Row** LE16 21 B8
**Burghley Cl**
Corby NN18 36 F4
Desborough NN14 51 A4
Market Harborough LE16 32 A3
**Burghley Dr** NN18 36 F5
**Burghley St** NN16 72 C4
**Burham Cl** NN4 175 E5
**Burkitt Rd** NN17 21 F3
**Burleigh Ho** 7 NN10 132 B2
**Burleigh Rd** NN2 141 C1
**Burleigh Terr** NN29 164 D3
**Burlington Apartments** NN1 160 A7

Burmans Way NN7 161 E6
Burnell Cl NN14 95 B3
Burnham Pl NN13 224 B8
Burnmill Rd LE16 31 E5
Burns Cl NN6 144 F4
Burns Dr NN17 36 D8
Burns Rd
  Daventry NN11 135 B4
  Kettering NN16 72 C5
  Wellingborough NN8 129 C4
Burns St NN1 159 E7
BURROW'S BUSH 130 B6
Burrows Cl NN11 119 E1
Burrows Ct NN3 142 E4
Burrows Farm La NN14 113 B8
Burrows Vale NN6 106 C2
Burryport Rd NN4 160 B2
Burton Cl NN11 135 C5
Burtone Cl NN14 90 A4
Burton Ho NN15 92 C2
BURTON LATIMER 92 A1
Burton Rd NN9 111 F6
Burton Terr NN29 164 D3
Burtram Cl NN3 142 E1
Burwell Hill NN13 233 F8
Burwell Hill Cl NN13 233 F8
Burwell Wlk NN18 36 C4
Burwood Rd NN3 142 B2
Bury Cl
  Cottingham LE16 20 C1
  Higham Ferrers NN10 132 C6
Bury Dyke NN6 101 A6
Bury Hill NN12 201 F6
Burystead Pl NN8 130 A4
Burystead Rise NN9 114 E7
Burywell Rd NN8 130 B6
Buscot Park Way 11 NN11 135 B7
Bushacre Ct NN16 71 F3
Bush Cl NN8 129 E5
Bushey Balk Cl NN18 36 B1
Bush Hill NN3 142 C2
Bushland Rd NN3 142 C2
Buswell Cl NN7 155 B3
Buswell Rise NN14 70 E7
Butcher's La
  Boughton NN2 125 C1
  Pattishall NN12 172 E1
  Pytchley NN14 90 F2
Butchers Paddock NN14 93 A7
Bute Cl NN17 36 B8
Butland Rd NN18 36 D2
Butler Gdns LE16 31 C1
Butlers Cl NN11 182 F2
Butlin Cl
  Daventry NN11 135 B3
  Rothwell NN14 70 B7
Butlin Ct NN8 130 C1
Butlins La NN7 191 D4
Buttercup Cl NN18 36 C2
Buttercup Rd NN14 51 A5
Butterfields NN8 129 F2
Buttermere NN8 129 C5
Buttermere Cl
  Kettering NN16 71 E3
  Northampton NN3 142 C3
Butterwick Wlk NN18 36 C4
Butt La LE17 45 E5
Buttmead NN7 190 D7
Butts Cl
  Aynho OX17 237 C7
  Culworth OX17 198 D2
Butts Croft Cl NN4 175 C6
Butts Hill Cres NN7 173 A8
Butts Rd
  Northampton NN4 175 C6
  Raunds NN9 114 E6
  Wellingborough NN8 129 F1
Butts The OX17 237 D8
Buxton Dr NN14 50 E4
Bycell Rd MK18 226 B3
BYFIELD 183 D7
Byfield Rd
  Chipping Warden OX17 196 F7
  Eydon NN11 184 C2
  Hinton NN11 184 B7
  Northampton NN5 159 A5
  Priors Marston CV47 166 E7
Byfield Sch NN11 183 C7
Bygones Mus* OX17 181 D1
By Pass Way NN7 178 B8
Byron Cl NN12 203 B5
Byron Cres
  Higham Ferrers NN10 132 A5
  Rushden NN10 131 E2
Byron Rd
  Corby NN17 36 D8
  Kettering NN16 72 C5
  Wellingborough NN8 129 D4
Byron St NN2 141 F1
Byron Wlk NN11 135 B3
BYTHORN 97 D4

## C

Cabot Cl
  Daventry NN11 135 C5
  Rothwell NN14 70 E6
Caernarvon Cl NN12 203 C4
Caesars Gate NN13 234 A6
Caistor Rd NN17 10 C1
Caldbeck Wlk 5 NN3 142 C4
CALDECOTE 189 B3
Caldecote Rd LE16 20 E6
CALDECOTT
  Corby 21 C8
  Higham Ferrers 133 C6
Caldecott Rd
  Chelveston NN9 133 B7
  Rockingham LE16 21 B5
Calder Cl NN17 21 D1
Calder Gn NN5 140 E1
Caledonian Ho 1 NN5 159 A6
Calke Ho 6 NN11 135 B7
Callcott Dr NN15 92 A8
Calstock Cl NN3 160 D7
Calvert Cl NN12 202 E8
Calvert Ct NN8 129 F8
CALVERTON 229 E3
Calverton Rd MK11 229 D4
Calvert Rd NN12 202 E8
Camberley Cl NN3 143 B2
Cambium Cl NN16 72 C6
Camborne Cl NN4 159 B2
Cambria Cres NN3 142 C1
Cambridge Ave NN17 36 B6
Cambridge St
  Kettering NN16 72 C3
  Northampton NN2 159 C8
  Rothwell NN14 70 D8
  Wellingborough NN8 130 A5
  Wymington NN10 148 A7
Cam Cl NN17 21 C1
Camden Sq NN29 164 D2
Camelot Way NN5 158 A7
Cameron Cl
  Daventry NN11 135 B1
  Northampton NN5 158 E7
Cameron Cres NN5 158 E7
Cameron Ct NN17 36 F5
Cameron Dr NN5 158 E7
Campaign Cl 9 NN4 175 E7
Campanula Cl NN3 160 C6
Campbell Cl
  Rushden NN10 148 D8
  Towcester NN12 203 C8
  Weedon Bec NN7 155 A4
Campbell Rd
  Corby NN17 36 F5
  Wellingborough NN8 130 A2
Campbell Sq 1 NN1 159 D6
Campbell St NN1 159 C7
Camp Cl NN7 173 A6
CAMP HILL 158 E2
Camp Hill NN7 173 A6
Campion Cl NN10 148 B8
Campion Ct NN3 143 B1
Campion Sch NN7 173 A8
Camp La NN7 157 D3
Camrose Rd NN5 159 A8
Camsdale Wlk LE16 35 C8
Canada Sq NN18 36 C3
Canal La MK19 228 E4
Canal Mus The* NN12 205 A8
Canalside
  Market Harborough LE16 31 D4
  Old Stratford MK19 229 C7
  Stoke Bruerne NN12 205 A8
Canberra Ho NN17 22 F1
Candace Ct NN5 158 E8
Candleford NN3 143 B4
Candleford Cl NN13 233 E8
Candleford Ct NN13 233 E8
Canford Gn NN18 36 A6
Cannam Cl LE16 20 B1
Cannock Rd NN17 36 F8
Cannon St NN8 130 A5
Canonbury NN8 129 C4
Canon Harnett Ct MK12 229 F6
CANONS ASHBY 185 D2
Canons Ashby* NN11 185 D2
Canons Ashby Ct NN11 185 B5
Canons Ashby Rd NN11 199 D7
Canon St NN16 72 B3
Canons Wlk NN2 141 B4
Canterbury Cl OX16 219 A7
Cantle Cl NN18 36 D3
Capell Gdns NN18 36 E4
Capell Rise NN7 155 E5
Cappenham Cl NN12 203 B6
Captain's Ct NN7 177 E1
Cardigan Cl 4 NN5 158 F8
Cardigan Ho NN17 36 E6
Cardigan Pl
  Corby NN17 36 E5
  Kettering NN16 72 D2
Cardigan Rd NN14 37 E2
Cardinal Cl NN4 175 B7
Cares Orch NN7 161 D3
Carey Cl NN3 126 B1
Carey Ct NN3 126 B1
Carey Dr NN17 36 C8
Carey Ho 2 NN16 72 B2
Carey Rd
  Hackleton NN7 177 A3
  Towcester NN12 203 C3
Careys Rd NN12 215 F7
Carey St
  Kettering NN16 72 C2
  Northampton NN1 159 E7
Carey Way NN10 132 D3
Carina Rd NN15 91 C5
Carisbrooke Cl NN15 91 F8
Carline Ct NN3 142 D4
Carlisle Cl NN18 36 D1
Carlow Rd NN14 95 A3
Carlow St NN14 95 A3
Carlton Cl NN10 148 A7
Carlton Gdns NN2 141 E2
Carlton Mews NN10 132 C5
Carlton Pl NN18 36 B6
Carlton Rd
  Northampton NN2 141 E2
  Wilbarston LE16 34 D5
Carlton St NN16 72 A3
Carlyle Ave NN5 158 E7
Carmarthen Way NN10 148 C8
Carnegie St NN10 132 A2
Carne The MK11 229 E5
Caroline Chisholm Sch NN4 175 F5
Carol Trusler Mews NN2 159 B7
Carousel Way NN3 160 F7
Carpetbeggar & Northants Aviation Mus* NN6 68 F3
Carradale Cl NN16 72 A6
Carrdus Sch The OX17 219 C8
Carriage Dr NN16 72 C6
Carriers Cl MK19 207 A2
Carrington Gdns 1 NN3 160 F8
Carrington St NN16 72 B2
Carron Cl NN17 21 C1
Carr's Way NN7 157 C6
Carsington Cl NN16 71 E3
Carter Ave NN14 90 A3
Carter Cl NN8 130 B4
Cartmel Pl NN3 142 C3
Cartmel Way NN10 132 D3
Cartrill St NN9 114 C6
Cartwright Cres NN13 233 D7
Cartwright Gdns OX17 237 D7
Cartwright Rd
  Charlton OX17 231 F5
  Northampton NN2 141 C1
Casterbridge Ct NN4 175 E7
Casterton Cl NN9 114 A5
Castilian St NN1 159 D5
Castilian Terr NN1 159 D5
Castillion Ct NN1 159 D5
CASTLE ASHBY 163 A3
Castle Ashby Craft Ctr* NN7 162 F3
Castle Ashby Gdns* NN7 163 B3
Castle Ashby Rd NN7 179 B7
Castle Ashby Rural Shopping Yd* NN7 162 F3
Castle Ave NN5 158 C8
Castle Bush NN5 158 C8
Castle Cl
  Corby NN18 36 A4
  Northampton NN5 158 C8
Castle Ct
  Rushden NN10 148 A8
  Wellingborough NN8 130 B4
Castlefields Cl NN10 132 C6
Castle Gdns NN14 54 B3
CASTLE HILL 233 E5
Castle Hill
  Daventry NN11 135 B1
  Rothwell NN14 70 D7
Castle La NN8 130 B4
Castle Mews NN8 130 B4
Castle Mound CV23 99 C2
Castle Mount NN13 233 E5
Castle Prim Sch NN1 159 D7
Castle Rd
  Lavendon MK46 180 F1
  Wellingborough NN8 130 B4
  Woodford Halse NN11 184 C6
Castle St
  Deddington OX15 236 A4
  Northampton NN1 159 C6
  Wellingborough NN8 130 B4
CASTLETHORPE 218 F6
Castlethorpe Fst Sch MK19 218 F5
Castlethorpe Rd MK19 206 F1
Castleton Rd NN14 50 E4
Castle View
  Barnwell PE8 59 B7
  Wellingborough NN8 130 B4
Castle Way
  Kettering NN15 91 F6
  Wellingborough NN8 130 A4
Caswell Rd NN4 160 B1
Catchland Cl NN18 36 C2
Catchpole Cl NN18 36 D3
Catesby Cl NN2 141 E4
Catesby End NN11 151 D1
Catesby Rd NN14 70 E7
Catesby St NN16 72 C3
Catlow Cl NN9 114 C8
Catterick Cl NN18 36 E1
Cattle End
  Farthingstone NN12 170 F3
  Silverstone NN12 214 C3
Cattle Hill NN3 143 C2
Cattle Market Rd NN1 159 C4
Catton Cl NN6 85 B8
Catton Cres NN2 140 F5
Cauldecott Cl NN4 158 D1
Causeway Rd NN17 21 E2
Causeway The
  Byfield NN11 183 E8
  Northampton NN3 161 C7
Causin Cl NN14 55 F8
Causin Way PE8 40 C6
Cavalry Dr NN11 135 B1
Cavalry Fields NN7 155 A4
Cavalry Hill NN7 155 A4
Cavendish Cl NN15 91 F5
Cavendish Ctyd NN17 22 E1
Cavendish Dr NN3 160 D6
Cawley Rd OX17 230 B5
Caxton Cl NN11 135 A4
Caxton St LE16 31 F1
Caythorpe Sq NN18 36 B6
Cecil Cl NN18 36 E4
Cecil Dr NN18 36 F4
Cecil Rd NN2 141 C2
Cecil St
  Kettering NN16 72 C4
  Rothwell NN14 70 D7
Cedar Cl
  Brackley NN13 222 F2
  Daventry NN11 135 C5
  Desborough NN14 51 C2
  Irchester NN29 147 A7
  Rushden NN10 148 A8
  Sywell NN6 143 D8
  Towcester NN12 203 C4
Cedar Ct
  Corby NN17 21 E1
  Northampton NN5 158 E8
Cedar Dr NN14 76 D1
Cedar Gate NN3 142 C7
Cedar Hythe NN6 124 D1
Cedar Rd
  Kettering NN16 72 C4
  Northampton NN1, NN3 142 A1
Cedar Rd E NN3 142 A1
Cedar Road Prim Sch NN3 142 A1
Cedar Way
  Higham Ferrers NN10 132 B6
  Wellingborough NN8 130 A7
Cedrus Ct NN2 140 F6
Celandine Cl NN10 148 C7
Celeborn Pl NN3 143 B5
Celtic Cl NN10 132 B7
Celtic Way NN6 100 C6
Cemetery La NN10 132 B6
Centaine Rd NN10 132 A1
Centec Ct MK19 229 B7
Central Ave
  Hinton NN11 184 A7
  Kettering NN16 72 D3
  Northampton NN2 141 B6
  Wellingborough NN8 129 E2
Central Mus & Art Gall* NN1 159 D5
Centre 2000 NN16 71 F4
Centre Par NN16 72 D4
Centurion Way NN4 175 F5
Chace Rd NN8 130 C4
CHACOMBE 208 F4
Chacombe CE Prim Sch OX17 208 F4
Chacombe Ho OX17 208 E3
Chacombe House Mews OX17 208 E3
Chacombe Priory OX17 208 D4
Chacombe Rd OX17 208 F1
Chadleigh Ct NN13 233 E6
CHADSTONE 162 E2
Chadstone Ave NN2 141 D6
Chadwick Gdns NN5 140 D1
Chaffinch Cl NN4 174 F7
Chaffinch Way NN13 222 E1
Chainbridge Ct NN14 76 C2
Chainbridge La PE28 97 F1
Chalcombe Ave NN2 141 C5
Chalcombe Rd NN2 141 C4
Chalfont Ct 14 NN1 159 C7
Chalk La NN1 159 B6
Chalon Cl NN8 129 F8
Chamberlain Ave NN8 129 E1
Chamberlain Rd CV21 99 B8
Chamberlain Way
  Higham Ferrers NN10 132 C5
  Raunds NN9 114 C5
Chambers Hill NN14 89 B4
Chambers Row NN6 64 E6
Chambers The NN1 159 E6
Champion Ct NN13 233 E8
Chancel Terr PE8 59 B5
Chancery La NN14 76 D2
Chandler Gdns NN14 76 E1
Chandlers Way NN17 36 E5
Channing St 8 NN16 72 C2
Chantelle Ct 1 NN11 135 B3
Chantry Cl NN3 143 B3
Chantry La NN12 203 C6
Chantry Rise MK46 195 F3
CHAPEL BRAMPTON 124 E2
Chapel Cl
  Clifton OX15 236 E4
  Great Addington NN14 94 B2
  Litchborough NN12 171 C1
  Rushden NN10 132 C3
  Silverstone NN12 214 D4
Chapel Ct PE8 8 B2
CHAPEL END 44 D4
Chapel End
  Croughton NN13 238 C8
  Great Gidding PE28 61 D2
  Piddington NN7 177 A2
Chapel Farm NN7 206 C6
Chapel Fields LE17 62 B3
Chapel Gn NN5 141 A2
Chapel Hill
  Higham Ferrers NN10 132 B7
  Irchester NN29 147 B8
  Islip NN14 76 B2
  Little Addington NN14 113 B7
  Silverstone NN12 214 D4
Chapel Ho NN4 159 B3
Chapel La
  Adderbury OX17 230 A4
  Badby NN11 153 A3
  Barrowden LE15 3 F5
  Blisworth NN7 190 D8
  Brafield-on-t-G NN7 161 E2
  Clipston LE16 66 F8
  Corby NN17 37 B6
  Crick NN6 101 A5
  Daventry NN11 135 C2
  Denford NN14 95 C6
  Elton PE8 28 C8
  Farthinghoe NN13 221 B4
  Flore NN7 155 F5
  Geddington NN14 54 A2
  Great Doddington NN29 145 E6
  Hackleton NN7 177 B2
  Ketton PE9 1 A5
  Lilbourne CV23 81 A6
  Lillingstone Lovell MK18 227 A1
  Little Harrowden NN9 110 C4
  Maidford NN12 186 D6
  Old NN6 107 C7
  Rushton NN14 52 C2
  Slapton NN12 201 E2
  Stanion NN14 37 E2
  Stanwick NN9 114 A3
  Stoke Albany LE16 34 B4
  Stoke Bruerne NN12 205 A8
  Turweston NN13 234 B7
  Whitfield NN13 223 D3
  Wilbarston LE16 34 C5
Chapel Pl 1 NN1 159 E6
Chapel Rd
  Greatworth OX17 210 E1
  Weldon NN17 38 A8
Chapel Row
  Northampton NN3 143 C2
  Souldern OX27 237 E3
Chapel St
  Charwelton NN11 168 A4
  Kilsby CV23 100 A2
  Ringstead NN14 95 A3
  Swinford LE17 62 B3
  Titchmarsh NN14 77 C4
  Warmington PE8 28 B3
Chapel View NN14 90 B5
Chaplins La NN14 51 A3
Chapman Cl NN12 203 C7
Chapman Gr NN17 36 E8
Chapmans Cl
  Irchester NN29 147 B8
  Stoke Albany LE16 34 B4
Chapmans Ct 11 NN16 72 C2
Chapmans Dr MK19 229 B7
Chapmans La OX15 236 A3
Chappell Ho 5 NN3 126 C1
Chardonnay Cl NN5 140 A2
Chariot Rd NN4 175 F5
Charity Cotts MK19 229 E2
Charlbury Cl NN8 145 E8
Charles Cl
  Higham Ferrers NN10 132 C7
  Long Buckby NN6 121 B3
  Old NN6 107 D7
Charlesfield Rd CV22 98 A8
Charles Robinson Ct NN8 129 E3
Charles St
  Corby NN17 36 F5
  Kettering NN16 72 B4
  Market Harborough LE16 31 D3
  Northampton NN1 159 D7
  Rothwell NN14 70 C6
  Thrapston NN14 76 E2
  Wellingborough NN8 129 E2
Charles Terr 8 NN11 135 C1
Charlotte Pl NN16 72 E4
Charlottes Row 6 NN10 132 A2
CHARLTON 231 F4
Charlton Cl NN2 141 C5
Charlton Rd OX17 237 C7
Charlton Way NN13 221 B4
Charnwood 1 NN8 130 A5
Charnwood Ave NN3 142 E2
Charnwood Cl 5 NN11 135 B4
Charnwood Ct NN3 142 E2
Charnwood Dr NN15 92 A5
Charnwood Rd NN17 36 F7
Charter Ct NN18 36 D2
Charter Gate NN3 142 B6
Charterhouse Cl NN13 233 E7
Charter Rd CV22 98 E8
Chartwell Ave NN3 142 C5
Chartwell Cl 13 NN11 135 B7
CHARWELTON 168 B5
Charwelton La NN11 167 D8

Charwelton Rd NN11 ... 169 C2
Chase Barn Cotts
OX27 ... 239 B3
Chase Cl NN14 ... 37 E3
Chase Farm NN14 ... 54 B2
Chase Hill NN14 ... 54 A3
Chase Park Rd NN7 ... 179 A5
Chaseport Cl MK46 ... 194 D2
Chase The
Long Buckby NN6 ... 121 B4
Pitsford NN6 ... 125 D4
Chase View Rd NN14 ... 54 B3
Chaston Pl NN16 ... 72 E5
Chatellerault Ct NN17 ... 36 D8
Chater Cl LE16 ... 32 A6
Chater La PE9 ... 1 A7
Chater Mews PE9 ... 1 A7
Chater St NN3 ... 126 D1
Chatsworth Ave
Kettering NN15 ... 91 C5
Northampton NN3 ... 142 F5
Chatsworth Dr
Market Harborough
LE16 ... 32 B3
Wellingborough NN8 ... 129 C7
Chatsworth Rd NN18 ... 36 D1
Chaucer Ct NN2 ... 141 F1
Chaucer Ho NN2 ... 141 F2
Chaucer Rd
Rugby CV22 ... 98 A7
Wellingborough NN8 ... 129 D4
Chaucer St NN2 ... 141 F1
Chaucer Way NN11 ... 135 B2
Cheaney Dr NN4 ... 175 E2
Cheddar Cl NN5 ... 158 D7
Cheddar Wlk NN18 ... 36 A6
Chedington Cl NN15 ... 92 A5
Chedworth Cl NN3 ... 143 D2
Cheese La [5] NN8 ... 130 A4
Chelfham Cl NN3 ... 160 D7
Chelmorton Vale NN14 ... 50 E4
Chelmscote Row
OX17 ... 208 F8
Chelmsford Cl NN4 ... 159 A2
Cheltenham Cl NN10 ... 148 C8
Cheltenham Rd NN18 ... 36 E1
CHELVESTON ... 133 C8
Chelveston Cres NN9 ... 133 D5
Chelveston Dr NN17 ... 36 B7
Chelveston Rd
Higham Ferrers NN10 ... 132 E7
Raunds NN9 ... 114 C4
Stanwick NN9 ... 114 B3
Chenderit Sch OX17 ... 209 A1
Cheney Ct OX17 ... 208 F1
Cheney Gdns OX17 ... 208 F2
Chepstow Cl
Kettering NN15 ... 91 F8
Northampton NN5 ... 159 A7
Chepstow Dr NN8 ... 129 C7
Chepstow Rd
Corby NN18 ... 36 D1
Corby NN18 ... 36 E1
Chequers Cl NN18 ... 36 E2
Chequers La
Grendon NN7 ... 163 E5
Ravensthorpe NN6 ... 103 D1
Wellingborough NN8 ... 130 A5
Chequers The MK19 ... 218 F5
Cheriton Cl NN11 ... 135 C6
Cheriton Rd NN18 ... 36 F4
Cheriton Way NN1 ... 160 C6
Cherradene Ct NN9 ... 114 D6
Cherry Ave NN8 ... 130 A7
Cherry Blossom Cl
NN3 ... 143 B2
Cherry Cl NN3 ... 142 C2
Cherry Ct NN9 ... 112 E1
Cherry Hill NN6 ... 107 E6
Cherry Lodge Rd NN3 ... 143 B3
Cherry Orch
Olney MK46 ... 195 E4
Rushden NN10 ... 132 C1
Cherry Rd NN16 ... 72 D4
Cherry St
Irthlingborough NN9 ... 112 E1
Ringstead NN14 ... 95 B3
Cherry Tree Cl
Desborough NN14 ... 51 B2
Husbands Bosworth
LE17 ... 45 E5
Cherry Tree La NN4 ... 160 E3
Cherrytree Wlk NN6 ... 143 D8
Cherry Wlk NN9 ... 114 B5
Cherwell Banks OX17 ... 231 A6
Cherwell Gn NN5 ... 140 F1
Cherwell Terr NN11 ... 184 C6
Cherwell The NN11 ... 134 F1
Cherwell Wlk NN17 ... 21 C1
Chesham Rise NN3 ... 143 B4
Chesil Wlk NN18 ... 36 A6
Chester Ave NN7 ... 157 B6
Chester Ct NN15 ... 91 B6
Chester Ho NN3 ... 161 B8
Chester Rd
Irchester NN29 ... 131 A1
Rushden NN10 ... 131 F2
Wellingborough NN8 ... 130 C4
Chestnut Ave
Corby NN17 ... 21 D1
Kettering NN15 ... 72 C1
Northampton NN4 ... 175 D5
Chestnut Cl
Hinton NN11 ... 184 A6
Long Buckby NN6 ... 121 B3
Milton Malsor NN7 ... 174 E4
Rushden NN10 ... 131 F3
Stony Stratford MK11 ... 229 D5
Chestnut Cl *continued*
Wymington NN10 ... 148 B5
Chestnut Ct
Northampton NN3 ... 142 A2
Raunds NN9 ... 114 D7
Chestnut Dr
Brackley NN13 ... 222 F1
Desborough NN14 ... 51 C2
Thrapston NN14 ... 76 D1
Chestnut Gn NN13 ... 223 E4
Chestnut Gr LE16 ... 67 A8
Chestnut Rd
Northampton NN3 ... 142 A1
Yardley Gobion NN12 ... 217 F6
Chestnuts The
Castlethorpe MK19 ... 218 F5
Clifton OX15 ... 236 E4
Hinton-in-t-H NN13 ... 232 F6
Chestnut Terr NN3 ... 142 A2
Chettle Pl NN12 ... 217 E2
Chetwode OX17 ... 219 C6
Cheviot Cl NN16 ... 72 B7
Cheviot Ct NN4 ... 158 E3
Cheviot Ho NN2 ... 141 C5
Chewton Cl NN5 ... 158 D7
Cheyne Wlk
Kettering NN15 ... 91 E8
Northampton NN1 ... 159 E5
Chichele Cl NN10 ... 132 B5
Chichele Coll* NN10 ... 132 B6
Chichele Ct NN10 ... 132 B3
Chichele St NN10 ... 132 C6
Chicheley Cotts NN14 ... 76 D2
Chichester Cl
[1] Daventry NN11 ... 135 D1
Rothwell NN14 ... 70 E6
Chieftan Bsns Pk
NN8 ... 129 A6
Child's St NN14 ... 95 C6
Chiltern Ave NN5 ... 158 D8
Chiltern Cl
Market Harborough
LE16 ... 31 F5
Northampton NN5 ... 158 D8
Chiltern Ct [3] NN10 ... 132 A2
Chiltern Prim Sch
NN5 ... 158 E8
Chiltern Rd
Daventry NN11 ... 135 B5
Kettering NN16 ... 72 B6
Chiltern Way NN5 ... 158 E8
Chilwell Ct [3] NN3 ... 160 F8
CHIPPING WARDEN ... 196 F6
Chipping Warden Sch
OX17 ... 196 F7
Chipsey Ave
Bugbrooke NN7 ... 172 F8
Northampton NN1 ... 160 B6
Chisholm Cl NN4 ... 175 F5
Choakles The NN4 ... 176 B6
Chowns Mill Bsns Pk
NN9 ... 113 B1
Christchurch Dr
NN11 ... 153 B7
Christchurch Rd NN1 ... 160 A7
Christie Way NN15 ... 90 F8
Christine Ct NN9 ... 114 D6
Christopher Ct NN6 ... 64 D5
Christopher Rawlins CE
Prim Sch OX17 ... 230 A4
Christopher Reeves Lower
Sch NN29 ... 147 E1
Chulmleigh Wlk NN3 ... 160 C7
Church Ave OX17 ... 230 F5
Church Bank LE16 ... 20 D7
CHURCH BRAMPTON
... 140 C8
CHURCH CHARWELTON
... 168 C3
Church Cl
Adderbury OX17 ... 230 A3
Braybrooke LE16 ... 49 E6
Caldecott LE16 ... 21 B8
Clipston LE16 ... 67 A8
Hartwell NN7 ... 192 D2
Milton Malsor NN7 ... 174 F4
Wardington OX17 ... 196 E1
West Haddon NN6 ... 102 C5
Wicken MK19 ... 228 B3
Wymington NN10 ... 148 B5
Churchcroft NN7 ... 191 D4
Church Dr NN18 ... 53 C8
CHURCH END ... 183 D7
Church End NN13 ... 238 D8
CHURCH END ... 207 A2
Church End
Piddington NN7 ... 177 A2
Potterspury NN12 ... 217 E3
Roade NN7 ... 191 D4
Syresham NN13 ... 224 C8
Church Farm Cl
NN29 ... 164 D3
Church Farm Way
LE16 ... 68 C7
Churchfield Cl NN2 ... 141 E4
Church Fields NN11 ... 152 C7
Church Gdns NN6 ... 103 E1
Church Gn
Badby NN11 ... 153 A2
Barnwell PE8 ... 59 B6
Northampton NN5 ... 140 F2
Woodford NN14 ... 94 D6
Church Hall Rd NN10 ... 131 F1
Church Hill
Badby NN11 ... 152 F2
Barnwell PE8 ... 59 B6
Finedon NN9 ... 111 E4
Geddington NN14 ... 54 A3
Church Hill *continued*
Hollowell NN6 ... 104 B4
Moulton NN3 ... 126 C1
Northampton NN4 ... 175 E6
Ravensthorpe NN6 ... 103 D1
Churchill Ave
Irthlingborough NN9 ... 113 B5
Northampton NN3 ... 142 B4
Wellingborough NN8 ... 129 E7
Churchill Cl NN14 ... 70 E7
Churchill Rd
Earls Barton NN6 ... 144 F4
Welton NN11 ... 135 E8
Churchill Way
Brackley NN13 ... 233 F6
Burton Latimer NN15 ... 92 B2
Daventry NN11 ... 153 E7
Kettering NN15 ... 72 F1
Church La
Adderbury OX17 ... 230 A3
Alderton NN12 ... 204 F2
Barnwell PE8 ... 59 B6
Barrowden LE15 ... 3 F4
Blisworth NN7 ... 190 D7
Bozeat NN29 ... 164 D3
Brafield-on-t-G NN7 ... 161 E2
Broughton NN14 ... 89 F6
Bugbrooke NN7 ... 172 E7
Burton Latimer NN15 ... 92 C2
Bythorn PE28 ... 97 D4
Caldecott LE16 ... 21 B8
Chacombe OX17 ... 208 E4
Church Brampton NN6 ... 140 B8
Claydon OX17 ... 181 D1
Clipston LE16 ... 67 A8
Cold Ashby NN6 ... 84 A5
Cold Higham NN12 ... 188 C8
Covington PE18 ... 116 C2
Cranford St John NN14 ... 93 B7
Croughton NN13 ... 238 D8
Deanshanger MK19 ... 228 E4
Denford NN14 ... 95 C6
Dingley LE16 ... 33 A4
Duddington PE9 ... 5 B6
East Carlton LE16 ... 34 F7
East Carlton LE16 ... 35 A7
East Haddon NN6 ... 122 D4
Evenley NN13 ... 233 F3
Grafton Regis NN12 ... 205 D2
Great Doddington
NN29 ... 145 E6
Harlestone NN7 ... 139 E6
Harrington NN6 ... 69 B6
Hellidon NN11 ... 151 C1
Husbands Bosworth
LE17 ... 45 E5
Kislingbury NN7 ... 157 D3
Lillingstone Lovell
MK18 ... 227 A6
Lyddington LE15 ... 9 D6
Maidford NN12 ... 186 D6
Middleton Cheney
OX17 ... 208 F1
Morcott LE15 ... 3 A6
Nether Heyford NN7 ... 156 B2
Newton Bromswold
NN10 ... 149 D8
Northampton, Bellinge
NN3 ... 161 A8
Northampton NN1 ... 159 C6
Pitsford NN6 ... 125 D5
Potterspury NN12 ... 217 E3
Slapton NN12 ... 201 E2
Slipton NN14 ... 75 A3
South Kilworth LE17 ... 63 C8
South Luffenham LE15 ... 3 E8
Spratton NN6 ... 105 B1
Stanford on A NN6 ... 62 F2
Stibbington PE8 ... 8 D2
Stoke Bruerne NN12 ... 205 A8
Stoke Doyle PE8 ... 41 D1
Sywell NN6 ... 127 E3
Thornby NN6 ... 84 D4
Thorpe Langton LE16 ... 17 A5
Walgrave NN6 ... 108 A4
Warmington PE8 ... 28 B3
Welford NN6 ... 64 E5
Wicken MK19 ... 228 B3
Wilby NN8 ... 129 B1
Wollaston NN29 ... 146 D3
Wymington NN10 ... 148 B5
Yardley Hastings NN7 ... 179 B7
Yelden MK44 ... 133 F3
Church Leys NN13 ... 233 E3
Church Mount NN6 ... 103 F6
Church Piece Cotts
NN13 ... 221 B4
Church Pk PE8 ... 7 D8
Church Rd
Brackley NN13 ... 233 F7
Braunston NN11 ... 118 B1
Greatworth OX17 ... 210 E1
Hargrave NN9 ... 115 F1
Ketton PE9 ... 1 A5
Piddington NN7 ... 177 A2
Pytchley NN14 ... 91 A1
Spratton NN6 ... 124 B8
Upper Boddington
NN11 ... 182 C7
Church Row PE8 ... 42 F3
Church Sq [6] LE16 ... 31 E3
Church St
Blakesley NN12 ... 187 B1
Boughton NN2 ... 141 C8
Brigstock NN14 ... 55 F7
Brixworth NN6 ... 106 B3
Broughton NN14 ... 90 B4
Burton Latimer NN15 ... 92 C3
Church St *continued*
Byfield NN11 ... 183 D7
Charwelton NN11 ... 168 B4
Clifton u D CV23 ... 80 A5
Cogenhoe NN7 ... 162 A6
Cottingham LE16 ... 20 D1
Crick NN6 ... 100 F6
Easton o t H PE9 ... 2 A6
Finedon NN9 ... 111 E4
Hargrave NN9 ... 115 E2
Helmdon NN13 ... 211 F3
Husbands Bosworth
LE17 ... 45 E5
Irthlingborough NN9 ... 112 F2
Isham NN14 ... 91 F1
Long Buckby NN6 ... 121 B4
Market Harborough LE16 ... 31 E3
Mears Ashby NN6 ... 128 B2
Moulton NN3 ... 126 C1
Naseby NN6 ... 85 B8
Nassington PE8 ... 15 F5
Nether Heyford NN7 ... 156 B2
Newnham NN11 ... 153 E4
Olney MK46 ... 195 F3
Oundle PE8 ... 42 A5
Pattishall NN12 ... 172 E1
Polebrook PE8 ... 42 F3
Raunds NN9 ... 114 E7
Ringstead NN14 ... 95 B3
Rothersthorpe NN7 ... 174 A6
Rushden NN10 ... 132 B2
Sibbertoft LE16 ... 47 A2
Silverstone NN12 ... 214 D5
Stanwick NN9 ... 114 A3
Staverton NN11 ... 152 C7
Stony Stratford MK11 ... 229 D5
Sulgrave OX17 ... 210 F7
Titchmarsh NN14 ... 77 C4
Wadenhoe PE8 ... 58 A3
Warmington PE8 ... 28 B2
Watford NN6 ... 120 C6
Weedon Bec NN7 ... 155 C3
Weldon NN17 ... 38 B7
Wellingborough NN8 ... 130 A4
Wilbarston LE16 ... 34 C5
Woodford Halse NN11 ... 184 C6
Woodford NN14 ... 94 D6
CHURCH STOWE ... 171 D8
Church View
Brackley NN13 ... 234 A7
Broughton NN14 ... 90 A4
Burton Latimer NN15 ... 92 C3
Ecton NN6 ... 143 F4
Greens Norton NN12 ... 202 E8
Keyston PE28 ... 97 A3
Moulton NN3 ... 126 C2
Northampton NN4 ... 175 E5
Raunds NN9 ... 114 D7
Walgrave NN6 ... 108 A5
Weldon NN17 ... 38 B7
Church View Rd NN14 ... 51 B2
Churchway NN3 ... 160 D8
Church Way
Denton NN7 ... 178 B8
Ecton NN6 ... 143 F4
Grendon NN7 ... 163 D5
Northampton NN3 ... 160 E7
Preston Capes NN11 ... 169 D2
Thorpe Malsor NN14 ... 71 A3
[1] Wellingborough
NN8 ... 130 A4
Whittlebury NN12 ... 215 C5
Church Way Ct NN3 ... 160 D8
Church Wlk
Barby CV23 ... 99 C1
Bozeat NN29 ... 164 D3
Corby NN17 ... 37 B6
Daventry NN11 ... 135 C2
Denford NN14 ... 95 C6
[5] Irthlingborough
NN9 ... 112 F2
Kettering NN16 ... 72 B2
Kilsby CV23 ... 100 A3
King's Cliffe PE8 ... 13 E7
Little Addington NN14 ... 113 B8
Lubenham LE16 ... 30 F3
Market Harborough
LE16 ... 32 A2
Newton Bromswold
NN10 ... 149 D8
Northampton NN3 ... 143 B2
Ringstead NN14 ... 95 B3
Weldon NN17 ... 38 B7
Cider Cl LE15 ... 3 F5
Cinnamon Cl [5] NN4 ... 175 D6
Circus End NN5 ... 140 C1
Circus Gr PE8 ... 42 F2
Cirrus Pk NN3 ... 142 A7
Cissbury Rd NN4 ... 158 F4
Clailey Ct MK11 ... 229 F5
Clannell Rd NN4 ... 175 A8
Clare Ave NN11 ... 135 C2
Clare Cl NN6 ... 144 F3
Clare Cres NN12 ... 203 B5
Clare Dr NN14 ... 76 E3
Claregate NN4 ... 175 B8
Claremont Ave MK11 ... 229 E4
Claremont Ct [13] NN1 ... 159 C6
Claremont Dr LE16 ... 32 A3
Clarence Ave NN2 ... 141 C2
Clarence Ct NN10 ... 148 A8
Clarence Rd
Kettering NN16 ... 72 C3
Stony Stratford MK11 ... 229 E5
Clarence St LE16 ... 31 F3
Clare Rd NN8 ... 129 C3
Clare St
Northampton NN1 ... 159 E7
Clare St *continued*
Raunds NN9 ... 114 D6
Clare Wlk NN10 ... 132 B5
Clark Cres NN12 ... 203 C8
Clarke Cl
Kettering NN16 ... 72 A4
Little Addington NN9 ... 113 B4
Clarke Ct NN6 ... 144 F4
Clarke Ho NN1 ... 160 A8
Clarke Rd
Corby NN17 ... 36 D8
Northampton NN1 ... 160 A8
Clarkes Dale LE16 ... 20 D6
Clarke St LE16 ... 31 D3
Clarkes Way
Brackley NN13 ... 233 D7
Welton NN11 ... 135 D8
Clarks La NN13 ... 221 A3
Claudius Way NN8 ... 130 E2
Claughton Rd NN4 ... 159 D3
CLAY COTON ... 82 A6
CLAYDON ... 181 D1
Claydon Cl NN8 ... 129 E5
Clayfield Cl NN3 ... 142 B6
Clay La NN17 ... 10 B1
Clayland Cl NN29 ... 164 C2
Claylands The NN7 ... 161 E6
Clay Pit La MK46 ... 195 F3
Claystones NN4 ... 158 D2
Clearway House Ind Est
OX16 ... 219 A7
Cleaver Ct NN15 ... 72 A1
Cleavers La NN6 ... 107 D7
Cleburne Cl NN9 ... 114 A4
Clee Rise NN5 ... 158 D8
Cleeve Way NN8 ... 129 D1
Clement Bois NN13 ... 233 E8
Clevedon Ct [1] NN11 ... 135 B7
Cleveland Ave NN16 ... 72 C6
Cleveland Pl NN4 ... 159 A2
Clickers Dr NN5 ... 158 D4
Clickers Pl NN5 ... 158 C4
Clickers Yd MK46 ... 195 F4
Clifden Terr NN6 ... 122 D4
Cliffe Rd PE9 ... 2 A3
CLIFTON ... 236 D4
Clifton Cl
Kettering NN15 ... 72 C1
Long Buckby NN6 ... 121 C4
Clifton Dr PE8 ... 41 E5
Clifton Gr NN15 ... 72 C1
Clifton Rd OX15 ... 236 B4
Clifton Sq NN17 ... 36 E8
CLIFTON UPON
DUNSMORE ... 80 A6
Cliftonville NN1 ... 159 E5
Cliftonville Ct [11] NN1 ... 159 F6
Cliftonville Rd NN1 ... 159 F5
Clinton Rd NN4 ... 159 B3
CLIPSTON ... 66 F8
Clipstone Ct NN14 ... 70 C6
Clipston Endowed Prim
Sch LE16 ... 67 A8
Clipston Field Pl [7]
NN3 ... 143 C2
Clipston La LE16 ... 48 E3
Clipston Rd
East Farndon LE16 ... 48 B4
Great Oxendon LE16 ... 48 D2
Clipston St LE16 ... 31 F1
Clipston Way NN5 ... 140 D1
Clive Cl NN15 ... 72 E1
Clock Mdw NN11 ... 183 C7
Clock Tower Ct NN3 ... 142 E6
Cloisters The
Daventry NN11 ... 135 D2
Priors Hardwick CV47 ... 166 A5
Rushden NN10 ... 132 B2
Wellingborough NN8 ... 130 B3
CLOPTON ... 78 E5
Close Rd NN7 ... 156 B1
Close The
Chipping Warden
OX17 ... 196 F6
Eastcote NN12 ... 188 F8
Easton o t H PE9 ... 1 F4
Greatworth OX17 ... 210 E1
Irthlingborough NN9 ... 112 F1
Kettering NN15 ... 91 B8
Northampton NN2 ... 141 C4
Roade NN7 ... 191 D4
Swinford LE17 ... 62 B4
Weston Underwood
MK46 ... 195 A1
Cloutsham St NN1 ... 159 E7
Clovelly Ct NN18 ... 36 F4
Clover Dr
Rushden NN10 ... 148 C8
Thrapston NN14 ... 76 D2
Clover Field NN4 ... 175 F2
Clover Gdns NN16 ... 72 B4
Clover La NN2 ... 141 B5
Club La NN14 ... 94 D6
Club St NN16 ... 72 C3
Clumber Ct NN18 ... 36 B6
Clumber Dr NN3 ... 160 E7
Clun Wlk NN17 ... 21 C1
Clwyd Wlk NN17 ... 21 C1
Clydesdale Rd NN17 ... 36 D7
Coach Ho The NN3 ... 160 B7
Coaching Wlk NN3 ... 142 D2
Coach Yd NN12 ... 217 E3
Coales Gdns LE16 ... 31 D5
Coalport Cl NN14 ... 50 F3
Cobblers Cl NN12 ... 187 B1

Cobbler's Pl NN29 164 D2
Cobblestone Ct NN4 158 D2
Cobbs Gdn MK46 195 F4
Cobb's La NN29 146 D3
Cobden St NN16 72 A3
Cob Dr NN4 158 B1
Cobley Cl NN11 184 D6
Cockbrook La PE28 79 C2
Cockerell Rd NN17 37 B8
Cockerill's Mdw CV21 99 A8
Cockley Rd NN13 221 C6
Codlin Cl NN3 143 B1
Coffee Tavern La [9] NN10 132 B2
Cofferidge Cl MK11 229 D5
Cogan Cres NN14 70 B6
COGENHOE 161 E5
Cogenhoe Mill Cvn Cite NN7 162 A7
Cogenhoe Prim Sch NN7 161 F5
Coggins Cl NN9 114 C6
COLD ASHBY 84 B5
Cold Ashby Rd
 Guilsborough NN6 103 E7
 Thornby NN6 84 D4
Coldermeadow Ave NN18 36 A3
COLD HIGHAM 188 C8
Coldstream Cl NN11 135 B1
Coldstream La NN4 175 E8
Cole Ct
 Kettering NN16 72 B4
 Raunds NN9 114 C5
Coleman Cl NN6 101 A6
Coleman St NN9 114 D6
Coleraine Cl NN2 141 A5
Coleridge Way NN17 36 C8
Coleridge Wlk NN11 135 B4
Coles Cl NN15 92 B2
Coles Rise NN13 233 D7
Cole St NN10 131 E4
College Field Cl NN3 143 C3
College Fields OX17 237 C7
College Grounds The NN3 126 B1
College Rd CV23 117 E3
College St Mews [28] NN1 159 C6
College St
 Higham Ferrers NN10 132 C6
 Irthlingborough NN9 112 F2
 Northampton NN1 159 C6
 Rushden NN10 132 B2
 Wellingborough NN8 129 E4
 Wollaston NN29 146 D2
Colley Rise LE15 9 C7
Collingcroft Cl NN4 175 A7
Collingdale Rd NN3 142 D2
Collingham Cl NN9 114 A5
COLLINGTREE 175 B4
Collingtree CE Prim Sch NN4 175 C4
Collingtree Ct NN4 175 B3
COLLINGTREE PARK 175 C5
Collingtree Rd NN4, NN7 175 A4
Collingwood Ave NN17 36 A7
Collingwood Bsns Ctr NN1 159 C6
Collingwood Rd NN1 141 F1
Collingwood Way NN11 135 E3
Collins Cl NN12 203 C7
Collins Hill NN7 155 E6
Collins St NN1 159 F7
Collmead Ct NN3 143 B4
Collswell La NN12 187 B1
Collyns Way PE9 1 D2
COLLYWESTON 1 D2
Collyweston Cross Rds PE8 6 A6
Collyweston Rd NN3 143 C5
Colmar Cl NN11 135 A4
Colne Cl NN17 21 C1
Colne Way NN5 140 E1
Colonial Dr NN4 175 C5
Colseed Rd NN14 89 B4
Colsons Way MK46 195 F5
Coltsfoot Rd NN10 148 C7
Columbus Cres NN14 70 E6
Columbus Ct NN11 135 B5
Colwell Rd NN8 130 C4
Colwyn Rd NN1 159 E8
Colyers Ave NN18 36 B3
Comfrey Cl NN10 148 B7
Commercial Rd
 Corby NN17 37 B6
 Kettering NN16 72 B2
Commercial St
 Higham Ferrers NN10 132 B5
 Northampton NN1 159 C5
Commercial Way NN8 130 A4
Common St MK46 194 D1
Compton Gn NN18 36 A6
Compton Ho NN1 159 B6
Compton Pl NN16 72 E2
Compton Rd NN8 130 C5
Compton St
 Desborough NN14 51 A3
 Northampton NN1 159 B6
Compton Way NN6 144 E3
Coneygree NN4 175 F8
Coneygree Ct NN3 143 B1
Coneywell Ct NN3 142 F1
Conifer Rise NN3 142 E1
Coniston Ave NN3 142 B3
Coniston Cl
 Daventry NN11 135 B2
 Higham Ferrers NN10 132 B8
 Wellingborough NN8 129 C5
Coniston Rd NN16 71 F2
Connaught Rd LE16 31 F4
Connaught St
 Kettering NN16 72 D3
 Northampton NN1 159 D7
Connegar Leys NN7 190 E7
Connell Cl LE16 30 F3
Connell Ct NN17 36 F5
Connolly Cl NN14 70 F7
Connolly Dr NN14 70 F7
Connolly Rd NN5 157 F8
Constable Dr
 Kettering NN15 92 A7
 Wellingborough NN8 129 F7
Constable Rd
 Corby NN18 36 E5
 Rugby CV21 80 B1
Constable Wlk NN14 94 D7
Conway Cl
 Northampton NN5 140 E2
 Rushden NN10 148 A8
 Wellingborough NN8 129 C6
Conway Dr
 Burton Latimer NN15 92 B2
 Thrapston NN14 76 F2
Conway Wlk NN17 21 D1
Conyngham Rd NN3 142 F2
Cony Wlk NN4 175 F3
Cook Cl
 Daventry NN11 135 C5
 Rothwell NN14 70 E6
Cooks Cl NN7 205 F8
Cooks Rd NN17 37 F8
Cook's Terr NN6 121 A3
Cook's Way NN6 121 A3
Coomb Rd NN18 36 D1
Co-operative Row NN10 132 B1
Cooper Cl NN12 203 C8
Cooper Ct NN14 76 D1
Cooper Dr NN8 129 F8
Copelands Rd NN14 51 C3
Copenhagen Rd NN18 36 A1
Copperfield Cl NN16 72 C6
Copper Leaf Cl NN3 142 C6
Coppertree Wlk NN14 76 D1
Coppice Cl
 Burton Latimer NN15 92 C4
 Daventry NN11 153 C8
Coppice Dr NN3 142 A5
Coppice The NN14 76 D1
Copse Cl
 Burton Latimer NN15 92 C3
 Northampton NN2 140 F5
Copymoor Cl NN4 176 A6
Cora Rd NN16 72 E4
Corbieres Cl NN5 140 A2
CORBY 36 E3
Corby Com Coll NN17 36 F6
Corby Com Hospl NN17 36 D6
Corby Gate NN17 22 F1
Corby Gate Bsns Pk NN17 22 F1
Corby Rd
 Cottingham LE16 35 E8
 Gretton NN17 22 B6
 Stanion NN14 37 E3
 Weldon NN17 38 A7
Cordon Cl NN3 143 B3
Cordon Cres NN6 144 F4
Cordwainer Gr NN14 76 D1
Cordwainer Ho NN5 159 A5
Cordwainers NN10 132 C1
Corfe Cl NN18 36 E2
Corner Cl NN29 147 E1
Cornfield Cl NN2 141 B5
Cornfield Way NN15 92 C1
Cornflower Cl NN4 175 F2
Cornhill Cl NN5 140 C3
Corn Kiln Cl NN7 161 F6
Corn La [7] NN8 130 A4
Cornwall Cl NN17 36 C6
Cornwall Rd NN16 72 D3
Cornwell Bsns Pk NN4 160 B2
Coronation Ave
 Rothwell NN14 70 D7
 Rushden NN10 131 E1
Coronation Cres PE8 39 E7
Coronation Rd
 Newnham NN11 153 D4
 Stony Stratford MK11 229 E5
Corporation St NN17 36 E6
Corran Cl NN5 158 E8
Cory Gdns NN7 157 C7
COSGROVE 218 D2
Cosgrove L Pk★ MK19 218 F1
Cosgrove Rd
 Northampton NN2 141 C5
 Old Stratford MK19 229 C7
Cosgrove Village Prim Sch MK19 218 E2
Cosgrove Way NN2 141 C5
Cosy Nook NN14 76 C2
COTON 103 E4
Coton Manor Gdns★ NN6 103 E4
Coton Rd
 Guilsborough NN6 103 F5
 Ravensthorpe NN6 103 E1
 Rugby CV21 80 A1
Cotswold Ave
 Kettering NN16 72 B5
 Northampton NN5 158 D8
Cotswold Cl NN11 135 B5
Cotswold Ct OX27 237 E3
Cotswold Dr NN8 129 D1
Cottage Cl NN2 141 A4
Cottage Gdns
 Northampton NN3 143 B3
 Rushden NN10 148 C7
Cottages The NN13 224 C5
Cottagewell Ct NN3 142 F1
COTTARVILLE 142 D1
Cottarville NN3 142 D1
COTTERSTOCK 27 A2
Cotterstock Rd PE8 41 F7
COTTESBROOKE 104 F8
Cottesbrooke Gdns NN4 175 D7
Cottesbrooke Grange NN6 105 A8
Cottesbrooke Hall★ NN6 105 A8
Cottesbrooke Hall Gdns★ NN6 105 A8
Cottesbrooke Pk NN11 135 A5
Cottesbrooke Rd NN17 36 B7
Cottesloe Ct MK11 229 F5
Cottesmore Ave NN15 92 A5
Cottesmore Cl NN5 140 B1
Cottesmore Way NN8 129 D4
COTTINGHAM 20 D1
Cottingham CE Prim Sch LE16 20 C1
Cottingham Dr NN3 142 B7
Cottingham Rd
 Corby NN17 36 E6
 Corby NN18 36 B7
 Rockingham LE16 21 A4
Cottingham Way NN14 76 C2
COTTISFORD 239 E3
COTTON END 159 C4
Cotton End
 Long Buckby NN6 121 D4
 Northampton NN4 159 C4
Cotton Mdw NN5 158 E7
Cottons The
 Rockingham LE16 21 B4
 Wellingborough NN8 129 D7
Coulon Cl NN29 147 A7
Coulthard Cl NN12 203 D8
Council Hos
 Farthingstone NN12 170 E3
 Guilsborough NN6 103 F7
 Hannington NN6 108 C3
 Podington NN29 147 E1
Council Ho's LE16 48 B8
Council Hos The
 Long Buckby Wharf NN6 136 E7
 Upper Wardington OX17 208 F8
Council Houses NN6 106 F6
Council St
 Bozeat NN29 164 D4
 Wollaston NN29 146 D2
Countess Ct NN5 159 A7
Countess Rd NN5 159 A7
Countryman Mews LE16 32 A5
Countryside NN11 118 B1
Counts Farm Rd NN18 36 F4
County Rd NN13 234 A6
County View OX15 236 D4
Courier Rd NN17 37 B8
Court Cnr MK46 195 E4
Court Dr NN16 72 B6
COURTEENHALL 191 E7
Courteenhall Cl NN2 141 D5
Courteenhall Rd NN7 191 A7
Court House Cl NN6 104 F4
Court La NN6 64 D3
Courtman Rd NN9 114 A4
Court Mews NN8 130 B4
Courtney Rd NN10 132 A1
Court Rd [11] NN1 159 C5
Courtwood NN9 114 A3
Courtyard La NN11 153 A3
Courtyard The
 Ecton NN6 143 F4
 Islip NN14 76 B3
 [4] Kettering NN16 72 C3
 Middleton Cheney OX17 219 D5
 Northampton NN3 142 C1
Courtyard Workshops LE16 31 E1
Coventry Rd LE16 31 D3
Coverack Cl NN4 159 B1
Coverdale NN2 140 F5
Covert Cl NN2 141 A6
COVINGTON 116 D2
Covington Gr NN8 130 A6
Covington St NN1 160 A7
Cowbeck Cl NN4 175 E5
Cowgill Cl NN3 143 B3
Cowley Cl NN4 175 D6
Cowley Rd NN11 135 B3
Cowley Way CV23 99 F2
Cowper Cl
 Earls Barton NN6 145 A4
 Irthlingborough NN9 112 D1
Cowper Factory NN1 159 E7
Cowper & Newton Mus The★ MK46 195 F3
Cowper Rd
 Daventry NN11 135 B2
 Wellingborough NN8 129 C4
Cowpers Orch MK46 195 A1
Cowper St
 Kettering NN16 72 B4
 Northampton NN1 159 E7
Cowper Terr NN2 141 F1
Cowslip Cl
 Corby NN18 36 D2
 Rushden NN10 148 C8
Cowslip Hill NN14 89 B5
Cow Yd NN2 141 B3
Cox Gdns NN12 202 E8
Cox's Cl NN6 121 B3
Cox's La NN14 90 A5
Cox's La NN11 151 C1
Crab Apple Way NN14 76 E1
Crabb St NN10 132 B1
Crabb Tree Dr NN3 143 A7
Crabtree Cl
 Hartwell NN7 192 E2
 Wellingborough NN8 129 F2
Crab Tree Cl MK46 195 E5
Crabtree Ho [8] NN11 135 C2
Crabtree La NN6 84 B5
Cracknuts La NN4 160 E2
Craddock Ct NN29 147 B8
Cragside NN8 129 C6
Craigie NN8 129 C4
Cranbrooke Rd NN2 141 C1
Crane Cl
 Broughton NN14 90 A5
 Rushden NN10 132 B4
 Wellingborough NN8 130 A2
Cranesbill Cl NN14 51 A4
Crane Wlk NN3 142 E6
Cranford CE Prim Sch NN14 93 B7
Cranford Ho [1] NN2 141 C3
Cranford Rd
 Burton Latimer NN15 92 D4
 Great Addington NN14 94 A4
 Kettering NN15 92 C6
 Northampton NN2 141 C3
CRANFORD ST ANDREW 93 A8
CRANFORD ST JOHN 93 A7
Cranford Terr [6] NN2 141 C3
Cranleigh Rd NN15 91 B7
Cranmere Ave NN1 160 B6
Cransley Ct NN14 89 B3
Cransley Gdns NN17 36 B7
Cransley Hill NN14 90 A4
Cransley Rd NN14 70 E1
Cransley Rise NN14 89 B4
Cranstoun St NN1 159 D7
Craven St NN1 159 D7
Crawford Ave NN5 158 E7
Crawford Gr NN17 36 E8
Crawley Ave NN8 129 D7
Craxford Rd NN17 10 B1
Creampot Cl OX17 196 A2
Creampot La OX17 196 A2
CREATON 104 E4
Creaton Rd NN6 104 D5
Crediton Cl NN3 160 D7
Creed Rd PE8 41 E7
Creighton Cres NN15 91 F6
Crescent Cl LE16 31 F4
Crescent The
 Burton Latimer NN15 92 C4
 Easton o t H PE9 1 F5
 Flore NN7 155 F6
 Hackleton NN7 177 A3
 Kettering NN15 91 B8
 Ketton PE9 1 A7
 Market Harborough LE16 31 F4
 Moulton NN3 126 D1
 Northampton NN1 159 F8
 Pattishall NN12 172 E1
 Rothwell NN14 70 C6
 Rushden NN10 131 E2
 Twyford OX17 230 A5
 Wellingborough NN8 129 D7
 Whittlebury NN12 215 C5
Creslow Ct MK11 229 F5
Cresswell Rd NN10 131 F2
Crestline Ct NN3 143 A5
Crestwood Gdns NN3 142 F5
Crestwood Rd NN3 142 F5
Creswell Wlk NN17 21 C1
CRICK 101 A5
Crick Cl NN17 22 A1
Cricketers Gn NN17 38 C8
Cricklade Cl NN3 160 D6
Crickley Cres NN4 158 E3
Crick Prim Sch NN6 100 F6
Crick Rd
 Rugby CV21, CV23 99 D7
 West Haddon NN6 102 A5
 Yelvertoft NN6 82 A2
Crimea Cl [2] NN4 175 F7
Crispian Ct NN10 132 A2
Crispian Ho NN1 159 D7
Crispin Cotts NN6 108 A4
Crispin Ho NN1 159 B6
Crispin Pl [14] NN16 72 B2
Crispin St
 [14] Northampton NN1 159 C6
 Rothwell NN14 70 E7
Crispin Way St NN9 114 C8
Crocket Cl NN2 141 E2
Crockwell Hill NN11 119 F1
Crocus Way NN10 148 B7
Croft Cl NN8 129 C5
Crofters Cl NN4 175 B7
Croft La
 Adderbury OX17 230 A4
 Roade NN7 191 D4
 Staverton NN11 152 B7
Croftmeadow Ct NN3 143 B4
Croft The
 Daventry NN11 153 C8
 Hanging Houghton NN6 106 C8
 [1] Northampton NN5 140 F1
 Rugby CV21 99 A8
Croft Way
 Rushden NN10 132 D3
 Weedon Bec NN7 155 A3
Cromarty Ct NN17 36 F5
Cromarty Ho NN17 36 F5
Crome Cl NN8 129 F8
Cromer Rd NN9 111 F4
Cromwell Cl NN14 51 A3
Cromwell Cres LE16 31 D1
Cromwell Ct NN8 130 B5
Cromwell Ho NN8 130 B4
Cromwell Rd
 Kettering NN16 72 A2
 Rushden NN10 132 C2
Cromwell St [15] NN1 159 C7
Cronin Ctyd NN18 37 E7
Cronin Rd NN18 37 E7
CROPREDY 196 A2
Crosby Rd LE16 31 F1
Cross Bank LE16 20 D6
Cross Brooks NN4 175 F6
Cross Ct NN16 72 A3
Crosse Cl NN7 155 C4
Cross Hill NN6 106 B3
Crosshills MK11 229 D4
Cross Keys Ct NN13 233 F7
Cross Keys Dr NN14 76 C2
Cross La
 Aldwincle NN14 57 E1
 Braunston NN11 118 C1
 Helmdon NN13 212 A5
 Weston Underwood MK46 195 B2
Cross Rd NN8 130 B6
Cross St
 Covington PE18 116 D2
 Daventry NN11 135 B2
 Kettering NN16 72 A3
 Market Harborough LE16 31 F2
 Moulton NN3 126 C1
 Rothwell NN14 70 E7
Cross The
 Great Houghton NN4 160 E2
 Gretton NN17 10 B1
Cross Tree Rd MK19 228 B3
Cross Waters Cl NN4 175 F6
Cross Way NN9 131 D8
Crouch Rd NN9 112 F1
CROUGHTON 238 D8
Croughton All Saints CE Prim Sch NN13 238 C8
Croughton Cl NN2 141 C5
Croughton Rd OX17 237 D7
Crowberry Ave NN3 142 C6
CROWFIELD 223 F8
Crow La NN3 161 C7
Crown Apartments [13] NN16 72 B2
Crown Ct
 Corby NN18 36 E5
 Oundle PE8 42 A5
Crown Ct NN10 131 E3
Crown La
 Barrowden LE15 3 F5
 Rothwell NN14 70 C7
 West Haddon NN6 102 C4
Crownsmead NN4 158 D1
Crown St NN16 72 B3
Crown Way NN10 131 E4
Crowthorp Rd NN3 143 C5
Croxdale Cl NN2 140 F5
Croxen Cl NN15 92 C2
Croyde Ave NN18 36 F4
Croyland Hall Her Ctr Mus★ NN8 130 A4
Croyland Prim Sch NN8 129 E3
Croyland Rd NN8 129 F3
Crucible Rd NN17 37 B7
Crystal Ct NN16 72 D3
Cubleigh Cl NN3 142 C6
Cuckoo Cl LE15 3 E5
Cukow Cl NN14 89 B4
Cullahill Ct NN4 158 E2
Culloden Ct NN17 36 F5
Culloden Dr NN15 91 F8
Culme Cl PE8 41 E7
Culross Wlk NN18 36 C3
CULWORTH 198 C3
Culworth CE Sch OX17 198 C2
Culworth Cres NN2 141 D5
Culworth Ho OX17 198 D2
Culworth Rd OX17 197 B6
Cumberland Ave NN9 114 A4
Cumberland Cl NN3 142 A3
Cumbrae Dr NN3 143 C2
Cunliffe Dr NN16 72 A4
Cunliffe Rd Ind Est NN16 72 A4
Cunningham Cl
 Daventry NN11 135 E2
 Higham Ferrers NN10 132 B5
Cupar Cres NN17 36 F5
Curgenven Cl NN11 183 E7
Curlbrook Cl NN4 176 A6
Curlew Way NN11 135 C3

urrie Rd NN2 141 C1
urtis Mews NN8 129 C7
urtlee Hill NN4 175 F5
urver Way NN17 22 D1
yclamen Cl NN3 160 C6
ypress Cl NN14 50 F3
ypress Ct NN3 142 E3
yril St NN1 159 E6
ytringen Cl NN15 91 A7

# D

ADFORD 225 D1
adford Rd NN12, MK18 225 D5
affodil Dr NN10 148 B7
ag La NN29 164 D2
agnall Rd MK46 195 E3
ahlia Rd NN16 72 D4
aimler Cl
  Daventry NN11 135 A3
  Northampton NN3 143 D4
ainty Gr NN4 175 E3
airy Cl
  Brixworth NN6 106 A1
  West Haddon NN6 102 D4
airy Cotts LE17 45 A4
airy Field NN6 103 D1
airy Ground OX17 231 A6
airymeadow Ct NN3 142 F6
airy Way NN9 131 E8
aisy Bank Ave NN14 70 C7
aisy Cl NN18 36 C2
aisy Croft NN10 148 C8
akin Cl PE8 13 F8
'albini Cl LE16 34 B4
alby Cl NN16 72 A6
ale Ave NN8 129 C5
ale Cl
  Brackley NN13 234 A7
  Daventry NN11 135 B5
  Mears Ashby NN6 128 C2
  Wellingborough NN8 129 C5
ale Farm Cotts NN6 128 C2
ale Ho 1 NN8 129 F4
ale St
  Corby NN17 36 D7
  Wellingborough NN8 129 F4
alestones NN4 158 D2
aleswood Rise PE8 13 E7
ale The NN8 129 C5
alkeith Ave 20 NN16 72 B2
alkeith Pl NN16 72 B2
alkeith Rd NN8 129 F1
allacre Dr LE16 34 C4
allacre Farm LE16 34 D4
ALLINGTON 158 F8
allington Cl NN14 54 A2
allington Ct NN5 158 F8
allington Gn 2 NN5 158 F8
allington Haven 5 NN5 158 F8
allington Park Rd NN5 158 F8
allington Rd NN5 159 A7
allison Cl LE16 48 E8
ALSCOTE 173 B1
alston Wlk 6 NN3 142 C4
Dalton Rd NN17 21 E2
Damherst Piece NN6 106 C2
Damson Cl NN14 76 E1
Damson Dell NN3 161 A8
Dance Way NN8 129 F8
Dando Cl NN29 146 D1
Dands Cl OX17 220 A8
Dands Dr OX17 220 A8
Dane Ct NN11 118 C1
Danefield Rd NN3 142 B1
Daneholme Ave NN11 135 C4
Dane Ridge NN5 158 C6
Danes Backside NN2 141 B3
Danes Camp Way NN4 158 E3
Danesholme Jun & Inf Sch NN18 36 A2
Danesholme Rd NN18 36 A2
Danes Way NN6 100 C7
Danetre Dr NN11 135 D2
Danetree Gdns NN3 142 B2
Danetre Hospl NN11 153 C8
Danetre Sch NN11 135 E1
Danewood Gdns NN3 142 B2
Danford Cl PE8 41 F4
Danfords PE8 41 F5
Daniaud Ct NN13 233 E8
Daniell Wlk NN18 36 D5
Daniels Rd NN8 130 C1
Dapplestone Cl NN4 158 D2
Darby Cl NN8 129 A5
Dardis Cl 2 NN2 141 E1
Darenth Ct 16 NN1 159 C7
Darescroft LE16 20 B1
Dark La
  Braunston NN11 118 D1
  Great Harrowden NN9 110 D2
Darley Cl NN16 72 C6
Darley Dale Rd NN17 36 D8
Dart Cl NN17 21 D2
Dartford Cl 2 NN4 159 A2
Dartmouth Rd MK46 195 F4
Dartmouth Row 3 NN11 135 D1
Darwin Ct NN17 37 C8
Darwin Ho NN17 22 F1
Darwin Rd NN17 37 C8
Darwin Wlk NN5 140 C1
Dash Farm Cl NN17 38 A8
DAVENTRY 135 D3
Daventry Abbey Jun Sch The NN11 135 D1
Daventry Cty Pk* NN11 135 D5
Daventry Cty Pk Visitor Ctr NN11 135 D5
Daventry Rd
  Banbury OX16 208 A2
  Barby CV23 118 C8
  Kilsby CV23 100 A1
  Newnham NN11 153 D4
  Norton NN11 136 C5
  Staverton NN11 152 B7
  Staverton NN11 152 C7
  Willoughby CV23 117 C7
Daventry Tert Coll NN11 153 B8
Daventry William Parker Sch NN11 135 C3
Davey Rd NN17 37 C8
Davies Cl
  Kettering NN15 90 F8
  Market Harborough LE16 31 D5
Da Vinci Cl NN5 158 C5
Davis Cl NN14 70 E6
Davis Ct NN17 37 A6
Davy Cl NN8 129 A6
Dawkins Ct NN14 90 A4
Dayrell Rd NN4 158 F2
Dayrell Sq 5 NN4 158 F2
Dayton St NN10 132 A2
Deacon Cl
  Market Harborough LE16 31 D5
  Rushden NN10 132 D3
Deacons Ct NN3 143 C4
Deal Ct NN1 159 D7
Deal St NN1 159 C7
Dean Cl
  Raunds NN9 114 D7
  Rushden NN10 148 A8
Deancourt Dr NN5 140 A1
Deane Par CV21 99 A8
Deane Rd CV21 99 B8
DEANSHANGER 228 D4
Deanshanger Dr NN12 216 F1
Deanshanger Prim Sch MK19 228 E3
Deanshanger Rd
  Old Stratford MK19 229 B6
  Wicken MK19 228 B3
Deans Row NN7 173 E2
Deansway NN3 143 C4
Dean Wlk 6 NN11 135 B4
Debbs Cl MK11 229 E5
Debdale Rd
  Northampton NN3 142 D2
  Wellingborough NN8 129 F5
Deben Rd NN17 21 D1
De Capel Cl NN14 94 D6
DEDDINGTON 236 A4
Deddington Castle Earthworks* OX15 236 A4
Deeble Rd NN15 72 F1
DEENE 23 F6
Deene Cl
  Adderbury OX17 230 B4
  Corby NN17 36 E7
  Market Harborough LE16 32 A3
Deene End NN17 38 C8
Deene Pk* NN17 23 E5
Deene Rd
  Deene NN17 11 D3
  Harringworth NN17 10 F7
Deeneside NN17 38 B8
DEENETHORPE 24 B4
Deenethorpe La NN17 24 B5
Deepdale LE16 20 D7
Deep Side PE9 1 F4
Deer Cl NN4 175 F2
Deerings Rd CV21 99 A8
Deer Park Rd NN3 142 A6
Dee Wlk NN11 135 A1
De Ferneus Dr NN9 114 D7
Delamere Dr NN15 92 A5
Delamere Rd NN4 159 C2
Delapre Abbey* NN4 159 D3
Delapre Cres NN4 159 C3
Delapre Crescent Rd NN4 159 C3
Delapre Ct NN4 159 C2
Delapre Pl NN18 36 A3
Delapre Prim Sch NN4 159 B3
Delapre St NN4 159 B3
De Lisle Cl LE16 31 D2
Dell Cres NN3 143 B5
Dell Pl NN10 132 C2
Dells MK46 195 F4
Dells Cl PE28 61 D2
Dell The NN6 144 E4
Delta Way NN2 141 A5
Delves The NN9 114 C6
De Montfort Ct NN13 222 E1
Dempsey Dr NN14 70 F6
Demswell NN6 106 C2
Denbeigh Ho 5 NN10 132 B2
Denbigh Rd NN3 160 D6
Denby Dale NN8 129 D7
Dencora Bsns Pk NN8 129 A4
Dene Cl
  Kettering NN16 72 A5
Dene Cl *continued*
  Wellingborough NN8 129 C6
Denfield Park Jun Sch NN10 132 C3
DENFORD 95 C5
Denford Dr NN15 91 F5
Denford Rd
  Corby NN17 36 B8
  Ringstead NN14 95 C4
  Thrapston NN14 95 D8
Denford Way NN8 129 D7
Denington Ct NN8 130 A2
Denington Ind Est NN8 130 B2
Denington Rd NN8 130 A2
Denman Cl LE16 34 A4
Denmark Cl NN18 35 F3
Denmark Ct NN10 132 C1
Denmark Rd
  Northampton NN1 159 E6
  Rushden NN10 132 C1
Denne Cl NN18 36 C1
Denney Cres NN11 135 B2
Denston Cl NN4 159 B1
Dent Cl NN5 157 F7
DENTON 178 A8
Denton Cl
  Irchester NN29 147 B8
  Rushden NN10 132 C3
Denton Ct NN15 92 B2
Denton Prim Sch NN7 178 C8
Denton Rd NN7 178 B6
De Quincey Cl NN13 222 E1
Derby Mews NN1 159 F8
Derby Rd NN1 159 F8
Dering Cotts OX17 210 E2
Derling Dr NN9 114 E6
Derngate NN1 159 D5
De Roos Way LE16 34 B4
Derry The NN6 100 F5
Derwent Cl
  Daventry NN11 135 A1
  Northampton NN5 140 F1
  Wellingborough NN8 129 C6
Derwent Cres NN16 71 F2
Derwent Dr NN5 140 F2
Derwent Ho PE8 42 A6
Derwent Wlk NN17 21 D2
DESBOROUGH 51 C2
Desborough Rd
  Arthingworth LE16 49 F1
  Braybrooke LE16 49 F5
  Rothwell NN14 70 C7
  Rushton NN14 52 B2
  Stoke Albany LE16 34 B3
De Vere Rd NN14 76 D2
Deveron Wlk NN17 21 D1
Devon Dr NN15 91 D6
Devon Ox Rd CV23 99 F2
Devonshire Cl
  Boughton NN2 141 C8
  Wellingborough NN8 129 E6
Devonshire Ho 6 NN5 159 A6
Devon Way NN3 142 A5
Devon Wlk NN10 132 C1
Dewar Dr NN11 135 A4
Dexter Way PE8 28 B3
Diamond Dr NN9 131 E8
Diamonds Bsns Ctr NN9 113 A3
Diamond Way NN9 113 A2
Diana Ho NN8 129 D5
Diana Way NN15 92 B1
Dibbin Cl NN17 38 B8
Dickens Dr
  Kettering NN16 72 B6
  Old Stratford MK19 229 B6
Dickens Spinney MK46 195 E4
Dick's Hill LE16 47 C5
Dickson Cl 4 NN4 158 F3
Digby St NN16 72 C3
Dimock Sq NN4 158 F2
Dinglederry MK46 195 F4
Dingle Rd NN10 131 E2
Dingle The
  Daventry NN11 153 C8
  Rugby CV21 99 B8
DINGLEY 33 A4
Dingley La LE16 32 F6
Dingley Rd LE16 32 B6
Dingley Terr LE16 31 F3
Disbrowe Ct NN9 133 C7
Diswell Brook Way MK19 228 E5
Ditchford Cl NN4 175 F6
Ditchford Rd NN8 131 C5
Dixon Rd NN2 141 E6
Dixon Wlk NN17 37 A6
Dobbins Cl OX17 231 A6
Dobson Cl NN4 160 F2
Dobson Wlk NN18 36 D5
Dockham Way NN6 100 E6
Docklewell Cl NN12 203 A4
Doctors La
  Eydon NN11 184 C1
  Great Doddington NN29 145 E6
Doddington Ct NN8 129 F2
Doddington Rd
  Earls Barton NN6 145 A4
  Great Doddington NN8 145 F8
  Wellingborough NN8 129 F2
  Wilby NN8 145 B8
Doddridge 1 NN1 159 C5
Doddridge Ho 21 NN1 159 C6
Doddridge Rd 1 LE16 31 E4
Doddridge St 24 NN1 159 C6
DODFORD 154 F6
Dog La
  Napton on t H CV47 150 A7
  South Kilworth LE17 63 C8
Dolben Ave NN9 113 F4
Dolben Cl NN9 111 E4
Dolben Sq NN9 111 F4
Dolver Cl NN18 36 C2
Donald Greaves Ho NN17 21 D1
Donaldson Ave NN14 90 A3
Don Cl NN17 21 D1
Donellan Gn NN3 142 F6
Donne Cl
  Higham Ferrers NN10 132 A5
  Kettering NN16 72 C6
Donovan Ct NN3 160 E8
Dorcas Rd OX16 219 A6
Dorchester Ct NN5 140 B2
Dore Cl NN3 143 B5
Doris Rd NN16 72 E4
Dorking Wlk NN18 36 C3
Dorman Cl NN3 142 B4
Dorothy Rd NN16 72 E3
Dorset Gdns NN2 141 D3
Dorset Rd
  Corby NN17 36 C6
  Northampton NN2 141 D3
Doubles The NN11 135 B1
Douglas Ct NN15 91 E8
Douglas Rd NN5 157 F8
Douglass Dr LE16 31 F4
Doulton Cl NN14 50 F3
Dove Cl NN12 203 C3
Dovecote Cl
  Barrowden LE15 3 F5
  Kettering NN15 91 F7
  Raunds NN9 114 E7
  Weston by W LE16 18 B3
  Yarwell PE8 16 A8
Dovecote Dr
  Denton NN7 162 B1
  Little Addington NN14 113 B7
Dovecote Rd NN7 191 C4
Dovecote The
  King's Cliffe PE8 13 F7
  Pitsford NN6 125 D5
Dovecote Yd NN14 110 A5
Dove Cotts OX17 210 A6
Dovedale Gr NN14 50 E4
Dovedale Rd NN17 36 E7
Dovehouse Cl
  Brackley NN13 233 F7
  Stanwick NN9 113 F3
  Welford NN6 64 E6
Dovehouse Ct MK19 228 E4
Dover Cl NN10 132 D1
Dovercourt NN5 159 B5
Dove's La NN3 126 D1
Downing Way NN11 153 C7
Downs The NN9 110 E1
Downsway NN4 175 B6
Downwood Cl NN3 143 C3
Dowthorpe End NN6 144 F4
Dowthorpe Hill NN6 144 F3
Drake Cl
  Corby NN17 36 B8
  Daventry NN11 135 E1
  Rothwell NN14 70 E7
Drake Lee Mews NN16 72 B1
Draper's Cl PE8 28 C3
Drapery NN1 159 C6
DRAUGHTON 87 E6
Draughton Rd NN6 87 B7
Draycott Cl NN3 160 D7
Draymans Wlk NN13 233 E6
Drayson La NN6 100 F6
DRAYTON
  Corby 20 A5
  Daventry 135 A2
Drayton Cl
  Corby NN18 36 B4
  Islip NN14 76 B3
  Rushden NN10 148 A8
Drayton Fields Ind Est NN11 135 A5
Drayton Leys CV22 98 A7
Drayton Pk NN11 135 B5
Drayton Pl NN9 112 F3
Drayton Rd
  Bringhurst LE16 20 B5
  Drayton LE16 19 D7
  Irthlingborough NN9 112 F3
  Lowick NN14 75 E6
  Medbourne LE16 19 A5
Drayton Way NN11 135 A5
Drayton Wlk NN2 141 D4
Dresden Cl NN18 35 F2
Driffield Gr NN17 36 F7
Drift The
  Collyweston PE9 1 D2
  Sutton PE5 8 F3
Drift Way MK46 195 F5
Drill Hall Ct NN15 72 A1
Drive The
  Horton NN7 177 E1
  Kettering NN15 72 B1
  Northampton, Duston NN5 158 A7
  Northampton, Phippsville NN1 141 F1
  Rushden NN10 132 C1
  Wellingborough NN8 130 A3
Droue Ct NN14 70 C7
Drovers Wlk NN2 141 A5
Drove The
  Collyweston PE9 1 D1
  Nassington PE8 15 E5
Druce End NN12 217 E6
Druids Way NN3 141 F5
Drum La 30 NN1 159 C6
Drumming Well La PE8 42 A5
Drummond Cl NN6 125 D4
Drydale Ave NN3 142 B3
Dryden Ave NN11 135 B2
Dryden Cl NN11 184 A7
Dryden Rd
  Northampton NN5 158 F7
  Towcester NN12 203 C5
  Wellingborough NN8 130 C5
Dryden's Cl NN14 77 C4
Dryden St
  Kettering NN16 72 B3
  Raunds NN9 114 C6
Dryden Way
  Corby NN17 36 C8
  Higham Ferrers NN10 132 B5
Dryland Rd NN3 142 C2
Dryland St NN16 72 B2
Dryleys Ct NN3 143 B5
Drywell Ct NN3 143 A1
Duchess Cl NN16 72 B4
Duchess End NN6 128 C2
Duchess Gdns NN12 217 D3
Duchy Cl
  Chelveston NN9 133 B8
  Higham Ferrers NN10 132 C5
Duck End
  Cranford St John NN14 93 B7
  Denford NN14 95 D6
  Hinton-in-t-H NN13 232 F6
  Wollaston NN29 146 D3
Duck La
  Harpole NN7 157 C6
  Oundle PE8 42 A5
Duck St
  Elton PE8 16 D1
  Rushden NN10 132 B2
Duckworth Dell NN3 142 F6
Duckworth Rd NN17 36 B7
DUDDINGTON 5 B6
Duffy Pl CV21 99 A8
Dugdale Cl NN14 76 D2
Dukelands NN7 155 A3
Dukes Ct NN15 92 C2
Dukes Green Rd NN7 157 D3
Duke St
  Burton Latimer NN15 92 B2
  Kettering NN16 72 B3
  Northampton NN1 159 D7
  Polebrook PE8 42 F3
  Wellingborough NN8 129 E1
Dulce Rd NN5 158 C8
Dulley Ave NN8 129 F1
Dulverton Rd NN3 160 D7
Dumas Cul-De-Sac NN13 233 E8
Dumble Cl NN18 36 D2
Dunbar Ct NN15 91 F8
Duncan Cl NN3 141 F7
Duncan Ct NN8 129 D3
Duncan Rd NN17 36 B7
DUNCOTE 188 E2
Dundee St NN5 158 F6
Dunedin Rd NN18 36 C2
Dungee Rd MK43 165 E2
Dunkirk Ave NN14 51 B3
Dunmore Rd LE16 32 A1
Dunn Cl NN6 101 A6
Dunnock La NN4 175 F3
Dunnock Rd NN18 36 E3
Dunslade Cl LE16 32 B2
Dunslade Gr LE16 32 B2
Dunslade Rd LE16 32 A2
DUNSMORE 80 C6
Dunsmore Ave CV22 98 E8
Dunster St NN1 159 D6
Durban Rd NN16 72 D2
Durham Cl NN17 36 B6
Durness Cl NN15 91 E8
Dusthill Rd NN14 55 D8
DUSTON 158 C7
Duston Cl NN11 135 A3
Duston Eldean Prim Sch NN5 140 B1
Duston Mill La NN5 158 D4
Duston Rd NN5 158 E6
Duston Sch The NN5 158 A8
Duston Wildes NN5 140 A2
Dybdale Cres NN8 129 E5
Dychurch La
  Bozeat NN29 164 E3
  Northampton NN1 159 D6
Dyson Cl CV21 80 A1
Dyson Dr NN16 72 A4

# E

Eady Cl NN3 126 E1
Eady Rd NN15 92 B1
Eady's Row NN14 94 D7
Eagle Dr NN4 159 F2
Eaglehurst NN6 106 C2
Eagle La NN14 71 B1
Eaglesfield NN11 136 C4
Eaglethorpe PE8 28 B4

EAKLEY LANES 193 D2
Ealing Terr NN10 132 A3
EARLS BARTON 144 F3
Earls Barton Inf Sch NN6 144 E4
Earls Barton Jun Sch NN6 144 E4
Earls Barton Mus* NN6 144 E4
Earls Barton Rd
Great Doddington NN29 145 C5
Mears Ashby NN6 128 B2
Earlsfield Cl NN4 176 A6
Earl's La OX15 236 A4
Earl Spencer Prim Sch NN5 159 A8
Earl St NN1 159 D7
Earlstrees Ct NN17 21 F2
Earlstrees Ind Est NN17 21 E2
Earlstrees Rd NN17 21 F2
EAST ADDERBURY 230 B4
East Ave
Burton Latimer NN15 92 B3
Corby NN17 36 F5
Kettering NN15 72 D2
East Bank NN3 142 E6
Eastbourne Ave NN18 36 B5
Eastbrook NN18 36 B4
Eastbrook Hill NN14 51 C3
East Butterfield Ct NN3 142 F5
EAST CARLTON 35 A7
East Carlton Countryside Pk* LE16 35 B8
East Carlton Pk LE16 35 B7
East Cl NN15 72 D2
EASTCOTE 189 A8
Eastcote Rd NN7 189 D8
East Cres
Rushden NN10 131 F2
Weldon NN17 38 C8
East Dr NN15 72 E2
EAST END 230 B4
East End NN6 106 F5
Eastern Ave N NN2 141 D4
Eastern Ave S NN2 141 D3
Eastern Cl NN2 141 D5
Eastern Way NN11 135 C2
EAST FARNDON 48 B7
Eastfield NN7 190 D7
Eastfield Cl NN5 140 C1
Eastfield Cres
Finedon NN9 112 A5
Yardley Gobion NN12 217 F5
Eastfield Dr MK19 207 A3
Eastfield Prim Sch NN3 142 B3
Eastfield Rd
Brixworth NN6 106 B1
3 Irthlingborough NN9 112 F2
Northampton, Duston NN5 158 B8
Northampton, Far Cotton NN4 159 C3
Wellingborough NN8 130 C6
Wollaston NN29 146 E2
Eastfields NN11 118 C1
Eastfields Cres PE8 15 E6
East Gr NN10 132 B3
EAST HADDON 122 D5
East Haddon CE Prim Sch NN6 122 D5
East Haddon Rd NN6 122 D8
Easthill Cl NN13 233 F7
East Hunsbury Prim Sch NN4 175 B6
Eastlands Rd NN9 112 A5
East Langham Rd NN9 114 D7
Eastleigh Rd NN15 91 D7
East Leys Ct NN3 142 C7
Eastmead Ct NN3 143 A1
Easton Garford CE Sch PE9 2 A5
Easton La NN29 164 C3
EASTON MAUDIT 163 F2
EASTON ON THE HILL 2 A4
Easton Way NN7 163 E4
Easton Wlk NN17 37 B6
East Oval NN5 140 F2
East Paddock Ct NN3 143 A4
East Park Par NN1 159 F8
East Priors Ct NN3 143 A4
East Rd PE8 42 A5
East Rising NN4 175 D7
East St
Irchester NN29 147 B8
Long Buckby NN6 121 D4
Market Harborough LE16 31 D3
Northampton NN1 159 F6
Olney MK46 195 F4
Stanwick NN9 114 A3
East View OX17 210 E2
East Wlk NN15 72 E2
Eastwood Gr CV21 99 C8
Eastwood Rd PE8 42 A5
Eaton Rd NN5 158 A8
Eaton Wlk NN10 132 B2
Ebbw Vale Rd NN9 131 E8
Ebenezer Pl 16 NN16 72 B2
Ebony Ct NN11 184 D5
Eccles Rd PE8 7 D8
Eckland Lodge Bsns Pk NN14 50 D6
ECTON 143 F4
ECTON BROOK 143 D2
Ecton Brook Prim Sch NN3 143 D2
Ecton Brook Rd NN3 143 D2
Ecton Hall NN6 143 F4
Ecton La NN6 127 D2
Ecton Leys CV22 98 A7
Ecton Park Rd NN3 143 C3
Ecton St 11 NN1 159 E6
Ecton Village Prim Sch NN6 143 F4
Edale Gn NN14 50 E4
Eden Cl
Daventry NN11 135 A1
Northampton NN3 142 B4
Eden Ct NN6 120 C6
Eden St NN16 72 B2
Edgar Mobbs Way NN5 158 E5
Edgar Rd NN16 72 D3
EDGCOTE 197 A4
Edgcote Drive Cotts OX17 197 A4
Edgehill Dr NN11 135 D6
Edgehill Rd NN5 140 D1
Edgell St NN16 72 C2
Edgemead Cl NN3 142 E7
Edgemont Rd NN3 142 E1
Edges Ct NN3 142 C7
Edgewood NN13 222 F1
Edinburgh Cl
Market Harborough LE16 31 F4
Rothwell NN14 70 C6
Edinburgh Ho NN5 158 C8
Edinburgh Mews NN2 141 C2
Edinburgh Rd
Kettering NN16 72 D3
Northampton NN2 141 C2
Wellingborough NN8 129 E1
Edinburgh Sq 3 NN11 135 B3
Edison Cl NN8 129 A6
Edison Ct NN8 129 A6
Edison Ctyd NN17 21 F3
Edison Dr NN5 158 D4
Edith Rd NN16 72 E4
Edith St NN1 159 E6
Edmonds Cl NN8 130 A2
Edmonds Dr PE9 1 A5
Edmund St NN16 72 D2
Edward Cl
Higham Ferrers NN10 132 C7
Kettering NN15 91 C7
Edwardian Cl NN4 175 E7
Edward Rd
Irchester NN29 147 B7
Kettering NN15 91 C7
Market Harborough LE16 31 D5
Edwards Cl NN11 183 D7
Edwards Dr NN8 129 D5
Edward Watson Cl NN2 141 B5
Edwinstowe Cl NN3 160 E7
Egerton Cl NN13 234 A7
Egmont Ave MK11 229 E4
Eider Cl
Burton Latimer NN15 92 A2
Daventry NN11 135 C3
Eismann Way NN17 37 C7
Ekins Cl NN3 142 D2
Elan Ct NN10 131 E3
Eldean Rd NN5 140 B1
Elderberry Ct NN3 143 C3
Elder Dr NN11 135 C4
Eldon Cl NN6 100 E6
Eldon Way NN6 100 E6
Eleanor Ct NN6 102 C5
Eleonore Ho NN3 142 C3
Elgin St NN5 158 F6
Eliot Cl NN16 72 C6
Elizabeth Cl
Earls Barton NN6 144 E5
Wellingborough NN8 129 D2
Elizabeth Ct NN10 132 C7
Elizabeth Rd
Daventry NN11 135 B3
Kettering NN16 72 D3
Rothwell NN14 70 C6
West Haddon NN6 102 C5
Elizabeth St
Corby NN17 36 E6
Northampton NN1 159 F6
Elizabeth Way
Earls Barton NN6 144 E5
Higham Ferrers NN10 132 C7
Irthlingborough NN9 131 E8
Elizabeth Wlk 6 NN1 159 F6
ELKINGTON 83 A5
Elkington La CV23 99 B1
Elkington Rd NN6 82 B4
Elkins Cl NN6 82 B4
Ellen Cl NN6 100 F6
Ellesmere Ave
Brackley NN13 233 F8
Northampton NN5 158 E7
Ellesmere Cl NN13 222 F1
Ellesmere Cres NN13 222 F1
Ellesmere Ct NN13 233 F8
Ellesmere Rd NN13 222 F1
Ellfield Ct NN3 142 F3
Elliot Ho 1 NN10 132 A2
Elliot Way NN10 132 A5
Ellis La NN14 89 B4
Ellison Cl NN9 114 C7
Elm Cl
Brafield-on-t-G NN7 161 D2
Hargrave NN9 115 F2
Elm Ct NN14 76 D1
Elm Dr
Brackley NN13 222 F1
Deanshanger MK19 228 D5
Hinton NN11 184 A6
Market Harborough LE16 31 C2
Elmfield Cl NN12 217 D3
Elm Gr NN4 176 A6
Elmhurst Ave NN3 142 A2
Elmhurst Ct NN3 142 A2
Elmington Cotts PE8 42 C8
Elmington Rd NN3 143 C5
Elmlea Dr MK46 195 F4
Elm Rd
Burton Latimer NN15 92 C4
Kettering NN15 72 D1
Elms Dr CV22 98 F8
Elms Dyke NN11 135 E8
Elm St
19 Northampton NN1 159 C7
Wellingborough NN8 129 F5
Elm Way NN7 177 C3
Elm Wlk
Corby NN17 21 D1
Higham Ferrers NN10 132 B6
Elmwood Wlk NN5 140 A1
Elsden Rd NN8 130 C5
ELTON 28 E8
Elton CE Prim Sch PE8 28 D8
Elton Cl
Desborough NN14 50 E3
Northampton NN3 143 B5
Elton Hall* PE8 28 D6
Elton Rd PE8 16 C7
Elwes Way NN3 143 B2
Elysium Terr NN2 159 C8
Embankment NN8 130 C2
EMBERTON 195 F1
Emberton Ctry Pk & Visitor Ctr* MK46 195 E1
Emerald Way NN1 159 B5
Emerton Gdns MK11 229 D5
Emery Cl NN11 135 E8
Emley Cl NN3 142 F1
Emmanuel Cl NN11 153 C8
Encon Ct NN3 141 F7
Enfield Cl NN5 157 F8
English Martyrs RC Prim Sch CV21 99 A7
Ennerdale Cl
Daventry NN11 135 A2
Kettering NN16 72 A2
Northampton NN3 142 A3
Ennerdale Rd
Corby NN17 21 E1
Northampton NN3 142 A4
Rushden NN10 132 D3
Ensleigh Cl NN15 92 C1
Enstone Ct NN8 129 E1
Enterprise Cl NN16 71 F4
Enterprise Ct NN8 129 B6
Enterprise Ind Pk NN17 22 F1
Enterprise Rd NN9 114 D7
Entwood Dr NN3 143 B5
Epping Cl NN15 92 A5
Epping Wlk 4 NN11 135 B4
Epsom Cl NN10 148 D8
Epsom Wlk NN18 36 C3
Equestrian Way NN7 155 B4
Ericsson Cl NN11 135 C5
Ermine Rd NN3 143 C5
Ermont Way OX16 219 A7
Erskin Wood NN6 105 B1
Esher Ct NN3 142 D4
Eskdaill Pl NN16 72 B3
Eskdaill St NN16 72 B3
Eskdale Ave
Corby NN17 36 E7
Northampton NN3 142 B3
Eskdale Cl NN8 129 C6
Essenden Ct MK11 229 F5
Essen La CV23 100 A3
Essex Cl NN17 36 B6
Essex Gdns LE16 31 D1
Essex Pl NN15 91 D6
Essex Rd NN10 132 C1
Essex St NN2 159 C8
Essex Terr NN2 159 C8
Ethel St NN1 159 E6
Eton Cl NN7 155 C4
Eton Ct 3 NN2 141 C3
Ettrick Cl NN16 72 A6
Euro Bsns Pk LE16 32 B4
Euro Hub NN18 37 A4
Euston Rd NN4 159 C3
Evans Cl NN11 135 E1
Eva Rd NN16 72 E3
Evelyn Way NN29 147 C7
Evelyn Wlk NN9 114 D6
EVENLEY 233 E2
Evenley Rd
Mixbury NN13 234 D1
Northampton NN2 141 C5
Evensford Wlk NN9 131 D8
Everard Cl CV23 80 A5
EVERDON 170 B8
Everdon Cl
Northampton NN2 141 E4
Rugby CV22 98 E8
Everdon Pk NN11 135 A5
Everdon Rd NN12 170 E3
Everdon Stubbs Nature Trail* NN11 170 C6
Everdon Stubbs Woodland Trust Wood* NN11 170 D6
Everest Ho NN17 36 E6
Everest La NN17 36 E6
Evergreen Dr NN14 113 B7
Everitt Cl NN8 130 B2
Evesham Cl NN8 129 E1
Evesham Ct NN3 143 A7
Evison Ct NN14 70 C6
Evison Rd NN14 70 C6
Ewenfield Rd NN9 111 F4
Excalibur Cl NN5 158 A7
Excelsior NN8 129 B4
Excelsior Ct NN9 112 E2
Excelsior Gdns NN5 157 F8
Exeter Cl NN11 153 C8
Exeter Inf Sch NN18 36 F5
Exeter Pl NN1 159 E7
Exeter St NN16 72 C5
Exmoor Cl NN3 160 D7
Exmouth Ave NN18 36 F4
Express Cl NN9 131 E8
Express Pk
Kettering NN16 71 F3
Rushden NN10 131 D3
Eyam Cl NN14 50 E3
EYDON 184 C1
Eyeletter Ho 7 NN5 159 A6
Eynard Impasse NN13 222 E1
Eynon Cl NN3 126 B1


## F


Factory La 9 LE16 31 E3
Fairfax Rd LE16 31 E1
Fairfax Rise NN6 85 B8
Fairfield NN7 174 B2
Fairfield Rd
Isham NN14 91 E1
Market Harborough LE16 31 D4
Northampton NN2 141 F2
Paulerspury NN12 216 B7
Fairfields Sch NN2 141 E1
Fairground Way NN3 160 E7
Fairhurst Way NN6 144 F4
Fair La NN14 76 E3
Fairlight Ct 3 NN18 36 B5
Fairmead Cres NN10 147 F8
Fairmead Rise NN2 140 F6
Fair Mile NN2 141 A6
Fairoaks Dr NN9 114 C7
Fairoaks The NN3 160 F8
Fairway
Market Harborough LE16 31 D4
Northampton NN2 141 E2
Fairway The
Daventry NN11 135 F2
Kettering NN15 91 A8
Wellingborough NN9 110 E1
Faith Terr MK19 207 A2
Falcon Dr MK19 229 B7
Falconers Cl NN11 135 C3
Falconer's Hill Com Jun & Inf Schs NN11 135 C3
Falconers Rise NN4 175 A8
Falcon View NN12 202 D8
Falcon Way NN13 222 D2
FALCUTT 212 A2
Falcutt Way NN2 141 D5
Falkner's Cl OX17 230 A4
Fallowfield NN9 129 E8
Fallowfields NN6 101 A6
Fallow Wlk NN2 141 A6
Falmer Wlk NN18 36 B4
Falster Cl NN18 36 A2
Faracre Ct NN3 143 B1
Faraday Cl
Daventry NN11 135 A4
Northampton NN5 158 D5
Wellingborough NN8 129 A6
Faraday Ct
Thrapston NN14 76 E2
Wellingborough NN8 129 A6
Faraday Gr NN17 37 A8
Faramir Pl NN3 143 B6
Far Brook NN6 125 B8
FAR COTTON 159 B3
Farebrother Cl NN11 183 D7
Fareham Ave CV22 98 E8
Far End NN5 158 F6
Faringdon Ct NN3 143 A7
Farmbrook Ct NN3 142 F5
Farm Cl
Brigstock NN14 55 F7
Holcot NN6 126 E8
Northampton NN2 141 B4
Farmclose Rd NN4 175 E6
Far Meadow Ct NN3 142 E5
Farmers Cl NN4 175 E5
Farmers Dr NN13 233 D8
Farmfield Ct NN15 91 F4
Farm Field Ct NN3 142 E5
Farmhill Rd NN3 143 A6
Farm Rd
Brackley NN13 234 A6
Wellingborough NN8 129 E8
Farmstead Rd NN18 36 A5
Farm Stile NN11 182 C8
Farmyard The NN7 163 A3
Farnborough Cl
Corby NN18 36 E1
Farnborough Cl *continued*
Kettering NN15 91 D5
Farnborough Dr 8 NN11 135 B7
Farndale Ave NN17 36 E7
Farndale View LE16 31 C2
FARNDISH 147 B4
Farndish Cl NN10 131 F2
Farndish Rd NN29 147 B7
Farndon Cl NN3 142 F6
Farndon Ct LE16 31 D2
Farndon Fields Prim Sch LE16 48 E8
Farndon Rd
Great Oxendon LE16 48 D4
Hinton NN11 184 A5
Lubenham LE16 30 F2
Market Harborough LE16 31 D1
Marston Trussell LE16 47 D7
Farnham Dr NN10 147 F8
Farnworth Cl NN5 140 C1
Farraxton Sq NN4 158 E2
Farrer Cl NN13 223 D4
Farthing Ct CV21 99 B8
FARTHINGHOE 221 B4
Farthinghoe Cl NN13 233 D7
Farthinghoe Prim Sch NN13 221 B4
Farthinghoe Rd OX17 231 F5
FARTHINGSTONE 170 F2
Farthingstone Rd
Litchborough NN12 171 B2
Weedon Bec NN7 155 B1
Faugere Cl NN13 233 F8
Favell Way NN3 160 D8
Fawsley Leys CV22 98 A7
Fawsley Rd
Everdon NN11 170 A8
Northampton NN4 159 C2
FAXTON 88 C3
Faxton Cl NN2 141 D4
Faxton End NN6 107 D7
Fay Cl NN11 184 A7
Feast Field Cl NN29 146 D1
Featherbed La
Geddington NN18 37 B1
Rugby CV21 80 A1
Federation Ave NN14 50 F2
Fegans Ct MK11 229 D6
Fellmead Rd NN3 143 C5
Fellows Cl NN29 146 C3
Fellows Way CV21 98 F8
Fell Wlk NN8 129 D6
Fengate Cl NN3 143 C5
Fenn Cl PE8 15 E5
Fennel Ct NN4 175 D5
Fenners Cl NN10 132 D2
Fenny Compton Rd OX17 181 D1
Fenton Rise NN13 233 D7
Fenwick Dr CV21 99 A8
Ferguson's Cl PE8 43 A3
Fermoy Ct NN7 138 B4
Fermyn Cl NN14 55 F8
Fermyn Pl NN18 36 A3
Fermyn Woods Ctry Pk* NN14 56 A7
Fern Dale Cl NN14 54 B3
Ferndale Rd NN3 142 D2
Ferne Furlong MK46 195 F5
Fernfield Cl LE16 32 B4
Fernie Chase LE16 17 A6
Fernie Cl NN15 92 A5
Fernie Ct LE17 45 E6
Fernie Field NN3 142 C6
Fernie Rd LE16 31 F3
Fernie Way NN8 129 D4
Fern Ley Cl LE16 32 B2
Fernmoor Dr NN9 112 F2
Fern Rd NN10 131 E3
Ferrers Ct NN10 132 C7
Ferrers Specialist Arts Coll The NN10 132 C5
Ferrestone Rd NN8 130 A6
Ferris Row NN3 160 F7
Ferro Fields NN6 106 C3
Fessey Rd NN11 183 D8
Festival Cl NN9 113 B5
Festival Rd NN12 172 D1
Fetter St NN1 159 D5
Fettledine Rd NN9 113 B5
Field Cl NN6 102 C4
Field Cotts NN18 53 B8
Fieldgate Cl NN4 175 F6
Fieldhead Cl LE16 31 C3
Fieldmill Rd NN3 143 B1
Field Rose Sq 4 NN3 143 C2
Field St NN16 72 B3
Field Street Ave NN16 72 B3
Fields View NN8 130 B4
Field View
Brackley NN13 233 D7
Braunston NN11 118 C1
Marston St Lawrence OX17 210 B2
Fieldway NN3 142 B1
Field Way NN13 212 A5
Fiennes Ct NN11 135 B6
Fiensgate NN4 158 D1
Fife St NN5 158 F7
Fifth Ave NN13 238 E7
Fifth St E NN13 238 E7
Fifth St NN13 238 E7
Filey Ct NN18 36 B4
Filleigh Way NN3 160 C7
Finch Dr NN15 92 A6
Finch-Hatton Dr NN17 10 C1

FINEDON 111 E4
Finedon Hall NN9 111 E4
Finedon Inf Sch NN9 111 F5
Finedon Mulso CE Jun Sch NN9 112 A5
Finedon Rd
Burton Latimer NN15 92 B1
Irthlingborough NN9 112 E3
Wellingborough NN8 130 B6
Finedon Road Ind Est NN8 130 B8
Finedon St NN15 92 B1
Finedon Station Rd NN9 111 A6
Fineshade Cl
Kettering NN15 92 A5
King's Cliffe PE8 13 E7
Fineshade Gr NN17 36 E7
Finland Way NN18 36 A2
Finney Dr NN4 175 E3
Firbank Cl NN3 160 F8
Firdale Ave NN10 132 B4
Fire Quarters The NN7 155 C4
Fir Rd NN16 72 D2
Firs Ct NN4 175 F8
First Ave NN8 129 D3
Firs The
Daventry NN11 135 C3
Market Harborough LE16 31 C3
First La NN5 158 F6
First St NN13 238 F6
Firsview Dr NN5 140 C1
Fir Tree Gr NN29 164 D2
Firtree La LE17 62 C3
Fir Tree Wlk
Market Harborough LE16 31 E4
Northampton NN3 142 E2
Fisher Ave CV22 98 E8
Fisher Cl NN14 76 E1
Fishermans Cl MK46 195 E4
Fishers Cl
Kilsby CV23 99 F2
Northampton NN3 143 B1
Fishpond Cl NN7 162 B1
Fishponds Rd NN3 143 B1
Fish St NN1 159 D6
Fishton Cl NN15 91 C7
Fitzroy Ct NN6 102 B4
Fitzroy Pl NN1 159 B6
Fitzwilliam Ct
4 Rushden NN10 132 A2
Wymington NN10 148 A7
Fitzwilliam Dr NN15 92 A5
Fitzwilliam Leys NN10 132 B7
Fitzwilliam Rd NN9 112 F3
Fitzwilliam St NN10 132 A2
Five Acres Fold NN4 158 F3
Five Cotts MK18 226 D4
Fiveways NN6 104 C1
Fjord Wlk NN18 36 A2
Flaggs Mdw MK46 195 E4
Flamingo Gardens & Zoo Pk* MK46 195 B3
Flatford Cl NN18 36 D1
Flatlets The NN9 112 F2
Flavius Gate NN13 234 A7
Flaxland Cl LE16 32 B3
Flaxlands Ct NN3 142 F3
Flaxwell Ct NN3 160 F8
Fleet St NN16 72 A2
Fleetwind Dr NN4 175 D7
Fleetwood Cl LE16 31 D1
Fleetwood Gdns LE16 31 D1
Fleming Cl NN8 129 B7
Fleming Rd NN17 22 A2
Flensburg Cl NN18 36 B2
Fletcher Gdns NN14 76 D1
Fletcher Rd NN10 132 A3
Fletton Way PE8 41 F6
Fleur Cl NN11 184 C6
Flintcomb Rise NN3 143 B3
Flinters Cl NN4 175 F7
Flitton Ct MK11 229 F5
Flora Thompson Dr NN13 233 E8
FLORE 155 F4
Flore CE Prim Sch NN7 155 E5
Flore Hill NN7 155 D5
Florence Rd NN1 159 F7
Floribunda Dr NN4 158 F2
Florin Pl CV21 99 A8
Flowerhill Dr NN8 130 B6
Flying Dutchman Way 2 NN11 135 A3
Fog Cotts NN6 120 B5
Folly La
Hartwell NN7 206 C8
Little Brington NN7 138 B4
Folly Rd MK19 228 D4
Fontwell Cres NN18 36 E1
Foot La NN9 133 C8
Ford Bank LE16 20 D6
Ford Dr NN13 233 D8
Ford St NN16 72 C2
Forest App PE8 13 F7
Forest Cl NN15 92 D3
Forest Ct NN10 132 D3
Foresters Pl CV21 99 B7
Forest Gate Rd NN17 36 E7
Forest Glade
Hartwell NN7 192 D2
Kettering NN16 72 C6
Forest Rd
Hanslope MK19 207 A6
Hartwell NN7 192 D2
Northampton NN4 159 C3
Piddington NN7 177 A1
Forest View NN7 192 D2
Forfar St NN5 158 F7
Forge Ho NN14 70 D7
Forge The NN10 132 B1
Forrester Dr NN13 222 E1
Forrester Gr NN14 76 E1
Forresters The NN9 114 D5
Forstal Cl NN18 36 D3
Fort Pl NN1 159 B6
Forty Foot La MK44 149 A1
Fosberry Cl NN4 175 F6
FOSCOTE 202 B3
Foskett Cl NN10 132 A3
Foskitt Ct NN3 143 B1
Fosse Cl NN8 129 D1
Fosse Gn NN10 132 C3
Foster Cl NN15 90 F8
Foster Ct NN18 36 E5
FOSTER'S BOOTH 188 D8
Foster's Booth Rd NN12 172 D1
Fothergill Cl LE16 32 B3
FOTHERINGHAY 27 D7
Fotheringhay Castle* PE8 27 E6
Fotheringhay Ct NN14 76 E2
Fotheringhay Mews PE8 42 A5
Fotheringhay Rd
Corby NN17 36 B8
Nassington PE8 15 F4
Foundry Ct 5 NN11 135 C1
Foundry Pl NN11 135 C1
Foundry St 13 NN1 159 C5
Foundry Wlk
4 Daventry NN11 135 C1
Thrapston NN14 76 C1
Fountain Ct MK46 195 F3
Four Crosses Ho CV23 117 E3
Fourth Ave
Croughton NN13 238 E6
Wellingborough NN8 129 D3
Fourth St NN13 238 E6
Fowey Cl NN8 129 C6
Fox Cl CV21 80 B1
Fox Covert Dr NN7 191 E3
Foxcovert Rd NN3 143 B6
Fox Coverts NN14 89 A4
Foxendale Sq NN3 143 D2
Foxfield Way NN4 175 F2
Foxford Cl NN4 174 F8
Foxglove Ave NN11 184 B6
Foxglove Cl
Corby NN18 36 E2
Northampton NN4 175 F2
Rushden NN10 148 C8
Foxglove Rd NN14 51 A5
Foxgoles Cl MK19 228 F5
Foxgrove Ave NN2 141 B4
Foxhill MK46 195 E5
Foxhill La OX27 237 E3
Foxhill Rd NN6 102 B3
Fox Hill Rd NN3 143 D2
Fox La
Brackley NN13 233 E7
Souldern OX27 237 E3
Foxlands NN14 51 B2
FOXLEY 187 D4
Fox St NN14 70 C7
FOXTON 30 E8
Foxton Canal Mus* LE16 30 C8
Foxton Ct NN15 72 A1
Foxton Locks Ctry Pk* LE16 30 C8
Foxton Prim Sch LE16 30 D8
Foxton Rd
Foxton LE16 30 B7
Lubenham LE16 30 D5
Foxwell Sq NN3 142 F7
Foxwood Cl NN10 131 E2
Fox Yd 7 LE16 31 E3
Franciscan Cl NN10 147 F8
Francis Ct NN10 131 E3
Francis Dickins Cl NN29 146 E3
Francis Row NN7 171 E6
Francis St
8 Northampton NN1 159 C7
Raunds NN9 114 B4
Francis Terr NN9 114 B4
Frank Large Wlk NN5 158 A7
Franklin Cres NN5 158 D7
Franklin Ct NN5 159 A6
Franklin Fields NN17 37 A8
Franklin's Cl NN6 143 F4
Franklin St NN5 158 F6
Franklin Way NN11 135 B5
Frankston Ave MK11 229 E5
Fraser Cl NN11 135 D2
Fraser Rd NN3 142 D6
Freehold St NN2 159 C8
Freeman's Endowed CE Jun Sch NN8 129 E4
Freeman's La NN14 95 C6
Freeman Way NN9 112 B5
Freeschool St 9 NN1 159 C5
Fremeaux Terr NN2 141 B2
French Dr NN15 72 F1
Frensham Cl 2 NN4 158 F3
Friar's Ave NN4 159 C1
Friars Cl NN8 130 A3
Friar's Cl NN4 159 B1
Friar's Cres NN4 159 C1
Friars Sch NN8 130 A3
Friary Cl NN11 135 D2
Friary The NN1 159 D6
Frinton Cl NN10 147 F8
Frisby La LE15 3 D8
Friston Cl NN15 92 A5
Frobisher Cl NN11 135 E2
Frog Hall
Brixworth NN6 106 A2
Silverstone NN12 214 D5
Frog La NN11 182 C7
Front St NN14 95 C6
Frost Cl NN14 51 B4
Frost Ct NN29 145 D6
Frosts Ct NN4 175 E5
Frosty Hollow NN4 175 C6
Froxhill Cres NN6 106 A1
Froxhill Wlk NN6 106 A1
Fuchsia Cl NN3 160 C6
Fuchsia Way NN10 148 B7
Fulford Dr NN2 141 E3
Fullen La NN17 22 D8
Fullerburn Ct 2 NN3 142 E3
Fuller Rd NN3 142 C8
Fullers Cl NN14 76 F8
Fuller St NN16 72 C2
Fullingdale Rd NN3 142 B2
Fullwell Rd NN29 164 D4
Fulmar La NN8 130 A8
Fulwell Ave NN17 10 C1
Furber Ct NN3 142 D4
Furlong Rd NN14 51 C3
Furlongs The LE16 32 B3
Furnace Cotts NN9 111 A5
Furnace Dr
Daventry NN11 135 A4
Thrapston NN14 76 D1
Furnace La
Finedon NN9 111 A5
Kettering NN16 72 A5
Nether Heyford NN7 172 A8
Furnace Lane Ind Est NN9 111 B5
Furnells Cl NN9 114 D7
FURTHO 218 A3
Furtho Ct MK19 229 B7
Furtho La NN12 217 E3
Furze Ct 5 NN4 159 A3
Furze Rd NN7 161 D2
Furze Wlk NN2 141 E2
Fusilier Rd NN11 135 B1
Fusilier Way NN7 155 A4
Fydell Row LE15 3 A6
Fyfe Rd NN17 36 B8
Fylingdale NN2 140 F5

G

Gable Cl NN11 135 B1
Gable Court Mews NN3 142 D1
Gables The NN15 72 B1
Gadesby Ct NN3 142 E3
Gainage Cl NN18 36 C1
Gainsborough Ave NN15 92 A7
Gainsborough Cres CV21 80 B1
Gainsborough Ct NN18 36 D5
Gainsborough Dr NN8 129 F7
Gainsborough Rd NN18 36 C4
Gainsborough Way NN11 135 C6
Gains La PE28 61 D2
Galahad Ct NN5 158 A8
Galane Cl NN4 158 D1
Gallery Cl NN3 143 A6
Gallery La PE8 42 A5
Gallery The* PE8 42 A5
Galley Hill MK11 229 F5
Gallfield Ct NN3 161 C8
Galliard Ct NN1 159 F7
Gallow Field Rd LE16 30 E7
Gallowhill Rd NN4 160 B1
Gambrel Rd NN5 158 D6
Gamston Wlk NN18 36 B6
Gander Cl NN17 38 A7
Gannet La NN8 130 A8
Ganton Cl NN11 135 F3
Gapstile Cl NN14 51 A4
Gap The NN29 146 E2
Gardenfield NN10 132 B5
Gardenfields Cl NN9 113 B5
Garden Fields Ct NN29 147 C8
Gardens The
East Carlton LE16 35 A7
Kettering NN16 72 A4
Whilton NN11 137 D6
Gardiner St LE16 31 C3
Gardner Cl NN9 114 C7
Gardner Rise NN13 233 D7
Garfield Cl NN2 141 C3
Garfield Ho NN2 141 B3
Garfield St
Kettering NN15 91 B8
Northampton NN2 141 B3
Garford La PE9 2 A5
Garners Way NN7 157 C7
Garrard Way NN16 71 F3
Garrick Rd NN1 160 B7
Garrow Cl NN9 112 E3
Garsdale NN2 140 F5
Garston Rd NN18 36 C1
Gas St 14 NN1 159 C5
Gatcombe Ho 3 NN10 132 B2
Gateford Ct NN18 36 B6
Gatehouse Cl CV21 99 A8
Gatehouse La LE16 20 F6
Gate La NN14 90 B5
Gatelodge Cl NN3 142 E6
Gates Cl NN9 112 E3
Gateway Cl NN4 175 F6
Gaultney The NN14 51 A3
Gawaine Ct NN5 158 A7
Gaydon Ho NN17 22 C1
Gayhurst Cl NN3 142 B7
GAYTON 173 F2
Gayton CE Prim Sch NN7 173 E2
Gayton Rd
Blisworth NN7 190 C8
Eastcote NN12 172 F1
Tiffield NN12 189 C6
GEDDINGTON 54 B3
Geddington CE Prim Sch NN14 54 B2
Geddington Rd NN18 37 D5
Gedling Cl NN3 160 F8
Gees Farm Cl NN7 179 A5
GEESTON 1 B4
Geeston Rd PE9 1 B5
Geldock Rd NN3 143 A1
Genner Rd NN17 22 B1
Gentian Cl NN10 148 C8
George Blackall Ct NN17 36 C8
George Nutt Ct NN4 159 C2
George Row NN1 159 C5
Georges Ave NN7 173 A7
Georges Cl NN7 173 A7
Georges Dr NN4 175 E3
George St
Burton Latimer NN15 92 D3
Corby NN17 36 E6
Higham Ferrers NN10 132 C7
Irthlingborough NN9 112 E1
Kettering NN16 72 B1
Rushden NN10 132 B2
Wellingborough NN8 130 A5
George Yd MK11 229 D5
Gerandria Ct CV22 98 E8
Gerrard Gdns LE16 48 D8
Gervase Sq NN3 143 C1
Gharana Nivas NN8 130 B5
Gibbons Dr NN14 70 E7
Gibbsacre Ct NN3 143 C1
Gibraltar Ct 23 NN1 159 C7
Gibson Dr
Rugby CV21 80 A1
Upper Benefield PE8 39 F7
Gibson La NN5 158 F8
Giffard Ct
Market Harborough LE16 31 D3
Northampton NN5 159 A5
Gifford Ct NN5 158 C8
Gilbert Cl LE16 32 B2
Gilbert Scott Ct NN12 203 B6
Gilbey Cl NN9 110 E1
Gilchrist Ave NN17 37 A8
Gillingham Rd NN15 90 F8
Gillitts Rd NN8 129 E3
Gillsway NN2 141 A4
Gilson's Cl LE15 3 A6
Gingles Ct CV21 99 A8
Gipsy La
Irchester NN29 146 E8
Kettering NN16 71 E2
Gipsy Lane Turn NN29 146 F7
Gisburne Rd NN8 130 A6
Glade Cl
Burton Latimer NN15 92 C3
Northampton NN3 143 B1
Glades The NN4 175 F2
Glade The NN9 110 E1
Gladiator Cl NN4 175 F5
Gladstone Cl NN5 141 A1
Gladstone Ct 7 NN16 72 C2
Gladstone Rd NN5 159 A8
Gladstone St
Desborough NN14 51 A4
Kettering NN16 72 C2
Market Harborough LE16 31 F2
Raunds NN9 114 D6
Ringstead NN14 95 C3
Rothwell NN14 70 D7
Glaisdale Cl NN2 140 F5
Glaister Pl NN16 72 D2
Glamis Cl NN10 132 D1
Glan y Mor Terr NN2 141 C5
GLAPTHORN 26 C2
Glapthorn CE Lower Sch PE8 26 B2
Glapthorn Rd PE8 41 F6
Glasgow St NN5 158 F6
Glassbrook Rd NN10 132 A2
Glassthorpe La NN7 157 A6
Glastonbury Cl NN15 91 F8
Glastonbury Rd
Corby NN18 36 A6
Northampton NN4 159 C1
Glaston Rd LE15 3 A5
Glebe Ave
Broughton NN14 90 B4
Kettering NN15 91 B8
Northampton NN4 175 E8
Glebe Cl
Holcot NN6 126 E8
Glebe Cl *continued*
Northampton NN4 175 E8
Glebe Ct PE8 58 A4
Glebe Dr NN13 234 A7
Glebe Farm Cl NN4 175 C4
Glebe Farm Ct NN29 145 E6
Glebe La
Great Houghton NN4 160 E2
Hanslope MK19 206 E5
Harlestone NN7 139 E7
Pitsford NN6 125 D5
Staverton NN11 152 C7
Glebeland Cres NN5 159 A8
Glebeland Gdns NN5 140 F1
Glebeland Rd NN5 158 F8
Glebelands NN6 105 B1
Glebeland Wlk 1 NN5 158 F8
Glebe Rd
Burton Latimer NN15 92 A2
Cogenhoe NN7 161 E6
Deanshanger MK19 228 E5
Market Harborough LE16 32 A2
Mears Ashby NN6 128 B2
Glebe Rise OX17 231 A5
Glebe The
Aynho OX17 237 D7
Badby NN11 153 A2
Daventry NN11 153 C8
Glebe Way
Cogenhoe NN7 161 E6
Northampton NN4 175 E8
Glen Ave NN7 174 B2
Glen Bank NN8 130 A4
Glen Baulk Rd NN14, NN16 71 C4
Glencoe Dr NN15 91 E8
Glendale Ct NN3 143 C1
Glendon Rd NN14 70 E7
Glendower Cl NN11 135 A4
Gleneagles Cl
Daventry NN11 135 E3
Kettering NN15 91 F8
Gleneagles Dr NN8 129 D7
Glenfield Cl NN10 131 F2
Glenfield Dr NN29 145 D5
Glengary NN3 142 D7
Glenshee Cl NN15 91 E8
Glenville NN3 142 B4
Gloucester Ave NN4 159 B1
Gloucester Cl
2 Kettering NN16 72 C2
Northampton NN4 159 B2
Weedon Bec NN7 155 B4
Gloucester Cres
Northampton NN4 159 B2
Rushden NN10 132 C3
Gloucester Ct NN14 70 C6
Gloucester Ho NN4 159 C2
Gloucester Pl NN8 130 A4
Glover Ct LE16 20 C1
Glovers Cl NN9 131 E8
Glovers La
Middleton Cheney OX17 208 F1
Raunds NN9 114 C5
Glyndebourne Gdns NN18 36 A4
Goadby's Yd 9 NN16 72 B2
Gocker Wood Cl NN18 36 B1
Goddard Ct 5 LE16 31 E4
Godwin Ct NN13 233 E6
Godwin Rd NN17 21 F3
Godwin Wlk NN5 140 D2
Goffs Yd NN29 164 D2
Goldcrest Ct NN3 143 A5
Goldcrest Rd NN13 222 D1
Goldenash Ct NN3 142 F5
Golding Cl NN11 135 C2
GOLDINGS 143 A5
Goldings Rd NN3 143 A5
Goldsmith Dr NN17 36 D8
Goldsmith Rd NN8 129 C4
Gold St
Clipston LE16 66 F8
Desborough NN14 51 A3
Hanslope MK19 207 A2
Kettering NN16 72 B2
Northampton NN1 159 C5
Podington NN29 147 E2
Walgrave NN6 108 A5
Wellingborough NN8 130 A6
Gold Street Mews 6 NN1 159 C5
Golf La NN6 140 C8
Goodacre Cl CV23 80 A5
Goodens La NN29 145 F6
Goodhew Cl NN15 90 F8
Good Shepherd RC Prim Sch The NN2 141 C3
Goodwin Cl NN8 130 A8
Goodwood Ave NN3 141 F5
Goodwood Cl
Corby NN18 36 E1
Market Harborough LE16 32 B3
Goodwood Rd NN10 148 D8
Goose Gn NN13 233 E6
Goosemere MK19 228 E4
Goran Ave MK11 229 E4
Gordon Rd
Oundle PE8 42 A6
Wellingborough NN8 130 B5
Gordon St
Kettering NN16 72 C2

**Gordon St** *continued*
Northampton NN2 159 C8
Rothwell NN14 70 D6
Rushden NN10 131 F2
**Gordon Terr** NN14 74 F2
**Gores La** LE16 32 A3
**Gorricks** MK11 229 D4
**Gorse Cl** NN2 141 B6
**Gorseholm Ct** [10] NN9 112 F2
**Gorse Rd**
Hinton NN11 184 B7
Kettering NN16 72 E4
Spratton NN6 124 B8
**Gosforth** NN8 129 C4
**Goslar The** NN8 129 B3
**Gotch Cl** NN15 91 F4
**Gotch Rd** NN15 91 F5
**Gough Cl** NN15 72 E1
**Goughs Cotts** NN5 158 C7
**Gould Cl** NN11 118 B1
**Goulsbra Rd** NN10 148 D8
**Goward St** LE16 31 E3
**Gower Cl** NN15 91 C6
**Gowerton Rd** NN4 176 C8
**Grace Ct** NN15 92 B1
**Gracelands** LE16 31 C2
**Graeme Rd** PE5 8 F2
**Grafton Cl**
Hartwell NN7 192 D2
Potterspury NN12 217 E3
Wellingborough NN8 129 D7
**Grafton Ct** NN7 193 A8
**Grafton Dr** NN17 36 B8
**Grafton Ho** NN1 159 B6
**Grafton Pl** [10] NN1 159 C7
**Grafton Rd**
Brigstock NN14 55 E4
Cranford St John NN14 93 A7
Geddington NN14 54 B2
Roade NN7 191 C4
Rushden NN10 132 D2
Yardley Gobion NN12 217 F6
**GRAFTON REGIS** 205 D2
Grafton St Ind Est
NN1 159 B7
**Grafton St**
Kettering NN16 72 A4
Northampton NN1 159 C7
**Grafton View** NN4 175 E6
**Grafton Way**
Northampton NN5 140 B2
Rothersthorpe NN7 174 A7
**Graham Hill** NN12 214 D4
**Graham Hill Rd** NN12 203 C7
**Granary Cl** LE16 31 F6
**Granary Ct** NN4 175 C7
**Granary Rd** NN4 175 C7
**Granby Cl** NN18 36 B6
**Grandborough Cl**
NN6 106 C1
**Grange Ave** NN5 140 B1
**Grange Cl**
Denton NN7 162 B1
Earls Barton NN6 144 E5
Irchester NN29 147 B7
Grange Com Sch NN16 72 E3
**Grange Ct**
Brixworth NN6 106 B2
Horton NN7 177 D1
Stony Stratford MK12 229 F6
**Grange La**
Pitsford NN6 125 E6
Thorpe Langton LE16 17 A5
**GRANGE PARK** 175 E3
**Grange Pl** NN16 72 E4
**Grange Rd**
Broughton NN14 90 B5
Geddington NN14 53 F2
Islip NN14 76 B1
Kettering NN16 72 A3
Northampton NN3 142 C3
Stanion NN14 37 E2
Stanwick NN9 114 A3
Wellingborough NN9 110 E1
Grange Road Workshops
NN14 53 F2
Grange Sch The
NN11 135 A1
**Grangeway** NN10 148 A8
**Grange Way** NN29 147 B7
**Grangewood** NN4 175 A7
**Grant Cl** NN15 90 F7
**Grantham Wlk** NN18 36 B4
**Grantown Cl** NN15 91 E8
**Grant Rd** NN8 130 B5
**Granville St**
Kettering NN16 72 C2
Market Harborough LE16 31 F2
**Grasmere Gn** NN8 129 B4
**Grasmere Rd** NN16 71 F2
**Grasmere Way** NN10 132 B8
**Graspin La** NN3 160 D8
**Grass Cl** NN12 203 B7
**Grasscroft** NN2 141 A4
**Grass Croft** NN6 121 A3
**Grassmere Ave** NN3 142 E2
**Grass Slade** NN6 106 C2
**Gravel Hill** NN11 199 D7
**Gravely St** NN10 131 F2
**Gray Cl** NN6 145 A4
**Grays Cl** NN12 216 D8
**Gray's Cl** NN17 36 E8
**Grays Dr** NN14 37 E3
**Grays La**
Paulerspury NN12 216 D8
**Grays La** *continued*
Yardley Gobion NN12 217 E6
**Gray St**
Irchester NN29 147 A7
Northampton NN1 159 E7
**Greasley Wlk** NN18 36 B6
**GREAT ADDINGTON** 94 B2
Great Addington CE Prim
Sch NN14 94 B3
**GREAT BILLING** 143 C3
**Great Billing Way**
NN3 143 C4
**GREAT BOWDEN** 32 A6
Great Bowden CE Prim
Sch LE16 32 A6
**Great Bowden Hall**
LE16 31 E7
**Great Bowden Rd** LE16 32 A4
**GREAT BRINGTON** 138 D7
Great Central Walk Nature
Trail★ CV22 98 D6
**Great Central Way**
NN11 184 C7
**Great Cl** NN6 124 D1
**GREAT CRANSLEY** 89 F6
Great Creaton Prim Sch
NN6 104 F4
**GREAT DODDINGTON**
145 D5
Great Doddington Prim
Sch NN29 145 E6
**GREAT EASTON** 20 E7
**Great Easton Rd**
Bringhurst LE16 20 C6
Caldecott LE16 21 A7
Drayton LE16 20 A5
Great Easton LE16 20 F6
**Great Field Ct** NN3 142 E5
**Great Folds Rd** NN18 35 F1
**GREAT GIDDING** 61 D3
Great Gidding CE Prim
Sch PE28 61 D3
**Great Ground Wlk**
NN4 175 F2
**Great Gull Cres** NN3 142 F6
**GREAT HARROWDEN**
110 D2
**Great Holme Ct** NN3 142 E5
**GREAT HOUGHTON** 160 F2
**Great La**
Bugbrooke NN7 172 F7
Hackleton NN7 177 B3
**Greatmeadow** NN3 143 C4
**Greatmeadow Rd**
NN3 143 B4
**Great North Rd**
Stibbington PE8 8 C2
Wothorpe PE9 2 B8
**GREAT OAKLEY** 53 B8
**GREAT OXENDON** 48 E3
**Great Park St** NN8 130 A5
**Great Russell St** NN1 159 D7
**GREATWORTH** 210 E2
Greatworth Prim Sch
OX17 210 E2
**Grebe Cl**
Hinton NN11 184 B6
Thrapston NN14 76 E3
**Greenacre Dr**
Rushden NN10 148 B8
Stanion NN14 37 E2
**Green Acres Cvn Pk**
LE16 31 C6
**Greenaway Cl** NN7 190 E7
**Greenbank Ave** NN15 72 D1
**Greenbank Terr** NN14 95 B3
**Green Cl**
Irthlingborough NN9 131 D8
Wellingborough NN8 129 C7
**Green Dale Sq** [8]
NN3 143 C2
**Green End** NN2 141 B2
**Green End La** MK19 207 A3
**Green Farm** OX17 230 A4
**Green Farm Cl** CV23 81 A6
**Greenfield Ave**
Kettering NN15 71 F1
Northampton NN3 142 B3
**Greenfield Rd** NN3 142 A2
Greenfields Sch NN2 141 B5
**Greenfield Way** NN10 132 A1
**Greenfinch Dr** NN3 142 C6
**Greenglades** NN4 158 E1
**Greenhill Cres** NN11 135 B3
**Greenhill Ct** NN6 121 A3
**Greenhill Rd**
Elton PE7 29 B6
Elton PE8 28 F8
Kettering NN15 91 A8
Long Buckby NN6 121 A3
**Greenhill Rise** NN18 36 B5
**Greenhills Cl** NN2 141 B6
**Greenhills Rd** NN2 141 B6
**Greening Rd** NN14 70 C7
**Green La**
Ashley LE16 18 F2
Braybrooke LE16 49 F5
Charlton OX17 231 E5
Desborough NN14 50 D3
Duddington PE9 5 B6
Husbands Bosworth
LE17 45 E5
Kettering NN16 72 B2
Market Harborough LE16 31 E1
Northampton NN4 175 E5
Silverstone NN12 214 D4
Stanwick NN9 113 F3
Stoke Albany LE16 34 B4
**Green La** *continued*
Thrapston NN14 76 D2
Towcester NN12 203 A5
Weston by W LE16 18 C6
**Greenland Wlk** NN18 36 A2
**Greenlaw** NN8 129 B4
Green Oaks Prim Sch
NN2 141 D4
**Green Rd** NN7 161 E2
**Greenside**
Blisworth NN7 190 D7
Northampton NN3 142 B3
Wappenham NN12 213 B8
**Greenslade Cl** NN15 91 A8
**GREENS NORTON** 202 D8
Greens Norton CE Prim
Sch NN12 202 E8
**Green St**
Milton Malsor NN7 174 E4
Northampton NN1 159 B5
Wollaston NN29 146 E2
**Greensward The**
OX17 196 E1
**Green The**
Abthorpe NN12 201 F2
Adderbury OX17 230 A4
Barby CV23 99 C1
Blakesley NN12 187 B1
Brafield-on-t-G NN7 161 E2
Braunston NN11 118 C1
Byfield NN11 183 D7
Caldecott LE16 21 B8
Chelveston NN9 133 C8
Church Stowe NN7 171 D7
Clipston LE16 67 A8
Cosgrove MK19 218 F2
Cranford St John NN14 93 A6
Culworth OX17 198 C3
Deanshanger MK19 228 E4
Dodford NN7 154 E6
Evenley NN13 233 F2
Everdon NN11 170 A8
Flore NN7 155 F5
Great Bowden LE16 32 B6
Great Brington NN7 138 D7
Great Houghton NN4 160 E2
Guilsborough NN6 103 E7
Hanslope MK19 207 A2
Harlestone NN7 139 D4
Hellidon NN11 151 C1
Helmdon NN13 211 F4
Hollowell NN6 104 B4
Husbands Bosworth
LE17 45 E5
Kislingbury NN7 157 D3
Lilbourne CV23 81 A6
Little Addington NN14 113 B8
Lower Boddington
NN11 182 B5
Lubenham LE16 30 E3
Lyddington LE15 9 D7
Marston St Lawrence
OX17 210 B1
Mawsley Village NN14 89 B4
Nether Heyford NN7 156 B1
Newnham NN11 153 D4
Northampton, Grange Park
NN4 175 F3
Northampton, Hardingstone
NN4 175 F8
Northampton, Kingsthorpe
NN2 141 B3
[10] Northampton NN1 159 C5
Orlingbury NN14 110 A5
Paulerspury NN12 216 B7
Priors Marston CV47 166 D7
Roade NN7 191 D4
Staverton NN11 152 B7
Titchmarsh NN14 77 C4
Turweston NN13 234 C8
Twywell NN14 75 A1
Wadenhoe PE8 58 A4
Weedon Lois NN12 200 C3
West Haddon NN6 102 B4
Weston by W LE16 18 B3
Whilton NN11 137 D6
Woodford NN14 94 D6
**Greenview Dr**
Northampton NN2 141 E3
Towcester NN12 203 B6
**Greenway**
Braunston NN11 118 B1
Eastcote NN12 173 A1
Northampton NN3 160 C8
**Greenway Ave** NN3 142 D4
**Greenway The** NN11 153 C8
**Greenwood Cl**
Byfield NN11 183 C7
Moulton NN3 142 C8
**Greenwood Rd** NN5 159 A6
**Greenyard The** NN7 179 B7
**Greeve Cl** NN18 36 C1
**Greeves Cl** NN5 139 F1
**Gregory St** [8] NN1 159 C5
**Gregory Wlk** NN18 36 D4
**Grenadier Rd** NN11 135 B1
**GRENDON** 163 E5
**Grendon Ave** NN17 36 B7
Grendon CE Prim Sch
NN7 163 D5
Grendon Lakes
Watersports Ctr★
NN7 145 C1
**Grendon Rd** NN6 144 E1
**Grendon Wlk** NN3 141 F5
**Grenville Cl**
Corby NN17 36 A8
Daventry NN11 135 E1
**Grenville Cl** *continued*
Rothwell NN14 70 E6
**Grenville Gdns** LE16 31 D1
**Gresham Dr** NN4 158 E2
**Gresley Cl** NN11 135 A4
**GRETTON** 10 C1
**Gretton Brook Rd**
Corby NN17 21 E3
Corby NN17 22 C4
**Gretton Ct** NN8 129 D7
Gretton Prim Sch
NN17 22 C8
**Gretton Rd**
Corby NN17 22 F3
Harringworth NN17 10 E7
Lyddington LE15 9 D5
Rockingham LE16 21 B5
Weldon NN17 38 A8
Gretton Road Ind Est
NN17 38 A8
**Greville Ave** NN3 142 A4
**Greville Cl** NN2 141 C8
**Greyfriars** NN1 159 C6
**Greyfriars Rd** NN11 153 B8
**Greys The** NN7 155 B4
**Grieg Wlk** NN18 36 A2
**Griffin Cl** OX17 230 A5
**Griffin Rd** LE16 49 E4
**Griffiths Cl** NN5 157 F8
**Griffith St** NN10 132 B1
**Grimmer Wlk** NN9 131 D8
**Grimsby Cl** NN18 36 C4
**GRIMSCOTE** 188 B8
**Grindleford Cl** NN14 50 E3
**Grizedale Cl**
Corby NN17 36 D8
Kettering NN16 72 A6
**Grombold Ave** NN9 114 C6
**Grooms La** NN6 105 A4
**Grosvenor Cl** NN15 92 A5
Grosvenor Ctr NN1 159 D6
**Grosvenor Gdns** NN2 141 D4
**Grosvenor Ho** NN2 141 D4
**Grosvenor Pl** NN13 233 E7
**Grosvenor Rd** NN15 92 A5
**Grosvenor Way** NN15 91 F5
**Groundwell Ct** [1]
NN3 142 F1
**Grovebury Dell** NN2 141 A4
**Grove Farm Cl** NN6 121 D4
**Grove Farm La** NN3 126 D2
**Grove La** NN12 199 F3
**Grovelands** NN11 153 A8
**Grove Pl** NN9 114 D5
**Grove Rd**
Brafield-on-t-G NN7 161 D3
Northampton NN1 159 E7
Rushden NN10 132 C2
Thrapston NN14 76 D1
**Grove St**
Higham Ferrers
NN10 132 C6
Raunds NN9 114 D5
Wellingborough NN8 129 E4
**Grove The**
Corby NN18 37 C6
Kettering NN15 72 B1
Moulton NN3 126 C2
Ringstead NN14 95 A3
Roade NN7 191 E3
Wollaston NN29 146 D1
**Grove Way** NN9 111 E3
**Grove Works** NN1 159 E7
**Grundy Ct** NN15 91 B8
**Guildhall Rd** NN1 159 D5
**Guillemot La** NN8 130 A7
**GUILSBOROUGH** 103 E6
Guilsborough CE Prim Sch
NN6 103 E7
**Guilsborough Hill**
NN6 104 B5
**Guilsborough Rd**
Ravensthorpe NN6 103 D1
West Haddon NN6 102 C5
Guilsborough Sch
NN6 103 D8
**Guinea Orch** MK46 195 E4
**Gullet La** LE16 18 F2
**Gumley Rd** LE16 30 C7
**Gunnell Cl** NN15 90 F8
**Gunnsbrook Cl** LE16 32 A6
**Gunthorpe Pl** NN18 36 B6
**Gurston Rise** NN3 143 C4
**Gynwell** NN6 85 B8

## H

**Hachenburg Pl** NN10 132 C5
**HACKLETON** 177 C3
Hackleton Prim Sch
NN7 177 A3
**Hackwood Rd** NN11 153 E8
**Haddon Cl**
Rushden NN10 132 A1
Wellingborough NN8 129 D8
**Haddon Ct** NN6 122 C5
**Haddonian Rd** LE16 31 F1
Haddonstone Show Gdn★
NN6 122 D4
**Hadfield Cl** CV23 80 A5
**Hadleigh Ho** [4] NN10 132 B2
**Hadrian's Gate** NN13 234 A7
**Hafod Cl** NN18 36 C2
**Hagley Cl** LE16 32 B3
**Haigh Dr** NN15 72 E1
**Hailsham Ct** OX17 220 B8
**Haines Rd** NN4 159 C3
**Hale Ave** MK11 229 E5
**Halfmoon Mews** PE8 42 A5
**Halford St** NN14 76 C1
**Halford Way** NN11 135 E8
**Halfway Thorn** NN6 124 C1
**Halifax Sq** NN18 36 B5
**Hallam Cl** NN3 142 B7
**Hallaton Rd** LE16 18 F7
**Hall Ave** NN10 132 A1
**Hall Cl**
Arthingworth LE16 68 C7
Harpole NN7 157 B6
Kettering NN15 90 F8
Kilsby CV23 100 A3
Kislingbury NN7 157 D4
Naseby NN6 66 B1
Northampton NN5 158 C6
Old Stratford MK19 229 B6
Weston by W LE16 18 B4
**Hall Dr**
Finedon NN9 111 E4
Long Buckby NN6 121 C4
**Hall Farm Cl** NN6 106 B3
**Hall Gdns**
East Haddon NN6 122 D5
Loddington NN14 70 C1
Polebrook PE8 43 A3
**Hall Hill** NN14 55 F7
**Hall La**
Ashley LE16 18 E2
Drayton LE16 20 A5
Kettering NN15 90 F8
South Luffenham LE15 3 E8
Welford NN6 64 D6
Wittering PE8 7 C8
**Hall Mead Ct** NN7 172 E6
Hall Meadow Prim Sch
NN15 90 F7
**Hall Piece Cl** NN3 143 C3
**Hall's Cl**
Geddington NN14 54 B3
Weldon NN17 38 A8
**Hall's La** NN13 233 E6
**Hallwood Rd** NN16 72 C5
**Hall Yd**
Collyweston PE9 1 C2
King's Cliffe PE8 13 F7
**HALSE** 222 B5
**Halse Rd** NN13 222 F1
**Halswell Ct** NN3 142 D4
**Hambledon Rise** NN4 158 E3
**Hamblin Ct** NN10 132 B2
**Hamilton Ct** NN6 124 D1
**Hamilton Ho**
Corby NN17 36 E5
Northampton NN2 141 C5
**Hamilton La** NN7 138 D6
**Ham La** NN14 95 A4
**Hamlet Gn** NN5 158 F8
**Hammas Leys** NN6 121 C4
**Ham Meadow Dr** NN3 143 C2
**Hammerstone La**
NN4 158 F3
**Hammond Way** LE16 31 E4
**Hampden Cres** NN16 72 D3
**Hampton Court Cl**
NN12 203 B5
**Hampton Ct** LE16 31 F3
**Hampton Dr** OX17 230 F6
**Hampton Ho** [1] NN10 132 B2
**Hampton St** NN1 159 B7
**Hamsterly Pk** NN3 143 A6
**Hanbury Cl** NN11 135 B6
**Handcross Ct** NN18 36 B4
**Handcross Way** NN10 132 C5
**Handley Cl** NN5 140 A1
**Hanemill Ct** NN3 143 C1
**Hangerfield Ct** NN3 142 F4
**HANGING HOUGHTON**
106 C8
**HANNINGTON** 108 C2
**Hanover Cl** NN15 92 A7
**Hanover Ct** NN3 143 B4
**Hanover Dr** NN13 233 E7
**Hans Apel Dr** NN13 233 D7
**HANSLOPE** 207 B3
Hanslope Comb Sch
MK19 207 A3
**Hanslope Rd** MK19 218 F7
**Harbidges La** NN6 121 A4
**Harborough Rd**
Braybrooke LE16 49 D7
Brixworth NN6 106 C3
Clipston LE16 48 A2
Desborough LE16, NN14 50 D7
Dingley LE16 32 D5
Dingley LE16 32 E1
Dingley LE16 33 A3
East Farndon LE16 48 C8
Great Oxendon LE16 48 F4
Kelmarsh NN6 67 F5
Lubenham LE16 31 A3
Maidwell NN6 87 B4
Market Harborough
LE16 31 C7
Marston Trussell LE17 30 A1
Northampton NN2 141 C4
Rushden NN10 132 C1
Stoke Albany LE16 34 B4
Theddingworth LE17 46 D8
**Harborough Rd N**
NN2 141 B6
**Harborough Way**
NN10 132 C1
**Harcourt Sq** NN6 144 E4
**Harcourt St**
[9] Kettering NN16 72 C2

Harcourt St *continued*
Market Harborough LE16 31 D3
Raunds NN9 114 D6
Harcourt Way NN4 158 E3
Hardays La NN6 102 B4
Harden Cl NN18 53 A8
Harding Cl NN15 72 F1
HARDINGSTONE 175 E8
Hardingstone La NN4 175 D8
Hardingstone Prim Sch NN4 175 E7
Harding Terr NN1 159 C7
Hardlands Rd NN5 158 C8
Hardwater Rd NN29 145 D4
HARDWICK 128 D8
Hardwick Cl NN8 129 E5
Hard wick Hall Way 10 NN11 135 B7
Hardwick Jun & Inf Sch NN8 129 C5
Hardwick Rd
Gretton NN17 10 B1
Little Harrowden NN9 110 B3
Northampton NN4 175 C8
Priors Marston CV47 166 D7
Wellingborough, Hatton Park NN8 129 D6
Wellingborough, Hatton Park NN8 129 E5
Wellingborough NN8 129 A7
Hardy Dr NN4 175 F7
Harebell Sq 1 NN3 143 D2
Harefield Rd NN3 143 B5
Harefoot Cl NN5 158 B8
Haresmoor Dr NN12 203 C4
Hares Run NN14 89 C5
HARGRAVE 115 E2
Hargrave Ct NN9 112 E1
Harksome Hill NN4 158 E2
Harlech NN18 36 C3
Harlech Ct NN14 76 F2
HARLESTONE 139 D5
Harlestone Ct NN5 158 F7
Harlestone Ho NN5 159 A7
Harlestone Prim Sch NN7 139 E5
Harlestone Rd
Church Brampton NN6 124 D1
Harlestone NN7 139 F6
Northampton NN5 140 B2
Harley Way
Brigstock NN14 56 C8
Lower Benefield PE8 40 D3
Harmans Way NN7 155 B4
Harnett Dr MK12 229 F6
Harold St 10 NN1 159 E6
Harpers Cl NN18 53 B8
Harper's Ct NN14 55 F7
HARPOLE 157 D6
Harpole Prim Sch NN7 157 D6
Harrier Pk NN4 175 B8
HARRINGTON 69 B4
Harrington Rd
Desborough NN14 50 F3
Kelmarsh NN6 67 F3
Loddington NN14 70 D1
Old NN6 107 D7
Rothwell NN14 70 C6
HARRINGWORTH 10 F7
Harringworth Rd NN17 10 C2
Harris Cl
Brackley NN13 233 D8
Northampton NN4 175 F7
Raunds NN9 114 D7
Harrison Cl
Market Harborough LE16 48 D8
Rugby CV21 99 B8
Wellingborough NN8 129 D5
Harrison Ct NN7 172 F7
Harris Rd NN17 21 C1
Harrod Dr LE16 32 A4
Harrogate Ct NN18 36 B4
Harrold Rd NN29 164 D3
Harrowden Rd
Finedon NN9 111 D3
Northampton NN4 160 B2
Orlingbury NN14 110 A5
Wellingborough NN8 129 F6
Harrowick La NN6 144 E4
Harrow La NN11 135 D6
Harrow Way NN2 140 F6
Harry Cl NN6 121 B3
Harry Potter Ho NN15 72 B1
Hartburn Cl NN3 161 C8
Hartland Dr LE16 32 B3
Hartley Dr NN15 92 A7
Hartley Ho NN13 233 F6
HARTWELL 192 D1
Hartwell CE Prim Sch NN7 192 D1
Hartwell Cl NN2 141 D5
Hartwell Rd
Ashton NN7 205 F8
Hanslope MK19 206 E4
Roade NN7 192 A2
Hartwood Croft NN16 72 C6
Harvest Cl
Burton Latimer NN15 92 C2
Daventry NN11 135 D6
Harvest Way NN2 140 F5
Harvey Cl NN9 114 B5
Harvey Dr MK46 195 F1
Harvey La NN3 142 B8
Harvey Rd
Rushden NN10 148 B7
Wellingborough NN8 129 E3
Harvey Reeves Rd NN5 159 A5
Harwood Dr NN16 72 A6
HASELBECH 86 A8
Haselrig Sq 4 NN4 158 F2
Hassocks Hedge NN4 158 C2
Hastings MK11 229 E5
Hastings Rd NN2 141 D3
Hastings Wlk 4 NN18 36 B5
Hatchdoyle La PE8 41 D1
Hatfield Cl
Corby NN18 36 E3
6 Northampton NN4 175 C8
Wellingborough NN8 129 C7
Hatherley Cl NN6 101 A6
Hathersage Cl NN14 50 E4
Hatton Ave NN8 129 F5
Hatton Cl NN3 142 A6
Hatton Hall 5 NN8 129 F5
Hatton La NN17 10 B1
HATTON PARK 129 E6
Hatton Park Rd NN8 129 F5
Hatton St NN8 129 F5
Hautboy La PE8 28 B3
Havelock Cotts PE8 42 A5
Havelock Ho 4 NN16 72 C4
Havelock Jun & Inf Schs NN14 51 A3
Havelock Mews NN16 72 B3
Havelock St
Desborough NN14 51 A3
Kettering NN16 72 C3
Wellingborough NN8 130 A5
Haven Cl NN5 159 A7
Haweswater Rd NN16 71 E3
Hawfinch Gn NN14 51 B4
Hawke Rd NN11 135 E1
Hawkesbeard Pl 3 NN3 143 C2
Hawkins Cl
Brackley NN13 233 D7
Corby NN17 21 B1
Daventry NN11 135 E2
Rothwell NN14 70 E7
Stony Stratford MK11 229 D5
Hawk Ridge NN4 158 F1
Hawkshead NN8 129 B3
Hawksmoor Way NN5 140 D1
Hawksnest NN4 175 A8
Hawkstone Cl NN5 158 D7
Hawkswood MK46 195 F5
Hawkwell Est MK19 229 B7
Hawson Cl NN15 91 C7
Hawthorn Ave NN14 89 C5
Hawthorn Cl NN15 92 B1
Hawthorn Com Prim Sch NN15 91 B8
Hawthorn Dr
Brackley NN13 222 F1
Daventry NN11 135 C3
Thrapston NN14 76 D1
Towcester NN12 203 C8
Hawthorne Cl NN11 184 B6
Hawthorne Rd NN9 112 A4
Hawthorne Wlk NN17 21 E1
Hawthorn Rd
Burton Latimer NN15 92 B1
Kettering NN15 91 B8
Northampton NN3 142 A1
Hawthorns The
Desborough NN14 51 C2
Higham Ferrers NN10 132 B6
Silverstone NN12 214 D3
Hawthorn Way NN8 129 E5
Hay Cl
Corby NN18 53 B8
Rushden NN10 148 B8
Haycroft Wlk NN2 141 A5
Hayden Ave NN9 112 A5
Hayden Rd NN10 132 C2
Hayden Wlk NN10 132 C2
Haydock Cl NN18 53 E8
Haydown Gn NN5 158 D8
Hayes Rd MK19 228 F5
Hayes Wlk PE8 16 D1
Hayeswood Rd NN3 142 F4
Hay La NN9 112 E1
Hayman Rd NN13 233 D7
Haynes La NN6 105 B1
Haynes Rd NN16 72 D2
Hayride The NN4 175 A7
Haystack The NN11 135 D6
Hayway
Irthlingborough NN9 112 E1
Rushden NN10 132 A4
Hayway Inf Sch NN10 132 B3
Hazeland Ho NN14 51 A3
Hazel Cl
Brackley NN13 222 F1
Hartwell NN7 192 E2
Hazel Copse NN4 175 F1
Hazel Cres NN12 203 B5
Hazel Croft NN11 118 C1
Hazelden Cl NN29 146 D1
Hazeldene Rd NN2 141 F3
Hazel Leys Prim Sch NN18 36 D4
Hazel Rd NN15 72 C1
Hazelwood NN12 214 C4
Hazelwood Ct 1 NN16 72 B1
Hazelwood La NN16 72 B1
Hazelwood Rd
Corby NN17 36 E7
Northampton NN1 159 D5
Headingley Rd NN10 132 D2
Headlands
Desborough NN14 51 C3
Kettering NN15 91 B8
Headlands Prim Sch NN3 142 C2
Headlands The
Market Harborough LE16 31 F4
Northampton NN3 142 C2
Wellingborough NN8 129 F6
Headway NN18 53 A8
Healey Cl NN3 143 D4
Hearndon Ct NN8 129 E3
Hearth St LE16 31 D3
Heart Of The Shires Sh Village NN7 136 F2
Heathcote Gr NN14 50 E4
HEATHENCOTE 204 A3
Heatherbreea Gdns NN10 131 F3
Heather Ct
Northampton NN4 159 A2
Rushden NN10 132 A2
Heatherdale Way NN2 141 E3
Heather La NN3 142 E4
Heather Rd NN16 72 D4
Heathers The NN29 146 E2
Heathfield Way NN5 141 A1
Heathfield Wlk NN18 36 B4
Heath Gn NN5 140 F1
Heath Rise NN8 129 D6
Heath Terr NN12 203 C6
Heathville NN5 140 F1
Heath Way
Burton Latimer NN15 92 C3
Rugby CV22 98 D8
H E Bates Way NN10 132 A2
Hecham Way NN10 132 B7
Hedge End NN4 175 C6
Hedgely Ct NN4 159 A2
Hedgerow Dr NN2 141 A5
Hedgerow La NN14 89 C5
Hedgerow Way NN11 135 C6
Hedges The NN10 132 C4
Hedgeway NN4 175 C6
HELLIDON 151 D1
Hellidon Cl NN2 141 E4
Hellidon Rd CV47 166 D7
HELMDON 211 F4
Helmdon Cres NN2 141 C4
Helmdon Prim Sch NN13 211 F4
Helmdon Rd
Greatworth OX17 210 E2
Northampton NN2 141 C5
Sulgrave OX17 210 F7
Wappenham NN12 213 A8
Weston NN12 199 F2
Helmsley Way NN18 36 B5
Hemans Rd NN11 135 B3
Hembury Pl NN4 158 F3
Hemery Way NN15 90 F8
HEMINGTON 60 E7
Hemington Rd PE8 42 F2
Hemmingwell Rd NN8 130 A7
Hempland Cl NN18 53 B8
Hemplow Dr NN6 64 B2
Henders MK11 229 E5
Henley Cl
Kettering NN15 91 F5
Wellingborough NN8 129 C6
Henley Ct NN6 120 C6
Henley Ho NN17 36 E6
Henry Bird Ct NN4 159 D4
Henry Bird Way NN4 159 D4
Henry Chichele Prim Sch NN10 132 B7
Henry Gotch Prim Sch NN15 72 D1
Henry Smith Ho 2 NN11 135 B3
Henry St NN1 159 E7
Henshaw Rd NN8 129 E3
Hensmans La NN29 164 D3
Henson Cl NN16 71 F5
Henson Pk NN16 71 F5
Henson Way NN16 71 E4
Herbert Gdns NN12 203 D8
Herbert St NN1 159 C6
Hereford Cl NN14 51 C4
Hereward Rd NN4 159 B2
Herford Cl NN18 36 A2
Heritage Ct NN16 72 B1
Heritage Way
Corby NN17 22 B2
Raunds NN9 114 E7
Hermitage Rd LE16 33 E3
Hermitage Way NN4 175 D7
Herne Hill Ct NN4 158 E2
Herne Rd PE8 42 B4
Heron Ave NN14 76 E3
Heron Cl
Burton Latimer NN15 92 A2
Hinton NN11 184 B6
Towcester NN12 203 C3
Wellingborough NN8 130 A7
Heron Ct NN11 135 C3
Heron Dr NN13 222 D1
Heronsford NN4 174 E8
Herons Wood Cl PE8 41 E5
Herrieffs Farm Rd NN13 233 F6
Herriotts Ct 11 NN8 130 A5
Herriotts La NN8 130 A5
Hertford Ct
Daventry NN11 153 C7
Northampton NN3 143 A1
Hertford Rd NN15 91 C6
Hervey Cl NN3 142 D2
Hervey St NN1 159 E7
Hesketh Cres NN12 203 C4
Hesketh Rd NN12 217 E6
Hesperus NN8 129 B4
Hester St NN2 159 C8
Hever Cl
Rushden NN10 148 C8
Thrapston NN14 76 E2
Hewlett's Cl NN29 164 D2
Hexham Ct NN4 159 A2
Heyford Rd NN5 157 F7
Heygate St LE16 31 E4
Hiawatha NN8 129 B4
Hibiscus Cl NN3 160 C6
Hickman Cl OX17 210 D2
Hickmire NN29 146 D3
Hicks Ct NN12 203 D4
Hicks Rd NN12 203 C4
Hidcote Cl
Corby NN18 36 E2
Northampton NN4 175 C7
Wellingborough NN8 129 D2
Hidcote Way 3 NN11 135 B7
Hield Cl NN18 36 C1
Higgins Sq NN4 158 F2
HIGHAM CROSS 206 D3
Higham Cross Rd MK19 206 E4
HIGHAM FERRERS 132 D6
Higham Ferrers Jun & Inf Schs NN10 132 B6
Higham Park Rd NN10 149 A5
Higham Rd
Burton Latimer NN15 92 C1
Chelveston NN9 133 B7
Little Irchester NN8, NN29 130 D1
Rushden NN10 132 B4
Stanwick NN9 113 F3
High Barns Cl NN4 175 E2
Highbridge Rd NN12 213 A8
Highbrook NN18 36 B4
Highcroft LE17 45 E6
Highcroft Cl NN12 217 E6
Highcross St LE16 31 C3
Highdown Cl NN4 158 E3
Highfield
Duddington PE9 5 B7
Woodford NN14 94 C7
Highfield Cotts LE15 3 E8
Highfield Court Mews NN13 233 E6
Highfield Cres NN15 91 C6
Highfield Ct NN13 233 E6
Highfield Gr NN17 36 F7
Highfield Pk NN6 104 D4
Highfield Rd
Daventry NN11 135 B3
Irthlingborough NN9 112 F2
Kettering NN15 91 B7
Mears Ashby NN6 128 C4
Northampton NN1 142 A1
Rushden NN10 131 F1
Thrapston NN14 76 E2
Wellingborough NN8 130 B5
Highfields
Polebrook PE8 42 F3
Towcester NN12 203 C3
Highfields Com Prim Sch NN15 91 B7
Highfield St
Finedon NN9 112 B5
Market Harborough LE16 31 D3
Highfield Way NN7 179 B6
HIGHGATE 28 D8
Highgate Gn PE8 28 D8
High Gn NN2 141 B3
High Greeve NN4 176 A6
Highgrove Ct 2 NN10 132 B2
High Hill Ave NN14 70 C7
Highlands Ave NN3 142 A4
Highlands Dr NN11 135 B5
High Leys The NN6 100 F4
High March NN11 153 E8
High March Cl NN11 153 E8
Highpoint NN13 233 F5
High St Mews 4 NN8 129 F4
High St N NN12 189 D5
High St Pl NN8 129 F4
High St S
Olney MK46 195 F3
Rushden NN10 132 B1
Tiffield NN12 189 D4
High St The NN6 103 D1
High Slade NN6 125 C8
High St
Adderbury OX17 230 A4
Astcote NN12 188 F7
Blakesley NN12 187 A1
Blisworth NN7 190 D7
Bozeat NN29 164 D2
Brackley NN13 233 F7
Braunston NN11 118 B1
Brigstock NN14 55 F8
Brixworth NN6 106 B3
Broughton NN14 90 A4
Bugbrooke NN7 172 F7
Burton Latimer NN15 92 C2
Byfield NN11 183 D7
Charwelton NN11 168 A4
High St *continued*
Chelveston NN9 133 C8
Clipston LE16 67 A8
Collyweston PE9 1 D2
Corby NN17 37 A6
Cottingham LE16 20 C1
Cranford St John NN14 93 A6
Creaton NN6 104 F4
Crick NN6 100 F5
Croughton NN13 238 C8
Culworth OX17 198 C3
Daventry NN11 135 C2
Deanshanger MK19 228 E4
Denford NN14 95 C6
Desborough NN14 51 A3
Duddington PE9 5 B6
Earls Barton NN6 144 E4
Easton o t H PE9 2 A5
Ecton NN6 143 F3
Everdon NN11 170 A8
Eydon NN11 184 C1
Finedon NN9 111 F5
Flore NN7 155 E5
Gayton NN7 173 E2
Great Doddington NN7 145 E6
Great Easton LE16 20 D7
Great Houghton NN4 160 E2
Greens Norton NN12 202 D8
Gretton NN17 10 C1
Guilsborough NN6 103 F6
Hanslope MK19 207 A2
Harpole NN7 157 C6
Harrington NN6 69 A5
Higham Ferrers NN10 132 B5
Husbands Bosworth LE17 45 E5
Irchester NN29 147 B8
Irthlingborough NN9 112 E2
Islip NN14 76 B2
Kettering NN16 72 B2
Ketton PE9 1 A6
Kislingbury NN7 157 D4
Lamport NN6 87 D2
Little Addington NN14 113 B8
Long Buckby NN6 121 C4
Market Harborough LE16 31 E3
Middleton Cheney OX17 219 F8
Milton Malsor NN7 174 E4
Morcott LE15 3 A6
Moulton NN3 126 C1
Naseby NN6 85 B8
Northampton, Collingtree NN4 175 C4
Northampton, Great Billing NN3 143 C2
Northampton, Hardingstone NN4 175 F8
Northampton, Kingsthorpe NN2 141 B3
Northampton, Weston Favell NN3 142 D1
Northampton, Wootton NN4 175 E6
Olney MK46 195 F4
Paulerspury NN12 216 C8
Pitsford NN6 125 C4
Podington NN29 147 E2
Potterspury NN12 217 D3
Preston Capes NN11 169 D2
Pytchley NN14 90 F2
Raunds NN9 114 D7
Ringstead NN14 95 B3
Roade NN7 191 D4
Rothwell NN14 70 C7
Rugby CV21 99 A8
Rushden NN10 132 B2
Rushton NN14 52 C2
Scaldwell NN6 106 F5
Shutlanger NN12 190 D1
Silverstone NN12 214 D4
Souldern OX27 237 E3
Spratton NN6 105 B1
Stanion NN14 37 E2
Stanwick NN9 113 F3
Stony Stratford MK11 229 D6
Swinford LE17 62 B3
Syresham NN13 224 B8
Thrapston NN14 76 D2
Titchmarsh NN14 77 D4
Twywell NN14 74 F1
Walgrave NN6 108 A5
Wappenham NN12 213 B8
Weedon Bec NN7 155 B4
Weedon Lois NN12 200 C2
Weldon NN17 38 B8
Welford NN6 64 E6
Wellingborough NN8 129 F5
Welton NN11 119 E1
West Haddon NN6 102 C4
Weston NN12 199 F2
Weston Underwood MK46 195 B2
Whittlebury NN12 215 C4
Wollaston NN29 146 D2
Woodford Halse NN11 184 C6
Woodford NN14 94 D7
Wymington NN10 148 B5
Yardley Gobion NN12 217 F6
Yardley Hastings NN7 179 B6
Yelvertoft NN6 82 B3
High Stack NN6 121 C3
High View
Deanshanger MK19 228 E5
Northampton NN4 175 E6

High Woods NN6 143 D8
Hilda Pl NN16 72 E4
Hillary Cl NN11 135 B5
Hillary Rd NN10 131 F1
Hillberry Rise NN3 143 D4
Hill Cl
Northampton NN5 140 C2
Walgrave NN6 107 F5
Hill Crest NN7 174 C1
Hillcrest Ave
Burton Latimer NN15 92 B1
Kettering NN15 72 D1
Market Harborough LE16 31 D4
Northampton NN3 142 A3
Hillcrest Cl NN14 76 E3
Hillcrest La LE17 45 E5
Hillcrest Rd NN7 173 E1
Hillcroft View NN12 187 B1
Hilldrop Rd NN4 175 B7
Hill Farm Est NN14 113 C7
Hill Farm Rise NN4 175 A8
Hillfield Rd PE8 41 E6
Hill Gdns LE16 31 C3
Hill Ho OX17 219 C6
Hill House Ct NN12 172 D1
Hill House Gdns NN9 113 F3
Hillmorton La
Clifton u D CV23 80 A4
Lilbourne CV23 80 F5
Yelvertoft NN6 82 A4
Hillmorton Prim Sch CV21 99 B8
Hill Rd NN11 182 C5
Hill Row NN11 134 C8
Hillside
Chelveston NN9 133 B8
Daventry NN11 135 E2
Great Harrowden NN9 110 E4
Hartwell NN7 192 D2
West Haddon NN6 102 B4
Hillside Ave
Kettering NN15 91 C8
Silverstone NN12 214 E5
Hillside Cl NN29 164 D2
Hillside Cotts PE28 97 A4
Hillside Cres
Nether Heyford NN7 156 C1
Weldon NN17 38 A7
Hillside Rd
Flore NN7 155 D6
Market Harborough LE16 31 F4
Nether Heyford NN7 156 C1
Piddington NN7 177 B1
Wellingborough NN8 130 C7
Hillside Terr NN16 72 A2
Hillside Way NN3 160 C8
Hill St
Brackley NN13 233 F7
Kettering NN16 72 A3
Raunds NN9 114 D6
Wellingborough NN8 129 F4
Hillstone Ct NN9 113 F3
Hill The
Aynho OX17 237 C7
Great Houghton NN4 160 E2
Middleton LE16 35 B8
Pury End NN12 215 F7
Syresham NN13 224 B8
Hilltop
Blisworth NN7 174 C1
Dodford NN7 154 F5
Great Harrowden NN9 110 E5
HILL TOP 141 D4
Hill Top NN2 141 D4
Hilltop Ave
Desborough NN14 50 F4
Kettering NN15 91 F5
Hilltop Cl
Brixworth NN6 106 B1
Desborough NN14 50 F4
Hill Top Rd NN9 110 D4
Hill View NN11 184 C1
Hilmorton Rd CV22 98 F8
Hind Stile NN10 132 B5
HINTON 184 A6
Hinton Ave NN18 36 A4
Hinton Cl
Hinton NN11 184 B6
Northampton NN2 141 C5
HINTON-IN-THE-HEDGES 232 F6
Hinton Manor Ct NN11 184 B6
Hinton Rd
Brackley NN13 233 E6
Hinton NN11 184 B5
Northampton NN2 141 C5
Hinton's Cl NN13 211 F3
HINWICK 165 D7
Hinwick Cl NN15 91 D5
Hinwick Hall Coll of F Ed NN29 147 C1
Hinwick Rd
Podington NN29 147 D1
Wollaston NN29 146 E1
Hipwell Ct MK46 195 F3
Hirondelle Cl NN5 139 F1
Hobbs Hill NN14 70 C6
Hobby Cl NN4 175 B8
Hocknell Cl NN4 175 F6
Hockney Ave NN15 92 A7
Hodge Cl NN12 188 F6
Hodges La NN7 157 D4
Hodge Way NN16 72 D2
Hodnet Cl NN4 175 C7
Hoe Way NN7 191 C4
Hogarth Cl NN8 129 F7
Hogarth Dr NN15 92 A7
Hogarth Wlk NN18 36 E5
Hogg End OX17 196 F6
Hogg La OX17 231 F5
Holback La MK18 226 A5
Holbein Gdns NN4 174 E8
Holbein Wlk NN18 36 D5
Holbush Way NN9 112 E3
HOLCOT 126 E8
Holcot Cl NN8 129 E8
Holcot La
Scaldwell NN6 107 A5
Sywell NN6 127 E4
Holcot Leys CV22 98 A7
Holcot Rd
Brixworth NN6 106 D2
Moulton NN3 126 C5
Walgrave NN6 107 F4
Holcutt Cl NN4 175 F7
HOLDENBY 123 D3
Holdenby
Holdenby NN6 123 D4
Kettering NN15 91 D5
Holdenby Cl LE16 32 B3
Holdenby House Gdns & Falconry Ctr★ NN6 123 C4
Holdenby Rd
East Haddon NN6 122 E5
Northampton NN2 141 E4
Spratton NN6 124 B8
Holden Gr NN11 135 B2
Holdgate Cl NN13 222 E1
Holes La MK46 195 F4
Holiday La MK19 206 F4
Holkham Cl NN18 36 D2
Holland Rise OX17 230 F4
Hollands Dr NN15 92 C2
Hollies The
Higham Ferrers NN10 132 B5
Moulton NN3 126 B2
Wellingborough NN8 129 E5
Hollingside Dr NN2 141 F3
Hollington Rd NN9 114 D6
Holloway The CV47 166 D7
Hollow Bank NN3 142 C6
HOLLOWELL 104 B5
Hollowell Cl NN10 148 D8
Hollowell Ct 3 NN8 129 F4
Hollowell Rd NN6 104 E4
Hollow The
Ravensthorpe NN6 103 E1
Stanwick NN9 114 A3
Hollow Way
Aynho OX17 237 C7
Eydon NN11 184 B1
Hollow Wood MK46 195 E3
Holly Bush La CV47 166 D7
Holly Cl
Brackley NN13 222 F1
Market Harborough LE16 31 E4
Hollyhill NN12 203 B4
Holly La NN14 90 A6
Holly Lodge Dr NN2 141 D6
Holly Rd
Kettering NN16 72 C4
Northampton NN1 159 F8
Rushden NN10 131 E3
Holly Wlk NN9 111 D4
Holman Cl NN3 142 D2
Holm Cl NN7 155 A2
Holme Cl
Wellingborough NN9 110 E1
Wilbarston LE16 34 D5
Holmecross Rd NN3 142 E5
Holmes Ave NN9 114 E5
Holmes Dr PE9 1 B5
Holme Way CV23 99 D1
Holmfield Dr NN9 114 E6
Holmfield Terr NN6 121 A4
Holmfield Way NN3 160 C8
Holmfirth Wlk NN18 36 C4
Holmleigh Cl NN5 158 C7
Holmwood Cl NN5 140 A1
Holt Rd LE16 19 C8
Holt View LE16 20 D7
Holyoake Rd NN29 146 D2
Holyoake Terr NN6 121 C4
Holyrood Ct NN5 158 F7
Holyrood Rd NN5 158 F7
Holyrood Wlk NN18 36 C3
Home Acre NN7 161 B4
Home Cl
Blisworth NN7 190 D7
Corby NN18 36 B1
Dingley LE16 33 A3
Eastcote NN12 188 F8
Greens Norton NN12 202 D8
Irthlingborough NN9 131 E8
Middleton Cheney OX17 220 B8
Northampton NN4 175 E2
Silverstone NN12 214 D4
Staverton NN11 152 C8
Towcester NN12 203 C5
Home Ct NN14 76 D2
Home Farm OX17 219 E7
Home Farm Cl
Corby NN18 53 B8
Creaton NN6 104 F5
East Farndon LE16 48 B7
Northampton NN3 161 B8
Weedon Bec NN7 154 F2
Home Farm Ct
Adderbury OX17 230 B4
Norton NN11 136 C4
Home Farm Gr LE16 68 C7
Home Farm La NN6 125 C4
Home Farm Rd NN14 37 E2
Home Farm Yd NN6 104 B5
Homefield NN11 153 C8
Homestead Cl NN3 126 D1
Homestead Ct NN2 141 E1
Homestead Dr NN7 173 A7
Homestead Rise NN4 175 E6
Homestead The NN14 74 F1
Homestead Way
Northampton NN2 141 E1
Potterspury NN12 217 E3
Homewelland Ho LE16 31 D4
Honey Hill Dr MK19 228 E5
Honey Holme NN6 106 A1
Honeypot La LE17 45 E5
Honeystones NN3 126 C1
Honeysuckle Rd NN14 51 A5
Honeysuckle Way NN3 160 C6
Honiton Gdns NN18 36 E4
Hood Ct NN17 36 B8
Hood Rd NN11 135 E1
Hood St NN1 159 E7
Hood Wlk NN15 91 D8
Hookhams Path NN29 146 E2
Hopes Pl NN2 141 B3
Hope St NN29 164 D4
Hopmeadow Ct 2 NN3 143 B4
Hoppet Cl NN18 53 A8
HOPPING HILL 140 C1
Hopping Hill Gdns NN5 140 D1
Hopping Hill Prim Sch NN5 158 C8
Hopton Cl NN11 135 D6
Hopton Fields LE16 48 D8
Hornbeam Cl
Podington NN29 147 E2
Wellingborough NN8 129 E5
Hornbeam Ct
Desborough NN14 51 D3
Northampton NN3 142 D3
Hornby Rd NN6 144 E5
Horncastle Cl NN11 135 C6
Horne Cl CV21 99 B8
Horn La MK11 229 D5
Horrell Ct NN10 132 A2
Horrock's Way NN15 72 F1
Horsefair Cl LE16 31 D4
Horsefair Gn MK11 229 D5
Horse La NN17 11 F5
Horselease Cl NN18 53 A8
Horse Market
Kettering NN16 72 B2
Northampton NN1 159 C6
Horsemoor Sq 6 NN3 143 C2
Horsepool The CV23 81 A7
Horseshoe Cl
Brixworth NN6 106 C2
Creaton NN6 104 F4
Horse Shoe La LE16 32 B6
Horseshoe St NN1 159 C5
Horse Well Ct NN3 142 C7
Horsham Wlk NN18 36 B5
Horsley Rd NN2 141 C1
HORTON 177 D1
Horton Cl OX17 220 A7
Horton Cres OX17 220 A8
Horton Dr OX17 220 A8
Horton Pk NN7 177 E2
Horton Rd
Brafield-on-t-G NN7 177 D7
Hackleton NN7 177 C2
Middleton Cheney OX17 220 A7
Hortonsfield Rd NN12 217 F5
Hortons' La NN14 76 D2
Hoskyn Cl CV21 98 F8
Hospital Bungalow NN6 126 D7
Hospital Hill NN14 70 D7
Hothorpe Rd LE17 46 D8
Houghton Hill NN4 160 A1
Hove Rd NN10 132 C2
Hove St NN18 36 B4
Howard Ave NN17 36 B7
Howard Biley Gdns NN3 142 C3
Howard Cl NN11 135 D1
Howard Ct 3 NN8 130 B5
Howard La NN2 141 C8
Howard Rd NN29 146 D2
Howard's Ct NN29 146 D2
Howards Mdw PE8 13 F7
Howard St NN16 72 A2
Howard Way LE16 31 D1
Howcut La NN7 178 E3
Howden Gn NN14 50 E4
Howe Cres
Corby NN17 36 A7
Daventry NN11 135 E1
Hoxton Cl NN3 142 E6
Hoylake NN8 129 C7
Hoylake Dr NN2 141 F3
Hoy Wlk NN17 21 C1
Hubble Rd NN17 21 F1
Hudson Cl
Corby NN18 36 C3
Daventry NN11 135 C5
Hudson Dr NN4 158 E1
HULCOTE 189 F1
Hulcote NN12 203 F8
Hulme Way NN8 129 E7
Humber Cl
Daventry NN11 134 F4
Northampton NN5 140 F2
Humber Gdns NN8 129 C6
Humber Wlk NN17 21 D2
Humfrey La NN2 141 C8
Humphries Dr NN13 233 D8
Hunsbarrow Rd NN4 158 E4
Hunsbury Cl NN4 158 F1
Hunsbury Gn NN4 158 D2
HUNSBURY HILL 158 F1
Hunsbury Hill Ave NN4 158 E3
Hunsbury Hill Ctry Pk★ NN4 158 F1
Hunsbury Hill Rd NN4 158 E1
Hunsbury Ironstone Railway Mus★ NN4 158 E2
Hunsbury Park Prim Sch NN4 158 F2
Hunslet La NN4 158 E2
Hunt Cl
Brixworth NN6 106 B2
Towcester NN12 203 C7
Wellingborough NN8 129 F8
Hunters Cl
Husbands Bosworth LE17 45 E6
Northampton NN2 141 D6
Hunters Rd NN17 22 F1
Hunter St NN1 159 D7
Hunters' Way NN6 106 B2
HUNTGATE END 206 D2
Huntingdon Cl NN18 36 E1
Huntingdon Gdns LE16 31 E1
Huntingdon Rd NN14 76 E2
Hunting Way PE8 14 C4
Huntsham Cl NN3 160 D7
Huntsmead NN3 143 D4
Hunt St NN18 36 D5
Hurst Cl NN15 92 C4
HUSBANDS BOSWORTH 45 D5
Husbands Bosworth CE Prim Sch LE17 45 E5
Hussar Cl NN11 135 B1
Hutchinson Ave NN14 90 B3
Hutts Cl NN11 183 D7
Huxley Cl NN8 129 A4
Huxloe Rise NN3 142 E6
Huxlow Science Coll NN9 112 E3
Hyacinth Way NN10 148 B7
Hyde Cl NN7 191 C4
Hyde Dr NN9 112 A5
Hyde Rd NN7 191 C4

## I

Ibsen Wlk NN18 36 A2
Ibstock Cl NN3 143 A6
Icknield Dr NN4 158 E1
Ickworth Cl 12 NN11 135 B7
Ideal Bldgs 17 NN1 159 C7
Ilex Cl NN4 159 F1
Ilmor Ave NN6 106 C3
Imperial Ct NN10 132 A2
Independent St CV23 100 A3
Indmere Cl NN4 158 C1
Ingleborough Way NN5 158 D8
Inglewood Ct NN3 143 C1
Inham Cl NN18 36 C2
Inkerman Way PE8 41 F5
Inlands Cl NN11 135 D1
Inlands Rise NN11 135 D1
Inlands The NN11 135 D1
Inn Yard Ct LE16 68 C7
Insignia Cl 7 NN4 175 E7
Inwood Cl NN18 36 C2
io Centre The NN5 140 C2
Iona Rd NN17 36 C8
IRCHESTER 147 B7
Irchester Com Prim Sch NN29 147 A8
Irchester Country Pk Trail★ NN8 130 D1
Irchester Country Pk Visitor Ctr★ NN29 130 D1
Irchester Ctry Pk★ NN29 130 F1
Irchester Narrow Gauge Rly Mus★ NN8 130 D1
Irchester Rd
Podington NN10 147 B4
Rushden NN10 131 F2
Wollaston NN29 146 F3
Irchester Turn NN29 131 A2
Ireton Rd LE16 31 D2
Iron Cross NN11 167 B2
Irondale Cl NN4 158 E3
Iron Duke Cl NN11 135 B4
Iron Pikes NN6 106 C1
Ironstone Ct NN9 111 F4
Ironstone La NN4 158 E3
Ironstone Way NN6 106 C3
Ironwood Ave NN14 51 A4
IRTHLINGBOROUGH 112 D2
Irthlingborough Inf Sch NN9 112 E2
Irthlingborough Jun Sch NN9 112 E2
Irthlingborough Rd
Finedon NN9 112 B4
Little Addington NN14 113 B7
Wellingborough NN8 130 E4
Irvine Dr NN12 203 D8
Irving Gr NN17 36 E8
Isebrook Ct NN15 92 A2
Isebrook Hospl NN8 130 B3
Isebrook Sch NN15 91 E7
Ise Com Coll NN15 72 D1
Ise Rd NN15 72 D1
Ise Vale Ave NN14 51 B3
Ise View Rd NN14 51 B3
ISHAM 91 E1
Isham CE Prim Sch NN14 91 F1
Isham Cl NN2 141 D5
Isham Rd
Orlingbury NN14 110 A5
Pytchley NN14 91 B3
Islay Wlk NN17 36 C8
Isley Valley Ind Est NN8 130 D7
Islington NN14 77 B4
Islington Ct NN12 203 D5
Islington Rd NN12 203 D5
ISLIP 76 B3
Ivens La NN12 171 C1
Ivy Ct NN11 135 B1
Ivydene Terr NN14 90 A4
Ivy La NN9 111 F4
Ivy Rd
Kettering NN16 72 D4
Northampton NN1 159 F8
Ixworth Cl NN3 142 F5

## J

Jackdaw Cl NN3 161 C8
Jacklin Ct NN8 129 C7
Jack Parnell Cl NN5 158 B6
Jackson Cl
Market Harborough LE16 48 E8
Northampton NN2 141 E6
Jackson Rd CV21 80 A1
Jackson's La NN8 129 F5
Jackson's Lane Flats 1 NN8 129 F5
Jackson Way NN15 90 F8
Jacorrin Cl NN2 141 E6
Jacques Rd NN15 92 C1
Jamb The NN17 37 A6
James Lewis Ct NN3 142 C2
James Rd NN8 130 A2
James St NN29 147 B7
James Watt Ave NN17 37 A8
James Watt Cl NN11 135 A4
Jardine Cl NN3 142 D1
Jarretts Yd NN4 175 E6
Jarvis Ct NN13 233 F8
Jasmine Ct NN16 72 D5
Jasmine Gdns NN10 148 B7
Jasmine Ho NN4 159 A2
Jasmine Rd
Kettering NN16 72 D4
Northampton NN3 143 C5
Jasper Wlk NN3 142 D6
Javelin Cl NN5 158 C8
Jay Rd NN18 36 E3
JBJ Bsns Pk NN7 174 D2
Jean Rd NN16 72 E3
Jellicoe Cl NN11 135 E1
Jenkinson Rd NN12 203 D4
Jenkins Rd CV21 80 A1
Jenner Cres NN2 141 B5
Jennings Cl
4 Daventry NN11 135 D1
Higham Ferrers NN10 132 B5
Jersey Cl NN8 130 B6
Jersey Ct NN3 142 F1
Jervis Cl NN11 135 E1
Jerwood Way LE16 31 F2
Jesus Hospl NN14 70 D7
Jetty The
Creaton NN6 104 F4
Hackleton NN7 177 B3
Wappenham NN12 213 B8
Wardington OX17 196 E1
Jeyes Cl NN3 126 B1
Jibwood NN14 89 B5
Jitty The NN14 89 B4
Joan Pyel Cl NN9 131 E8
Job's Yd NN16 72 B2
John Beverly Mews NN14 70 C6
John Clare Cl NN13 222 F1
John Clare Ct NN16 72 C6
John Clare Way NN17 36 D8
John Clark Way NN10 132 C3
John Eagle Cl NN9 113 F4
John Gray Rd NN29 145 D6
John Hellins Prim Sch NN12 217 D3
John Lea Way NN8 130 A1
John Pyel Rd NN9 112 E1
John Smith Ave NN14 70 E7
Johnson Ave
Brackley NN13 233 C8
Wellingborough NN8 130 A1
Johnson Cl NN11 135 B3
Johnson Ct NN4 159 D4
Johnsons Field MK46 195 E4
Johns Rd NN7 157 A1
John St
Rushden NN10 132 B2
Thrapston NN14 76 E2
John White Cl The NN10 132 C6
Jones Cl NN13 233 D8
Jordan Cl LE16 32 A3

Joseph Priestley Ct 6
NN11 135 C1
Joshua Sq NN4 158 F2
Jowett Cl NN15 92 A8
Jubilee Ave NN18 36 D5
Jubilee Cl
Byfield NN11 183 D7
Islip NN14 76 B3
Long Buckby NN6 121 A4
Northampton NN4 158 F3
Jubilee Cres NN8 129 F2
Jubilee Ct PE8 39 E7
Jubilee Dr NN6 108 B5
Jubilee Gdns
Market Harborough
LE16 31 F4
Rushden NN10 148 C8
Jubilee Rd NN11 135 B2
Jubilee St
Irthlingborough NN9 112 E1
Rothwell NN14 70 D6
Jubilee Terr
Isham NN14 110 F8
Stony Stratford MK11 229 E5
Judes Ct NN15 72 A1
Judges Ct NN6 104 F4
Judith Rd NN16 72 E4
Julian Way NN2 141 A3
Junction Rd NN2 141 E1
Juniper Cl NN12 203 B4
Juniper Ct NN3 143 D3
JUNIPER HILL 239 E6
Juniper Thorn NN6 106 C1
Jura Cl NN17 36 B8
Justin Park Cvn Site
LE16 48 F7
Jutland Way NN16 72 A2

## K

K2 Ho NN5 141 A1
Kane Wlk NN17 36 E8
Kangaroo Spinney
NN8 130 E3
Karlstad Cl NN18 36 A2
Kathleen Dr NN16 72 E4
Katrine Cl NN17 21 B1
Kealdale Rd NN3 142 A4
Keating Cl NN15 92 A8
Keats Cl
Earls Barton NN6 144 F4
Great Houghton NN4 160 F1
Keats Dr
Kettering NN16 72 C6
Towcester NN12 203 B5
Keats Rd
Daventry NN11 135 B3
Wellingborough NN8 129 D4
Keats Way
Corby NN17 36 C8
Higham Ferrers NN10 132 A5
Rushden NN10 131 E3
Keble Cl NN11 153 B8
Keble Ct NN8 129 F4
Keble Rd NN13 233 D8
Kedleston Cl 3 NN4 175 C8
Keebles Cl NN14 37 E2
Keepers Cl NN4 175 F3
Kelburn Cl NN4 175 B7
Keld Cl NN18 36 D2
KELMARSH 67 F3
Kelmarsh Hall* NN6 67 F4
Kelmarsh Rd
Arthingworth LE16 68 C7
Clipston LE16 67 A7
Corby NN17 36 C7
Kelmscott Cl NN3 143 A5
Kelsall Cl NN5 158 B8
Kelthorpe Cl PE9 1 A4
Kelvin Gr NN17 37 A7
Kemp Ho NN17 21 F3
Kemps Cl NN14 89 B4
Kemps Rd OX17 230 A5
Kempton Cl NN18 53 E8
Kendal Cl
Northampton NN3 142 D4
Rushden NN10 132 D1
Wellingborough NN8 129 D6
Kendalls Cl LE16 34 D5
Kenilworth NN18 36 C3
Kenilworth Cl
Daventry NN11 135 B1
Northampton NN5 158 B8
Rushden NN10 132 C1
Kenilworth Dr NN15 91 F8
Kenilworth Gdns NN14 76 F2
Kenmore Dr NN14 51 B2
Kenmuir Ave NN2 141 F2
Kenmuir Cres NN2 141 F2
Kenmuir Gdns NN2 141 F2
Kenmuir Rd NN9 111 F4
Kennedy Cl NN11 135 E1
Kennel Hill NN14 55 F7
Kennel Rd NN12 215 C3
Kennels Dr NN12 216 E3
Kennel Terr NN6 106 B2
Kennet Cl NN8 129 C6
Kennet Gn NN5 140 F2
Kensington Cl
Kings Sutton OX17 230 F6
Rushden NN10 131 E3
Towcester NN12 203 B4
Kensington Gdns NN15 91 B8
Kensington Pl MK46 195 F5
Kensington Wlk NN18 36 C3
Kent Cl
Corby NN17 36 C7
Kent Cl *continued*
Northampton NN5 158 C6
Kentford Cl NN4 175 B8
Kenton Ct NN15 92 A8
Kent Pl NN15 91 D6
Kent Rd
Northampton, Duston
NN5 158 B6
Rushden NN10 132 C3
Wellingborough NN8 129 F1
Kentstone Cl NN2 140 F4
Kent The CV21 80 A2
Kerley Cl NN14 90 A3
Kerrfield Est NN5 158 C7
Kestian Cl LE16 31 D5
Keston Way NN9 114 B5
Kestrel Cl NN3 142 D1
Kestrel Cres NN13 222 E1
Kestrel La NN8 130 A7
Keswick NN8 129 B5
Keswick Dr
Northampton NN3 142 C4
Rushden NN10 132 D3
Keswick Rd MK19 207 B2
Ketco Ave PE9 1 B7
KETTERING 72 E3
Kettering Gdns 2
NN1 159 E6
Kettering General Hospl
NN16 71 F2
Kettering Parkway
NN15 91 D5
Kettering Rd
Broughton NN14 90 B5
Burton Latimer NN15 92 B3
Geddington NN14 54 A1
Great Harrowden NN9 110 E4
Isham NN14 91 E1
Islip NN14 75 E1
Market Harborough LE16 32 B2
Moulton NN3 126 F2
Northampton NN1 159 E8
Northampton, Spinney Hill
NN3 142 A3
Pytchley NN14 90 F2
Rothwell NN14, NN16 70 E5
Stanion NN14 37 E2
Walgrave NN6 108 C6
Weldon NN17 38 B7
Woodford NN14 94 B8
Wothorpe PE9 2 C8
Kettering Rd N NN3 142 C5
Kettering Sta NN15 72 A1
Kettering Town FC
NN16 72 B5
Kettle End NN12 200 C3
KETTON 1 A6
Kettonby Gdns NN15 91 B8
Ketton CE Prim Sch
PE9 1 A5
Ketton Rd PE9 1 C3
Keyham Ct NN3 143 A5
Keys Cl NN11 135 D1
Keys La CV47 166 E8
KEYSTON 97 A4
Keystone NN4 158 C1
Keyston Rd PE18 116 D2
Keyte's Cl OX17 230 A4
KG House Bsns Ctr 4
NN5 140 F1
Kielder Ct NN15 92 A4
Kieldsen Cl OX17 210 B1
Kiel Wlk NN18 36 A2
Kilborn Cl NN8 129 E7
Kilborn Rd NN8 129 E6
Kilburn Pl NN10 132 B4
Kilby Cl NN8 129 E3
Kiln La
Litchborough NN12 171 C1
Welton NN11 135 E8
Kiln Way NN8 129 D4
KILSBY 100 A3
Kilsby CE Prim Sch
CV23 100 A3
Kilsby La CV21 99 C7
Kilsby Rd
Barby CV23 99 C1
Crick NN6 100 F2
Watford NN6 120 B7
Kilvey Rd NN4 160 B2
Kilworth Rd
Husbands Bosworth
LE17 45 D4
Rugby CV21 99 B7
Swinford LE17 62 C4
Kimble Cl NN4 175 B8
Kimbolton Ct NN14 76 E2
Kimbolton Rd
Chelveston NN9 133 D8
Higham Ferrers NN10 132 C6
Kinewell Cl NN14 95 A3
Kinewell Lake Nature
Trail* NN14 95 A3
King Cup Cl NN10 148 C7
King Edward Rd NN1 160 A7
Kingfisher Cl
Hinton NN11 184 B6
Northampton NN4 175 A7
Ringstead NN14 95 A3
Kingfisher Ct NN6 143 D8
Kingfisher Rd NN13 222 E2
Kingfisher Way NN15 92 A2
King George Cres
MK11 229 E6
King John Sch The
NN14 76 D1
Kingmaker Way NN4 159 A2
King Richard Ct NN4 175 C6
Kings Arms La PE8 42 F3
Kings Ave NN10 132 C7
Kingsbrook NN18 36 B3
Kingsbrook Sch MK19 228 F4
Kings Cl NN4 175 F3
KING'S CLIFFE 13 E8
King's Cliffe Endowed
Prim Sch PE8 13 F7
Kings Cliffe Rd PE8 14 C4
Kings Corner Cl
NN11 184 C6
Kingscroft Ct NN3 143 C1
Kings Ct NN14 51 B3
King's Ct 2 LE16 31 E4
Kingsfield Bsns Pk
NN5 141 A1
Kingsfield Cl NN5 141 A1
Kingsfield Piece
NN12 215 C4
Kingsfield Way NN5 141 A1
King's Forest PE8 13 F7
Kings Gn NN11 153 C7
King's Head Pl LE16 31 E3
KING'S HEATH 140 E2
King's Heath Prim Sch
NN5 140 F2
Kingshill Dr MK19 228 E5
Kings La
Barrowden LE15 3 F5
Pury End NN12 215 F7
Yelvertoft NN6 82 B4
King's La
Flore NN7 155 F5
Little Harrowden NN9 110 B3
Kingsland Ave NN2 141 D3
Kingsland Cl NN2 141 D3
Kingsland Gdns NN2 141 C3
Kingsley Ave
Daventry NN11 135 B1
Kettering NN16 72 B5
Rugby CV21 98 F8
Kingsley Dr NN17 36 D8
Kingsley Gdns 3
NN2 141 E1
KINGSLEY PARK 141 F2
Kingsley Park Mid Sch
NN2 141 D1
Kingsley Park Terr
NN2 141 F1
Kingsley Prim Sch
NN2 141 F2
Kingsley Rd
Northampton NN2 141 E1
Rothwell NN14 70 C7
Silverstone NN12 214 E5
Kingsley Sch NN15 72 F1
Kingsmead
King's Cliffe PE8 13 F8
Northampton NN2 141 A5
Kings Meadow La
NN10 132 B7
Kings Meadow Sch
NN3 142 C7
Kingsmead Pk NN10 148 C7
Kingsmith Dr NN9 114 E6
Kings Park Rd NN3 141 F6
Kings Pk NN7 155 A3
Kings Pl NN10 132 C2
Kings Rd
Oundle PE8 42 A6
Rushden NN10 132 C2
Weldon NN17 38 B7
King's Rd LE16 31 E3
Kings St NN8 130 A5
Kings Stile OX17 208 F1
KINGS SUTTON 231 A4
Kings Sutton Prim Sch
OX17 231 A5
Kings Sutton Sta
OX17 230 E5
King St
Desborough NN14 51 B3
Earls Barton NN6 144 E5
Kettering NN16 72 C3
Long Buckby NN6 121 B4
Maidford NN12 186 D5
Northampton NN1 159 C6
Stony Stratford MK11 229 E6
Kingsthorne Distribution
Pk NN16 71 E4
KINGSTHORPE 141 C3
Kingsthorpe Ave NN17 36 B7
Kingsthorpe Bsns Ctr
NN2 141 B2
Kingsthorpe Com Coll
NN2 141 E5
Kingsthorpe Gr NN2 141 C2
Kingsthorpe Grove Prim
Sch NN2 141 C2
Kingsthorpe Ho NN2 141 C5
KINGSTHORPE HOLLOW
141 D1
Kingsthorpe Mid Com Sch
NN2 141 B4
Kingsthorpe Rd NN2 141 C1
Kingsthorpe Sh Ctr 2
NN2 141 C3
Kingsthorpe Village Prim
Sch NN2 141 B3
Kingston Ave MK11 229 E5
Kingston Cl
Blakesley NN12 187 B1
Daventry NN11 135 B3
Long Buckby NN6 121 C4
Middleton Cheney
OX17 220 A7
Kingston Way LE16 31 E6
King Style Cl NN6 100 F6
Kingsway
Northampton NN2 141 B4
Wellingborough NN8 129 E2
Kingswell Rd NN2 141 B3
Kingswell St NN1 159 C5
Kingswood Pl NN18 36 A3
Kingswood Prim Sch
NN18 36 C3
Kingswood Sch The
NN18 36 A3
Kinross Cl NN3 142 A4
Kipling Dr NN12 203 B5
Kipling Rd
Corby NN17 36 D8
Kettering NN16 72 C5
Kippell Hill MK46 195 F5
Kipton Cl NN14 70 E7
Kipton Field NN14 70 E7
Kirby Cl
Corby NN18 36 A3
Northampton NN4 175 F7
Kirby Ct NN15 91 C5
Kirby Hall* NN17 23 B6
Kirby Ho LE16 31 F3
Kirby La NN17 23 C5
Kirby Rd NN17 10 C1
Kirkby Rd CV21 98 F8
Kirkhams Cl NN6 82 C3
Kirkstone Wlk 7
NN3 142 C4
Kirkwall NN17 21 C1
Kirton Cl NN3 143 B5
Kirton End NN3 143 B4
KISLINGBURY 157 E4
Kislingbury Prim Sch
NN7 157 D4
Kislingbury Rd
Bugbrooke NN7 173 A8
Rothersthorpe NN7 174 A7
Kitchener Cl NN11 135 B4
Kitchen Gdns NN14 89 F6
Kitelee Cl MK19 207 A3
Kites Cl NN4 175 A8
Kits Cl NN7 192 D2
Knaphill Cres NN4 158 F4
Knibb Pl NN15 91 F6
Knibb St NN16 72 C2
Knightlands Rd NN9 112 F3
Knightley Cl NN11 183 D7
Knightley Rd NN2 141 C1
Knighton Cl NN5 140 A3
Knightons Way NN6 106 C1
Knights Cl
Bozeat NN29 164 D2
Corby NN18 36 A5
Earls Barton NN6 144 E4
Knightscliffe Way
NN5 140 D1
Knights Ct
Northampton, Little Billing
NN3 143 B1
Northampton NN1 159 F8
Wellingborough NN8 129 F5
Knight's End Rd LE16 32 B6
Knights Hill NN6 85 B8
Knight's La NN2 141 B3
Knights Mews NN10 132 C1
Knob The OX17 231 A5
Knock La NN7 190 F5
Knoll Ct NN16 72 B4
Knoll St LE16 31 C3
Knoll The
Brixworth NN6 106 C2
Grendon NN7 163 D5
KNOTTING 149 E3
KNOTTING GREEN 149 F1
Knowle Cl NN3 160 C6
Knowles Cl NN10 132 D3
Knowle Way 2 NN11 135 B7
Knox Ct NN8 130 B4
Knox Rd NN8 130 B5
KNUSTON 131 D1
Knuston Dr NN10 131 F2
Knuston Spinney
NN10 131 E1
Knutsford La NN6 121 C4
Kylesku Cres NN15 91 E8
Kynnesworth Gdns
NN10 132 C6
Kyoto Cl NN3 142 A6

## L

Laburnum Cl
Hinton NN11 184 B6
Wellingborough NN8 129 E5
Laburnum Cres
Kettering NN16 72 D4
Northampton NN3 142 A3
Laceby Wlk NN3 142 F5
Lacemakers Ct NN10 148 C8
Lace Mews MK46 195 F4
Lacock Ho 7 NN11 135 B7
Laddermakers Yd
NN7 172 E7
Ladybower Cl NN16 71 E3
Ladybridge Dr NN4 174 E8
Lady Cl NN11 153 D3
Lady Croft NN11 135 B1
Lady Hollows Dr NN4 176 A6
Ladymead Cl NN4 158 D1
Lady's La
Mears Ashby NN6 128 B2
Northampton NN1 159 C6
Lady Smock Cl NN4 175 F2
Ladywell Ct NN8 130 A7
Ladywell Mews NN14 70 D7
Lady Winefride's Wlk
NN3 143 B2
Lahnstein Ct 12 NN16 72 B2
Lake Ave NN15 90 F8
Lake Cres NN11 135 A2
Lakeside
Irthlingborough NN9 131 D7
Northampton NN3 143 A7
Lakeside Bglws NN15 91 E6
Lakeside Cl NN14 76 D3
Lakeside Dr NN3 143 D3
Lakeside Lodges NN3 143 A7
Lakeview Gn NN3 142 C4
Lake Wlk
Adderbury OX17 230 B4
Northampton NN4 175 C4
Lalgates Ct NN5 158 F8
Lambert's Cl LE15 3 A6
Lambourne Way
OX17 230 B4
Lambrook Dr NN4 175 C7
Lammas Cl
Husbands Bosworth
LE17 45 E5
Orlingbury NN14 110 A5
Lammas Ctyd NN17 23 A1
Lammas Rd NN17 23 A1
LAMPORT 87 D2
Lamport Cl NN15 91 D5
Lamport Ct NN11 135 A5
Lamport Dr NN11 135 A5
Lamport Hall* NN6 87 D1
Lamport Rd
Draughton NN6 87 E6
Old NN6 107 C7
Lamva Ct MK11 229 F5
Lancaster Cl NN29 146 C3
Lancaster Dr
Brackley NN13 233 E8
Thrapston NN14 76 F2
Lancaster Rd
Kettering NN16 72 C3
Rothwell NN14 70 E7
Lancaster St NN10 132 C7
Lancaster Way
Northampton NN4 159 A1
Rushden NN10 132 C3
Lancers Way NN7 155 B4
Lanchester Way NN11 134 F3
Lancum Ho NN8 129 E5
Landcross Dr NN3 160 C7
Landimore Rd NN4 176 A7
Landor NN8 129 C4
Landor Cl NN17 21 D1
Landsdown Dr NN3 142 E2
Landseer Cl
Rugby CV21 80 B1
Wellingborough NN8 129 F8
Landseer Ct NN18 36 D5
Lanercost Wlk
Northampton NN3 142 C4
8 Northampton NN3 142 C4
Laneside Hollow NN4 175 C6
Lane The
Ashby St L CV23 119 B5
Denton NN7 178 B8
Eastcote NN12 173 A1
Easton o t H PE9 2 A5
Grafton Regis NN12 205 D2
Rothersthorpe NN7 174 B6
Wappenham NN12 213 B8
Weston by W LE16 18 B4
Langdale NN14 50 F3
Langdale Ct NN8 129 D5
Langdale Gr NN17 36 D8
Langdale Rd NN2 141 D3
Langdale Wlk LE16 31 E1
Langdon Cl NN11 135 B5
Langford Dr NN4 175 D5
Langham Cl NN6 104 F5
Langham Pl
Northampton NN2 159 C8
Walgrave NN6 108 A5
Langham Rd NN9 114 D7
Langley Cl NN4 158 E3
Langley Cres NN9 113 B5
Langley Ct NN15 92 B2
Langley Way NN15 91 C6
Langley Wlk NN18 36 D5
Langport Gn NN18 36 B6
Langsett Cl
Kettering NN16 71 E3
Northampton NN3 142 F1
Langton Ct
Corby NN18 36 B6
Market Harborough LE16 31 F3
Langton Pl NN14 91 E1
Langton Rd LE16 32 A7
Langton Rise NN11 137 C6
Lansdown Cl NN11 135 D5
Lansom Cl NN15 92 C3
Lapford Rd NN18 36 E4
Lapland Wlk NN18 36 B2
Lapstone Ho NN5 159 A5
Lapwing Cl NN4 175 A7
Larch Cl
Hinton NN11 184 A6
Irchester NN29 147 A7
Larch Dr NN11 135 C5
Larch La NN5 140 B2
Larch Rd
Corby NN17 21 D1
Kettering NN15 72 C1
Larchwood Cl NN8 129 E5
Larkhall La NN7 157 D6

Larkhall Way NN7 157 C7
Larkhill NN10 132 A4
Larkin Gdns NN10 132 A5
Lark La NN4 175 F4
Lark Rise
Brackley NN13 233 E8
Northampton NN3 143 B4
Larkwood Cl NN16 72 C6
Larratt Rd NN17 38 A8
Larwood Cl NN2 141 A5
Lasham Ct NN3 143 C1
Latham Rd PE8 41 F7
Latham's Hospl PE8 59 B6
Latham St NN14 55 F7
Lathbury Rd NN13 233 D8
Lathkill St LE16 31 F1
Latimer MK11 229 E4
Latimer Cl
Burton Latimer NN15 92 C2
Gretton NN17 10 C1
Latimer Com Arts Coll NN15 92 A6
Latimer Cres LE16 31 F2
Latimer Rd NN17 36 E8
Lattimore Cl NN6 102 C5
Latymer Cl LE16 49 E5
Latymer Ct 4 NN1 159 C6
Lauda Way NN12 203 C8
Lauderdale Ave NN4 159 A2
Laud's Rd NN6 101 A5
Laughton Rd LE16 30 C4
Launcelot Ct NN5 158 A7
Launde Pk LE16 32 A2
Laundry Rd PE8 14 C4
Laurel Ct
Northampton NN3 142 E3
4 Wellingborough NN8 130 B5
Laurel Pl NN12 203 D5
Laurel Rd NN16 72 C4
Laurels The
Ecton NN6 143 F3
Moulton NN3 126 B2
Laurel Valley NN4 175 D4
Lavant Wlk NN3 141 F5
Lavender Cl
Corby NN18 36 D2
Thrapston NN14 76 D2
Lavender La NN7 177 D1
Lavender Way NN10 148 C8
Lavendon Ct NN15 92 A5
Lavenham Cl NN3 142 F5
Lavery Ct NN18 36 D5
Lawns The
Corby NN18 36 A4
Kettering NN16 72 A1
Kilsby CV23 100 A2
Northampton NN5 158 E8
Lawrence Cl
Kettering NN15 92 A8
Raunds NN9 114 B5
Lawrence Ct
Corby NN18 36 D5
Long Buckby NN6 121 B4
22 Northampton NN1 159 C7
Laws Croft NN13 233 D7
Laws La NN9 111 F4
Law's La PE8 13 F7
Lawson Cres NN3 143 C1
Lawson St
Kettering NN16 72 C3
Raunds NN9 114 D6
Lawton Rd NN10 132 C3
Lawyers Cl NN13 233 E2
LAXTON 11 F5
Laxton Cl NN17 36 B8
Laxton Ct NN15 92 A5
Laxton Dr PE8 42 B7
Laxton Jun Sch PE8 42 A5
Laywood Cl NN9 114 C7
Laywood Way NN9 131 E8
Leafields NN3 160 F8
Leah Bank NN4 159 A2
Leah Cl NN18 53 A8
Lealand The LE16 48 B8
Leamington Way NN11 135 A2
Leam The NN11 134 F1
Lea Rd NN1 159 F8
Leatherland Ct 18 NN16 72 B2
Lea Way NN8 129 D3
Leben Sq NN3 143 C5
Leckhampstead Rd MK19 228 A3
Ledaig Way NN3 142 A4
Ledbury Rd NN15 91 F5
Leeds Cl NN18 36 F2
Lees Cl NN12 215 C4
Leeson Cres NN15 91 F6
Leeson Ct NN12 203 D4
Leeson Rd NN12 203 C4
Lees St NN9 112 E1
Lee's Way NN14 54 A3
Lee Way NN9 114 D7
Legg Rd PE8 7 D8
Legion Cres NN16 71 F3
Leicester Cl NN16 72 A3
Leicester La LE16 31 D7
Leicester Par NN2 159 C8
Leicester Rd
Husbands Bosworth LE17 45 D7
Market Harborough LE16 31 D5
Leicester St
Kettering NN16 72 A3
Northampton NN1 159 C7
Leicester Terr 2 NN2 159 C7
Leighton Cl NN8 129 F8
Leighton Pl NN8 129 F4
Leighton Rd NN18 36 D5
Leith Ct NN4 158 E3
Lely Ct NN18 36 D5
Lennon Cl CV21 99 C8
Lennox Wlk NN5 140 D2
Lensway NN14 89 B5
Lenthall Sq LE16 31 E1
Lenton Cl NN14 90 A3
Leonard La 1 NN3 126 C1
Leonardo Ct NN18 36 D5
Lerwick Way NN17 36 C8
Leslie Rd NN2 159 B7
Lesson Rd NN6 106 B1
Lester Cl OX17 230 A6
Letts Rd NN4 159 B3
Leven Way NN17 21 B1
Lever Rd CV21 80 A1
Levitts Rd NN7 173 A8
Lewin Cl NN14 70 B7
Lewin Rd NN18 36 B1
Lewis Ho NN14 91 E1
Lewis Rd
Kettering NN15 91 C7
Northampton NN5 159 A7
Lexden Cl NN4 175 F7
Lexton Gdns OX17 220 B8
Leyland Dr NN2 141 A5
Leyland Trad Est NN8 130 D4
Leyland View NN8 130 D4
Leys Ave
Desborough NN14 51 C3
Rothwell NN14 70 C7
Leys Cl
Denton NN7 162 B1
Long Buckby NN6 121 C4
Leys Gdns NN8 130 B6
Leyside Ct NN3 143 B5
Leys La NN4 160 F1
Leys Rd
Earls Barton NN6 144 D4
Pattishall NN12 172 D1
Rugby CV21 99 C7
Wellingborough NN8 130 B6
Leys The
Bugbrooke NN7 172 E6
Denton NN7 162 B1
Long Buckby NN6 121 C4
Northampton NN2 141 B2
Orlingbury NN14 110 A5
Roade NN7 191 D4
Upper Boddington NN11 182 C8
Welford NN6 64 E5
Woodford NN14 94 D7
Yardley Hastings NN7 179 A6
Leyswell Ct 4 NN3 161 A8
Liberty Dr NN5 140 C1
Lichfield Cl NN7 157 D3
Lichfield Dr NN4 175 B7
Liddington Way NN2 141 B5
Lightfoot La LE16 20 B1
Lilac Cl NN14 76 D3
Lilac Ct NN8 129 E5
Lilac Gr NN10 148 B7
Lilac Pl NN15 72 D1
LILBOURNE 81 A6
Lilbourne Rd CV23 80 C5
LILFORD 58 E4
Lilford Pl NN16 72 D3
Lilford Rd NN14 77 C8
Liliput Rd NN4 160 C3
Lilley Homes The NN8 129 F2
Lilley Terr NN9 112 F2
LILLINGSTONE DAYRELL 226 E4
LILLINGSTONE LOVELL 227 A5
Lillington Ct NN18 36 B6
Lillycourt Ho NN16 72 A2
Lilly Hill MK46 195 F5
Lime Ave
Eydon NN11 184 C1
Long Buckby NN6 121 C4
Northampton NN3 142 A1
Oundle PE8 41 F7
Lime Cl
Broughton NN14 90 B4
Hartwell NN7 192 E2
Lime Ct NN9 112 F2
Lime Farm Way NN4 160 F2
Limefields Way NN4 175 D6
Lime Gr
Bugbrooke NN7 173 A7
Rushden NN10 132 B4
Wellingborough NN8 130 A7
Limehurst Cl NN5 140 C1
Limehurst Rd NN5 158 C8
Limehurst Sq NN5 158 C8
Lime Rd
Kettering NN16 72 D4
Yardley Gobion NN12 217 E6
Lime St
Irthlingborough NN9 112 F2
Olney MK46 195 F3
Rushden NN10 132 B4
Limes The
9 Daventry NN11 135 C1
11 Irthlingborough NN9 112 F2
Stony Stratford MK11 229 E5
Limes The *continued*
Thorpe Langton LE16 17 A5
Thrapston NN14 76 E2
Lime Terr NN9 112 F2
Lime Tree Mews NN15 72 B1
Lime Trees Gr NN17 37 A6
Limlow Cl NN4 158 E3
Limoges Ct NN5 140 A2
Linacre Cl NN3 142 F6
Lincoln Ct
Brackley NN13 233 F5
Hanslope MK19 207 A2
Market Harborough LE16 31 F5
Lincoln Ho NN5 159 A5
Lincoln Pk NN13 233 F5
Lincoln Rd NN5 159 A5
Lincoln St NN2 141 C3
Lincoln Way
Corby NN18 36 C4
Daventry NN11 153 C8
Lindale Cl NN3 142 B3
Linden Ave
Higham Ferrers NN10 132 B7
Kettering NN15, NN16 72 D1
Linden Cl NN15 72 D1
Linden Gr PE28 97 A2
Linden Rd NN3 142 A1
Lindens The
Northampton NN1 159 E5
Towcester NN12 203 C6
Lindisfarne Dr NN15 91 F8
Lindisfarne Rd NN17 21 C1
Lindisfarne Way
Northampton NN4 175 C8
Thrapston NN14 76 F2
Lindrick Cl NN11 135 E2
Lindsay Ave NN3 142 B2
Lindsay St NN16 72 B3
Lindsay Terr NN3 142 A2
Lindsey Cl PE8 14 F1
Lindsey Gdns LE16 48 D8
Lingfield Terr NN2 141 F2
Lingfield Wlk NN18 36 C2
Lings Prim Sch NN3 142 F4
Lings Way NN3 143 A4
Lingswood Pk NN3 143 A3
Link La NN14 89 B4
Link Rd
Northampton NN2 141 B6
Rushden NN10 148 B7
Links Rd NN8 130 C8
Links The NN15 91 B8
Link Way
Bugbrooke NN7 173 A7
Towcester NN12 203 C5
Linley Dr NN14 50 F4
Linley Gn NN5 158 D8
Linnell Way NN16 71 F4
Linnet Cl NN8 130 A7
Linnet Dr NN15 92 A6
Linnet Rd NN12 203 C3
Linnetts La NN10 132 B5
Lion Ct NN4 159 D4
Lismore Cl NN3 143 C2
Lismore Wlk NN17 21 C1
Lister Cl NN17 22 A1
Lister Dr NN4 158 E1
Lister Rd NN8 130 A5
LITCHBOROUGH 171 D1
Litchborough Rd
Farthingstone NN12 170 F3
Grimscote NN12 188 A7
Litchfield Cl
Brixworth NN6 106 B2
Kettering NN16 72 C6
Litchfield La NN6 104 F4
LITTLE ADDINGTON 113 B7
Little Back La NN11 151 D1
LITTLE BILLING 143 B1
Little Billing Way NN3 143 A1
LITTLE BOWDEN 32 A2
Little Bowden Manor LE16 31 F3
Little Bowden Sch LE16 31 F2
LITTLE BRAUNSTON 118 D1
LITTLE BRINGTON 138 C4
Little Cl
Bozeat NN29 164 C2
Chapel Brampton NN6 124 D1
LITTLE CRANSLEY 90 A5
LITTLE CREATON 105 A3
Little Cross St NN1 159 B6
Littledale NN8 129 D6
LITTLE EVERDON 154 A1
Little Field NN4 175 F4
Little Field Cl NN12 189 A8
Little Gn PE8 28 B3
Little Greeve Way NN4 176 A6
Little Gull Cl NN3 142 F6
LITTLE HARROWDEN 110 B4
Little Harrowden Com Prim Sch NN9 110 C4
Little Horton Ho NN7 177 E2
Little Horton House Dr NN7 177 E2
LITTLE HOUGHTON 161 A3
LITTLE IRCHESTER 130 C1
Little La
Aynho OX17 237 C7
Blisworth NN7 190 D8
Great Houghton NN4 160 E2
Ravensthorpe NN6 103 D1
Stanion NN14 37 E3
Wollaston NN29 146 D3
Little La *continued*
Yardley Hastings NN7 179 A7
Little London
Deanshanger MK19 228 E4
Silverstone NN12 214 D5
Little Mdw NN18 36 B1
LITTLE OAKLEY 54 A8
Little Park St 6 NN8 130 A5
Little Priel Rd NN7 155 B4
Little St
Rushden NN10 132 C1
Sulgrave OX17 211 A8
Yardley Hastings NN7 179 B6
Littlewood Cl NN5 159 A8
Littlewood St NN14 70 E7
LITTLEWORTH 188 E1
LITTLE WYMINGTON 148 A7
Livingstone Cl NN14 70 F7
Livingstone Rd NN11 135 C4
Llewellyn Wlk NN18 36 D5
Lloyd Cl NN8 130 B8
Lloyd's Rd NN17 37 B7
Loach Ct NN3 142 A6
Loatlands Prim Sch NN14 50 F3
Loatland St NN14 50 F3
Lobelia Rd NN16 72 C4
Lockcroft Sq 6 NN3 143 D2
Lock La MK19 218 E2
Locks Gn PE8 16 A8
Locks The CV21 80 B1
Locktons Cl NN12 201 E2
Lockwood Cl NN2 141 C4
LODDINGTON 70 C2
Loddington CE Prim Sch NN14 70 D1
Loddington Rd NN14 89 F7
Loddington Way NN14 89 B4
Lodge Ave NN4 175 C4
Lodge Cl
Little Houghton NN7 161 B3
Northampton, Hopping Hill NN5 140 B1
Northampton NN4 175 F3
Lodge Ct 1 NN8 130 B5
Lodge Farm Ct MK19 218 F6
Lodge Farm Ind Est NN5 140 C2
Lodge Flats NN6 122 D5
Lodge Green Rd NN17 36 E8
Lodge La NN6 121 F3
Lodge Park Tech Coll NN17 21 B1
Lodge Pk NN12 215 C4
Lodge Rd
Daventry NN11 135 C2
Little Houghton NN7 161 A3
Rushden NN10 148 A8
Lodge The OX17 198 D2
Lodge Way
Irthlingborough NN9 131 E8
Northampton NN5 140 C3
Lodore Gdns NN3 142 C3
Logan Cres LE16 31 C4
Logan Ct LE16 31 D4
Logan St LE16 31 D3
Logwell Ct NN3 142 F1
Loire Cl NN5 140 A2
Lombard Way OX16 219 A6
Lombardy Ct NN3 142 D3
Lomond Cl NN17 21 C1
Lomond Dr NN15 91 F8
London End
Earls Barton NN6 144 D4
Irchester NN29 147 B8
Titchmarsh NN14 77 D3
Upper Boddington NN11 182 C8
London Ho MK11 229 D5
London Rd
Bozeat NN29 164 C3
Braunston NN11 118 A1
Daventry NN11 153 D8
Kettering NN15 91 C8
Little Irchester NN8 130 C1
Northampton, Far Cotton NN4 159 C2
Northampton, Wootton NN4 175 D5
Old Stratford MK19 229 C6
Raunds NN9 114 C6
Roade NN7 191 C4
Stony Stratford MK11 229 E5
Towcester NN12 203 D5
Wansford PE8 8 B3
Wellingborough NN8 130 B3
Willoughby CV23 117 E3
Wollaston NN29 146 D1
Wothorpe PE9 2 F7
Lone Pine Ct NN6 106 B2
Long Acre NN7 161 D3
Long Acres 4 NN4 175 B8
Long Acres Dr NN9 112 E3
Long Barrow OX17 196 F7
Long Breech NN14 89 B5
Long Brimley Cl LE16 32 B3
LONG BUCKBY 121 B4
Long Buckby Inf Sch NN6 121 B4
Long Buckby Jun Sch NN6 121 B3
Long Buckby Pocket Pk★ NN6 121 A4
Long Buckby Rd NN6 120 E5
Long Buckby Sta NN6 121 A2
LONG BUCKBY WHARF 136 E7
Longburges OX17 220 B8
Long Cl NN18 36 B1
Longcroft La NN12 216 C8
Long Croft Rd NN14, NN18 37 C3
Longdown La CV23 118 B7
Longfellow Dr NN16 72 C6
Longfellow Rd NN8 129 B4
Longford Ave NN3 161 A8
Long Furlong CV22 98 A8
Long La
Olney MK46 195 F4
Warmington PE8 28 B2
Longland Ct NN3 142 B2
Longland Rd NN3 142 C2
Longlands The LE16 32 B3
Longleat Cl LE16 32 B3
Longleat Ct 5 NN4 175 C8
Longleat Gr NN15 91 C5
Long Mallows Rise 9 NN3 143 C2
Long March NN11 153 D8
Long March Ind Est NN11 153 D8
Long Marsh NN8 130 B2
Long Marsh Sq NN3 143 A6
Long Massey MK46 195 E5
Long Mdw NN4 176 B6
Longmead Ct NN3 143 B4
Longmynd Dr NN5 158 D8
Long Row
Leckhampstead MK18 227 E1
Woodford NN14 94 D7
Long Row Cl NN11 170 A8
LONG STREET 206 E4
Long Street Rd MK19 207 A3
Longueville Ct NN3 142 E4
Long Wall NN13 233 E6
Longwell NN12 186 D5
Lonsborough Dr NN15 90 E8
Lonsdale Rd NN15 91 B7
Loop Rd PE28 97 A3
Lordswood Cl NN4 176 A6
Lorne Ct NN17 36 F6
Lorne Rd NN1 159 C7
Lorraine Cres NN3 142 B5
Lorraine Dr NN3 142 C5
Loseby Cl NN10 148 A8
Lotus Ct NN15 72 B1
Louisa Dr NN16 72 E4
Louisa Lilley Homes The 7 NN9 112 F2
Louisburg Cl 4 NN4 175 E7
Louise Rd NN1 159 D7
Lounts Cres LE16 20 D7
Lovap Way NN18 36 B1
Lovat Dr NN5 158 E7
Lovell Cl NN9 114 A4
Lovell Ct 12 NN9 112 F2
Lovers La PE5 8 F2
Lovett Rd NN11 183 D8
Lowbury Ct NN4 158 E3
Lower Adelaide St NN2 159 C7
Lower Bath St NN1 159 B6
LOWER BENEFIELD 40 C6
LOWER BODDINGTON 182 D5
LOWER CATESBY 151 D4
Lower Cross St NN1 159 B6
Lower Ecton La NN3 143 D1
Lower End NN12 201 F5
LOWER END
Brafield-on-the-Green 161 E3
Grendon 163 E7
Hartwell 192 C1
Lower End
Hartwell NN7 192 C1
Pytchley NN14 91 A1
Lower Farm Rd NN3 141 F7
LOWER GREEN
Blakesley 200 F6
Willoughby 117 A5
Lower Harding St 11 NN1 159 C6
LOWER HARLESTONE 139 E5
Lower Hester St NN2 159 C8
Lower Hilmorton Rd 5 CV21 80 A1
Lower King St NN14 51 B3
Lower Lea Pl CV21 99 B8
Lower Meadow Ct NN3 142 E5
LOWER MIDDLETON CHENEY 220 B8
Lower Mounts NN1 159 D6
Lower Pastures NN18 53 A8
Lower Priory St NN1 159 B7
Lower Rd
Milton Malsor NN7 174 E4
Stoke Albany LE16 34 B5
Lower St
Desborough NN14 51 A3
Great Addington NN14 94 B2
Great Doddington NN29 145 E6
Kettering NN16 72 A2
Pury End NN12 216 A7
Rugby CV21 99 C8
Twywell NN14 75 A1
Willoughby CV23 117 D4
Lower Stable Yd NN12 203 D5
Lower Steeping NN14 51 B2
Lower Thrift St NN1 159 F6
Lower Weald MK19 229 E2

LOWER WEEDON 155 A3
Low Farm Pl NN3 141 F7
Low Greeve NN4 176 A6
LOWICK 75 F6
Lowick Cl NN8 129 D7
Lowick Ct NN3 142 C7
Lowick La NN14 76 F7
Lowick Rd
 Aldwincle NN14 76 E7
 Islip NN14 76 B3
Lowlands Cl NN3 143 C5
Low March NN11 153 D7
Lowood NN1 159 F5
Lowry Cl
 Corby NN18 36 D4
 Northampton NN3 142 B4
 Wellingborough NN8 129 E7
Loxton Cl NN5 140 C1
Loyd Rd NN1 160 A6
LUBENHAM 30 E3
Lubenham All Saints CE Prim Sch LE16 30 F3
Lubenham Hill LE16 31 C2
Lubenham Rd
 East Farndon LE16 31 B1
 Marston Trussell LE16 30 D1
Lucas Cl NN9 131 E8
Lucas La NN7 177 B3
Lucas Rd NN6 121 A3
LUDDINGTON IN THE BROOK 61 B4
Luddington Rd PE8, PE28 61 C3
Ludlow Cl NN3 143 A7
Ludlow Wlk NN18 36 E1
Luffenham Rd LE15 3 F6
Lukes Cl NN13 212 A5
Lulworth Wlk NN18 36 A6
Lumber La NN12 216 B7
Lumbertubs La NN3 142 D5
Lumbertubs Prim Sch NN3 142 F3
Lumbertubs Rise NN3 142 D5
Lumbertubs Way NN3 142 E3
Lunchfield Ct NN3 126 C1
Lunchfield Gdns NN3 126 C1
Lunchfield La NN3 126 C1
Lunchfield Wlk 7 NN3 126 C1
Lundie Cl NN9 114 D7
Lundy Ave NN18 36 E4
Lupin Cl NN16 72 D4
Lutterworth Rd
 Northampton NN1 160 A6
 Swinford LE17 62 B6
LUTTON 44 C4
Lutton Rd PE8 43 C3
LYDDINGTON 9 C7
Lyddington Rd
 Caldecott LE15, L16 9 D2
 Gretton NN17 10 A1
Lydia Ct NN10 132 A2
Lyle Ct NN8 129 C7
Lyncrest Ave NN5 158 E7
Lyncrest Prim Sch NN5 158 E7
Lyncroft Way NN2 141 B1
Lyndhurst Rd CV21 98 F8
Lyneford Way NN10 147 F8
Lyne Wlk NN7 177 B3
Lynmore Cl NN4 158 C1
Lynmouth Ave NN3 160 C7
Lynmouth Pl NN18 36 E4
Lynton Ave NN2 141 C6
Lynton Gr NN18 36 F4
Lynwood Cl NN16 72 B5
Lytham Cl NN2 141 E3
Lytham Ct NN8 129 C7
Lyttleton Rd NN5 159 A7
Lyveden New Bield★ PE8 57 A7
Lyveden Pl NN16 72 D3
Lyveden Rd
 Brigstock NN14 55 F7
 Northampton NN4 160 A1
Lyveden Way NN18 36 E2


## M


Macadam Cl NN11 134 F5
Macadam Rd NN17 22 A1
McGibbon Wlk NN9 131 D8
McInnes Way NN9 114 D7
Mackenzie Rd NN9 114 C5
Mackintosh Ct NN15 92 B1
Mackworth Dr NN9 111 E4
Mackworth Gn NN9 111 F4
Maclean Cl NN3 160 C7
Macmillan Way NN3 142 B4
Macon Cl NN5 139 F2
Madams Gdns NN14 70 D7
Madams Hill NN14 70 D7
Madeline Cl LE16 32 A5
Madison Apartments NN16 72 A3
Magdalen Cl
 Daventry NN11 153 B8
 Stony Stratford MK11 229 D6
 Syresham NN13 224 C8
Magdalen College Sch (St John's) NN13 233 F6
Magdalen College Sch (Waynflete) NN13 233 E7
Magdalene Cl NN14 54 B3
Magdalen Ho MK11 229 D6
Magdalen Mdws NN13 222 E1
Magdalen Rd CV23 117 E3
Magee St NN1 159 F7
Magellan Cl
 Daventry NN11 135 C5
 Rothwell NN14 70 E6
Magnolia Cl NN3 160 D6
Magnolia Dr
 Daventry NN11 135 C4
 Rushden NN10 148 B7
Magpie La NN13 233 E6
Magpie Rd
 Sulgrave OX17 210 E7
 Towcester NN12 203 C3
Maida Cl NN4 175 E7
Maidencastle NN3 143 B3
MAIDFORD 186 D6
Maidford Rd
 Corby NN17 36 C7
 Farthingstone NN12 170 D1
MAIDWELL 87 B7
Maidwell Hall (Prep Sch for Boys) NN6 87 B6
Maidwell Prim Sch NN6 87 B6
Maidwell Rd
 Haselbech NN6 86 B8
 Maidwell NN6 87 D7
Main Dr NN12 217 B2
Main Rd
 Collyweston PE9 1 D2
 Crick NN6 100 F5
 Dingley LE16 32 F3
 Earls Barton NN6 144 D6
 Farthinghoe NN13 221 B4
 Grendon NN7 163 D6
 Hackleton NN7 177 B3
 Kelmarsh NN6 67 F3
 Kilsby CV23 99 F3
 Middleton Cheney OX17 220 A8
 Northampton, Duston NN5 158 B7
 Northampton, Far Cotton NN4 159 B3
 Shutlanger NN12 204 D8
 Syresham NN13 224 C7
 Upper Heyford NN7 156 D4
 Wilby NN8 129 B1
Main St
 Abthorpe NN12 201 F2
 Aldwincle NN14 76 F8
 Apethorpe PE8 14 C4
 Ashby St L CV23 119 C5
 Ashley LE16 18 F2
 Aston le W NN11 182 F2
 Badby NN11 152 F2
 Barnwell PE8 59 B5
 Barrowden LE15 3 F5
 Bradden NN12 201 F5
 Bythorn PE28 97 D4
 Caldecott LE16 21 B8
 Charlton OX17 231 F4
 Church Stowe NN7 171 E8
 Claydon OX17 181 D1
 Clifton u D CV23 80 A5
 Cold Ashby NN6 84 B5
 Cosgrove MK19 218 E2
 Cottesbrooke NN6 105 A8
 Denton NN7 162 B1
 Drayton LE16 20 A5
 East Farndon LE16 48 B7
 East Haddon NN6 122 D5
 Farthingstone NN12 170 E3
 Foxton LE16 30 A8
 Great Addington NN14 94 B2
 Great Bowden LE16 32 A6
 Great Brington NN7 138 D7
 Great Gidding PE28 61 D3
 Great Oxendon LE16 48 E3
 Hannington NN6 108 C3
 Hellidon NN11 151 D1
 Holcot NN6 126 E8
 Little Brington NN7 138 C4
 Little Harrowden NN9 110 C4
 Loddington NN14 70 C1
 Lowick NN14 75 F6
 Lubenham LE16 30 F3
 Lyddington LE15 9 C7
 Mawsley Village NN14 89 B4
 Medbourne LE16 19 A7
 Middleton LE16 35 C8
 Orton NN14 70 A3
 Polebrook PE8 43 A3
 Rockingham LE16 21 B4
 Slipton NN14 75 A3
 Southwick PE8 26 B5
 Stoke Dry LE15 9 A7
 Sudborough NN14 56 D1
 Sutton Bassett LE16 18 A1
 Tansor PE8 27 D2
 Theddingworth LE17 46 D8
 Thorpe by Water LE15 10 A5
 Thurning PE8 60 D3
 Turweston NN13 234 C8
 Upper Stowe NN7 171 F6
 Wadenhoe PE8 58 A4
 Wakerley LE15 4 A4
 Watford NN6 120 C6
 Wilbarston LE16 34 C5
 Willoughby CV23 117 E3
 Woodend NN12 200 F7
 Woodnewton PE8 14 E1
 Yarwell PE8 15 F8
Makepeace Ho NN11 118 C1
Malabar Fields NN11 153 B8
Malaslea NN14 89 B4
Malborough Way NN12 217 F5
Malcolm Ct NN17 36 F6
Malcolm Dr NN5 158 E7
Malcolm Rd NN2 141 F2
Malcolm Terr NN2 141 F2
Malham Ct NN8 129 D6
Malham Dr NN16 72 A5
Mallard Cl
 Earls Barton NN6 144 F5
 Higham Ferrers NN10 132 C8
 Northampton NN4 158 F2
 Thrapston NN14 76 D3
Mallard Dr
 Burton Latimer NN15 92 A2
 Hinton NN11 184 B6
Mallery Cl NN10 132 D3
Mallets Cl MK11 229 E5
Mallory Way NN11 135 C5
Mallory Wlk NN3 141 F5
Mallows Dr NN9 114 C7
Mallows Yd NN29 164 D3
Mall The NN16 72 B2
Malmo Cl NN18 36 A2
Malpas Dr NN5 158 B8
Malthouse Cl
 Irthlingborough NN9 112 F2
 Northampton NN4 159 D4
Malthouse Ct NN12 203 C6
Malting La NN14 54 A3
Maltings Cl NN17 10 B1
Maltings Field MK19 218 F5
Maltings Rd NN17 10 B1
Maltings The
 Ashley LE16 18 F3
 10 Market Harborough LE16 31 E3
 Rothwell NN14 70 C7
 Wollaston NN29 146 D3
 Wothorpe PE9 2 E8
Malting Way NN7 192 D1
Malt La NN13 224 C8
Malt Mill Cl CV23 100 A2
Malt Mill Gn CV23 100 A2
Malton Wlk NN18 36 B5
Malvern Cl
 Kettering NN16 72 B7
 Wellingborough NN8 129 D1
Malvern Dr MK11 229 F4
Malvern Gr NN5 158 D8
Malzor La NN7 174 E4
Manchester Rd NN29 146 C3
Mander Cl NN5 157 F8
Mandeville Cl NN3 142 B4
Manfield Rd NN1 160 A7
Manfield Way NN3 142 B4
Manitoba Cl NN18 36 B3
Manitoba Pl NN11 184 C1
Manitoba Way NN11 184 C1
Manna Ho NN1 159 D6
Manning Ct NN3 142 C7
Manningham Rd NN9 114 A4
Manning Rd NN3 142 C7
Mannings Rise NN10 132 C1
Manning St NN10 132 C1
Mannington Gdns NN4 175 C7
Mannock Rd NN8 129 E3
Manor Cl
 Bozeat NN29 164 D3
 Charwelton NN11 168 A4
 Cosgrove MK19 218 E2
 Great Addington NN14 94 B2
 Great Harrowden NN9 110 D2
 Hanslope MK19 207 A2
 Harpole NN7 157 C6
 Hinton NN11 184 B7
 Irchester NN29 147 B8
 Isham NN14 110 F8
 Middleton Cheney OX17 220 B7
 Roade NN7 191 E4
 Sulgrave OX17 210 F8
 Thrapston NN14 76 D2
Manor Ct
 Brackley NN13 233 F8
 Cottingham LE16 20 C1
 Grendon NN7 163 D5
 Little Harrowden NN9 110 C4
 Northampton NN2 141 B3
 Rushden NN10 148 C8
 2 Wellingborough NN8 130 B5
Manor Dr
 Corby NN18 36 A4
 Irthlingborough NN9 113 A2
Manor Farm
 Apethorpe PE8 14 C4
 Hannington NN6 108 C3
Manor Farm Cl
 Barby CV23 99 C2
 Broughton NN14 90 B4
 Walgrave NN6 108 A5
Manor Farm Cotts NN13 238 C8
Manor Farm Ct
 Cogenhoe NN7 162 A6
 Titchmarsh NN14 77 C4
Manor Farm Rd
 Northampton NN3 143 B2
 Raunds NN9 114 E6
Manorfield Cl NN3 161 B8
Manorfield Rd NN3 161 B8
Manorfields Rd MK19 229 B6
Manor Gdns
 Farthingstone NN12 170 F3
 Norton NN11 136 C4
 Pytchley NN14 90 F2
Manor Gdns *continued*
 Stanwick NN9 114 A3
Manor Ho The NN14 76 D2
Manor House Cl NN6 144 E5
Manor House Gdns NN9 114 D6
Manor House Mus★ NN16 72 B1
Manor La
 Clifton u D CV23 80 A5
 Farthinghoe NN13 221 B4
 Newnham NN11 153 E4
 Whilton NN11 137 D6
 Wymington NN10 148 A5
Manor Pk
 Claydon OX17 181 D1
 Nether Heyford NN7 156 C2
Manor Pl NN15 91 B8
Manor Rd
 Brackley NN13 233 E7
 Daventry NN11 135 D1
 Earls Barton NN6 144 E5
 Great Bowden LE16 32 A6
 Grendon NN7 163 D5
 Grimscote NN12 188 A8
 Hanging Houghton NN6 106 C8
 Hinton NN11 184 B6
 Kilsby CV23 100 A3
 Mears Ashby NN6 128 B2
 Medbourne LE16 19 A7
 Moulton NN3 142 C8
 Northampton NN2 141 B3
 Pitsford NN6 125 D5
 Rothwell NN14 70 B7
 Rushden NN10 148 B8
 Rushton NN14 52 C2
 Spratton NN6 105 B1
 Stanion NN14 37 E2
 Staverton NN11 152 B7
 Sulgrave OX17 210 F8
 Sutton PE5 8 F2
 Weedon Bec NN7 155 B3
Manor Sch & Sports Coll NN9 114 E6
Manor St NN9 114 D6
Manor The NN11 199 C7
Manor View PE9 1 A6
Manor Way
 Higham Ferrers NN10 132 C5
 Yardley Gobion NN12 217 E6
Manor Wlk
 Hanging Houghton NN6 106 C8
 Market Harborough LE16 31 E3
 Nether Heyford NN7 156 C2
Mansard Cl NN5 158 E6
Manse Cl
 Rushden NN10 132 C3
 Stony Stratford MK11 229 D6
Mansefield Cl NN14 51 A3
Mansel Cl MK19 218 D2
Mansell Cl NN12 203 C8
Mansfield Ct NN12 202 D8
Mansfield St NN9 113 F4
Mansfield Way NN29 147 A8
Manshead Ct MK11 229 F5
Mansion Cl NN3 142 A6
Mansion Hill OX17 219 F8
Mantlefield Rd NN18 36 B6
Manton Ct NN10 132 C2
Manton Rd
 Corby NN17 22 A2
 Irthlingborough NN9 112 E2
 Rushden NN10 132 C1
Manton Spinney NN10 131 E2
Maple Cl
 Brackley NN13 222 F1
 Braunston NN11 118 D1
 Bugbrooke NN7 172 F7
 Hinton NN11 184 A6
 Towcester NN12 203 B4
Maple Ct NN17 21 E1
Maple Dr NN8 129 E5
Maplefelds Sch NN18 36 D5
Maple Rd
 Kettering NN16 72 D4
 Rushden NN10 132 C2
Maples The NN11 135 D1
Mapletoft St NN9 114 C5
Maple Wood NN10 148 B7
Mapperley Dr NN3 160 F8
Marchwood Cl NN3 142 F6
Marconi Ctyd NN17 22 B1
Marecroft LE16 66 F7
Mare Fair NN1 159 C5
Margaret Ave NN8 129 E2
Margaret House Ctyd NN13 233 F6
Margaret Rd
 Kettering NN16 72 E3
 Twyford OX17 230 B5
Margaret St NN1 159 D7
Marion Sq NN16 72 E3
Maritime Way NN11 135 E1
Marjoram Cl 6 NN4 175 D6
Market Cross NN9 112 F2
MARKET HARBOROUGH 31 C2
Market Harborough CE Prim Sch LE16 31 D3
Market Harborough District Hospl LE16 31 D3
Market Harborough Mus★ LE16 31 E3
Market Harborough Sta LE16 32 A3
Market Hill NN14 70 D7
Market Pl
 Brackley NN13 233 E6
 Kettering NN16 72 B1
 Long Buckby NN6 121 B4
 Olney MK46 195 F3
 Oundle PE8 42 A5
Market Rd NN14 76 D2
Market Sq
 3 Daventry NN11 135 C2
 Hanslope MK19 207 A2
 Higham Ferrers NN10 132 C6
 Northampton NN1 159 C6
 Stony Stratford MK11 229 D5
 3 Wellingborough NN8 130 A4
Market St
 Kettering NN16 72 B2
 Northampton NN1 159 E7
 Wellingborough NN8 130 A4
Market Street Mews 10 NN16 72 B2
Market Wlk NN1 159 E7
Markham Cl NN5 140 C1
Markham Wlk NN18 36 B5
Marks Cl NN9 114 A3
Marlborough Ave NN8 129 D7
Marlborough Cl
 Kettering NN15 72 F1
 Kings Sutton OX17 230 F6
Marlborough Croft NN13 233 F6
Marlborough Rd NN5 159 A6
Marlborough Way LE16 31 E5
Marlow Cl
 Daventry NN11 135 B1
 Rothwell NN14 70 C6
Marlow Ct
 Corby NN18 36 B5
 Medbourne LE16 19 A8
Marlowe Cl NN4 175 B7
Marlow Rd NN12 203 D5
Marlstones NN4 158 D2
Marnock Sq 3 NN4 158 F2
Marquee Dr NN3 160 F7
Marriots Rd NN6 121 C3
Marriott Cl NN9 131 E8
Marriott St NN2 159 C8
Marseilles Cl NN5 139 F1
Marshall Ct 2 LE16 31 F2
Marshalls Ct NN9 114 D6
Marshall's Rd NN9 114 C6
Marsh Cl NN6 101 A5
Marsh La NN9 113 B3
Marshleys Ct NN3 143 B5
Marsh The NN6 101 A5
Marshwell Ct 5 NN3 161 A8
Marsons Dr NN6 100 F5
Marston Hill
 Marston St Lawrence OX17 210 B3
 Priors Marston CV47 166 E7
Marston La LE16 48 A7
Marston Rd
 Greatworth OX17 210 E2
 Lubenham LE16 30 D2
MARSTON ST LAWRENCE 210 A1
MARSTON TRUSSELL 47 C8
Marston Trussell Rd LE16 47 F7
Marston Way NN11 135 D6
Martel Cl NN5 157 F8
Martha Wallis Ct 1 NN16 72 B2
Martial Daire Bvd NN13 233 E8
Martin Cl NN10 132 B4
Martindale NN2 140 F5
Martin Rd NN15 91 C7
Martins La NN4 175 E8
Martins Rd NN7 177 A1
Martins Yd NN5 159 B7
Martlet Cl NN4 175 E5
Martonia 1 NN1 159 F7
Marvills Mill Rd NN4 159 C4
Marwood Cl NN3 160 C7
Masefield Cl NN8 129 C4
Masefield Dr NN10 131 E3
Masefield Rd NN16 72 C5
Masefield Way
 Corby NN17 36 D8
 Northampton NN2 141 E2
Mason Cl
 Oundle PE8 42 A5
 Thrapston NN14 76 D1
Massey Cl NN4 175 E8
Matchless Cl NN5 140 A1
Matlock Way NN14 50 E4
Matson Cl NN14 70 B6
Matson Ct NN9 114 E7
Matthew Clarke Ho 4 LE16 31 E4
Matthews Cl NN14 52 C3
Mauduit Cl MK19 207 A3
Maunsell Rise NN14 70 B6
Mauntley Ave NN14 55 F7
Maurice Rd LE16 48 D8
Mawsley Chase NN14 89 C5
Mawsley Cres NN16 71 F2
Mawsley La NN14 89 C8
Mawsley Lo NN14 89 B3

Mawsley Prim Sch
NN14 . . . 89 B5
**MAWSLEY VILLAGE** . . . 89 A4
**Maxwell Wlk** NN18 . . . 36 E5
**May Bank** NN11 . . . 153 B8
**Maybush Wlk** MK46 . . . 195 E5
**May Cl** NN10 . . . 148 C7
**Maye Dicks Rd** NN10 . . . 148 C8
**Mayfield Rd**
Daventry NN11 . . . 135 C3
Desborough NN14 . . . 51 C3
Northampton NN3 . . . 142 B3
**Maylan Rd** NN17 . . . 21 F3
**Mays Way** NN12 . . . 217 D3
**Mazewood Gate** PE8 . . . 13 E7
**Meacham Cl** NN14 . . . 90 A3
**Meadow Cl**
Daventry NN11 . . . 135 D6
Higham Ferrers NN10 . . . 132 B6
Market Harborough LE16 . . . 31 F4
Northampton NN5 . . . 140 B2
Ringstead NN14 . . . 95 A3
Wellingborough NN8 . . . 130 D8
**Meadow Ct**
6 Kettering NN16 . . . 72 B2
Ravenstone MK46 . . . 194 D2
Towcester NN12 . . . 203 C5
Meadowdale Prim Sch
LE16 . . . 32 B4
**Meadow Dr** NN10 . . . 132 B6
**Meadow Farm Cl** NN7 . . . 155 F5
**Meadow Gate** PE8 . . . 14 E2
**Meadow La**
Denford NN14 . . . 95 C6
Little Houghton NN7 . . . 161 A4
Raunds NN9 . . . 114 A6
Thornhaugh PE8 . . . 7 F5
Thrapston NN14 . . . 76 D2
**Meadowlands** NN9 . . . 110 B3
**Meadow Rd**
Kettering NN16 . . . 72 A2
Rothwell NN14 . . . 70 C6
**Meadow Rise** NN12 . . . 189 D4
Meadowside Inf Sch
NN15 . . . 92 B2
Meadowside Jun Sch
NN15 . . . 92 B2
**Meadow St** LE16 . . . 31 E4
**Meadows The**
Northampton NN4 . . . 175 F1
Northampton NN4 . . . 175 F2
Old Stratford MK19 . . . 229 B6
Wellingborough NN9 . . . 110 E1
**Meadow Sweet Rd**
NN10 . . . 148 C7
**Meadowsweet Wlk**
NN4 . . . 175 F2
**Meadow The** NN3 . . . 142 C1
**Meadowvale** NN9 . . . 112 F1
**MEADOW VIEW** . . . 140 F6
**Meadow View**
Adderbury OX17 . . . 230 A4
Great Addington NN14 . . . 94 C3
Higham Ferrers NN10 . . . 132 A6
Potterspury NN12 . . . 217 D3
**Meadow Way** NN9 . . . 112 F1
**Meadow Wlk**
Higham Ferrers NN10 . . . 132 B6
9 Irthlingborough
NN9 . . . 112 F2
**Mead Rd** NN15 . . . 90 F8
**Meads Ct** NN15 . . . 92 B1
**Meadslade** NN7 . . . 192 D2
**Meadway**
Bugbrooke NN7 . . . 172 F7
Northampton NN3 . . . 160 D8
**Meadway Cl** NN15 . . . 91 D8
**MEARS ASHBY** . . . 128 C2
Mears Ashby Prim Sch
NN6 . . . 128 B2
**Mears Ashby Rd**
Earls Barton NN6 . . . 144 C6
Wilby NN8 . . . 129 A1
**MEDBOURNE** . . . 18 F6
**Medbourne Cl** NN3 . . . 142 B7
**Medbourne Rd**
Ashley LE16 . . . 18 E4
Drayton LE16 . . . 19 E4
Medbourne LE16 . . . 18 C8
**Medellin Hill** NN3 . . . 142 F6
**Medinah Cl** NN4 . . . 175 D5
**Medina Rd** NN17 . . . 21 C1
**Medlicott Cl** NN18 . . . 53 A8
**Medway Cl**
Market Harborough
LE16 . . . 32 A3
Northampton NN5 . . . 140 E2
**Medway Dr**
Northampton NN5 . . . 140 F2
Wellingborough NN8 . . . 129 C6
**Medway Ho** PE8 . . . 42 A6
**Medway The** NN11 . . . 135 A1
**Medwin** NN8 . . . 129 B4
**Meeting La**
Burton Latimer NN15 . . . 92 C2
Corby NN17 . . . 37 B7
Irthlingborough NN9 . . . 112 F2
15 Kettering NN16 . . . 72 B2
Northampton NN5 . . . 158 C7
Rothwell NN14 . . . 70 C6
Towcester NN12 . . . 203 C6
**Meissen Ave** NN14 . . . 50 F3
**Melbourne Ho**
Corby NN17 . . . 22 F1
4 Northampton NN5 . . . 159 A6
**Melbourne La** NN5 . . . 158 C6
**Melbourne Rd** NN5 . . . 158 F6
**Melbourne St** 3 NN1 . . . 159 F6
**Melbourne Wlk** 4
NN1 . . . 159 F6
**Melbury La** NN3 . . . 143 B3
**Melbury Pl** NN3 . . . 143 B3
**Melchbourne Rd**
MK44 . . . 149 F4
**Melchester Cl** NN4 . . . 175 E7
**Meldon Cl** NN4 . . . 175 C8
**Melford Cl** NN18 . . . 36 D2
**Mellor Rd** CV21 . . . 99 B8
**Melloway Rd** NN10 . . . 131 E2
**Melrose Ave** NN5 . . . 158 E7
**Melrose Cl** NN15 . . . 91 F8
**Meltham Cl** NN3 . . . 142 F1
**Melton Rd** NN8 . . . 130 C5
**Melton Rd N** NN8 . . . 130 B5
**Melton St** NN16 . . . 72 B3
**Melville St** NN1 . . . 159 F7
**Membris Way** NN11 . . . 184 A6
**Memorial Gn** NN7 . . . 191 E4
**Mendip Cl** NN16 . . . 72 B5
**Mendip Ct** NN11 . . . 135 B5
**Mendip Rd** NN5 . . . 158 D7
**Meon Cl** NN17 . . . 21 C1
**Meon Way** NN5 . . . 158 D8
**Mercer Ct** CV22 . . . 98 F8
**Mercer's Row** 3 NN1 . . . 159 C5
**Mercia Gdns** NN3 . . . 142 C1
**Mercury Cl** NN11 . . . 135 A4
**Mercury Dr** NN4 . . . 160 A2
**Mere Cl**
Brafield-on-t-G NN7 . . . 161 D2
1 Northampton NN4 . . . 175 B8
Mere Farm Bsns Units
NN6 . . . 108 D4
**MEREFIELD** . . . 175 B7
**Merefields** NN9 . . . 112 E3
**Merestone Hos** OX17 . . . 210 B1
**Merestone Rd** NN18 . . . 36 D3
**Mere Way** NN4 . . . 175 C8
Mereway Com Coll
NN4 . . . 159 B1
**Merlin Gr** 5 NN4 . . . 175 B8
**Merrivale Cl** NN15 . . . 90 F7
**Merrycot La** NN6 . . . 82 B4
**Merrydale Sq** NN3 . . . 143 A6
**Merryhill** NN4 . . . 158 E2
**Merry Tom La** NN6 . . . 124 D4
**Mersey Cl** NN4 . . . 159 A2
**Mersey Gn** NN17 . . . 21 C1
**Mershe Cl** NN4 . . . 175 F7
**Merthyr Rd** NN5 . . . 159 A8
**Merton Cl** NN13 . . . 233 D8
**Merton Rd** NN11 . . . 153 B7
**Mescalero** NN2 . . . 141 C4
**Meshaw Cres** NN3 . . . 160 B7
**Methodist Homestead** 4
NN2 . . . 141 E1
**Mews Cotts** LE16 . . . 48 E3
**Mews The**
Brixworth NN6 . . . 106 B2
Brockhall NN11 . . . 137 C2
Great Bowden LE16 . . . 31 E7
Long Buckby NN6 . . . 121 B4
Northampton NN3 . . . 160 D8
4 Rugby CV21 . . . 80 A1
**Michaelmas Cl** OX17 . . . 208 F1
**Michael's Wlk** LE16 . . . 21 B4
**Mickleborough Cl**
LE16 . . . 18 B3
**Mickle Hill** PE18 . . . 116 D7
**Micklewell La** NN3 . . . 142 F6
**Middlebrook Gn** LE16 . . . 32 A4
**Middledale Rd** LE16 . . . 32 A3
**Middlefield Cl** NN14 . . . 95 B3
**Middle Grass** NN9 . . . 112 E3
**Middle Greeve** NN4 . . . 176 A6
**Middle La** LE16 . . . 34 B4
**Middlemarch** 5 NN3 . . . 143 B4
**Middle March** NN11 . . . 153 D8
**Middlemead Ct** NN3 . . . 143 A1
**Middlemore** NN3 . . . 142 F6
**Middle St**
Elton PE8 . . . 28 D8
Foxton LE16 . . . 30 E8
Isham NN14 . . . 110 F8
Kilsby CV23 . . . 100 A3
Nether Heyford NN7 . . . 156 C2
**Middlethorpe** NN12 . . . 200 B2
**MIDDLETON** . . . 35 B8
**MIDDLETON CHENEY**
. . . 209 A1
Middleton Cheney Com
Prim Sch OX17 . . . 219 F8
**Middleton Cl**
Banbury OX16 . . . 219 A7
Northampton NN2 . . . 141 C5
**Middleton Rd**
Ashley LE16 . . . 19 B3
Banbury OX16 . . . 219 A7
Bringhurst LE16 . . . 20 C4
Chacombe OX17 . . . 208 E4
**Middle Weald** MK19 . . . 229 E1
**Middlewell Ct** 2 NN3 . . . 142 F1
**Middlewich Cl** NN11 . . . 135 C6
**Midfield Ct** NN3 . . . 142 E5
Midland Bsns Ctr
NN10 . . . 132 C6
Midland Bsns Units
NN8 . . . 130 C6
**Midland Cotts** NN14 . . . 52 C3
**Midland Rd**
Higham Ferrers
NN10 . . . 132 C6
Olney MK46 . . . 195 F5
**Midland Rd** *continued*
Raunds NN9 . . . 114 E7
Rushden NN10 . . . 132 A3
Thrapston NN14 . . . 76 C1
Wellingborough NN8 . . . 130 B4
Midland Works Bsns Ctr
NN8 . . . 130 D6
**Midway**
Blisworth NN7 . . . 174 B2
Middleton Cheney
OX17 . . . 209 A1
**Milbury** NN6 . . . 144 F3
**Milby La** NN14 . . . 54 A2
**Mildmay Cl** PE8 . . . 41 E5
**Miles Cl** NN9 . . . 114 B5
**Miles La** NN6 . . . 121 C4
**Mile St** NN29 . . . 164 D3
**Milestone Mews** LE16 . . . 20 C1
**Miles Well Ct** NN3 . . . 142 D3
**Milford Ave** MK11 . . . 229 E4
**Military Rd** NN1 . . . 159 D7
**Militia Cl** NN4 . . . 175 E7
**Milking Slade La** PE28 . . . 61 F3
**Millais Rd** NN18 . . . 36 E5
**Millbank** NN3 . . . 143 D2
**Millbrook Cl** NN5 . . . 159 A4
Millbrook Inf Sch
NN15 . . . 91 F8
Millbrook Jun Sch
NN15 . . . 91 F8
**Millburn Dr** NN5 . . . 158 A6
**Mill Cl**
Braunston NN11 . . . 118 B1
Corby NN18 . . . 36 B1
Raunds NN9 . . . 114 C6
**Milldale Gdns** NN15 . . . 91 D8
**Mill Dale Rd** NN15 . . . 91 D8
**Millenium Cl** NN15 . . . 91 A7
**Millennium Way**
NN11 . . . 135 C2
**Miller Cl**
Kettering NN15 . . . 91 C6
Thrapston NN14 . . . 76 E1
**Miller Hill** NN4 . . . 158 E2
**Miller Rd** NN15 . . . 92 B1
**Millers Cl**
Lower Boddington
NN11 . . . 182 C5
Rushden NN10 . . . 131 F2
**Miller's Cl**
Finedon NN9 . . . 112 A5
Kislingbury NN7 . . . 157 D2
**Millers Gdns** LE16 . . . 31 B2
**Millers La** NN8 . . . 145 F8
**Millers Pk** NN8 . . . 130 A1
**Miller St** NN9 . . . 114 D7
**Millers Way** NN4 . . . 175 F3
**Miller's Yd** 5 LE16 . . . 31 E3
**Mill Est** NN10 . . . 148 B7
Mill Farm Ctyd MK19 . . . 229 B1
**Millfield Ave** LE16 . . . 20 D1
**Millfields** PE8 . . . 41 F6
**Mill Fields** NN10 . . . 132 B7
**Millfields Ave** CV21 . . . 98 F8
**Millglade The** NN14 . . . 91 F1
**Mill Greene Ct** 3
NN16 . . . 72 C4
**Mill Hill**
Corby NN18 . . . 53 B7
Lubenham LE16 . . . 30 E3
**Mill Hill Rd** LE16 . . . 31 F3
**Mill Ho**
Brackley NN13 . . . 233 E5
6 Northampton NN2 . . . 159 C7
**Millholm Rd** NN14 . . . 51 B2
**Millhouse Ct** NN5 . . . 159 B5
**Millies La** NN17 . . . 12 C1
**Mill La**
Adderbury OX17 . . . 230 A3
Barrowden LE15 . . . 4 A5
Brackley NN13 . . . 234 A6
Brigstock NN14 . . . 55 F7
Caldecott LE16 . . . 21 B8
Chipping Warden OX17 . . . 196 F6
Cogenhoe NN7 . . . 162 A7
Croughton NN13 . . . 238 C7
Earls Barton NN6 . . . 145 A3
Greens Norton NN12 . . . 202 E7
Grimscote NN12 . . . 172 B1
Isham NN14 . . . 91 F1
Islip NN14 . . . 76 C3
Ketton PE9 . . . 1 A5
Kings Sutton OX17 . . . 230 F4
Kislingbury NN7 . . . 157 D3
Lowick NN14 . . . 75 F6
Northampton, Kingsthorpe
NN2, NN5 . . . 141 B2
Northampton NN2 . . . 159 B7
Old NN6 . . . 88 E3
Oundle PE8 . . . 27 B1
Stoke Bruerne NN12 . . . 191 A1
Stony Stratford MK11 . . . 229 D5
Wadenhoe PE8 . . . 58 A3
Westbury NN13 . . . 234 F4
**Mill Marina Cvn Pk**
NN14 . . . 76 C1
**Mill Mdw** NN2 . . . 141 D5
**Mill Rd**
Bozeat NN29 . . . 164 C2
Cottingham LE16 . . . 20 C2
Great Gidding PE28 . . . 61 E3
Gretton LE15, NN17 . . . 9 F2
Irthlingborough NN8 . . . 131 B7
Islip NN14 . . . 76 B3
Kettering NN16 . . . 72 C2
Kislingbury NN7 . . . 157 D3
Northampton NN2 . . . 159 C7
Oundle PE8 . . . 41 F4
**Mill Rd** *continued*
Wellingborough NN8 . . . 130 B5
Whitfield NN13 . . . 223 E4
Woodford NN14 . . . 94 C7
Yarwell PE8 . . . 16 A7
Mill Rd Ind Est NN8 . . . 130 C6
**Mill Road Pas** 5 NN16 . . . 72 C2
**Mills Cl** NN6 . . . 144 F4
**Millside Cl** NN2 . . . 141 D5
**Mill St** PE9 . . . 5 B6
**Millstone Cl** NN4 . . . 158 D2
**Millway** NN5 . . . 158 C6
Millway Prim Sch
NN5 . . . 158 D6
**Millwood Way** PE8 . . . 13 E7
**Milner Rd** NN9 . . . 111 F4
**MILTHORPE** . . . 200 B2
**Milthorpe** NN12 . . . 200 B2
**Milton Ave** NN8 . . . 129 C3
**Milton Bridge** NN4 . . . 176 A6
**Milton Ct**
Kettering NN16 . . . 72 C5
Milton Malsor NN7 . . . 174 E3
**MILTON MALSOR** . . . 174 E4
Milton Parochial Prim Sch
NN7 . . . 174 E4
**Milton Rd**
Corby NN17 . . . 36 C8
Daventry NN11 . . . 135 B2
Gayton NN7 . . . 173 F2
Little Irchester NN8 . . . 130 C1
Oundle PE8 . . . 41 F5
**Milton St N** NN2 . . . 141 E1
**Milton St**
Higham Ferrers NN10 . . . 132 B5
Northampton NN2 . . . 141 F1
**Milton Terr** PE8 . . . 44 C4
**Milverton Cres** NN3 . . . 160 D7
**Mimosa Cl** NN3 . . . 160 C6
**Minden Cl** NN18 . . . 35 F2
**Minehead Cl** NN18 . . . 36 A6
**Minerva Way** NN8 . . . 129 D5
**Minster Ho** 2 NN1 . . . 159 D6
**Minton Cl** NN14 . . . 50 F3
**Mirfield Cl** NN18 . . . 36 C5
**Mistletoe Pl** NN3 . . . 142 C1
**Mitchell Cl** NN5 . . . 140 D2
**Mitchell Rd** NN17 . . . 22 B2
**Mitchell St** NN16 . . . 72 C5
**Mitchison Cl** CV23 . . . 118 C8
**MIXBURY** . . . 234 D1
**Mixbury Rd** NN13 . . . 233 F2
**Moat Farm Dr** CV21 . . . 99 A7
**Moat La** NN12 . . . 203 C6
**Moat Pl** NN1 . . . 159 B6
**Moat Yd** NN12 . . . 203 C6
**Mobbs Miller Ho** NN1 . . . 160 A7
**Moffatt Terr** NN8 . . . 130 A5
**Molesworth Bglws** PE9 . . . 1 A6
**Monarch Ctyd** NN4 . . . 160 A2
**Monarch Rd** NN2 . . . 141 C1
**Monarch Terr** NN2 . . . 159 C8
Monkfield Coll NN14 . . . 50 E2
**Monk's Hall Rd** NN1 . . . 159 F7
**Monks Park Rd** NN1 . . . 159 F7
**Monks Pond St** NN1 . . . 159 B6
**Monks Rd** NN29 . . . 146 D3
**Monks Way**
Corby NN18 . . . 36 A4
Crick NN6 . . . 101 A6
Wellingborough NN8 . . . 130 A3
**Monkswood** NN12 . . . 214 C4
**Monmouth Cl** NN14 . . . 76 F2
**Monmouth Rd** NN5 . . . 159 A7
**Monroe Cl** LE16 . . . 31 D5
**Monson Way** PE8 . . . 41 E7
**Montabaur Rd** NN13 . . . 234 A7
**Montagu Ct** NN15 . . . 91 D5
**Montague Cres** NN5 . . . 140 D2
**Montague Ct** NN14 . . . 76 D2
**Montague Dr** CV23 . . . 100 A3
**Montague St** NN10 . . . 132 A2
Montagu Sch NN16 . . . 72 D5
**Montagu St** NN16 . . . 72 C2
**Montagu Terr** PE8 . . . 59 B6
**Montcalm Cl** NN15 . . . 72 F1
**Monterly Gate** NN14 . . . 55 F7
**Montfort Cl** NN5 . . . 158 E6
**Montgomery Cl** NN15 . . . 72 E1
**Montgomery Way**
NN4 . . . 175 D7
**Montrose Cl** LE16 . . . 31 D1
**Montrose St** NN17 . . . 36 F6
Montsaye Com Coll
NN14 . . . 70 B7
**Moonshine Gap** NN6 . . . 128 D6
**Moore Cl**
Corby NN17 . . . 36 D8
Kettering NN15 . . . 92 A7
**Moor End** PE8 . . . 60 D3
**MOOR END** . . . 217 D6
**Moorend Rd** NN12 . . . 217 E6
**Moores Cl** NN7 . . . 172 F7
**Moores Hill** MK46 . . . 195 F5
**Moore St** NN2 . . . 141 F1
**Moor Field** NN12 . . . 203 B5
**Moorfield Gn** NN14 . . . 70 B6
**Moorfield Rd** NN14 . . . 70 B6
**Moorfield Sq** NN3 . . . 143 A6
**Moorhouse Way** NN15 . . . 90 E8
**Moorings The** NN14 . . . 94 E6
**Moor La** CV23 . . . 117 D3
**Moorland Cl** NN3 . . . 142 E2
**Moorlands** NN8 . . . 129 D7
**Moorlands The** NN10 . . . 132 B4
**Moor Rd** NN10 . . . 132 A2
**Moors Cl** MK19 . . . 228 E4
**Moors Dr The** OX17 . . . 219 F8
**Moors La** CV21, CV23 . . . 99 D8
**Morby Ct** NN15 . . . 92 B1
**MORCOTT** . . . 3 A5
**Morcott Rd** LE15 . . . 3 D5
**Mordaunt Cl** NN14 . . . 75 E6
**Mordaunt La** NN5 . . . 140 D1
**Morehay La**
King's Cliffe PE8 . . . 13 E6
King's Cliffe PE8 . . . 13 F7
**More Rd** NN11 . . . 135 B4
**Moreton Ave** NN8 . . . 129 D2
**MORETON PINKNEY** . . . 199 D7
**Moreton Rd** NN11 . . . 184 C1
**Moreton Way** NN2 . . . 141 C5
**Morgan Cl** NN3 . . . 143 C4
**Morgan Dr** NN6 . . . 106 C3
**Morgans Cl** PE8 . . . 43 A3
**Moriston Cl** NN17 . . . 21 C1
**Morland Rd** NN18 . . . 36 E5
**Morley St**
Kettering NN16 . . . 72 C4
Market Harborough
LE16 . . . 31 D3
**Morley Wlk** NN17 . . . 36 C8
**Morning Star Rd** 1
NN11 . . . 135 A3
**Morris Ave** NN10 . . . 131 F1
**Morris Cl** NN8 . . . 129 A6
**Morrison Park Rd**
NN6 . . . 102 C5
**Morris Rd**
Daventry NN11 . . . 134 F3
Northampton NN2 . . . 141 D3
**Morse Way** NN14 . . . 51 B4
**Mortar Pit Rd** NN3 . . . 143 C5
**Mortimer Cl** NN4 . . . 159 A2
**Morton Ct** CV22 . . . 98 F8
**Mortons Bush** NN4 . . . 176 A6
**Moss Cl** NN12 . . . 203 C8
**Moss Ct** NN16 . . . 72 B3
**Moss Wlk** NN18 . . . 36 A2
**Motala Cl** NN18 . . . 36 A2
**Motherwell Ho** NN17 . . . 37 A8
**Motspur Dr** NN2 . . . 141 B1
**Motts The** NN7 . . . 157 B6
**Moulds La** LE16 . . . 20 D7
**MOULTON** . . . 126 C2
Moulton Coll NN3 . . . 126 C1
**Moulton Crossing**
NN3 . . . 142 E8
**Moulton La** NN2, NN3 . . . 141 D8
**MOULTON PARK** . . . 142 A6
Moulton Park Bsns Ctr
NN3 . . . 142 A6
Moulton Prim Sch
NN3 . . . 126 C1
**Moulton Rd**
Holcot NN6 . . . 126 D7
Pitsford NN6 . . . 125 D3
Moulton Sch & Science
Coll NN3 . . . 126 B1
**Moulton Way** NN3 . . . 142 C6
**Moulton Way N** NN3 . . . 142 C6
**Moulton Way S** NN3 . . . 142 C6
**Mountbatten Dr** NN14 . . . 95 C3
**Mountbatten Ho**
NN11 . . . 153 E8
**Mountbatten Way**
NN9 . . . 114 E6
**Mountclair Ct** NN3 . . . 160 E8
**Mountfield Rd**
Irthlingborough NN9 . . . 112 F3
Northampton NN3 . . . 142 A3
**Mount Hill Ave** MK19 . . . 229 B7
**Mount Pleasant**
Earls Barton NN6 . . . 144 F4
Harpole NN7 . . . 157 C7
Morcott LE15 . . . 3 A6
Wardington OX17 . . . 196 E1
Woodford Halse NN11 . . . 184 D6
Yardley Gobion NN12 . . . 217 F6
**Mount Pleasant Rd**
LE15 . . . 3 A6
Mounts Bsns Ctr NN1 . . . 159 D7
**Mounts Ct** 1 NN3 . . . 142 E3
**Mounts La** NN11 . . . 153 E4
**Mounts The** NN6 . . . 121 B3
**Mow Mead** MK46 . . . 195 F5
**Mowsley Ct** LE17 . . . 45 E6
**Mowsley Rd**
Husbands Bosworth
LE17 . . . 45 E6
Theddingworth LE16 . . . 46 C8
**Moyeady Ave** CV22 . . . 98 E8
**Muirfield Dr** NN11 . . . 135 E2
**Muirfield Rd** NN8 . . . 129 C7
**Mulberry Cl**
Desborough NN14 . . . 51 A5
Northampton NN5 . . . 158 F7
Wellingborough NN8 . . . 129 E5
**Mulberry Ct** LE16 . . . 20 A5
**Mull Dr** NN17 . . . 36 C8
**Mullions The** NN4 . . . 175 E5
**Mulso Rd** NN9 . . . 112 A4
**Mumford Dr** NN7 . . . 174 A7
**Muncaster Gdns** NN4 . . . 175 D7
**Muncaster Way** NN6 . . . 102 C5
**Murcott** NN6 . . . 121 A4
**Murcott Cl** NN6 . . . 121 A4
**Murray Ave** NN2 . . . 141 D1
**Murray Ho** NN1 . . . 160 A8
**Murray Wlk** NN18 . . . 36 E5
**Mursley Ct** MK11 . . . 229 F5
**Murswell Cl** NN12 . . . 214 D4
**Murswell La** NN12 . . . 214 D4
**MUSCOTT** . . . 137 B3
**Muscott La** NN5 . . . 158 C6
**Muscott St** NN5 . . . 159 A6

Mus–Oba 257


Museum Way NN3 160 F7
Musgrave Cl NN4 175 F7
Mushroom Field Rd
NN3 143 D2
Musk Cl LE16 20 D7
Musott Cl NN7 155 E6
Musson Cl NN9 112 E2
Myers Cl OX17 231 F5
Myers Rd CV21 99 C8
Myers Way OX17 231 F5
Myrtle Rd NN16 72 D4

## N

Nags Head La NN9 115 F2
Nansen Cl
  Daventry NN11 135 C5
  Rothwell NN14 70 E6
Nansen Wlk NN18 36 B2
Nantwich Dr NN11 135 D6
Naomi Cl NN3 142 F1
Napier Cl
  Daventry NN11 153 D8
  Wellingborough NN8 129 A4
NAPTON ON THE HILL 150 A7
Narvik Rd NN18 36 A2
NASEBY 66 B1
Naseby Battle & Farm Mus★ NN6 85 B7
Naseby CE Prim Sch NN6 66 B1
Naseby Cl
  Market Harborough LE16 31 E2
  Wellingborough NN8 129 D7
Naseby Dr NN11 135 C6
Naseby Ho NN16 71 F3
Naseby Rd
  Clipston LE16 66 F8
  Corby NN17 36 C7
  Haselbech NN6 85 F8
  Kettering NN16 72 E3
  Sibbertoft LE16 46 F2
  Thornby NN6 84 E4
  Welford NN6 65 C5
Naseby Sq LE16 31 E2
Naseby St NN2 159 C8
Nash Ct NN15 92 A8
Nasmith Ave NN17 37 A8
Nasmyth Rd NN11 134 F5
NASSINGTON 15 E5
Nassington Prim Sch PE8 15 F5
Nassington Rd
  Woodnewton PE8 14 F1
  Yarwell PE8 15 F7
Navigation Row NN1 159 C4
Navisford Cl NN14 76 E3
NBC Depot NN2 141 E3
Neale Ave NN16 72 B5
Neale Cl
  Northampton NN3 160 E8
  Wollaston NN29 146 C3
Near Side NN5 158 F6
Near The Church LE16 17 A5
Needham Rd NN9 113 F4
Neene Ct 13 NN9 112 F2
Nelson Ave NN11 184 B6
Nelson Cl NN11 135 E2
Nelson Dr NN14 70 E7
Nelson Rd NN17 36 B8
Nelson St
  Kettering NN16 72 C3
  Market Harborough LE16 31 D3
  24 Northampton NN1 159 C7
Nelson's Yd NN12 203 C6
Nene Cl
  Kettering NN15 92 A5
  Raunds NN9 114 D7
  Wansford PE8 8 A3
  Wellingborough NN8 129 C6
Nene Cres NN17 21 C1
Nene Ct
  Thrapston NN14 76 D2
  Wellingborough NN8 130 C3
Nene Dr NN5 140 F2
Nene Ent Ctr NN2 159 C8
Nene La NN12 203 A6
Nene Park (Rushden & Diamonds FC) NN9 113 A2
Nene Pl NN5 141 A2
Nene Rd
  Burton Latimer NN15 92 A2
  Higham Ferrers NN10 132 B5
Nene Rise NN7 161 F6
Neneside Cl NN7 155 B3
Nene Side Cl NN11 152 F3
Nene Univ Coll Northampton NN2 141 E5
Nene Valley Bsns Pk PE8 42 B5
Nene Valley Ret Pk NN1 159 B4
Nene Valley Way NN3 160 D5
Nene View
  Irthlingborough NN14 112 F2
  Islip NN14 76 B3
  Oundle PE8 41 F6
Nene Way
  Kislingbury NN7 157 C3
  Northampton NN5 141 A2
  Oundle PE8 41 F7
  Sutton PE5 8 F2
Nene Whitewater Ctr★ NN4 160 B3
Nene Wlk
  Daventry NN11 135 A1
  Northampton NN5 140 F2
Nepcote Cl NN15 91 D8
Nesbitt Cl NN3 160 E8
Nest Farm Cres NN8 130 A8
Nest Farm Rd NN8 130 A7
Nest La NN8 130 B7
Nether Cl NN13 234 A7
NETHERCOTE 219 B7
Netherfield Gr NN17 36 F8
Netherfield Rd NN15 91 C7
Nether Gn LE16 67 A8
NETHER HEYFORD 156 B1
Nether Jackson Ct 3 NN3 143 B4
Nether La NN7 155 F4
Nethermead Ct NN3 142 F4
Nethertown Way NN14 89 B4
Nettle Gap Cl NN4 175 F6
Neuville Way NN14 50 F3
Nevill Cl MK19 207 B2
Neville Day Cl PE9 1 F5
Neville Ho NN17 36 E6
NEVILL HOLT 19 D8
Nevill Holt Rd LE16 19 F6
Nevis Cl NN17 21 C1
Newark Dr NN18 36 C6
NEW BARTON 144 F5
Newbery Dr NN13 233 D8
New Bldgs 7 NN16 72 B2
Newbold Cl PE8 41 E6
Newbolt Cl NN12 216 B8
NEWBOTTLE 231 E7
Newbottle & Charlton CE Prim Sch OX17 231 F5
Newbridge NN6 136 D8
Newbridge La NN9 114 A3
Newbury Cl
  Corby NN18 36 D1
  Rushden NN10 132 D3
Newbury Dr NN11 135 C6
Newby Ct NN3 142 C3
New College Farm NN6 127 A6
Newcombe Rd NN5 159 A7
Newcombe St LE16 31 E2
Newcomen Rd NN8 130 B5
New Croft NN7 155 B3
NEW DUSTON 140 B2
Newell Rd NN14 95 B3
New Forest Way NN11 135 B4
NEW HACKLETON 177 A3
New Hall NN11 153 B7
Newham Cl NN14 70 C7
Newington Rd NN2 141 C4
New La PE8 8 C1
Newland NN1 159 C6
Newland Rd NN6 108 A5
Newlands
  Brixworth NN6 106 B2
  3 Daventry NN11 135 C1
  Kings Sutton OX17 231 A6
  Naseby NN6 66 C1
Newlands Ctr NN16 72 B2
Newland Sq NN2 141 C4
Newlands Rd NN6 64 E5
Newland St
  Braybrooke LE16 49 E5
  Kettering NN16 72 B2
Newland Wlk 5 NN1 159 D6
Newlife Apartments 15 NN1 159 C6
Newman St
  Burton Latimer NN15 92 B2
  Higham Ferrers NN10 132 C7
  6 Kettering NN16 72 C2
Newmarket Cl NN18 36 D1
NEWNHAM 153 E4
Newnham Dr NN11 135 A5
Newnham Prim Sch NN11 153 D4
Newnham Rd NN2 141 D3
Newnham Windmill★ NN11 153 D7
Newport Pagnell Rd
  Horton NN7 177 D1
  Northampton NN4, NN7 176 A7
Newport Pagnell Rd W NN4 175 D8
Newport Rd
  Hanslope MK19 207 B2
  Northampton NN5 159 A7
New Post Office Sq NN17 36 E6
New Rd
  Brackley NN13 233 E6
  Castlethorpe MK19 218 F5
  Collyweston PE9 1 C2
  Easton o t H PE9 2 A5
  Farthinghoe NN13 221 A4
  Geddington NN14 54 A2
  Greens Norton NN12 202 D8
  Maidford NN12 186 D6
  Northampton NN4 175 E6
  Oundle PE8 42 A6
New South Bridge Rd NN4 159 C4
New St
  Brixworth NN6 106 A2
  Daventry NN11 135 C1
  Desborough NN14 51 A3
  Earls Barton NN6 144 F4
  Irchester NN29 147 B8
New St *continued*
  Irthlingborough NN9 112 F2
  Oundle PE8 42 A5
  Rothwell NN14 70 D7
  Stony Stratford MK11 229 D5
  Weedon Bec NN7 155 C3
  Wellingborough NN8 130 A5
Newstead Cl NN3 143 D3
Newstead Ct NN15 91 C5
Newstone Cres NN4 158 E4
New Street Ct NN29 147 B8
New Terr NN11 183 D7
NEWTON 53 E3
NEWTON BROMSWOLD 149 D8
Newton Cl
  Daventry NN11 135 A4
  Rushden NN10 132 D1
  Wellingborough NN8 129 B6
Newton Ct CV23 80 A8
Newton Gr NN17 22 A1
Newton Manor La CV23 80 A8
Newton Rd
  Clifton u D CV23 80 A7
  Geddington NN14 54 A3
  Higham Ferrers NN10 132 E5
  Kettering NN15 91 F5
  Northampton NN5 158 D8
  Rushden NN10 132 E1
  Wollaston NN29 146 D2
Newton Road Com Prim Sch NN10 132 C2
Newton St MK46 195 F4
Newton Way LE16 49 F6
Newtown
  Brigstock NN14 55 E8
  Woodford NN14 94 D7
New Town PE9 2 A5
Newtown Rd
  Little Irchester NN8 130 C1
  Raunds NN9 114 E5
New Town Rd 2 NN1 159 F6
Newtown St NN14 94 D7
Nibbits La NN11 118 C1
Nicholas Hawksmoor Prim Sch NN12 203 B5
Nicholas La NN9 112 E1
Nicholas Rd NN9 112 E1
Nicholas Way NN10 131 F3
Nicholls Ct NN3 142 E5
Nicholls Ho 1 NN4 159 A3
Nichols St NN14 51 A4
Nichols Way NN9 114 C7
Nielson Rd NN8 130 C8
Nigel Ct NN13 234 A5
Nightingale Cl
  Brackley NN13 222 E2
  Daventry NN11 135 D6
Nightingale Ct NN2 141 D1
Nightingale Dr
  Desborough NN14 51 B4
  Towcester NN12 203 C3
Nightingale La NN8 130 B7
Nine Arches Way NN14 76 C2
Niort Way NN8 129 C8
Nippendale NN10 132 C2
Nithsdale Ave LE16 31 F2
Nithsdale Cres LE16 31 F2
Nithsdale Rd NN17 36 D7
Noble Ave NN9 113 A5
Nobold Ct LE16 66 F8
NOBOTTLE 138 E2
Noel Mews NN3 142 B4
Nook The
  Corby NN17 37 B6
  Cottingham LE16 20 D1
  Easton o t H PE9 2 A5
Norbury Cl LE16 31 D3
Norfolk Cl NN17 36 C7
Norfolk St NN2 159 C8
Norfolk Terr NN2 159 C8
Norman-D-Gate NN1 159 E5
Norman-D-Gate Ind Est NN1 159 E5
Normandy Lo NN13 233 E8
Norman Rd NN3 142 B1
Norman Way
  Irchester NN29 147 C8
  Wellingborough NN8 129 D2
Normead Sq 4 NN3 143 D2
Norris Acre NN13 232 F6
Norris Cl NN15 92 A8
Norris Way NN10 131 E3
Norris Way Ind Est NN10 131 E3
Norse Wlk NN18 36 A2
Northall NN6 108 A5
Northall Mews NN16 72 A2
Northall St NN16 72 B3
Northam Ct NN16 72 B4
NORTHAMPTON 159 E4
Northampton Acad NN3 142 F2
Northampton Christian Sch NN1 160 A8
Northampton Coll
  Northampton NN1 159 D6
  Northampton, The Arbours NN3 142 D3
Northampton General Hospl NN1 159 E5
Northampton High Sch NN4 175 E8
Northampton Ho 7 NN1 159 D6
Northampton La N NN3 142 C8
Northampton La S NN3 142 C7
Northampton Prep Sch NN4 160 E3
Northampton Rd
  Blisworth NN7 174 D1
  Brackley NN13 223 A1
  Brixworth NN6 106 B1
  Broughton NN14 90 A3
  Chapel Brampton NN6 124 E1
  Cosgrove MK19 217 F7
  Denton NN7 178 B8
  Earls Barton NN6 144 D5
  Ecton NN6 143 F4
  Harpole NN7 157 C5
  Kettering NN15 71 F1
  Litchborough NN12 171 E2
  Market Harborough LE16 31 F3
  Orlingbury NN14 109 F5
  Roade NN7 191 D5
  Rushden NN10 131 E4
  Towcester NN12 203 C7
  Welford NN6 64 E4
  Wellingborough NN8 129 D3
  West Haddon NN6 102 C4
  Yardley Hastings NN7 179 A6
Northampton Sch for Boys NN1 160 A6
Northampton Sch for Girls
  Northampton NN3 142 A4
  Northampton NN3 142 A5
Northampton Science Pk NN3 141 F6
Northamptonshire Fire & Rescue HQ NN3 142 C6
Northamptonshire Gram Sch NN6 125 D4
Northampton Sta NN1 159 B5
Northampton (Sywell) Airport NN6 127 E5
Northampton Town FC NN5 158 E5
Northamton & Lamport Rly★ NN6 124 F1
Northants County Cricket Club★ NN1 160 A8
Northants Ent Pk NN2 141 E6
North Ave NN15 92 B3
Northbank LE16 31 E3
Northbrook NN18 36 B4
North Cape Wlk NN18 36 A2
North Cl NN11 118 D1
Northcote St NN2 159 C7
Northend MK46 194 E3
North End NN10 132 B7
Northen Way NN8 129 F8
Northern Cl NN17 22 B8
Northern Way NN11 135 D4
Northfield Ave
  Kettering NN16 72 A3
  Ringstead NN14 95 B3
North Field Cl NN16 72 A4
Northfield Gn NN6 122 D5
Northfield La PE8 15 E5
Northfield Point NN16 72 A4
Northfield Rd
  Broughton NN14 71 C1
  Northampton NN5 140 B1
Northfield Way NN2 141 B4
North Folds Rd NN18 35 F1
Northgate NN12 203 C7
Northgate Sch NN2 141 C2
North Hayes Ct NN3 142 F5
North Hill MK18 225 D2
North Holme Ct NN3 142 D5
NORTH KILWORTH 45 A3
North La LE16 30 D8
North Lea LE16 18 B3
Northleigh Gr LE16 31 D4
North Leys Ct NN3 142 C7
North Luffenham Rd LE15 3 B8
North Meadow View NN5 157 F7
North Oval NN5 140 F2
North Paddock Ct NN3 142 F4
North Park Dr NN16 72 C5
North Portway Cl NN3 142 F7
North Priors Ct NN3 143 A4
North Rd
  Clifton u D CV23 80 A6
  Earls Barton NN6 144 E5
  Northampton NN3 141 F6
  South Kilworth LE17 63 D8
North St
  Castlethorpe MK19 218 F5
  Daventry NN11 135 C2
  Kilsby CV23 99 F3
  Mears Ashby NN6 128 B2
  Oundle PE8 42 A5
  Raunds NN9 114 E7
  Rothersthorpe NN7 174 B6
  Rushden NN10 132 B3
  Swinford LE17 62 B4
  Titchmarsh NN14 77 C4
  Wellingborough NN8 129 F5
Northumberland Cl NN15 91 D6
Northumberland Rd NN15 91 D6
Northumbria Gdns NN3 142 B1
North Way
  Deanshanger MK19 228 E5
  Potterspury NN12 217 E2
North Western Ave NN2 141 A4
Northwood Rd NN3 142 B2
Nortoft NN6 103 F7
NORTON 136 C4
Norton Cl NN11 135 D2
Norton Cres NN12 203 B6
Norton Leys CV22 98 A6
Norton Rd
  Corby NN17 36 C7
  Daventry NN11 135 D2
  Northampton NN2 141 C3
Norton St NN14 70 E7
Norway Cl NN18 36 A3
Norwood Rd NN5 157 F8
Notre Dame Mews 3 NN1 159 D6
Nuffield Cl NN13 233 D8
Nunneley Way LE16 31 F5
Nunnery Ave NN14 70 C7
Nunn Mills Rd NN1 159 E4
Nuns La NN6 121 B4
Nurseries The
  Horton NN7 177 D1
  3 Moulton NN3 126 C1
  Northampton NN1 159 F5
Nursery Cl
  Little Houghton NN7 161 A4
  Maidwell NN6 87 B7
Nursery Ct NN6 128 B2
Nursery Dr NN8 130 B7
Nursery End LE16 31 C2
Nursery Gdns NN9 112 E2
Nursery La NN2 141 C3
Nutcote NN6 85 B8
Nuthall Cl NN3 160 F8

## O

Oak Ave NN7 174 B1
Oak Cl
  Broughton NN14 90 B4
  Hartwell NN7 192 E2
  Irchester NN29 147 A7
  Market Harborough LE16 31 F4
  Towcester NN12 203 C4
Oakdown Cres MK46 195 F3
Oak Dr NN11 184 B6
Oakfield NN10 132 A4
Oak Gr NN11 135 C5
Oakgrove Pl NN4 175 D6
Oakham Cl
  Desborough NN14 50 F4
  Northampton NN3 142 B7
  Rushden NN10 148 A8
Oakham La NN11 152 B7
Oak La NN6 100 F6
Oaklands
  Bugbrooke NN7 173 A7
  Weedon Bec NN7 155 A2
Oaklands Dr NN3 142 E1
Oaklands Pk 4 LE16 31 F2
Oakleas Rise NN14 76 D1
Oaklee Cl PE8 58 A3
Oakleigh Cl NN9 114 C7
Oakleigh Dr NN5 140 C1
Oakley Ct NN18 36 A1
Oakley Dr
  Moulton NN3 126 D1
  Wellingborough NN8 129 D3
Oakley Hay Ind Est NN18 36 A1
Oakley Mews LE16 31 D3
Oakley Pond NN18 53 B8
Oakley Rd
  Corby NN17 37 A6
  Corby NN18 36 C3
  Pipewell NN14 52 D8
  Rushden NN10 131 F3
  Rushton NN14 52 E5
Oakley St
  Kettering NN16 72 B4
  Northampton NN1 159 D7
Oakmont Cl NN4 175 C5
Oakpark Cl NN3 143 A6
Oakpits Way NN10 132 C1
Oak Rd
  Brackley NN13 222 F1
  Kettering NN15 72 D1
Oaks Dr NN10 132 B6
Oak St
  20 Northampton NN1 159 C7
  Rushden NN10 132 B4
  Weedon Bec NN7 155 A2
Oaks The NN4 175 F3
Oak Terr 6 NN9 112 F2
Oak Tree Cl NN14 50 F3
Oaktree Ct 2 NN16 72 B1
Oak Tree Ct NN14 76 F8
Oak View NN9 110 F1
Oakway NN8 129 F7
Oak Way NN9 112 F2
Oakway Jun & Inf Sch NN8 130 A7
Oakwood Cl PE8 27 D2
Oakwood Rd NN1 142 A1
Oathill Cl NN6 106 B1
Oat Hill Dr NN3 143 D2
Oat Hill Rd NN12 203 C4
Oathill Rise NN15 92 C2
Oban Cl NN15 91 E8

**Obelisk Cl** NN2 ......... 141 C8
**Obelisk Rd** NN9 ......... 112 A5
**Obelisk Rise** NN2 ....... 141 C6
**Occupation Rd**
Corby NN17 ............. 36 F7
Middleton LE16 .......... 20 B2
Oundle PE8 ............. 42 A7
**Octagon The** NN17 ....... 37 A8
**Octagon Way** NN3 ...... 142 F2
**Octavian Way** NN13 ..... 234 A7
**Odeon Bldgs** NN17 ....... 37 A7
**OLD** ................. 107 D7
**Old Barn Ct** NN3 ........ 142 F3
**Old Brewery Wlk**
NN13 ................. 233 F6
**Old Brickyard The**
NN6 .................. 102 C4
**Old Carpenters Cl**
NN3 .................. 143 C2
**Old Cl** NN4 ............. 175 E2
**Old Coach Ho The**
LE16 .................. 35 A7
**Old Coffee Mills The** [6]
LE16 .................. 31 F2
Old Dairy Farm★
NN7 .................. 171 E6
Old Depot The NN7 ..... 155 B4
**Old Dry La** NN14 ......... 55 F8
**Olde Forde Cl** NN6 ...... 106 B1
**Olde Hall Cl** NN6 ........ 105 B1
**Oldenburg Rd** NN18 ...... 35 F3
**Old End** NN7 ............ 177 A1
**Oldenmead Ct** NN3 ..... 142 F3
**Olden Rd** NN3 .......... 143 C5
**Old Farm** PE8 ............ 41 C1
**Old Farm La** NN14 ....... 76 B3
**Old Forge Dr** NN6 ....... 102 C4
**Old Forge La** NN11 ...... 169 C2
**Old Gn** LE16 ............. 18 F6
**Old Gorse Way** NN14 ..... 89 A4
**Old Gram School The**
NN6 .................. 103 F6
**Old Great North Rd** PE8 ... 8 C2
**Old Greens Norton Rd**
NN12 ................. 203 B7
**Old Hall La** LE16 ......... 30 F3
**Old Holt Rd** LE16 ......... 19 A7
**Old La** NN13 ............ 221 A4
**Oldland Rd** NN18 ........ 36 D3
**Old Leicester Rd** PE8 ...... 8 A3
**Old Manor Ct** NN11 ..... 135 E8
**Old North Rd** PE8 ......... 8 A4
**Old Oak Dr** NN12 ....... 214 D4
**Old Oundle Rd** PE8 ........ 7 A6
**Old Quarry Ct** NN3 ...... 142 E4
**Old Rd**
Braunston NN11 ........ 134 C8
Scaldwell NN6 .......... 107 A7
Stanion NN14 ........... 37 E2
Walgrave NN6 .......... 107 F5
**Old Rectory Dr** PE8 ....... 8 A6
**Old Rickyard The**
NN11 ................. 199 D7
**Old School Cotts**
NN6 .................. 105 A8
**Old School La** NN12 ..... 187 A1
**Old School Mews** LE16 ... 31 E3
**Old Stable Yd** MK19 ..... 229 C7
**OLD STRATFORD** ....... 229 B7
Old Stratford Prim Sch
MK19 ................. 229 B6
**Old Sulehay Rd** PE8 ...... 15 F8
**Old Tiffield Rd** NN12 .... 203 C8
**Old Towcester Rd**
NN4 .................. 159 C4
**OLD TOWN** ............. 234 A7
**Old Town** NN13 ......... 234 A7
**Old Vineyard The**
NN10 ................. 132 B6
**Old Woodyard The**
NN12 ................. 214 D4
**Old Yew Ct** NN2 ........ 141 B3
**Oleander Cres** NN3 ..... 143 C4
**Oliver Cl** NN10 .......... 132 C2
**Oliver St** NN2 ........... 141 E1
**Ollerton Wlk** NN18 ....... 36 C5
**Ollis Cl** NN17 ............ 36 E8
**OLNEY** ................ 195 E4
Olney Inf Sch MK46 ..... 195 E3
Olney Mid Sch MK46 .... 195 F5
**Olney Rd** MK46 ......... 195 F1
**Olympia Cl** NN4 ......... 175 B8
**Olympic Way**
Kettering NN15 .......... 91 A7
Wellingborough NN8 ..... 129 C5
**ONLEY** .................. 98 D2
**Onley La** CV22 ........... 98 D6
**Onley Pk** CV23 .......... 117 C8
**Oransay Cl** NN3 ......... 143 C2
**Orchard Cl**
Badby NN11 ........... 152 F3
Desborough NN14 ........ 50 E3
East Haddon NN6 ....... 122 D5
Finedon NN9 ........... 111 F5
Hannington NN6 ........ 108 C3
Hollowell NN6 .......... 104 B5
Milton Malsor NN7 ...... 174 E4
Northampton NN4 ....... 175 E6
Orlingbury NN14 ........ 110 A5
Oundle PE8 ............. 41 F6
Ringstead NN14 .......... 95 C3
Rushden NN10 .......... 131 F3
Spratton NN6 ........... 124 B8
Towcester NN12 ........ 203 C4
Walgrave NN6 .......... 107 F5
**Orchard Cl** *continued*
Warmington PE8 .......... 28 B3
Weedon Bec NN7 ........ 155 C3
Weldon NN17 ............ 38 B8
Wilbarston LE16 .......... 34 C5
Wollaston NN29 ......... 146 D3
Yardley Gobion NN12 ..... 217 F6
Yelvertoft NN6 ........... 82 B4
**Orchard Cotts** NN6 ...... 125 C5
**Orchard Cres**
Kettering NN16 .......... 72 C4
Woodnewton PE8 ......... 14 E2
**Orchard Ct**
Pattishall NN12 ......... 172 D1
Woodford NN14 .......... 94 C7
**Orchard Est** NN14 ........ 90 F2
**Orchard Field** NN14 ...... 93 A6
**Orchard Gn** NN3 ........ 142 C2
**Orchard Hill** NN3 ....... 143 A1
**Orchard Ho** NN17 ........ 38 B8
**Orchard La**
Denton NN7 ............ 162 B1
Gretton NN17 ........... 10 C1
King's Cliffe PE8 ......... 13 E7
Woodnewton PE8 ......... 14 E2
**Orchard Pl** NN29 ........ 147 A8
**Orchard Rd**
Finedon NN9 ........... 111 F5
Raunds NN9 ............ 114 B5
**Orchard Rise**
Long Buckby NN6 ....... 121 D4
Olney MK46 ............ 195 F3
Orchard Sch The NN16 ... 72 B5
**Orchard St**
Daventry NN11 ......... 135 B2
Market Harborough LE16 .. 31 E4
[3] Northampton NN5 .... 159 A6
**Orchards The** NN6 ...... 103 D1
**Orchard Terr**
Finedon NN9 ........... 111 F5
Welford NN6 ............ 64 E6
Wellingborough NN8 ..... 129 F5
**Orchard The**
Apethorpe PE8 ........... 14 C4
Bozeat NN29 ........... 164 D3
Flore NN7 .............. 155 F5
Kislingbury NN7 ........ 157 D3
Potterspury NN12 ....... 217 C3
Sibbertoft LE16 .......... 47 A2
Staverton NN11 ......... 152 B7
Upper Boddington
NN11 ................. 182 C7
**Orchard Way**
Cogenhoe NN7 .......... 161 F6
Easton o t H PE9 ........... 1 F6
Harpole NN7 ........... 157 C6
Kings Sutton OX17 ...... 231 A5
Northampton NN5 ....... 158 C6
Roade NN7 ............. 191 D4
Thrapston NN14 .......... 76 E1
**Orchid Cl** NN14 .......... 51 A4
**Ordnance Ho** NN7 ...... 155 A4
**Ordnance Rd** NN7 ....... 154 F3
**Oriel Rd** NN11 .......... 153 C7
**Oriel Way** NN13 ......... 233 D8
**Orient Ho** NN1 .......... 159 E6
**Orient Way** NN8 ........ 130 A4
**Orion Way** NN15 ......... 91 C5
**Orkney Wlk** NN17 ........ 36 B8
**ORLINGBURY** ........... 110 A5
**Orlingbury Rd**
Great Harrowden
NN9 ................. 110 D2
Isham NN14 ............ 110 C7
Little Harrowden NN9 ... 110 B4
Pytchley NN14 ........... 90 F1
**Ormond Pl** NN14 ........ 110 E8
**Orson Leys** CV22 ......... 98 A7
**ORTON** ................. 70 A3
**Orton Pl** NN8 ........... 129 D7
**Orton Rd**
Kettering NN15 .......... 91 F5
Loddington NN14 ......... 70 D2
**Orwell Cl**
Clifton u D CV23 ......... 80 A5
Raunds NN9 ............ 114 D7
Wellingborough NN8 ..... 129 C6
**Osborn Cl** NN8 .......... 129 E3
**Osborne Cl** NN10 ........ 132 D4
**Osborne Rd** NN2 ........ 141 C2
**Osborn's Ct** MK46 ....... 195 F3
**Osbourne Cl** NN18 ....... 36 E2
**Osier Bed La** NN17 ....... 24 B5
**Osiers The** NN14 ......... 51 D2
**Osier Way** NN14 .......... 76 C1
**Osler Cl** NN2 ............ 141 B5
**Oslo Gdns** NN18 ......... 36 A3
**Osmond Dr** NN3 ......... 143 A5
**Osprey Dr** NN11 ......... 135 C3
**Osprey La** NN8 .......... 130 B7
**Osprey Rise** NN4 ........ 175 B8
**Osprey View** [6] NN4 ..... 175 B8
**Ostlers La** MK11 ........ 229 D6
**Ostlers Way** NN15 ........ 91 B7
**Oswald Rd** NN10 ......... 132 C2
**Osyth Cl** NN4 ........... 160 B2
**Oulton Rise** NN3 ........ 141 F4
**OUNDLE** ................ 42 A6
Oundle CE Prim Sch
PE8 ................... 41 F5
**Oundle Dr** NN3 .......... 142 B7
Oundle & Kings Cliffe Mid
Sch PE8 ................ 41 E7
Oundle Mus★ PE8 ........ 41 F5
**Oundle Rd**
Elton PE8 .............. 16 F1
Thrapston NN14 .......... 76 E2
Weldon NN17 ............ 38 E7
**Oundle Rd** *continued*
Woodnewton PE8 ......... 14 F1
Oundle Sch PE8 .......... 42 A5
Our Lady of Walsingham
RC Prim Sch NN17 ...... 36 F7
Our Lady & Pope John RC
Sch NN18 .............. 36 A4
Our Lady's Convent Prep
Sch NN15 .............. 71 F1
Our Lady's RC Jun & Inf
Sch NN8 .............. 129 D3
**Ousebank Way** MK11 .... 229 D5
**Ouse Cl** NN8 ........... 129 C6
**Ouse La** NN12 .......... 203 A6
**Outlaw La** NN8 ......... 129 F5
**Oval Cres** NN10 ......... 132 D2
**Oval Rd**
Rugby CV22 ............. 98 D8
Rushden NN10 .......... 132 D2
**Oval The**
Kettering NN15 .......... 91 B8
Market Harborough LE16 .. 31 E4
**Overdale Cl** LE16 ......... 32 A3
**OVER END** .............. 28 E7
**Overfield Ave** LE16 ....... 31 F5
**Overhills** MK46 ......... 195 E4
**Overleys Ct** NN3 ........ 143 B5
**Overmead Rd** NN3 ...... 143 D2
**Overslade Cl** NN4 ....... 175 A8
**Overslade Ho** NN4 ...... 175 A8
**OVERSTONE** ............ 127 B1
**Overstone Cl** NN3 ....... 126 E1
**Overstone Cres** NN6 .... 127 B1
**Overstone Hts** NN6 ..... 127 D3
**Overstone La** NN6 ...... 126 F1
**Overstone Lakes Cvn Pk**
NN6 .................. 143 D8
**OVERSTONE LODGE** ..... 143 B5
Overstone Park Sch
NN6 .................. 143 B8
Overstone Prim Sch
NN6 .................. 127 A1
**Overstone Rd**
Moulton NN3 ........... 126 D1
Northampton NN1 ....... 159 D7
Sywell NN6 ............ 127 D3
**OVERTHORPE** .......... 219 D6
Overthorpe Ind Est
OX16 ................. 219 A7
Overthorpe Prep Sch
OX17 ................. 219 C8
**Overthorpe Rd** OX16 .... 219 B6
**Ovett Cl** NN15 ........... 90 F8
**Owen Cl** NN8 ........... 129 B5
**Owen Mews** NN8 ........ 129 B5
**Owen Way** NN10 ........ 132 A5
**Owl Cl** NN3 ............. 141 F7
**Owl End La** NN11 ....... 182 C5
**Owl End Way** NN11 ..... 182 C5
**Oxburgh Ct** [7] NN4 ..... 175 C8
**Oxendon Hall** LE16 ....... 48 E3
**Oxendon Rd**
Arthingworth LE16 ........ 49 A1
Braybrooke LE16 ......... 49 D5
Clipston LE16 ............ 48 B1
East Farndon LE16 ........ 48 B5
**Oxfield Park Dr** MK19 ... 229 C7
**Oxford Cl**
Daventry NN11 ......... 135 C1
Earls Barton NN6 ....... 144 F3
**Oxford Ct** NN13 ......... 233 F5
**Oxford Rd**
Adderbury OX17 ........ 230 A3
Corby NN17 ............. 36 C6
Evenley NN13 .......... 233 E5
**Oxford St**
Daventry NN11 ......... 135 C1
Finedon NN9 ........... 112 B5
Kettering NN16 .......... 72 A3
Northampton NN4 ....... 159 B3
Rothwell NN14 ........... 70 D8
Stony Stratford MK11 ... 229 D5
Wellingborough NN8 ..... 129 F4
Wymington NN10 ........ 148 A7
**Oxleys** MK46 ........... 195 E4
**Oxwich Cl** NN4 ......... 160 A1

## P

**Packer Rd** NN15 .......... 90 E8
**Packwood Ave** CV21 ...... 99 C8
**Packwood Cl** [9] NN11 .... 135 B7
**Paddock Cl** NN6 ......... 103 D1
**Paddock Ct** LE16 .......... 31 E3
**Paddock End** NN14 ....... 89 B4
**Paddock La**
Desborough NN14 ........ 51 A3
Mears Ashby NN6 ....... 128 B2
Medbourne LE16 ......... 19 D8
**Paddock Mews** NN14 ..... 51 A3
**Paddock Mill Ct** [1]
NN3 .................. 143 B4
**Paddocks Cl** NN6 ....... 108 A5
**Paddocks Rd** NN10 ...... 131 F3
**Paddocks The**
Brixworth NN6 .......... 106 B3
Bugbrooke NN7 ......... 172 F7
Moulton NN3 ........... 126 C1
Orlingbury NN14 ........ 109 F5
Shutlanger NN12 ........ 204 D8
Souldern OX27 .......... 237 E3
Stanion NN14 ............ 37 F3
Yelvertoft NN6 ........... 82 A5
**Paddocks Way** NN3 ..... 143 A1
**Paddock The**
Crick NN6 ............. 100 F5
**Paddock The** *continued*
Lower Boddington
NN11 ................. 182 C5
Raunds NN9 ............ 114 C4
Weedon Lois NN12 ...... 200 B2
Welton NN11 ........... 135 E8
Woodnewton PE8 ......... 14 E2
**Paddox Cl** CV22 .......... 98 F8
**Paddox Ct** CV23 ........ 100 A3
Paddox Prim Sch
Rugby CV22 ............. 98 D8
Rugby CV22 ............. 98 E8
**Padmans Cl** NN14 ........ 89 B4
**Padwell Ct** [2] NN3 ...... 161 A8
**Pagent Ct** NN15 .......... 91 A7
**Pages Wlk** NN17 .......... 37 B6
**Paget Cl** NN4 ........... 160 E2
**Paget Ho** NN5 ........... 140 E1
**Paget Rd** LE16 ........... 30 E3
**Pagnell Ct** NN4 ......... 176 A7
**Palace Ct** [8] NN10 ...... 132 B2
**Palk Rd** NN8 ............ 130 B4
**Palmer Ave** NN9 ........ 113 B4
**Palmer Cl** NN8 .......... 129 D7
**Palmer Ct** NN8 .......... 129 F5
**Palmer's Cl** CV21 ......... 99 B8
**Palmer Sq** NN3 ......... 143 C1
**Palmerston Ct** [5]
NN1 .................. 159 E6
**Palmerston Ho** [4]
NN1 .................. 159 E6
**Palmerston Rd** NN1 ..... 159 E6
**Palm Rd** NN10 .......... 131 E3
**Pantell Way** NN10 ....... 132 A7
**Panters La** NN14 ......... 75 A1
**Parade Bank** NN3 ....... 126 C1
**Parade The** NN1 ........ 159 C6
**Paradise Ave** NN15 ....... 91 D6
**Paradise Ho** [2] NN8 ..... 129 F5
**Paradise La** NN15 ........ 91 D6
**Pargeter Cl** OX17 ....... 210 E2
**Park Ave**
Kettering NN16 .......... 72 B4
Northampton, Abington
NN1 .................. 160 A8
Northampton NN5 ....... 140 B1
Raunds NN9 ............ 114 E5
Rushden NN10 .......... 132 A2
**Park Ave N** NN3 ........ 142 A1
**Park Ave S** NN3 ........ 160 B7
**Park Cl**
Badby NN11 ........... 153 A3
Brafield-on-t-G NN7 ..... 161 E2
Cosgrove MK19 ......... 218 F2
Earls Barton NN6 ....... 144 D4
Isham NN14 ............ 110 F8
King's Cliffe PE8 ......... 14 A8
Northampton NN5 ....... 140 A1
Sywell NN6 ............ 127 D2
Watford NN6 ........... 120 C6
Whittlebury NN12 ....... 215 C4
**Park Cnr** NN5 ........... 158 F6
**Park Cres** [8] NN8 ....... 130 A5
**Park Cres E** NN5 ........ 140 F2
**Park Cres W** NN5 ....... 140 F1
**Park Dr**
Market Harborough
LE16 .................. 31 E4
Northampton NN5 ....... 140 F1
**Park End** NN13 ......... 238 D8
Park End Works
NN13 ................. 238 D7
**Parker Rd** PE8 ............ 7 D8
**Parkers Terr** NN9 ....... 111 F4
**Parker Way** NN10 ....... 132 B7
**Park Farm Barns** NN7 ... 139 E6
**Park Farm Ct** NN14 ....... 77 C4
Park Farm Ind Est
NN8 .................. 129 A5
**Park Farm Way** NN8 ..... 129 A3
**Parkfield Ave** NN4 ...... 159 C1
**Parkfield Cres** NN4 ..... 159 C2
**Parkfield Rd**
Brixworth NN6 .......... 106 A1
Long Buckby NN6 ....... 121 A4
Parkham Ind Est
NN10 ................. 131 D3
**Park Hill Rd** NN3 ....... 142 D3
**Park Ho** LE16 ............ 31 E4
Park Jun Sch
Kettering NN16 .......... 72 C4
Wellingborough NN8 ..... 130 A5
**Park La**
Earls Barton NN6 ....... 144 D4
Gayton NN7 ............ 173 E2
Harpole NN7 ........... 157 C6
Hartwell NN7 ........... 192 C1
Northampton NN5 ....... 140 A2
Paulerspury NN12 ....... 216 B7
Sulgrave OX17 .......... 210 F7
Watford NN6 ........... 120 C6
**Parklands**
Crick NN6 ............. 100 C7
Stanwick NN9 .......... 113 F3
Sywell NN6 ............ 127 D1
**Parklands Ave** NN3 ..... 142 A5
**Parklands Cl** NN14 ....... 70 D1
**Parklands Cres** NN3 .... 142 A5
Parklands Mid Sch
NN3 .................. 142 A5
Parklands Prim Sch
NN3 .................. 142 A4
**Park Leys** NN11 ......... 135 C1
**Park Lo** NN17 ............ 36 E6
**Park Mews**
Market Harborough
LE16 .................. 31 E4
Towcester NN12 ........ 203 C6
**Park Mews** *continued*
Wellingborough NN8 ..... 130 A5
**Park Pl** NN10 ........... 132 B2
**Park Rd**
Burton Latimer NN15 ..... 92 B2
Hanslope MK19 ......... 207 B1
Hartwell NN7 ........... 192 C1
Irthlingborough NN9 ..... 112 F1
Kettering NN16 .......... 72 C4
Raunds NN9 ............ 114 E6
Rushden NN10 .......... 132 C1
Stony Stratford MK11 ... 229 D5
Titchmarsh NN14 ......... 77 C4
Wellingborough NN8 ..... 130 A5
**Parkside** NN3 ........... 143 D2
**Park Spinney Cl** NN6 ..... 84 A5
**Park Sq** NN5 ............ 140 F2
**Park St**
Earls Barton NN6 ....... 144 D4
King's Cliffe PE8 ......... 13 F7
Raunds NN9 ............ 114 E6
Towcester NN12 ........ 203 C6
Wollaston NN29 ......... 146 E2
**Park The** PE28 ........... 97 A3
**Park View**
Kettering NN16 .......... 72 B4
Moulton NN3 ........... 142 E8
Northampton NN5 ....... 158 E8
Thrapston NN14 .......... 76 D2
Wellingborough NN8 ..... 130 B4
**Park View Cl** NN3 ....... 126 E1
**Park View Ho** NN10 ..... 132 A3
**Park View Rd** NN12 ..... 203 D5
**Parkway**
Nassington PE8 .......... 15 F5
Northampton NN3 ....... 142 D1
**Parkway Cl** PE8 .......... 15 F5
**Park Wlk**
Brigstock NN14 .......... 55 E7
Easton o t H PE9 .......... 2 A6
Northampton NN5 ....... 140 F2
**Parkwood St** NN5 ....... 159 B5
**Parnell Cl** NN6 .......... 102 C5
**Parracombe Way**
NN3 .................. 160 C7
**Parsons Cl**
Ecton NN6 ............. 143 F4
Nether Heyford NN7 ..... 156 C2
**Parsons' Cl** NN7 ........ 163 D5
**Parsons Gr** NN17 ......... 22 A1
**Parsons Meade** NN4 ..... 158 E2
**Parsons Rd**
Daventry NN11 ......... 134 F5
Irchester NN29 ......... 147 B8
**Parsons St**
Adderbury OX17 ........ 230 A4
Woodford Halse NN11 .... 184 C6
**Partridge Cl**
Charwelton NN11 ....... 168 A5
Northampton NN2 ....... 141 A5
**Partridge La** NN11 ...... 184 C1
**Parva Ct** NN3 ........... 142 E3
**Pascoe Cres** [1] NN11 .... 135 A4
**Pashler Gdns** NN14 ...... 76 D2
**PASSENHAM** ........... 229 C3
**Pasteur Cl** NN2 ......... 141 B5
**Pasteur Ctyd** NN17 ....... 37 B8
**Pasture End** NN14 ....... 89 C5
**Pasture Mobile Home Pk**
NN14 .................. 51 C8
**Pastures The**
Market Harborough
LE16 .................. 31 C3
Northampton NN2 ....... 141 A5
Wellingborough NN9 ..... 110 E1
**Pasture The** NN11 ....... 135 C1
**Paterson Rd** NN8 ....... 130 B8
**Patrick Cl** NN15 .......... 91 C6
**Patrick Rd**
Corby NN18 ............. 36 D4
Kettering NN15 .......... 91 C6
**Patricks La** MK19 ....... 228 E4
**Patrick St** LE16 ........... 31 F2
**Patterdale Wlk** [1]
NN3 .................. 142 C4
**Patterson Cl** NN3 ....... 142 E1
**PATTISHALL** ............ 172 E1
Pattishall CE Prim Sch
NN12 ................. 188 F8
**PAULERSPURY** .......... 216 C8
Paulerspury CE Prim Sch
NN12 ................. 216 B8
**Pavilion Dr**
Northampton NN4 ....... 159 F1
Oundle PE8 ............. 41 E6
**Pavillons Way** NN13 .... 233 E8
**Paxford Cl** NN8 ......... 129 E1
**Paxton Cl** MK46 ......... 195 F3
**Paxton Rd** NN3 ......... 142 D4
**Payne's La** LE16 .......... 18 F7
**Peace Cl** NN4 ........... 158 F3
**Peace Hill** NN7 ......... 172 E7
**Peacock Dr** NN14 ........ 95 B3
**Peacock Pl** [6] NN1 ...... 159 D6
**Peacock's Cl** OX17 ...... 220 A8
**Peake Cl** LE16 ............ 35 B8
**Peak The** NN7 .......... 156 C1
**Pearmain Ave** NN8 ...... 129 F7
**Pearmain Ct** NN3 ....... 143 A2
**Pearson Mews** NN29 .... 146 D2
**Peartree Cl** NN11 ....... 135 C4
**Pear Tree Cl**
Bozeat NN29 ........... 164 D3
Northampton NN3 ....... 143 A2
**Pear Tree Gdns** LE16 ..... 31 D2
**Peaselands** NN14 ........ 50 F4
**Pebble Cotts** LE17 ....... 46 D8
**Pebbleford Rd** NN15 ..... 91 D8

- Pebble La
  - Brackley NN13 233 F7
  - 4 Wellingborough NN8 130 A4
- Pebody Pl MK46 195 F3
- Peck Way NN10 132 B4
- Pegasus Ct NN13 233 F7
- Pegasus Way NN10 131 E4
- Peg's La
  - Clipston LE16 66 F8
  - Denford NN14 95 C6
- Pelham Ct NN3 142 D4
- Pell Ct NN3 142 E3
- Pells Cl NN6 103 E7
- Pemberton St NN10 132 A3
- Pembroke Cl
  - Rushden NN10 132 C1
  - Thrapston NN14 76 E2
- Pembroke Cres NN5 159 B8
- Pembroke Gdns NN5 159 A8
- Pembroke Ho MK46 195 F3
- Pembroke Rd NN5 159 B8
- Pembroke Way NN11 153 B7
- Penarth Rd NN5 159 A8
- Pen Ct NN1 159 D4
- Pendered Rd NN8 130 A1
- Pendle Ave NN16 72 A6
- Pendle Rd NN5 158 C8
- Penfold Cl NN2 141 B4
- Penfold Dr NN3 143 B3
- Penfold Gdns NN3 143 C3
- Penfold La NN3 143 C3
- Pen Gn La NN17 37 A8
- Peninsular Cl 12 NN4 175 E7
- Penistone Rd NN3 142 E3
- Penistone Wlk 3 NN3 142 E3
- Pennard Cl NN4 160 B2
- Penn Gdns NN4 175 B7
- Pennine Ct NN11 135 B5
- Pennine Way
  - Kettering NN16 72 B6
  - Northampton NN5 158 D7
- Pennycress Pl NN3 143 D1
- Penny La NN9 114 D7
- Penrhyn Cl NN18 36 F3
- Penrhyn Ct NN14 76 E2
- Penrhyn Rd NN4 159 C3
- Penrith Dr NN8 129 D6
- Pentelowes The PE18 116 D2
- Penthorne Cl NN12 188 A8
- Pentlands MK11 229 F4
- Penvale Rd NN4 175 B7
- Pepper Alley OX15 236 E4
- Peppercorn Way NN4 175 D6
- Perceval Cl NN5 140 D1
- Perch Cl NN11 135 B6
- Percival Rd CV22 98 D8
- Percy Rd
  - Northampton NN1 159 F7
  - Woodford Halse NN11 184 C6
- Peregrine Pl NN4 175 A8
- Perkins Cl LE16 31 F4
- Perkins Ct 4 NN8 130 A5
- Perkins Rd NN9 131 E8
- Perkins Way NN11 153 E4
- Perry Cl NN15 91 A7
- Perry St NN1 159 F7
- Pershore Cl NN8 145 E8
- Perth Ho NN17 22 F1
- Peterborough Rd
  - Morcott LE15 3 D6
  - Wansford PE8 8 A3
  - Warmington PE8 28 C4
- Peters La NN6 106 F5
- Pether Ave NN13 233 C8
- Petherton Ct NN16 72 B3
- Pettiver Cres 2 CV21 80 A1
- Petworth Dr LE16 32 B2
- Petworth Gdns NN18 36 B5
- Pevensey Cl NN10 132 D1
- Pevensey Wlk 2 NN18 36 B5
- Peverel Cl NN10 132 C6
- Peverel's Way NN5 158 E6
- Peveril Rd
  - Greatworth OX17 210 E2
  - Northampton NN5 158 C7
- Pevers La MK46 195 A1
- Pevrel Pl NN14 50 E4
- Pexley Ct PE8 41 E5
- Pheasant Way NN2 141 A5
- Pheonix Parkway NN17 37 B8
- Philip Way NN10 132 C7
- Phillips Way NN6 121 C4
- Phipps Rd NN11 184 B6
- PHIPPSVILLE 141 F1
- Phoenix Ct NN8 130 B3
- Phoenix Parkway NN17 22 B2
- Phoenix St 23 NN1 159 C6
- Piccadilly Bldgs 3 NN16 72 B1
- Piccadilly Cl NN4 158 F2
- Pickering Ct NN18 36 B4
- Pickerings The NN6 106 C1
- Picks Cl LE16 32 B3
- PIDDINGTON 177 B2
- Piddington La NN7 177 A2
- Piddington Roman Villa Mus* NN7 177 B2
- Piece The
  - Cogenhoe NN7 161 F6
  - Spratton NN6 105 B1
- Pie Cnr NN6 127 D3
- Pied Bull Cl PE9 1 A6
- Pierce Cres PE8 28 C3
- Pigeon Hill NN12 189 D3
- Pightles Terr NN10 132 C1
- Pightles Wlk NN10 132 C1
- Pigott's La NN15 92 C2
- Pike La NN1 159 C6
- Pikemead Ct NN3 143 B4
- Pike Rd NN18 36 A1
- Pilgrims La NN7 173 A7
- Pilgrims Pl NN4 159 C2
- Pilgrim Way NN8 129 F3
- Pilot Rd NN17 37 C8
- PILTON 58 C5
- Pilton Cl NN3 143 C5
- Pilton Rd PE8 58 A4
- PIMLICO 223 F6
- Pincet La LE17 45 A6
- Pindar Rd NN8 129 E2
- Pindar Rise NN3 142 E6
- PINDON END 206 C4
- Pine Ave NN6 127 D1
- Pine Cl
  - Desborough NN14 51 C2
  - Irchester NN29 147 A7
  - Northampton NN4 175 F3
  - Rushden NN10 148 A8
- Pine Copse Cl NN5 140 A2
- Pine Cres NN6 127 D1
- Pine Ct NN7 138 C4
- Pine Gr CV21 80 A1
- Pineham Ave NN2 141 D6
- Pine Rd NN15 72 D1
- Pine Ridge NN3 142 F7
- Pines The LE16 32 A6
- Pine Tree Ct NN14 76 B3
- Pine Trees NN3 142 D1
- Pinetrees Cl NN7 177 B3
- Pine Wlk NN17 21 E1
- Pinewood Cl NN16 72 B6
- Pinewood Rd NN3 142 B3
- Pinfold Cl LE15 3 E8
- Pinfold Gn NN11 152 F3
- Pinfold La LE15 3 E8
- Pingle La LE15 3 B6
- Pioneer Ave
  - Burton Latimer NN15 92 B2
  - Desborough NN14 50 F2
- Pioneer Cl 10 NN4 175 E7
- Piper Cl NN8 129 F8
- Pipers Cl
  - Irthlingborough NN9 112 F2
  - Kettering NN15 72 C1
- Piper's Hill Rd NN15 91 C8
- PIPEWELL 52 C8
- Pipewell Rd
  - Desborough NN14 51 C4
  - East Carlton LE16 35 B3
- Pippin Cl
  - Cogenhoe NN7 161 E5
  - Rushden NN10 131 E3
  - Wellingborough NN8 129 F4
- Pippin La NN3 143 A2
- Pitchers La LE16 20 D7
- Pit La PE9 1 A7
- PITSFORD 125 D5
- Pitsford & Brampton Sta* NN6 124 E2
- Pitsford Prim Sch NN6 125 D5
- Pitsford Rd
  - Chapel Brampton NN6 124 E1
  - Moulton NN3 126 B2
- Pitstone Rd NN4 158 E3
- Pittams Cl NN6 121 B3
- Pittams La NN12 213 B8
- Pittoms La CV23 99 C1
- Pitt St NN8 129 E4
- Plank Hos NN12 203 C5
- Plantagenet Cl NN13 233 E8
- Plantagenet Sq 7 NN4 158 F2
- Playford Cl NN14 70 F7
- Plaza 2& 4 The 1 NN1 159 E7
- Pleasant Row NN14 94 D7
- Plessey Cl NN12 203 D5
- Pleydell Gdns NN4 159 C2
- Pleydell Rd NN4 159 C2
- Plough Cl
  - Daventry NN11 135 D6
  - Rothwell NN14 70 D7
- Plough La NN2 141 A6
- Ploughmans Way NN4 175 F3
- Ploughmans Wlk NN2 141 B5
- Ploughmans Yd 11 LE16 31 E3
- Plough Mews NN13 233 F7
- Plover Cl NN12 203 C3
- Plowden Cl NN11 182 F2
- Plum Park La NN12 216 D8
- PLUMPTON 200 B5
- Plumpton Ct NN18 36 B5
- PLUMPTON END 216 D7
- Plumpton La NN11 199 D7
- Plumpton Rd
  - Weston NN12 200 A2
  - Woodend NN12 200 F6
- Plumtree Ave NN8 130 A7
- Poachers Cl NN4 175 F3
- Poachers Way NN2 141 B5
- Pochin Dr LE16 31 F5
- PODINGTON 147 E2
- Podington Rd NN10 148 A4
- Podmore Way NN14 90 A3
- Poets Way NN11 153 E5
- Poitiers Ct NN5 139 F1
- Pokas Cotts NN9 133 C8
- Polar Star Cl NN11 135 A4
- POLEBROOK 43 A3
- Polebrook Airfield Nature Reserve* PE8 43 F3
- Polebrook CE Prim Sch PE8 43 A3
- Polebrook Ct PE8 42 F3
- Polegate Ct NN18 36 B5
- Police Flats NN17 36 E6
- Pollards Cl LE15 3 F5
- Pollard St NN16 72 B4
- Polopit NN14 77 D3
- Polwell La NN15 92 A4
- Pomfret Arms Cl NN4 159 C4
- Pomfret Rd NN12 203 C6
- Pond Bank NN7 190 D8
- Ponder St NN14 70 D7
- Pond Farm Cl NN5 158 C7
- Ponds Cl NN9 114 D6
- Pond Wood Cl NN3 142 B6
- Pool Cl NN12 188 D8
- Poole St NN1 159 D7
- Pool Farm Ct NN11 184 A5
- Pool St NN11 184 B5
- Pope Rd NN8 129 C3
- Popham Cl NN9 114 C7
- Poplar Cl
  - Daventry NN11 135 C5
  - Irchester NN29 147 A7
  - Rushden NN10 148 A8
  - Towcester NN12 203 C4
- Poplar Ct NN3 142 D5
- Poplar Pl
  - Wellingborough NN8 129 F4
  - Wollaston NN29 146 E2
- Poplar Rd
  - Burton Latimer NN15 92 C4
  - Corby NN17 21 D1
  - Finedon NN9 112 A5
  - Kettering NN16 72 D2
- Poplar Rise NN12 213 B8
- Poplars Cl
  - Blakesley NN12 187 B1
  - Middleton Cheney OX17 220 A8
  - Raunds NN9 114 C6
- Poplars Ct
  - Market Harborough LE16 31 D4
  - Scaldwell NN6 106 F6
- Poplar's Farm Rd NN15 92 B8
- Poplars La NN6 126 E8
- Poplars Rd OX17 208 F4
- Poplar St NN8 130 A5
- Poplars The
  - Guilsborough NN6 103 E7
  - Long Buckby NN6 121 B3
  - Northampton NN1 159 C7
- Poppy Cl NN10 148 C8
- Poppyfield Ct
  - Northampton NN3 142 F4
  - Thrapston NN14 76 D3
- Poppy Fields NN16 71 F3
- Poppy Leys NN6 125 B8
- Porlock Cl NN5 158 E8
- Portchester Gdns 4 NN3 160 F8
- Porter's Cl MK19 228 E4
- Porter's La PE9 2 A5
- Portland Cl NN5 135 D1
- Portland Pl NN1 159 E6
- Portland Rd
  - Irthlingborough NN9 112 F3
  - Rushden NN10 132 B2
- Portlow La NN6 100 F6
- Port Rd NN5 140 A2
- Portree Wlk NN17 36 C8
- Portstone Cl NN5 140 A2
- Portway
  - Aynho OX17 237 D7
  - Croughton NN13 238 E7
- Portway Cres NN13 238 E7
- Portway Dr NN13 238 D7
- Portway Gdns OX17 237 D7
- Portwey Cl NN6 106 C1
- Postle Cl CV23 99 F2
- Post Office Cl NN17 37 B6
- Potter Ct NN9 114 A4
- Potters End NN11 183 D7
- POTTERSPURY 217 D3
- Potterspury Lodge Sch NN12 217 A6
- Pound Cl
  - Corby NN18 36 B2
  - Ringstead NN14 95 B3
  - Wicken MK19 228 A4
- Pound Ct NN3 126 B1
- Poundfield Rd NN12 217 E2
- Pound La
  - Badby NN11 152 F3
  - Bugbrooke NN7 173 A7
  - Eastcote NN12 172 F1
  - Moulton NN3 126 C1
  - Northampton NN3 143 C2
- Pound Pl NN9 111 F4
- Pound The
  - Great Brington NN7 138 D6
  - Horton NN7 177 E1
  - Nether Heyford NN7 156 B1
  - Syresham NN13 224 B7
- Powys Cl NN18 36 E2
- Poyntz Gdns NN5 158 E8
- Poyntz La NN5 158 E8
- Pratt Rd NN10 132 C2
- Prebendal Gn PE8 15 F8
- Premier Ct NN3 142 A7
- Premier Way NN9 131 E8
- Prentice Ct NN3 143 A5
- Prentice Wlk NN17 37 A6
- Prescott Cl NN3 143 C4
- Presland Way NN9 112 D1
- Pressland Dr NN10 132 C6
- Prestbury Rd NN5 140 A1
- Prestidge Row NN11 199 C7
- PRESTON CAPES 169 D2
- Preston Ct
  - Burton Latimer NN15 92 C3
  - Northampton NN3 142 E3
- PRESTON DEANERY 176 E4
- Preston Deanery Rd NN7 176 B1
- Preston Dr NN11 135 C6
- Preston Hedges Prim Sch NN4 175 F6
- Preston Rd NN11 184 C2
- Prestwold Way NN3 143 B5
- Pretoria Cotts NN9 114 C1
- Prices Way NN13 222 D1
- Pride Pl LE16 31 D2
- Pridmore Cl PE8 14 E2
- Priestley Ct NN17 22 D1
- Priestwell Ct NN6 122 D5
- Primrose Cl
  - Corby NN18 36 C2
  - Kettering NN16 72 D4
- Primrose Gdns NN9 114 D5
- Primrose Hill
  - Daventry NN11 135 C2
  - Northampton NN2 159 C8
  - Raunds NN9 114 D6
- Primrose Pl NN8 130 C5
- Primrose Wlk
  - Hinton NN11 184 B6
  - Northampton NN4 175 F2
- Primula Cl NN3 160 C6
- Primula Ct NN2 159 C8
- Prince Cl NN11 135 B3
- Prince Of Wales Row NN3 126 D1
- Prince Rupert Ave NN14 50 F3
- Princes Ave NN14 51 B3
- Princes Cl NN7 155 A3
- Princes Ct NN16 72 B3
- Princess Anne Bldg NN2 141 C4
- Princess Cl NN3 160 B6
- Princess Marina Hospl NN5 158 B6
- Princes St NN16 72 C3
- Princess Way NN8 129 E2
- Prince St NN8 144 E5
- Princes Wlk 4 NN1 159 D6
- Princethorpe Dr OX16 219 A7
- Prince William Rd PE8 41 E5
- Prince William Sch PE8 42 B4
- Princewood Rd NN17 21 E3
- Printers Yd NN16 72 B2
- Priors Cl NN10 147 F8
- Priors Ct
  - Corby NN17 23 A1
  - Priors Marston CV47 166 D7
- PRIORS HARDWICK 166 A5
- Priors Hardwick Rd NN11 182 B8
- Priors Haw Rd NN17 23 A1
- PRIORS MARSTON 166 E8
- Priors Marston Rd
  - Byfield NN11 167 B8
  - Hellidon NN11 151 C1
- Priors Sch The CV47 166 D8
- Priory Cl
  - Daventry NN11 135 D1
  - Northampton NN3 160 B6
- Priory Cres NN7 191 C4
- Priory Ct
  - Geddington NN14 54 A2
  - Weedon Bec NN7 155 A2
- Priory Ho NN1 159 B6
- Priory Rd
  - Wellingborough NN8 129 F3
  - Wollaston NN29 146 D3
- Pritchard Cl NN3 143 C6
- Probyn Cl NN3 143 A6
- Promenade The NN8 129 E6
- Prospect Ave
  - Irchester NN29 147 A7
  - Rushden NN10 132 B4
- Prospect Cl NN29 146 D3
- Prospect Ct NN12 217 F6
- Prospect Pl MK19 218 F5
- Prospect Rd MK11 229 C5
- Prospect Way NN11 134 F3
- Provence Ct NN5 139 F1
- Pudding Bag La NN29 164 D3
- Puddledock NN12 214 D5
- Pumping Station Cott LE16 21 A7
- Pump Pl MK19 229 B7
- Purbeck Rd NN10 131 D2
- Purse La MK16 207 F8
- Purser Rd NN1 159 F8
- Purvis Rd NN10 132 A2
- PURY END 215 F8
- Pury Hill Bsns Pk NN12 204 E1
- Pury Rd NN12 205 A3
- PUXLEY 228 D7
- Puxley Rd MK19 228 D5
- Pye Ct CV23 117 D4
- Pyghtles The
  - Daventry NN11 135 B1
- Pyghtles The *continued*
  - Wollaston NN29 146 D1
- Pyghtle The
  - Earls Barton NN6 144 E5
  - Olney MK46 195 F3
  - Wellingborough NN8 129 F6
- Pyghtle Way NN4 175 A7
- Pyket Way NN3 160 E8
- Pyke Way NN6 101 A6
- Pym Cl NN8 130 B6
- Pyramid Cl NN3 142 E2
- PYTCHLEY 90 F2
- Pytchley Cl NN6 106 B2
- Pytchley Ct
  - Corby NN17 36 B8
  - West Haddon NN6 102 C4
- Pytchley Dr NN6 121 B4
- Pytchley Endowed CE Prim Sch NN14 90 F2
- Pytchley La NN15 91 C5
- Pytchley Lodge Ind Est NN15 91 C6
- Pytchley Lodge Rd NN15 91 C5
- Pytchley Rd
  - Kettering NN15 91 C6
  - Orlingbury NN14 109 F5
  - Rugby CV22 98 C8
  - Rushden NN10 131 F3
- Pytchley Rise NN8 129 D3
- Pytchley St NN1 159 E6
- Pytchley View NN3 126 D1
- Pytchley Way
  - Brixworth NN6 106 B2
  - Northampton NN5 140 B2
- Pywell Ct NN17 22 E2
- Pywell Rd NN17 22 E2


## Q


- Quakers Cl NN7 172 F7
- Quantock Cl
  - Daventry NN11 135 B5
  - Kettering NN15 92 A5
- Quantock Cres NN5 158 D8
- Quarry Green Cl MK19 228 B3
- Quarry Park Cl NN3 142 B6
- Quarry Rd
  - Brixworth NN6 106 C3
  - Northampton NN5 140 B2
- Quartercroft NN3 142 E2
- Quarterstone NN4 158 D1
- Quebec Cl
  - Corby NN18 36 C2
  - 5 Northampton NN4 175 E7
- Queen Eleanor Prim Sch
  - Northampton NN4 159 B2
  - Stony Stratford MK11 229 F4
- Queen Eleanor Rd
  - Geddington NN14 54 A3
  - Northampton NN4 159 C2
- Queen Eleanor St MK11 229 E6
- Queen Eleanor Terr NN4 159 C2
- Queensberry Rd NN15 72 B1
- Queensbury Ct NN15 72 B1
- Queens Cl LE16 34 C5
- Queens Cres NN2 141 D2
- Queensland Gdns NN2 141 D2
- QUEEN'S PARK 141 C1
- Queens Park Ind Est NN2 141 B1
- Queen's Park Par NN2 141 C2
- Queen's Pk NN7 155 A3
- Queens Rd
  - Daventry NN11 135 B3
  - Wilbarston LE16 34 D5
  - Wollaston NN29 146 D2
- Queen's Rd
  - Northampton NN1 159 E7
  - Towcester NN12 203 C6
- Queen's Sq NN17 36 E5
- Queens St
  - Culworth OX17 198 D2
  - Farthinghoe NN13 221 B4
  - Wellingborough NN8 130 A5
- Queen St
  - Bozeat NN29 164 C2
  - Desborough NN14 51 B3
  - Earls Barton NN6 144 F5
  - Geddington NN14 54 A2
  - Irthlingborough NN9 112 E2
  - Kettering NN16 72 B2
  - Market Harborough LE16 32 A2
  - Middleton Cheney OX17 219 F8
  - Rushden NN10 132 B2
  - Stony Stratford MK11 229 E6
  - Thrapston NN14 76 E2
  - Weedon Bec NN7 155 A2
- Queensway
  - Burton Latimer NN15 92 B1
  - Higham Ferrers NN10 132 C5
  - Wellingborough NN8 129 C4
  - Wellingborough NN8 129 D3
- Queenswood Ave NN3 142 D5
- Quernstone La NN4 158 E3
- QUINBURY END 187 A1

**QUINTON** 176 B1
**Quinton Green Cotts** NN7 192 C7
Quinton House Sch NN5 158 B5
**Quinton La** NN11 184 C6
**Quinton Rd** NN4 175 F5
**Quintonside** NN4 175 F3
**Quorn Cl**
Kettering NN15 92 A5
Wellingborough NN8 129 D4
**Quorn Rd** NN10 132 A3
**Quorn Way** NN1 159 B7

## R

**Racecourse Rd** PE9 2 D5
**Racedown** NN8 129 B3
**Radleigh Cl** NN4 159 A2
**Radleigh Ct** NN2 141 E1
**Radnor Way** NN15 92 A5
**RADSTONE** 222 F6
**Radstone** NN13 222 F6
**Radstone Rd** NN13 222 F2
**Radstone Way** NN2 141 C5
**Raeburn Rd** NN2 141 F2
Raeburn Sch NN2 141 F2
**Raglan Cl** NN10 132 D1
**Raglan St** NN1 159 E6
**Ragsdale Ct** NN14 70 E7
**Ragsdale St** NN14 70 E7
**Ragsdale Wlk** NN3 142 E6
**Railport App** NN6 100 B6
**Railside La** NN17 37 A6
**Railway Cotts**
Church Brampton NN6 140 A7
Kilsby CV23 100 A6
Nether Heyford NN7 172 A8
**Railway View** NN16 72 A2
**Raincliffe Cl** OX17 237 C7
**Rainsborough Cres** NN4 158 F4
**Rainsborough Gdns** LE16 48 D8
**Rainsbrook Ave** CV22 98 E8
Rainsbrook Valley Rly★ CV22 98 C6
**Raisins Field Cl** NN3 143 C3
**Rakestone Cl** [4] NN4 175 D6
**Raleigh Cl**
Corby NN17 36 A8
Rothwell NN14 70 E7
**Raleigh Ct** NN11 135 B5
**Ramsay Cl** NN9 114 C7
**Randall Cl** NN9 131 E8
**Randall Ho** NN1 159 F7
**Randall Rd** NN2 141 E1
**Rands Way** NN9 114 E5
**Ranelagh Rd** NN8 130 B4
**Rankine Ho** NN17 36 D8
**Rannoch Cl** NN15 91 E8
**Rannoch Way** NN17 21 C1
**Ransome Rd** NN4 159 D3
**Rate's La** PE8 13 F7
**Rathbone Cl** CV21 99 A8
**Rathlin Cl** NN17 36 C8
**RAUNDS** 114 C6
Raunds Park Inf Sch NN9 114 E6
**Raunds Rd**
Chelveston NN9 133 C8
Stanwick NN9 114 A4
**Raven Dr** NN15 92 A6
**Ravensbank** NN10 132 B4
**Ravenscourt** NN17 36 F8
**Ravens Croft** NN4 175 A7
**RAVENSTHORPE** 103 E1
**Ravensthorpe Rd** NN6 122 D5
**RAVENSTONE** 194 D2
**Ravens Way** NN3 161 C8
**Rawley Cres** NN5 140 A1
**Rawlings Cl** [2] NN11 135 D1
**Rawlins Cl** OX17 230 A5
**Ray Cl** PE8 41 F7
**Raymond Cl** NN29 146 E1
**Raymond Rd** NN5 159 A7
**Raynsford Rd** NN5 158 F8
**Rea Cl** NN4 175 C7
**Rectory Cl**
Barby CV23 99 C1
Crick NN6 100 F5
Stanwick NN9 113 F4
Swinford LE17 62 C4
**Rectory Ct** LE16 48 B6
**RECTORY FARM** 143 C4
**Rectory Farm Ct** PE8 28 D8
**Rectory Farm Mews** PE8 28 D8
Rectory Farm Prim Sch NN3 143 C5
**Rectory Farm Rd** NN3 143 D4
**Rectory Gdns** NN9 112 E2
**Rectory Hill** NN14 93 A7
**Rectory La**
Barby CV23 99 C1
Holcot NN6 126 E8
Market Harborough LE16 32 A2
Medbourne LE16 19 A7
Middleton Cheney OX17 208 F1
**Rectory La** *continued*
Milton Malsor NN7 174 E3
Orlingbury NN14 110 A5
Walgrave NN6 108 A4
Woodford NN14 94 D6
Yardley Hastings NN7 179 A7
**Rectory Rd** NN10 132 B2
Rectory Road Bsns Ctr NN10 132 B3
**Rectory Way** NN12 213 B8
**Rectory Wlk** NN15 91 F7
**Redbourne Ct** MK11 229 F5
Redbourn Pk NN4 160 B3
**Redding Cl** NN10 148 A7
**Redgrave Cl** NN15 90 F7
**Redgrave Ct** NN8 129 F8
**Red Hill Cres** NN29 146 D3
**Redhill Way** NN9 110 E1
**Red House La** NN6 108 E4
**Redhouse Rd** NN14 109 C4
**Red House Rd** NN3 142 B7
**Red House Wharf** NN7 155 C4
**Redland Cl** LE15 3 F5
**Redland Dr** NN2 141 A4
**Redliech Cl** LE16 32 B3
**Red Lion St** OX17 230 F5
**Red Lodge Rd** NN17 12 A1
**Redmile's La** PE9 1 A5
**Redmoor** NN12 203 B4
**Red Row** NN9 114 D6
**Redruth Cl** NN4 159 B1
**Redwell Ct** NN8 129 F6
Redwell Jun & Inf Sch NN8 129 E7
Redwell L Ctr NN8 129 E7
**Redwell Rd** NN8 129 F6
**Redwing Ave** NN3 142 C6
**Redwood Cl** NN29 147 A7
**Red Wood Cl** NN14 51 C2
**Reedham Cl** NN5 140 C1
**Reedhill** NN4 158 E1
**Reedway** NN3 142 A4
**Reffield Cl** NN12 203 D5
**Regal Cl** NN3 141 F6
**Regal Ct** NN10 132 C1
**Regal Dr** NN16 72 C6
**Regency Cl** NN7 155 B4
**Regency Ct**
[5] Daventry NN11 135 C2
Finedon NN9 112 A5
Rushden NN10 132 B3
**Regent Cl** NN15 92 A2
**Regent Rd** NN15 92 A2
**Regents Hall** MK11 229 D6
**Regent St**
Desborough NN14 51 B3
Finedon NN9 111 F4
Kettering NN16 72 C3
Northampton NN1 159 C6
Wellingborough NN8 130 A5
**Regent Way** NN7 177 D1
**Regiment Cl** NN4 175 E7
**Reigate Wlk** NN18 36 B3
**Reims Ct** NN5 140 A2
**Remus Gate** NN13 234 A6
**Rendelsham Cl** NN16 72 A6
**Rennishaw Way** NN2 141 F3
**Repton Ct** NN3 142 D4
**Reservoir Cl**
Irthlingborough NN9 131 E8
Stanion NN14 37 E3
**Reservoir Hos** NN6 125 D5
**Reservoir Rd** NN16 72 B4
**Resthaven Rd** NN4 175 D6
**Restormel Cl** NN10 132 D1
**Retford Ct** NN3 142 F4
**Retreat The**
Easton o t H PE9 1 F5
Stony Stratford MK11 229 D5
**Reynard Pk** NN13 233 F5
**Reynard Way** NN2 141 D6
**Reynolds Cl**
Kettering NN15 92 A8
Rugby CV21 80 B1
Wellingborough NN8 129 F7
**Reynolds Rd** NN18 36 E5
**Reynoldston Cl** NN4 160 C1
**Rhodes Cl**
Daventry NN11 135 C5
Market Harborough LE16 31 C2
**Rhosili Rd** NN4 160 A2
**Rhymer Cl** MK19 206 F4
**Rhymer Ho** NN2 141 D5
**Ribble Cl**
Northampton NN5 140 F2
Wellingborough NN8 129 D6
**Ribblesdale Ave** NN17 36 E7
**Richard Cl** NN15 91 C6
**Richardsons La** NN14 70 D2
**Richardson Way** NN9 114 E7
**Richmond Ave** NN15 91 F8
**Richmond Cl** NN10 132 C1
**Richmond Ct** NN12 203 C5
**Richmond Rd**
Corby NN17 36 E6
Towcester NN12 203 C6
**Richmond St** OX17 231 A5
**Richmond Terr** NN5 159 B6
**Rickyard Rd** NN3 142 E3
**Rickyard Wlk** NN4 175 F2
**Ridding Cl** NN18 36 D3
**Rides Ct** NN3 142 C7
**Ridge Rd** NN14 76 C4
**Ridge The** NN29 145 E7
**Ridge View** LE16 31 E5
**Ridgeway**
Northampton NN3 160 D8
Stony Stratford MK11 229 F4
Wellingborough NN8 129 F7
Ridgeway Prim Sch LE16 31 F5
**Ridgeway The**
Barby CV23 118 E8
Kilsby CV23 100 A1
Market Harborough LE16 31 F5
Welton NN11 119 E1
**Ridgeway W** LE16 31 E5
**Ridgmont** MK19 228 E5
**Ridgmont Cl** MK19 228 E5
**Ridgway Rd** NN15 92 B8
**Riding Ct** NN13 233 F5
**Riding Rd** NN13 233 F5
**Ridings The**
Brixworth NN6 106 C2
Desborough NN14 50 E4
Northampton, Grange Park NN4 175 E2
Northampton NN1 159 D6
Roade NN7 191 C4
**Riding The** MK19 228 D5
**Ridley Ct** [1] NN11 135 C2
**Ridley St** NN16 72 A4
**Riggall Cl** NN14 90 A3
**Riley Cl**
Daventry NN11 134 F4
Market Harborough LE16 31 B2
Northampton NN3 143 C5
**Riley Rd** NN16 71 E4
**Rillwood Ct** NN3 142 E4
**RINGSTEAD** 95 B3
Ringstead CE Prim Sch NN14 95 B3
**Ringstead Cl**
Corby NN17 36 B8
Kettering NN15 91 F5
**Ringstead Rd**
Denford NN14 95 C5
Great Addington NN14 94 C2
**Ringtail Cl** NN9 131 E8
**Ring The** OX17 208 E4
**Ring Way** NN4 159 A3
**Ringwell Cl** NN9 112 E3
**Ringwood Cl** NN2 141 A5
**Ripley Cl** LE16 32 B3
**Ripley Rd** LE16 20 D1
**Ripley Wlk** NN18 36 C3
**Ripon Cl** NN4 159 A2
**Risdene Ct** [11] NN10 132 B2
**Rise The**
Northampton NN2 141 B3
Twyford OX17 230 A5
**Ritchie Pk** LE16 48 E8
**Rivercrest Rd** MK19 229 B6
**River La** PE8 28 C8
**Riverside** LE16 32 A4
Riverside Bsns Pk NN3 160 E7
**Riverside Cl** PE8 42 A4
**Riverside Ct**
Kislingbury NN7 157 D4
Market Harborough LE16 31 D2
Weedon Bec NN7 155 B3
**Riverside Dr** NN7 155 B3
Riverside Ind Est LE16 32 A4
**Riverside Maltings** PE8 42 A6
**Riverside Spinney** PE8 8 A3
**Riverside Way**
Islip NN14 76 B2
Northampton NN1 159 F5
Riverside Way Ind Est NN1 159 F5
**Riverstone Way** NN4 158 D2
**Riverview** NN15 111 B8
**Riverview Gdns** NN14 95 C6
**Riverwell** NN3 143 D2
**Rivetts Cl** MK46 195 E4
**Rixon Cl** NN3 142 E1
**Rixon Rd** NN8 130 C7
RNIB Rushton Hall Sch NN14 52 B2
**ROADE** 191 E4
**Roade Hill** NN7 191 F1
Roade Prim Sch NN7 191 E4
Roade Sch Sports Coll NN7 191 C3
**Roadins Cl** NN15 91 A7
**ROAD WEEDON** 155 C4
**Robbins Ct** CV22 98 F8
**Robb's La** NN14 75 F6
**Roberson Cl** NN12 203 C4
**Robert Hill Cl** CV21 80 A1
**Roberts Cl** MK19 228 E4
**Roberts Field** NN7 156 B1
**Robert's La** PE8 42 F2
Robert Smyth Sch The LE16 31 E5
**Robertson Cl** CV23 80 A5
**Roberts St**
Bozeat NN29 164 C2
Rushden NN10 132 C2
Wellingborough NN8 129 E4
**Robert St** NN1 159 D7
**Robin Cl**
Kettering NN15 92 A6
Towcester NN12 203 C3
**Robinia Cl** NN4 158 E3
**Robin La** NN8 130 A7
**Robin Ride** NN13 222 E1
**Robins Cl** NN7 192 C1
**Robins Field** PE8 8 A4
**Robinson Cl** NN16 71 F4
**Robinson Dr** NN13 233 D7
**Robinson Ho** NN3 142 E4
**Robinson Rd** NN10 132 C2
**Robinson Way**
Kettering NN16 71 F4
Northampton NN4 176 A6
**Robinswood** PE8 8 A4
**Roche Cl** NN11 153 C8
**Rochelle Way** NN5 140 A2
**Rochester Cl** NN15 91 F7
**Rochester Gdns** LE16 31 D1
**Rochester Rd** NN18 36 E2
**Rochester Way** OX17 230 B5
**Roche Way** NN8 129 F6
**Rockcroft** [3] NN4 175 D6
**Rock Hill** NN14 70 D7
**Rockhill Rd** NN6 121 A3
**ROCKINGHAM** 21 B4
Rockingham Castle & Gdns★ LE16 21 B3
**Rockingham Cl**
[1] Daventry NN11 135 B4
Thrapston NN14 76 E2
**Rockingham Ct** NN10 148 A8
**Rockingham Hills** PE8 41 E7
Rockingham Ind Est LE16 32 B3
**Rockingham Mews** NN17 37 A7
Rockingham Motor Speedway★ NN17 22 E4
**Rockingham Paddocks** NN16 72 B6
Rockingham Prim Sch NN17 37 A8
**Rockingham Rd**
Caldecott LE16 21 B6
Corby, Great Oakley NN14 53 A3
Corby NN17 21 E2
Cottingham LE16 20 E2
Gretton LE16, NN17 21 E7
Kettering NN16 72 A5
Market Harborough LE16 32 B4
Northampton NN4 159 C2
**Rockleigh Cl** NN9 112 A5
**Rock Rd**
Finedon NN9 112 A5
Oundle PE8 41 F6
**Rock St** NN8 129 F5
**Roderick Ct** [9] NN11 135 B4
**Roderick Way** [7] NN11 135 B4
**Rodewell Ho** NN14 70 D7
**Rodney Cl** NN11 135 E1
**Rodney Dr** NN17 36 B8
**Roe Rd** NN1 160 A8
Rokeby Inf Sch CV22 98 A8
Rokeby Jun Sch CV22 98 A8
**Rokeby Wlk** NN5 140 D1
**Roland Way** NN10 132 B6
**Rolfe Cres** NN7 156 B1
**Rolleston Cl** LE16 32 A3
**Roman Cl**
Northampton NN4 175 F5
Weldon NN17 38 B8
**Roman Dr** PE8 8 D2
**Roman Way**
Brackley NN13 234 A7
Daventry NN11 135 C5
Desborough NN14 51 B2
Higham Ferrers NN10 132 B7
Irchester NN29 147 B7
Market Harborough LE16 31 E4
Northampton NN4 175 E4
Raunds NN9 114 E6
Thrapston NN14 76 E3
**Romany Rd** NN2 141 E2
**Romney Rd** NN18 36 E5
**Romulus Cl** NN4 175 F5
**Romulus Way** NN13 234 A6
Rookery Farm★ NN12 191 B1
**Rookery La**
Northampton NN2 141 A5
Stoke Bruerne NN12 191 B1
**Rookery The** NN4 175 E3
**Rookwell Dr** LE16 31 F1
**Roper Cl** CV21 99 A8
**Rose Ave**
Rushden NN10 131 F1
Weldon NN17 38 B8
**Rosebay Rd** NN14 51 A5
**Rosebery Ave** NN5 158 F6
**Rosebery St**
Burton Latimer NN15 92 B1
Kettering NN16 72 C2
Ringstead NN14 95 B3
**Rose Cl**
Broughton NN14 90 B5
Corby NN18 36 E2
Hartwell NN7 192 E2
Rothwell NN14 70 E6
**Rose Cotts** NN14 113 B7
**Rose Ct**
Irchester NN29 147 B8
Olney MK46 195 F3
Weldon NN17 38 B8
**Rose Dale** LE17 45 A4
**Rosedale Ave** NN17 36 E6
**Rosedale Rd** NN2 141 D3
**Rose Dr** NN13 233 D8
**Rose Hall La** OX17 220 A8
**Rose Hill** NN9 112 A5
**Rose Hill Way** NN14 89 C5
**Roseholme Rd** NN1 160 A8
**Rose La** MK19 206 E6
**Rosemoor Cl** LE16 32 B3
**Rosemoor Dr** NN4 175 C7
**Rosemount Dr** NN15 91 C7
**Rosenella Cl** [3] NN4 158 F3
**Rose Paddock** NN14 94 D7
**Roses Cl** NN29 146 C3
**Rose Terr** NN14 94 D7
**Rosette Cl** NN5 158 C8
**Rosewood Ave** CV22 98 A8
**Rosewood Cl** NN11 135 C5
**Rosewood Ct** NN8 130 C3
**Rosewood Pl** NN16 72 C4
**Rosgill Pl** NN3 142 B2
**Rossendale Dr** NN15 92 A5
**Rossetti Rd** NN18 36 E5
**Rossiter Ho** NN13 233 E6
**Ross Rd** NN5 158 E6
**Rotherhithe Cl** [9] NN4 158 F2
**ROTHERSTHORPE** 174 A7
**Rothersthorpe Ave** NN4 159 A3
Rothersthorpe CE Prim Sch NN7 174 A6
**Rothersthorpe Cres** NN4 159 A3
**Rothersthorpe Rd**
Kislingbury NN7 157 E2
Northampton NN4 159 A3
**Rothesay Rd** NN2 141 F2
**Rothesay Terr** NN2 141 F2
**ROTHWELL** 70 D8
**Rothwell Grange Cotts** NN16 71 B5
**Rothwell Grange Ct** NN16 71 B5
Rothwell Jun Sch NN14 70 D7
**Rothwell Rd**
Desborough NN14 51 A2
Harrington NN6 69 B5
Kettering NN16 71 D4
Kettering NN16 71 F3
Rothwell Victoria Inf Sch NN14 70 D7
**Rotten Row** NN29 146 D2
**Rotton Row** NN9 114 D7
**Roughton Cl** NN15 91 B6
**Round Cl** NN11 119 E1
**Roundel The** NN6 143 B6
**Roundhill Cl** LE16 32 B2
**Roundhill Rd** NN15 91 C8
**ROUND SPINNEY** 142 E7
**Round The** NN14 89 B4
**Roundtown** OX17 237 C7
**Roundway The** NN11 135 D6
**Roundwood Way** NN5 157 F8
**Roveley Ct** MK11 229 F5
**Rowallen Way** [2] NN11 135 A4
**Rowan Ave**
Market Harborough LE16 31 E1
Mawsley Village NN14 89 B4
Northampton NN3 142 C5
**Rowan Cl**
Brackley NN13 222 F1
Northampton NN4 175 E2
Towcester NN12 203 B4
Wellingborough NN8 129 E5
**Rowan Ct** NN17 21 E1
Rowan Gate Prim Sch NN8 130 B6
**Rowans The** NN11 135 C4
**Rowan Way** NN11 184 B6
**Rowe Cl** CV21 99 C8
**Rowell Way** PE8 42 B4
**Rowlandson Cl** NN3 142 E1
**Rowlett Cl** NN10 132 C5
Rowlett Com Prim Sch NN17 37 B6
**Rowlett Rd** NN17 36 D8
**Rowley Way** NN2 141 E6
**Rowtree Rd** NN4 175 B6
**Roxton Cl** NN15 92 A5
**Royal Cl** NN11 135 B3
**Royal Gdns** NN14 50 F2
Royal Oak Ind Est NN11 134 F3
**Royal Oak La** OX17 220 A8
**Royal Oak Way N** NN11 134 F3
**Royal Oak Way S** NN11 134 F2
**Royal Star Dr** NN11 135 A4
**Royal Terr** NN1 159 C7
**Royce Cl** NN17 21 F1
**Rubens Wlk** NN18 36 E5
**Rubicon Ho** NN1 159 C7
**Ruddington Cl** NN3 160 E7
**Rudge Mews** NN5 157 F8
**Rudgeway** NN13 233 F2
**Rufford Ave** NN3 160 E7
**Rufford Cl** NN15 92 A5
**Rufford Wlk** NN18 36 C6
**RUGBY** 99 A7
**Rugby Cl** LE16 31 D2
**Rugby Rd**
Barby CV23 99 C1
Kilsby CV21, CV23 99 E5
Lilbourne CV23 80 F6
South Kilworth LE17 62 E6
Swinford LE17 62 B3
**Ruins The** NN12 203 C6
**Runnell La** PE8 15 F5
**Runneymede Gdns** [5] NN3 142 F1
**Rupert Rd** LE16 31 E1
**Rush Cl** NN7 192 E2

RUS–Sch 261


RUSHDEN ... 132 E2
Rushden Com Coll The NN10 ... 132 A4
Rushden Hospl NN10 ... 148 B8
Rushden Rd
Newton Bromswold NN10 ... 149 C7
Wymington NN10 ... 148 A6
Rushden Station Transport Mus★ NN10 ... 132 B3
Rushes La LE16 ... 30 F3
Rushes The NN15 ... 111 B8
Rushmere Ave NN1 ... 160 B6
Rushmere Cl
Islip NN14 ... 76 B3
Raunds NN9 ... 114 C5
Rushmere Cres NN1 ... 160 B6
Rushmere Rd NN1 ... 160 B5
Rushmere Way
Northampton NN1 ... 160 B6
Rushden NN10 ... 132 B4
Rushmills NN4 ... 160 B3
RUSHTON ... 52 C2
Rushton Prim Sch NN14 ... 52 C2
Rushton Rd
Desborough NN14 ... 51 C3
Rothwell NN14 ... 70 E8
Wilbarston LE16 ... 34 C4
Rushton Triangular Lo★ NN14 ... 52 A2
Rushwell Cl NN14 ... 94 B3
Rushy End NN4 ... 175 B6
Ruskin Ave NN8 ... 129 C4
Ruskin Jun & Inf Sch NN8 ... 129 C3
Ruskin Rd
Daventry NN11 ... 153 C8
Northampton NN2 ... 141 C4
Russell Ct NN10 ... 132 B2
Russell Hill PE8 ... 8 A6
Russell Rise NN7 ... 155 E5
Russell Sq NN3 ... 142 C6
Russell St
Kettering NN16 ... 72 C2
Stony Stratford MK11 ... 229 D5
Russell Street Sch MK11 ... 229 D5
Russell Way NN10 ... 132 B6
Russet Dr NN3 ... 143 A2
Russett Cl LE16 ... 31 F5
Rutherford Ct NN17 ... 22 B1
Rutherford Dr NN8 ... 129 A5
Rutherford Way NN11 ... 134 F4
Rutherglen Rd NN17 ... 36 F7
Ruth Gdns NN16 ... 72 E3
Rutland Cl NN17 ... 36 B7
Rutland Ct NN14 ... 50 F4
Rutland St NN16 ... 72 C3
Rutland Wlk
Market Harborough LE16 ... 31 F5
Northampton NN3 ... 142 B7
Rycroft Cl NN8 ... 129 D5
Rydal NN8 ... 129 B3
Rydal Mount NN3 ... 142 C3
Rydalside
Kettering NN15 ... 72 D1
Northampton NN4 ... 158 F3
Ryder Ct NN18 ... 52 F8
Ryder View NN8 ... 129 C7
Ryeburn Way NN8 ... 129 E5
Ryebury Hill NN8 ... 111 E2
Rye Cl
Burton Latimer NN15 ... 92 C2
Rushden NN10 ... 148 C8
Ryefields NN6 ... 124 B8
Ryehill Cl
Irthlingborough NN9 ... 131 E8
Isham NN14 ... 91 E1
Long Buckby NN6 ... 121 A3
Northampton NN5 ... 140 C2
Ryehill Ct NN5 ... 140 C2
Ryehill Rd NN3 ... 142 F3
Ryeland MK11 ... 229 E6
Ryeland Rd NN5 ... 158 A8
Ryeland Way NN5 ... 140 A1
Ryland Rd
Moulton NN3 ... 142 C8
Northampton NN2 ... 141 E2
Rylands Cl LE16 ... 32 B3
Ryle Dr NN8 ... 129 A4
Rylstone The NN8 ... 129 B4
Ryngwell Cl NN6 ... 106 B1


## S


Sackville St
Kettering NN16 ... 72 A4
Raunds NN9 ... 114 D6
Thrapston NN14 ... 76 D2
Sacrewell Farm & Ctry Ctr★ PE8 ... 8 B5
Saddleback Rd NN5 ... 158 D6
Saddlers Sq NN3 ... 142 F6
Saddlers The NN4 ... 175 F3
Saddlers Way NN9 ... 114 B5
Saffron Cl NN4 ... 175 D5
Saffron Rd NN10 ... 132 B6
Sage Cl NN3 ... 142 E4
Saimon Cl NN13 ... 233 E8
St Alban's Cl
Kettering NN15 ... 73 A1
Northampton NN3 ... 142 B3
St Albans Pl NN29 ... 146 D2
St Alban's Rd NN3 ... 142 B3
St Amandas Cl NN15 ... 72 F2
St Andrews CE Prim Sch NN3 ... 143 C2
St Andrew's CE Prim Sch NN16 ... 72 A4
St Andrews Cl
Broughton NN14 ... 90 B4
Great Easton LE16 ... 20 D7
St Andrew's Cl NN14 ... 77 D3
St Andrews Cres
Rugby CV22 ... 98 A8
Wellingborough NN8 ... 129 E2
St Andrews Ct NN1 ... 159 C6
St Andrew's Ct NN14 ... 90 B4
St Andrews Dr NN11 ... 135 E3
St Andrew's Ho 9 NN1 ... 159 F6
St Andrew's Hospl NN1 ... 159 F6
St Andrews La NN14 ... 77 D4
St Andrew's La NN14 ... 93 A7
St Andrew's Rd
East Haddon NN6 ... 122 D5
Northampton NN2 ... 159 B7
St Andrew's St
Kettering NN16 ... 72 B3
Northampton NN1 ... 159 C6
St Andrews Way NN14 ... 90 B4
St Andrew's Wlk NN17 ... 37 B6
St Annes Cl
Brackley NN13 ... 233 D8
Daventry NN11 ... 153 C8
St Anne's Rd NN15 ... 73 A1
St Ann's Ct PE8 ... 41 F5
St Anthonys Cl NN11 ... 153 B8
St Anthony's Hill NN14 ... 51 A2
St Anthony's Rd NN15 ... 72 F1
St Augustine's Cl NN15 ... 73 A1
St Augustin Way NN11 ... 135 D1
St Barnabas CE Sch NN8 ... 129 F4
St Barnabas' Cl NN15 ... 73 A1
St Barnabas Ho 10 NN1 ... 159 C6
St Barnabas St NN8 ... 129 F4
St Bartholemews Ho 5 NN1 ... 159 C6
St Bartholomew's Cl NN15 ... 73 A1
St Benedicts Mount NN4 ... 158 E2
St Bernards Ct NN15 ... 72 F1
St Botolphs Gn PE8 ... 28 E7
St Botolph's Rd NN15 ... 91 F7
St Brendan's RC Inf Sch NN18 ... 36 B6
St Catharine's Rd NN15 ... 73 A1
St Catherines Cl NN11 ... 153 B8
St Cecilia's Cl NN15 ... 72 F1
St Chad's Cl NN15 ... 73 A1
St Christopher's Cl NN15 ... 73 A1
St Christopher's Dr PE8 ... 42 B4
St Christopher's Wlk NN3 ... 160 B7
St Clements Ct NN15 ... 91 B7
St Crispin Ave NN8 ... 129 F2
St Crispin Cl NN15 ... 92 C3
St Crispin Cres NN5 ... 157 F8
St Crispin Dr NN5 ... 158 A7
St Crispin Rd NN6 ... 144 F4
St Davids Cl NN6 ... 106 B1
St David's Cl NN15 ... 72 F1
St David's Ct NN13 ... 234 A8
St Davids RC Mid Sch NN2 ... 141 C3
St David's Rd
Brixworth NN6 ... 106 A1
Northampton NN2 ... 141 C2
Rushden NN10 ... 131 D3
St Dunstan's Cl NN15 ... 91 F8
St Dunstans Rise NN4 ... 158 E1
St Edmunds Cl NN11 ... 153 C7
St Edmund's Hospl NN1 ... 159 E7
St Edmund's Rd NN1 ... 159 E6
St Edmund's St NN1 ... 159 E6
St Edward's RC Prim Sch NN15 ... 91 E7
St Emilion Cl NN5 ... 139 F1
St Francis Ave NN5 ... 159 A8
St Francis' Cl NN15 ... 73 A1
St Georges Ave CV22 ... 98 A8
St George's Ave NN2 ... 159 D8
St Georges Cl NN12 ... 203 C5
St Georges Ho 2 NN1 ... 159 C6
St George's Pl NN2 ... 159 C8
St George's St NN1 ... 159 C7
St George's Way NN10 ... 131 F3
St Giles' Cl NN15 ... 73 A1
St Giles Mews MK11 ... 229 D6
St Giles's Cl NN14 ... 51 A3
St Giles' Sq NN1 ... 159 D5
St Giles' St NN1 ... 159 D6
St Giles' Terr NN1 ... 159 D6
St Gregory's RC Prim Sch NN3 ... 142 D3
St Gregory's Rd NN3 ... 142 D3
St Helens Cl NN6 ... 84 D4
St Hilda's Cl NN11 ... 153 C8
St Hughes Cl NN11 ... 153 C8
St James' CE Prim Sch NN5 ... 159 A7
St James Cl
2 Daventry NN11 ... 135 C1
Hanslope MK19 ... 207 A2
St James' Cl
Kettering NN15 ... 92 A8
Rushden NN10 ... 132 C4
St James' Cres NN14 ... 76 E2
ST JAMES' END ... 159 A5
St James Inf Sch NN11 ... 135 C1
St James' Lake Nature Reserve★ NN13 ... 233 E6
St James' Mill Rd NN5 ... 159 A4
St James Mill Rd E NN1 ... 159 B4
St James' Park Rd NN5 ... 159 A6
St James Rd
Brackley NN13 ... 233 F5
Corby NN18 ... 37 A6
St James' Rd NN5 ... 159 A5
St James Ret Pk NN1 ... 159 B5
St James St NN11 ... 135 C1
St Johns Ave CV22 ... 98 E8
St John's Ave NN2 ... 141 C6
St Johns Cl
Daventry NN11 ... 153 B8
Rothersthorpe NN7 ... 174 A6
St Johns Ct NN1 ... 159 D5
St John Ho
8 Northampton NN1 ... 159 C6
3 Wellingborough NN8 ... 129 F5
St John's La MK19 ... 228 B4
St John's Pl NN17 ... 37 B6
St Johns Rd NN12 ... 189 E4
St John's Rd NN15 ... 91 F8
St John's Sq NN11 ... 135 C2
St John's St
Northampton NN1 ... 159 D5
Wellingborough NN8 ... 129 F5
St John's Terr NN1 ... 159 D5
St John's Way NN7 ... 177 A2
St John's Wlk NN3 ... 142 D1
St Josephs Cl MK46 ... 195 F4
St Joseph's Cl NN15 ... 73 A1
St Joseph's RC Prim Sch LE16 ... 31 E3
St Julien Cl NN5 ... 140 A2
St Katharine's Way NN29 ... 131 B1
St Katherine's Ct 25 NN1 ... 159 C6
St Katherine's Sq 27 NN1 ... 159 C6
St Katherine's St 2 NN1 ... 159 C5
St Laurence Way NN9 ... 113 F4
St Lawrence CE Jun Sch NN12 ... 203 C5
St Lawrence CE Lower Sch NN10 ... 148 A5
St Lawrence Ct 12 NN1 ... 159 E6
St Lawrence Ho 3 NN1 ... 159 C6
St Lawrence Rd NN12 ... 203 C5
St Lawrence Rd S NN12 ... 203 C4
St Lawrence Wlk NN10 ... 148 B5
St Leonards Cl CV47 ... 166 D8
St Leonard's Cl NN15 ... 72 F1
St Leonards Ct NN4 ... 159 C3
St Leonard's Rd NN4 ... 159 C3
St Loys CE Prim Sch NN12 ... 200 B2
St Luke's CE Prim Sch NN5 ... 158 C6
St Lukes Cl
Northampton NN5 ... 157 F8
Spratton NN6 ... 105 B1
St Luke's Cl NN15 ... 92 A8
St Luke's Ho 12 NN1 ... 159 C6
St Luke's Hospl LE16 ... 31 D5
St Luke's Rd NN18 ... 37 A5
St Magdalenes Rd NN15 ... 72 F2
St Margarets Ave NN10 ... 132 A1
St Margaret's Gdns 3 NN5 ... 140 F1
St Mark's Cl
Kettering NN15 ... 73 A1
Rushden NN10 ... 131 E2
St Mark's Cres NN2 ... 141 B6
St Marks Ho 7 NN1 ... 159 C6
St Mark's Rd NN18 ... 37 A5
St Martins Cl NN2 ... 141 C4
St Martins Ho 1 NN1 ... 159 C6
St Martins Yd 3 LE16 ... 31 E3
St Martyn's Way NN7 ... 155 B3
St Mary & St Giles CE Jun Sch MK11 ... 229 E6
St Mary's Ave
Finedon NN9 ... 111 F5
Rushden NN10 ... 132 B1
Stony Stratford MK11 ... 229 E6
St Mary's CE Prim Sch
Burton Latimer NN15 ... 92 C2
Kettering NN16 ... 72 C2
St Marys Cl
Thrapston NN14 ... 76 F3
Woodnewton PE8 ... 14 E2
St Mary's Cl
Nassington PE8 ... 15 E5
Priors Hardwick CV47 ... 166 A5
St Marys Ct NN7 ... 173 F2
St Mary's Ct
Finedon NN9 ... 111 E5
Market Harborough LE16 ... 32 A4
22 Northampton NN1 ... 159 C6
St Marys Hill PE8 ... 14 E2
St Mary's Hospl NN15 ... 72 C1
St Mary's Paddock NN8 ... 130 C4
St Mary's Pl LE16 ... 31 F3
St Mary's RC Prim Sch
Aston le W NN11 ... 182 F2
Northampton NN5 ... 140 F1
St Marys Rd NN29 ... 146 E2
St Mary's Rd
Bozeat NN29 ... 164 D2
Kettering NN15 ... 72 C1
Market Harborough LE16 ... 31 F3
St Mary's St NN1 ... 159 C6
St Mary's Way
Nassington PE8 ... 15 E5
Roade NN7 ... 191 D5
Weedon Bec NN7 ... 155 B3
St Matthew's Par NN2 ... 141 F1
St Matthew's Rd NN15 ... 73 A1
St Matthew's Sch NN3 ... 142 A1
St Michael's Ave NN1 ... 159 E7
St Michael's Ct NN7 ... 205 F8
St Michaels Gdns NN15 ... 91 C8
St Michael's La NN29 ... 146 D2
St Michael's Mount NN1 ... 159 E7
St Michael's Rd
Kettering NN15 ... 91 C8
Northampton NN1 ... 159 D6
St Nicholas Cl
Kettering NN15 ... 72 F2
Market Harborough LE16 ... 31 F2
St Nicholas Ct NN29 ... 145 E6
St Nicholas Rd NN29 ... 145 D6
St Nicholas Way
Islip NN14 ... 76 B3
Market Harborough LE16 ... 31 F2
St Oswald's Cl NN15 ... 91 F8
St Osyths La PE8 ... 42 A5
St Patrick's RC Prim Sch NN18 ... 36 D4
St Patrick St 11 NN1 ... 159 C7
St Paul's Ct
Kettering NN15 ... 72 B1
Stony Stratford MK11 ... 229 D6
St Pauls Gdns NN14 ... 76 D2
St Paul's Rd NN2 ... 159 C8
St Paul's Terr NN2 ... 159 C8
St Peter's Ave
Kettering NN16 ... 72 C1
Kettering NN16 ... 72 C2
Rushden NN10 ... 131 F3
St Peter's CE Jun Sch NN9 ... 114 E6
St Peters Cl NN11 ... 153 B8
St Peter's Cl NN14 ... 37 F2
St Peters Ct NN9 ... 114 D6
St Peter's Gate NN13 ... 234 A7
St Peter's Gdns NN3 ... 142 D1
St Peter's Ho 20 NN1 ... 159 C6
St Peter's Ind Sch NN3 ... 143 A3
St Peter's Mews 12 NN16 ... 72 C2
St Peters Rd PE8 ... 41 F7
St Peter's Rd NN13 ... 233 F8
St Peter's Sch NN15 ... 91 B8
St Peters Sq 12 NN1 ... 159 C5
St Peter's St NN1 ... 159 B5
St Peters's Way NN9 ... 112 F2
St Peters Way NN7 ... 161 F6
St Peter's Way
Corby NN17 ... 37 A6
Northampton NN1 ... 159 C5
Weedon Bec NN7 ... 155 B3
St Peters Wlk 5 NN1 ... 159 C5
St Philip's Cl NN15 ... 73 A1
St Rochus Dr NN8 ... 130 A1
St Rumbolds Dr OX17 ... 231 A5
St Saviour's Rd NN15 ... 73 A1
St Simon's Cl NN15 ... 73 A1
St Stephens Ho 9 NN1 ... 159 C6
St Stephen's Rd NN15 ... 73 A1
St Swithins Cl NN15 ... 72 F2
St Theresa's Cl NN15 ... 72 F1
St Thomas Ho NN1 ... 159 D6
St Thomas More RC Prim Sch NN16 ... 71 F1
St Thomas Rd NN7 ... 161 D3
St Valentine's Cl NN15 ... 72 F1
St Vincents Ave NN15 ... 72 F2
St Wilfrids Rd PE8 ... 41 F7
Salcey Ave NN7 ... 192 D2
Salcey Cl
2 Daventry NN11 ... 135 B4
Hartwell NN7 ... 192 E2
Kettering NN15 ... 92 A5
Salcey Forest Trail★ NN7 ... 192 F4
Salcey Forest Trail (Rose Copse)★ NN7 ... 193 B2
SALCEY GREEN ... 207 B7
Salcey Rise NN7 ... 177 B1
Salcey St NN4 ... 159 C2
Salcombe Rd NN18 ... 36 E4
Salem Cl NN6 ... 121 A3
Salem La 9 NN8 ... 130 A5
Salen Cl NN15 ... 92 B5
Salford Cl NN6 ... 64 E6
Salisbury Rd NN8 ... 130 C5
Salisbury St
Kettering NN16 ... 72 C4
Northampton NN2 ... 159 C8
Salisbury Wlk NN18 ... 36 E1
Sallow Ave NN3 ... 143 C3
Sallow Rd NN17 ... 22 E1
Salmons La OX17 ... 220 B8
Salthouse Rd NN4 ... 160 C2
Salt Pikes NN6 ... 125 B8
Saltwell Sq 5 NN3 ... 143 C2
Samuel Pl NN17 ... 37 A8
Samuels Cl NN9 ... 113 F3
Samwell Way NN4 ... 158 C1
Sandby Rd NN18 ... 36 E4
Sanders Cl
Braunston NN11 ... 118 B1
Wellingborough NN8 ... 111 B1
Sanders La NN12 ... 217 D3
Sanders Lodge Ind Est NN10 ... 131 D3
Sanderson Cl NN15 ... 91 A8
Sanders Rd NN8 ... 111 B1
Sanders Terr NN6 ... 121 B4
Sandfield Cl NN3 ... 142 B6
Sandhill Rd 2 NN5 ... 159 A6
Sandhills NN6 ... 105 A1
Sandhills Cl NN2 ... 141 B6
Sandhills Rd NN2 ... 141 B6
Sandhurst Cl NN4 ... 175 B8
Sandiland Rd NN3 ... 142 B2
Sandlands Ave NN14 ... 55 F7
Sandlands Cl NN14 ... 55 F7
Sandover NN4 ... 175 D6
Sandown Cl NN18 ... 36 E1
Sandpiper Cl NN15 ... 92 A2
Sandpiper La NN8 ... 130 A7
Sandringham Cl
Brackley NN13 ... 233 E7
Northampton NN1 ... 160 B7
Rushden NN10 ... 132 A1
Towcester NN12 ... 203 C4
Wellingborough NN8 ... 129 E2
Sandringham Ct NN15 ... 91 D5
Sandringham Rd
Kings Sutton OX17 ... 230 F5
Northampton NN1 ... 160 A7
Sandringham Way LE16 ... 32 B3
Sandringham Wlk NN18 ... 36 E2
Sands Cl NN12 ... 172 D1
Sandy Cl NN8 ... 129 F6
Sandy Hill La NN3 ... 126 E2
Sandyhome Rd NN12 ... 203 C5
Sandy La
Church Brampton NN6 ... 140 D8
Harpole NN7 ... 157 E7
Northampton NN5 ... 139 F2
Saneco La NN6 ... 106 B3
Sansom Ct NN3 ... 142 D4
Sansome Cl NN7 ... 177 B3
Saplings The NN16 ... 72 C6
Sapphire Cl NN15 ... 72 C1
Sarek Pk NN4 ... 174 F7
Sargeants La NN4 ... 175 C4
Sargent Rd NN18 ... 36 E4
Sarjeant Ct NN14 ... 70 D7
Sarrington Rd NN17 ... 36 F8
Sartoris Rd NN10 ... 131 F2
Saruman La NN3 ... 143 B6
Sassoon Cl NN8 ... 129 C6
Sassoon Mews NN8 ... 129 B6
Saunders Cl NN16 ... 72 B1
Savill Cl NN4 ... 175 C7
Sawyers Cres NN9 ... 133 B8
Saxby Cres NN8 ... 130 C4
Saxilby Cl NN18 ... 36 C4
Saxon Acre NN13 ... 233 F7
Saxon Ave NN4 ... 175 E3
Saxon Cl
Desborough NN14 ... 51 A3
Higham Ferrers NN10 ... 132 B7
Market Harborough LE16 ... 31 F4
Saxon Dale NN16 ... 72 C6
Saxon Ho NN6 ... 106 B2
Saxon Hts NN6 ... 125 B8
Saxonlea Cl NN10 ... 131 E3
Saxon Rise
Earls Barton NN6 ... 144 E3
Irchester NN29 ... 147 C8
Northampton NN5 ... 158 B7
Saxon St NN3 ... 142 B1
Saxon Way NN9 ... 114 E6
Saxon Way E NN18 ... 53 A8
Saxon Way W NN18 ... 52 F8
Sayers Cl NN12 ... 214 D3
SCALDWELL ... 106 F6
Scaldwell Rd
Brixworth NN6 ... 106 D4
Old NN6 ... 107 C7
Scapa Rd NN17 ... 36 C8
Scarborough St NN9 ... 112 E2
Scarborough Wlk NN18 ... 36 B4
Scarletwell St NN1 ... 159 B6
Scarplands The NN5 ... 158 C6
Scharpwell NN9 ... 112 E3
Scholars Ct NN1 ... 159 D5
Scholars Row NN14 ... 89 B4

School Cl
Braunston NN11 118 D1
Greens Norton NN12 202 D8
Yelvertoft NN6 82 A4
School End OX17 237 C7
School Farm Yd LE16 18 B3
School Gdns CV21 80 A1
School Hill
Irchester NN29 147 B8
Middleton LE16 35 C8
Newnham NN11 153 D4
School La
Abthorpe NN12 202 A2
Adstone NN12 186 B3
Badby NN11 152 F3
Barrowden LE15 3 F5
Braybrooke LE16 49 F5
Bythorn PE28 97 D4
Castlethorpe MK19 218 F5
Cottingham LE16 20 C1
Denford NN14 95 C6
Elton PE8 28 D8
Evenley NN13 233 F2
Everdon NN11 170 A8
Eydon NN11 184 C1
Greens Norton NN12 202 D8
Hannington NN6 108 C2
Harpole NN7 157 B6
Hartwell NN7 192 D2
Higham Ferrers NN10 132 B7
Husbands Bosworth LE17 45 E5
Irchester NN29 147 A8
Islip NN14 76 B2
Kettering NN16 72 B2
Kislingbury NN7 157 D4
Little Harrowden NN9 110 C4
Lubenham LE16 30 F3
Market Harborough LE16 31 E3
Morcott LE15 3 A6
Moulton NN3 126 C1
Naseby NN6 85 B8
Northampton NN4 175 E3
Priors Marston CV47 166 D8
Quinton NN7 176 B1
Rothwell NN14 70 D7
Scaldwell NN6 106 F6
Swinford LE17 62 B4
Titchmarsh NN14 77 C4
Wappenham NN12 213 B8
Warmington PE8 28 B3
Weldon NN17 38 B8
Wilbarston LE16 34 C5
Yardley Gobion NN12 217 E6
Yelvertoft NN6 82 B4
School Pl NN18 36 D5
School Rd
Gretton NN17 10 B1
Irchester NN29 147 A8
Mawsley Village NN14 89 B4
Pattishall NN12 188 F8
Spratton NN6 105 B1
School St
Daventry NN11 135 A2
Rugby CV21 80 A1
Sulgrave OX17 210 F7
Woodford Halse NN11 184 C6
School Wlk NN8 130 A1
Scirocco Cl NN3 141 E6
Scoborough Rd LE16, LE17 30 A1
Scotgate NN17 10 F7
Scotia Cl NN4 160 C2
Scotland End LE16 31 F1
Scotland Rd LE16 32 A2
Scotland St NN16 72 C3
Scotney Cl 1 NN4 175 C8
Scotney Way NN14 76 E2
Scots Mere NN9 112 D3
Scott Ave NN14 70 E7
Scott Cl
Daventry NN11 135 C4
Market Harborough LE16 31 E5
Ravensthorpe NN6 103 D1
Scotter Wlk NN18 36 C4
Scott Rd
Corby NN17 37 A6
Kettering NN16 72 C5
Wellingborough NN8 129 C3
Scotts La LE16 34 C5
Scriveners La NN12 216 A8
Scrivens Hill NN11 184 D6
Scully Cl 8 NN4 175 E7
Scythe Rd NN11 135 C6
Seaford Wlk NN18 36 B5
Seagrave Ct NN3 143 B5
Seagrave St NN15 91 C8
Sears Cl NN7 155 E6
Sears Ho NN1 159 F7
Seaton Cres NN18 36 E4
Seaton Dr NN3 142 F1
Seaton Rd
Barrowden LE15 3 C4
Harringworth NN17 10 E8
Second Ave NN8 129 D3
Second Drift PE9 2 D8
Second La NN5 158 F6
Second St NN13 238 E6
Sedbergh Rd NN18 36 C4
Sedge Cl NN14 76 C1
Sedgemoor Ct NN11 135 C6
Sedgemoor Way NN11 135 C6
Sedgwick Ct NN3 142 F3
Sedlescombe Pk CV22 98 A8
Seedfield Cl NN3 142 E1
Selby Cl LE16 48 E8
Selby Ct NN15 91 F8
Selby Gdns NN29 164 C2
Selby Wlk NN18 36 C4
Selsey Rd NN18 36 B5
Selston Wlk NN3 160 D7
Selwyn Cl NN11 153 C7
SEMILONG 159 D8
Semilong Ho 4 NN2 159 C7
Semilong Rd NN2 159 C8
Senna Dr NN12 203 C8
Sentinel Rd NN4 158 E1
Sentry Cl 6 NN4 175 E7
Senwick Dr NN8 130 C4
Senwick Rd NN8 130 C4
Setchells Yd PE8 41 F5
Settlers Fields NN15 91 A7
Seven Sisters Cl NN13 221 B4
Severn Cl NN8 129 C6
Severn Ct NN15 92 B2
Severn Dr NN5 140 F2
Severn Ho PE8 42 A6
Severn The NN11 135 A1
Severn Way NN16 72 A5
Severn Wlk NN17 21 C1
Sewter Gdns PE8 15 E6
Sexton Cl NN11 135 B3
Seymour Pl PE8 41 E7
Seymour St NN5 159 A6
Shackleton Cl NN14 70 E7
Shackleton Dr NN11 135 C5
Shadowfax Dr NN3 143 C5
Shaftesbury Ho NN8 130 A3
Shaftesbury Rd NN18 36 B6
Shaftesbury St NN16 72 C2
Shakespeare Ave NN11 135 B2
Shakespeare Dr NN15 92 A2
Shakespeare Ho 2 NN1 159 E7
Shakespeare Rd
Kettering NN16 72 B5
Northampton NN1 159 E7
Rushden NN10 131 E2
Wellingborough NN8 129 C4
Shakespeare Way NN17 36 D8
Shale End NN5 140 A3
Shannon Cl NN10 132 D3
Shannon Ct NN18 36 E4
Shannon Way NN15 92 B2
Shap Gn NN3 142 C4
Shard Cl NN4 175 D6
Sharman Cl NN11 135 C5
Sharman Rd
Northampton NN5 159 A5
Wellingborough NN8 129 F4
Sharmans Cl NN7 162 A6
Sharman Way NN14 70 F7
Sharpes La NN6 121 B4
Sharplands NN7 163 D5
Sharrow Pl 7 NN3 143 D2
Sharwood Terr NN29 147 B8
Shatterstone 2 NN4 175 D6
Shaw Cl NN8 129 B5
Shawell Rd LE17 62 A4
Shaw The MK18 227 F1
Sheaf Cl NN5 140 B2
Sheaf St NN11 135 C1
Shearwater La NN8 130 A7
Shedfield Way NN4 175 C6
Sheep St
Kettering NN16 72 B1
Northampton NN1 159 C6
Wellingborough NN8 130 A4
Sheerwater Dr NN3 143 D3
Sheffield Ct NN9 114 C5
Sheffield Way NN6 144 E3
Sheffield Wlk NN18 36 B4
Sheila Pl NN16 72 E4
Sheldons La NN6 108 A5
SHELFLEYS 174 E8
Shelford Cl NN3 143 B5
Shelland Cl LE16 32 C2
Shelley Cl
Daventry NN11 135 B2
Towcester NN12 203 B5
Shelleycotes Rd NN6 106 A1
Shelley Dr
Corby NN17 21 D1
Higham Ferrers NN10 132 B5
Shelley Rd
Kettering NN16 72 C5
Wellingborough NN8 129 B4
Shelley St NN2 141 F1
Shelmerdine Rise NN9 114 D6
Shelsley Dr NN3 141 F4
Shelton Ct
Corby NN17 22 E2
Wollaston NN29 146 D2
Shelton Rd
Corby NN17 22 E2
Raunds NN9 114 E4
Shepherd Cl NN2 141 A5
Shepherds Hill NN29 146 F1
Shepherds Wlk
Bugbrooke NN7 173 A8
Harpole NN7 157 C6
Sheppard Way NN12 213 B8
Shepperton Cl
Castlethorpe MK19 218 F5
Northampton NN3 143 C2
Sheppey La NN7 177 B3
Shepton Ct NN18 36 A6
Sheraton Cl NN3 142 C2
Sheraton Mews NN3 142 C2
Sherborne Way NN14 76 E2
Sherborne Wlk NN18 36 A6
Sheriff Ho NN9 112 E1
Sheriff Rd NN1 159 F7
Sherrard Rd LE16 31 E5
Sherwood Ave NN2 140 F6
Sherwood Cl NN17 36 E8
Sherwood Dr
Daventry NN11 135 B4
Kettering NN15 91 F5
Shetland Way NN17 21 C1
Shieling Ct NN18 36 A1
Ship La PE8 41 F4
Shipton Way NN10 131 C3
Shire Pl NN3 143 C5
Shire Rd NN17 21 C1
Shires Bsns Pk The NN13 234 A6
Shires Rd NN13 234 A6
Shirley Rd NN10 132 B3
Shoal Creek NN4 175 C5
Shoe Maker Cl NN12 188 F7
Shoemakers Ct NN10 132 B3
Shop La NN7 179 B6
Shoreham Ct NN18 36 B5
Short Cl PE8 28 B3
Short La
Cogenhoe NN7 162 A6
Thorpe Malsor NN14 71 B3
Wellingborough NN8 129 F5
Shortlands Cl NN13 211 F3
Shortlands The NN9 113 B5
Short Massey MK46 195 E5
Short Stocks NN10 132 D2
Shortwoods Cl NN9 114 D5
SHOTLEY 11 B7
Shotwell Mill La NN14 70 D8
Showsley Rd NN12 204 D8
Shrewsbury Ave LE16 32 B2
Shropshire Cl LE16 31 E4
Shropshire Pl LE16 31 E4
Shrubberies The NN14 94 D7
Shrubfield Gr NN17 36 F8
Shuckburgh Cres CV22 98 D8
Shuckburgh Rd CV47 166 D8
Shurville Cl NN6 144 F3
SHUTLANGER 204 D8
Shutlanger Rd NN12 190 F1
SIBBERTOFT 46 F2
Sibbertoft Rd
Clipston LE16 47 E1
Husbands Bosworth LE17 45 F2
Marston Trussell LE16 47 B6
Sibley Rd NN9 112 B4
SIBSON 16 F8
Siddeley Way NN11 134 F3
Siddons Cl PE8 41 E7
Siddons Way NN3 126 D1
Sidebrook Ct NN3 142 F5
Sidegate La NN8 130 F8
Sidings Ind Ctr The NN13 234 A8
Sidings The NN9 131 D8
Sidlaw Ct MK11 229 F4
Sidmouth Wlk NN18 36 F4
Sidney Rd
Rugby CV22 98 D8
Woodford Halse NN11 184 C6
Silkweavers Mews NN14 70 D7
Sillswood MK46 195 E4
Silverdale Gr NN10 131 E2
Silverdale Rd NN3 142 D2
Silver St N OX17 208 E4
Silver St
Abthorpe NN12 201 F2
Brixworth NN6 106 B3
Broughton NN14 90 A5
Chacombe OX17 208 E4
Kettering NN16 72 B2
Northampton NN1 159 C6
Stony Stratford MK11 229 D5
Walgrave NN6 108 A5
Wellingborough NN8 130 A4
SILVERSTONE 214 D4
Silverstone CE Jun Sch NN12 214 D4
Silverstone Cl NN2 141 D5
Silverstone Inf Sch NN12 214 D5
Silverstone Motor Racing Circuit* NN12 225 E8
Silverstone Tech Pk NN12 214 E2
Silverwood Ct NN15 91 C8
Silverwood Rd NN15 91 C8
Simborough Way LE16 32 B3
Simon de Senlis Ct NN1 159 D7
Simon de Senlis Prim Sch NN4 175 B8
Simon's Wlk
17 Northampton NN1 159 C6
Pattishall NN12 172 D1
Simpson Ave NN10 132 C7
Simpson Barracks NN4 175 D6
Sinclair Dr NN8 129 B6
Sir Christopher Hatton Sch NN8 130 A6
Sir Georges La OX17 230 A4
Sir John Brown Ct NN16 72 A2
Sir John Pascoe Way NN5 158 C8
Sissinghurst Dr NN14 76 F2
Siward View NN5 140 D2
Six Cotts MK18 226 E5
Sixth St NN13 238 E7
Six Willows NN9 110 B3
Skagerrak Cl NN18 36 A2
Skawle Ct NN3 142 F3
Skeffington Cl NN14 54 A2
Skegness Wlk NN18 36 C4
Skelton Wlk 4 NN3 142 C4
Sketty Cl NN4 160 C1
Skiddaw Wlk NN3 142 C4
Skinner Ave NN5 158 D5
Skinner's Hill NN10 132 B2
Skin Yard La NN6 121 B4
Skippon Cl LE16 31 D2
Skippons Ct NN6 85 B8
Skipton Cl
Corby NN18 36 B4
Northampton NN4 175 B7
Skittle Alley OX17 237 C7
Skye Rd NN17 36 B8
Slade Cl NN14 54 B3
Slade Cres NN15 91 B7
Slade Hill NN13 234 D1
Slade Ho NN11 153 C8
Slade Leas OX17 220 B8
Sladeswell Ct 1 NN3 161 A8
Slade The
Daventry NN11 153 C8
Silverstone NN12 214 E5
Slade Valley Ave NN14 70 F7
SLAPTON 201 D2
Slapton Pre Prep Sch NN12 201 E2
Slate Drift PE9 1 E3
Slaters Cl NN10 132 D2
Slawston Rd
Medbourne LE16 18 E7
Welham LE16 17 F6
Slim Cl NN15 72 F1
Slips The NN9 110 E2
Slip The NN6 106 C2
SLIPTON 75 A3
Slipton La
Slipton NN14 75 A3
Sudborough NN14 56 C1
Sloe La NN14 89 C5
Smart's Cl NN13 233 D8
Smarts Est CV23 100 A3
Smith Cl NN7 177 A1
Smith Ct NN9 114 D5
Smitherway NN7 173 A8
Smithfield Pl NN9 114 D6
Smithland Ct NN12 202 D8
Smiths Ct NN4 159 D4
Smith St NN6 105 A1
Smiths Yd NN9 110 B3
Smithy The
Deanshanger MK19 228 E4
Northampton NN3 142 D1
Rushden NN10 132 B1
Smyth Cl LE16 31 E5
Smyth Ct NN3 142 E3
Snetterton Cl NN3 141 F4
Snowbell Sq 1 NN3 143 C2
Snowshill Cl 4 NN11 135 B7
Soane Cl NN8 129 F8
Soar Gn NN17 21 C1
Solly's Way NN12 203 C5
Somerford Rd NN8 129 E6
Somerset St NN1 159 E7
Somerton Ct NN18 36 A6
Somerville Ct OX17 230 D3
Somerville Rd
Brackley NN13 233 D8
Daventry NN11 153 B8
Sondes Cl PE8 41 E7
Sondes Rd NN17 22 E2
Sopwith Way NN11 135 B5
Sorrel Cl
Isham NN14 91 F1
Northampton NN4 175 E5
Sorrels The NN14 91 F1
Sotheby Rise NN3 143 D3
Soudan Ave NN13 233 E8
SOULDERN 237 E3
Sourton Pl NN11 135 D6
Southall Rd NN17 37 B6
Southampton Rd NN4 159 C3
Southam Rd CV47 166 D7
South Ave NN15 92 B3
South Bank NN13 234 B7
South Bridge Cl PE8 41 F4
Southbrook NN18 36 B3
Southbrook Jun & Inf Schs NN11 135 E1
South Cl
Braunston NN11 118 D1
Greatworth OX17 210 D1
Long Buckby NN6 121 B3
Rushden NN10 132 C1
South Copse NN4 175 B7
Southcourt NN3 142 C7
Southcrest NN4 158 F1
South End Jun & Inf Schs NN10 148 B8
Southfield Ave NN4 159 D3
Southfield Ct NN13 233 E6
Southfield Dr NN15 91 F4
Southfield Prim Sch NN13 233 E6
Southfield Rd
Gretton NN17 10 C1
Northampton NN5 158 B6
SOUTHFIELDS 143 A7
Southfields NN10 132 C1
Southfield Sch for Girls NN15 91 C7
South Fields Dr NN6 101 A5
South Folds Rd NN18 35 F1
Southgate Dr
Kettering NN15 72 D2
Towcester NN12 203 D5
South Gr NN10 148 B5
South Holme Ct NN3 142 E5
SOUTH KILWORTH 63 D8
South Kilworth CE Prim Sch LE17 63 C8
South Kilworth Rd NN6 64 B5
Southlands NN15 72 B1
Southleigh Gr LE16 31 D4
SOUTH LUFFENHAM 3 D8
South March NN11 153 D8
South Meadow View NN5 158 A6
South Oval NN5 140 F1
South Paddock Ct NN3 142 F4
South Pk NN10 132 B1
South Pl NN11 135 B1
South Portway Cl NN3 142 F6
South Priors Ct NN3 143 A3
South Rd
Clifton u D CV23 80 A5
Corby NN17 37 B6
Oundle PE8 42 A4
South St
Castlethorpe MK19 218 F5
Isham NN14 110 F8
Northampton NN1 159 F6
Weedon Bec NN7 155 C3
Wollaston NN29 146 D2
Woodford Halse NN11 184 C6
South Terr
Greens Norton NN12 202 E8
Northampton NN1 159 F6
South Vale NN7 179 A5
South View
Brixworth NN6 106 B1
Harpole NN7 157 E5
Nether Heyford NN7 156 B1
Roade NN7 191 D4
Whilton NN11 137 C6
South Way NN11 135 D1
SOUTHWICK 26 B5
Southwick Hall* PE8 26 C5
Southwood Hill NN4 159 A3
Southwood Ho NN8 130 A3
Sovereign Ct
Northampton NN3 142 F6
Rushden NN10 132 B3
Sovereign Pk LE16 31 F1
Sovereigns Ct NN16 72 C6
Sower Leys Rd NN18 36 C4
Spalding Rd NN18 36 C4
Spanslade Rd NN3 143 A1
Sparke Cl NN8 129 D7
Spartan Cl NN4 175 F5
Spectacle La NN3 125 F1
Speedwell Rd NN14 51 A4
Speke Dr NN11 135 C5
Spelhoe St NN3 142 F6
Spencelayh Cl NN8 129 F7
Spencer Bridge Rd NN5 159 A7
Spencer Cl
Bugbrooke NN7 173 A8
Chapel Brampton NN6 124 D1
Earls Barton NN6 144 F4
Evenley NN13 233 F2
Spencer Ct
Corby NN17 36 E5
Rushden NN10 132 A3
West Haddon NN6 102 C4
Spencer Gdns
Bozeat NN29 164 D2
Brackley NN13 233 E6
Spencer Haven NN5 159 A7
Spencer Par
Northampton NN1 159 D6
Stanwick NN9 113 F3
Spencer Rd
Irthlingborough NN9 112 E1
Long Buckby NN6 121 B3
Northampton NN1 159 E7
Rushden NN10 132 A3
Stanion NN14 37 E3
Wellingborough NN8 130 A1
Spencer St
Burton Latimer NN15 92 B2
Kettering NN16 72 B4
Market Harborough LE16 31 D3
Northampton NN5 159 A5
Raunds NN9 114 E6
Ringstead NN14 95 B3
Rothwell NN14 70 D8
Spencer Wlk NN18 36 E5
Spendlove Dr NN17 10 C1
Spenfield Ct NN3 142 F3
Spenser Cres NN11 135 A3
Spens Ho NN2 141 D5
Spey Cl NN8 129 C6
Spiers Dr NN13 233 D7
Spilsby Cl NN18 36 C4
Spinners Cotts OX17 210 F7
Spinney Bank OX17 230 F5
Spinney Cl
Boughton NN2 141 C7
Market Harborough LE16 31 C3
Rushden NN10 131 F2

Spi–Swe 263

Spinney Cl *continued*
Thrapston NN14 ... 76 D1
Towcester NN12 ... 203 C3
Warmington PE8 ... 28 B2
Spinney Dr
Kettering NN15 ... 91 D7
Northampton NN4 ... 175 C4
Spinney Gr NN17 ... 36 E7
SPINNEY HILL ... 142 A3
Spinney Hill NN11 ... 118 D1
Spinney Hill Cres NN3 ... 142 A4
Spinney Hill Rd
Northampton NN3 ... 142 A4
Olney MK46 ... 195 E3
Spinney La
Kettering NN15 ... 91 D7
Wellingborough NN8 ... 129 C2
Spinney Rd
Burton Latimer NN15 ... 92 C3
Irthlingborough NN15 ... 112 F2
Rushden NN10 ... 131 F1
Weldon NN17 ... 38 C7
Spinney Rise
Daventry NN11 ... 135 C1
Denford NN14 ... 95 C6
Spinney St NN9 ... 114 D6
Spinney Terr [8] NN9 ... 112 F2
Spinney The NN4 ... 175 E2
Spinney Way NN3 ... 142 A5
Sponne House Sh Ctr NN12 ... 203 C6
Sponne Sch Tech Coll NN12 ... 203 B6
Sponnes Rd NN12 ... 203 C5
Spotted Cow La NN11 ... 136 D5
SPRATTON ... 105 C1
Spratton CE Prim Sch NN6 ... 105 B1
Spratton Hall Sch NN6 ... 105 B1
Spratton Rd NN6 ... 106 A2
Spring Bank LE16 ... 18 F7
Springbanks Way [2] NN4 ... 175 B8
Spring Cl
Boughton NN2 ... 125 C1
Brackley NN13 ... 233 F7
Daventry NN11 ... 153 C8
Hollowell NN6 ... 104 B4
Irthlingborough NN9 ... 112 F2
Kilsby CV23 ... 100 A2
Springer Straight [1] NN4 ... 158 F3
Springfield
Flore NN7 ... 155 E5
Northampton NN4 ... 175 E7
Springfield Ave NN14 ... 76 E3
Springfield Cl NN15 ... 91 C7
Springfield Ct
[1] Market Harborough LE16 ... 31 F2
Northampton NN3 ... 142 F3
Springfield Gdns MK19 ... 228 E4
Springfield Gr NN17 ... 36 F8
Springfield Rd
Kettering NN15 ... 91 C7
Olney MK46 ... 195 F4
Oundle PE8 ... 41 F7
Rushden NN10 ... 148 D8
Walgrave NN6 ... 107 F5
Wilbarston LE16 ... 34 C4
Springfields NN12 ... 203 B5
Springfield St LE16 ... 31 F2
Springfield Way NN13 ... 233 E8
Spring Gdns
Burton Latimer NN15 ... 92 C3
Earls Barton NN6 ... 144 F4
Higham Ferrers NN10 ... 132 B6
Northampton NN1 ... 159 D5
Rothwell NN14 ... 70 D7
Towcester NN12 ... 203 D5
Wellingborough NN8 ... 129 F4
Springhill Gdns LE16 ... 31 C2
Springhill Hos CV22 ... 98 C8
Spring Ho [2] NN8 ... 129 F4
Spring La
Alderton NN12 ... 204 F2
Flore NN7 ... 155 E5
Northampton NN1 ... 159 B6
Olney MK46 ... 195 F3
[8] Wellingborough NN8 ... 130 A4
Spring Lane Prim Sch NN1 ... 159 B6
SPRING PARK ... 141 A5
Spring Rise NN15 ... 91 C7
Spring St [4] NN9 ... 112 F2
Springs The
Northampton NN4 ... 159 A3
Swinford LE17 ... 62 C4
Spring Terr
Irthlingborough NN9 ... 112 F2
Medbourne LE16 ... 19 A6
Springwell Cl NN4 ... 175 F3
Springwood Ct NN3 ... 142 F5
Spruce Ct
Kettering NN16 ... 72 C4
Northampton NN3 ... 142 E3
Spurlings PE8 ... 41 F5
Spyglass Hill NN4 ... 175 B6
Square The
Aynho OX17 ... 237 C7
Earls Barton NN6 ... 144 E4
Greatworth OX17 ... 210 E1
Square The *continued*
Holdenby NN6 ... 123 D4
Kings Sutton OX17 ... 230 F5
Market Harborough LE16 .. 31 E3
Moreton Pinkney NN11 ... 199 C7
Northampton NN4 ... 175 F3
Pitsford NN6 ... 125 C4
Raunds NN9 ... 114 D6
South Luffenham LE15 ... 3 D8
Thorpe Malsor NN14 ... 71 B3
Welford NN6 ... 64 E6
Yardley Hastings NN7 ... 179 A6
Squire Cl NN18 ... 36 A4
Squires Wlk NN3 ... 142 B3
Squirrel Cl NN4 ... 175 F2
Squirrel La NN5 ... 158 C7
Stable Ct
Brackley NN13 ... 233 F7
[4] Northampton NN2 ... 141 C3
Pitsford NN6 ... 125 D4
Stablegate Way LE16 ... 32 A3
Stable Hill NN14 ... 55 F7
Stable Mews NN29 ... 147 D1
Stables La NN6 ... 140 B8
Stables The PE8 ... 8 A3
Stable Yd
Loddington NN14 ... 70 C1
Thenford OX17 ... 220 E8
Stadtpeine Cl NN17 ... 36 C7
Staffa Wlk NN17 ... 36 B8
Stafford Cl NN11 ... 135 D5
Stafford Pl NN3 ... 141 F7
Stafford Rd NN17 ... 22 C8
Staffords La NN6 ... 102 B4
Stagshaw Cl [2] NN4 ... 175 C8
Staines Cl NN5 ... 158 E6
Stalbridge Wlk NN18 ... 36 A6
Stamford Cl LE16 ... 31 E2
Stamford La PE8 ... 28 B3
Stamford Rd
Corby NN14, NN18, NN17 ... 37 E4
Deenethorpe NN17 ... 23 E2
Duddington PE9 ... 5 C7
Easton o t H PE9 ... 2 B5
Geddington, Little Oakley NN14 ... 54 B5
Geddington NN14 ... 54 A1
Kettering NN16 ... 72 E5
Ketton PE9 ... 1 C8
South Luffenham LE15 ... 3 D7
Weldon NN17 ... 38 A6
Stamford Wlk NN18 ... 36 C4
Stanbridge Ct MK11 ... 229 F5
Standens Barn Prim Sch NN3 ... 160 F8
Standens Barn Rd NN3 ... 142 F1
Standing Stones NN3 ... 143 B3
Standside NN5 ... 158 F6
Stanfield Rd NN5 ... 158 C6
Stanford Cl NN6 ... 84 A5
Stanford Hall* LE17 ... 62 F3
STANFORD ON AVON ... 62 F2
Stanford Rd
Cold Ashby NN6 ... 84 A5
Swinford LE17 ... 62 D3
Stanford Way NN4 ... 175 C8
Stanhill Row NN12 ... 201 F1
Stanhope Rd NN2 ... 141 D1
Stanier Cl NN16 ... 72 A3
Stanier Rd NN17 ... 21 F1
STANION ... 37 F2
Stanion CE Prim Sch NN14 ... 37 E3
Stanion La
Corby NN18 ... 37 B6
Corby NN18 ... 37 D5
Stanion Rd NN14 ... 38 C1
Stanley Boddington Ct NN15 ... 91 C8
Stanley Ct MK46 ... 195 F3
Stanley Mews [5] NN8 ... 130 B5
Stanley Rd
Northampton NN5 ... 159 A6
Wellingborough NN8 ... 130 B5
Stanley St
Northampton NN2 ... 159 C8
Rothwell NN14 ... 70 E7
Stanley Way NN11 ... 135 C5
Stannard Way NN6 ... 106 B2
Stanton Ave NN3 ... 142 A4
Stanton Cl
Desborough NN14 ... 51 B4
Wellingborough NN8 ... 111 B1
Stanway Cl LE16 ... 32 A3
Stanwell Cl OX17 ... 209 A1
Stanwell Dr OX17 ... 209 A1
Stanwell Lea OX17 ... 209 A2
Stanwell Way NN8 ... 129 C3
STANWICK ... 113 E4
Stanwick Prim Sch NN9 ... 114 A3
Stanwick Rd
Higham Ferrers NN10 ... 132 C8
Raunds NN9 ... 114 B4
Star Cnr CV23 ... 99 C1
Starmers La NN7 ... 157 D4
Starmer's Yd NN5 ... 158 C7
Starvold Cl NN6 ... 105 A1
Station Cl
Daventry NN11 ... 135 D2
Ecton NN3 ... 143 C1
Long Buckby NN6 ... 121 B3
Station Cotts NN18 ... 53 D7
Station Ct NN11 ... 184 C6
Station Gdns NN11 ... 184 C6
Station Mews NN3 ... 143 C2
Station Rd
Aynho OX15, OX17 ... 237 A6
Blisworth NN7 ... 174 B2
Brixworth NN6 ... 106 A4
Burton Latimer NN15 ... 92 A2
Castlethorpe MK19 ... 218 F5
Clifton OX17 ... 236 F5
Cogenhoe NN7 ... 161 E6
Corby NN17 ... 37 A6
Cottesbrooke NN6 ... 105 A7
Desborough NN14 ... 51 A4
Earls Barton NN6 ... 144 E3
Earls Barton NN6 ... 144 F1
Finedon NN9 ... 111 D6
Great Bowden LE16 ... 32 A6
Gretton NN17 ... 10 B1
Helmdon NN13 ... 211 F4
Husbands Bosworth LE17 ... 45 D3
Irchester MK44 ... 147 C8
Irthlingborough NN9 ... 113 A2
Kettering NN15 ... 72 B1
Ketton PE9 ... 1 A5
King's Cliffe PE8 ... 13 F7
Lilbourne CV23 ... 81 A7
Little Houghton NN7 ... 161 C5
Long Buckby NN6 ... 121 A2
Morcott LE15 ... 3 B6
Nassington PE8 ... 15 F5
Northampton NN3 ... 143 C1
North Kilworth LE17 ... 45 A4
Oundle PE8 ... 42 A6
Raunds NN9 ... 115 B7
Ringstead NN14 ... 94 F2
Rushden NN10 ... 132 A3
Rushton NN14 ... 52 C2
Theddingworth LE17 ... 46 D8
Watford NN6 ... 120 C5
Welton NN11 ... 119 E1
West Haddon NN6 ... 102 B4
Woodford Halse NN11 ... 184 C6
Station Yard Ind Est OX17 ... 230 A2
Stavanger Cl NN18 ... 36 A2
Staveley Way NN6 ... 106 C3
STAVERTON ... 152 C7
Staverton CE Prim Sch NN11 ... 152 C7
Staverton Leys CV22 ... 98 A7
Staverton Rd NN11 ... 135 B1
Steadfold La PE9 ... 1 C8
Steane View NN13 ... 233 D7
Steel Cl NN14 ... 76 D1
Steele Rd NN8 ... 129 D4
Steel Rd NN17 ... 22 E2
Steene St NN5 ... 159 A6
Stefen Way NN11 ... 153 B7
Stenhouse Cl NN6 ... 121 D4
Stenson St NN5 ... 159 A6
Stent Mews NN4 ... 175 F8
Stephen Bennett Cl NN5 ... 158 C8
Stephenson Cl NN11 ... 134 F4
Stephenson Ct
Kilsby CV23 ... 99 F2
Roade NN7 ... 191 C4
Stephenson Way NN17 ... 37 A8
Sterling Bsns Pk NN4 ... 160 C2
Sterling Ct NN14 ... 70 C1
Sterndale Cl NN14 ... 50 E4
Stevens Ct NN6 ... 144 F5
Stevenson St NN4 ... 159 C2
Stevens St LE16 ... 31 D3
Stewart Cl NN3 ... 126 B2
Stewart Dr NN12 ... 214 D4
Stewarts Rd NN8 ... 130 B8
Steyning Cl NN18 ... 36 A5
STIBBINGTON ... 8 D2
Stilebrook Rd MK46 ... 195 F6
Stile Cl NN11 ... 135 A2
Stimpson Ave NN1 ... 159 F7
Stimpson Avenue Prim Sch NN1 ... 159 F7
Stinford Leys LE16 ... 32 B3
Stirling Cl NN18 ... 36 E2
Stirling St NN5 ... 158 F6
Stirrup Ho NN5 ... 159 B5
Stitchman Ho [8] NN5 ... 159 A6
Stockbridge Rd NN17 ... 22 A1
Stocken Cl MK46 ... 195 E4
Stockerston La LE16 ... 20 D8
Stockholme Cl NN18 ... 36 A2
Stocking Cl NN7 ... 192 D1
Stocking Green Cl MK19 ... 207 A3
Stockley St [6] NN1 ... 159 E6
Stockmead Rd NN3 ... 161 A8
Stocks Gn PE8 ... 28 C8
Stocks Hill
Finedon NN9 ... 111 E4
[8] Moulton NN3 ... 126 C1
Silverstone NN12 ... 214 D5
Stock's Hill PE9 ... 1 A5
Stock's La NN17 ... 37 B6
Stocks The MK19 ... 218 E2
Stockwell Ave NN4 ... 175 D5
Stockwell Cl LE16 ... 32 B3
Stockwell La
Hellidon NN11 ... 151 D1
Sulgrave OX17 ... 210 F8
Stockwell Rd NN7 ... 174 F4
Stockwell Way NN7 ... 174 F4
Stockwood Dr NN17 ... 21 F1
STOKE ALBANY ... 34 A4
Stoke Albany Rd LE16 ... 18 E1
STOKE BRUERNE ... 205 B8
Stoke Bruerne CE Prim Sch NN12 ... 205 A8
STOKE DOYLE ... 41 C1
Stoke Doyle Rd PE8 ... 41 D4
Stoke Firs Cl NN4 ... 175 F6
Stoke Hill
Oundle PE8 ... 41 F5
Stoke Albany LE16 ... 34 A4
Stoke Rd
Ashton NN7 ... 205 E8
Blisworth NN7 ... 190 E4
Desborough NN14 ... 51 A7
Lyddington LE15 ... 9 C7
Stokes Rd NN18 ... 36 D4
Stonebridge Ct NN3 ... 142 F3
Stone Circle Rd NN3 ... 142 E7
Stone Cl
Wellingborough NN8 ... 129 F8
Wollaston NN29 ... 146 D2
Stone Hill Ct NN3 ... 142 E4
Stonehill Way NN6 ... 125 B8
Stonehouse Ct CV23 ... 81 A6
Stone House Mews NN6 ... 84 E4
Stonehurst Cl NN7 ... 192 C1
Stonelea Rd NN6 ... 127 D3
Stoneleigh Chase NN5 ... 140 D1
Stonemasons Cl MK46 ... 195 F3
Stone Pit Cl MK46 ... 195 E3
Stonepit Dr LE16 ... 20 D1
Stoneway
Badby NN11 ... 152 F2
Hartwell NN7 ... 192 E2
Stone Way NN5 ... 158 B7
Stonewold Cl NN2 ... 141 A4
Stoney Fields NN14 ... 89 B4
Stoneyhurst NN4 ... 158 F3
Stoney Piece Cl NN29 ... 164 C2
Stony Hill NN12 ... 216 C8
STONY STRATFORD ... 229 E5
Stony Stratford Nature Reserve* MK11 ... 229 D7
Stook The NN11 ... 135 C6
Storefield Cotts NN14 ... 53 A4
Stornoway Rd NN17 ... 21 C1
Stotfold Ct MK11 ... 229 E4
Stourhead Dr NN4 ... 175 C7
Stour Rd
Corby NN17 ... 21 D1
Northampton NN5 ... 158 F6
Stour The NN11 ... 153 A8
Stourton Cl NN8 ... 129 D1
Stow Cl NN8 ... 129 D1
Stowe Wlk NN3 ... 141 F5
Stradlers Cl NN4 ... 175 E5
Stratfield Way NN15 ... 91 D5
Stratford Arc MK11 ... 229 D5
Stratford Dr NN4 ... 175 D6
Stratford Rd
Cosgrove MK19 ... 218 D1
Deanshanger MK19 ... 228 F4
Roade NN7 ... 191 C3
Stony Stratford MK12 ... 229 F6
Strathay Wlk NN17 ... 21 C1
Strath Cl CV21 ... 99 A7
Stratton Cl
Market Harborough LE16 ... 31 D1
Northampton NN3 ... 160 D7
Stratton Dr NN13 ... 233 D7
Strawberry Hill NN3 ... 143 C3
Strawberry Hill Cotts MK44 ... 149 F2
Straws Cl NN9 ... 112 E1
Stream Bank Cl NN8 ... 129 D4
Streambank Rd NN3 ... 142 E6
Streatfield Rd NN5 ... 159 A8
Streather Ct NN9 ... 114 C5
Streather Dr NN17 ... 36 E7
Streeton Way NN6 ... 144 E5
Street The LE15 ... 3 E8
Strelley Ave NN3 ... 160 F8
Stringer's Hill NN14 ... 90 F2
STRIXTON ... 164 C8
Strixton Manor Bsns Ctr NN29 ... 164 C8
Strode Rd NN8 ... 130 B5
Stronglands Ct PE8 ... 41 F6
Stuart Cl
Kettering NN16 ... 72 C2
Northampton NN4 ... 174 F7
Stuart Cres LE16 ... 30 F7
Stuart Rd
Brackley NN13 ... 233 E8
Corby NN17 ... 36 F6
Market Harborough LE16 .. 31 E2
Stubbing End NN18 ... 53 B8
Stubble Cl NN2 ... 141 A6
Stubbs Cl NN8 ... 129 F7
Stubbs La NN15 ... 92 A8
Stubbs Rd NN11 ... 170 B7
STUCHBURY ... 211 A5
Studfall Ave NN17 ... 36 E8
Studfall Ct NN17 ... 36 E7
Studfall Inf Sch NN17 ... 36 E8
Studfall Jun Sch NN17 ... 36 D8
Stud Farm Cl OX17 ... 196 E1
Studland Rd NN2 ... 141 B1
Sturdee Cl NN11 ... 135 D1
Sturgess Ct NN15 ... 92 C2
Sturminster Way NN18 ... 36 A6
Sturton Wlk NN18 ... 36 C4
Styles Pl NN6 ... 82 B3
SUDBOROUGH ... 56 C1
Sudborough Rd
Brigstock NN14 ... 56 A4
Sudborough Rd *continued*
Slipton NN14 ... 75 A6
Suffolk Pl NN15 ... 91 D6
SULBY ... 65 B8
Sulby Hall Old Dr NN6 ... 46 B1
Sulby Rd
Northampton NN3 ... 142 E6
Welford NN6 ... 65 A8
Sulehay Rd PE8 ... 7 C1
SULGRAVE ... 210 F8
Sulgrave Dr NN17 ... 36 C7
Sulgrave Manor* OX17 ... 211 A8
Sulgrave Rd
Culworth OX17 ... 198 D1
Northampton NN5 ... 158 F7
Summerfield Rd NN15 ... 91 C8
Summerfields NN4 ... 158 E2
Summerhouse Rd NN3 ... 142 A6
Summerlee Mews NN9 ... 111 F4
Summerlee Rd NN9 ... 111 F4
Summer Leys Nature Res* NN29 ... 145 F4
Summers Cl OX17 ... 230 A5
Summers Way LE16 ... 31 D2
Summit Rise NN4 ... 175 D7
Sunderland St NN5 ... 159 A6
Sundew Ct NN4 ... 158 D1
Sun Hill NN14 ... 70 C7
Sunley Ct NN15 ... 91 C8
Sunningdale Cl NN2 ... 141 E2
Sunningdale Dr
Daventry NN11 ... 135 E3
Rushden NN10 ... 148 D8
Sunny Bank
Arthingworth LE16 ... 68 C7
Holcot NN6 ... 126 E8
SUNNYSIDE ... 141 D5
Sunnyside
Ecton NN6 ... 143 F4
Northampton NN4 ... 175 E6
Woodford NN14 ... 94 D7
Sunny Side NN6 ... 144 D4
Sunnyside Prim Sch NN2 ... 141 D6
Sunny View NN7 ... 179 B6
Sunset Ct NN3 ... 143 A2
Sun Yd NN12 ... 203 D5
Surfleet Cl NN18 ... 36 C4
Surrey Cl NN17 ... 36 C6
Surrey Rd NN15 ... 91 D6
Surtees Way NN12 ... 203 C7
Sussex Cl NN5 ... 158 C6
Sussex Ct [6] NN1 ... 159 C6
Sussex Pl NN10 ... 132 B4
Sussex Rd NN15 ... 91 C6
Sutcliffe Rd PE8 ... 7 D8
Sutherland Rd NN18 ... 36 D4
SUTTON ... 8 F2
Sutton Acre NN7 ... 155 E5
SUTTON BASSETT ... 18 A1
Sutton Cl
Aston le W NN11 ... 182 F3
Northampton NN2 ... 141 D6
Sutton Ct LE16 ... 31 E1
Sutton Heath Rd PE5, PE8, PE9 ... 8 D6
Sutton Rd
Great Bowden LE16 ... 32 B6
Oundle PE8 ... 42 B4
Sutton Bassett LE16 ... 32 E7
Weston by W LE16 ... 18 B3
Sutton St NN7 ... 155 F5
Sutton's Wlk NN12 ... 188 F7
Swain Ct NN3 ... 142 E3
Swale Cl
Corby NN17 ... 21 D1
Roade NN7 ... 191 C3
Swale Dr
Northampton NN5 ... 140 F3
Wellingborough NN8 ... 129 C6
Swallow Cl
Brackley NN13 ... 222 E1
Kettering NN15 ... 92 B6
Northampton NN4 ... 175 A7
Swallow Dr NN10 ... 132 B5
Swanage Ct NN18 ... 36 A6
Swan Ave NN14 ... 55 E8
Swan Cl
Brackley NN13 ... 222 D2
Burton Latimer NN15 ... 92 A2
Hinton NN11 ... 184 B6
Middleton Cheney OX17 ... 219 F8
Thrapston NN14 ... 76 D3
Swan Ct NN6 ... 87 D1
Swanhill PE8 ... 8 A4
Swann Dale NN11 ... 135 D1
Swann Dale Cl NN11 ... 135 D1
Swansea Cres NN5 ... 159 A7
Swansea Rd NN5 ... 159 A8
Swansgate Ctr The [9] NN8 ... 130 A4
Swans La [6] NN8 ... 130 A4
Swanspool Ct NN8 ... 130 A4
Swanspool Par NN8 ... 130 A3
Swan St NN1 ... 159 D5
Swans Way NN10 ... 132 C8
Swan Terr MK11 ... 229 D5
Swan Valley Way NN4 ... 174 C8
Swedish Hos NN7 ... 139 D4
Sweetacre Cl NN7 ... 163 D4

Swift Cl NN4 175 F3
Swift Way NN13 222 E1
Swinburne Cl NN16 72 C6
Swinburne Rd NN8 129 B4
Swinfen's Yd MK11 229 D5
SWINFORD 62 C3
Swinford CE Prim Sch LE17 62 B4
Swinford Cnr LE17 62 A8
Swinford Hollow NN3 161 A8
Swinford Rd LE17 62 A8
Swingbridge St LE16 30 E8
Swinnertons La NN6 82 B4
Swinneyford Rd NN12 203 C5
Swyncombe Gn NN7 192 C1
Sycamore Ave NN11 184 B6
Sycamore Cl
Corby NN17 21 E1
Daventry NN11 135 C5
Kettering NN16 72 D4
Rushden NN10 132 C2
Towcester NN12 203 C4
Sycamore Dr
Desborough NN14 51 D2
Sywell NN6 143 D8
Sycamore Rd
Greens Norton NN12 202 E8
Northampton NN5 158 C7
Sycamores The LE17 63 D8
Sycamore Yd NN12 187 B1
Sydenham Cl OX17 230 B4
Sydney St NN16 72 D2
Syers Green Cl NN6 121 A4
Syers Green La NN6 121 A4
Sykes Ct NN17 37 A8
Syke The NN14 55 F7
Syles Cl NN6 102 B5
Sylmond Gdns NN10 148 A7
Sylvanus Ho NN8 129 D5
Symington St NN5 159 A7
Symington Way LE16 31 E3
SYRESHAM 224 B8
Syresham St James CE Prim Sch NN13 224 C7
Syresham Way NN2 141 C5
SYWELL 127 D3
Sywell Airport Bsns Pk NN6 127 F4
Sywell Ave NN8 129 D6
Sywell CE Prim Sch NN6 127 D3
Sywell Ctry Pk* NN6 144 A7
Sywell Rd
Holcot NN6 126 F8
Mears Ashby NN6 128 A1
Overstone NN6 127 B1
Wellingborough NN8 129 C6
Sywell Way NN8 129 D6


## T


Taborley Cl NN3 142 E1
Tadcaster Cl NN11 135 C6
Taggies Yd NN14 109 F5
Tailby Ave NN16 72 A5
Tainty Cl NN9 111 E5
Talan Rise NN3 143 C5
Talavera Cl NN11 135 B1
Talavera Way NN3 142 D6
Talbot Rd
Northampton NN1 159 E7
Rushden NN10 131 F1
Wellingborough NN8 130 C5
Talbot Rd N NN8 130 C5
Talbots Hyde MK46 195 E4
Talbot Yd LE16 31 E3
Tall Trees Cl NN4 174 F8
Tallyfield End NN4 158 E3
Tally-Ho Cotts PE8 60 E7
Tamar Cl NN5 140 E2
Tamar Gn NN17 21 D1
Tamarisk Dr NN3 142 C6
Tamar Sq NN11 135 A1
Tancred Cl 1 NN4 175 E7
Taney Ct PE8 42 A5
Tanfield La NN1 160 C5
Tanfields Gr NN17 36 E8
Tanglewood NN4 175 D4
Tanner's La NN16 72 B2
Tanner St NN1 159 C5
Tannery The LE15 4 A5
Tann Rd NN9 111 F5
Tanser Cott LE17 63 C8
TANSOR 27 D2
Tansor Cl NN17 36 B8
Tansy Cl NN4 158 D1
Tantree Way NN6 106 C2
Tapeley Gdns NN4 175 D7
Taper Way NN11 135 B3
Tarn Croft NN3 142 B3
Tarragon Way NN4 175 D6
Tarrant Cl NN3 126 D1
Tarrant Way NN3 126 D1
Tarrys End NN6 82 B4
Tasman Way NN14 70 E6
Tate Gr NN4 175 F7
TATHALL END 207 D2
Tattersall Cl NN3 142 A5
Taunton Ave
Corby NN18 36 B6
Northampton NN3 160 C7
Tavern La 1 NN11 135 C1
Tavern Wlk NN18 36 A4
Tavistock Cl 3 NN3 143 D2
Tavistock Rd NN15 92 A5
Tavistock Sq NN18 36 F4
Tay Cl NN17 21 D1
Taylor Ave NN3 142 C1
Taylor Cl NN8 129 C7
Taylors Gn PE8 28 B2
Teal Cl
Burton Latimer NN15 91 F2
Daventry NN11 135 C4
Higham Ferrers NN10 132 C8
Northampton NN4 174 E8
Teal La NN8 130 B7
Teasel Cl NN10 148 C7
Teasel Dr NN14 51 A4
Tebbitt Cl NN6 121 B4
Tebbutt Cl NN14 70 F7
Tebbutt's Yd NN6 144 E4
Tees Cl NN8 129 C6
Teesdale NN3 142 F6
Teesdale Rd NN17 36 D7
TEETON 104 D1
Teeton La NN6 104 E3
Teeton Rd
Guilsborough NN6 103 F5
Ravensthorpe NN6 103 E1
Telfords La NN17 37 A8
Telford Way
Kettering NN16 71 F4
Northampton NN5 158 D4
Temperance Terr MK11 229 C6
Templar Dr NN2 141 A4
Templar Rd NN15 72 F1
Temple Bar 21 NN1 159 C7
Temple Ct NN10 132 B7
Tenbury Way NN14 70 F7
Tenby Rd NN5 159 A8
Ten Cotts
Church Brampton NN6 140 B8
Wormleighton CV47 181 B8
Tenlands OX17 219 F8
Tennyson Cl
3 Northampton NN5 158 F8
Towcester NN12 203 B5
Tennyson Dr NN17 36 D8
Tennyson Rd
Daventry NN11 135 B3
Kettering NN16 72 B2
Rothwell NN14 70 C7
Rushden NN10 131 F2
Wellingborough NN8 129 D3
Tennyson Road Inf Sch NN10 131 F2
Ten Pines NN3 142 F7
Tenter Cl NN10 132 B5
Tenter La NN9 111 F5
Tenter Rd NN3 141 F7
Tentsmuir Cl NN16 72 A6
Terrace The NN13 224 C5
Terrington Cl NN13 233 E7
Test Gn NN17 21 D1
Tettenhall Cl NN18 36 A1
Teviot Cl
Corby NN17 21 D1
Northampton NN5 140 E2
Tewkesbury Cl
Northampton NN4 159 A1
Wellingborough NN8 129 D6
Tewkesbury Dr NN10 148 D8
TEW'S END 216 C8
Tews End La NN12 216 C8
Thackers Cl PE8 8 A4
Thames Ct NN15 92 B2
Thames Rd
Daventry NN11 135 A1
Northampton NN4 175 C7
Wellingborough NN8 129 C6
Thames Rise NN16 72 A4
Thames Wlk NN17 21 D1
Thatch Meadow Dr LE16 32 B3
Thatchwell Ct NN3 160 F8
THE ARBOURS 142 C3
Theatre Ct NN1 159 D5
Thebwell Rd 3 NN3 142 F1
THEDDINGWORTH 46 C8
Theddingworth Rd
Husbands Bosworth LE17 46 A6
Lubenham LE16 30 C2
Marston Trussell LE16 47 B8
THENFORD 220 E8
Thenford Rd OX17 209 D1
Thenford St NN1 159 E6
Thetford Cl NN18 36 B1
Third Ave NN8 129 D3
Third St NN13 238 E6
Thirlestane Cres NN4 159 B3
Thirlestane Rd NN4 159 B3
Thirlmere NN8 129 C5
Thirlmere Ave NN3 142 C3
Thirlmere Cl
Daventry NN11 135 A2
Kettering NN16 71 E3
Thirlmere Flats NN16 71 E3
Thirsk Rd NN18 36 C5
Thistle Ct 3 NN4 159 A3
Thistle Dr NN14 51 A5
Thistleholme Cl NN2 141 E3
Thoday Cl NN14 90 A3
Thomas Becket RC Sch NN3 142 B5
Thomas Chapman Gr NN4 159 C4
Thomas Cl
Byfield NN11 183 D6
Thomas Cl *continued*
Corby NN18 36 D4
Crick NN6 101 A6
Thomas Crewe Cl NN13 233 F7
Thomas Flawn Rd NN9 131 D8
Thomas Rd NN15 91 C7
Thomas Rippin Cl NN14 54 A2
Thomas St
Northampton NN1 159 D7
Wellingborough NN8 130 B5
Thomas Webb Cl 10 NN11 135 C2
Thompson Cl NN5 158 A6
Thompson Way NN15 90 F8
Thorburn Rd NN3 160 E8
Thoresby Ct NN18 36 C5
Thornapple Cl NN3 143 C4
Thornborough Cl LE16 32 A2
Thornbridge Cl NN10 132 A1
THORNBY 84 E4
Thornby Dr NN2 141 B3
Thornby Rd
Cold Ashby NN6 84 B5
Naseby NN6 85 B8
Thorn Cl NN16 72 B6
Thorne Ct NN18 36 C5
Thornfield NN3 143 C4
Thorngate St NN16 72 C2
THORNHAUGH 7 F5
Thornhill OX17 208 F4
Thorn Hill NN4 159 A3
Thornlea Croft MK46 195 F3
THORNTON 235 C4
Thornton Cl
Crick NN6 101 A6
Flore NN7 155 F5
Newnham NN11 153 D3
Thornton Coll MK17 235 C5
Thornton Park Farm MK17 235 D4
Thornton Rd
Northampton NN2 141 B1
Thornton MK17 235 F2
Thoroughsale Rd NN17 36 E7
THORPE BY WATER 10 A6
Thorpe Cl
Banbury OX16 219 A6
Wellingborough NN8 129 C5
Thorpe Ct NN14 77 C7
Thorpe Dr OX16 219 A6
THORPE LANGTON 17 A5
Thorpe Langton Rd LE16 17 D6
THORPE MALSOR 71 B3
THORPE MANDEVILLE 210 B7
Thorpe Rd
Chacombe OX17 208 E4
Earls Barton NN6 144 E2
Lyddington LE15 9 D6
Northampton NN4 159 C3
Thorpe Waterville NN14 77 A8
Upper Wardington OX17 208 F8
Thorpe St NN9 114 D5
THORPE UNDERWOOD 69 C7
Thorpeville NN3 142 D7
THORPE WATERVILLE 77 C8
Thorplands Prim Sch NN3 142 E5
Thor Wlk NN18 36 A2
THRAPSTON 76 E1
Thrapston Prim Sch NN14 76 D1
Thrapston Rd
Finedon NN9, NN14 93 C2
Woodford NN14 94 D8
Three Shires Hospl NN1 159 F5
Thrift Mews 13 NN1 159 F6
Thrift St
Higham Ferrers NN10 132 B5
Irchester NN29 147 A7
Wollaston NN29 146 D2
Thrupp Bridge NN4 176 A6
Thrush La NN8 130 B6
Thruxton Dr NN3 141 F4
Thurburn Cl NN14 90 B5
THURNING 60 D2
Thurning Rd PE8, PE28 79 F7
Thursby Rd NN1 160 B7
Thurso Wlk NN17 21 D1
Thurspit Pl 8 NN3 143 D2
Thurston Dr NN15 91 A8
Thyme Ct NN3 142 E3
Tibbs Way NN7 173 A6
Tideswell Cl
Desborough NN14 50 E4
Northampton NN4 174 F8
Tiffany Gdns NN4 175 C6
TIFFIELD 189 D4
Tiffield CE Prim Sch NN12 189 D3
Tiffield Rd NN7 189 E8
Tilbury Rd NN6 122 C5
Tilbury Rise NN6 122 C5
Tilley Hill Cl PE8 41 E7
Timken Ho 3 NN11 135 A4
Timken Lo NN11 135 A4
Timken Way NN11 135 A4
Timor Ct MK11 229 D6
Timpson Cl NN16 72 C5
Timson Cl LE16 31 D5
Tingdene Rd NN9 111 F5
Tinkers Cres NN6 128 B2
Tinsley Cl NN3 143 B3
Tintagel Cl NN10 132 D1
Tintern Ave NN5 159 A7
Tintern Ct NN15 91 F8
Tippings La LE15 3 F5
Tiptoe Cl NN3 143 C3
TITCHMARSH 77 D4
Titchmarsh CE Prim Sch NN14 77 C4
Tithe Barn Cl NN9 114 E7
Tithe Barn Rd NN8 130 A4
Tithe Barn Way NN4 174 B8
Tithe Cl
Holcot NN6 126 E8
Ringstead NN14 95 A3
Tithe La OX15, OX17 236 C6
Tithe Rd NN7 155 A2
Tithe Way NN7 191 D5
Titley Bawk Ave NN6 144 F6
Titty Ho NN9 114 C5
Tiverton Ave NN2 141 C7
TIXOVER 4 E5
Tixover Grange PE9 4 F8
Todd's Hill PE9 5 B6
Todmorden Cl NN18 36 C5
Tofts Cl NN14 77 D4
Tollbar NN10 132 B5
Toll Bar La PE28 97 B4
Toll Bar Rd NN14 76 B2
Toller Pl NN15 91 F6
Toller St NN16 72 C3
Tollgate Cl NN2 141 B2
Tollgate Pl NN18 37 B6
Tollgate Way NN5 158 D6
Tompson Cl NN11 118 C1
Toms Cl
Northampton NN4 175 C3
Theddingworth LE17 46 D8
Tonmead Rd NN3 142 E3
Top Cl NN14 76 F3
Top Dysons NN14 92 F7
Top End
Little Addington NN14 113 B7
Pytchley NN14 90 F2
Top Farm Ct NN11 184 B6
Top Farm La NN29 145 E7
Top Lo NN17 5 A1
Top Station Rd NN13 234 A8
Top Station Road Ind Est NN13 234 A8
Topwell Ct NN3 143 A1
Top Yard Farm LE16 31 F6
Torch Way LE16 48 F8
Tordoff Pl NN16 72 B2
Torksey Cl NN18 36 A1
Torridge Cl NN16 71 F4
Torridon Cl NN17 21 C1
Torrington Cres NN8 129 D6
Torrington Gn NN8 129 E6
Torrington Rd NN8 129 E6
Torville Cres NN15 91 A8
Totnes Cl NN18 36 F4
Toulouse Cl 11 NN4 175 E7
Touraine Cl NN5 139 F2
Tove La NN12 203 A6
Tovey Dr NN11 135 D1
TOWCESTER 203 B3
Towcester Cl NN18 36 E1
Towcester Dr NN12 217 B3
Towcester Inf Sch NN12 203 C5
Towcester Rd
Blisworth NN7 190 B6
Greens Norton NN12 188 E1
Litchborough NN12 171 C1
Milton Malsor NN7 174 E5
Northampton NN4 159 B2
Old Stratford MK19 229 B7
Silverstone NN12 214 E4
Towcester NN12 203 A8
Whittlebury NN12 215 C5
Tower Cl NN9 112 A4
Tower Ct
Lubenham LE16 30 F3
Northampton NN6 143 B7
Wollaston NN29 146 F3
Tower Field Sq NN3 143 A6
Tower Hill Cl NN4 158 E3
Tower Hill Rd NN18 36 A4
Tower Sq NN5 158 F6
Tower St NN1 159 C6
Town Cl NN9 110 C3
Town Cnr NN5 158 F6
Townley Way NN6 144 E5
Townsend
Hinton NN11 184 B6
Maidford NN12 186 D6
Towns End NN6 121 C4
Townsend Cl
Hanging Houghton NN6 106 C8
Wellingborough NN8 129 F4
Townsend Ct PE8 39 E7
Townsend La
Thorpe Mandeville OX17 209 F6
Upper Boddington NN11 182 B8
Townsend Leys NN10 132 B8
Townsend Rd NN6 107 F5
Townson Cl NN6 107 D7
Townwell La NN29 147 B8
Towrise OX17 210 F8
Towton Ct NN4 159 A1
Trafalgar Rd NN16 72 A2
Trafalgar Rd Ind Est NN16 72 A2
Trafalgar Way NN11 135 D1
Trafford Rd NN10 132 D2
Trailli La NN14 94 D6
Treen Cl NN14 76 F2
Treetops NN3 143 A5
Trefoil Cl NN10 148 C7
Trelawney NN8 129 B5
Trenery Way NN4 159 D4
Trengothal Ct NN13 223 D4
Trent Cl
Northampton NN5 140 F2
Wellingborough NN8 129 C6
Trent Cres NN15 92 B1
Trentham Cl NN4 175 C7
Trent Ho PE8 42 A6
Trent Rd
Corby NN17 21 D1
Kettering NN16 72 A5
Wittering PE8 7 D8
Trent Wlk NN11 135 A1
Tresham Gn NN5 140 D1
Tresham Inst
Corby NN17 36 E6
Kettering NN15 72 C1
Kettering NN15 91 D8
Tresham Inst (Wellingborough Campus) NN8 130 A5
Tresham St
Kettering NN16 72 C3
Rothwell NN14 70 D7
Trevithick Rd NN17 37 C8
Trevor Cl NN5 158 E7
Trevor Cres NN5 158 E7
Trimley Cl NN3 160 D6
Trinity Ave NN2 141 D1
Trinity CE Lower Sch NN14 76 F8
Trinity Cl
Daventry NN11 153 B8
Old Stratford MK19 229 B7
Trinity Ct NN14 70 C6
Trinity Ctr NN8 129 A7
Trinity Rd NN14 70 C6
Trinity Way OX17 230 D3
Trinity Wlk NN18 36 E4
Triumph Gdns NN5 139 F1
Trojan Ctr NN8 130 B8
Tromso Cl NN18 36 A2
Troon Cres NN8 129 C7
Troutbeck Wlk NN3 142 C4
Trussell Rd NN3 143 C1
Tudely Cl NN4 175 F7
Tudor Ct 4 NN16 72 C2
Tudor Gdns MK11 229 E4
Tudor Rd NN1, NN2 142 A2
Tudor Way
Brackley NN13 233 E8
Wellingborough NN8 129 E7
Tudor Wlk NN10 132 C3
Tulbrook Stones OX17 220 B7
Tulip Dr NN10 148 B7
Tungstone Way LE16 31 E1
Tunnel Hill Cotts NN4 159 A2
Tunwell La NN17 37 B7
Turnberry Ct NN8 129 C7
Turnberry La NN4 175 C5
Turnbrook Cl NN9 112 E3
Turnells Mill La NN8 130 A1
Turner Cl
Kettering NN15 92 A8
Rugby CV21 99 B8
Turner Rd
Corby NN18 36 E5
Wellingborough NN8 129 F7
Turners Ct NN4 175 D7
Turners Farm Cl NN6 108 C2
Turner St NN1 159 F7
Turners Yd PE8 41 F5
Turn Furlong NN2 141 A5
Turnpike Cl LE16 31 D5
Turvins Mdw CV47 166 D8
TURWESTON 234 C8
Turweston Manor NN13 234 C8
Turweston Rd NN13 223 A1
Tweed Cl
Burton Latimer NN15 92 B2
Daventry NN11 153 A8
Tweed Rd NN5 158 E6
Twickenham Ct 5 NN18 36 B5
Twigden Rd NN7 157 D3
Twistle The NN11 183 C7
Twitch Hill NN12 204 D8
TWYFORD 230 B5
Twyford Ave
Raunds NN9 114 C7
Twyford OX17 230 A6
Twyford Cl 7 NN3 161 A8
Twyford Gdns OX17 230 A6
Twyford Gr OX17 230 A6
Twyford Rd OX17 230 C7
TWYWELL 75 A1
Twywell Hills & Dales Nature Res* NN14 93 F8
Tyebeck Cl NN2 141 B3
Tyes Ct NN3 142 F3
Tyler Way NN14 76 E1
Tymecrosse Gdns LE16 31 D5
Tynan Cl NN15 92 A8
Tyne Cl NN8 129 C6

**Tyne Rd**
Corby NN17 ............. 21 D1
Daventry NN11 ......... 153 A8
Northampton NN5 ....... 158 E6
**Tyringham Cl** NN3 ...... 142 D1
**Tyrrell Way** NN12 ....... 203 C8
**Tyson Ctyd** NN18......... 37 E7
**Tythings The** OX17...... 208 F2

## U

**Uist Wlk** NN17 ........... 21 C1
**Ullswater Cl**
Higham Ferrers NN10..... 132 B8
Wellingborough NN8..... 129 C5
**Ullswater Rd** NN16....... 71 E2
**Underbank La** NN3....... 142 C6
**Underwood Rd** NN14..... 70 C7
**Union St**
Desborough NN14........ 51 B3
Finedon NN9 ........... 112 A5
Kettering NN16 .......... 72 A3
**Unity Cl** NN29........... 146 C3
Unity Coll NN2........... 141 D1
**Unity St** NN14 ........... 51 A2
Univ Coll Northampton
NN2.................... 141 D1
Univ of Leicester
(Northampton Ctr)
NN2.................... 159 C8
**Upland Rd** NN3 ......... 142 C2
**UPPER ASTROP** ......... 231 C7
**Upper Astrop Rd**
OX17 .................. 231 A5
**Upper Bath St** NN1...... 159 C6
**UPPER BENEFIELD** ....... 39 F7
**UPPER BODDINGTON**
......................... 182 D8
**UPPER CATESBY** ........ 151 F4
**Upper Cross St** 18
NN1 ................... 159 C6
**Upper Dane** NN14........ 50 E3
**Upperfield Gr** NN17...... 36 E8
**Upper George St**
NN10 .................. 132 C7
**Upper Glen Ave** NN7 .... 174 B2
**Upper Gn** NN11.......... 199 D7
**Upper Green Pl** LE16..... 32 A6
**UPPER HARLESTONE**
......................... 139 D4
**Upper Havelock St** 7
NN8 ................... 130 A5
**UPPER HEYFORD** ....... 156 D3
**Upper Higham La**
NN10 .................. 133 C3
**Upper High St** NN7...... 157 C7
**Upper Kings Ave**
NN10 .................. 132 C7
**Upper Mounts** NN1 ..... 159 D6
**Upper Park Ave** NN10 ... 131 F1
**Upper Priory St** 7
NN1 ................... 159 C7
**Upper Queen St**
NN10 .................. 132 C3
**Upper St** NN16........... 72 A2
**Upper Steeping** NN14 .... 51 B2
**UPPER STOWE** ......... 171 E6
**Upper Thrift St** NN1..... 159 F6
**UPPER WARDINGTON**
......................... 196 F1
**UPPER WEEDON** ........ 155 A2
**Uppingham Rd**
Caldecott LE16........... 9 B2
Corby NN17 ............. 36 A7
Medbourne LE16 ......... 19 A8
**Uppingham St** NN1 ..... 159 B7
**UPTON** ................ 158 C5
**Upton Cl** NN2........... 141 D6
**Upton Way** NN4, NN5 .... 158 D3
**Usher Ho** NN2 .......... 141 C5

## V

**Vale Cl** CV21............. 99 A8
**Valentine Way** NN3 ..... 143 C3
**Vale St** NN16 ............ 72 A3
**Vale The** NN1........... 141 F1
**Valley Cl** NN13.......... 234 A8
**Valley Cres**
Brackley NN13........... 234 A8
Northampton NN3 ....... 143 B1
**Valley End** NN12........ 172 D1
**Valley Rd**
Brackley NN13........... 234 A8
Northampton NN3 ....... 143 B1
Wellingborough NN8 ..... 129 F1
Weston by W LE16......... 18 B3
**Valley Rise**
Brackley NN13........... 233 F8
Desborough NN14......... 51 B2
**Valley Way** LE16 ......... 32 B4
**Valley Wlk** NN16 ......... 72 E2
**Vancouver Cl** NN18 ...... 36 B2
**Vantage Mdw** NN3....... 143 D3
**Vara Cl** NN18 ............ 36 B2
**Vardon Cl** NN8........... 129 C7
**Varley Cl** NN8 ........... 129 E8
**Vaughan Cl** LE16.......... 48 E8
**Vaux Rd** NN8 ............ 111 A1
**Velbert Ho** NN17.......... 21 E1
**Velocette Way** NN5 ...... 140 A1
**Venture Cl** NN17.......... 22 F1
**Verdant Vale** 1 NN4 .... 175 D6
**Vermont Standing** 3
NN16 .................... 72 C3
**Vernier Cl** NN11 ........ 135 A3
**Vernon Ave** CV22 ........ 98 E8
**Vernon Cl** NN11......... 153 E8
Vernon Ct NN16 .......... 71 F5
**Vernon Ct** 10 NN1....... 159 F6
**Vernon Rd** NN12 ........ 203 D5
**Vernon St** NN1 ......... 159 F6
**Vernon Terr** NN1 ....... 159 F6
Vernon Terrace Prim Sch
NN1.................... 159 F6
**Vernon Wlk** 7 NN1 ..... 159 F6
**Verwood Cl** NN3........ 142 F5
**Veteran Cl** NN4......... 175 E7
**Vian Way** NN17 .......... 36 B8
**Vicarage Cl**
Hackleton NN7.......... 177 A3
Northampton NN2 ....... 141 A3
Wellingborough NN8..... 129 D6
Whittlebury NN12 ....... 215 C5
Yardley Gobion NN12..... 217 E6
**Vicarage Ct** MK19....... 207 B2
**Vicarage Farm Rd**
NN8 ................... 129 D6
**Vicarage Hill** NN11...... 153 A2
**Vicarage La**
Denton NN7............ 178 B8
East Haddon NN6 ....... 122 D5
Mears Ashby NN6 ....... 128 B2
Northampton NN2 ....... 141 B3
Podington NN29 ........ 147 E2
Priors Marston CV47..... 166 E8
**Vicarage Rd**
Northampton NN5 ....... 159 A7
Rushden NN10........... 132 C3
Stony Stratford MK11 .... 229 D6
**Vicarage Rise** NN12..... 200 C3
**Vicarage Wlk** MK11 ..... 229 D6
**Vicar La** NN11 .......... 135 D2
**Viceroy Cl** NN9 ......... 114 E6
**Vickers Cl** NN14 ......... 70 F7
**Victoria Ave** LE16......... 31 D5
Victoria Bsns Pk NN5 ... 159 B6
**Victoria Cl**
Earls Barton NN6........ 144 E5
Rushden NN10........... 132 B3
West Haddon NN6....... 102 C5
**Victoria Ct**
10 Kettering NN16 ....... 72 C2
Rothwell NN14........... 70 D7
Rushden NN10........... 132 B3
Woodford NN14........... 94 C7
**Victoria Gdns** NN1 ...... 159 D5
**Victoria Ho** NN1 ........ 159 E6
Victoria Pk NN8 ......... 130 B2
Victoria Prim Sch
NN8.................... 130 B6
**Victoria Prom** NN1...... 159 D5
**Victoria Rd**
Cogenhoe NN7.......... 161 E5
Finedon NN9 ........... 111 F5
Northampton NN1 ....... 159 E6
Oundle PE8 ............. 42 A6
Rushden NN10........... 132 B3
Wellingborough NN8 ..... 130 B4
**Victoria St**
Burton Latimer NN15 ..... 92 B2
Desborough NN14......... 51 A3
Earls Barton NN6........ 144 F5
Irthlingborough NN9...... 112 E1
Kettering NN16 .......... 72 B2
Northampton NN1 ....... 159 D6
**Vienne Cl** NN5.......... 157 F8
**Viking Cl** NN16 .......... 72 C6
**Viking Way** NN18 ........ 36 B1
**Villa Gdns** NN15 ......... 92 B1
**Villagers Cl** NN4 ........ 175 E5
**Villa La** NN9............ 113 F3
**Villa Rise** NN10 ......... 132 B7
**Villa Way** NN4 .......... 175 F5
**Vincent Cl** NN5 ......... 157 F8
**Vinco Terr** PE8 .......... 28 D8
**Vine Cl** PE8.............. 42 A5
**Vine Hill Cl** NN10 ....... 132 A6
**Vine Hill Dr** NN10....... 132 B6
**Violet Cl** NN18........... 36 D2
**Violet La**
Creaton NN6 ........... 104 F4
Rothwell NN14, NN16 ..... 71 C6
**Viscount Rd** NN3 ....... 143 C6
**Vislok Cl** LE16 ........... 31 E1
**Vivian Rd** NN8 .......... 130 B5
**Vokes Cl** NN3........... 143 A1
**Volunteer Cl** NN4 ....... 175 E6
**Vulcan Cl** NN11 ......... 135 A3
**Vyse Rd** NN2 ........... 141 C8

## W

**Wadcroft** 3 NN16 ....... 72 B2
**Wadd Close La** NN11.... 137 D6
**Wade Meadow Ct**
NN3 ................... 142 F4
**WADENHOE** ............. 58 A4
**Wadenhoe La** PE8 ....... 57 F4
**Wadenhoe Rd** NN14...... 57 E1
**Wades Cl** PE8 ........... 14 F1
**Wadham Ct** NN11 ....... 153 C7
**Waggoners Way** NN7 ... 173 A7
**Wagstaff Way** MK46...... 195 F3
**Wagtail Cl** NN3 ......... 142 C7
**Waingrove** NN3.......... 143 B4
**Wainwright Ave** NN14.... 76 D1
**Wake Cl** NN8 ........... 130 A1
**Wakefield** NN8 .......... 129 C4
**Wakefield Dr** NN6 ....... 64 D5
**Wakefield Rd** NN2 ...... 141 D4
**Wakefield Way** NN7..... 156 C1
**Wakehurst Dr** NN4...... 175 C7
**WAKERLEY** ............... 4 A3
**Wakerley Cl** PE8 ......... 41 D5
Wakerley Great Wood
Forest Trail★ LE15 ....... 4 C2
Wakerley Great Wood
Orienteering Course★
LE15 ..................... 4 B2
**Wakerley Rd**
Barrowden LE15 .......... 4 A4
Harringworth NN17....... 10 F7
**Wake Way** NN4 ......... 175 F3
**Walcot Cl** PE8 ........... 41 E7
**Walcote Rd** LE17......... 63 C8
**Walcot Rd** LE16.......... 31 E2
**WALES** ................ 230 F5
**Wales St**
Kings Sutton OX17....... 230 F5
Rothwell NN14........... 70 C7
**Walford Pl** CV22 ......... 98 F8
**WALGRAVE** ............ 108 B5
**Walgrave Cl** NN3 ....... 161 B8
Walgrave Prim Sch
NN6.................... 108 A5
**Walgrave Rd**
Holcot NN6 ............ 107 E1
Old NN6................ 107 E6
Walgrave NN6 .......... 108 B4
**Walker Dr** NN12 ........ 203 C8
**Walkers Acre** NN6 ...... 108 A5
**Walkers Field** PE8 ....... 13 F8
**Walkers La** NN6 ........ 140 B8
**Walker's La** 5 NN16 ..... 72 B2
**Walker Sq** NN8 ......... 129 C7
**Walkers Way** NN4....... 175 E5
**Walker's Way** NN9 ...... 111 F4
**Walks The** PE9 ............ 1 D2
**Walk The** NN6 .......... 124 B8
**Wallace Gdns** NN2...... 141 F2
**Wallace Rd** NN2 ........ 141 F2
**Wallace Terr** NN2....... 141 F2
**Wallbeck Cl** NN2........ 141 C4
**Walledwell Ct** 4 NN3 ... 142 F1
**Wallingford End** 6
NN3 ................... 161 A8
**Wallis Cl** NN8........... 129 A4
**Wallis Cres** NN15 ........ 91 C8
**Wallis Rd** NN15 .......... 91 C8
**Wallwin Cl** NN7......... 191 C4
**Walmer Cl** NN10 ........ 132 D1
**Walnut Cl**
Brackley NN13.......... 222 F1
Braunston NN11 ........ 118 D2
Clifton OX15............ 236 E4
Culworth OX17 ......... 198 D2
Silverstone NN12........ 214 D4
Weldon NN17............ 38 B8
**Walnut Cres** NN16 ....... 72 D4
**Walnut Gdns** OX17...... 181 D1
**Walnut Gr** NN3 ......... 142 C1
**Walnut Tree Cl** NN14..... 94 D6
**Walnut Tree Ct** NN10.... 132 B7
**Walsingham Ave** NN15 ... 91 F8
**Waltham Cl** NN17 ........ 36 D8
**Waltham Gdns** OX16 .... 219 A6
**Walton Ave** OX17 ....... 230 B5
**Walton Heath Way**
NN2 ................... 141 E3
**Walton Pl** NN18.......... 36 B6
**Wansell Rd** NN17 ........ 37 F8
**WANSFORD** ............... 8 B4
**Wansford Pl** NN17 ....... 36 B8
**Wansford Rd**
Elton PE8 ............... 16 E3
Yarwell PE8 .............. 7 F2
Wansford Sta★ PE8...... 16 E8
**Wansford Wlk** NN3 ..... 142 E6
**Wantage Cl**
Hackleton NN7.......... 177 B3
Moulton NN3 ........... 126 E1
**Wantage Pl** NN29........ 147 B8
**Wantage Rd**
Irchester NN29 ......... 147 B8
Northampton NN1 ....... 160 A8
**WAPPENHAM** .......... 213 A8
**Wappenham Rd**
Abthorpe NN12 ......... 201 F1
Helmdon NN13 ......... 212 A5
Syresham NN13......... 213 C2
**Wardens Lo** 2 NN11 .... 135 C2
**WARDINGTON** .......... 196 D2
**Wardington Rd** OX17.... 208 D6
**Wardle Ct** NN16 ......... 72 B3
**Wardle's Cl** NN7 ........ 138 C7
**Wardlow Cl** NN4 ........ 174 F8
**Ward Rd** NN13.......... 234 A5
**Wards La** NN6 ........... 82 C3
**Wareham Gn** NN18........ 36 B6
**Warehouse The** LE16..... 31 D4
**Wareing La** NN7 ........ 178 B8
**Ware Orch** CV23 ......... 99 C2
**Ware Rd** CV23 ........... 99 C2
**WARKTON** .............. 73 A4
**Warkton La** NN15, NN16... 73 B2
**Warkton Way** NN17 ...... 36 B8
**WARKWORTH** .......... 219 D5
**Warkworth Rd** OX17 .... 219 E7
**WARMINGTON** ........... 28 C3
Warmington Sch PE8 .... 28 B3
**Warminster Cl** NN18 ..... 36 A7
**WARMONDS HILL** ....... 132 A6
**Warmonds Hill** NN10..... 132 B5
**Warners Hill** NN29 ...... 164 D2
**Warnham** NN8.......... 129 B5
**Warren Bridge** PE8 ...... 41 E5
**Warren Cl** NN29 ........ 147 C7
**Warren End**
Desborough NN14......... 51 B4
Mawsley Village NN14..... 89 A4
**Warren Hill** NN16 ........ 71 E3
**Warren La**
Bythorn PE28............. 97 D4
Clopton NN14 ........... 78 F1
**Warren Rd**
Northampton NN5 ....... 158 F7
Stanion NN14............ 37 E3
Wothorpe PE9 ............ 2 E7
Yardley Gobion NN12..... 217 F6
**Warrens Cl** NN9 ........ 112 F2
**Warren The**
Northampton NN4 ....... 175 F8
Thorpe Mandeville
OX17 .................. 210 A6
**Warren Yd** MK12........ 229 F6
**WARRINGTON** .......... 180 B1
**Warrington Rd** MK46.... 195 F5
**Warth Park Way** NN9 .... 114 B7
**Wartnaby St** LE16........ 31 D3
**Warwick Ave** NN14....... 37 E3
**Warwick Cl**
Market Harborough
LE16 .................... 31 F5
Northampton NN5 ....... 158 B8
Raunds NN9............. 114 D5
**Warwick Ct**
Daventry NN11 ......... 135 B1
Kettering NN15 .......... 91 F8
**Warwick Gdns** NN14 ..... 76 F2
**Warwick Ho** NN5 ....... 158 F7
Warwick Prim Sch
NN8.................... 129 F1
**Warwick Rd**
Hanslope MK19......... 207 A3
Upper Boddington
NN11.................. 182 C7
Wellingborough NN8..... 130 A2
**Warwick St** NN11 ....... 135 B1
**Warwick Way** NN17 ...... 36 C6
**Washbrook Cl** NN3...... 143 B1
**Washbrook La** NN6 ..... 143 F5
**Washbrook Rd** NN10.... 132 A3
**Washingley La** PE7........ 44 F6
**Washington Ct** NN14..... 76 E3
**Washington Sq** NN16..... 72 D3
**Washington St** NN2...... 141 C3
**Washle Dr** OX17 ........ 220 B7
**Water Cl** MK19.......... 229 B7
**Waterfall Way** LE16 ...... 18 F6
**Waterfield Pl** LE16 ....... 31 E5
**Waterhouse Gdns**
NN15 ................... 92 A7
**Watering La** NN4 ....... 175 C3
**Water La**
Adderbury OX17 ........ 230 A3
Bradden NN12........... 201 F5
Chelveston NN9......... 133 B8
Cottingham LE16 ......... 35 D8
Northampton NN4 ....... 175 E6
Shutlanger NN12........ 204 D8
Towcester NN12 ........ 203 C5
Weldon NN17............ 38 A8
**Waterlee Furlong**
NN6 ................... 106 C1
**Waterloo** NN11 ......... 135 C1
**Waterloo Way** NN9 ..... 131 D8
**Waterlow Bridge** NN9... 111 F5
**Water Meadow Cl**
NN18 ................... 36 B1
**Watermeadow Dr**
NN3 ................... 142 F6
**Watermill Cl** NN14 ....... 51 D3
**Waterpike** NN6 ......... 106 C2
**Waterpump Ct** NN3 ..... 142 F5
**Waters Edge** PE8 ........ 16 B8
**Waterside Way** NN4..... 160 B4
**Waters La** OX17......... 209 B1
**Watersmeet** NN1 ....... 160 C6
**Water St** NN16........... 72 C2
**Watervill Way** NN14...... 113 B8
**Waterworks Way** LE17 ... 45 F5
**Watery La**
Brackley NN13.......... 234 A7
Nether Heyford NN7 ..... 156 C2
**WATFORD** ............. 120 C6
**Watford Rd**
Crick NN6 .............. 101 A2
West Haddon NN6....... 102 B3
**Watkin Ct** NN1.......... 159 D7
**Watkin Terr** NN1........ 159 D7
**Watling St E**
Pattishall NN12 ......... 188 D8
Towcester NN12 ........ 203 C6
**Watling St W**
Pattishall NN12 ......... 188 D8
Towcester NN12 ........ 203 C6
**Watling St**
Kilsby CV23 ............ 100 A3
Potterspury NN12 ....... 217 D3
Weedon Bec NN7........ 155 C4
**Watson Ave** LE16 ........ 48 D8
**Watson Cl**
Corby NN17 ............. 21 E2
Oundle PE8 ............. 41 E7
Wellingborough NN8..... 129 C7
**Watson Rd** NN6......... 121 B2
**Watts Cl** MK19.......... 207 A3
**Watts La** CV21 ........... 99 B8
**Watts Way** NN6 ......... 121 C3
**Wavell Cl** NN15 .......... 72 E1
**Waveney Cl** NN11 ....... 153 A8
**Waveney Way** NN5...... 140 F1
**Waver Cl** NN18 .......... 36 D3
**Waverley Ave** NN17 ...... 37 A6
**Waverley Cl** OX17....... 230 F5
**Waverley Rd**
Kettering NN15 .......... 91 D8
Northampton NN2 ....... 141 E1
**Waverley Rd** *continued*
Rugby CV21............. 80 A1
**Waynflete Ave** NN13 .... 233 E7
**Waynflete Cl** NN13...... 233 E7
**Waypost Ct** NN3 ........ 142 F3
**Wayside Acres** 3
NN4 ................... 175 B8
**Weares Cl** LE15............ 3 B5
**Weaver Cl** NN16 ......... 72 B6
**Weavers End** MK19 ..... 207 B2
**Weavers Rd** NN8........ 129 D4
Weavers Sch NN8........ 129 D4
**Weavers The** NN4....... 175 C6
**Webb Cl** PE8 ............ 42 B5
**Webb Rd** NN9 .......... 114 C7
**Webbs Factory** NN2..... 141 D1
**Webbs La** NN6.......... 127 D3
**Webster Cl** NN9 ........ 114 D7
**Weddell Way** NN4 ...... 160 C2
**Wedgwood Cl** NN14...... 50 F3
**Wedmore Cl** NN5 ....... 158 D7
**Wedmore Ct** NN18 ....... 36 B6
**WEEDON BEC** .......... 155 A3
Weedon Bec Prim Sch
NN7.................... 155 B3
**Weedon La** NN11 ....... 136 C4
**WEEDON LOIS** .......... 200 C2
**Weedon Rd**
Farthingstone NN12 ..... 170 F3
Kislingbury NN7......... 157 D5
Nether Heyford NN7 ..... 156 B2
Newnham NN11......... 153 E4
Northampton NN5 ....... 158 D5
**WEEKLEY** ............... 72 F6
**Weekley Glebe Rd**
NN16 ................... 72 D5
**Weekley Wood La**
NN16 ................... 72 E6
**Weekly Cl** NN14......... 113 B8
**Weggs Farm Rd** NN5.... 139 F1
**Weighbridge Way**
NN9 ................... 114 C5
**Weinahr Cl** LE16 ......... 34 C5
**Weir Cl** NN8 ............ 129 F7
**Weir The** 14 NN11....... 135 B7
**Welbeck Ct**
Corby NN18 ............. 36 C5
Kettering NN15 .......... 91 F8
**Welbourne Cl** NN9...... 114 C6
**WELDON** ............... 38 C8
Weldon CE Prim Sch
NN17.................... 38 A8
**Weldon Cl** NN8 ......... 129 D7
Weldon North Ind Est
NN17.................... 22 F1
**Weldon Rd** NN17......... 37 C7
**Weldon St** 2 NN16 ...... 72 C3
**WELFORD** .............. 64 E5
**Welford Ave** NN9 ....... 113 B5
**Welford Cl** NN9......... 113 B5
**Welford Gr** NN17 ........ 36 C7
**Welford Rd**
Husbands Bosworth
LE17 ................... 45 E3
Northampton NN2 ....... 141 B4
Sibbertoft LE16 .......... 46 D2
South Kilworth LE17 ...... 63 D7
Spratton NN6........... 124 A8
Thornby NN6 ............ 84 D4
Welford NN6 ............ 64 E7
Welford Sibbertoft &
Sulby Endowed Sch
NN6..................... 64 E5
**WELHAM** ............... 17 E5
**Welham La**
Great Bowden LE16....... 32 C8
Welham LE16............ 17 E8
**Welham Rd**
Great Bowden LE16....... 32 B8
Thorpe Langton LE16...... 17 B5
Welham LE16............ 18 A8
Weston by W LE16......... 18 A4
**Welland Ave** LE16........ 30 E7
Welland Bsns Pk LE16.... 32 B4
**Welland Cl**
Caldecott LE16........... 21 C8
Daventry NN11 ......... 152 F8
Gretton NN17 ........... 22 B8
Raunds NN9............. 114 C7
**Welland Ct**
Burton Latimer NN15 ..... 92 B2
Desborough NN14......... 51 A3
3 Market Harborough
LE16 .................... 31 F2
Market Harborough
LE16 .................... 32 A4
**Welland Gn** NN5 ........ 140 F2
**Welland Mdws** PE9 ........ 4 F8
Welland Park Com Coll
LE16 .................... 31 E2
**Welland Park Rd** LE16.... 31 E2
**Welland Rd** NN16 ........ 72 A5
**Welland Rise** LE16 ....... 46 F2
**Welland Vale Rd** NN17 ... 21 E1
**Welland View Rd** LE16 ... 20 D1
**Welland Way** NN5 ...... 141 A2
**Welland Wlk** NN5....... 140 F2
**Well Hill Cl** NN6 ........ 100 F5
**WELLINGBOROUGH** ..... 130 D6
Wellingborough Jun Sch
NN8.................... 130 B3
**Wellingborough Rd**
Broughton NN14 ......... 90 B3
Earls Barton NN6........ 144 F6
Finedon NN9 ........... 111 F4

**Wellingborough Rd** *continued*
Great Harrowden NN9 110 E1
Irthlingborough NN9 131 C8
Isham NN14 110 F8
Little Harrowden NN9 110 B3
Mears Ashby NN6 128 C2
Northampton, Cottarville NN3 142 E1
Northampton NN1 159 F6
Olney MK46 195 F5
Rushden NN10 131 F3
Sywell NN6 127 F4
Wellingborough NN8 111 E1
Wellingborough Sch
Wellingborough NN8 130 B3
Wellingborough NN8 130 B4
Wellingborough Sta NN8 130 C5
**Wellington Pl** 18 NN1 159 C7
**Wellington Rd** NN9 114 C5
**Wellington St**
Kettering NN16 72 C3
Northampton NN1 159 D6
**Wellington Terr** NN14 76 B2
Wellington Wks 1 NN16 72 C3
**Well La**
Barnwell PE8 59 B7
Everdon NN11 170 A8
Guilsborough NN6 103 F6
Rothwell NN14 70 D7
Staverton NN11 152 B7
Welton NN11 119 E1
**Wells Cl**
Husbands Bosworth LE17 45 E5
Kettering NN15 90 F8
**Wells Ct** NN3 142 C8
**Wells Gn** NN18 36 B6
**Wellspring** NN7 190 D7
**Well St** NN9 111 F5
**Wells The** NN9 111 F5
**Well Yd** NN2 141 B3
**Welsh Rd**
Aston le W NN11 182 C8
Chipping Warden OX17 197 C6
**WELTON** 119 E1
Welton CE Prim Sch NN11 119 E1
**Welton La** NN11 135 D6
**Welton Pk** NN11 119 E1
**Welton Pl** CV22 98 D8
**Welton Rd**
Braunston NN11 118 D1
Daventry NN11 135 C3
**Wenlock Way** NN5 140 D1
**Wensleydale** NN2 140 F5
**Wensleydale Pk** NN17 36 D8
**Wentin Cl** NN18 36 C1
**Wentworth Ave** NN8 129 C7
**Wentworth Cl** NN11 135 E3
**Wentworth Cotts** MK18 227 A5
**Wentworth Dr** PE8 41 E7
**Wentworth Rd**
Finedon NN9 112 A5
Rushden NN10 132 A2
**Wentworth Way**
Northampton NN2 141 E3
Stoke Bruerne NN12 204 F8
**Weskers Cl** LE16 67 A7
**Wesley Ct** NN9 114 D6
**Wesley Pl** OX17 208 E4
**Wesley Rd** CV21 99 A8
**Wessex Cl** NN16 72 B6
**Wessex Way** NN3 142 B1
**West Ave** NN15 92 B3
**West Bank** NN3 142 E6
**Westbrook** NN8 129 B4
**West Brook**
Blisworth NN7 190 D8
Newnham NN11 153 D4
**WESTBURY** 234 F4
**Westbury Cl** NN5 158 D7
**Westbury Mill** NN13 234 F4
**Westbury Wlk** NN18 36 B6
**West Cotton Cl** NN4 159 C4
**Westcott Way**
Corby NN18 36 D5
Northampton NN3 160 E7
**West Cres** NN10 131 E2
**West Ct** NN11 135 C1
**West End**
Bugbrooke NN7 172 E7
Scaldwell NN6 106 F5
Silverstone NN12 214 C4
Welford NN6 64 D4
West Haddon NN6 102 B4
**Westerburgh Sq** NN11 153 C8
**Westerdale** NN2 140 F5
**Western Ave**
Daventry NN11 153 B8
Easton o t H PE9 1 F5
Market Harborough LE16 31 D1
Nether Heyford NN7 156 B1
**Western Cl** NN11 135 B2
**Western Dr** MK19 207 A3
**Western View** NN1 159 B5
**Western Way** NN8 129 D3
**West Farm Cl** NN6 108 C3
**West Farm Dr** LE15 3 E5
**WEST FARNDON** 183 F3
**Westfield Ave**
Deanshanger MK19 228 D5
Raunds NN9 114 B4
Rushden NN10 131 F2
**Westfield Barns** CV47 166 D7
**Westfield Cl** LE16 31 C3
**Westfield Cres** NN6 64 E6
**Westfield Ct** NN6 102 C4
Westfield Ctr NN13 233 E8
**Westfield Dr** NN9 114 B4
**Westfield Ho** 8 NN16 72 B2
**Westfield Pl** NN10 131 F2
**Westfield Rd**
Northampton, Duston NN5 158 B8
Northampton NN5 158 F6
Wellingborough NN8 129 E4
**Westfields**
Little Harrowden NN9 110 B3
Wellingborough NN8 130 D3
**West Fields** PE9 1 F5
**Westfields Ave** NN10 132 B5
**Westfields Rd** NN17 36 E8
**Westfields St** NN10 132 B5
**Westfields Terr** NN10 132 B5
**West Furlong** NN15 71 F1
**Westgate La** LE16 30 E3
**Westgate Rd** NN5 158 D6
**West Glebe Rd** NN17 36 F7
**WEST HADDON** 102 C4
West Haddon Endowed CE Prim Sch NN6 102 B4
**West Haddon Rd**
Cold Ashby NN6 84 A5
Crick NN6 101 B6
Guilsborough NN6 103 D7
Ravensthorpe NN6 103 C1
Watford NN6 120 D7
**Westhaven** PE9 2 A5
**Westhill Ave** NN13 233 E7
**Westhill Cl**
Brackley NN13 233 E7
Kettering NN15 71 F1
**Westhill Dr** NN15 71 F1
**Westhill Gdns** NN13 233 D7
**WESTHORP** 183 C7
**Westhorp** OX17 210 E2
**Westhorpe**
Ashley LE16 18 E2
Sibbertoft LE16 46 F2
**Westhorpe La** NN11 183 C7
**Westhorpe Mews** NN11 183 C6
**Westland Cl** LE16 30 E3
**Westlea Rd** NN6 127 D3
**Westleigh Cl** NN1 159 F8
**Westleigh Pk** NN3 141 E6
**Westleigh Rd** NN15 92 B8
**Westley Cl** NN15 92 B1
**West Leys Ct** NN3 142 C7
West Lodge Rural Ctr* NN14 51 C6
**West March** NN11 153 D7
**Westmead Ct** NN3 142 F1
**West Mill** PE9 1 F4
**Westminster Cl** NN13 234 A7
**Westminster Cres** NN13 234 A7
**Westminster Croft** NN13 233 F7
**Westminster Dr** NN15 91 F7
**Westminster Rd**
Brackley NN13 233 F6
Wellingborough NN8 129 E7
**Westminster Wlk** NN18 36 C4
**Westmoreland Cl** PE8 15 E5
**Westmorland Dr** NN14 51 C4
**WESTON** 200 A2
**WESTON BY WELLAND** 18 A3
**Westone Ave** NN3 142 E1
**WESTON FAVELL** 160 E8
Weston Favell CE Prim Sch NN3 142 D1
Weston Favell Ctr NN3 142 F2
Weston Favell Sch NN3 142 D3
**Weston Mill La** NN3 160 E6
**Weston Rd**
Ashley LE16 18 D3
Olney MK46 195 D3
Ravenstone MK46 194 E2
Sulgrave OX17 211 A8
Sutton Bassett LE16 18 A2
Welham LE16 17 F5
**WESTON UNDERWOOD** 195 A2
**Westonville** PE9 1 D2
**Weston Way** NN3 160 C8
**Weston Wlk** NN18 36 C6
**West Oval** NN5 140 F1
**Westover Rd** NN15 71 F1
**West Paddock Ct** NN3 142 F4
**West Priors Ct** NN3 143 A4
**West Ridge** NN2 141 D3
**West Rising** NN4 175 D7
**West Side Rise** MK46 195 F4
**West St**
Broughton NN14 90 A5
Earls Barton NN6 144 E4
Easton o t H PE9 2 A5
Ecton NN6 143 F4
Geddington NN14 54 A3
Kettering NN16 72 B1
King's Cliffe PE8 13 E7
**West St** *continued*
Long Buckby NN6 121 A4
Moulton NN3 126 C1
Northampton NN1 159 F6
Olney MK46 195 F4
Oundle PE8 41 F5
Raunds NN9 114 D6
Rushden NN10 132 B2
Stanwick NN9 113 E3
Weedon Bec NN7 155 B3
Welford NN6 64 E6
Wellingborough NN8 129 F4
Woodford NN14 94 C7
**West View**
Corby NN17 37 B7
Daventry NN11 135 B1
**Westvilla Cotts** NN8 129 F4
**West Villa Rd** NN8 129 F4
**Westway** NN15 71 F1
**West Way**
Earls Barton NN6 144 D5
Weedon Bec NN7 155 B3
**Westway The** NN11 153 D8
**Westwood Rd** CV22 98 F7
**Westwood Way** NN3 142 D1
**Westwood Wlk** NN18 36 C5
**Wetenhall Rd** NN9 114 A4
**Wetheral Cl** NN3 142 C4
**Weymouth Cl** NN18 36 B6
**Whaddon Cl** NN4 158 E1
**Whaddon Field** NN6 106 C1
**Whalley Gr** NN7 161 F6
**Wharf Cl** MK19 229 B7
**Wharfedale Rd** NN17 21 E1
**Wharfe Gn** NN5 140 F2
**Wharf La**
Old Stratford MK19 229 C7
Souldern OX27 237 B4
**Wharf Rd** NN10 132 B6
**Wharton Cl** NN8 129 F5
**Wheat Cl** NN11 135 C6
**Wheatcroft Gdns** NN10 132 C2
**Wheatens Cl** NN6 125 C8
**Wheatfield Dr** NN15 92 C2
**Wheatfield Gdns** NN3 142 B1
**Wheatfield Rd** NN3 142 B1
**Wheatfield Rd N** NN3 142 B2
**Wheatfield Rd S** NN3 142 B1
**Wheatfield Terr** NN3 142 B1
**Wheatley Ave** NN17 36 F6
**Wheeler's Rise** NN13 238 C8
**Wheel La** LE15 3 F5
**Wheelwright Cl** NN9 114 E7
**Wheelwright Ho** NN14 70 D7
**Wheelwrights Way** MK19 229 C7
**Wheelwrights Yd** NN29 164 D2
**Whernside** NN8 129 D6
**Whernside Way** NN5 158 C8
**WHILTON** 137 D6
**Whilton Lo** NN11 136 D8
**WHILTON LOCKS** 136 F6
Whilton Mill* NN11 137 C6
**Whilton Rd**
Great Brington NN7 138 C7
Northampton NN2 141 D4
**Whistlefield Cotts** NN6 143 C7
**Whistlets Cl** NN4 158 D1
**WHISTON** 162 D6
**Whiston Rd**
Cogenhoe NN7 162 C6
Denton NN7 162 B2
Northampton NN2 141 D4
**Whitby Cl** NN15 91 F8
**Whitecroft Gdns** NN11 184 B7
**White Delves** NN8 129 E7
**White Doe Dr** NN3 142 C7
**Whitefield Rd** NN5 140 C1
**Whitefield Way** NN9 114 C7
**Whiteford Dr** NN15 91 C7
**Whitefriars** NN10 131 F1
Whitefriars Jun & Inf Schs NN10 147 F8
**Whitegates** NN4 158 D1
**Whiteheart Cl** NN3 143 B2
**Whitehill** MK46 195 E5
**Whitehill Rd** NN14 50 E3
**WHITE HILLS** 141 B6
**White Hills Cres** NN2 141 B6
Whitehills Prim Sch NN2 141 A6
**White Hills Way** NN2 141 B6
**White Horse Yd**
Stony Stratford MK11 229 D5
Towcester NN12 203 C6
**White House Ct** NN10 132 C1
White House Ind Est NN6 144 D6
**Whiteland Rd** NN3 142 C2
**Whiteman La** NN14 70 C7
**White Post Ct** NN17 21 E2
**Whitesands Way** NN4 158 C2
**Whites Rise** NN9 112 E1
**Whitethorns Cl** LE17 62 B3
**White Way** NN6 144 E5
**WHITFIELD** 223 E3
**Whitfield Way** NN2 141 D5
**Whiting Ct** NN3 142 C8
**Whitmees Cl** MK46 195 E4
**Whitmore Ct** NN12 214 D5
**Whitney Cl** NN9 114 C5
**Whitney Rd** NN15 92 B1
**Whitsundale Cl** NN9 111 F4
**Whittall St** OX17 230 F5
**Whittam Cl** NN9 114 C7
**Whittemore Rd** NN10 132 D3
**WHITTLEBURY** 215 C4
Whittlebury CE Prim Sch NN12 215 C4
**Whittlebury Cl** NN2 141 D5
**Whittlebury Ct** NN12 215 C5
**Whittlebury Rd** NN12 214 E5
**Whittle Cl**
Daventry NN11 135 A5
Wellingborough NN8 129 B6
**Whittle Rd** NN17 37 B8
**Whittles Cross** NN4 176 A6
**Whittlesea Terr** NN14 94 D6
**Whitton Cl** OX17 210 E2
**Whittons La** NN12 203 C6
**Whitwell Cl** PE8 41 E5
**Whitworth Ave** NN17 37 A8
**Whitworth Cres** NN6 144 E5
**Whitworth Rd**
Northampton NN1 159 F7
Wellingborough NN8 130 C5
**Whitworth Way**
Irthlingborough NN9 131 E8
Wellingborough NN8 130 B2
**Whytewell Rd** NN8 129 F6
**Wick Cl** NN18 36 D3
**WICKEN** 228 A3
**Wicken Park Rd** MK19 228 B1
**Wicken Rd** MK18 227 E1
**Wickery Dene** NN4 176 A6
**Wicksteed Cl** NN15 91 C6
Wicksteed L Pk* NN15 91 D6
**Wiggins Cl** CV21 99 B8
**WIGSTHORPE** 59 B2
**Wigston Rd** 3 CV21 80 A1
**WILBARSTON** 34 D5
Wilbarston CE Prim Sch LE16 34 C5
**Wilbarston Rd** LE16 34 B4
**Wilberforce St** 3 NN1 159 E6
**WILBY** 129 A1
Wilby CE Prim Sch NN8 129 B1
**Wilby Cl** NN17 36 B8
**Wilbye Grange** NN8 129 D2
**Wilby La** NN29 145 D6
**Wilby Park Mobile Home Pk** NN8 129 C2
**Wilby Rd** NN6 128 D2
**Wilby St** NN1 159 F6
**Wilby Way** NN8 129 D1
**Wilce Ave** NN8 130 A1
**Wildacre Rd** NN10 131 E2
**Wild Cherry Cl** NN11 184 B6
**Wildern La** NN4 175 C5
**Wilford Ave** NN3 160 F8
**Wilkie Cl** NN15 90 F8
**Wilkie Rd** NN8 129 F8
**Wilks Wlk** NN4 175 E3
**Willetts Cl** NN17 36 E8
**Willey Ct** MK11 229 F4
**William Rd** NN6 121 B3
**Williams Cl** MK19 206 F3
**WILLIAMSCOT** 208 C8
**Williamscot Hill** OX17 208 B6
Williamscot Road Ind Ctr OX17 196 A1
**William St**
Burton Latimer NN15 92 B2
Finedon NN9 112 A4
Kettering NN16 72 B4
Northampton NN1 159 D7
**William Steele Way** NN10 132 C5
**Williams Terr** NN11 135 B2
**Williams Way**
Higham Ferrers NN10 132 B5
Northampton NN4 175 E3
**William's Way** NN29 146 E1
**William Trigg Cl** NN9 131 E8
**Willis Way** NN12 203 C5
**Williton Cl** NN3 160 D7
**Willmott Rd** NN10 148 C8
**WILLOUGHBY** 117 C3
**Willoughby Cl** NN11 135 B3
**Willoughby Pl** CV22 98 D7
**Willoughby Rd** LE15 3 A6
**Willoughby Way** NN7 177 A1
**Willowbrook Appartments The** NN8 130 B4
Willowbrook East Ind Est NN17 22 E2
**Willow Brook Rd** NN17 36 C8
**Willow Brook Sq** NN3 143 D2
**Willow Cl**
Desborough NN14 51 C3
Hinton NN11 184 A6
Spratton NN6 124 A8
Towcester NN12 203 C3
**Willow Cres**
Great Houghton NN4 160 F2
Market Harborough LE16 31 C2
**Willow Ct** NN1 160 A7
**Willow Gr** MK19 229 B6
**Willow Herb Cl** NN10 148 C7
**Willow Herb Wlk** NN14 51 A4
**Willow La**
Great Houghton NN4 160 E2
King's Cliffe PE8 13 F7
Stanion NN14 37 F2
Stony Stratford MK11 229 C5
**Willow Rd**
Brackley NN13 234 A6
Kettering NN15 72 C1
**Willow Rise** NN3 161 B8
**Willows Hill** NN12 201 F5
**Willows The**
Daventry NN11 135 C3
Kings Sutton OX17 231 A6
Little Harrowden NN9 110 B3
Silverstone NN12 214 C5
Thrapston NN14 76 C1
**Willow Tree Gdns** CV21 99 A8
**Willow View** NN7 157 C3
**Wills Cl** NN6 103 E7
**Willson Cl** LE16 32 A3
**Wilmington Wlk** 1 NN18 36 B5
**Wilson Cl** NN11 135 A4
**Wilson Cres** NN9 112 E1
**Wilson Rd** 5 NN10 132 A2
**Wilson Terr** NN16 72 B4
**Wilson Way** NN6 144 E3
**Wilton Cl** NN14 51 A2
**Wilton Rd** NN15 91 F8
**Wimbledon St** NN5 159 A6
**Wimborne Cl** NN3 143 D3
**Wimborne Pl** NN11 135 C5
**Wimborne Wlk** NN18 36 A7
**Wimpole** NN8 129 C4
**Wimpole Ho** 5 NN11 135 B7
**Wincanton Ct** NN18 36 B6
**Wincely Cl** NN11 135 C6
**Winchester Cl** NN4 159 C1
Winchester House Sch NN13 233 F7
**Winchester Rd**
Northampton NN4 159 C1
Rushden NN10 132 C1
**Winchilsea Dr** NN17 10 B1
**Windermere Cl** NN11 135 B2
**Windermere Dr**
Higham Ferrers NN10 132 B8
Wellingborough NN8 129 C6
**Windermere Rd** NN16 71 F2
**Windermere Way** NN3 142 C4
**Windflower Pl** 2 NN3 143 D2
**Windgate Way** PE8 8 A6
**Windingbrook La** NN4 175 C5
**Winding Way** NN14 76 E2
**Windmill Ave**
Blisworth NN7 190 E7
Kettering NN15, NN16 72 D2
Raunds NN9 114 D6
**Windmill Banks** NN10 132 C7
Windmill Bsns Ctr 7 NN10 132 A2
**Windmill Cl**
Cottingham LE16 20 D1
Wellingborough NN8 129 E2
Wollaston NN29 146 E2
**Windmill Cotts** NN15 92 D4
**Windmill Ct** NN16 72 D3
**Windmill Gdns** NN11 152 C7
**Windmill Glade** NN6 106 A1
**Windmill Gr** NN9 114 D6
**Windmill La**
Denton NN7 178 B8
Raunds NN9 114 D7
Staverton NN11 152 C7
Windmill Prim Sch NN9 114 C7
**Windmill Rd**
Irthlingborough NN9 112 E1
Rushden NN10 132 A2
**Windmill Rise** LE16 20 D1
**Windmill Terr** NN2 141 D4
**Windmill Way**
Greens Norton NN12 202 D8
Lyddington LE15 9 D6
**Windmill Wlk** NN15 72 D1
**Windrush Rd** NN4 175 F8
**Windrush Way** NN5 141 A2
**Windsor Ave** NN14 50 F2
**Windsor Cl**
Daventry NN11 135 B1
Kings Sutton OX17 230 F6
Long Buckby NN6 121 B3
Towcester NN12 203 B4
Weedon Bec NN7 155 B4
Wilbarston LE16 34 C4
**Windsor Cres** NN5 158 E6
**Windsor Ct**
Market Harborough LE16 31 D4
Northampton NN3 143 C2
**Windsor Dr**
Brackley NN13 233 E8
Thrapston NN14 76 E2
**Windsor Gdns** NN16 72 A2
**Windsor Ho** NN5 158 C8
**Windsor Pl** NN17 36 E5
**Windsor Rd**
Rushden NN10 132 C3
Wellingborough NN8 129 F1
**Windyridge** NN2 141 D3
**Winemar Cl** MK19 207 A3
**Wingate Cl** NN15 72 E1
**Wing Rd** LE15 3 A6
**Winnington Cl** NN3 143 C5
**Winsford Way** NN3 160 D7
**Winsland Ct** NN6 126 E8
**Winstanley Rd** NN8 130 B5
**Winston Cl**
Nether Heyford NN7 156 B1

Winston Cl *continued*
  Northampton NN3 . . . . . . . 142 C5
  Woodford Halse NN11 . . . 184 D5
Winston Cres NN13 . . . . . . . 233 F6
Winston Dr NN14 . . . . . . . . 91 D1
Winter Bourne Ct
  NN18 . . . . . . . . . . . . . . . . . . . . 36 B6
Winterburn Ct NN16 . . . . 71 E3
Winthorpe Way NN18 . . . 36 C6
WINWICK . . . . . . . . . . . . . . 102 B8
Winwick Rd PE28 . . . . . . . 61 D1
Winwood Cl MK19 . . . . . 228 E5
Wire La LE16 . . . . . . . . . . . 19 D2
Wisley Cl NN4 . . . . . . . . . 175 C7
Wisteria Cl NN10 . . . . . . . 148 B7
Wisteria Way NN3 . . . . . . 160 C6
Witham Gn NN5 . . . . . . . . 140 E2
Witham Ho NN2 . . . . . . . . 141 E1
Witham The NN11 . . . . . . 134 F1
Witham Way NN5 . . . . . . . 140 F1
Witham Wlk NN5 . . . . . . . 140 F2
Witheys The NN4 . . . . . . . 175 F2
WITTERING . . . . . . . . . . . . . 7 D8
Wittlich Rd NN8 . . . . . . . . 130 B6
Witton Rd NN5 . . . . . . . . . 158 C8
Woburn Cl LE16 . . . . . . . . 32 A3
Woburn Ct NN10 . . . . . . . 148 A8
Woburn Gate NN3 . . . . . . 143 D3
Wodhams Dr NN13 . . . . . 222 E1
Wold Farm Ind Pk
  NN6 . . . . . . . . . . . . . . . . . . . 107 D7
Wold Rd NN15 . . . . . . . . . 92 E2
Wolfe Cl NN15 . . . . . . . . . 72 F1
WOLLASTON . . . . . . . . . . 146 F2
Wollaston Com Prim Sch
  NN29 . . . . . . . . . . . . . . . . . 146 D2
Wollaston Mus* . . . . . . . . 146 D2
Wollaston Rd
  Bozeat NN29 . . . . . . . . . . 164 C5
  Irchester NN29 . . . . . . . . . 146 F6
Wollaston Sch NN29 . . . . 146 E2
Wollaton Gdns **2**
  NN3 . . . . . . . . . . . . . . . . . . . 160 F8
Wollongong Ho NN17 . . . . 36 E8
Wolsey Cl NN4 . . . . . . . . . 101 A6
Wolverton Rd MK11 . . . . 229 E6
Wood Avens Cl NN4 . . . . 158 E1
Woodbine Cotts NN6 . . . 108 A5
Woodborough Gdns **5**
  NN3 . . . . . . . . . . . . . . . . . . . 160 F8
Woodbreach Dr LE16 . . . . 32 B3
WOOD BURCOTE . . . . . 203 C2
Woodcock St NN15 . . . . . 92 D3
Woodcote Ave NN3 . . . . . 142 A5
Woodcroft Cl NN12 . . . . . 203 C3
Woodcroft Way NN15 . . . . 91 F5
WOODEND . . . . . . . . . . . . 200 F7
WOODEND GREEN . . . . 200 E6
Woodfield PE9 . . . . . . . . . . 1 D1
Woodfield Gr NN17 . . . . . . 36 E7
WOODFORD . . . . . . . . . . . 94 C6
Woodford CE Prim Sch
  NN14 . . . . . . . . . . . . . . . . . . 94 D6
Woodford Chase NN6 . . . 127 C2
Woodford Cl NN15 . . . . . . 91 F5
Woodford Glebe NN6 . . . . 64 E5
WOODFORD HALSE . . . . 184 C6
Woodford Halse CE Sch
  NN11 . . . . . . . . . . . . . . . . . . 184 D6
Woodford La NN14 . . . . . . 75 E6

Woodford Rd
  Byfield NN11 . . . . . . . . . . 183 D7
  Eydon NN11 . . . . . . . . . . . 184 B2
  Great Addington NN14 . . . 94 C1
  Little Addington NN14 . . . 94 C3
Woodford St **7** NN1 . . . 159 E6
Woodford Wlk **9**
  NN1 . . . . . . . . . . . . . . . . . . . 159 E6
Woodgate LE16 . . . . . . . . . 30 E8
Woodgate Cl LE16 . . . . . . 32 B2
Woodgate Rd NN4 . . . . . 175 F6
WOOD GREEN . . . . . . . . 224 F1
Woodhall Cl NN4 . . . . . . . 158 D1
Wood Hill NN1 . . . . . . . . . 159 D5
Woodhill Rd NN5 . . . . . . . 140 C1
Wood La
  Hartwell NN7 . . . . . . . . . . 192 E2
  King's Cliffe PE8 . . . . . . . . 13 E7
  Oundle PE8 . . . . . . . . . . . 41 D4
  Weston Underwood
    MK46 . . . . . . . . . . . . . . . . 195 A2
Woodland Ave
  Kettering NN15 . . . . . . . . . 92 A5
  Northampton NN3 . . . . . . 142 A1
  Overstone NN6 . . . . . . . . 127 B1
Woodland Cl NN5 . . . . . . 140 B1
Woodland Dr NN15 . . . . . 92 C4
Woodland Hospl The
  NN16 . . . . . . . . . . . . . . . . . . 71 B5
Woodland Rd NN10 . . . . . 132 A3
Woodlands NN4 . . . . . . . . 175 E1
Woodlands Ave NN17 . . . . 21 F1
Woodlands Cl NN14 . . . . . 55 F7
Woodlands Ct
  **1** Kettering NN16 . . . . 72 C4
  Watford NN6 . . . . . . . . . . 120 C6
Woodlands Grange
  NN6 . . . . . . . . . . . . . . . . . . 145 A4
Woodlands La NN18 . . . . . 53 C8
Woodlands Mews
  NN14 . . . . . . . . . . . . . . . . . . 55 F7
Woodlands Rd
  Irchester NN29 . . . . . . . . 147 A7
  Weldon NN17 . . . . . . . . . . 38 C7
Woodlands The
  Geddington NN14 . . . . . . 54 B3
  Market Harborough
    LE16 . . . . . . . . . . . . . . . . . 31 C4
  Silverstone NN12 . . . . . . 214 D4
  Stanwick NN9 . . . . . . . . . 114 A3
  Staverton NN11 . . . . . . . . 152 B7
Woodland View Prim Sch
  NN4 . . . . . . . . . . . . . . . . . . . 175 E3
Woodland Wlk NN3 . . . . 143 B6
Woodleigh Pl NN17 . . . . . 36 E6
Woodley Chase NN5 . . . . 140 B1
Woodmans Cl MK19 . . . . 228 E4
WOODNEWTON . . . . . . . . 14 F2
Woodnewton Inf Sch
  NN17 . . . . . . . . . . . . . . . . . . 36 C8
Woodnewton Rd PE8 . . . 15 D4
Woodnewton Way
  NN17 . . . . . . . . . . . . . . . . . . 36 C7
Woodpecker Cl NN13 . . . 222 D1
Woodpecker Way NN4 . . 174 F7
Wood Rd PE8 . . . . . . . . . . 13 F7
Woodroffe Rd PE8 . . . . . . 7 D8
Woodrush Way NN3 . . . . 142 C7
Woods Ct
  Brackley NN13 . . . . . . . . 233 D7
  Rushden NN10 . . . . . . . . 132 B3

Woodsfield NN6 . . . . . . 106 A2
Woodside
  Stony Stratford MK11 . . . 229 E6
  Sywell NN6 . . . . . . . . . . . 127 D1
Woodside Ave NN3 . . . . 142 D4
Woodside Cres NN3 . . . . 142 D4
Woodside Gn NN5 . . . . . 140 F1
Woodside Pk NN17 . . . . . 38 C7
Woodside Way NN5 . . . . 140 F1
Woodside Wlk NN5 . . . . 140 E1
Woods La NN12 . . . . . . . 217 E3
Wood St
  Corby NN17 . . . . . . . . . . . 36 E6
  Geddington NN14 . . . . . . 54 B3
  Higham Ferrers NN10 . . . 132 C5
  Kettering NN16 . . . . . . . . 72 C4
  Northampton NN1 . . . . . 159 D6
  Wellingborough NN8 . . . 129 F4
Woodstock **12** NN1 . . . 159 F6
Woodstock Cl NN8 . . . . 129 E7
Woodvale Prim Sch
  NN3 . . . . . . . . . . . . . . . . . . 143 A5
Woodville Cres NN12 . . . 217 E6
Woodward Cl NN11 . . . . 135 E1
WOODWELL . . . . . . . . . . . 94 A8
Woodwell Cotts NN14 . . . 94 A8
Woodwell Hill NN14 . . . . 50 F2
Woodyard Cl NN14 . . . . . 55 F8
Woodyard The NN7 . . . . 163 A3
Wooldale Rd NN4 . . . . . 175 A4
Woolmans MK11 . . . . . . 229 F4
Woolmonger St **4**
  NN1 . . . . . . . . . . . . . . . . . 159 C5
Woolrich Gdns MK11 . . . 229 E5
Woolscott Rd CV23 . . . . 117 C4
Woolston Ct NN17 . . . . . . 10 C1
WOOTTON . . . . . . . . . . . . 175 F5
Wootton Brook Cl
  NN4 . . . . . . . . . . . . . . . . . 175 C6
Wootton Ct NN12 . . . . . 203 D5
WOOTTON HALL . . . . . 175 C6
Wootton Hall Pk NN7 . . 175 C5
Wootton Hill Farm
  NN4 . . . . . . . . . . . . . . . . . 174 F8
Wootton Hope Dr
  NN4 . . . . . . . . . . . . . . . . . 175 F6
Wootton Prim Sch
  NN4 . . . . . . . . . . . . . . . . . 175 E6
Wootton Rd NN7 . . . . . . 176 A2
Wootton Trad Est
  NN4 . . . . . . . . . . . . . . . . . 175 F6
Worcester Cl
  Corby NN18 . . . . . . . . . . . 36 E1
  Northampton NN3 . . . . . 143 B2
  West Haddon NN6 . . . . . 102 C5
Worcester Dr LE16 . . . . . 31 E5
Worcester Way NN11 . . . 153 C7
Wordsworth Ave NN17 . . 21 D1
Wordsworth Cl
  Brackley NN13 . . . . . . . . 222 F1
  Towcester NN12 . . . . . . 203 B5
Wordsworth Rd
  Daventry NN11 . . . . . . . 135 B3
  Kettering NN16 . . . . . . . . 72 C5
  Wellingborough NN8 . . . 129 B3
Worksop Gdns NN8 . . . . 36 B6
Works The **8** NN1 . . . . 159 E6
WORMLEIGHTON . . . . . 181 B8
Wormleighton Way
  NN14 . . . . . . . . . . . . . . . . . 54 A3
Worthing Rd NN18 . . . . . 36 B5

WOTHORPE . . . . . . . . . . . . 2 D8
Wothorpe Hill PE9 . . . . . . 2 C7
Wothorpe Villas PE9 . . . . 2 D8
Wrekin Cl NN4 . . . . . . . . 158 E3
Wrenbury Rd NN5 . . . . . 140 A1
Wren Cl
  Brackley NN13 . . . . . . . . 222 D1
  Corby NN18 . . . . . . . . . . . 36 E3
  Kettering NN15 . . . . . . . . 92 A6
  Northampton NN4 . . . . . 175 F3
  Towcester NN12 . . . . . . 203 C3
Wrendyke Cl LE15 . . . . . . 3 A6
Wrenn Sch
  Wellingborough NN8 . . . 130 A3
  Wellingborough NN8 . . . 130 B3
Wren Spinney Com Specl
Sch
  NN15 . . . . . . . . . . . . . . . . . 71 F1
Wrightons Hill NN13 . . . 211 F4
Wright Rd NN6 . . . . . . . . 121 B3
Wroe Cl NN18 . . . . . . . . . . 36 C1
Wroe The NN10 . . . . . . . 132 B7
Wyatt St NN16 . . . . . . . . . 72 C2
Wyatt Way PE8 . . . . . . . . 41 E6
Wychwood Cl NN5 . . . . 140 A1
Wyckley Cl NN9 . . . . . . . 112 E3
Wycliffe Rd NN1 . . . . . . . 160 A6
Wye Cl NN8 . . . . . . . . . . . 129 C6
Wye The NN11 . . . . . . . . 153 A8
Wykeham Rd NN10 . . . . 132 C7
Wyman Cl NN29 . . . . . . . 164 D2
Wymersley Cl NN4 . . . . . 160 F2
WYMINGTON . . . . . . . . . 148 B5
Wymington Pk NN10 . . . 132 B1
Wymington Rd
  Podington NN29 . . . . . . 147 E3
  Rushden NN10 . . . . . . . . 148 B8
Wyndham Way NN16 . . . . 71 E4
Wysall Rd NN3 . . . . . . . . 143 B5

**Y**

Yaffle Cres NN14 . . . . . . . 51 B4
Yardley Cl NN17 . . . . . . . . 21 D1
Yardley Ho NN2 . . . . . . . 141 D6
YARDLEY GOBION . . . . 217 E5
Yardley Gobion CE Prim
  Sch NN12 . . . . . . . . . . . 217 E6
YARDLEY HASTINGS . . 179 B6
Yardley Hastings Prim Sch
  NN7 . . . . . . . . . . . . . . . . . 179 A7
Yardley Rd
  Cosgrove MK19 . . . . . . . 218 D2
  Grendon NN7 . . . . . . . . . 163 D4
  Olney MK46 . . . . . . . . . . 195 F5
  Yardley Gobion NN12 . . 217 F4
Yarrow NN8 . . . . . . . . . . . 129 B3
Yarrow Cl NN10 . . . . . . . 148 C2
Yarrow Ho NN2 . . . . . . . 141 C5
YARWELL . . . . . . . . . . . . . 16 A8
Yarwell Ct NN15 . . . . . . . 91 C6
Yarwell Junc* PE8 . . . . . . 16 B7
Yarwell Rd PE8 . . . . . . . . 8 A3
Yarwell Sq NN4 . . . . . . . 158 F2
Yateley Dr NN15 . . . . . . . 92 A5
YELDEN . . . . . . . . . . . . . . 133 F3
Yelden Cl NN10 . . . . . . . 131 F2
Yeldon Ct NN8 . . . . . . . . 111 B1
YELVERTOFT . . . . . . . . . . 82 C4

Yelvertoft Prim Sch
  NN6 . . . . . . . . . . . . . . . . . . 82 B4
Yelvertoft Rd
  Crick NN6 . . . . . . . . . . . . 101 A8
  Lilbourne CV23 . . . . . . . . 81 D6
  Northampton NN2 . . . . . 141 C3
  West Haddon NN6 . . . . . 102 B5
Yeoman Cl NN14 . . . . . . . 95 A3
Yeoman Dr NN2 . . . . . . . 141 B5
Yeoman Mdw NN4 . . . . 174 F8
Yeomanry Cl NN11 . . . . . 135 B1
Yeomanry Ct LE16 . . . . . 31 E3
Yeomanry Way NN11 . . . 135 B1
Yeomans Cl NN13 . . . . . 234 A8
Yeomans Ct NN15 . . . . . 92 C2
Yew Cl NN17 . . . . . . . . . . 21 E1
Yew Tree Cl
  Kettering NN15 . . . . . . . . 91 C8
  Middleton Cheney
    OX17 . . . . . . . . . . . . . . . 220 A8
Yewtree Ct NN3 . . . . . . . 142 D5
Yew Tree Gdns NN7 . . . 155 F5
Yew Tree Gr NN11 . . . . . 153 B8
Yew Tree La NN6 . . . . . . 124 B8
Yew Tree Rise NN13 . . . 238 D8
York Ave NN7 . . . . . . . . . 161 F6
York Cl
  Higham Ferrers
    NN10 . . . . . . . . . . . . . . . 132 C7
  Towcester NN12 . . . . . . 203 C4
York Ct NN12 . . . . . . . . . 203 C5
York Dr NN13 . . . . . . . . . 233 E8
Yorke Cl NN9 . . . . . . . . . 111 E5
York Ho NN1 . . . . . . . . . 159 F6
York Rd
  Corby NN18 . . . . . . . . . . . 36 C5
  Higham Ferrers NN10 . . . 132 C7
  Kettering NN16 . . . . . . . . 72 B2
  Northampton NN1 . . . . . 159 E6
  Rushden NN10 . . . . . . . . 132 C1
  Stony Stratford MK11 . . . 229 D5
  Wellingborough NN8 . . . 130 B5
  Wollaston NN29 . . . . . . . 146 D3
York Ride NN7 . . . . . . . . 155 B4
York St LE16 . . . . . . . . . . 31 F3
York Way NN9 . . . . . . . . 114 C7

**Z**

Zion Hill NN6 . . . . . . . . . 108 A5

# Addresses

| Name and Address | Telephone | Page | Grid reference |
|---|---|---|---|
| | | | |

| | | | | | |
|---|---|---|---|---|---|
| NG | NH | NJ | NK | | |
| NM | NN | NO | NP | | |
| NR | NS | NT | NU | | |
| | NX | NY | NZ | | |
| | SC | SD | SE | TA | |
| | SH | SJ | SK | TF | TG |
| SM | SN | SO | SP | TL | TM |
| SR | SS | ST | SU | TQ | TR |
| SW | SX | SY | SZ | TV | |

Any feature in this atlas can be given a unique reference to help you find the same feature on other Ordnance Survey maps of the area, or to help someone else locate you if they do not have a Street Atlas.

The grid squares in this atlas match the Ordnance Survey National Grid and are at 500 metre intervals. The small figures at the bottom and sides of every other grid line are the National Grid kilometre values (**00** to **99** km) and are repeated across the country every 100 km (see left).

To give a unique National Grid reference you need to locate where in the country you are. The country is divided into 100 km squares with each square given a unique two-letter reference. Use the administrative map to determine in which 100 km square a particular page of this atlas falls.

The bold letters and numbers between each grid line (**A** to **F**, **1** to **8**) are for use within a specific Street Atlas only, and when used with the page number, are a convenient way of referencing these grid squares.

## Example The railway bridge over DARLEY GREEN RD in grid square B1

**Step 1:** Identify the two-letter reference, in this example the page is in **SP**

*Eastings (read from left to right along the bottom) come before Northings (read from bottom to top). If you have trouble remembering say to yourself Along the hall, THEN up the stairs !*

**Step 2:** Identify the 1 km square in which the railway bridge falls. Use the figures in the southwest corner of this square: Eastings **17**, Northings **74**. This gives a unique reference: **SP 17 74**, accurate to 1 km.

**Step 3:** To give a more precise reference accurate to 100 m you need to estimate how many tenths along and how many tenths up this 1 km square the feature is (to help with this the 1 km square is divided into four 500 m squares). This makes the bridge about **8** tenths along and about **1** tenth up from the southwest corner.

This gives a unique reference: **SP 178 741**, accurate to 100 m.

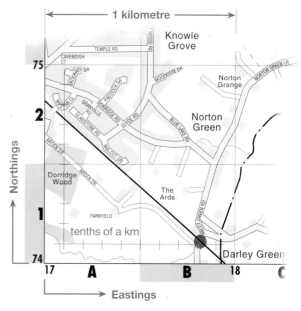

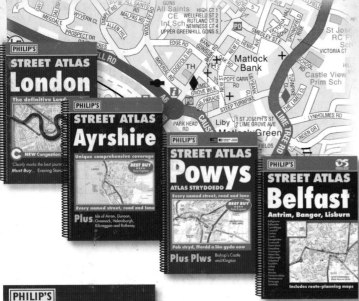